# The Quest for
# Democracy
# in Iran

# The Quest for Democracy in Iran

A Century of Struggle against Authoritarian Rule

**Fakhreddin Azimi**

Harvard University Press

Cambridge, Massachusetts

London, England

2008

*Library of Congress Cataloging-in-Publication Data*

Azimi, Fakhreddin.
The quest for democracy in Iran : a century of struggle
against authoritarian rule / Fakhreddin Azimi.
p.   cm.
Includes bibliographical references and index.
ISBN-13: 978-0-674-02778-7 (alk. paper)
ISBN-10: 0-674-02778-7 (alk. paper)
1. Democracy—Iran.   2. Iran—Politics and
government—20th century.   I. Title.
JQ1789.A15A95   2008
955.05—dc22      2007038345

*For Talat, Arman, and Saman*

# Contents

# Preface

The quest for democracy in Iran is traceable to the nineteenth century, and my concern with the topic dates from my undergraduate days at Tehran University in the 1970s. I began thinking about this book several years ago, in anticipation of the centennial of the Iranian Constitutional Revolution of 1906, a revolution that Iranians widely regard as epitomizing the genesis of their struggle for democracy. The writing of this book coincided with an escalating chorus of ideological casuistries in the United States regarding democracy in the Middle East. The unfolding tragedy in Iraq would not deter bellicose circles in the United States from engaging in ominous saber rattling in their confrontation with Iran, while continuing to profess support for the spread of "democracy." Given such a situation, the prominence of the term "democracy" in the book's title requires some explanation. Like so many noble ideals, democracy has not been immune from abuse; it has been cynically invoked, to further agendas detrimental to it. The seemingly earnest but ultimately hypocritical advocacy of democracy—most recently and notably by American neoconservatives—has harmed and degraded those in countries such as Iran who have for decades striven for or advocated democratic values and practices—those whose efforts long precede the current appropriation of "democracy" for purposes of propaganda.

The experiences of Iranians through the twentieth century have made them increasingly appreciative of the ideal of democratic self-rule. The struggle for democracy in Iran must not be denigrated by those who have supported and benefited from authoritarian arrangements. It must not, and indeed cannot, be hijacked by propaganda from abroad; nor can it be tainted by attempts to associate it with other states' imperial adventures. Every political ideal is susceptible to perversion, and democracy is no exception. However, concepts such as democracy are too central to making sense of and shaping the human longing for a decent sociopolitical order to be shunned because of abuse. The interrelated notions of democracy, citizenship, and civil society are constitutive of the very definition of modern civility. Rather than being abandoned to cynical abuse or unenlightened detraction, they should be intellectually rehabilitated and conceptually invigorated; without them the analytical and normative language of politics will be impoverished.

I have attempted in this book to chart the trajectory of both the suppression of democracy in Iran and the sustained quest for it. In 1906 Iran became a pioneer in the nonwestern world in seeking to establish a constitutional representative democracy of citizens. Henceforth Iranian politics would consist largely of struggles to fulfill, partially accommodate, or circumvent the political and civic ideals associated with the Constitutional Revolution. These ideals would continue to dominate the Iranian public sphere, and, in defiance of political constraints, the Iranians would persist in seeking to act as citizens. In historically situating my analysis of authoritarian rule I have been cognizant not only of the state's suppressive role but also of its impact on shaping and transforming society, and of the structural requirements of its viability. What I have particularly sought to underline has been the significance of a *democratic* state—committed to respecting and promoting the equal political and civic rights of citizens—in the political struggles, aspirations, and discourses in Iran of the last 100 years. It is only such a state that can claim real legitimacy or command extensive public support. As Ronald Dworkin has argued, only those states that treat the fate of all their citizens with equal concern can claim their allegiance and be construed as legitimate.

This book does not attempt to explore or identify in any depth the theoretical preconditions or underpinnings of democracy. Viewing democracy as a global trend and as the only effective way of legitimizing political authority, I consider it to be intrinsically linked with rationality. However, I contend that the very struggle to craft democracy and make it succeed—even in a society in which its philosophical or cultural preconditions may not be firmly in place or adequate—can itself more than any other factor contribute to democracy's resonance and ultimate success. It is not a set of abstract notions or a predisposed and congenial culture that makes democracy possible, but the trials and errors, and the sense of dedication and determination involved in attaining it. It is the historical experience of grappling with alternative modes of governance that generates cumulative interest in democracy and determination to achieve it.

The process of crafting democracy creates citizens who are both its creators and its creatures. In this process citizens tend to identify themselves increasingly with the nation-state and with a polity that facilitates their real empowerment. They seek to organize themselves freely to affirm, protect, and promote their formally stipulated political and civic rights and entitlements. More crucially, citizens require opportunities and resources that will empower them to act upon and enjoy their formal rights. Such empowerment entails a permissive and supportive sociocultural and economic environment, and an institutionalized constitutional order that is conducive to both effective governance and wide-ranging freedom. The negative liberties of a liberal capitalist provenance are inadequate; citizens must also have the opportunity to fulfill their capabilities, or, as Amartya Sen has maintained, have the "capacities" to act as citizens.

In societies not susceptible to mobilized sectarian prejudice or traumatized by civil strife, and where a democratic constitution exists to serve as a national covenant, identity tends to transcend ethnic, religious, tribal, and communal loyalties in favor of national and civic solidarity. In a democracy the locus of citizens' identity shifts from assumed primordial ties to attachment to the principles of equal treatment and just empowerment within the boundaries of the nation-state. Those ties—in the case of Iran, primarily Shi'ite Islam—will of course continue to be among the salient ingredients of the majority of citizens' sense of self. The relation between Shi'ism and Iranian culture is, however, more subtle and complex than is often assumed. Iranian cultural identity, nationalism, and Shi'ism have existed in a relationship characterized by both tension and complementarity; in recent decades they have come to be mutually reinforcing. Iranian culture must not, however, be reduced to religion; a reductionist and essentialist approach to identity, culture, and religion must be avoided, and none should be construed as monolithic or static. No tradition, religious or otherwise, can survive without reflective reformulation of its values and approaches, intellectual renewal, and adaptation to changing circumstances and the demands of citizens. Many writers have stressed the extent to which Iranian Islam has experienced a process of introspection and change, and also the way in which Islamic precepts have been recast in the language of social protest. But to identify a set of often rigidly narrow principles as Islamic and to assume a facile correlation between them and the behavior of Iranians, and of other Muslims, or to see the lives of all Muslims as in every sense saturated and determined by "Islam," is dangerously simplistic.

In attempting to situate the main themes of this book securely in the broader context of Iranian history over the last 100 years, I have inevitably faced dilemmas about what to include or exclude. I have devoted less space than I ordinarily would have to the important period 1941–1953 because I have treated it at length in other writings. The chapters dealing with the prelude to and aftermath of the revolution of 1978–1979 combine research with personal observation and elements of autobiography. They also involve personal engagement of an intellectual but also emotional nature. I have grappled with the fact that recounting the story of Iran since my student days in Tehran is a voyage of introspection that both defies detachment and demands it.

I have drawn on a variety of archival and other primary sources and have also consulted many secondary works. In my notes I refer mainly to primary sources and less frequently to secondary ones, but this approach reflects the constraints of space and not any lack of appreciation for the large number of existing scholarly works of high quality on modern Iran. It also reflects my hope that this book will be accessible to students and general readers as well as to fellow scholars.

While thinking about and writing this book I have benefited from the intellectual support of Iraj Afshar, Abbas Amanat, Ali Amini-Najafi, Mohsen Ashtiany, Daryush Ashuri, Edmund Burke III, Ann Enayat, Mark Gasiorowski, John Gurney, Houshang Keshavarz-Sadr, William Roger Louis, Ali Mirzaie, Hossein Modarressi, Roger Owen, the late Mostafa Rahimi, Eugene Rogan, Ehsan Yarshater, and Mahmud Zand-Moqaddam. I would like to record my gratitude to a number of individuals whom I was able to interview before their deaths: most notably, former premier Ali Amini, former ministers Gholam-Hosein Sadiqi and Ali Ardalan (who allowed me access to his collection of documents), parliamentarians Karim Sanjabi and Mozaffar Baqa'i, academic Mehdi Haeri-Yazdi, and ambassador Sir Denis Wright, who also made some of his personal papers available to me and graciously responded to my queries. I would also like to thank Nosratollah Khazeni, a high-ranking member of the office of the prime minister under Mohammad Mosaddeq, former ambassador Iraj Amini, and prominent civic-nationalist activists Houshang Keshavarz-Sadr, Hosein

Mahdavi, and Amir Pichdad. The staff of several archives and libraries in Iran, Britain, and the United States deserve special thanks. For his friendship, I owe Jamshid Marvasti more gratitude than he can imagine.

My colleagues in the History Department at the University of Connecticut, particularly Richard D. Brown, Roger Buckley, Frank Costigliola, John A. Davis, Robert Gross, and Shirley Roe, have been exceptionally supportive over the years. Various grants from the university's Research Foundation and the Office of the Chancellor enabled me to travel, conduct research, and devote time to completion of this book. An intellectually enriching year as a fellow of the Humanities Institute at the University of Connecticut (2004–2005) gave me an invaluable opportunity to move forward in my research, thinking, and writing. I would like to thank the institute's director, Richard Brown, associate director Françoise Dussart, and other fellows for their support, encouragement, and friendship.

I consider myself fortunate to have had the opportunity to get to know and to learn from scholars and teachers such as the late Hamid Enayat, John Gurney, the late Albert Hourani, and Roger Owen. While a graduate student at Oxford, I counted among my intellectually formative experiences—and pleasures—participating in inspiring seminars organized by Steven Lukes at Balliol College, and attending lectures by thinkers such as Charles Taylor and visiting scholars such as Jürgen Habermas and the late Clifford Geertz.

I wish to thank the editorial staff of Harvard University Press for their help throughout the book's production; Kathleen McDermott, Editor, History and Social Sciences, was steadily encouraging and supportive; I am indebted to Christine Thorsteinsson, and particularly to Ann Hawthorne for her meticulous editorial attention to the manuscript. I am also grateful to the anonymous readers engaged by the Press for their helpful comments.

My deepest gratitude goes to my family, whose patience and unfailing emotional and intellectual support sustained me over the long period of writing this book. My wife read many drafts with inexhaustible good humor and offered invaluable help. My two sons, both avid readers, shared with me their passion for words and for nuances of meaning, and eagerly awaited the moment when I could spend more time with them.

Without all the generous advice, support, and encouragement I have received while working on this book, it would have been poorer. Needless to say, I alone am responsible for how I have interpreted what I have learned from others and for any shortcomings of this work.

# Note on Transliteration

The system of transliteration used in this book is a modified version of the one used by *Encyclopaedia Iranica*, minus diacritical marks except an apostrophe (') in the middle of certain words to indicate a *hamza* or the letter *ain*.

# The Quest for
# Democracy
# in Iran

# Prologue:
# In Search of a National Covenant

*What experience and history teach is this—that people and governments
never have learned anything from history, or acted on principles.*
　　　　　　　—G. W. F. Hegel, *The Philosophy of History*

*The constitutional movement was carried forward by two groups: the elite,
who rarely acted with integrity, and the ordinary folks, who rarely acted
without it.*
　　　　　　　—Ahmad Kasravi, *Tarikh-e mashruteh-ye Iran*

　　　　The political history of Iran in the last 100 years has been an intricate
narrative of struggle to craft a modern, institutionalized, impersonal, and
accountable state—a legally constituted state whose legitimacy would rest
on meaningful constitutional representative procedures. The aspirations
permeating this struggle involved the conviction that by embodying popular sovereignty the state would be more committed to promoting the public
interest and more empowered to safeguard national sovereignty. Despite
the Iranian Constitutional Revolution of 1906, the persistence of authoritarian rule, albeit intermittently in retreat, provoked a crisis of legitimacy, and
of representation in its broad political as well as sociocultural sense, which
marred Iranian public life. The Constitutional Revolution marked the genesis not only of this crisis but also of a resilient movement to overcome it. In
the following pages I explore the contours of constitutional politics since its
emergence, the obstacles it encountered, the aspirations it nurtured, and
the underlying causes of the political malaise that it attempted to eradicate.

I

Devoting special attention to the Pahlavi era (1925–1979), I investigate the domestic and external factors that permitted and facilitated the ascendancy of authoritarian rule. Following an analysis of the revival of constitutional politics (1941–1953), I focus on the changing structure of the Pahlavi state, particularly in the aftermath of the coup of August 1953, and explore the configuration of forces sustaining and opposing the state. Finally, I discuss the constitution—the makeup and structure—of governance and the trajectory of democratic aspirations following the fall of the monarchy in 1979.

As a complex movement for political transformation and adaptation, the Constitutional Revolution embodied both continuity and change. Retention of the monarchy, despite its associations with absolutism, amounted to an affirmation of traditional institutions that could not be easily discarded or replaced. In addition to the monarchy, many old institutions and mores, entrenched hierarchies, the influence of old networks of patronage, of clusters of well-placed notables and senior clerics, persisted. Privileged families continued to dominate the upper echelons of the civil service. In a society with limited urbanization and literacy and an inadequate infrastructure, and in a domestic and international environment that was inhospitable to effective democratic self-rule, authoritarian power could be apparently displaced but not radically uprooted. Inevitably pulled in opposite directions by the emotional weight and visceral grip of tradition and the intellectual allure of modernity—with its Promethean ethos, inspirational notions, and novel ideas about social organization—the political and public culture evolved a hybrid character as adaptation and resistance uneasily coexisted. An old self-conscious civic culture geared to inner virtues and cultivated manners, and underpinned by traditionally sanctioned internalized values, persisted alongside new modes of conduct informed by modern values. The result was a dynamic intermixture of the old and the new, the renewed and the invented, the indigenous and the borrowed.

In the long run, the impulses for change proved more appealing and significant. The Constitutional Revolution marked a break with the past in crucial respects. A new conception of citizens as bearers of equal political and civil rights began to emerge. A novel understanding of governance, sovereignty, law, justice and fairness, protest and redress, nation and national self-reliance, the separation of powers, and governmental accountability was explicitly or implicitly embodied in the Constitution and became increasingly salient in the culture of politics. The growth of print culture facilitated this process. Change was not confined to the political arena, but permeated the social and cultural realms. How people thought about society and the vocabulary of both sociopolitical transformation and analysis were gradually transformed. A wide spectrum of coexisting ideologies, a restless associational life, a shift in conceptions of the private and the public spheres and in perceptions of the state and its duties pervaded the political arena. The very idea of a constitution as a foundational covenant of a national community and a legally binding framework for decent governance became an indelible component of Iranian political life.

Through its institutions, rituals, and public emblems—elections, parliamentary acts and debates, the press, political and civic associations—the Constitution became a crucial signifier of change as well as its catalyst. The constitutional demystification of monarchy meant that the shahs could no longer claim to be shadows of God on earth, fully entitled to their patrimonial fiefdom. They were pronounced to be in effect no more than ceremonial appendages to the constitutional order. Their refusal to abide by their prescribed role was resented and whenever possible strongly opposed. As the source and bearers of sovereignty, collectively empowered to determine the country's political destiny, the people and their uncoerced consent became the basis of legitimacy. Regardless of the extent of its realization, this proved to be the most far-reaching, emblematic, and resonating legacy of the Constitutional Revolution, persisting beyond the revolution of 1978–1979 and becoming a canonical principle difficult to ignore. Kings, and oligarchs of any description, even self-appointed custodians of the public good, were obliged to pay homage to it. Anyone in a formal position of political leadership, if not freely elected by popular vote or validly and democratically mandated by the people or their representatives, was widely perceived as illegitimate and a usurper of office.

On the practical level, the political arrangements envisaged by the constitutionalists involved a bureaucratically viable centralized state capable of safeguarding and developing the national community but unable to expropriate the citizens' political life. The state thus envisioned had to be an orderly, equitable, and decent polity responsive to public expectations and demands, and at the same time sensitive to cultural, moral, and religious sensibilities. The constitutionalists faced the enormous challenge of forging a political system in which the imperatives of promoting freedom and order, accountability and authority, socioeconomic development and political and civic vibrancy, were delicately balanced and reconciled, and the calamities of dictatorship, disorder, and stalemate avoided. They had to enhance the viability of the constitutional framework and reduce its vulnerability to the onslaught of forces and trends inimical to it. They needed to reconcile effective political leadership with deliberative decision making and to ensure that the idea of the separation of the branches of government did not conflict with their necessary coordination. They had to create an executive vested with sufficient institutional authority to act independently of the royal court without intruding upon the prerogatives of the parliament.

Of the three branches of government envisaged by the constitutionalists—inspired by the legacy of Montesquieu—most attention was understandably paid to the parliament, while the institutional foundations and authority of the executive remained ill defined. The political system thereby introduced was a parliamentary one in which the directly elected parliament was supposed to act as the pivotal institution, while the cabinet, chosen by the parliament but without any sustained organizational links with a majority of parliamentarians, lacked security of tenure or effective authority and could easily be unseated by the parliament or eclipsed and manipulated by the court. If, instead of a constitutional monarchy, a republican system had been set up with a directly elected president as the head of the executive branch, legitimately empowered to govern, the crisis of governance afflicting Iranian politics could to a large extent have been avoided, and the emergence of a viable democratic polity facilitated.

From the very outset the constitutionalists encountered serious difficulties in their key goal of recasting the monarchy as a *constitutional* entity reconciled with popular sovereignty and the rule of law. This undertaking proved to be perpetually elusive; monarchy remained essentially irreconcilable with meaningful constitutionalism. As a political regime, monarchism, together with its underlying discursive apparatus, retained much of its preconstitutional prerogatives and acquired considerably greater military and political power. Contrary to the prevailing assumptions, monarchy was not merely a notional form of government but an entrenched institutional complex closely linked to loci of privilege and sustained by patronage. Regardless of its incumbent, the monarchy was bound to dominate, if not undermine, the nascent, institutionally fragile parliamentary order, and take advantage of or exacerbate the disarray of constitutionalist forces.

Monarchism entailed royal supremacy unhindered by constitutional constraints. Needing to justify or render palatable its defiance of the Constitution, from the 1920s on the monarchy would seek to act as the chief promoter of modernization. However, by subverting democratic politics it came to symbolize politically what in a different context has been dubbed "regressive modernity."[1] Socially, too, the monarchy, representing hierarchy, unmerited or unearned privilege, ascriptive values, and archaic mores, was incongruent with the culture of modernity. Nor was it consonant with the notion of popular sovereignty, which entailed a republican undercurrent, albeit tenaciously occluded by the royalist-clerical subculture and the nexus of vested interests sustaining it. Clearly, a contradiction lingered at the heart of Iranian modernity: the broadly egalitarian ethos of the Constitutional Revolution also affirmed the inherently inegalitarian monarchy.

The protagonists of constitutional arrangements in Iran were not able, and had insufficient opportunity, to resolve the numerous problems they faced. The Constitution, an outcome of an intricate process of compromise, inevitably reflecting the diverse demands of powerful sociopolitical forces, was ambiguous. It was meant to be a code of fundamental rights, a blueprint for establishing the rule of law, and a framework for viable governance; yet from the outset it became a contested document. Most ardent constitutionalists saw it as unequivocally sanctioning representative government. Monarchists saw it as an impediment to effective rule, ignored it, or portrayed and used it as primarily affirming the centrality of the monarchy. Some saw it as a malleable set of rules, while for others it acquired the status of a reified and rigid code. Inevitably, fear of subversion of the Constitution or its radical revision was never far from the surface. Its democratically minded proponents engaged in a prolonged struggle to define and defend it, to retrieve its spirit, and above all to establish a measure of consensus as to its contours. Their efforts were ultimately thwarted.

Reza Shah (1925–1941) bypassed the Constitution without formally tampering with its key clauses. His son, Mohammad Reza Shah (1941–1979), relentlessly seeking to enhance his prerogatives, arranged for the Constitution's amendment through a proto-coup in 1949, and thereby acquired the right to dissolve the parliament. To most constitutionalists this represented a dangerous step in formally rolling back the constitutional objective of harnessing the monarchy. The royalist ascendancy was reaffirmed as a result of the coup of August 1953, the fourth coup to be launched against the fragile constitutional order by its opponents. In a reversal of the constitutionalists' objectives, from 1953 until 1979 monarchism increasingly came to define constitutionalism.

Even if blessed with a better-crafted constitution, in the absence of permissive structural conditions advocates for a constitutional order lacked the means of implementing it. The questions of how monarchs could be obliged to assume essentially ceremonial roles, or be plausibly expected to exercise benevolent moral authority without succumbing to the temptation of abusing their privileged position, remained unanswered. Some constitutionalists gave in to disillusionment, even to cynicism. Discerning constitutionalists could not have naively assumed that it would be easy to harness the monarchy, yet they continued to maintain that a viable constitutional polity in which the monarchy had a role was not only desirable but possible. The consolidation of such a polity required time, effort, a process of adaptation, patient trial and error. It needed, and also generated, political experience and maturity. The monarchists persisted, however, in regarding the country as unprepared for constitutional governance. Occasionally, when forced to do so by circumstances, they tolerated a controlled measure of representation. Though retaining constitutional rituals, they refused to acknowledge that legitimacy could be generated only through the constitutional-democratic process. This refusal precipitated prolonged periods of crisis; it provoked the latent or open resistance of the politically disenfranchised public and corroded the vestiges of the monarchy's authority.

The widening gulf between ardent constitutionalists and committed monarchists in one way or another sealed the fates of all four monarchs of the post-1906 era. Mohammad Ali Shah Qajar (1907–1909) was removed and forced into exile as a result of his efforts to roll back constitutionalism. His son, Ahmad Shah (1914–1925), the last reigning Qajar, and his successor, Reza Shah, the first Pahlavi monarch, also died in exile as a result of factors related to the ongoing crisis of constitutionalism. Mohammad Reza Shah, the second and last Pahlavi king, was overthrown and exiled following a revolutionary upheaval, largely as a result of his persistent and conspicuous disregard of constitutionalism and its underlying aspirations. Undoubtedly the political conduct of the monarchs was significantly affected by their traits of character. More importantly, the monarchy remained institutionally and structurally geared to the perpetuation of monarchical rule. The weakness of the constitutional arrangements, which both reflected and contributed to the institutional strength of the monarchy, helped to encourage and facilitate the monarchs' autocratic proclivities. Such proclivities were also underpinned by the persistent authoritarian components of the political culture, and by foreign imperial determination to maintain hegemony in Iran.

The constitutionalists faced their greatest challenge in the task of reinventing the state as both authoritative and accountable. The state structure that emerged after the Constitutional Revolution resisted the demands of accountability. It was eventually able to deflect social pressures and public expectations, particularly the civic and political aspirations of a nascent modern middle class that sustained the vibrant civil society of the pre-Pahlavi era. By the early 1930s those segments of the middle class involved in trade, finance, and industrial enterprises became economically and politically subordinated to the state. Other middle-class elements also increasingly became employees of the state or subject to its control. This situation, particularly in the economic field, was relaxed in the 1940s with the revival of parliamentary politics, which allowed a cluster of political forces, including those representing the middle classes, to reclaim or establish their constituencies. Political parties, trade unions, and associations emerged, along with a lively civic and secular culture; but the notables also reclaimed their networks of kinship and patronage, while the court remained able to play a crucial political role. After the coup of 1953, the political emasculation of the middle classes and the forces representing them, such as the Mosaddeqists, gained momentum. Political society, or a space for political activity and debate immune from the illegitimate interventions of the state, began to erode. By the 1960s foreign support and oil wealth gave the regime considerable leverage for purchasing elite loyalty and for cronyism and co-optation. As a result the state enjoyed virtual independence from domestic social forces and reliance on tax revenues, and was thereby able to pursue its development agenda, further subordinate the middle classes, and ignore or dismiss the political and civic aspirations and demands of the public.

The Pahlavi state under Mohammad Reza Shah was militarily strong but politically precarious; in terms of ideological power it remained particularly weak, unable to justify the Shah's personalized rule in any terms other than professed dedication to socioeconomic reform. Its invocation of the Constitution as synonymous with monarchism, its appeal to the "imperial system" or other invented traditions, and its promise of a "great civilization" failed to furnish it with a sustainable ideological legitimacy. Increasingly identified with the person of the Shah—whose limited capacity for leadership was further corroded by paranoia and hubris—and resting on the connivance of a self-seeking elite, the seemingly invincible Pahlavi regime remained structurally fragile. It failed to mask or normalize its authoritarian paternalism by successfully reinventing itself or by reproducing its contrived counternarrative of reformist beneficence. The unintended and unanticipated consequences of its socially dislocating and culturally insensitive policies would come to provoke deep disaffection among the disenfranchised citizenry.

Evidently the constraints of constitutionalism, no matter how eroded, and the rhetoric of the rule of law, human rights, and norms of modern civilization could not be entirely disregarded. The authoritarian monarchy under Mohammad Reza Shah was not as resolutely absolutist as it appeared, yet it revealed little structural capacity for credible political reform. Its intransigence toward moderate secular constitutionalist forces paved the way for increasingly radicalized leftist and Islamist opponents. Growing oppositional radicalism in turn helped to diminish the regime's capacity for timely accommodation. The specific configuration of authoritarian rule, particularly in the last fifteen years of the Pahlavi dynasty, rendered it essentially unreformable. The state showed itself to be devoid of the structural capacity to tolerate, manage, and survive a credible level of political liberalization. Its vulnerability demonstrably increased as its opponents formed a coalition of diverse forces united primarily by hostility to the monarchy. This hostility was relentlessly preached by Ayatollah Khomeini, a charismatic populist leader myopically written off by the regime.

But it was not merely the leadership of Khomeini that transformed and immeasurably broadened the movement against the Shah. Authoritarian rule had helped to engender forces whose political genealogy and purpose it failed to comprehend. The role of the lay intelligentsia in opinion formation and even moral leadership had increased thanks to the growth of print culture and a modernist ethos. Such an ethos also invigorated the reactive or countervailing role of the pulpit, which simultaneously attempted to roll back modernity while selectively appropriating it. Lay segments of the educated middle class, having long succumbed to alienation from the regime, instigated a movement of protest that soon engulfed nearly the entire urban population, and in which the Islamist forces gained the upper hand. Charisma, political dexterity, amplified ambiguity, the invocation of laudable ideals—which soon went awry—and an unflinching repudiation of the Shah enabled Khomeini to dominate, if not entrance, the public. Repudiating the Shah was increasingly to be perceived as an affirmation of every noble aspiration that he had quashed; it furnished the *raison d'être* of revolutionary solidarity; it even enabled the Shah's illiberal or antidemocratic opponents to assume a progressive posture. The Shah undoubtedly played a crucial role in the process that culminated in the regime's collapse. He was sometimes compared to Louis XIV, but as it turned out, Louis XVI provided a better comparison. As Emmanuel Le Roy Ladurie observes in the case of the French Revolution: "A despot, enlightened or otherwise, a strong hand and a steady head, might perhaps have delayed (although perhaps not avoided altogether), might have tamed or domesticated the Revolution. Louis XVI, on the other hand, became one of its handmaids; a not entirely involuntary midwife to Revolution."[2]

The fabric of the old regime, and the worldview sustaining it, were torn apart as a result of the revolution of 1978–1979, which despite its subsequent trajectory began as a massive endeavor to accomplish what the earlier revolution had failed to bring about. Given the unmistakably republican and intensely antimonarchist tenor of the revolutionary struggle, the system of governance adopted after the fall of the Shah could only be republican. However, the spirit of a monarchical style of domination persisted. To many, hereditary monarchy was replaced by an avowedly nonhereditary oligarchy—a regime with little regal aura and splendor, with more subdued paraphernalia and rituals of investiture, but no less monarchic in approach. Indeed it radically transcended the mundane claims of the monarchy by invoking divine sanction. The "Guardianship of the Islamic Jurist," the arcane institution that replaced the monarchy, was formally empowered to wield far greater power than its predecessor, combining military, political, and ideological-spiritual powers. Nevertheless, despite relentless suppression, efforts to reverse the drastic shrinkage of popular sovereignty and retrieve the republican objectives of the revolution continued to grow in scale and intensity.

Before the revolution of 1978–1979, religion had been overshadowed by a process of secularization spearheaded by a politically repressive but socially permissive state. Later, social liberties were drastically curtailed, equal rights for women denounced, and politics eclipsed by a state-enforced politicized religiosity. Seeking to unravel secularity, the revolution's heirs attempted to eradicate the line of demarcation between the private and the public spheres. Developments after 1979 were not congenial to a flourishing civil society, which nevertheless received a strong impetus from social forces refusing to submit to a highly intrusive state. The appeal and urgency of democracy increased, as did the prerequisites for its eventual success. The revolutionary process had inevitably engendered ideologies, interest groups, movements, and political forces with large constituencies, a state of affairs that made authoritarian control difficult to sustain. Charismatic leadership, ideological power, unhesitant suppression, and exploitation of the exigencies of the war that engulfed the country from 1980 to 1988 held the regime together, but in the interest of self-preservation it was forced to relent in the face of uncontainable social pressures.

In crucial respects the outcome of the revolution both dashed and boosted democratic aspirations, as the regime felt itself unable either to disown or to embrace them. Such aspirations could not be indefinitely ignored, but the regime failed to develop a capacity to accommodate them. It feared the prospect of losing political control, its hold on the sources of wealth maintaining its privileged nexus of bureaucratic functionaries and retainers, and its vast complex of patronage. Only the naive or the deluded could underestimate the Islamic regime's capacity for reinventing itself, resorting to force and fraud or mobilizing its base of support, sustained by belief or material reward or both to keep itself afloat. Yet in their refusal to embrace an inclusive politics and go beyond a restricted and flawed form of participatory arrangements, the rulers could not suppress the growing public conviction that the Islamic regime was as impervious to real political reform as its predecessor had been. This conviction augured ill for the oligarchs, particularly in the context of the demographic transformation of Iranian society, increasing literacy, a broadened culture of nationalism, new means of communication, and the expectations and demands of the young and the growing middle class. Despite all the odds, an irrepressible public sphere and a resilient civil society remained poised to move toward an inclusive representative democracy.

Charting the trajectory of the quest for democracy in Iran largely involves an explanation of the revolution that overthrew the monarchy. In analyzing the concept of revolution, the English political theorist John Dunn makes two points: first, "the most important of twentieth-century revolutions have gained their importance not from the undeniable drama of their commencement but from the scale of their long-term consequences"; second, "the key experience which turned the term 'revolution' into a central category of modern political discourse was the unexpected collapse of an absolutist order of some longevity in the face of the angry political energy of its subjects."[3] The pertinence of Dunn's observations is borne out by an analysis in the following chapters of the process and consequences of the collapse of the Iranian monarchy. I first explore the sociogenesis of the revolution, by which, following the German-British historical sociologist Norbert Elias, I mean the processes of social development and transformation of Iranian society that paved the way for the revolution.

This study combines a thematic with a chronological, and a problem-oriented with a narrative approach. The explanatory framework I employ is pluralistic; it rejects monocausal explanations. It is both structural and interpretive, mindful of causes as well as reasons and meanings. I explore the configuration of authoritarian rule, which in the Iranian context denotes a system of governance favoring, and seeking to enforce, unquestioning obedience to the authority of the government, particularly that of the Shah— or, after 1979, the Leader—at the expense of a meaningful constitutional process, the rule of law, democratic deliberation, and political and civic liberties. Much of my analysis focuses on the conduct of the rulers and their key supporters and opponents, although I do not intend to reduce a highly complex history to the foibles of a few men. Nor do I ignore vexed theoretical issues pertaining to agency and structure, subscribe to methodological individualism, or disregard fundamental structural factors or circumstances that constrain or enable well-placed individuals. Following Max Weber, I view society as consisting of a delicately balanced multiplicity of opposing forces. Such a balance can be undermined in favor of a certain outcome by a variety of structural and contingent factors—a war, a revolution, a severe economic downturn, a charismatic leader or an inept one.[4] The question of which factor or set of factors should be given greater analytical weight can be answered only in the specific historical circumstances of a particular society.

Far from being a political history in the narrow sense, this book investigates how public alienation, resentment, resistance, and demands for change were articulated or expressed, violently or otherwise, at specific junctures; how the state's indifference to a politics of recognition reduced its capacity to contain public disaffection; how a culture of confrontation between the state and its opponents was reinforced at the expense of a public space of dialogue. I also explore how structures of rule are underpinned: what their institutional foundations are; what factors, whether domestic sociopolitical forces or foreign interests, help to sustain them; and what the mechanisms involved in this process of sustaining are. Dealing with such issues clearly impinges on the question of power. Influenced by the English social theorist Steven Lukes, I conceive of power both as observable coercion and as barely visible machinations, inculcations, and manipulations that result in the subjects' not realizing how or to what extent their wants and expectations, their perceptions of their interests, and indeed their consciousness are shaped by it.[5] Unlike Lukes, I deal mainly with the power of the state or organized collectivities, but find his conception of power helpful in making sense of how certain issues and agendas are promoted and others demoted or occluded, how claims are advanced about what is in the best interest of the public or the nation, and who is best capable—if not mandated by history or God—of determining and promoting those interests.

At the time of writing, the U.S. government claims to want to promote democracy in the Middle East. In Iran, efforts to this end began 100 years ago, and one of the major factors militating against them was imperialism, whether Russian, British, or, later, American. In the early 1950s, under the auspices of the British and U.S. secret services, a protracted campaign was launched to thwart Iranian democratic aspirations, undermine struggles to promote Iranian national sovereignty, and roll back efforts to harness the authoritarian impulses of the monarch. The campaign involved insidious machinations to manipulate, exploit, and undermine Iranian democratic institutions and procedures. The primary aim was to retain control over Iranian oil and to ensure that Iran remained a dependent state of the Western alliance. It is my contention that the campaign that culminated in the coup of August 1953 crucially reinvigorated and indeed transformed the waning Pahlavi monarchy, enabling it to defy democratic principles and neutralize constitutional struggles. Without the coup Iran might well have escaped the cataclysmic later revolution. The long nourishment of Pahlavi authoritarianism by foreign imperial interests deeply affected the Iranian culture of politics. Iranians have good reason to be wary of foreign interventions and intentions, real or perceived meddling, and sententious pronouncements about the virtues of democracy.

The rhetoric of "democracy" has recently become a replica of the Cold War–era discourse of "the free world." Certain advocates of the U.S. system of rule have self-righteously presented it as the culmination of history, an ideal model to be emulated by the whole of humanity. Conversely, critics have viewed the paradigm of democracy in the United States as falling far short of the ideals it claims to uphold. The prevailing political establishment in the United States, its critics maintain, privileges market freedom more than political and civil liberties, possessive individualism more than civic interdependence. Conceiving of liberty in a narrowly negative sense, it dedicates few resources to its citizens' self-development. It thrives on public apathy, routinely panders to special interests, and tolerates lucrative networking; it abhors egalitarian and distributive agendas, and encourages a culture of greed that reduces social interaction to business transactions. The neoliberal democracy as practiced in the United States will not work in societies with strong collectivist or communitarian cultures, where notions of social justice continue to resonate with large segments of the populace. Moreover, force and coercion or an assumed moral influence sustained by military and economic power is not an appropriate means to promote democracy. Nor is it plausible to take for granted the susceptibility of an emerging democracy to undue U.S. influence. Invoking the discourse of human rights as self-evidently represented by the West, or cynically using it to bully unfriendly regimes while ignoring it in the process of propping up friendly ones, is counterproductive. In an age of more intensely mobilized collective identities and solidarities—nationalist, religious, ethnic—the residual dreams of empire are bound to be resisted.

The sovereignty of nations remains the only framework in which a viable system of international law can be sustained. Yet human beings now live in an interconnected world in which physical borders and cultural boundaries have become porous, individual autonomy has become a defining feature of modernity, and normative standards of civility have increasingly assumed a cross-cultural character. In such a world, accountability has become both domestic and global; states can no longer invoke the principle of sovereignty to ill-treat their citizens with impunity or to ignore fundamental rights that are constitutive of the very notion of a person and of civilized humanity. Democratic self-rule within the framework of a rational political covenant has to be inclusive, affirm as wide a range of entitlements as possible, and view all citizens as entitled to equal respect and concern. It must also consider genuine commitment to human rights and social justice as emblematic of democracy and integral to its legitimation. Political democracy in a minimal sense cannot involve anything less than citizens' having the ability and the opportunity freely to elect those who govern and represent them from among real alternatives offered by those competing for the popular vote. It is a mode of politics characterized less by majority rule than by the protection of minorities. It creates an environment in which a variety of values, aspirations, and interests can legitimately coexist and represent themselves in the sociopolitical field.[6]

The issue of the feasibility of democratic rule in societies such as Iran has sometimes been approached on grounds other than the specific historical circumstances of these societies. Orientalists such as Bernard Lewis, and even social theorists such as Ernest Gellner, have considered "Muslim" society inhospitable to any form of government other than the autocratic. According to Lewis: "That there is a pre-disposition to autocratic government among Muslim peoples is clear enough," though their "inherent incapacity for any other is yet to be proved."[7] In the same spirit, for Gellner, "Muslims do not seem too outraged if the control of the state remains a matter of conflict between rival patronage networks, or if political loyalty remains personal, rather than being directed towards abstract institutions and principles, which survive temporary power-holders."[8] Such essentialist generalizations are not only empirically untenable and historically reductive but can be construed as culturalist fallacies tantamount to stating that the problem with Muslims is that *they are Muslim*. Such assumptions purport to explain not only why a large portion of humanity has failed to enjoy the benefits of democracy or decent governance but also why it should continue to do so. The explanation they provide is inattentive to the specific and complex histories of different "Islamic" societies.

Regarding Iran, some commentators, both Iranian and foreign, have derided the ideals of the Constitutional Revolution as either opaque or half-hearted, or as impractical and premature. Some have dismissed interludes of hectic parliamentary politics as periods of chaos. Others have maintained a simplistic antithetical contrast between a perfect democracy—which exists nowhere—and a gratuitously authoritarian rule. The reality is that all democratic societies have evolved over time, have started with a haphazard and limited form of participation, and have encountered numerous obstacles. The insouciant royalist apologists of authoritarian rule discredited the very procedures that were meant to lend legitimacy to the political process, and cynically invoked such procedures when it suited them. The clerical-Islamist rulers have maintained a truncated form of procedural participation, have not publicly disparaged representative institutions, and have paid lip service to accountability and transparency; at the same time they have resisted a freely competitive electoral politics and have shown little appreciation of the core components of real republican governance and of the civic virtues that it requires and nurtures. They have ignored the public resonance of a politics of recognition dedicated to inclusive civic and political egalitarianism and meaningful republican sovereignty.

In the modern world, every state is purportedly committed to sustaining a secure environment for a fulfilling and dignified life for its citizens. Every state claims to strive to enable its citizens to engage in endeavors aimed at promoting national well-being and overcoming sociopolitical, economic, and natural predicaments. In such endeavors, meaningful sociocultural, managerial, and cognitive resources and skills are fused. A state that enjoys the support of its people is more capable of sustaining its claims. It does not appear stronger than society or at odds with it; it is committed to justifying its actions rationally and transparently, and to fostering political, civic, and cultural institutions as well as a healthy and viable associational life. Such a state has a far better chance of creating real conviction that it is effective, competent, deservedly in power, and legitimately so; it can present itself as demonstrably capable not of suppression and exploitation but of dedication to the common good.

In Iran, as in any society with strong democratic aspirations, without the inclusive involvement of citizens and the real public engagement of politically discerning and skilled citizens, politics will continue to lack a clear direction and a reasoned sense of purpose. In the absence of democratic legitimacy and rational political and bureaucratic norms, it will continue to be marred by an incubating or full-blown crisis of authority. Deluded by illusions of cohesion or strength, the rulers will miss one opportunity after another until it is too late. In nondemocratic regimes, failings and errors are solely the responsibility of the rulers, whereas in a democratic society the burden of responsibility is shared by the rulers and those who have elected them. Representative democracies can degenerate into favoring a dispersed and depoliticized citizenry; they all fall far short of the ideals they claim to embody. Yet, no matter how unsatisfactory, they possess greater capacity and resources for self-correction; their failings are fewer than those of feasible alternatives. As thinkers such as John Rawls and Jürgen Habermas have argued, only a politically liberal and deliberative democracy can constitute a rational mode of governance.[9]

# Part I

# Constituting
# a National Community

## (1906–1953)

The safety of the people, requireth further, from him, or them that have the sovereign power, that justice be equally administered to all degrees of people; that is, that as well as the rich and mighty, as poor and obscure persons, may be righted of the injuries done to them; so as the great, may have no greater hope of impunity, when they do violence, dishonor, or any injury to the meaner sort, than when one of these, does the like to one of them: for in this consisteth equity; to which, as being a precept of the law of nature, a sovereign is as much a subject, as any of the meanest of his people.

—Thomas Hobbes, *Leviathan*

The political community monopolizes the legitimate application of violence for its coercive apparatus and is gradually transformed into an institution for the protection of rights.

—Max Weber, *Economy and Society*

# 1

# Constitutional Trial and Error

## Capacities and Constraints

The sociopolitical processes that culminated in the formation of the National Consultative Assembly (referred to here as the parliament or the lower house of parliament) and the adoption of a constitution in the first parliament were inspired by a strong, if insufficiently articulated, desire for the creation of a constitutional representative democracy. In contrast to *estebdad* (despotic rule), *mashruteh* (constitutional rule) denoted more than merely a constitutional form of government. This connotation is borne out by the antiautocratic, modern, and cautiously secular content and subtext of the Constitution, as well as the deliberations of the first parliament, not to mention the public debate at large.[1]

In spite of the imprecision, inconsistencies, and inadequacies of the Constitution, which reflected the circumstances of its genesis and the constraints to which its authors were subject—particularly a desire to deflect or minimally accommodate royal and clerical objections—monarchical prerogatives were pronounced to be essentially ceremonial. Monarchs were not politically accountable and therefore could not meaningfully exercise executive authority. Such authority was vested in the government, which was responsible to the parliament. The parliament, composed of representatives chosen through competitive elections, would be legitimately empowered to legislate and determine policy, which would be executed by the government. The judiciary, institutionally infused with a secular tenor, would be independent of the legislative and executive branches of the government, and the political and civil rights and duties of the citizens, as well as their equality before the law, would be guaranteed. In short, the legitimacy of the state would rest primarily on democratic validation.

There were, of course, fundamental problems that could not be easily addressed: How would the shahs be constrained to comply with their constitutional role? How was the political authority of the prime minister and the cabinet to be secured vis-à-vis both the court and the legislature? How was a system of checks and balances or institutionalized legal restraints that could avoid stalemate and paralysis to be established? How was a structurally secure and authoritative state, committed to the promised rights and liberties of citizens, to be constitutionally created and sustained? The Constitution itself offered little help in addressing or overcoming these and similar problems bedeviling the nascent Iranian movement toward constitutionalism. Its ardent proponents perceived it as marking a rupture with the past and ushering in a new era: in place of subjects with mere duties and obligations, citizens with rights and entitlements would exercise sovereignty through their elected representatives in the parliament, which would serve as the chief locus of the constitutional polity. The Constitution stipulated that the parliament alone was responsible for authoritative interpretation of laws—and, by implication, the Constitution itself. In the face of contrary pressures from forces opposed to and supportive of constitutionalism, and fearing possible future tampering with the Constitution, its authors had provided no specific procedures for its amendment. The resolution of disagreements regarding seemingly inconsistent clauses remained problematic. Moreover, the Constitution failed to invest the executive branch with a measure of authority commensurate with its tasks.

More significantly, without the structural prerequisites and permissive conditions, democratic aspirations and legalistic blueprints could not easily be translated into functioning arrangements. A hierarchical society, with a deeply embedded consciousness of status and rank, would find it difficult to reconcile itself with democratic political egalitarianism. The predominantly rural and pastoral-nomadic makeup of the population, widespread illiteracy, and the vulnerability of peasants and nomads to landowning notables, chieftains, and government officials, whether civilian or military, militated against meaningful political participation. A politically informed citizenry or urban middle class capable of creating and sustaining a democratic polity could emerge only gradually. Political experience and prudence and civic responsibility and pride could not develop without sustained practice.

Those with a vested interest in denigrating or undermining the fledgling deliberative procedures depicted minor obstacles as insurmountable impediments. They portrayed the diatribes and clamor of journalists, activists, and parliamentarians as endangering political order, if not the territorial integrity of the country or the very moral fabric of society. Those whose privileges were threatened by the erosion of traditional political restraints sought to arouse popular anxieties by capitalizing on any real or perceived abuse of freedom. Such abuses often manifested themselves in vitriolic outbursts in the press, which at the same time appealed to the underprivileged. It was also possible to portray the requirements of an effective, bureaucratically centralized state, capable of maintaining order and suppressing local rebels and bandits, as incongruent with the inevitably slow parliamentary processes. More immediately, the authoritarian royalist subculture and the monarchy's intrinsic penchant for autocracy exacerbated the undeniable but by no means insuperable shortcomings of the parliamentary institutions and procedures. Not surprisingly these shortcomings would invariably be invoked to further strengthen the monarchy.

For more than forty of the seventy-three years of constitutional monarchy in Iran, the spirit of democratic constitutionalism was overshadowed and hampered by monarchism; the remaining period amounted to a prolonged crisis of political authority and sovereignty as the monarchy relentlessly circumvented its constitutionally prescribed role. The monarchy's institutional strength and persistence enhanced its opportunity to foster loyalty or subservience to the crown, promote a court-centered system of patronage, and employ a variety of means to control the elite. Whether motivated by strong beliefs or, as is more likely, by pragmatic or opportunistic concerns, large segments of the elite were all too willing to accept and cling to office as little more than servants of the Shah. Having often succumbed to corrosive cynicism, they rarely publicly questioned the monarch's perilous course of action. They played a crucial role in helping to empty constitutionalism of any meaningful content. Foreign powers, too, helped bolster the monarchy; at critical junctures these powers, and more specifically Britain and later the United States, often by directly approaching the royal court rather than precarious governments, reaffirmed and enhanced its influence. Dealing with an autocrat was an easier way of doing business than having to negotiate with heads of governments who were answerable to the parliament and obliged to defer to it.

The parliament, even in barely permissive circumstances, was an institution of tremendous significance. Whenever parliamentary elections were not entirely rigged, or whenever the royal court was incapable of acting assertively, the parliament established itself as a credible forum for public deliberation on national issues, a focus of national loyalty, a vehicle for enhancing political consciousness, a protector of political and civil liberties and rights, the ultimate recourse, and a sanctuary for protesters. Despite vitiating factionalism, rigged elections, and foreign or domestic manipulation and pressure, it was able to establish a large measure of institutional and collective identity. Even when elections were largely fraudulent, the presence of a handful of credible figures could enliven the parliament, enabling it to play an important role in articulating and representing national wants and aspirations.

In the absence of real party politics and in view of the fluidity of its factional alignments, the parliament could not perform its tasks effectively. Other factors also hindered its proper legislative functioning. The quorum specified by the Constitution, requiring the presence of three-quarters of the deputies for a vote to be taken, could easily be prevented by the absence or departure from the chamber of a fairly small number of deputies. The brief term of office—two years—was also a hindrance, since many deputies spent considerable portions of this period on efforts to secure, or at least not jeopardize, their reelection. In May 1957 a joint session of the parliament and the Senate voted to amend the Constitution, abandoning the original quorum in favor of a simple majority of those deputies present in the chamber, and extending the term of office to four years. By then, however, eclipsed by monarchism, parliamentary politics had lost much of its vitality.

From its inception the parliament seldom proved capable of sustaining a majority stable enough to provide cabinets with consistent support, with the result that many cabinets sought foreign or royal backing or both. Enjoying no reliable and effective ideological or organizational link with the parliament, self-reliant cabinets were too vulnerable to function successfully. A small but vocal parliamentary group could significantly affect, and sometimes effectively disrupt, the operation of the parliament, which was also susceptible to a variety of outside pressures.

Press freedom was integrally linked with the continued vitality of parliamentary politics. Existing conceptions of free expression—often verging on the absence of rules—were, however, rarely informed by a developed understanding of civic responsibility. Inadequate laws regulating press freedom and the grudges, narrow agendas, and vested interests of individuals or groups that the press largely represented often resulted in sensational invective, disinformation, and malicious propaganda that harmed the parliamentary arrangements. Nor were these arrangements immune to the opposition of radical or traditionalist and right-wing forces. The attitude of radical left-wing activists to parliamentary democracy was predominantly utilitarian and their support for it often largely tactical. They regarded it as dominated by the upper classes and as serving their interests to the detriment of the subjugated masses. Traditionalist and right-wing religious forces, on the other hand, tended to view a parliament endowed with full legislative authority as incompatible with Islam, likely to erode traditional restraints and promote uncontrollable liberty, which they often confused with libertinism. They abhorred political and civic egalitarianism and feared secularism and communism. Many other right-wing and conservative groups, as well as royalists, regarded parliamentary governance as similarly distasteful, contrary to native traditions, susceptible to demagoguery, and likely to result in republicanism, anarchy, communism, and territorial disintegration.

The political culture that accompanied the erratic experiment with parliamentary democracy in Iran failed to nurture sufficiently internalized modern civic virtues and a reflective, self-confident liberal and tolerant ethos. The state continued to be mistrusted, viewed negatively, avoided if possible. Politics primarily denoted deception and mendacity geared to the pursuit of personal or narrow gains. It was rarely perceived as pertaining to collective cooperation for improving the quality of public life, to identifying and promoting the common good. No large disciplined political parties with elaborate programs for action, dedicated to the realization of liberal democratic ideals, emerged. Such ideals were opposed from both the left and the right as well as by foreign imperial interests. The modern urban middle class remained ideologically fragmented and politically emasculated. The vested interests of the privileged classes associated with the court militated against the effective rule of law, democratic accountability, and civic and political egalitarianism.

Yet even at the peak of authoritarian rule, the public spirit remained unbroken; beneath the shadow of the apparatuses of coercion a boisterous counterculture of resistance persisted. It expressed itself deftly and in a variety of ways—from positive acts of defiance, such as strikes or refusal to vote despite official pressure, to negative but no less potent gestures such as rebuffing official propaganda or mocking those in power. Whenever there was a tangible relaxation in the intensity of repression, the level of interest in establishing associations, societies, parties, and newspapers and in voicing opposition to tyranny was remarkable. These collective endeavors may have seemed fissiparous, maximalist, or naively unrealistic, and their protagonists may not have proffered readily practical solutions to the country's ills. Yet there was little doubt that their advocacy of change and rejection of authoritarian rule resonated with the public. Resuscitating democratic governance along the contours envisaged by the protagonists of the Constitutional Revolution remained a potent ideal; those who sincerely advocated it retained public support and respect. With the persistence of authoritarian rule, however, the disenfranchised public was eventually left with no effective alternative and little choice but to turn against what it widely perceived to be the ultimate culprit—not only the Shah, but the very system which he unmistakably symbolized—the deeply vacuous "constitutional" monarchy.

## Why a Constitutional Revolution?

Iran at the turn of the twentieth century had a population of barely ten million, some 20 percent of which was urban; the rest consisted of rural and pastoral-nomadic communities sparsely scattered through a semiarid land. The country was isolated, and forbidding deserts and mountains militated against ease of transportation and communication. Tribal and other decentralizing forces were strong, as were conservative, traditionalist, and clerical constellations opposing innovation and modernization. Most arable lands were irrigated by means of *qanats,* ingenious networks of interconnected

wells needing constant care and repair. The primarily agrarian society of
Iran, characterized by labor-intensive subsistence agriculture, did not generate an adequate surplus for investment purposes, the promotion of industry, or infrastructural projects. Landed and mercantile families, particularly
if associated with the state, enjoyed wealth and privilege, but the Islamic
system of inheritance contributed to the dispersal of wealth. Lower-order
extended families suffered a heavy burden of poverty.

The Qajar dynasty (1786–1925) had reunified the country after a century
of disorder, establishing Tehran as the capital. The authority of the Qajar
rulers remained fragile, however, for they failed to develop an effective administrative structure or a modern army. They lacked the vision and the
will to pursue reforms similar to those adopted in the Ottoman empire and
Egypt. More significantly, the means, conditions, and resources for effective
reform were absent. Attempts at state-sponsored reform remained limited
and were rarely sustained. The remarkable efforts and achievements of the
mid-nineteenth-century chief minister, Mirza Taqi Khan Amir-Kabir, unsettled many vested interests and cost him not only his position but his life.
The configuration of the essentially parasitic state was not conducive to
sustainable reform.

Modern means of communication such as the telegraph and a postal
system were introduced with foreign help, but Iran had to wait until the
later decades of the twentieth century to achieve many essential infrastructural prerequisites of modernity—adequate roads, railroads, a system
of primary and higher education, health and sanitation, a reasonable legal
system. The populace remained vulnerable not only to the often arbitrary
behavior of the rulers, but also to brigandage, disease and epidemics, nar-
cotic addiction, malnutrition, and famine. A devastating famine (1869–1872),
caused by chronic drought and the increasing cultivation of cash crops, particularly opium, resulted in extensive suffering and loss of life. In the absence of adequate roads and means of transportation, crop failure due to
drought or disease often resulted in localized famine. Farmers in certain regions suffered hardship because they could not transport and sell their surplus grain in other areas. "In fact," noted a Qajar politician and diarist as
late as 1918, "Iran's misfortune and lack of prosperity are due to nothing as
much as the absence of roads."[2]

The Qajar dynasty consisted of a vast nepotistic clan that with its retainers and cronies ruled mostly through manipulation and divisive tactics and the exploitation of local conflicts and rivalries. The Qajar rulers' exercise of power was largely arbitrary and personal, yet Orientalist assumptions emphasizing a persistent and unqualified "despotic" tradition in Iran are far from unproblematic. In fact throughout most of the nineteenth century the Qajar rulers' grip on power was tenuous. They had to negotiate their authority intricately in a rough political landscape, remaining constantly mindful of the vested interests of established notables, religious dignitaries, tribal magnates, a host of urban mercantile and other socioeconomic forces, complex networks of patronage, as well as British and Russian imperialism. The Qajar state had to defer, at least tacitly, to powerful forces in society such as the clerics *(ulama)*—a hierocratic group ranging from learned high-ranking divines to local preachers. As guardians, promoters, and scholars of Islam and a socially anchored and traditionally influential estate, the clerics, particularly their more prominent representatives, were among the most politically consequential and the least vulnerable subjects of the state.

Though occasionally blessed with the services of capable chief ministers and other officials, the Qajar state was incapable of engendering a sense of national purpose or an adequate measure of nationwide prosperity, order, and security. Sustained by nepotism and patronage, in the main the Qajar bureaucracy operated informally and through favoritism, bribery, and other abuses of office. Besides the influential women of the harem—most notably the Shah's mother and his favorite wives—the Qajar court consisted largely of sycophantic and superstitious officials who vied ceaselessly for the Shah's attention and conspired against one another and against competent and reform-minded officials. The shahs, "shadows of God on earth," differed in capability, intelligence, and piety but were invariably pleasure-loving, insular veterans of the harem, interested in poetry and art but devoid of any clear understanding of the rapidly changing world outside the confines of their sheltered domain. The lavish European trips of the later monarchs produced no result remotely commensurate with the strains put on the state treasury, which in turn exacerbated the mounting foreign debt. The traditional institutions, practices, and conceptions of governance, long in existence and rarely reconsidered, were no longer adequate at a time when a growing number of people were becoming aware of alternative modes of life and governance elsewhere. The political mentality of the rulers, imbued with the traditional wisdom imparted by the obsolete "mirrors for princes"—traditional manuals of princely conduct—was archaic and anachronistic.

The Qajar state proved particularly vulnerable to British and Russian imperial ambitions. With the intensification of Anglo-Russian rivalry after 1800 aimed at expanding their respective political influence and strategic and commercial interests, the authority of the Qajar state and its room for maneuver shrank severely, while the presence of foreign officials, agents, missionaries, and merchants became more tangible. Aggressive Russian policies resulted in two wars that ended in Iranian defeats, the loss of large areas of territory, and punishing and humiliating treaties (Golestan in 1813 and Turkamanchai in 1828). Concerned about the security of India, the British sought to counter Russian domination by enhancing their own influence, which was on the rise, particularly in southern and eastern areas adjacent to British India. In the 1850s Iran lost the eastern city of Herat to the British, and after the opening of the Suez Canal in 1869 Britain's commercial and military presence in the Persian Gulf rapidly increased.

Foreign domination also had a crucial impact on the Iranian economy. In the 1840s an Anglo-Russian agreement reducing tariffs for their merchants increased the volume of cheap foreign goods arriving in Iran to the detriment of domestic products, provoking the resentment of local merchants and manufacturers. Iranian merchants felt increasingly vulnerable to competition from their intrusive European counterparts relying on greater financial resources, the support of their consular officials, and privileges resulting from capitulations. Such privileges, enjoyed by European nationals in other places, including the Ottoman empire, entitled them to significant immunities and exemption from local jurisdiction. Foreign domination also facilitated the extraction of lucrative concessions from the Qajar state, deepening existing resentments and provoking strong public resistance. The 1872 Reuter concession—giving a British subject extensive rights over Iranian natural resources and development projects for seventy years—was widely opposed and thwarted, as was the 1891 concession that gave the control of tobacco production to a British subject.

While the Russians built alliances in northern Iran, the British did likewise in the south. The two powers also used various inducements to cultivate political figures, acquire clients, and recruit agents and informers in the capital. Anglophiles and russophiles constituted powerful segments of the political elite. Russian and British influence and meddling in Iranian affairs increased local impediments to change but also created new incentives for it. Exploiting Anglo-Russian rivalry enabled Iran to escape formal colonization and maintain nominal sovereignty. Yet, with the two powers pursuing their objectives virtually unhampered, the legitimacy of the ineffective Qajar state continued to erode. Beset by political disarray, administrative incompetence, and corruption, the state's remedies proved inadequate, while capable officials continued to fall victim to the intrigues and vested interests of courtiers and others.

In the last decades of the nineteenth century the increasingly tangible repercussions of dramatic socioeconomic developments in western Europe, which also accounted for rampant European, particularly British, imperialism, further destabilized the traditional socioeconomic and political fabric of Iranian society and eventually brought about the Constitutional Revolution. The structural causes of the revolution were rooted in the growing rift between the changing Iranian society and the virtually stagnant Qajar state. This rift was in turn integrally linked to dislocations in Iranian society caused by European capitalist and imperialist penetration, as well as Iran's unsettling exposure to European sociopolitical and cultural influences. The revolutionary fervor arose from the distress and resentments of a society suffering from domestic misrule and from subjugation or manipulation by imperial powers. It stemmed from growing awareness of the inadequacy of the prevailing modalities of the political, judicial, and administrative conduct of the state, the inequities of the existing socioeconomic order, and a belief that relief required collective action.

The greater visibility of foreign influence was also related to measures aimed at reforming the administration, including efforts to revitalize the revenue-generating customs department and the collection of taxes through employing Belgian officials. Those steps failed to remedy the situation and created new problems for the financially and politically bankrupt state. The victory of Japan—an Asian country that had adopted a constitution—over Russia in the Russo-Japanese War of 1904–1905, as well as the revolution that followed Russia's defeat, contributed to the agitation for change in Iran. The impotence of the Qajar state vis-à-vis foreign interests and nationals and its consequent loss of face contrasted sharply with its coercive and humiliating treatment of its own subjects. The state's demonstrated lack of protective capacity and inability to maintain order, uphold justice, and retrieve its credibility gave rise to a growing crisis of political authority, which emboldened large segments of the urban populace to voice their disquiet and disapproval of the existing apparatus of misrule. The protests arising from their cumulative resentments, expectations, and demands gained momentum as a direct result of the marked incapacity of the rulers to contain or adequately respond to them.

A complex and multifaceted struggle, the Constitutional Revolution involved several major cities and various social classes and groups. A host of reformist thinkers and activist dissenters, religious and lay, Muslim and non-Muslim, contacts with political and cultural trends in Europe, the Ottoman empire, Russia and India, together with Persian-language papers published abroad and smuggled into the country, broadened Iranian intellectual horizons, enhancing public awareness and engagement. Reformist intellectuals familiar with European thought played an important role in furnishing a new vocabulary and infusing the old political idiom with a new content. The enriched discourse of change provided a more pertinent vocabulary to formulate and articulate demands. The revolution started in a haphazard, spontaneous, improvised manner. Ideologically inchoate, it initially appeared more as a revulsion against injustice and oppression than as an affirmation of clear goals; yet it soon assumed the shape of a purposive movement for political and sociocultural change. Justice figured prominently in the political vocabulary of the protesters; it resonated in terms of both traditional Islamic and modern secular sensibilities. Justice clearly implied the rule of law, which required enactment and impartial implementation of just laws and an end to the arbitrary behavior of the state. Indeed, the revolution was triggered by an instance of the last—the public bastinadoing of two prominent sugar merchants on the orders of the governor of Tehran in December 1905. The broader aims of the revolution were the creation of a decent socioeconomic order and the establishment of a viable and law-abiding government responsive to the demands and expectations of the Iranian people and capable of asserting Iranian national sovereignty.

The goal of sustaining national sovereignty, which also implied resisting imperialism, was a driving force in the revolutionary movement. Acquiring a distinctly modern connotation thanks to the rapid spread of print culture

after 1906, "nation" *(mellat)* came increasingly to denote a community defined by a common culture and entitled to self-rule. Crafting a modern nation-state became an integral and crucial component of the Constitutional
Revolution. The fact that Iran was formally independent helped a powerful
manifestation of Iranian nationalism to assume a more distinctly civic, inclusive, reformist, and antidespotic character. Another strain of nationalism
embraced a nostalgic longing for the glories of the ancient past, combined
with chauvinistic lionization of the "Aryan" Iranians and denigration of the
legacy of Arab and Turkic invaders. The emerging, more mainstream nationalism embodied a consciousness of the continuity, distinct character,
and richness of national culture; its central tenet was that Iranians must become real masters of their own destiny and territory in order to deserve
and achieve national regeneration and a society that could satisfy their sense
of national self-worth.

## Clerical Clout

Nationalism, with its implicitly secular tenor, appealed primarily to the intelligentsia. Nevertheless, many clerics shared the wider revulsion at the increasing subjugation of Iran, the helplessness of its rulers vis-à-vis the Europeans, and their continued mistreatment of their own subjects. Clerical
reaction, clearly overlapping with nationalist concerns and demands, was
expressed in religious terms. Certain prominent clerics maintained ties with
the Qajar state in order, among other things, to influence its conduct and
policies; they could, in fact, significantly constrain the state. At the same
time, most high-ranking clerics traditionally owed their prestige and popular credibility to their pursuit of a life of piety and conspicuous frugality. By
maintaining a safe distance from the rulers, they enlisted public respect and
confidence, a circumstance that enabled them to maintain close links with
the middle classes and to represent them and the more vulnerable segments
of the population, to intercede on their behalf with the government, and to
attempt to protect them from injustice and victimization. Enjoying autonomy from the rulers and having their own sources of revenue increased
their ability to act as spokesmen for those who resented foreign influence
and the inability of the state to counter it.

The defeat of Iran by Russia in the wars of the first half of the nineteenth century damaged the standing of those leading clerics who had un-successfully attempted to mobilize the population for holy war against the Russians; but the blow to the Qajar state was more severe. The Qajars could claim no religious legitimacy, and were thus vulnerable in their relations with the clerics, who in the nineteenth century grew more cohesive. An anti-Sufi campaign by a leading cleric in the first half of the century marked a reassertion of the formal scripturalist Shi'ism of the clerical elite versus popular Shi'ism. Moreover, following the doctrinal debates and frictions of the eighteenth century—regarding governance, legitimacy, and particularly the nature and scope of religious authority in the absence of the Hidden Imam—by the nineteenth century most leading clerics supported the need for living religious authorities of high learning and rank *(mojtaheds)* who en-joyed considerable latitude in interpreting the corpus of Shi'ite traditions and exercising independent judgment. They would provide authoritative guidance for the less learned and lay faithful, or act as models to be emu-lated by them in matters pertaining to religion. This development contrib-uted to the consolidation of a de facto clerical hierarchy.

The rise of Babism, a messianic religious movement with roots in eso-teric Shi'ite teachings and strong overtones of social protest, was viewed by the clerics with particular alarm. Founded in the 1840s by Sayyed Ali-Mohammad Shirazi (1819–1850), who assumed the title Bab (the "gateway" to the Hidden Imam), Babism challenged or threatened both the Shi'ite es-tablishment and the Qajar state. Bab was tried and executed for heresy, as he had violated a fundamental Islamic tenet that the prophet Mohammad was the last of God's messengers. In 1852, after an attempt on the life of Naser al-Din Shah Qajar, many Babis were executed or imprisoned. The Babi movement would eventually give way to Baha'ism.

Babism awakened the clerics to the need to defend their collective inter-ests in alliance with or opposition to the Qajar state; the concerted cam-paign to suppress the new religious movement enabled them to play a more prominent sociopolitical role. The successful tobacco boycott of 1891–1892, which sought to thwart both the Qajar state and foreign interests, revealed the influence of the clerics and the readiness of some of them to support movements of opposition and resistance. Taking advantage of the Shah's growing need for funds, a British subject won a fifty-year concession to con-trol the production, sale, and export of Iranian tobacco, a widely used commodity. The concession affected all classes of society. Several clerics, including the leading reformer Sayyed Jamal al-Din al-Afghani (Asadabadi), played a role in launching opposition to it. A religious edict (*fatwa*) attributed to a high-ranking divine, Mirza Hasan Shirazi, led to a near-universal boycott of tobacco. This action, together with growing public restlessness, forced the Shah to revoke the concession, a move that involved the Iranian government's payment of half a million pounds sterling in compensation, thus increasing the country's burden of debt. The successful tobacco boycott confirmed the clerics' self-image and demonstrated the effectiveness of organized protest as well as the vulnerability of the state.

The Qajar state, though generally viewed as despotic, had not developed an absolutist character in the European sense. The emergence of the centralized absolutist state in sixteenth- and seventeenth-century Europe was largely a result of intense interstate competition for power that rested on, and was exacerbated by, the growth of powerful armies. These armies could be sustained only by the levying of more and more taxes, which they themselves helped extract. The Qajar state had long lacked the military power and resources to assert itself domestically, let alone ward off its powerful imperial neighbors. Moreover, unlike the absolutist governments of Europe, the Qajar state had not evolved in response to intense religious wars and conflicts such as those that accompanied or followed the sixteenth-century Reformation.

European absolutism rested on a clearly indivisible notion of sovereignty exclusive of and inimical to ecclesiastical power. In contrast, the Shi'ite clerics in Iran maintained their considerable sociopolitical power, which constrained the authority of the state. In its attitude to the clerics, the state pursued a context-dependent or situationally specific strategy of appeasement, manipulation, avoidance, or a combination of these. In the Ottoman empire the clerics were in effect part of the state structure; religion and the Sunni clerics were later identified with the old order, defeat, and imperial collapse. In contrast, the economic and political autonomy of the Shi'ite clerics in Iran enabled them to exercise much greater sociopolitical influence. Many of them resided in Ottoman-controlled Iraq, and living outside the jurisdiction of the Iranian state gave them greater room for political maneuver. The tobacco boycott had revealed the scale of clerical power, making them a more appealing ally to other advocates of change; it indi-

*Proconstitutionalist protesters taking sanctuary* (bast) *in the compound of the British Legation during the Constitutional Revolution.* (Courtesy of the Institute for the Study of Contemporary Iranian History, Tehran)

cated that they could not be readily identified with reactionary forces opposing change or condoning unpopular policies of the state. Concomitantly, the clerics' role in the Constitutional Revolution, and the fact that in most cases at least a segment of them appeared to side with oppositional or popular causes, made it difficult to undermine either them or their sociopolitical status and influence.

The clerics could not afford to remain passive in the face of the popular resentments and protests that culminated in the emergence of constitutionalism, but they were divided about how to respond to the movement for change. The clerics' political activism, which was rooted in their opposition to foreign influence as well as a desire to enhance their public standing and affirm their popular leadership roles, together with the imperative of responding to pressure from their constituencies, in particular the merchants, with whom they had close social and often kin ties, led many to support the Constitutional Revolution. Though uncertain about the meaning and implications of constitutionalism, by supporting it they hoped to be able to control or influence the course of events to their own advantage, and to forestall radicalism and secular tendencies. Prompted by their followers, the clerics assumed, or felt obliged to assume, an important role in antidespotic protests. Several high-ranking clerics, as well as a number of politicized preachers, spearheaded activities aimed at mobilizing protests, including the highly effective practice of organizing sit-ins or seeking sanctuary *(bast)* in sacred or inviolable spaces. Religious venues, rituals, symbols, as well as vocabulary, which increasingly acquired political overtones, were widely deployed to galvanize the public.

High-ranking clerical supporters of constitutionalism included Molla Mohammad-Kazem Khorasani and Sheikh Abdollah Mazandarani, both residing in Najaf, Iraq. Inside Iran, an indispensable role in promoting and defending constitutionalism was played by Sayyed Mohammad Tabataba'i, renowned for his integrity and sincerity but not exceptional political skills, and by Sayyed Abdollah Behbahani, a dynamic, fearless, and politically astute cleric who supported the constitutionalists despite his links with the state. The most cogent religious justification for constitutional representative government would be provided by the eminent divine Mirza Mohammad-Hosein Na'ini in a tract written in Najaf in 1909. The active constitutionalist clerics initially enjoyed the support of the equally prominent Sheikh Fazlollah Nuri, who later changed his position and sided with the opponents of constitutionalism, seeking to refute it on religious grounds. The clerical opponents of constitutionalism, by attempting to salvage the discredited edifice of royal rule, undermined their popular standing.

Following the establishment of constitutional government, many of its clerical supporters grew disillusioned. Fearing the future direction of constitutionalism, others continued to intervene to prevent any policy or course of action injurious to their collective interests and concerns. Cooperating with Mohammad Ali Shah Qajar, certain clerics had ensured that the Constitution not only left the Shah with considerable residual power but also stipulated that a body of five qualified clerics would supervise the process of parliamentary legislation in order to ensure conformity with Islamic principles. This provision was the closest to meeting the clerics' demand that no parliamentary legislation should contravene Islamic law. Although it amounted to a clerical veto over legislation in violation of democratic principles, in practice the provision remained defunct; the clerics did not succeed in, or emphatically insist on, enforcing it. Curiously, in 1953 the CIA and its British counterpart, in their zeal to overthrow the secular government of Mohammad Mosaddeq, were prepared to help revive clerical oversight of parliamentary legislation in exchange for the support of leading clerics in unseating Mosaddeq.[3] Though failing to establish formal control over the legislative process, the clerics remained the guardians of the constitutionally sanctioned official religion, which militated against the explicitly inclusive, religiously neutral notions of citizenship and civic equality. With its secular premises and implications, political and civic egalitarianism was anathema to clerical beliefs and influence.

Yet despite their shared interests and concerns, the sociopolitical attitudes of the clerics, and their interpretive perspectives on Islamic law or the interests of the community, differed markedly. As a result Islam would continue to be invoked both in support of constitutionalism and in opposition to it. As before, the motives and incentives of the clerics who continued to support constitutionalism remained varied and complex. Many of them viewed a constitutional government as beneficial to Islam and the country, and unlikely to prove inimical to their interests. Others were moved by pressure from their peers or followers, personal ambition, fear of marginalization, or a desire to remain capable of responding to actual or perceived expectations. Others hoped to exercise a restraining influence.

Though implicitly secular in substance and ethos, the Constitution was unambiguous in its commitment to Islam. It clearly reflected the circumstances of its emergence, most notably the clerics' determination to oppose the rise of an avowedly secular polity. They remained particularly averse to any move seen as likely to undermine Shi'ism as the official state religion. Yet in practice, the officially affirmed religion only broadly defined the parameters of constitutional politics; it was not regarded as the chief source or primary determinant of legislation. The legislative authority of the parliament was not narrowly defined in terms of ensuring strict conformity with Islamic religious norms. With the ascendancy of secular forces, the growing appeal of modern ideas and trends—regarding education, legal order, political and civic egalitarianism, the status of minorities, and the position and role of women, together with the rise of cultural nationalism—threatened to undermine the privileged status and traditional role of the clerics.

Many clerics turned to quietism or resignation. Many others sought to reaffirm traditions, practices, and beliefs that they viewed as threatened or targeted by secular trends. Local preachers, with their hold on the popular imagination and their ability to manipulate emotions and mobilize fears, prejudices, and superstitions, would continue to play an important role, benefiting from widespread illiteracy, particularly of the rural or semirural population, while accommodationist or more worldly clerics would try to adapt to the tempo and exigencies of a changing world. Many resisted or only partially condoned processes such as the adoption of a modern legal code. Others understood that modernization and some form of socio-political secularity were inevitable and not necessarily inimical to religion as an indispensable component of the inherited culture, inseparably linked to moral notions and spiritual needs.

The first parliament benefited considerably from the presence of a number of modern-minded and learned men of religion, such as Mirza Taher Tonekaboni and Sheikh Ali Nuri, distinguished scholars of Islamic philosophy, as well as Fazl-Ali Tabrizi, who developed a sophisticated discourse on the meaning of constitutionalism. Sheikh Mohammad-Ali Tehrani, Sheikh Hosein Falak al-Ma'ali, and Sheikh Ebrahim Zanjani made valuable contributions to the parliamentary debates and processes and played a key role in the modernization of traditional discourses. Zanjani, as revealed by his trenchant memoirs, was a perceptive critic of clerical bigotry, obscurantism, and abuse of position.[4] Another clerical deputy, Sheikh Mohammad-Taqi Vakil al-Ro'aya, had the temerity to advocate extension of the franchise to women.

Such an ambitious measure was, however, barely conceivable at the time, when even many European countries had not yet enfranchised women. Not only the whole clerical establishment but also an array of other conservative forces were deeply opposed to any such move. Sayyed Hasan Modarres, a politically astute cleric and skilled parliamentarian, echoed such opposition when he strongly objected in the second parliament to a parliamentary committee considering the issue of enfranchising women. In the traditionalist view of Modarres, any consideration of giving women the right to vote or treating them as equal with men was to be rejected:

> God has not endowed them [women] . . . with the competence to enjoy the right to choose . . . moreover, in Islam women are subject to guard-

*Members of the first parliament, 1906.* (Courtesy of the Institute for the Study of Contemporary Iranian History, Tehran)

ianship, men are predominant over women . . . and our official religion
is Islam. They are to have guardians and shall not ever have the right to
choose; others must protect the rights of women.[5]

Despite their differences, whenever they were able to do so the clerics relentlessly opposed measures likely to diminish their influence and the grip
of the faith. Chief among such measures, they considered, were efforts
aimed at establishing or enhancing civic and gender equality or at slacken-
ing Islamic norms of female chastity. Spoken or unspoken assumptions
such as those invoked by Modarres also underlined clerical opposition to
any serious discussion of enfranchising women. Despite the clerics' unre-
mitting opposition, the franchise was eventually extended to women in
1963—later than in many other Muslim countries. It was not rescinded following the revolution of 1978–1979, as this would have been too regressive a
step to contemplate.

## Law or Order

The politics of Iran from 1906 until the coup of 1921, which paved the way
for the formal establishment of the Pahlavi dynasty, was characterized by
an arduous struggle by the parliamentarians to reconcile the requirements

of the nascent, institutionally precarious constitutional governance with the formally redefined role and prerogatives of the institutionally entrenched monarchy. The parliamentarians' primary objective was to ensure that the democratic components of constitutionalism found a real measure of practical and institutional expression. They faced the daunting challenge of creating both political order and political accountability in the absence of permissive circumstances and in the context of insurmountable domestic and international crises.

The deputies of the first parliament, though almost invariably unversed in parliamentary practices and procedures, displayed a keen, almost idealistic appreciation of their own role and responsibilities, and of the position of the parliament as the cornerstone of the new and evolving political arrangements.[6] Led by skillful politicians such as Morteza-Qoli Sani' al-Dauleh and Mahmud Ehtesham al-Saltaneh, and thanks to a sizable number of deputies with training in modern legal and political disciplines, the parliament's accomplishments were considerable.[7] It both acted as a revolutionary constituent assembly and took important steps to transform itself into a robust legislative body. It worked to promote the overall equality of citizens before the law; established freedom of expression and association; initiated legal, administrative, and financial reform; opposed granting concessions to foreigners or securing loans from Britain and Russia; and endeavored, inconclusively, to create a national bank. The parliament asserted its authority vis-à-vis the new monarch, Mohammad Ali Shah Qajar, who had assumed the throne in January 1907 soon after the death of his ailing father and six months after the late Shah had formally consented to the establishment of a constitutional government. The new Shah had only grudgingly acquiesced in the establishment of parliamentary arrangements, was unwilling to relinquish royal prerogatives, and used traditionalist forces, including amenable clerics, to derail constitutionalism or to supplant it with a system of rule based on Islamic law *(mashru'eh)*. These maneuvers were countered by dedicated parliamentarians such as the bold and compelling Mashhadi Baqer, who represented the trade guilds, one of six "classes" that elected deputies to the first parliament. The parliament resisted the intrusions of the Shah and emphatically maintained that royal prerogatives were determined by law and were largely ceremonial.[8]

One of the significant tasks of the parliament was to pursue the goal of

enhancing Iranian national sovereignty. The constitutionalists had been supported by Britain and opposed by Russia. However, the 1907 Anglo-Russian
Convention, prompted by the exigencies of European politics and the threat
of a powerful Germany, not only dampened the hopes of the constitutionalists but exacerbated their problems. For many years Iranian politicians
had benefited from Anglo-Russian rivalry, but now the baffling alliance of
the former foes formalized the division of Iran into two spheres of influence. This situation undermined traditional Iranian political and diplomatic
premises and room for maneuver, and further vitiated Iranian national sovereignty at the very moment of intense struggle to assert it.

A constitutional parliamentary government capable of exerting its authority in the face of foreign and domestic challenges clearly involved much
more than a deliberative and legislative body. Among other things, it required an executive apparatus headed by a cabinet and consisting of a bureaucratic structure capable of administering the country and implementing parliamentary legislation. The cabinet system took some time to evolve
and reconcile itself with the imperative of accountability to the parliament.[9]
It remained institutionally enfeebled and incapable of dealing effectively
with its numerous tasks, particularly the two key problems of maintaining
order and warding off financial bankruptcy. These two problems topped the
list of issues that plagued the eight cabinets formed by six prime ministers
during the twenty-one-month term of the first parliament.[10] Maintaining
political order proved no less difficult than tackling the country's financial
problems.

The birth of constitutional governance accompanied the appearance of
numerous political associations and societies *(anjomans)* and a flourishing
press. The prevailing atmosphere of anxious patriotic restlessness and reformist enthusiasm, of heated public debate and disagreement, whether
oral or printed, together with the growing significance of public opinion in
the larger urban centers, indicated the emergence of a civil society and the
beginnings of a vibrant public space of dialogue. Such a milieu could also
be seen or portrayed as indicating the absence of a real measure of political
consensus, political fragmentation, and the erosion of customary restraints.
Several societies, together with other radical elements, resorted to extremist
rhetoric and tactics likely to provoke, or be invoked by, the Shah and other
opponents of constitutionalism, and thereby harm the parliament.[11] Parlia-

mentary deputies resented and denounced extremism but failed to confront and contain it. Eventually Mohammad Ali Shah, having long awaited an opportunity to eliminate the constitutional process, resorted to violent action against the parliament.

Having led a cloistered life in provincial Tabriz, tutored by a reactionary Russian teacher, the Shah was "ignorant, superstitious, greedy, and surrounded by corrupt and stupid cronies."[12] Unable to reconcile himself with the fragile constitutional order, the uncouth, scheming, and ruthless Shah was willing to resort to any move to undermine or derail it. Lamenting the willingness of his father to make concessions to the constitutionalists, he had reportedly even sought, albeit unsuccessfully, to persuade his father's physician to pronounce the late Shah mentally unstable.[13] Temperamentally ill suited to accepting legal constraints on his powers, Mohammad Ali Shah tactically invoked religion and enlisted the support of a number of clerics to subvert constitutionalism or seriously dilute it. Assisted and encouraged by anticonstitutionalist royalist figures and forces, he saw no good reason to defer to or tolerate the prevailing problem-ridden constitutional arrangements. The parliamentarians, however, persisted in pressing him to comply with the role of a constitutional monarch.

In the hope of defusing the crisis and buying time, the Shah publicly affirmed his commitment to constitutionalism, but blamed and promised to punish "a handful of treasonous, self seeking, and corrupt elements."[14] Pronouncing the prevailing liberties to be detrimental to both Islam and the monarchy, the Shah accused his opponents of equating religiosity with superstition, of agitating and corrupting the minds of the common folk, and even of "encouraging women to form societies and discuss freedom." Considering the dangers facing Islam and "the foundation of the 6,000-year-old Iranian monarchy," he asserted, he could no longer remain "tolerant and silent." He offered to institute a religiously based constitutional government (*mashruteh-ye mashru'eh*).[15]

This alternative, supported by clerics such as Nuri, was repugnant to the radicalized proconstitutional forces, who intensified their activities. Pamphleteering had continued to function as an effective means of communicating views. A plethora of telegrams from the provinces indicated strong national concern for the fate of constitutionalism. Solidarity-generating acts of protest, including seeking sanctuary, continued to be as symbolically evo-

*Mohammad Ali Shah Qajar, flanked by courtiers and officials, a few days before the royalist bombardment of the parliament in June 1908.* (Courtesy of the Institute for the Study of Contemporary Iranian History, Tehran)

cative and prevalent as before. Recently formed open or secret societies, together with gatherings in religious venues, indicated an effective and active associational network in support of the Constitution. Lay and religious leaders, activists, orators, and preachers played key roles by mobilizing and channeling, as well as responding to, strong popular convictions and passions. Pulpits, secular platforms, and other intricate combinations of traditional and modern forms of mobilization and protest generated a resilient force of resistance.

The deepening of hostilities between the royalists and the constitutionalists led the Shah to unleash the Russian-commanded Cossack Brigade to unravel constitutionalism; he ordered the bombardment of the parliament, which was defended by proconstitutionalist forces. Although many constitutionalists escaped, many others were killed, executed, or detained and brutally treated. The two leading constitutionalist divines, Tabataba'i and Behbahani, were among the detainees. Thus began a period of thirteen months known as "the minor despotism" (June 1908–July 1909). But restoring the old order was no longer feasible. The royalist onslaught had helped generate greater tenacity of purpose among proconstitutionalist forces. They soon regrouped, and with the crucial help of militia forces from various parts of the country, particularly Azarbaijan, confronted the royalists, who had failed to consolidate their hold on power. The ensuing civil war resulted in the ignominious defeat of the Shah, who sought Russian protection and showed no intention of capitulating. The constitutionalists proceeded to replace him with his son, Ahmad Mirza, then a minor; a regent was appointed to perform royal duties; a number of royalist hardliners were tried and executed. The removal of Mohammad Ali Shah also resulted in the unprecedented public trial and execution of Nuri, who had maintained shady links, financial and otherwise, with the court as well as with the Russians. Nuri had publicly supported and aided the Shah's move against the constitutionalists; he was the chief spokesman of those clerics who contended that constitutionalism and Islam were incompatible.

After a recess of nearly seventeen months, the second parliament (1909–1911) was convened. It remained vulnerable to debilitating party and factional divisions with varying ideological commitment. The two major political parties, Democrats and Moderates, which dominated parliamentary politics, were spirited forces contributing both to formal associational life and to ideological and partisan rifts; they were vital ingredients of a dynamic political life but also contributed to its fragility. Despite the adverse effects of factionalism on its legislative capacity, the parliament worked toward creating a functioning administrative structure as well as a modern judiciary. It enacted universal male suffrage—an advanced measure by the standards of the time—and helped to defeat a serious Russian-backed royalist challenge. It also voted to create a gendarmerie, aimed at expanding and sustaining the authority of the government beyond the cities and establishing order in the often troubled remote areas of the country and on the roads. The gendarmerie, which would also function as a countervailing force to the anticonstitutionalist Cossack Division, was eventually formed with Swedish support and by 1921 numbered about 11,000.

William Morgan Shuster, who headed an American team of financial advisers employed in early 1911, worked diligently to reform Iranian government finances. He formed a treasury gendarmerie to collect taxes from landowners and notables, including those who enjoyed foreign protection. Both his measures and his denunciation of Anglo-Russian transgressions in Iran antagonized both powers. Backed by the British, the Russians issued an ultimatum demanding Shuster's expulsion. Having done much to bolster the anticonstitutionalist forces, they insisted that no foreign adviser be appointed without prior Anglo-Russian approval; they backed their saber rattling with military action and threatened to occupy Tehran. The parliament's brave, popularly backed resistance eventually proved unsustainable. Against a background of deteriorating political order and chronic financial crisis, the Iranian government—dominated by Bakhtiari tribal chieftains who secretly negotiated to appease the Russians and the British—and the Oxford-educated, conservative regent, Abolqasem Naser al-Molk, saw no alternative but to dissolve the recalcitrant parliament and give in to the Russian ultimatum. Anglo-Russian cooperation had facilitated flagrant Russian acts of aggression in northern Iran, in collusion with forces loyal to the deposed Shah. These acts included the hanging of eight constitutionalists, among them a high-ranking cleric in Tabriz in late 1911, and bombardment of the holy shrine in Mashhad in late March 1912 to eject constitutionalists who had taken refuge there.

The third parliament (1914–1915) followed a recess of three years, but Iran's embroilment in the First World War caused widespread disruption and seriously hampered the evolution of its parliamentary structures. Iran's declared neutrality was ignored by the British, Russian, German, French, and Ottoman imperial forces and agents. The belligerent powers pursued their war-related agendas irrespective of Iranian sovereignty. There were outbreaks of famine, severe shortages of foodstuffs, rampant lawlessness and brigandage. The populations of smaller towns were often at the mercy of marauding tribesmen. Many towns and villages in central areas were prey to bandits such as the notorious Nayeb Hosein of Kashan and his followers.

The disastrous repercussions of the First World War severely disrupted Iranian parliamentary politics, and successive governments proved incapable of alleviating mounting hardships. In 1917–1918, famine, together with the outbreak of infectious diseases such the influenza pandemic, left thousands dead. Shortages and the high price of foodstuffs, particularly wheat, were largely a result of disrupted transportation caused by disorder or by damaged roads and bridges. This situation rekindled Iranian aspirations for the creation of a powerful centralized state and an army capable of maintaining order. Hasan Vosuq (Vosuq al-Dauleh), prime minister from August 1916 to May 1917, showed exceptional ability in dealing with some of the existing problems and gained considerable domestic support. Equally impressed by his capabilities, in July 1918 the British helped secure Vosuq's reappointment as prime minister by agreeing to establish a monthly stipend for Ahmad Shah Qajar, who had come of age and assumed the throne four years earlier. The stipend would continue as long as the Shah supported Vosuq, who retained the premiership until June 1920.

Britain's primary purpose in supporting Vosuq's premiership was to secure the ratification of an agreement with the Iranian government that was finalized in August 1919 and was championed by Lord George Curzon, who soon afterward became foreign secretary. Curzon was, and saw himself as, an "imperialist, heart and soul";[16] he firmly believed that the British empire, or rather he, had a moral duty to save Iran. Doing so, Curzon believed, required exclusive domination over the country regardless of what the Iranians themselves wanted. Such domination would help the security of British India and the fortunes of the empire, soon to be augmented by colonial footholds in Iraq and Palestine. Taking advantage of Iran's political, military, and financial disarray and the erosion of Russian influence caused by the revolution of 1917, Curzon sought to impose an agreement that would have virtually established formal British tutelage over Iran. Among other measures adopted to promote the agreement, British officials paid a substantial sum to Vosuq and two of his key ministers, the Qajar princes Akbar Masu'd (Sarem al-Dauleh) and Firuz Firuz (Nosrat al-Dauleh). As prime minister, Vosuq worked vigorously to enhance the authority of the central government, combat famine, strengthen the gendarmerie, and restore order. He ordered the arrest and trial of members of the "punishment committee," a clandestine terrorist cell responsible for several murders. By April 1920 he had also had some 200 bandits rounded up and executed, including Nayeb Hosein and his son, Masha'allah Khan.[17] But Vosuq's premiership was marred by his close association with the 1919 agreement, which he had come to view as an antidote to the country's disintegration and a remedy for its intractable crisis of governance.

The British position in Iran was unrivaled. In 1901 William Knox D'Arcy, a British subject and son of an Irish lawyer who had made a fortune in Australia, extracted an oil concession from the Qajar state giving him comprehensive rights to Iranian oil in all areas except five northern provinces. The concession bore fruit in 1908 with the discovery of oil in commercial quantities; a year later the Anglo-Persian Oil Company (APOC) took over the D'Arcy concession. In 1914 the British navy converted to using oil instead of coal; this move rendered Iranian oil strategically indispensable to the British empire, prompting the British government's acquisition of 51 percent of shares in APOC, renamed the Anglo-Iranian Oil Company in 1933. As a result the Iranians, who received a mere 16 percent of the company's annual net profits as royalties, were dealing not with a private company but with a powerful empire. Aiming to safeguard their interests and influence in southern Iran and to protect the oil fields, the British maintained close links with and subsidized certain tribal chieftains; they also formed their own military unit, the South Persia Rifles, and maintained other military forces in the country. Along with the Russians, they played a key role in influencing the appointment of prime ministers and other key officials. Unlike the Russians, who had often pursued their objectives through naked force, the British tended to prefer covert measures, including bribing key individuals. With the collapse of the Ottoman empire, the British and the French were establishing themselves as rulers of virtually all the Arab Middle East, but Iran was to be an exclusively British domain. The nationalist sensibilities of the Iranians were offended by the fact that, like the Egyptians, they were prevented—mainly as a result of British opposition—from presenting their case (regarding damages Iran had incurred during its wartime occupation) at the 1919 Paris peace conference. The Anglo-Iranian agreement of the same year was a far greater blow to such sensibilities. Although the British had secured the support of the Shah and key ministers, growing Iranian nationalist opposition, together with international disapproval, prevented them from enforcing the agreement. The British minister in Tehran, Herman Norman (1920–1921), later described it as "an impossible and insane policy."[18]

Among other things, the agreement envisaged the establishment of an effective administrative machinery and a unified army through the employment of British advisers. The absence of such an army, efficient security forces, and a functioning administrative structure—in short, a viable central government—had continued to bedevil Iranian constitutionalism. The ineffectiveness of the prevailing constitutional arrangements not only resulted in increasing disappointment, both at the center and the periphery of Iranian politics, but provided an opportunity for the emergence of regional movements. Growing disquiet at British domination, together with a sense of national malaise and disorientation, contributed to this process. The regional movements purportedly aimed at revitalizing Iranian constitutionalism. In the wooded northern province of Gilan, Mirza Kuchek Khan "Jangali"—an idealist who espoused pan-Islamist, constitutionalist, and nationalist objectives—had since 1915 led a movement supported mainly by peasants. Surviving defeat by the British and backed by Soviet forces, in 1920 the movement formed an ill-fated alliance with Iranian Communists, which resulted in the formation of the Gilan-based "Soviet Socialist Republic of Iran." The ensuing tension between the Communist and noncommunist components of the movement led to splintering and paved the way for the movement's eventual disintegration. The Jangali movement has been described as "the most important post–World War I attempt to reestablish constitutional government in Iran, to promote progress and welfare, and to free the country from foreign domination."[19] Farther west, in Azerbaijan, a fertile ground for Iranian nationalism and constitutionalism, a movement seeking to revive Iranian constitutionalism but less socially rooted than the Jangali movement, was led by Sheikh Mohammad Kheiabani, a visionary constitutionalist cleric and former parliamentarian. Despite his authoritarian temperament, he proclaimed his "sole objective" to be the formation of "a democratic government" in the whole country, and called for the abolition of undue influences and privileges. "We say," Kheiabani declared, "there should be justice, equality and liberty . . . we want to be sons of our own century."[20]

The fragile central government was understandably suspicious of such claims; it was incapable of addressing the legitimate issues that they raised, and it feared the spread of Bolshevism and foreign-instigated separatism. The reputable constitutionalist prime minister, Hasan Pirnia (Moshir al-Dauleh), who succeeded Vosuq, felt unable to reach an accommodation with Kheiabani, whom he suspected of harboring secessionist aims. In contrast to the Jangali movement, eliminating Kheiabani's short-lived movement proved relatively easy. Abandoned by his disillusioned supporters, he was killed by government forces in September 1920.

The government of Pirnia resisted British pressure to implement any aspects of the 1919 agreement or to acknowledge its legitimacy. It maintained that any agreement had to be approved by the Iranian parliament. Pirnia's successor was less effective. With Soviet backing the Jangali insurgents were able with impunity to defy the central government, which had continued to suffer from political fragmentation, chronic cabinet instability, administrative incapacity, and lack of effective means and resources, particularly an adequate military force. The British officials in Tehran now sought a leader or leaders capable of hindering any southward march of Bolshevism and willing to implement the substance of the 1919 agreement. Their primary objective was the firm establishment of British hegemony over the country, regardless of formal ratification or rejection of the agreement. The lingering atmosphere of political crisis and frustration rooted in a sense of national impotence paved the way for the coup of February 1921, which was launched in the name of establishing the authority and credibility of the central government.

## Militarism

The coup took place during the long parliamentary hiatus, four months before the inauguration of the fourth parliament. Had there been a parliament in session, such a venture would have proved more difficult. The leaders of the coup were an ambitious pro-British journalist and political broker, Sayyed Zia al-Din Tabataba'i (henceforth referred to as Sayyed Zia), the thirty-one-year-old son of an anticonstitutionalist cleric, and Reza Khan, then a Cossack brigadier general in his early forties. Of modest origins, Reza Khan had joined the Cossacks at an early age, showing considerable promise. Although as a Cossack officer he harbored no positive sentiments toward constitutionalism, he belonged to a generation of men who had experienced and regretted the absence of effective central authority in the country. A desire for the creation of such an authority was at the core of Iranian nationalism, but few had any viable idea about how it could be accomplished. Sooner or later some kind of action, including a coup, was likely if not inevitable, but the extent of British influence and interests in the country made success unlikely without British support or acquiescence.

In fact a number of key British diplomats and military officers stationed in Iran encouraged or supported, if not instigated, the coup. Norman, the

British minister, was in contact with Sayyed Zia, while Major General Sir Edmund Ironside, commander of the British forces in northern Iran, cultivated Reza Khan, whom he viewed as uniquely capable of leading Iran out of the prevailing turmoil. Walter Smart, the Oriental secretary at the British Legation, together with two other colleagues, was extensively involved, as was Lieutenant Colonel Henry Smith, informally attached to the Cossack units stationed in the city of Qazvin that carried out the coup. These officials helped not only with the planning of the coup but also with its successful execution, consolidation, and the thwarting of possible countermeasures. The British government seems not to have been involved or even formally informed. Clearly both Sayyed Zia and Reza Khan took advantage of a favorable situation to advance their own political agendas. Reza Khan in particular was intent on using the British at least as much as they sought to use him.

In the wake of the march on Tehran of a Cossack force of some 3,000 led by Reza Khan, the Shah felt he had no choice but to appoint Sayyed Zia as prime minister. Soon thereafter Reza Khan became war minister and commander of the army; he concentrated his efforts on the interrelated objectives of consolidating his own position and creating a unified standing army. An anticommunist conservative and a reckless political operator of considerable ability, Sayyed Zia espoused a curious mixture of old-fashioned beliefs and modern reformist ideas. Aiming to demonstrate his authority as prime minister, he resorted to a number of drastic measures: as a populist gesture he denounced the "ruling class" and ordered the detention of a large number of senior statesmen and magnates, including some of the wealthiest and most influential men in the country, implicitly pronouncing them responsible for its existing ills.

Though publicly denouncing the 1919 agreement, Sayyed Zia proceeded, in effect, to implement some of its chief components, a move that he hoped would rally the British solidly in his support. He began recruiting British officers to key positions in the Cossack Division and asked for British officials to reorganize the financial administration; he had plans to absorb the South Persia Rifles, with a limited number of British officers, into the gendarmerie, and intended to seek advisers from other countries. He also envisaged reorganizing the Justice Ministry, instituting agrarian reform and financing these measures by fines imposed on the detained statesmen. He

*Ahmad Shah Qajar (center, with cane) and officials,*
*including War Minister Reza Khan on his right.*
(Courtesy of the Institute for the Study of Contemporary Iranian History, Tehran)

reduced the stipends of the Shah and royal princes and appointed a court minister to oversee the court and reduce its expenditure and corruption. He created a Health Ministry (which did not long survive him), banned the sale or public serving of alcoholic beverages, ordered the dismissal of opium-addicted government employees, and for the first time had electric lighting installed in a number of Tehran streets. Capitalizing on his links with Britain, his opponents, including journalists and political activists, denounced him; he in turn treated them harshly. Though himself a journalist, he showed little patience with press criticism; Yahya Reyhan, one journalist who vocally criticized Sayyed Zia, was summarily dispatched to a lunatic asylum.

The cabinet of the politically inexperienced and tactless Sayyed Zia lasted some three months; he had no domestic power base, and his British supporters failed to sustain him: by the last six weeks of his term of office, they had withdrawn their troops from Iran. At this point he had antagonized many influential people, and his deteriorating relations with the Shah precipitated his dismissal and exile from the country in the last week of May 1921. He had been increasingly eclipsed by the politically savvier Reza Khan, who collaborated with the Shah in his ouster. Reza Khan had vigorously opposed Sayyed Zia's policy of appointing British officers to positions of command in the Cossack Division and thwarted it, viewing it as detrimental to his own position and aims. Ahmad Qavam, one of Sayyed Zia's detainees, a consummate politician and brother of former prime minister Vosuq, was now appointed prime minister. Within a month, the fourth parliament (1921–1923) was convened after a hiatus of almost six years. The elections, however, had been largely manipulated by prime minister Vosuq in the hope of putting in place a parliament willing to ratify the 1919 agreement. Not surprisingly, and in the context of mobilized nationalist sentiments, the parliament strongly resisted British pressure; it also refused to allow the Shah to act outside the limits of his constitutional role.

As premier, Qavam faced an immediate challenge: the rebellion of Colonel Mohammad-Taqi Khan Pesian, commander of the gendarmerie in the eastern province of Khorasan. Admired by many who knew him as a brave and patriotic soldier, Pesian, whose relations with Qavam had been stormy, defied him. With mediation efforts failing, Pesian, feeling cornered, launched a rebellion in support of constitutionalist and anti-imperialist causes. Coinciding with the increasing radicalization of the Jangali movement in Gilan and the outbreak of several minor local rebellions, Pesian's venture provoked greater efforts by the central government to assert its authority. The rebellion cost Pesian his life. Though anathema to Pesian's sympathizers, Qavam had shown considerable capability as prime minister and remained a viable statesman. In the meantime no one was in a position to steal the limelight from War Minister Reza Khan. In mid-October 1921, two weeks after the death of Pesian, Reza Khan entered Rasht, the provincial capital of Gilan, personally commanding the government forces. This move marked the end of the increasingly isolated and fragmented Jangali movement, whose leader froze to death in the mountains less than two months later. The movement had been abandoned by the Soviet government, which had opted to support the central government. Following the Irano-Soviet agreement of February 1921, which established friendly relations between the two countries, the Soviets came to see Reza Khan as working to reduce British influence.[21] Conversely, the British viewed him as capable of saving Iran from Bolshevism. Reza Khan skillfully endeavored to foster and exploit both perceptions.

In early 1922 Reza Khan combined, restructured, and reorganized the existing disparate military units to form a unified army that, together with the police force, would sustain his power and advance his personal political objectives. Creating a unified military would not be an easy task; the Cossack Division, one of the two key segments of such an army, was Reza Khan's main constituency, while the other, the gendarmerie, whose officers were better educated and more liberal in outlook, was not uniformly supportive of him. These differences and their political implications complicated Reza Khan's task of establishing himself as the unchallenged commander of a unified army. However, few could deny that the creation of such an army was a vital move toward consolidating the authority of the central government and extending it to the whole country. Inevitably it ran counter to the influence of the Soviets in the north and provoked considerable British misgivings. Having maintained close ties with many southern tribal chieftains, British consular and oil company officials tended to view southern Iran as effectively outside the jurisdiction of the central government.

But the centralizing drive continued unabated. After the defeat of the Jangalis and Pesian, an abrupt occupation of Tabriz in February 1922 by a breakaway gendarmerie force was countered and defeated; its leader, Abolqasem Lahuti, a gendarmerie officer and activist poet, fled to the Soviet Union. The most significant immediate threat facing the country remained a rebellion among Kurdish tribesmen in the northwest led by Ismail Aqa Semitqu (Simko). By the summer of 1922 Semitqu had also been defeated and forced to flee Iran,[22] an event officially celebrated across the country and particularly in the capital, where Reza Khan himself organized an elaborate ceremony, at which he received much praise. The army now concentrated on subduing the tribesmen of Lorestan, who were disrupting traffic and communication between central Iran and Khuzestan. Relying on the army and capitalizing on its military achievements, War Minister Reza Khan was playing an increasingly active role in domestic politics irrespective of constitutional and legal strictures, and to the growing consternation of parliamentarians.

Mirza Mohsen Mo'tamed al-Tojjar, the deputy for Tabriz, audaciously vented such feelings in early October 1922. He forcefully criticized Reza

Khan's moves against the Constitution and his use of martial law to ban public meetings and to harass or silence supporters of freedom. Denouncing the suppression of newspapers and the imprisonment, banishment, or torture of journalists, he voiced regret that after seventeen years of constitutionalism and "so much sacrifice made for the sake of freedom, instead of fundamental reforms we must still complain about transgressions against the Constitution."[23] This criticism was reinforced by Modarres, a deputy whose modest life style, consistent candor, and championing of constitutionalism had ensured him broad popularity. Emphasizing the centrality of the parliament in a constitutional polity, Modarres asserted that the parliament had the authority to change the dynasty and to dismiss the prime minister and any other official, including Reza Khan. He expediently added, however, that the benefit to the country of having Reza Khan as war minister far outweighed the drawbacks and needed to be amplified.[24] In response Reza Khan, addressing a group of military officers, dismissed his critics as instigated by foreigners and as failing to recognize his services. Resorting to the maneuver of resigning, he resumed his position two days later following demonstrations in his favor by military units and threats against the parliament. He himself adopted a conciliatory posture; appearing before the parliament, he undertook in principle to lift martial law and to relinquish the War Ministry's control of indirect taxes and state lands, which was to be handed over to the Finance Ministry.

Reza Khan's retreat was only tactical; he had no intention of relenting in his strategy of subduing the parliament. In his contacts with Sir Percy Loraine, the new British minister (1921–1926), he presented this strategy, and his objective of turning the parliament into a subservient body by rigging elections, as a prerequisite of closer ties with Britain.[25] A compromise with the parliament, however, provided Reza Khan with additional opportunity to consolidate his position by extending the authority of the central government to the south. This task required the cooperation or acquiescence of the British. British diplomats differed in their assessments of the unfolding developments in the country. Loraine showed willingness to acknowledge the existence of an Iranian public opinion and growing nationalism. He saw an orderly, strong, and centralized Iran as posing no threat to Britain; a weak and fractious Iran might succumb to Soviet influence. In contrast to Curzon, Loraine perceived British interests as best served by supporting

Reza Khan and his army, whose achievements he praised. In May 1923, commenting on the defeat of various revolts, Loraine noted that "the Shahsevan have been cowed, disarmed without serious fighting and they have surrendered 34,000 rifles to the Government." The danger of "any general movement in Persian Kurdistan is ended. The Turkomans are being gradually reduced to order. Throughout North, North-West and North-East Persia, the Persian army organization has consolidated its position and prestige: all Russian influences there have suffered a severe setback and are being steadily combated." In the south and southwest less had been done, "but there has been no threat against the authority of central Government from this quarter." Considering it "incontestable" that the result of these changes "has been so far uniformly beneficial to British interests," Loraine noted that the credit went entirely to Reza Khan, who had accomplished these despite "every kind of handicap, with a chronically empty Treasury, with an incompetent civil Government, in the teeth of Russian displeasure." There was, he added, "a very genuine element of patriotism underlying all that Reza Khan does."[26]

Although not every British official dealing with Iran was as sympathetic to him as Loraine, Reza Khan continued to emphasize that what he was attempting to accomplish corresponded closely with what the British had hoped to bring about in Iran. While carefully avoiding any course of action that might turn the British against him, Reza Khan maintained that it was in the British interest to cultivate the friendship of a strong and unified Iran and not to be seen opposing the legitimate reassertion of Iranian sovereign rights. He intended to extend firm central government authority over the territory controlled by the Bakhtiari chieftains and the restless nomads of Lorestan, and particularly over the oil-rich and relatively inaccessible southern province of Khuzestan. He proceeded cautiously and concentrated on overcoming British opposition.

Reza Khan's efforts to establish the army as the custodian of a viable centralized state and to advance his own political career moved forward simultaneously. In October 1923 he left the increasingly perturbed and helpless Ahmad Shah with no choice but to appoint him prime minister despite having no confidence in him. Among the prime ministers who had preceded Reza Khan, Qavam may have been the only potential alternative. Qavam, however, had been implicated in a plot against Reza Khan shortly before the

*Reza Khan—prime minister, war minister, and commander of the armed forces—*
*and senior military commanders.* (Courtesy of the Institute for the Study of
Contemporary Iranian History, Tehran)

latter's assumption of the premiership; he was arrested but on the Shah's intercession was allowed to leave the country. He would not be allowed to return until March 1930. Reza Khan was an energetic prime minister: for instance, he ordered ministers to send him daily reports "showing work
accomplished on the previous day."[27] Above all, he concentrated on consolidating his exclusive control over the state's means of coercion, policing, and
intelligence gathering. Having increased the budget available to the prime
minister's office for the political secret service, he added it to the budget of
the military intelligence service. This fund amounted to the very considerable sum of 18,000 tomans a month.[28] The War Ministry had taken over the
gendarmerie from the Interior Ministry in the summer of 1921. The gendarmerie was abolished in early 1922, its Iranian officers and soldiers absorbed
into the Iranian army, and its Swedish officers dismissed. Reza Khan now
ended the Swedish control of the police *(nazmiyeh),* appointing one of his

protégés as police chief. This measure, previously resisted by politicians who feared that it would facilitate Reza Khan's dictatorial rule, considerably increased his opportunity to act virtually unhampered.

Within a week of Reza Khan's appointment as prime minister, the Shah left Iran for his third and final trip to Europe, where he would die seven years later aged thirty-two (February 1930). His brother, Crown Prince Mohammad-Hasan Mirza, remained as regent. Of negligible force of character, Ahmad Shah gratified his chief passion, the acquisition of wealth, by unhesitatingly selling honorific titles, demanding payments in exchange for lucrative appointments, and seeking stipends from the British while overburdening the meager financial resources of the government with his travel and other expenses. Evincing no commitment to maintaining the dignity of his inherited office and no real concern for his country, he had forfeited any justifiable claim to political and moral authority. Neither he nor his unimpressive brother had the capability or the means to outmaneuver Reza Khan.

Filling the vacuum, Reza Khan, who readily resorted to threats, bullying, or naked coercion and exuded an unusual air of authority, established himself as the strong man of Iranian politics. He had a flair not only for taking advantage of existing crises but also for manufacturing them in order to render himself indispensable to the country's political stability. Able to aggravate and exploit divisions among political notables, and aided by a number of capable men, he capitalized on the undeniable need for order, stability, and reform. Resolute and cunning in pursuing his aims, he showed considerable aptitude for tactical compromise, collusion, and the utilization of a variety of manipulative tactics. Seeking to forge alliances, mollify or neutralize would-be opponents, and augment and invigorate his supporters, he cultivated extensive contacts. His home and offices became focal points of considerable activity, as on a daily basis he received a large number of influential people, including a considerable number of senior clerics. Treating high-ranking clerics with special attention and deference, he endeavored to reassure them about his aims, win them over, or undermine their opposition. He skillfully used a variety of tactics to ensure that parliamentary factional alignments were rearranged to his benefit. He wooed tribal chieftains and played them off against one another. Dealing with foreign representatives with apparent candor and flexibility, he acted with the secure confidence of a man manifestly destined to rule the country. Opponents were increasingly marginalized, while avenues to negotiate with them and win them over remained open. To the detriment of his parliamentary and other opponents, he linked his personal success with any gains in enhancing the authority of the central government.

The elections for the fifth parliament (1924–1926) were effectively controlled by Reza Khan and his military commanders; only the Tehran elections were not manipulated. The predominant issue in the fifth parliament was Reza Khan's continuing efforts to enhance and perpetuate his authoritarian hold on power as his opponents grew increasingly powerless. Modarres, his chief parliamentary adversary, appealed to Loraine—who had dismissed the deputy as an "impecunious demagogue"—regarding "the desirability of less arbitrary actions," but was told that "only a strong government would prevent injurious agitation and noxious propaganda." Only such a government, Loraine and the British Foreign Office maintained, could establish order—a prerequisite of economic prosperity and stability—and ward off the Soviet threat.[29]

Dissatisfied with his status as premier and assisted by his supporters, Reza Khan gradually staged a republican campaign. Starting in January 1924 he sponsored a committee to organize a press campaign and plan other activities in favor of a republic. Although his achievements as war minister had helped to disarm many of his critics and earn him recognition, his cavalier attitude to constitutional processes did not augur well; his ultimate aims deeply worried his opponents and even some of those who wished to continue to support him. In opposing Reza Khan's bid for autocratic power—camouflaged as republicanism—some feared a radical reversal of constitutional achievements. With the example of Turkey in mind, and in the context of the elective affinity between monarchism and clericalism, the clerics in particular opposed a republican regime. Though far from unanimous in their views and approaches, they considered the secular ethos of republicanism inimical to their influence. In early March the leading clerics of Qom informed their counterparts in Tehran that they were opposed to a republic. Traditional segments of the population, ranging from the urban lower classes to peasants and pastoral nomads, generally felt a sense of attachment to the monarchy.

Provoking considerable real or manufactured public agitation, the issue dominated the fifth parliament as soon as it convened. While an organized barrage of telegrams from the provinces demanding a republic inundated the parliament, the outspoken Modarres concentrated on thwarting Reza Khan's ambitions, and was in the process assaulted in the parliament by a pro–Reza Khan deputy. This incident helped galvanize the opponents of republicanism. On March 22 an antirepublican crowd of some 10,000, converged before the parliament. Encountering Reza Khan in the precincts, they booed him, and he ordered soldiers to confront them; many were assaulted or arrested. The Speaker remonstrated with Reza Khan, demanding the release of those detained. Reza Khan acquiesced and apologized, realizing that public opposition would not allow his supporters in the parliament to advance his republican bid. His hasty and clumsy efforts to subdue the opposition by bullying had backfired, deepening the misgivings of his detractors and widening public, particularly clerical and mercantile, opposition to his republican plan.

Reza Khan had tried to co-opt certain clerics and had exploited the differences between those residing in Tehran and the shrine city of Qom, and the high-ranking Iranian clerics of Iraq, who had been expelled from there in 1923 and whose cause in returning to Iraq he had shown himself keen to support. In late March 1924 he went to Qom, ostensibly to bid them farewell but more to confer with and win over leading divines such as Ayatollahs Abolhasan Esfahani and Mohammad-Hosein Na'ini, who were returning to Iraq. Upon his return to the capital a few days later, Reza Khan announced that following discussions with the clerics he had decided against republicanism. Evidently, he renounced republicanism as effortlessly as he had espoused it. He pointedly did so in a conspicuous show of deference to the clerics, whom he was courting in the expectation of being able to rely on their implicit or explicit support or acquiescence in his future bid to assume the throne.

Soon after, aiming to show his dejection at the setback he had suffered and thus outwit his opponents, in a carefully choreographed maneuver (far better organized than his October 1922 move) Reza Khan resigned the premiership and threatened to leave the country. His supporters were again galvanized on his behalf, and military commanders, prompted to act, sent ominously threatening messages to the parliament. Reza Khan's reinstatement by the parliament was a clear blow to his constitutionalist and royalist opponents, while the Shah, who from the safety of Europe had attempted to replace him, suffered an irreversible setback. In the meantime the committee agitating for a republic, having tactically retreated, changed its strategy to concentrate on efforts to secure the Shah's removal.

The artificiality of the republican agitation indicated and reinforced Reza Khan's failure to foster popularity. His authoritarian conduct and that of his cronies, civilian or military, had provoked resentment and resistance throughout the country. His petulance and uncontrollable temper had become notorious in the capital; when driving through the city, if passersby failed to show the expected deference, he promptly stopped and personally abused and assaulted them.[30] His behavior was unlikely to endear him to the public. "Public criticism of the Prime Minister," reported the British military attaché in June 1924, "is becoming bolder and more outspoken, and it is indeed more dangerous to speak in his favour; a mullah, who attempted to praise him in the Masjed-e Shah, was roughly handled by the crowd; a small merchant used by Reza Khan as a propaganda agent in the bazaars, has been forced to leave Tehran owing to the hostility of the populace."[31]

Press criticism of Reza Khan had also increased. In early July, following the murder of Mohammad-Reza Mirzadeh-Eshqi, a journalist and poet who had denounced Reza Khan's republicanism as spurious, many journalists took sanctuary in the parliament. This crisis was, however, overshadowed by another two weeks later. A convoluted amalgam of political intrigues, religious fervor, popular fears, belief in miracles, mobilized prejudices, and anti-Baha'i agitation provided the context in which the inexperienced American consul, Robert Imbrie, was killed by a crowd after being seen taking photographs of a fountain believed to produce miraculous cures. The police and the army had not acted promptly, and the soldiers were, according to British accounts, "undoubtedly" among his assailants.[32] Regardless of how this incident unfolded and to what extent it was or was not manufactured, it politically benefited Reza Khan, who imposed martial law, suspended remaining liberties, and arrested some 300 people. Reza Khan's angered parliamentary opponents tabled a motion of interpellation against him, but bullying and physical assaults prevented them from attending parliament, and the motion was defeated.

Reza Khan's manner of dealing with opponents reinforced the belief that his republicanism would amount to little more than militaristic and authoritarian rule and the demise of existing laws and liberties. The Shah was not loved, but the public perceived him as providing a check on Reza Khan's dictatorial power, while Reza Khan knew that with the existence of another source of authority, and with opponents in the parliament and among journalists, he could not achieve his objective of formalized and unchallenged autocratic rule. Though failing to win over the public, he had the backing of those politicians and bureaucrats who saw him as the only available means of bringing about socioeconomic change or viewed their career interests as better served by supporting him. His primary bases of support were, however, the military and the police. Constituting Reza Khan's chief locus of power, the military treated rebels and the restless segments of the population in a manner that was often punishing and sometimes gratuitously brutal. The fame or notoriety it thus gained readily reflected on its commander. The military played a crucial role not only in silencing or threatening Reza Khan's opponents but also in collecting revenues, from which it amply benefited. Despite differences, for instance between Cossack officers who supported a republic and those formerly affiliated with the gendarmerie who opposed it, by May 1924 the military commanders had pledged full support for Reza Khan.

Reza Khan still needed to overcome his bitterness over the failure of his republican venture, and to compensate for it while also gaining a breathing space in which to prepare for replacing the Qajars. No move was more likely to help him in this than at last bringing Khuzestan into the orbit of central government authority by subjugating a British-backed regional opponent. Though not without its dangers, such a task would earn him further credit, undermine or muzzle his parliamentary opponents, demonstrate his determination and power, and underline his autonomy from Britain. Sheikh Khaz'al, the powerful ruler of Khuzestan, who had turned the province into a virtual British protectorate and enjoyed close links with the Bakhtiari tribal chieftains, had long felt threatened by Reza Khan's centralizing drive. By the end of 1923 Khaz'al had agreed to pay taxes to the central government, but by the summer of 1924 he was at loggerheads with Reza Khan. In contact with some of Reza Khan's parliamentary opponents, particularly Modarres, Khaz'al openly supported the Shah and invoked constitutionalism in order to justify his opposition to Reza Khan.

Some of Reza Khan's parliamentary opponents sought any ally who might help thwart his ambitions. Although Arthur Millspaugh, the American administrator general of finances in Iran from 1922 to 1927 (and again from 1943 to 1945), had not proved popular with the deputies, they were willing to tolerate him, as he could be used to restrain Reza Khan.[33] They were also willing to enlist the support of Khaz'al, in the hope of encumbering Reza Khan with an insurmountable challenge or driving a wedge between him and his British supporters. While they found it difficult to oppose Reza Khan's move against Khaz'al openly, opponents hoped that a solution endorsed by Britain would discredit Reza Khan while an outcome disagreeable to the British would turn them against him. The British, however, whose support had so far saved Khaz'al, no longer seemed willing to deter Reza Khan from acting against him. Loraine advocated qualified support for the extension of Reza Khan's centralization policies to the south, and the latter continued his efforts to allay British misgivings.[34] In November 1924, despite residual British objections, Reza Khan led a military force to Khuzestan. British efforts prevented a military confrontation; pressured by them, Khaz'al offered no resistance and was formally granted amnesty by Reza Khan in December. Four months later, however, he was summoned to Tehran, where he would be forced to reside for the rest of his life.[35]

Having maintained cordial relations with the British, Reza Khan had persuaded them that supporting the authority of the central government was politically more advantageous than protecting Khaz'al or subsidizing tribal chieftains; that the oil installations were better protected by central government forces than by local notables or tribesmen.[36] A corollary was further effective British commitment to Reza Khan. The removal of the recalcitrant Khaz'al crucially strengthened Reza Khan and dealt another blow to his opponents, including the Shah. After a pilgrimage to the Iraqi shrine cities of Najaf and Karbala to reaffirm his professions of religiosity, and to secure clerical support or approval for his moves against the Qajars, Reza Khan returned to Tehran in early January 1925 amidst lavish welcoming ceremonies. Taking advantage of his victory to consolidate his position further and gain additional concessions from his opponents, on February 8 he gave the parliament a virtual ultimatum that he would relinquish office unless his authority was increased within a few days.

After extensive debates and maneuvers, in a carefully worded resolution the parliament agreed to confirm Reza Khan as supreme commander of the defense and security forces of the country with full powers but acting within the limits of the Constitution and other laws; he could not be stripped of this position without parliamentary approval. Although the wording of the resolution was intended to avoid directly impinging on the nominal authority of the Shah as commander-in-chief of the armed forces, this position had in effect been appropriated by Reza Khan since the coup of February 1921. Nevertheless, the parliamentary formalization of Reza Khan's command over the armed forces marked an additional setback for the Shah and his supporters. Led by Modarres, they tactically supported the measure with the aim of depriving Reza Khan of any pretext to invoke the vulnerability of his position and in the hope of forestalling his efforts to depose the Shah. Before backing the resolution, Modarres had obtained Reza Khan's promise to invite the Shah to return to the country.

Ostensibly satisfied, Reza Khan now adopted a more cooperative approach to the parliament. He proposed that a committee of senior deputies be formed to advise him on drafting development bills to be submitted to the parliament, and announced measures to secure the Shah's return. At the same time, military commanders continued to issue dire warnings to the parliament against any moves to undermine Reza Khan, that is, to support the Shah. Press campaigns against the Qajars also continued to exhort the deputies and clerics not to impede "progress." Reza Khan was inching irresistibly toward his chief objective of deposing the Qajars and becoming Iran's foremost political boss; whether this could be achieved as president or as king made little difference. He had relinquished his republican bid only because the prospect of becoming king was more tantalizing and, among other things, thanks to the attitudes and actions of many of his opponents, particularly the clerics, events were moving in that direction.

In different circumstances the progressive aura of republicanism would have appealed widely to supporters of change and reform. What many people had opposed was not republicanism as such but Reza Khan himself;[37] they feared the disappearance of what had been achieved as a result of the Constitutional Revolution. Had Reza Khan succeeded in setting up a republican regime it would doubtless have been an authoritarian and unmistakably monarchical presidency. Yet even a formally republican rule based on a revised version of the Constitution and periodically punctuated by elections could potentially have allowed for a greater measure of politically beneficial change than would be possible under a monarchy. It could have resulted at least in a partial replacement of the ruling clique, and terminated or modified the dominance of a constitutionally entrenched dynastic political clan over the political process. Politically, even a formally republican governance would have been a major progressive step in contrast to the monarchy, which rested on unjustifiable heredity and archaic traditions.

Of course, many of those who thwarted Reza Khan's republican bid could not have imagined his *volte-face* in favor of assuming the throne, or else they overestimated their ability to restrain him. From mid-September 1925, though ostensibly welcoming the Shah's message regarding his imminent return, Reza Khan intensified maneuvers to prevent. He and his supporters and agents acted in a more coordinated manner. With the aim of lessening popular hostility to himself, Reza Khan announced that soldiers found to be ill-treating the people would be punished. He also capitalized on continued successes in subduing tribal rebels. In Lorestan, the brutal treatment of tribesmen and the treacherous execution of their leaders despite a promise of amnesty had resulted in unrest throughout 1924; but by April 1925, following reconciliation with a key tribal chieftain, tranquility had more or less returned. The autumn of 1925 saw the end of a rebellion among the Turkoman tribes of northeastern Iran, in the course of which aircraft had been used against the rebels. There was scarcely a contender in Tehran or beyond who could seriously worry Reza Khan.

Having increasingly overshadowed, snubbed, and rendered irrelevant the hapless Qajar prince regent, Reza Khan behaved less like a prime minister and more as the unchallenged ruler of the country. He continued intensive efforts to win over more supporters, build tactical alliances, and thwart the opposition. Clerics were among the wide cross-section of people whom he courted.[38] He also often secretly met and negotiated with his implacable and influential opponent Modarres, whose support he needed—and gained—to ensure parliamentary passage of measures such as the military conscription bill.[39] However, no sustained understanding between Modarres and Reza Khan proved possible, despite the temporary inclusion of two Modarres nominees in the cabinet. Reza Khan had also concentrated on enlisting British support or acquiescence in his efforts to end the Qajar dynasty. Despite the misgivings of Loraine, particularly about the impact on

Anglo-Iranian relations of Reza Khan's dictatorial tendencies, few British officials saw any advantage in taking steps to save the Qajar monarchy. Although Reza Khan suspected them of having opposed republicanism, the British had remained neutral, and they continued to pursue the same policy regarding the change of dynasty. A message to this effect from Austin Chamberlain, the Conservative British foreign secretary, conveyed by Loraine to Reza Khan, removed any residual hesitation he might have felt about proceeding with his plans.[40]

In addition to his covert maneuver, Reza Khan resorted to overt moves. On September 23 and 24, demonstrations were organized ostensibly to protest the shortage of bread. It was, however, widely believed and "hardly open to doubt" that Reza Khan "himself intended deliberately to provoke a disturbance." His agents had secured the closure of the bazaars and collected a crowd to engage in an anti-Shah demonstration, but this tactic backfired: the crowd, including a contingent of women, expressed strong sentiments and "approbation" in support of the Shah while abusing Reza Khan.[41] From early October, pressure on bazaar merchants and shopkeepers to close their shops and engage in activities and demonstrations against the Shah in front of the parliament had increased but "aroused little sympathy in the mass of the people."[42] Not having been actively involved in governing and widely viewed as unjustly victimized by Reza Khan, the Shah and the regent—who had continued to maintain a dignified composure—had garnered considerable popular sympathy.

Irrespective of public feeling, manufactured prorepublican demands gave way to an organized clamor, instigated mainly by the military, for ending the Qajar dynasty. During the second half of October the parliament was bombarded by telegrams sent from committees of what had been dubbed a "national movement" (nahzat-e melli). One such committee, in Tabriz, stridently threatened the parliament with severing relations with the central government and forming a force to march to the capital if the parliament failed to terminate the Qajar dynasty. Having failed to create a real popular movement, Reza Khan and his acolytes manufactured a "national movement" whose artificiality could not be disguised. In Tehran itself, in late October 1925, Reza Khan and his cronies marshaled their supporters and cajoled, bribed, or coerced the deputies congregated in the parliament. In an ominous atmosphere of intimidation, and overcome by a sense of inevitability, the deputies complied with Reza Khan's barely disguised directive to depose the Qajars, and thus paved the way for his assumption of the throne. Reza Khan's ascendancy had started with a coup and was formalized by a flagrant manipulation of the Constitution. The Constitution, the respected statesman Hasan Mostaufi (Mostaufi al-Mamalek) reportedly told Reza Khan, was the mother of the parliament; the parliament had violated its mother.

Reza Khan's coercion and manipulation of the parliament to depose the Qajars, and the measures he employed to accomplish this, left no doubt about the extent of his disrespect for procedures likely to generate legitimacy. The prince regent was promptly and unceremoniously escorted out of Iran. Now formally designated head of the provisional government and with an eye to further reassuring the clerics, Reza Khan declared his agenda as consisting of two principles: the implementation of Islamic law and the promotion of public welfare. In the face of these rapidly unfolding events, however, public reaction amounted to little more than apathy. Foreign governments with representatives in Iran, beginning notably with the British, promptly recognized the new regime. Wasting no time and assisted by those who for whatever reason had thrown in their lot with him, Reza Khan convened a barely credible constituent assembly to formalize his assumption of the throne and the establishment of the dynasty. Having accomplished this, in mid-December 1925 he swore allegiance to the Constitution as Reza Shah Pahlavi. His coronation followed on April 25, 1926.

As incumbent of the office of monarch, Ahmad Shah, the undistinguished last of the Qajar kings, had been able, despite British pressures and payments, to complicate the tasks even of prime ministers as capable as Vosuq. The Shah had acted as an obstacle to effective government;[43] his position enabled him to frustrate or discomfit prime ministers who were inattentive to his expectations. His initial indifference to the Constitution gave way to invoking it in his attempts to ward off Reza Khan's ascendancy.[44] He did not, however, lose his throne as a result of his undeniable failings or his inability to inspire an effective defense of constitutionalism. Even if he had stayed in the country and had possessed a different character, Ahmad Shah would, in all likelihood, have failed to avert the demise of the exhausted Qajar dynasty. The rise of Reza Shah demonstrated that the existing constitutional arrangements, in the absence of permissive conditions, were vulnerable to a variety of machinations, and less than viable. Despite the considerable sacrifices made to achieve and protect constitutionalism, the idealistic dedication and resilience of its proponents, and the desire of the urban populace to maintain it, the structures and forces militating against it were stronger. The rise of a militaristic autocracy was the consequence of a prolonged crisis of governance in which order, stability, and efficiency not only had come to appear more urgent than legality and liberty, but were falsely portrayed as irreconcilable with them. Reza Khan's takeover of the state was, of course, not the only possible alternative, let alone a desirable one, to the existing constitutional arrangements.

The unashamedly stage-managed action of the parliament in arranging for Reza Khan's assumption of the throne was bravely contested by a number of deputies. Among them was the Swiss educated lawyer Dr. Mohammad Mosaddeq, who provided the most cogent argument against such a move. As a capable war minister or prime minister, Reza Khan, Mosaddeq maintained, had achieved commendable results; were he to become king, however, he would be entitled, constitutionally speaking, to play only a largely ceremonial role. By helping Reza Khan to assume the throne, Mosaddeq argued, his protagonists had deprived the country of a capable statesman and had done the nation a disservice. Of course, Mosaddeq added, if Reza Khan were to become king and also to act as prime minister, that is, if he were to reign and rule simultaneously, the entire constitutional achievements and struggles of the Iranian people would be undermined. Iran would regress politically; it would be more backward than Zanzibar.[45] Ali Akbar Davar, the ardently pro–Reza Khan deputy, contested Mosaddeq's argument, retorting that such a regression was unthinkable; it could not happen.[46]

Reza Khan's assumption of the throne was a reversal for the country's constitutional evolution and a major setback for the development of a democratic public sphere; it marked the beginning of the end of a turbulent phase in Iranian politics, a period in which a host of societies, associations, parties, journalists, political activists, and parliamentarians heatedly debated the merits as well as the shortcomings of constitutionalism and how the latter could be overcome. A boisterous press, which helped to shape and inform as well as reflect public opinion in the cities, served as the chief vehicle for such debates. It did not survive the rise of the Pahlavi dynasty.

Veteran constitutionalists such as Hasan Pirnia, Hosein Pirnia (Mo'tamen al-Molk), Mostaufi, Modarres, and Mosaddeq, without denying the need for reform, emphatically regarded parliamentary and democratic procedures as indispensable safeguards of Iran's higher national interest. They viewed any serious tampering with these procedures, despite their frustrating inadequacies, to be incalculably dangerous and ultimately counterproductive. They did not offer readily practical remedies for strengthening the executive branch of the government, but maintained that such an aim did not require discrediting the legislature or the Constitution itself. In their eyes, the existing parliamentary arrangements, though flawed, constituted a major step in the right political direction.

Without embracing romantic populist sentiments, these parliamentarians, though different in character and political style, adhered to a tradition of Iranian civic virtues that valued trust, truthfulness, sincerity, and transparency of public conduct—values and practices that were publicly acclaimed and culturally sanctioned. Owing their popularity and prestige to demonstrated attachment to nationalist and constitutionalist causes, they were, in turn, able to enhance the popular credibility of the government. Regarding a genuine parliamentarian to be a public trustee, they advocated, and to varying degrees practiced, a style of politics that was responsive to ordinary people's sensibilities, desires, and expectations. In contrast, the arrogant elitist mentality shared and reinforced by the Pahlavis perceived the people as essentially a rabble, an unruly and treacherous multitude to be despised, manipulated, paternalistically treated, and subdued.

In the twenty-year interval between the granting of the Constitution and the accession of Reza Shah, nineteen prime ministers, all but two of whom were from the ranks of titled notables, had formed thirty-four cabinets that went through sixty reshufflings. Contrary to article 7 of the Constitution, which stipulated that constitutional arrangements could not be suspended, during this period the parliament was in session for less than eight and a half years, and could not therefore be held primarily responsible for causing political disarray and instability.

Instability could be only partially attributed to the prevailing parliamentary arrangements; it was more fully explicable as a consequence of the heightened impact of global economic, sociopolitical, and cultural developments on the traditional fabric of Iranian society. Iran had not been formally colonized; it had suffered from the ill effects of informal colonialism but had not, strictly speaking, experienced a solidarity-generating struggle for independence, although opposing foreign domination had been a crucial component of the Constitutional Revolution. The Qajar state was opposed not because it was an avowedly colonial entity, but because it was oppressive, administratively ineffective, and unable to protect its subjects; it was incapable of resisting foreign encroachments and coping with the changing circumstances of the modern world. It could not, however, be easily replaced by a modern state structure. The convulsions that followed the Constitutional Revolution and the political fragmentation of the country, worsened by foreign influence and the impact of the First World War, paved the way for the emergence of a ruler who, at the helm of a civilian and military elite, helped expedite the transformation of the ramshackle Qajar kingdom into a nation-state. The replacement of the Qajars by the Pahlavis inaugurated extensive change but did not drastically modify some of the essential features of governance. The resilient autocratic traditions continued to militate against the emergence of a depersonalized state. Autocracy in the past had been circumscribed by powerful social forces, old institutions, and religious and traditional restraints; under the Pahlavis, the state acquired a far greater capacity to act coercively and defy previously effective forces of restraint.

In Iran, demands for the creation of democratic accountability had coincided with the necessity of creating a centralized state strong enough to maintain order and security, resist outside pressures, and effect socioeconomic reform. Adherence to constitutional principles and procedures came increasingly to be regarded as subservient to action aimed at addressing the practical and urgent need for political order, administrative effectiveness, and socioeconomic modernization, which in Iran, in contrast to Turkey or Egypt, had been seriously delayed. Such a situation could partially account for a shift by segments of the elite and the intelligentsia away from democratic aspirations and toward support of the growing power of Reza Khan, who cultivated and relied on both domestic military and British backing and at least the acquiescence of the Soviet Union.

The quest for political order and socioeconomic development, even the idea of a modern army, had preoccupied Iranian parliamentarians from the outset and was not intrinsically incompatible with constitutional procedures. Constitutionalism and efforts to institutionalize and augment it would have strengthened the state by endowing it with democratic legitimacy. They could have crucially helped to bridge the gulf that traditionally separated the nation *(mellat)* from the state *(daulat)* and ensured their mutual animosity. Publicly trusted statesmen would have been able to enhance the state's popular credibility and legitimacy and defuse potentially dangerous resentments. Reza Shah's conception of governance and style of rule, however, resulted in the exclusion or elimination of credible statesmen and the retention of only the ceremonial veneer of constitutionalism. Reza Shah and his supporters, and indeed the Pahlavi dynasty, implicitly invoked the impracticability of a fully developed democracy in order to justify the eradication of any real measure of the rule of law and credible political accountability.

# 2

# Pahlavist Absolutism

## Consolidation

Although the Pahlavi state was unmistakably identified with the person of Reza Shah, the establishment of autocratic absolutism was gradual. Reza Shah initially needed and endeavored to enlist the cooperation of as many reputable politicians as possible. He resorted, among other things, to self-promotion, promising to investigate complaints against government officials and frequently visiting various parts of the country to inspect military and civilian installations and projects. Having recruited many "unsavory characters" to assist him in his bid to assume political ascendancy, he began to dissociate himself from some of them.[1] As the British military attaché noted, "The jackals whom the Shah used during the three or four years before his succession to the throne, for intrigues in the bazaars, and of whom some were, regrettably, his close companions, have in most cases been disappointed of the rewards they hoped would come their way when the tiger became king."[2] There was also a need to demonstrate that, with the establishment of the new dynasty, Iran had at last achieved not only a centralized bureaucratic state but also an assertively independent one. Foreign attempts to reduce the country to a protectorate or divide it into spheres of influence were declared to be a thing of the past. The foreign-controlled military units had ceased to exist; foreign-operated telegraph lines came under Iranian control; foreign debts were renounced, and the state appropriated revenues tied up for debt repayment.[3]

Reza Shah had done everything he could to win British confidence and support, but because of the lingering stigma of enjoying close ties with the British he could not afford to act in any way that compromised the independence of the country or contravened nationalist sensibilities. Robert Clive, the new British minister (1926–1931), showed little hesitation, or any of his predecessor's subtleties, in venting British imperial disdain for the country or disappointment with the new ruler. He denounced the Shah as neither "enlightened" nor "patriotic," adding that his "lack of vision, his complete lack of education, his lack of the more human qualities of honesty and kindness, seem all the more noticeable in the hard light that beats upon a throne." He regretted that the Persians' "incapacity for positive action remains undiminished, but their amiability has been rendered somewhat acid by the gall of militarism and nationalism." Describing the Persians as "feckless," "incompetent," and "conceited," he found their "ingratitude particularly disagreeable," adding that "to the passive indolence of the old Persia has been added the active self-conceit of the new. We have gained nothing by the advent of militarism and centralisation in Persia; it may well be that we have lost a great deal." He nevertheless considered Reza Shah "better than" the Qajars and "infinitely better than a republic," and bluntly stated:

> Although the Persians much dislike us, they are still sufficiently afraid of us not to go too far. They have attempted a few pin pricks, but they have not seriously endeavoured to attack our vital interests, The Imperial Bank, the telegraph, the Anglo-Persian Oil Company have prospered exceedingly. If the Russians have increased their influence in the north, our interests in the south have since 1925 been in no way seriously affected. The Capitulations are at the moment more or less intact. So long as our essential interests can be maintained there seems no real reason why His Majesty's Government (as distinct from His Majesty's Legation) need be unduly disturbed by the conditions in Persia.[4]

British "essential interests" did not in the long run prove as secure as Clive had assumed, and the abolition of capitulations received immediate attention as an important step to emphasize national sovereignty. It was announced in May 1927 that capitulatory rights would be formally abolished by May of the following year. These rights had been enjoyed for 100 years by the Russians and gradually also by other foreign nationals. Mosaddeq had been the first Iranian to advocate the abolition of capitulations, in a widely circulated pamphlet in 1914.[5] After the Soviet revolution of 1917 and the cancellation of concessions to and agreements with the old regime in Russia, the capitulations had in effect been abolished, but the extension of this measure to other countries enjoying capitulatory privileges in Iran had to wait until 1928. The abolition of capitulations provided additional impetus for the modernization of the Iranian judicial system. It could also be seen as part of the state's efforts to revive national self-confidence and channel it into the desired political direction.[6]

The Shah left the routine aspects of governance to the professional politicians and more specifically to a few capable ministers, and concentrated his own efforts on consolidating his hold on the state, strengthening the military and the security forces, and dealing with residual clerical, pastoral-nomadic, or other resistance to his rule. Despite owing much to the clerics, the Shah showed little willingness to tolerate their continued influence. In late October 1926 an attempt against the life of Modarres—Reza Khan's nemesis in his republican bid—left him injured. The failure of the clerics to act on his behalf, especially following his arrest in October 1928 and his imprisonment in a desolate area in eastern Iran (where he would be gruesomely killed nine years later), reflected a decline in clerical power. Policies such as instituting conscription had provoked the intense opposition of many clerics, who organized protests in the shrine city of Qom and elsewhere. The government was, however, able to neutralize or mollify the clerics and undermine their capacity to act effectively. Many senior clerical figures had died, and those who survived did not have sufficient clout or were quietist. There were few capable or willing leaders, and those who vocalized the resentments of the public were treated harshly. The law of December 1928, imposing a unified dress code and headgear—the "Pahlavi" hat—for men, with the qualified exception of bona fide and accredited clerics, signaled an intensification of measures aimed at undermining clerical influence. These measures, together with the failure to respect the sanctity of religious sites, caused deep clerical resentment. By the end of 1928 there were rumors of senior clerics emigrating en masse to Iraq, prompting the Iraqi government to introduce visa restrictions.

Of more immediate concern was the further pacification or subjuga-

*Male members of a provincial family of artisans, merchants, and clerics in the 1920s, before the imposition of the unified dress code.*
(Author's collection)

tion of the pastoral-nomadic population. Since the autumn of 1925 tranquillity had prevailed in the tribal areas, and in 1928, when the army defeated the rebellious tribesmen in Baluchestan, the authority of the central government appeared to be consolidated. Many southern tribal chieftains had cooperated with the new ruler in the maintenance of peace. However, chronic maladministration and ill-treatment of the tribal population, particularly by the military, had aggravated disaffection. When political subjugation of the tribes was followed by measures to transform the nomadic way of life, rebellion ensued. Resentment centered on the conduct of military governors, conscription, the disarming of civilians, the detention of chieftains, direct taxation, the government monopoly over commodities such as tea and sugar, tribal settlement or relocation policies, and other intrusive steps. By 1929 this situation, aggravated by the imposition of the new dress code, had united the southern tribes against the state, provoking widespread rebellion.[7]

Military campaigns, which involved the use of aircraft, though often bloody did not prove successful, and Reza Shah was forced to make a number of tactical concessions and resort to manipulatory moves. Accustomed to an active British interest in tribal affairs, and in some cases to British protection, several chieftains sought mediation by the British, whom the Shah primarily blamed for the rebellion;[8] he was unwilling to recognize the depth of tribal discontent or the possible spontaneity of any resistance. However, despite Iranian suspicions, vented privately but also in the officially sponsored press, by the late 1920s British links with the southern tribes had considerably diminished. By the summer of 1930, with a combination of force and tactical conciliation and the help and mediation of co-opted tribal chieftains, the government had overcome tribal unrest without abandoning its coercive measures. Many Lors were removed, together with their livestock, to be resettled in distant areas such as Qom and Khorasan. Large numbers of Kurds would also be resettled elsewhere. Reza Shah would await the opportunity to subdue and conclusively defeat those who had challenged him. In order to save face, he blamed the failure of the military campaigns or excessive casualties on commanding officers and key local officials.

In the wake of the military or political subjugation of the tribes, the policy of coercively transforming nomads into settled cultivators was intensified, and in the 1930s the sedentarization of the tribes was enforced with relentless brutality. Although nomadic people were among the most deprived of the Iranian population, many tribal chieftains had long been part of the political establishment; they supported modernization and a centralized state or felt obliged to assist or connive in the suppression of their fellow tribesmen. Reza Shah could not, however, tolerate a situation in which political notables enjoyed their own actual or potential power base. Thus not only did the tribes as a political force have to be eliminated, but the pastoral-nomadic way of life had to be uprooted. Reza Shah's attitude to the tribes was shared by the urban intelligentsia, who revealed little understanding of the country's highly diverse nomadic communities and the complexities of their lives, viewing them as an outright threat to the centralized state and the modernizing drive, and condoning the government policies toward them.[9]

Reza Shah's customary *modus operandi* was to respond with an iron fist to any move that he perceived as a challenge to the authority of the state.

When success seemed certain, the Shah himself led the operations; his projected image of fearless determination often demoralized the rebels, leading to their defeat or capitulation. Such a situation helped enhance his standing and reaffirm his belief in the efficacy of his tactics and policies. Military commanders, however, often dealing with more complicated situations, expected little respite in case of failure. Spectacular success in combat or popularity among the troops was equally troublesome and could result in early retirement or worse. Officers who resented their treatment always posed a threat, but Reza Shah ensured that their activities were carefully monitored. In any event, efforts within the military to resist or act against him were neutralized, as were attempts from outside, which were quelled by the military itself.[10] Officers who were implicated in anti-Shah activities by vengeful rivals or unscrupulous police chiefs suffered a variety of punishments. The execution in February 1928 of Colonel Mahmud Puladin, for allegedly conspiring to launch a coup, was meant to be a deterrent to others. Wanting Puladin summarily punished, the Shah only reluctantly agreed to his trial and eventually secured a death sentence. General Habibollah Sheibani, the chief of staff, was promptly replaced for his refusal to endorse the verdict. Puladin's alleged accomplices included Samuel Haim, representative of the Jewish community in the fifth parliament, who was later executed. He blamed the new regime and its police chief, General Mohammad Dargahi, for his failure to regain his parliamentary seat. The notoriously scheming Dargahi played a crucial role in manufacturing incriminating evidence and exaggerating the scale of the plot.[11]

While the Shah was preoccupied with overcoming resistance, rebellions, and other actual or perceived challenges to his rule, the task of governing the country was largely performed by the court minister, Abd al-Hosein Teymurtash, who overshadowed all other officials, including ineffective prime ministers, and was actively assisted by Firuz Firuz (Nosrat al-Dauleh) and Ali-Akbar Davar, capable ministers of finance and justice respectively.[12] A suave, Russian-educated *bon vivant*, compulsive gambler, drinker, and consummate womanizer, Teymurtash had played a crucial role in aiding Reza Shah's assumption of the throne and consolidation of power. He regularly attended cabinet sessions and enjoyed enormous influence, but held no formal cabinet position or responsibility and was accountable only to the Shah. A foremost driving force and a mastermind behind many state policies and

*Abd al-Hosein Teymurtash, Reza Shah's influential court minister
from 1926 to 1932.* (Courtesy of the Institute for the Study of
Contemporary Iranian History, Tehran)

projects, he had an unrivaled command of complex domestic and foreign
policy issues; he not only formulated policy but also oversaw its implementation. His many tasks included ensuring that the parliament acted as a cooperative instrument for endorsing government policies; he told the British
minister that "it will be essential, before long, to set definite limits to the
powers" of the parliament.[13]

In the early summer of 1927 Teymurtash created the New Iran (Iran-e
Nau) Party, which was committed to the Shah's leadership as the catalyst
of change. According to one account, in "his conception of the idea,"
Teymurtash was "undoubtedly influenced by the Fascist party in Italy."[14]
The party was intended to become a nationwide organization mobilizing

support for the Shah and acting as the party of government; it was to dominate the parliament and create a pool of acceptable candidates for parliamentary seats. Incorporating most existing parties and factions, it became unwieldy as aspirants to office showed great eagerness to join it. Considering it to be antireligious, the clerics instigated opposition to it. Other parties were formed to rival it; in the ensuing turmoil, the Shah intervened to dampen expectations. Within a few months the party became moribund and soon ceased to exit.[15] Teymurtash now took control of another formation, the Progress (Taraqqi) Party, created by deputies as a counterpart to the New Iran Party and broadly subscribing to similar ideas.

In the absence of real representation, debate, or choice, however, such parties were no more than spurious. As the parliament's significance radically waned, efforts aimed at controlling it or creating a semblance of formal party alignments dedicated to formulating and promoting policies became redundant. Yet the Progress Party continued to function as a vehicle for executing royal intentions as articulated by Teymurtash. Led and controlled by him, it remained a useful tool for discussing and refining bills before their adoption, as well as for keeping the deputies in line by promising them reelection. Not surprisingly, with the unexpected fall of Teymurtash in late 1932 the party melted away. Although the Shah continued to speak of the need for a national party, the idea remained unrealized.

The reign of Reza Shah encompassed the sixth to the twelfth terms of the parliament, of which only the sixth parliament (1926–1928) retained some credibility, since its elections were not wholly manipulated. Reza Shah's authoritarian rule and policies held little appeal for the electorate and certainly not for the inhabitants of the capital. In Tehran, those who cared to vote—which often meant the most politically discerning sections of the population—elected several deputies who were clearly opposed to or critical of Reza Shah. They thus showed a marked preference for the preservation of credible constitutional procedures. Modarres gained the highest number of votes, and Mosaddeq was also reelected.[16] Hosein Pirnia, Speaker of the third, fourth, and most of the fifth terms of the parliament and a critic of Reza Shah, was reelected as Speaker; the respected statesman Mostaufi served as prime minister.

The elections for the seventh parliament and its successors, however, were systematically controlled by the court and the military commanders to ensure the exclusion of recalcitrant deputies.[17] Even in cities such as Tehran and Tabriz, where elections traditionally mattered greatly to the population, the word "election" became a misnomer. Many deputies were virtually unknown to their constituencies. In line with its strategies of co-optation, the court sought to support the candidacy of statesmen such as Mostaufi and the Pirnia brothers in Tehran, but they declined the offer. After the demise of the Teymurtash-led Progress Party, an elaborate system was employed for the selection of parliamentary candidates. Their credentials were vetted through the coordinated work of local governors, army commanders, and the royal court. Their "election" was subsequently authorized by the Shah on the basis of demonstrated loyalty to the regime and also, in some cases, a measure of local standing.

The emergence of an autocratic centralized bureaucratic state as the vehicle for the effective monopolization of force involved a major shift in the traditional configuration and social basis of Iranian politics. Titled landowning notables, the Qajar nobility, tribal chieftains, religious dignitaries, as well as credible parliamentarians and other public figures, all helplessly witnessed the erosion of their power and influence. Established modes of political conduct and exercise of power, together with the diffuse and intricate, mutually reinforcing patronage networks that nourished them, were being replaced by a court-centered politics of autocratic control sustained by the military and security forces. Tribal chieftains who were not eliminated or imprisoned became tame courtiers.

As the chief dispenser of patronage and a wide range of political and symbolic rewards, the court became the sole locus of power to be cultivated by aspiring public figures. Notables who sought or were called upon to serve the regime were reduced to the status of expendable court retainers with no autonomous power base of their own, vulnerable to the whims of the Shah. The magnates' loss of status was symbolized by the July 1935 abolition of the honorific titles generously dispensed under the Qajars. In contrast to its Qajar predecessor, the Pahlavi state was no longer visibly constrained by the religious and traditional conceptions of justice or the implicit norms of a moral economy. The diminished influence of urban thugs and street leaders was a welcome development for the lower classes. Peasants too were no longer at the mercy of bandits or marauding nomads. The lower classes and peasants were, however, vulnerable to the predation or whims of military officers, petty but powerful bureaucrats, rapacious and corrupt urban and rural police, a burdensome array of taxes and dues, low wages and incomes, and the steadily eroding influence of those who might intercede on their behalf with the intrusive state.

There had long been traditional practices that, though susceptible to abuse, provided individuals and groups with a measure of protection from arbitrary arrest and an opportunity to express discontent or resist injustice. Chief among these was the practice of seeking sanctuary in places considered sacred or inviolable. This practice was first banned for military personnel and was later altogether prohibited. In March 1927, inadequate observance of the veil by the Shah's principal wife while visiting the shrine of Qom provoked a cleric's rebuke. Upon learning of this episode, the enraged Shah immediately departed for Qom with armored vehicles. Entering the shrine without any formalities and ill-treating and coercively removing a few who had taken sanctuary there, he had the offending cleric and several others arrested. Shocking the public and affronting the clerics, this conduct and the violation of the shrine's sanctity in effect marked the end of the time-honored practice of seeking sanctuary. Other traditional practices that would be proscribed included the widely prevalent closure of bazaars and shops as a sign of protest, and the intercession of leading clerics on behalf of those accused of wrongdoing or awaiting judicial punishment. Religious gatherings such as mourning ceremonies, which could convey a political statement, would also be restricted. From June 1935 onward such ceremonies would be confined to officially designated mosques and restricted to two hours.

## Reign of Fear

With the court becoming the locus of the state's commanding role as well as the chief repository of political spoils, the political elite, particularly ministers and other senior officials, exerted every effort to win over court employees, treating even the palace gardeners and other menial servants with deference; any attachment to the court conferred unusual influence.[18] The court minister, Teymurtash, continued to act as chief adviser to the Shah. The multilingual and well-traveled Teymurtash possessed qualities that the Shah visibly lacked and silently envied. He helped conceal the coarser aspects of the royal behavior and remained the primary channel of access to the Shah, which he jealously controlled. Being ultimately dependent on the Shah, however, Teymurtash's position was precarious. One event that revealed the extent of his vulnerability was the sudden arrest in late May 1929 of his closest friend, Firuz, a capable minister and son of the patrician Qajar prince Abd al-Hosein Mirza Farmanfarma (d. 1939), who had been a patron of Reza Khan and had initiated him into politics. Firuz, Teymurtash, and Davar had in effect acted as a triumvirate, contributing significantly to the consolidation of Reza Shah's rule and laying the groundwork for much of what was credited to him. Placed under house arrest, tried a year later for bribery and corruption, imprisoned for some time and released, Firuz was arrested again in October 1936, exiled, and eventually killed in prison in January 1938, aged fifty.

Coming in the wake of the southern tribal rebellion and some agitation among certain Qajar magnates, the arrest of Firuz was prompted, as the then prime minister Mehdi-Qoli Hedayat surmised, by the Shah's suspicion of his complicity with the rebel tribesmen.[19] Firuz's cousin Akbar Mas'ud (Sarem al-Dauleh), who was governor-general of Fars, was also arrested. Clive, the British minister, plausibly attributed the arrest of Firuz to the Shah's fear of an antidynastic move—a fear that Clive considered unfounded.[20] The arrest signaled the beginning of the end of the triumvirate. It had an adverse effect on government efficiency and sense of direction and the morale of senior officials; it increased their tendency to prevaricate, avoid taking initiatives, and deflect responsibility. Firuz's successor distinctly lacked his capabilities. The triumvirate had antagonized influential people and had many enemies within the elite and beyond. Embroiled in a web of court-centered struggles for influence, intrigues, and counterintrigues, they faced well-entrenched enemies such as Generals Dargahi and Karim Buzarjomehri, the chief of police and mayor of Tehran respectively, who enjoyed the backing of the Shah's principal wife.

Undoubtedly shaken but confident of his own indispensability and of the incompetence of his opponents, Teymurtash continued to exert tremendous influence. The impact of his friend's arrest was partially compensated by the dismissal and arrest of his archenemy Dargahi in December 1929, and by the near-farcical performance in office of Buzarjomehri, who had been elevated to ministerial rank. In 1931 the British legation, with some justification, characterized the Iranian government as a duarchy, "dependent on the health and life of two men." Teymurtash made "no attempt to put his finger on the military pie," while the Shah allowed him "a free hand in civil affairs."[21] Such "freedom," however, involved not only responsibility and credit but also danger. Being in control of foreign policy, Teymurtash attempted to negotiate the perilous path of optimizing Iranian interests by playing the Soviets and the British against each other. Though having employed a controlled version of such a strategy himself, the Shah now feared it, or the possibility that it could get out of control. In the context of well-entrenched British influence and in an atmosphere rife with intrigue and disinformation, in which the Shah's fears and suspicions could be easily stimulated by the anglophiles and others, such a strategy was hazardous. His opponents could portray Teymurtash as amenable to Soviet manipulation aimed at offsetting British influence in Iran, which in turn could provoke British countermeasures against the dynasty.

Teymurtash had for several years been seeking better terms for Iran from APOC and a more equitable share of its profits; he showed greater intransigence and independence vis-à-vis the company than did the Shah.[22] Not only more actively responsive to nationalist sensibilities than the Shah, Teymurtash was also less afraid of British machinations. He persisted in pressing the company and the British, while British officials in both Tehran and London considered him a major obstacle to a settlement satisfactory to them and to British interests in general. His hold on foreign policy was somewhat diminished when, in May 1930, Mohammad-Ali Forughi, who had spent several years abroad as ambassador, was appointed foreign minister. Forughi was trusted by the Shah and by the British, who regarded him as someone on whose support they could rely. As protracted negotiations bore no fruit, in late November 1932 the Shah ordered the cancellation of the 1901 oil concession. But he soon realized how dangerously such a move could backfire, and a month later, with the aim of cushioning the blow or deflecting responsibility and blame, he took the drastic step of abruptly dismissing Teymurtash and abolishing the court ministry.[23]

The Shah had grown increasingly averse to the high profile of his court minister, and, fearing his influence, intentions, and connections, he was also determined that Teymurtash should not survive him. Soon after his dismissal Teymurtash was arrested. He was tried on charges of bribery and embezzlement and was murdered in prison nine months later, aged fifty-two. "Reza Shah," commented a onetime minister, "deeply feared any man of capability." He would not shrink from eliminating anyone who might challenge or jeopardize his son's assumption of the throne.[24] Complicit in the consolidation of a regime intent on the elimination of its actual or perceived opponents, Teymurtash himself fell victim to it. He became the highest-ranking official disposed of by a ruthless dictator who combined immense self-confidence with compulsive paranoia.[25]

In addition to poignantly demonstrating the fragility of elevated office in a sultanist regime, the fate that befell Teymurtash and Firuz was intended to deter would-be plotters. It also indicated that the Shah's confidence in the continuation of his dynastic rule was shaky; otherwise he would have confined himself to incarcerating the alleged culprits. The Shah left little doubt that he was willing, if not determined, to eliminate not only potential opponents but also those who had proved indispensable in his rise to power. Indeed, in seeking to intimidate his officials, the Shah routinely used the words "I will eliminate you."[26] One official thus threatened was Davar, since 1927 a resourceful justice and then finance minister who had grown deeply demoralized, haunted especially by the fate of Teymurtash. Davar was the last member of the Teymurtash-led triumvirate to meet a tragic end. He had crucially aided Reza Shah's ascendancy and had continued to serve him loyally, viewing him as capable of implementing objectives long cherished by the intelligentsia. Davar was a guiding spirit behind many of the major reforms associated with the Reza Shah era and had cultivated and promoted some of the ablest officials ever to serve the country. Among other things, Davar dedicated himself to reorganizing and modernizing the judicial system despite enormous obstacles, including various vested interests and the relentless opposition of many clerics. Humiliated by the Shah and in the grip of unnerving fear, Davar was driven to take his own life in February 1937, aged fifty.

The process of elimination went beyond the triumvirate. Ja'far-Qoli Sardar As'ad, a Bakhtiari tribal chieftain, veteran war minister, and Reza Shah's confidant, had, among other things, played a major role in quelling or defusing tribal unrest, particularly in the south. He was uninterested in politics and uninformed about military matters, and it was perhaps for this reason that Reza Shah sardonically told him in 1930 that he truly deserved to

*Ali-Akbar Davar, reformist justice and finance minister from 1927 to 1937.*
(Courtesy of the Institute for the Study of Contemporary
Iranian History, Tehran)

be war minister for life.[27] In his capacity as war minister he facilitated Reza Shah's control over the Bakhtiaris, a powerful tribe of pastoral nomads with a cavalry force of 20,000.[28] As the last surviving senior confidant of the Shah, and perhaps his closest friend, Sardar As'ad felt secure enough in his position to try to intercede on Teymurtash's behalf, having often done so on behalf of others. He was, however, abruptly arrested in November 1933 soon after Teymurtash's murder, and killed in prison four months later. Isma'il Qashqa'i (Saulat al-Dauleh), a prominent Qashqa'i tribal chieftain who had also played a major role in helping to end the southern rebellion, had been eliminated in August 1933. In a 1928 diary entry the unsuspecting Sardar As'ad had noted:

In the course of five years since the rise of the Pahlavi star, great services in the areas of security, finance, armed forces, etc., have been rendered to the country. Reza Shah is therefore entitled to control the elections fully . . . when the people are endowed with knowledge, maturity,
and patriotism, imposed deputies will surely be abandoned. An informed nation needs no guardian [qayyem], but a nation like Iran does;
the Iranians need a tough and unyielding guardian.[29]

Reza Shah's determination to remain such a guardian and his overreaction
to any threats, real or perceived, had ensured that none of those suspected
of ill-will would be spared; they were killed, died in prison or in mysterious
circumstances, or were targeted in other ways. Some of those arrested for
political reasons suffered the indignity of being charged with financial corruption; this was a convenient ploy, since accusing them of conspiracy, treason, or improper links with foreigners would have attracted unwelcome foreign attention. Judges failing to find the alleged culprits guilty themselves
suffered.

The most ominous event in the daily lives of Iranians was to be summoned either by the court or by the police.[30] Combining ordinary police
and intelligence work with a vast array of extrajudicial activities, including
monitoring, intimidating, and if necessary framing those suspected of posing a threat to the Shah or the regime, the police had grown into a notorious organizational complex geared to deterrence, control, harassment, and
extortion. After the Shah, one observer maintained, the police chief was the
most important personage in the country; Reza Shah had once asserted: "I
am the police."[31] Structured primarily to act as an instrument for safeguarding the regime, the police ultimately and routinely reported to the Shah, reassuring him of his full control over the sinews of power. Though loyally
submissive to the Shah, the police chiefs were at the same time clearly in a
position to manipulate him or to influence his political views and perception of events and people. Yet even the most notorious chiefs of police, who
were the main functionaries and purveyors of the prevailing apparatus of
fear, feared for their lives. General Mohammad-Hosein Ayrom, police chief
since April 1931, was at one time "looked upon as having greater power than
any member of the Cabinet and to be the Shah's right-hand man."[32] Jealous
of the close relationship of Teymurtash and Sardar As'ad with the Shah,

Ayrom had played a role in turning the Shah against them. Having won the Shah's confidence, he used his position for every kind of personal abuse— venality, graft, extortion, smuggling, confiscation of property, framing the innocent, encouraging individuals to spy on one another. Suspecting a fate similar to that of other friends of the Shah, and having amassed considerable wealth, Ayrom successfully feigned illness in order to leave the country, never to return.[33]

Constitutionalist statesmen had long felt that they had no option but to shun politics. One of them, Mosaddeq, though in virtual exile in his remote estate outside the capital since 1936, was arrested in 1940 and imprisoned in an inhospitable area of the country for six months. He was allowed to return to his estate only through the mediation of the crown prince, Mohammad Reza. Other constitutionalists, such as Mostaufi and the Pirnia brothers, had gradually eased themselves out of politics, avoiding any move that might antagonize the Shah. Until his death in 1935, Hasan Pirnia turned entirely to the safety of scholarship, devoting himself to writing a monumental history of ancient Iran. Despite having opposed Reza Khan's assumption of the throne, the veteran constitutionalist Sayyed Hasan Taqizadeh later served the state in various capacities, including Finance minister. Iranian minister in France since late 1933, he lost his position in 1934 when the French press published criticism of the Shah. Recalled to Tehran, he chose not to return. He further provoked royal anger by publishing an article in the official journal of the Ministry of Education advocating a gradual rather than coercive revision of the Persian language. Foroughi, a dedicated facilitator of the rise of Reza Shah, twice prime minister and a prominent man of letters, lost his position as a result of royal pique and turned to scholarly pursuits.

Despite the unpredictability of political life, a host of resilient civil servants and public figures persevered in creating the administrative, cultural, legal, and economic institutions essential for a viable state. A body of high-ranking officials, steeped in traditional cultural and literary values, continued at various junctures to serve the state: they included statesmen such as Foroughi, before he fell out of favor in late 1935; Hedayat, who after more than six years as prime minister finally gave up active politics in September 1933; and the veteran parliamentary Speaker Hasan Esfandiari. Such men were demonstrably loyal and discreetly capable; prudently unquestioning and unobtrusively dutiful, they were neither particularly dynamic nor ambitious, neither threatening nor assertive. They were able to lend an air of re-spectability to the regime and tried to limit damage both to themselves and to the country; if circumstance permitted they could partially reduce, con-tain, or conceal the more senseless or vulgar aspects of state policies. Curi-ously, Hedayat and Esfandiari, two of the longest-serving officials of the Reza Shah era, were strongly imbued with traditional and religious values, when the ethos of the state seemed clearly at odds with such values. In his memoirs Hedayat sardonically expressed regret at the growing arbitrariness of autocratic rule and the superficiality of what the regime counted as civi-lization.[34] The avowedly religious Esfandiari did not find it difficult to recon-cile himself to changing circumstances. Ultimately these and others re-tained their positions as long as the Shah deemed it necessary. Cabinets, prime ministers, ministers, and other senior officials were appointed and dismissed at the royal behest. No individual had the luxury of refusing of-fice, and virtually none was allowed to resign his position without the Shah's acquiescence; senior officials were relieved of their duties whenever he decided. Deputies were summarily stripped of their parliamentary im-munity, to be detained or prosecuted.

Reza Shah's preference for docile loyalty and his aversion to capable and ambitious, but also conspicuously intelligent, men drove many officials to conceal their ambitions as well as their intelligence. Ministers with an inti-mate knowledge of his character and aware of his dislike for noticeably clever and cultivated officials feigned dimwittedness in order to preserve their positions and avert his suspicion.[35] It was widely known that the mere suspicion of opposing the Shah resulted in the elimination, imprisonment, exile, or persecution of many tribal chieftains, politicians, political activists, and journalists. The fate of Teymurtash and Sardar As'ad revealed the tragic consequences of too close an association with the ruler. There were also limits to how far actively serving officials could distance themselves from him. Sycophantic and self-serving henchmen of the Shah helped to reaffirm him in his self-righteous pursuits and reassure him in his hubris and grandiose illusions. His vanity was matched only by his paranoia, which was aggravated by his overzealous security and intelligence functionaries and which ensured that he was inordinately concerned with the activities and intentions of his subordinates, whose lives were consequently pervaded by an undercurrent of fear.

Having denounced the Shah in 1927 for the creation of "an atmosphere of uncertainty and fear," in 1929 the British minister again noted: "The Shah understands well that Persia can be ruled by fear rather than by kindness."[36] In 1933 another senior member of the British legation observed:

> How long even Persia can be run on fear of one man it is difficult to prophesy. Her history is a long record of tyrants varying in the degree of their ferocity, and Persians probably dislike oppression less than most people. The fact remains that the Shah's earlier popularity has long since vanished and he is now almost universally loathed and detested . . . it is difficult to believe that his dynasty can survive him.[37]

According to another British report, "the reign of terror" had "silenced even elements among the upper classes who formerly talked vague sedition."[38] The paralyzing effect of fear manifested itself in various ways. When reporting to the Shah, the terrified Mahmud Jam, prime minister from late 1935 to October 1939, sweated so profusely that upon returning home he was forced to take medications in order to recover his composure.[39] Baqer Kazemi, a cabinet minister from 1931 to 1936, would refrain from even privately discussing politics with his father-in-law.[40] Even Field Marshal Ahmad Amir-Ahmadi, the highest-ranking officer in the military, who had brutalized the nomadic peoples, particularly the Lors in the 1920s, constantly feared being eliminated on the Shah's orders.[41]

## The Cloistered Universe of an Autocrat

Reza Shah's considerable intelligence, unrivaled political instincts, prodigious memory, and remarkable ability to absorb details more than compensated for his inadequate formal education. His natural authority was accentuated by his physical stature. By the mid-1930s, however, immobility and opium addiction had left their marks on him.[42] Single-minded and cunning, he was a shrewd judge of character, with a legendary ability to conceal his simmering grudges until the opportune moment. Elusive, taciturn, irritable, and rarely courteous, he was habitually—but also theatrically— brusque, abrasive, and abusive in his language and conduct. He often humored himself by choreographed outbursts of anger and by the consequent real or feigned helplessness and humility of his cornered or chastised subordinates. Those who worked with or for him did their utmost to please him and avoided arousing his suspicion or provoking his anger. He enjoyed the discomfiture of his retinue and detested any self-assertion.[43] Unhesitant even to assault physically those who provoked his ire, he resembled a larger-than-life, vicious schoolmaster riding roughshod over cowed pupils. In the words of Charles Hart, the U.S. minister in Tehran (1930–1933), "there is no end to the stories one hears of Reza Shah's personal cruelties. Chauffeurs, butlers, cooks, personal servants, all tell the same poignant tales of how they have been brutalized by him, and not even Ministers have escaped his corporal wrath."[44]

The Shah lacked the cultivation and finesse associated with royalty. His personal life style, his eating and sleeping habits, remained traditional. Observing a strict daily routine, he slept on the floor and used the traditional Iranian bath rather than a modern shower.[45] Showing little enthusiasm for mastering the conventional etiquette of high society, he did not relish parties and was usually represented by Teymurtash, who, before his fall, together with other officials, had endeavored to create the courtly ambiance befitting a dignified kingship. Despite an air of indifference, Reza Shah enjoyed the trappings of power, the pomp and protocols of royalty; he did, however, retain his soldierly characteristics and felt comfortable only in a military uniform. He showed contempt for the effusive flattery ritually lavished on rulers, but in effect nurtured an inherently unctuous court culture. He was utterly unforgiving of any hints of disapproval at home, and intensely touchy about the slightest criticism in the foreign press or conduct deemed disrespectful of Iranian national dignity. Such criticism or conduct was often countered by a disproportionate diplomatic reaction.[46]

Reza Shah's paranoiac proclivities led him readily to attribute any outbreak of disorder or outburst of popular discontent to the machinations and intrigues of ill-intentioned individuals. Someone had to be held publicly responsible for virtually every unpalatable occurrence. In the manner of his Qajar predecessors, Reza Shah found it politically useful to make scapegoats of officials and subjects, to ensure that their treatment served as a lesson to others. Very much in the mold of a traditional sultan, with an inherent instinct for fostering authority based on fear, he instilled lingering dread in the hearts of his subordinates and covert opponents alike and, convinced of the fondness of the downtrodden for unflinching resolve, projected an image of brutal efficiency. For Reza Shah, being feared, together with unhesitant and remorseless punishment of real or imagined enemies, rivals, or friends suspected of disloyalty, was a routine modality of an effective ruler's political repertoire. The Shah seemed invested in the belief that fear produced order. But by committing himself to using fear as the chief instrument for inducing submission and destroying the will to resist, Reza Shah ensured that he himself also had much to fear. A British report assessing his strengths and weaknesses noted: "He is not popular but he is feared, and this in an oriental country, is the more advantageous . . . While feared by his subjects by reasons of his rough tongue and his rougher methods of treatment, he himself is not without fear, and it is said that he never goes to bed without having within reach several weapons, and that he frequently starts up from his sleep to grasp one of them."[47]

Coming from a background of relative poverty, Reza Shah was compulsively driven to amass wealth; he built a large personal fortune, particularly through the acquisition of prime agricultural lands, mostly in the northern provinces. He also accumulated shares in many state-run factories. Unhesitant in treating the country as a patrimonial fiefdom, or abusing office for self-enrichment, he once reportedly said that he had made Iran a prosperous country and was thus entitled to his share of the profits;[48] he saw his accumulation of wealth and his manner of doing so as perfectly in order. He even opened a restaurant in Shemiran, a salubrious district to the north of Tehran, forcing the closure of other restaurants in the area.[49] Almost on the eve of the Anglo-Soviet invasion of the country, he bought a large parcel of prime land in Tehran at one-tenth of its actual price for the construction of a modern hotel.[50] The enormous amount of land he came to own was rarely acquired without coercion or pressure, in clear violation of the regime's proclaimed adherence to the rule of law, and without regard for public opinion or damage to the image of kingship. He cultivated his lands with public funds, usually transported the produce in army trucks, and sold it at inflated prices. He built and maintained lavish dwellings for his sons and daughters with public money. His great wealth, however, contrasted sharply with his parsimony: on one occasion he angrily rebuffed Gholam-Reza, his son from his third and divorced wife, who had asked for a refrigerator to be purchased for himself and his mother.[51] In the words of

Hart, "He likes money, but evidently only for the love of counting it, because he is a man of no luxuries and no vices except his opium pipe."[52]

Maintaining an active and detailed interest in the affairs of the state and ongoing development projects, the Shah regularly visited various parts of the country, particularly the north. With the return from Switzerland of crown prince Mohammad Reza in the spring of 1936, the Shah appeared to have acquired a new buoyancy; accompanied by the prince, he traveled extensively, keenly inspecting civilian and military projects, and displayed an unusual exuberance. In October 1938, having organized a birthday celebration for the prince, to which foreign diplomats were also invited, Reza Shah was "the life and soul of the party."[53] In contrast to his earlier political career, however, he shunned foreign representatives except on formal or ceremonial occasions. Relegating such contacts to government channels was proper and had clear advantages. However, as the crisis resulting in the country's occupation would reveal, a secluded ruler who ultimately made all decisions was always in danger of acting without accurate information. Nor was the Shah better informed about the real feelings of the public, for the practice of submitting petitions to the throne had long ceased. He saw only ministers and a few officials such as the chief of police, but was otherwise out of touch with the world beyond the sheltered confines of the court.

Shielded by his courtiers and the police, particularly from the early 1930s onward, the increasingly aloof Shah grew more out of touch with public opinion and sentiments, and more readily succumbed to his phobias. He became increasingly jealous of anyone else receiving credit for the achievements of the regime or any public recognition. Hubris cast a dark shadow over his life: he saw himself, and was apparently seen by his supporters, as the regenerator of modern Iran who had endowed the country with a sense of national pride. Such pride and what it involved were assumed to be self-evident and beyond discussion; even a hint of dissent was taken as verging on sedition or treason. In Reza Shah's eyes, no one but himself could justifiably claim to be a patriot or possess the will and capacity to maintain national security. At the same time, he showed a singularly narrow understanding of meaningful law and order, and of the institutional requirements of a viable state capable of surviving an autocrat. Reza Shah, observed the veteran prime minister Hedayat, ensured security from brigands but not from rapacious state functionaries. Tribal chieftains and bandits were "eliminated but military commanders more or less replaced them; resources were centralized, but security [*amniyat*] was by no means achieved."[54]

No recognizable notion of constitutional constraints and no determinate conception of legal rights and entitlements had a place in Reza Shah's political mentality. He had crafted a psychologically effective strategy for eradicating or demoralizing opposition, but no effective way of winning genuine support or loyalty. He seemed convinced that there was no middle ground between establishing the authority of the state and coercively subjugating the people, or between dictatorship and disorder. Yet he gave little thought to the probability that the demise of a feared dictator would readily result in disorder. In 1935 he told the German minister that an authoritarian form of government was the only viable form of government; otherwise nations would succumb to communism.[55] Belief in the efficacy of power and its cognates—naked or disguised force, coercion, manipulation, and fraud—infused Reza Shah's political mentality and conduct. Yet, essentially a pragmatist, he espoused no elaborate political views; lacking the gift of oratory, he was uncomfortable speaking in public; he was, and wanted to be seen as, a man of action. He shared with the intelligentsia, who had assisted or favored his rise to power, a desire to modernize the country through state-sponsored measures, a barely disguised anticlericalism, and an attachment to nationalism. Pahlavi nationalism did not, however, acquire a popular, let alone civic, character; it sought to reshape society from above; it did not develop a politics of recognition, nor did it genuinely seek to generate or mobilize popular support for its aims or for anti-imperialist purposes.

## The Modernizing Mission

Ethnocultural nationalism and modernization, which came to be associated with the era of Reza Shah, had long preoccupied the Iranian intelligentsia, both at home and abroad, and were widely discussed in a number of influential journals and societies. *Kaveh,* published in Berlin from 1916 to 1924 by constitutionalist scholar-activists such as Taqizadeh, advocated Iranian sovereignty, modernity, the propagation of modern values, and the fostering of a consciousness of Iran's past as a basis for nationalism. *Iranshahr,* also published in Berlin (1922–1927) and widely read in Iran, attracted contributors who became part of the cultural elite of the Reza Shah era. It promoted modernist nationalism and the strengthening of the Iranian national identity. These issues were also among the central concerns of *Ayandeh,* which began publication in Tehran in 1925, edited by the Swiss-educated Dr. Mahmud Afshar. *Ayandeh* strongly advocated Iranian national unity and territorial integrity, which, it argued, required unanimity of language, dress, and mores and the elimination of difference and division. Afshar was a member of the Young Iran Society (Anjoman-e Iran-e Javan), which consisted of a number of Western-educated intellectuals who were to play significant roles in the country's politics and culture. They favored modernization of the country and elimination of the gulf separating it from Europe. According to one of them, in 1921, Reza Khan, then war minister, in a meeting with a number of the society's members had commended them on their agenda, which he said he fully shared and pledged to implement.[56]

As the salient component of the prevailing intellectual milieu, nationalism had a more tangible impact on the ethos of the new regime than any other idea. Taking its inspiration from the mythological repository of Iran's pre-Islamic heritage, the ascendant nationalism sought to revive real or imagined ancient traditions and symbols. In his early military expeditions and other trips, Reza Shah visited and was visibly moved by Persepolis and other monuments of ancient Iran. Conveniently forgetting that he had intended to establish a republic, he came to see himself as heir to the ancient kings of Persia. Among the grand public occasions in the reign of Reza Shah were the millenary celebrations in October 1934 of the birth of Abolqasem Ferdowsi, Iran's greatest epic poet, whose literary legacy was instrumental in keeping alive the sense of the country's cultural distinctiveness and a strong consciousness of its pre-Islamic past.[57] The celebrations included a conference attended by more than eighty renowned foreign and Iranian scholars, in the course of which the Shah dedicated a mausoleum erected on the poet's grave. Preparations for construction of the mausoleum had started a decade earlier; the idea for it had originated in the nineteen century. Nationalist orientations and pre-Islamic Zoroastrian, Achaemenid, and Sasanian motifs strongly influenced the officially sponsored architecture of major state buildings, including the Museum of Iranian Antiquities and the National Bank. The glorification of pre-Islamic

Iran also involved efforts to purge the Persian language of Arabic words and to encourage the adoption of names of Persian rather than Arabic provenance. The spirit animating such measures had contributed, in March 1925, to the parliament's reform and standardization of the solar (Iranian/Islamic) calendar, which had been gaining currency for official purposes. It revived the old Persian *(jalali)* names for solar months and discarded the Arabic astrological names; the Persianized solar calendar was officially adopted, but the use of the lunar Islamic calendar, particularly for religious purposes, continued. All official use of the lunar calendar was banned ten years later. In its more zealous manifestations, the nationalism of the Reza Shah era castigated the Arabs, and by implication Islam, for the destruction of pre-Islamic Iranian civilization, further aggravating clerical resentment.

The clerics had long realized that having consolidated his position, Reza Shah was abandoning his earlier policy of tactical appeasement and utilization of the clerics in favor of measures aimed at undermining their influence. Integrally linked to the prevailing nationalism, these measures intensified the tempo of the supple and piecemeal but by no means negligible process of secularization that had started with the Constitutional Revolution. That process had sought to redefine the public role of religion as a vital but unobtrusive component of the inherited culture compatible with the requirements of a constitutional polity and an avowedly pluralistic public sphere. Under Reza Shah, respect for "genuine" Islamic norms and values would be emphasized, but this would be viewed as in no way entailing unchecked clerical influence. Many of the state's policies, particularly the secularization of education and the legal system, directly encroached upon the privileges of the clerics. For example, the reorganization of pious endowments and the extension of state control over the revenue-generating shrine in Mashhad, with its vast endowment, severely restricted the clerical establishment's financial resources. In 1935 many historic religious sites were opened to non-Muslim foreign visitors; a year later it was announced that judges would in future be required to have a law degree from Tehran University or approved foreign institutions.

Quietist high-ranking clerics, such as Ayatollah Sheikh Abd al-Karim Ha'eri, remained undisturbed in establishing a major Shi'ite center of learning in Qom. Ha'eri's objections to the state policy of public prohibition of the veil, implemented in January 1936, strained his relations with the Shah, but his death in February 1937 was officially and extensively mourned. Despite such gestures, the regime had delivered its first major shock to the clerics in the form of the 1928 dress code. By delineating and regulating clerical or religion-related occupations, and by restricting the wearing of religious attire, it had threatened to diminish the size and thus the collective clout of the clerical estate. Pursuing a religious career was now generally dissuaded by the state, with the clear implication that it no longer entitled individuals to special privileges. The dress code, and particularly the banning of the veil, deeply distressed the clerics, who remained unable to mount a sustained opposition. Restrictions were not confined to the clerics; manifestations of popular Islam were also scrutinized and restrained. The traditional Moharram processions and ceremonies, previously widely observed, even by army units, and often involving violent clashes between participants from rival city quarters, were severely curtailed; certain rituals were completely banned. Many colorful relics of a seemingly fast-vanishing world—itinerant healers, wandering dervishes, fortune-tellers—were harassed or taken off the streets.

The policies of the state were aimed not only at restricting the activities and numbers of the clerics but also at curtailing their ability to shape and dominate the popular culture and imagination and at undermining their crucial role in the production of society's meaning-system. The clerics were clearly no longer as free as they had been to amplify and reproduce their symbolic or cultural capital, and they were barred from converting it into political capital. Though unable to pursue a formally secular agenda, the Pahlavi state was intent on being assertively secular in ethos. Reza Shah fashioned an absolutist state of a kind not previously experienced in Iran, a militarist state whose sovereignty was essentially unhampered by the influence of the clerical estate. His anticlerical strategy was, however, only partially successful; it failed to uproot the informal but institutionalized influence of the clerics or to dislodge them as a culturally embedded and socially influential and privileged status group. Policies such as the dress code purged and reduced their numbers but increased their distinct identity and cohesion. Islamic law remained an important component of the legal system, particularly of the civil code, and the significance of Shi'ism in the Iranian cultural identity persisted. Reza Shah's anticlericalism contrasted sharply with the accommodating approach of his Qajar predecessors; nevertheless, like them, he pursued a strategy that involved a considerable measure of avoidance and evasion. Subscribing to the conventional wisdom of the age, he hoped or expected that the ongoing modernization drive would drastically diminish the sociocultural role of the clerics.

In the summer of 1934 Reza Shah paid a successful visit to Turkey; save for a brief visit to Iraq's holy places earlier in his career, this was his only foreign trip. He admired the Turkish leader, Mustafa Kemal Atatürk, and sought to initiate reforms similar to his. To a considerable extent Atatürk's reforms represented the continuation of a cumulative process that had started in the nineteenth-century Ottoman empire; a comparable process of reform was largely lacking in Iran. Nevertheless, virtually all the reform measures undertaken during Reza Shah's rule had been in one form or another envisaged or advocated by earlier reformist thinkers, associations, or parties, and in certain significant cases were initiated by Iranian constitutionalists. But although he shared Atatürk's enthusiasm for change, Reza Shah lacked the breadth of vision of his Turkish counterpart. In his sultanist approach to politics and aversion to a broad-based form of governance, the Pahlavi autocrat saw no need to pay real attention to political institutions likely to strengthen and sustain the state. Despite efforts by aides such as Teymurtash, the Shah soon proved himself to be unreconciled with the idea of even state-sponsored political parties. He had come to perceive them as divisive and dangerous, or at best as expendable instruments of redundant criticism.[58]

Reza Shah's socioeconomic achievements were more considerable. Those who had lamented the country's vulnerability to rampant foreign encroachment and influence, the weakness and fragility of the state, the disarray and helplessness of politicians, the ineffectiveness of public servants, the unbridled influence of tribal chieftains and local notables, banditry and general disorder, welcomed the Pahlavi ruler's efforts to create an independent, centralized bureaucratic state, sustained by a standing army and the means for effective enforcement of law and order. Initiatives to create basic public amenities and infrastructure gained growing public support.

Initially enjoying the backing of an important segment of the intelligentsia, who saw him as capable of creating a viable state structure and implementing their reformist agenda, the Pahlavi state embarked upon or expedited measures intended to transform Iranian society. The expansion of education received increasing attention but like many other measures required more resources than were available.[59] The secular educational system became the chief vehicle for promoting the state's nationalist and assimilationist goals.[60] Selected high school graduates were more regularly and extensively than in the Qajar era sent to Europe at the state's expense to acquire much-needed technical and scientific expertise. Education ministers such as Sayyed Mohammad Tadayyon, Ali-Asghar Hekmat, and Esma'il Mer'at played important roles in the development of educational and cultural establishments. Various institutions of higher education were founded, and Tehran University, incorporating a number of existing institutions, was formally opened in March 1936 to become the country's premier cultural and educational center, with immense practical as well as symbolic significance. In 1938 female students were admitted to the university.

Departing from earlier laissez-faire policies, a state monopoly on the sale of tea and sugar had been introduced in May 1925, enabling the government to play an important role in determining the prices of these commodities. From 1930 on, the government resorted to more interventionist measures. The foreign trade monopoly law of 1931 established a government monopoly over all foreign trade, both imports and exports; masterminded mainly by Teymurtash, the measure produced mixed results. Enhancing the salience of the state, it ensured that state enterprises became predominant and the scope for private initiative remained limited; it did not have the desired effect on export trade and remained unpopular with merchants. The privileged and the well-connected were on the whole able to adapt themselves to government polices and even take advantage of them. Taxes, better accounting, and higher tariffs on imports helped increase government revenues. Development projects and manufacturing plants provided new employment opportunities, but in the absence of possibilities for organized action or protest, low incomes and wages, harsh taxation, and inflation increased the relative deprivation of the poor, both urban and rural. Having coercively disrupted the lives of nomadic communities, the state showed little appreciation of their needs or attention to their welfare.

A prestige project of enormous significance symbolizing the state's development drive was the construction of the trans-Iranian railroad. Largely financed by extra taxes on the importation of sugar and tea, the railroad was built over a period of a decade and formally opened in August 1938.

The construction of new roads and the improvement of old ones facilitated mobility and national integration and enabled motorized army units to reach distant areas. There were measures to extend electrification, modernize transportation and communications, construct ports, tunnels, and bridges, and establish civil aviation. There was a drive not only to encourage local handicrafts but to create manufacturing industries to produce a variety of commodities, including sugar and cloth. During the period 1930–1940, 265 new factories employing some 47,000 workers were created by both the public and the private sectors.[61] The desire for industrial self-sufficiency included the highly ambitious step to build a steel mill.[62]

Hospitals and clinics were also established, primarily in Tehran and other major cities. In 1928 there had been no adequate Iranian-run hospital in Tehran, but by the end of Reza Shah's rule Tehran had seven civilian government-run hospitals, although their combined number of beds barely exceeded 700. However, when in 1940 they came under the control of the Ministry of Education and were linked to Tehran University, they had a considerable impact on the training of doctors and the improvement of patient care. Little, however, was done by way of preventive medicine or combating infant mortality and epidemic diseases; preventable ailments continued to afflict the rural population, and malaria remained a major problem in the Caspian area, the Shah's favorite region of the country. Measures aimed at improving general health remained inadequate, and an essential component of this effort, the provision of clean water, received virtually no attention. Steps were also taken to enhance agricultural productivity by combating plant and animal diseases, but the improvement of the irrigation system was neglected.

Substantial efforts to modernize the institutions and procedures of justice, starting in the pre-Pahlavi era, together with the promulgation of new legal codes and the training of judges, placed the judicial branch of the government on a new footing. The cumulative development of the judiciary rendered it potentially a successful and effective branch of government. However, the prevailing intrusive authoritarian rule was anathema to meaningful legal security and the impartial administration of justice. There was also little possibility of redress for the victims of those closely associated with the regime. According to one observer, the Shah made no attempt to restrain Teymurtash, and later his own sons, from wantonly preying on the daughters and wives of other men.[63] In the words of Hedayat: "From the seventh or eighth year of Pahlavi rule, hopes had begun to turn into despair; general order in the affairs of the state, the establishment of factories, the construction of the railroads, and the widening of streets were conspicuous and doable; the foundations of justice were, however, eroded, and all achievements pale in the face of such a calamity."[64] Formal legal processes were used to lend a veneer of legality to the transgressions of those in power; dissenting judges were pressured into compliance, rendered ineffective, or punished. In 1930, for instance, the royal court obtained a judicial ruling seeking, on dubious grounds, to expropriate the lands of a group of farmers in the vicinity of Tehran. The ruling was rescinded by Ahmad Kasravi (1890–1946), a high-ranking, bold, and incorruptible judge, who was immediately suspended. As a reformer, Kasravi was not unsympathetic to many of the steps being undertaken to modernize the country. Yet he considered a real measure of credibility and integrity to be essential to a worthwhile legal system. Incurring the odium of Davar, whom he did not admire, as well as the disfavor of the court, ended Kasravi's career as a judge.[65]

The judiciary continued to be highly vulnerable to the dictates of the Shah and pressure from his entourage and other sources of influence; it was also not immune to mundane forms of corruption and inefficiency. Yet it did not totally lack opportunities to maintain a real measure of credibility. It contained many barely competent judges but also a sizable number of able and dedicated lawyers of high caliber and integrity. Its formal task of promoting the rule of law and impartial adjudication of disputes implied the negation of arbitrary and capricious rule, and the ultimate indispensability of constitutional legitimation. Even paying public lip service to the rule of law implied valuing it and had a constraining effect on the behavior of those in power.

Measures to promote social integration and create a homogeneous nation militated against the country's cultural diversity. Visible markers of division—local and other primordial loyalties, ethnicity, nomadism, religious affiliation, the rural-urban divide, even sartorially expressed differences of rank and status—would be eliminated or diminished in favor of national solidarity, homogeneity, and an officially sanctioned sense of identity. The Shah was deeply sensitive to the possibility that foreigners might view or sneer at the country as backward.[66] Modernity was conceived as involving a coercive shift in the threshold of public shame, a determined move away from traditional modes of dress and behavior officially designated as embarrassing and unacceptable. Identifying sociocultural heterogeneity and the colorful diversity of Iranian society with shameful backwardness, Reza Shah's policy of enforced cultural homogenization was most visibly exemplified by the 1928 dress code.

Though coercive, such measures, together with the symbolically significant abolition of honorific titles enacted by parliament in May 1925, which also required all Iranians to adopt surnames, could signify a modernist, equalizing trend. They could in some respects inadvertently help to affirm the constitutionally valued principle of equal treatment, a principle at odds with the prevailing culturally embedded attachment to social rank and status. Inevitably, steps of these kinds were resented as violating deeply held beliefs and customs, while measures such as the policy of settling the pastoral-nomadic population subverted traditionally rooted ways of life and ignored the ecological determinants of the pastoral-nomadic mode of life.[67]

In June 1935 men were ordered to discard the "Pahlavi" hat in favor of the rimmed hat or *chapeau*. Steps were also taken to extend the dress code and headgear stipulation to women. These moves triggered simmering opposition, which, in the context of resentments arising from measures such as overtaxation, resulted in a bloody confrontation in Mashhad in July involving protesters and government forces, a large number of arrests, and the exile of seventy clerics.[68] Undeterred, in January 1936 the regime formally extended the dress code to women, requiring them to discard the veil *(chador)* in public. Some women in Tehran had abandoned the veil long before, and many others did so as soon as the regime seemed to favor it. Educated women welcomed the move as eroding the social constraints of custom and tradition as well as barriers to their public service. Women in rural and pastoral-nomadic communities had of course always been an active part of the workforce and public life. Yet the majority of women and families, particularly in the provinces, were agonized by the regime's relentlessly pursued sartorial policy. The emotional distress and even the unavailability of appropriate outfits and hats in most parts of the country or their unaffordability were of little concern to the regime. Women who could not reconcile themselves to the new situation became virtually housebound; those who ventured out veiled or even wearing headscarves were harassed

*A group of members of Tehran's Society of Women after 1936 and public removal of the veil.* (Courtesy of the Institute for the Study of Contemporary Iranian History, Tehran)

by the police and barred from buses, taxis, bath houses, shops, and bazaars. Civil servants whose wives appeared veiled in public were promptly dismissed. Preachers who publicly opposed the policy risked banishment from their towns and villages.

Removal of the veil facilitated the social prominence and greater inclusion of privileged women in public life but traumatized poor and traditional women, accentuating their exclusion. Its educational consequences were mixed. The sartorial revamping of society by diktat widened the intelligibility gap between traditionalists and advocates of modernization, and undermined, obscured, or distorted many issues central to reflective modernity. But although such measures as the banning of the veil were socially radical by comparison with the gradualist approach to this issue pursued in Turkey, they were not as politically far-reaching as they appeared.[69] Reza Shah's steps to address gender inequality remained rudimentary; he affirmed the traditional view of women's primary role as managers of the household. In a speech on January 7, 1936 (17 Dey 1314), when public removal of the veil was formalized, the Shah asserted that the previously "deprived" half of the population had now actively joined public life and could serve the nation unhindered, while at the same time urging women to be frugal and avoid "luxury and wastefulness."[70] He did not follow Atatürk's 1934 step of extending voting rights to women.

In March 1935 the Foreign Ministry informed foreign embassies that they should refer to the country as Iran rather than Persia and to its inhabitants as Iranians rather than Persians.[71] Reflecting the prevailing nationalism, the Iranian Academy (Farhangestan), established a month later, sought to unearth old Persian words and coin new ones to replace foreign, mainly Arabic terms and, working together with Tehran University, enlisted the services of a generation of scholars steeped in the literature and culture of the past. These scholars continued pioneering work in editing and publishing the classics of Persian literature. Combined with studies by European Orientalists, their work created a cumulative body of knowledge about the Iranian past that in turn helped to lend substance to cultural nationalism.

Universal male conscription was met with a plethora of strategies to avoid it; the rich and the well-connected were better able to do so. In rural areas it was resisted because it drained the workforce available to peasant households. Yet it not only provided a reservoir of soldiers but also helped to integrate and socialize young men from remote rural areas, and different religious and ethnic affiliations, into nationalist values. Similarly, measures such as the introduction of identity cards and formal citizenship (tabe'iyat) contributed to a greater sense of identification with the nation-state. At the same time, these measures, along with the registration of births, deaths, and marriages, as well as of land and real estate, and conducting a census, helped, among other things, to extend the state's capacity for bureaucratic control. Indeed, the extent of the state's penetration into the lives of its citizens was unprecedented.

Out of the disparate military units in existence, Reza Khan and his fellow officers created a unified army, viewing it as the prerequisite of a viable state. He closely oversaw the choice and promotion of key officers on the basis of talent, but more significantly on the basis of loyalty. The required infrastructure for sustaining a modern standing army, including officer training facilities, was not neglected. Steps were also taken for the creation of a navy and an air force. The military primarily served and helped to

further the political ambitions of its royal commander by eradicating domestic challenges and consolidating the centralized authority of the state. It
proved effective in subduing regional rebels and countering or checking unrest; together with the gendarmerie it ensured a remarkable degree of security on the roads and in remote areas previously infested with bandits.

Senior officers shared Reza Shah's vested interest in enhancing the collective role and standing of the military. The fact that the ruler himself was an
officer, together with the extent of the regime's pampering of and reliance
on the military, gave it a distinct militaristic aura. Although officers were no
more secure in their careers or lives than civilian officials, by enjoying royal
patronage and taking advantage of condoned corruption the military's top
brass were able to amass considerable wealth and constituted a privileged
status group envied by civilians. According to the British legation, "That the
army holds first place in the [Shah's] affection is borne out by the demean-
our of the soldiery. They profit by their importance in the eyes of their
Royal master, and, though naturally timid, adopt a swashbuckling attitude
and strut about the streets of the capital shouldering their civilian brethren
into the gutter."[72]

The Turkish army, emboldened by its success in defending the territorial
integrity of the mainland in the wake of the collapse of the Ottoman empire, saw itself as a vigorous guardian of secular republicanism and the
Kemalist legacy; it would regularly intervene in politics when Kemalism
was endangered by political and ideological squabbles. The military in Iran,
on the other hand, though sharing the prevailing nationalism, was not imbued with any distinct ideological attachment to the Pahlavi state. Yet, developing a symbiotic relation with the state, the Iranian military constituted
its most effective organizational component, with a sociopolitical salience
that enabled it to play a significant role in areas ranging from governing
tribal regions to manipulating elections, or from the coinage of new words
to the development of Persian music.

Benefiting from Reza Shah's rule, the military in general sought to sustain it. By the end of 1926 the army was estimated to number 33,000, while
the military budget, excluding the police, represented 40 percent of the estimated revenues of the country.[73] Toward the end of Reza Shah's rule, the
military, comprising more than 100,000 men, absorbed up to 25 percent of
the national budget. It had clearly proved to be too costly, and had grown

too large for maintaining domestic order, while remaining inadequate for countering outside threats. Its speedy and ignominious collapse and virtual disintegration in the face of the Allied invasion of 1941 resulted in a devastating loss of stature.[74] Gradually rehabilitated, it remained the autocratic monarchy's ultimate power base, as well as its chief beneficiary.

## Sociocultural Milieu

Urbanization remained a slow process: between 1900 and 1940 the urban population increased by less than 2 percent; by 1938 only six cities in Iran had a population exceeding 100,000, and by 1941 urban dwellers constituted only 23 percent of the population. According to a census carried out in March 1940, Tehran had a population of some 531,000; of the country's urban centers, it saw the most change and attracted more migrants. Urban development involved tangible physical transformation and also disfigurement: the demolition of old city walls, the careless destruction of historic neighborhoods and sites, including city gates, to build straight streets and boulevards as manifestations of modernization. Scant attention was paid to the poorer inhabitants who lost their dwellings, and little or no compensation was assigned for demolished property. New streets and boulevards in Tehran, and indeed in many cities, were named or renamed after the Shah and the dynasty. The Shah's very name, and the heroic statues of him erected in the main urban centers, would become icons of a new era. In the capital, grand buildings were constructed, but the creation of parks was not a priority, and no steps were taken to supply clean water to the inhabitants. Nevertheless, the paving of many streets with asphalt, the increased presence of motorcars, and electrification, together with a building spree that sparked urban renewal, had a tangible impact on conceptions of life and sensibilities befitting modern city life. The appearance of boutiques, cafés, restaurants, clubs, and cinemas in Tehran and other major cities, frequented by both men and women dressed in European attire, indicated a noticeable shift from traditional to modern modes of socialization.

In its obsession with the more conspicuous trappings of modernity, the state showed no appreciation of its fundamental components and the deeper changes and expectations characterizing the modern ethos; it also ignored or belittled the traditional civic qualities of Iranian culture. The emerging albeit distorted modernity still signified and helped to expedite the structural transformation of Iranian society; it involved growing bureaucratization, industrialization, and consumerism; it affected attitudes to work, discipline, leisure, and time; it engendered new perceptions of self and individuality, and new approaches to privacy and sociability. Both the public and the private spheres of life, however, became more susceptible to intrusions by the state. The vibrant civil society of the pre–Reza Shah days, with its restless journalists, satirists, and poets and its many political parties and associations, had gradually given way to a dull and intolerant police state severely restricting freedom of expression and association.[75] The press served primarily as an instrument of propaganda for the regime as well as the internalization of nationalist values. Censorship, strictly enforced by the police, left the populace isolated and starved of information, and resulted in a vapid, laudatory press inimical to the emergence of an informed public.

Every small gathering, including traditional private meetings, became the target of police surveillance. The stifling atmosphere of fear created a politically passive urban population, with men of means seeking pleasure in drinking and womanizing.[76] Given the ubiquity of real or perceived police informers, people shunned discussion of politics even in private. Citizens were required to obtain special permits to travel within the country. The police monitored the postal service and personal correspondence. The regime even forbade the composition of melancholic poems, requiring poetry to express "satisfaction and contentment."[77] Similarly, it was official policy to ensure that Persian music ceased to be "saturated with sorrow."[78] The politically inquisitive had to rely on rumor and gossip. In the last few years of the regime, foreign broadcasts to Iran stimulated a widespread interest in the acquisition of radio sets and to some extent filled the news vacuum, leading to the belated establishment of the Tehran radio station in April 1940.

On the other hand, important steps were being taken to create the institutional prerequisites for a more modern cultural life. The rise in literacy, though modest, meant a larger readership for books and other printed matter, a growing need for more printing presses and bookshops, and a demand for more varied topics and subjects. The gradual return of state-sponsored students educated in European universities brought new expertise, ideas, and outlooks likely to broaden intellectual horizons. Bodies such as the Education Commission (komision-e ma'aref), established in 1924 and consisting of prominent public and literary figures, oversaw the publication of textbooks and facilitated the preparation, translation, and publication of important works in history and culture. Institutions of higher education, particularly Tehran University, together with museums, libraries, and other cultural establishments such as the Society for the Preservation of National Monuments (anjoman-e asar-e melli), furnished the institutional setting for the development of the national culture. A whole generation of eminent scholars and littérateurs linked to educational institutions emerged; the study and preservation of the literary, historical, and architectural legacy of the past proceeded, as did a growing interest in Persian music and even popular culture. Novelists, playwrights, and poets experimenting in new genres and able to circumvent censorship helped develop the expressive capacity of modern Persian. The expansion of education was bound to militate against insularity and promote inquisitiveness. The state's efforts to control the flow of information were countered by sociocultural trends fueled by growing literacy. State policies inadvertently and inevitably heightened public appreciation of absent political and civic liberties.

The period also witnessed an interesting reorientation in socioreligious thought in the work of maverick reformist thinkers such as Reza-Qoli Shari'at-Sangelaji (1890–1944) and Kasravi. Influenced by trends in Sunni reformism, Sangelaji developed an unorthodox approach to the reading of Islamic texts, sought to revise key assumptions of Shi'ite Islam, and extensively reinterpreted Shi'ite messianism. Emphasizing the need for active, independent reasoning as opposed to passive emulation, he maintained that the understanding of Islam could no longer ignore modern scientific thinking. He also advocated paying greater attention to religious precepts that promoted social justice. Unhampered in his preaching, as the state favored his modernist approach to religiosity, he attracted many followers who looked for a version of Shi'ism reconcilable with the modern world. While his opponents among traditionalist clerics and bazaar merchants denounced him, his supporters regarded him as "the great reformer" (mosleh-e kabir). It was in response to the writings of one of Sangelaji's clerical disciples that in 1941 the future ayatollah, Ruhollah Khomeini, wrote a rebuttal in which he also castigated the polices of Reza Shah.[79]

Kasravi's ideas would provoke more vehement clerical-traditionalist objections. Having abandoned his clerical roots, he became a scholar, a lawyer, a tireless visionary reformer, an inventive albeit eccentric thinker, a relentless denouncer of many religious and cultural beliefs and practices, a sharp critic of certain traditional literary canons. Torn between modern and premodern values, he espoused qualified nationalism and rejected mindless emulation of Europe. Although many of his more controversial tracts were published after the Reza Shah era, from November 1933 onward he edited the journal *Peyman*, in which, among other things, he advocated promoting "Iranism" *(Iranigari)* and combating superstition, illiteracy, and social divisions. This position, together with his abhorrence of creeds and mores that he viewed as conducive to intellectual sloth and social fragmentation, rendered him sympathetic to certain policies of the regime. Yet his attachment to constitutionalism, whose history he began chronicling in his journal, clearly contravened the spirit of the Reza Shah era.

Thinkers and writers whose work or activities did not impinge on the authority and interests of the state were tolerated, unlike those who promoted ideas inimical to the state's policies. Even the work of those who were supportive of the prevalent nationalism was hampered by rigid censorship, which became more intense as a result of the implementation in 1933 of the antisocialist law adopted two years earlier. In November 1938 fifty-three intellectuals and activists charged with having formed a Communist network were tried and most imprisoned. Taqi Arani, the leading member of the group, had developed an active interest in Marxism while in Berlin (1926–1932); he was also regarded as genuinely nationalistic.[80] After returning to Iran he worked as a high school teacher, and between February 1934 and June 1935 published the journal *Donya*, whose arcane "dialectical materialist" terminology eluded the censors. He died in prison in February 1940. Mohammad Farrokhi-Yazdi, a constitutionalist and left-wing nationalist poet, journalist, and one-term parliamentarian (1928–1930), had endured police harassment or imprisonment since 1933; he eventually died in prison in October 1939. The deaths of Farrokhi and Arani were treated as murder in post-1941 trials of Reza Shah's police officials.

From the early 1930s creative work in literature began to wane. Those poets who survived repression either succumbed to poverty and desolation—such as Abolqasem Aref (d. 1933)—or, like Mohammad-Taqi Bahar, Iran's greatest classical poet of the twentieth century, were forced to compose panegyrics for the Shah in order to survive or avoid prolonged incarceration or banishment. Sadeq Hedayat, who had gained some prominence since 1930, became a pioneering and original novelist, a writer of short stories, and a collector and explorer of folklore. The prevailing cultural nationalism resonated with his nostalgic interest in pre-Islamic Iran, his anticlericalism, and his uncompromisingly critical attitude to the country's Arabo-Islamic heritage. However, as a highly sensitive intellectual of leftist sensibilities, he abhorred authoritarianism and the repression of the regime, and after 1941 strongly denounced its official cultural policies.

## Constitutional Façade

Reformist measures, issuing directly or indirectly from the Shah or identified with him, further enhanced his power. Reza Shah's autocratic rule was facilitated by the authoritarian components of Iranian political culture; it also invigorated them. Reza Shah's state retained many of the characteristics of its Qajar predecessor, while he acquired the kind of power that none of the Qajar kings had possessed and would have envied. His power was constrained by neither the forces that had checked the prerogatives of the Qajars nor by the existing constitutional formalities. Not surprisingly, no preparations for the future were made, other than hoping for a smooth succession through the elimination of actual and potential contenders for power, and relying on the continued efficacy and loyalty of the amply rewarded military and the police.

Reza Shah's style of rule—the manner in which the lives and tenuous fortunes of civil and military officials had become dependent upon his whims, his paranoiac distrust of others, the Kafkaesque atmosphere of dread generated by his overzealous secret police—demoralized or alienated most of his supporters. Many of them tenaciously concentrated on pleasing the Shah or at least not incurring his odium; most opted to be as unobtrusive as possible or found it safer to resort to prevarication or concealment of the truth. The Shah claimed to expect nothing short of veracity from his subordinates, but his conduct systematically undermined such a claim. In their dealings with the Shah, his officials felt obliged or preferred to tell him what he wanted to hear. The prevailing climate of fear also ensured that, to the dismay of future historians, there would be few diaries and memoirs written by political figures of the period.

Reza Shah had tried to establish his claim to be the uncontested ruler of Iran by proving himself fully deserving of the role. He had attempted to achieve this by championing national independence and the creation of a state capable of extending its authority over the whole of the country, extricating it from a morass of administrative inefficiency, weakness, and backwardness. He benefited from a favorable geopolitical situation: the British, the most powerful foreign presence in Iran, considered their interests as compatible with his agenda and in effect facilitated his rise to power, as indeed did the Soviets. In the context of the virtual fragmentation of the country, the undeniable failure of the traditional politics of the notables, and the absence of the structural prerequisites for enhancing the authority of the state, there had seemed no viable alternative to Reza Khan. Moreover, in the view of his supporters, his personal ambitions in many respects converged with national aspirations.

A state that was either not authoritarian or less so would undoubtedly have pursued different socioeconomic priorities. Yet, regardless of the manner in which they were implemented or the shape they assumed, most of the modernizing steps of the Reza Shah era, and particularly those measures taken to achieve national independence and create a more modern state structure, were necessary. With the active help of many of those who were subsequently eliminated or marginalized, Reza Shah oversaw the emergence of a nation-state—one of the most cherished ideals of the constitutionalist reformers and a process that had in effect started with the Constitutional Revolution.

The crafting of a discernibly modern nation-state was the single most important achievement of the Reza Shah era; earlier in his political career, the pursuit of this objective had secured him recognition and legitimacy. It involved the creation of a centralized bureaucratic state that monopolized the means of violence, eradicated regional challenges, unified the country, established its authority domestically, and sought to act as sovereign vis-à-vis foreign powers. This was, however, accomplished at the cost of arresting the development of constitutionalism and deliberative politics. The key constitutionalist objectives of putting an end to the capricious exercise of power, establishing the rule of law, and ensuring a depersonalized exercise of state power were subverted.

Assuming an increasingly paternalistic aura, Reza Shah saw himself and was widely portrayed as being solely qualified and entitled to determine what was in the country's best interest.[81] He was inevitably credited for the successes of the regime and blamed for its failings. The lines of demarcation between loyalty and servility, between high-level public service and abject subservience to the ruler, between the maintenance of public order and capricious oppression became increasingly blurred. Civic confidence, patriotic responsibility, and attachment to principle fell prey to cultivated sycophancy and corrosive cynicism. Intolerance of any public criticism or scrutiny of the regime ensured that the main victim of the regime's ponderous propaganda was the regime itself. The establishment in the early winter of 1939 of the Organization for the Cultivation of Ideas (Sazman-e parvaresh-e afkar) in Tehran and other major cities was designed to promote official, or royalist, values and respect for state ordinances. This was not, however, an objective that could be accomplished by fiat. By ignoring the existing inconvenient realities, the regime's functionaries seemed more successful in self-deception than in deceiving the public.

No achievement of the regime necessitated the cavalier and unmitigated discrediting of constitutional institutions and principles; nor were there any grounds to maintain that the positive accomplishments of the regime required or necessitated its degeneration into a police state. Unimaginatively viewing any expression of dissent as detrimental to the authority of the state, Reza Shah and his acolytes eroded the country's political development and civic vitality by eliminating real parliamentary representation and debate, political parties and press freedom, viewing them as unsettling signs of political disorder. However, as thinkers as diverse as Machiavelli and the German sociologist Georg Simmel have observed, conflict is not to be dismissed as purely counterproductive. An indication of political vitality, discord and dissension can prove beneficial to the continuity of the existing order. No political order can endure without adequate safety valves. With his political insularity and military cast of mind, however, Reza Shah seemed convinced that political and particularly parliamentary tensions were dangerous and intolerable; they merely provided an opportunity for rabble-rousing and resulted in turmoil.

Reza Shah had no "link" with the Constitutional Revolution and "no solid identification, practical or sentimental, with the constitution."[82] Yet despite his "deep-rooted contempt" for parliamentary arrangements, as monarch Reza Shah did not attempt to amend the Constitution or to tamper openly with constitutional formalities.[83] The edicts and whims of the Shah, overriding in all matters of state, were invariably passed through the usual formalities of parliamentary procedures and camouflaged as parliamentary legislation. The customary parliamentary "vote of inclination" *(ra'-ye tamayol)*—the formality of seeking prior parliamentary approval for prime ministerial candidates—remained more or less operative throughout his reign, and in certain cases he allowed the deputies a measure of limited and innocuous freedom in debating, modifying, and even mildly criticizing government bills.

The fact that Reza Shah in many respects fastidiously adhered to the constitutional façade indicated a recognition of the legitimating function of the Constitution. He perceived of himself and wanted to be seen as a "constitutional monarch." In the course of a trip to northern Iran, enraged by the deplorable state of the roads, Reza Shah told the minister of roads, Rajab-Ali Mansur, who was accompanying him, "you must be thankful that I am a constitutional monarch; otherwise I would have had you decapitated right away."[84] Unlike the Qajar kings, who had invoked "the sword of the ancestors" and attributed their legitimacy to ancestral conquest of the country and dynastic patrimonial entitlement, Reza Shah had utilized or manipulated quasi-legal procedures to assume the throne. The legitimacy of his reign formally rested on constitutional provisions. By systematically undermining and discrediting such provisions, however, he unwittingly but ultimately undermined his own position. The manner of his removal starkly revealed that his self-inflicted erosion of legitimacy had made him deeply vulnerable. In the words of Mohsen Sadr, a high-ranking judge, a justice minister of the Reza Shah era, and later a prime minister:

> In my opinion, Reza Shah was evicted from Iran neither because of the threats of the Russians nor because of the tricks of the British; what resulted in his exile was his boundless hubris, and the enormous rift that separated him from the people. The people had grown estranged from him to such an extent that his removal by foreign forces resulted in no

adverse popular reaction, but rather, the people rejoiced in it and congratulated one another, and this should not be seen as an indication of the disloyalty of the Iranian people. At that point, the anger and animosity of the people toward him had reached such a pitch that they felt a sense of satisfaction in his humiliation.[85]

## Unforeseen Vulnerability

To enable Iran to act as a sovereign state pursuing an independent foreign policy was a goal that Reza Shah shared with other Iranian nationalists. While carefully avoiding measures that might antagonize the Russians and the British, Reza Shah had endeavored to contain their influence in Iran. Despite earlier British support, Reza Shah seemed not only to share most of his compatriots' mixed feelings of fear and distrust of the British but to do so more intensely. Such feelings came to the fore during the oil crisis of 1932–1933. Had Teymurtash remained on the scene, the trajectory of oil negotiations might have been different;[86] but after the cancellation of the 1901 oil concession and Teymurtash's removal, the Shah personally took charge of the oil negotiations, a situation that rendered him vulnerable. A ruler who had so confidently relied on a highly capable aide was now put in the spotlight; his lack of remotely comparable diplomatic guile and relevant skills, and his greater susceptibility to phobias and fears of possible British measures against him, could now be more easily exploited.

Reza Shah's cancellation of the concession proved to be at best a bungled exercise in brinkmanship. His subsequent intervention in the Anglo-Iranian negotiations—a move that his ministers did not welcome—resulted in the disadvantageous terms of the 1933 agreement, which renewed the sixty-year duration of the original concession and thereby extended the concessionary period by a further thirty-two years. This agreement—the result of intense British pressure and the Shah's fear of the consequences of intransigence—was lamented by nationalists at the time and particularly later. Reaffirming British influence and power, and the clear limitations of the Iranian state's room for maneuver, the new agreement constituted a setback for Reza Shah. Though able to conceal his humiliation, his dislike of the British became more intense; he would describe a meeting with the British minister in Tehran as a veritable ordeal.

During Reza Shah's rule, relations between Iranians and foreign nationals were subject to severe restrictions. In addition to the imperative of countering foreign espionage, such restrictions were justified in terms of past foreign meddling in Iran, as well as the need to counter the practice, common among certain Iranians, of seeking to cultivate the support and patronage of foreign embassies. Any unauthorized Iranian contact with foreign diplomats and other nationals was banned. A high-ranking general was imprisoned for having dined at the French embassy.[87] Watched by the police, Iranian citizens, particularly government employees, tried to avoid even a routine exchange of formalities with foreign diplomats. In the end, Reza Shah's fear of foreign designs seemed to become a self-fulfilling prophecy, for he lost his position as a result of foreign intervention.

Staunch opposition to Soviet Communism, together with other national interests and foreign policy considerations, effectively placed Iran in the British camp; Britain's imperial power and its strategic and particularly oil interests in Iran did not leave Iranians with much room for maneuver in this regard. Iran generally wished, however, to pursue as independent or neutralist a foreign policy as possible. Germany, an industrially advanced country with no history of imperial transgressions in Iran, continued to be regarded as a countervailing force against British and Russian/Soviet imperialism. Reza Shah had not been eager to employ foreign advisers, and when forced to do so he preferred to recruit them from countries seen as harboring no ill-will toward Iran. The National Bank had been established with the help of more than seventy German advisers.[88] Germany maintained growing economic and commercial ties with Iran, which sought and received German assistance for both civilian and military development projects. The Germans contributed to the construction of the railroad network, the development of aviation, and the establishment and running of several important industrial enterprises. Germany was the main provider of manufactured goods to Iran and a steady customer of Iranian goods.

None of these transactions, however, implied any particular commitment to Germany or neglect of economic and commercial ties with other European countries. At the outbreak of the Second World War in Europe, Iran opted for a policy of neutrality; with the outcome of the war uncertain, such a policy was considered least likely to bring harm. However, relations between Iran and Germany and the presence of Germans in Iran became a subject of growing British concern. No doubt Reza Shah preferred the anticommunist Nazis to the Weimar republic, whose press had been critical of him and whose political liberties and tolerance for communism had influenced Iranian students there; as his police chief, Ayrom, told the German minister, Reza Shah welcomed the rise to power of Hitler as heralding the end of communism.[89] Yet in his pro-German attitude, the Shah was motivated primarily by anti-Soviet and anti-British feelings. The British could not easily accuse him of being favorable to or favored by the Nazis; by May 1940 Persian broadcasts from Berlin had become critical of the Shah and later fiercely attacked him.[90]

In response to British pressure, the Iranian government expelled some Germans whose actions seemed suspicious and closely watched the rest, but there were many projects that were being run with German help. The British continued to view the size of the German community as disproportionate to the work it "professed to be doing."[91] They impressed upon the Iranian government, and indirectly the Shah, the dangers of a German fifth column and the possibility of a pro-German coup. These fears of undue German influence contributed to the removal toward the end of June 1940 of the government of Ahmad Matin-Daftari, whom the British regarded as pro-German. According to the Iranians, there were 2,590 British subjects, 690 Germans, and 390 Russians in the country; the British, however, kept referring to "numerous" Germans.[92] The Iranian government faced the delicate task of negotiating its desire to remain neutral; it had to avoid antagonizing any of the belligerents and persuade them to respect its neutrality. Expelling a large number of Germans would have violated this policy and harmed Iran economically. The government made some concessions but preferred prevarication while awaiting clarification of the outcome of the war in Europe.

Though willing to adopt some measures to allay British concerns regarding the German presence in Iran, the government was not willing to accept a substantial reduction in its share of the oil income for 1940, as demanded by the British. Since 1932 Iran's oil income had averaged more than £2 million a year, and in 1939 it had received over £4 million. During Reza Shah's rule oil revenues were not part of the national budget and were deposited in the state reserve fund, used for military purchases and occasionally railroad equipment.[93] At the end of September 1941 the parliament passed a bill authorizing the Ministry of Finance to take charge of the revenues from the Anglo-Iranian Oil Company (AIOC), as well as the reserve fund built up from past revenues.[94] Counting on steady revenues from oil and aware of the vulnerability of the beleaguered British empire, Reza Shah saw no reason to forgo demanding what the Iranians considered they were minimally entitled to.

When the Iranian government threatened to put a proposal for the cancellation of the oil concession before the parliament by July 7,[95] the AIOC relented, agreeing to pay up to £4 million for 1940 and for 1941, on the condition that this arrangement did not affect the terms of the concession or create a precedent. The Shah, however, informed the British that Iran reserved the right to modify the concession whenever it wished. Such conduct antagonized the British, particularly the hawkish new minister, Reader Bullard, who had taken up his post in December 1939.[96] The Shah, Bullard reported,

> was not interested to learn that the demand for oil had diminished because of the restrictions on the use of private cars in the United Kingdom, the necessity to carry oil by the quickest route (e.g., from America) because of shortage of tankers, and so on. What he wanted was to have at least as much money as he had counted on when he forced a new concession on the company in 1933; and since, by breaking his word and committing blackmail, he got what he wanted.[97]

Bullard was deeply prejudiced against the Iranians, whom he fiercely disparaged as a "race." "Persians," he wrote in 1942, "have so little moral courage that when a man who has the normal amount comes into conflict with them they tend to collapse. That is why Reza Shah was able to treat them like dogs for so long."[98]

While the Shah himself was deeply suspicious of the British,[99] German propaganda—that Britain was responsible for the Shah and his misdeeds—resonated with the public. "The Shah," reported Bullard,

> is still the only source of authority, but there is now a potential danger in the fact that the population have been persuaded, partly by active German propaganda, and partly by their own vanity, which will not ad-

mit that they can have deserved the Government they have got, that the British are responsible for all their troubles for having, it is alleged, placed the Shah on the throne and maintained him ever since.[100]

Their resentment against the regime mingling with anti-British sentiment, most people hoped for a German victory. In the words of one official, "everyone supported the Germans and hated the Russians and the British."[101] Fearing a Soviet invasion, the Iranians hoped that Germany would protect Iran. The German invasion of the Soviet Union in June 1941 and the subsequent formation of an Anglo-Soviet alliance represented the Iranians' worst nightmare and resurrected the ghost of the 1907 Anglo-Russian Convention. Despair and disorientation set in, contributing to the failure of Iranian politicians to show greater agility in dealing with the unfolding crisis.

The British were determined to reassert their hegemony in Iran as elsewhere in the region, to protect their strategic assets and interests, and to ensure that the country was secure against German designs or threats posed by anti-British sentiments manifesting themselves as support for Germany. Well before the occupation of Iran by Allied forces, investigations into the possible use of the Iranian transport system to supply Russia had already begun. Iran—with its recently completed railroad connecting the south of the country to the north—was viewed as the main all-weather route for sending military supplies to the Soviet Union in order to prevent its collapse. In early July 1941 the Soviet and British diplomatic representatives protested the growing German influence in Iran. Again on August 16, parallel Anglo-Soviet representations were made to the Iranian government to expel most Germans, particularly suspect ones, from the country, to provide a list of those expelled, and to bar those allowed to remain from working in sensitive installations. In its response on August 19, the Iranian government, having already given conciliatory informal assurances, offered to meet some of these demands.[102] Barely a week later, on August 25, the joint Anglo-Soviet invasion of the country started and proceeded despite the Shah's offer to meet Allied demands.[103] Clearly, planning and preparation for the invasion had long been under way, and demands were made in the anticipation that they would produce no "adequate" response and Iran would persist in its "intransigence." No ultimatum or unequivocal threats were issued, nor was a deadline; these omissions indicated that the invading powers wanted to preempt a response from Iran that could make the occupation more difficult to justify. The occupation of Iran followed the British occupation of Iraq in May 1941, and the occupation of Syria by the British and French Gaullist forces in June.

The question whether Iran could have escaped occupation cannot as yet be conclusively settled and requires greater archival exploration. Bullard later wrote: "If only the Iranian Government had agreed to get rid of all the Germans except a few in key positions (not railways though) who were not a danger to us, I believe the rest could have been arranged."[104] Similarly, senior officials such as Abbas-Qoli Golsha'ian, acting finance minister since May 1941, have maintained that the invasion could have been prevented, and that there were enough information and warnings—from diplomats such as Mohammad Sa'ed, Iran's ambassador to Moscow—to impel the government to act to ward off the invasion. Golsha'ian primarily blames Rajab-Ali Mansur, prime minister since June 1940, who falsely reassured the Shah, did not keep him adequately informed, and even kept his cabinet colleagues in the dark.[105] Conversely, Nasrollah Entezam—a capable diplomat who since March 1940 had acted as the court's grand master of ceremonies and was closely in touch with the Shah—recounts that with the German invasion of the Soviet Union, the Shah realized that he could no longer take advantage of Anglo-Soviet friction. He had shown considerable flexibility, but he could not abruptly change course: doing so would have confirmed existing assumptions that he was a British stooge. Following his firm stand regarding Iranian oil royalties, the British, Entezam explains, wanted to secure the Shah's removal; they considered control of Iran vital for the security of India and the rest of the Middle East, and the occupation therefore had to happen; "the alertness or negligence" of Reza Shah made no difference.[106]

Clearly, Reza Shah had failed to be sufficiently amenable to British pressures and demands, and it is therefore plausible to assume that the British decided that he had to be cut down to size or removed. Contrary to what they publicly maintained in their propaganda, it was not his cruel authoritarian rule that the British objected to but his insistence that Iran should be treated as a sovereign state. With British control of Iran's oil resources, the country's sovereignty was extremely tenuous. Domestically, the Iranian state lacked the means, both material and moral, for sustaining even its highly circumscribed sovereign status or warding off the looming dangers. Internationally and geopolitically, too, squeezed between the Soviet and British empires, circumstances were not favorable to Iran; nor were the promises of the Atlantic Charter of August 1941, asserting respect for the sovereignty and independence of nations, intended to apply to the non-European world.

Nevertheless, had the Iranian government and ministers enjoyed any real measure of authority and autonomy, Iran might have escaped the occupation. The Iranians might at least have been able to deprive the Allies of any ready pretext to invade the country; they might have persuaded them to pursue their objectives short of an invasion. Such an outcome would have required a government that was not in every respect overshadowed and hampered by the Shah, a government more alert in ascertaining the magnitude of the danger facing the country, capable of shouldering the burden of responsibility and initiating measures to avert confrontation and crisis—in short, a government that enjoyed and could rely on public support. Such a government—comprising not routinely interchangeable bureaucrats but statesmen, leaders endowed with principle, vision, and courage—would have done everything in its power to ensure that the Shah himself was spared the humiliation of forced abdication and exile, and that the country escaped the disastrous consequences of foreign occupation.

Yet, given the prevailing structure of authority and his traits of character, any significantly different behavior by the Shah and his government or ministers seems inconceivable; premised on unquestioning obedience, the regime had proved intrinsically inimical to the emergence or survival of leaders. The Shah, according to a high-ranking official, trusted no one, and everyone lied to him; his nervousness and paranoia intensified as the international situation deteriorated. He was barely aware of what was happening in the world, and no minister who might have appreciated the gravity of the dangers facing the country dared to approach and alert him. Thus critical days were wasted, while the deceptive façade of a powerful military capable of safeguarding the country's declared neutrality provided a false sense of reassurance.[107] The veiled threats of the British and Soviet diplomatic representatives were not taken sufficiently seriously or adequately conveyed to the Shah, who, in any case, treated them with an unjustifiable air of optimistic or dismissive incredulity.

Reza Shah lost the throne as a result of unforeseen circumstances. However, the configuration of his authoritarian rule ensured that even if no occupation had occurred, his demise, as some of his ministers feared, would have resulted in sociopolitical convulsion rather than an orderly succession and continuation of the Pahlavi monarchy.[108] The tragedy of the Pahlavi autocracy was that both its protagonist and his supporters seemed deeply averse to pondering the future political direction and shape of the country. They did not reflect on how the erosion of legitimizing institutions and the elimination of credible statesmen could mire the country in the calamity of ungovernability and political disorder. Proponents of autocracy, unwittingly or otherwise, ensured that its political alternative would involve collision, collusion, and shifting alliances among competing political clans and power fiefdoms that would inevitably mar the country's future political life. Such a situation was bound to breed social disaffection and political crisis, and prove detrimental to the coexistence of mutually reinforcing political order and political liberty.

# 3

# Restoration of Parliamentary Politics

## Occupation

The nightmare of the Anglo-Soviet invasion took the disoriented government and the incredulous and perplexed Shah by surprise. The fact that virtually no preparation had been made for resistance indicates that until the very end the Shah was confident that a full-scale attack would not materialize. The AIOC had ensured that the Iranian army units had no adequate fuel supply, but this was only one of many problems that plagued the ill-prepared, panic-ridden, and poorly supplied military. Resistance lasted no more than three days, deteriorating into confusion, collapse, and disintegration. Reza Shah was forced not only to abdicate but also to give up his immense wealth. According to one member of the cabinet, in the wake of the invasion Reza Shah shocked the ministers by revealing an inordinate concern for his estates in the north, which lay in the zone that would be occupied by the Soviets.[1] He did not return his wealth to the nation but bequeathed it to his heir.[2]

The Allied invasion had forced the reluctant Shah to call on Forughi—out of office and favor for the past six years but acceptable to the Allies—to form a cabinet. Not surprisingly, even at that critical moment in the country's history and in the last days of his rule, Reza Shah still sought the appointment of a prime minister who would be wholly at his disposal. His ministers, according to one of them, while apprehensive about the future, looked forward to the prospect of "the country being rid of a dictator who filled all ministers with terror."[3] Fearing the imminent occupation of the capital by Soviet forces, the Shah insisted on leaving Tehran. Displaying even greater anxiety, the crown prince also wished to accompany his father and join the royal family in the central city of Esfahan; both had to be persuaded by the ministers that their departure would have an adverse effect on the panic-ridden population and might provoke serious disorder.

Reza Shah agreed to stay, but his self-confidence and aura had irretrievably crumbled; he was able neither to provide leadership nor to reconcile himself to the new situation. Deeply dismayed by the growing assertiveness of the parliament, and aiming to salvage his fast-eroding authority, he announced, through Forughi and the press, that he intended henceforth to be a law-abiding constitutional monarch; thereafter he made a point of repeatedly invoking the Constitution. The cabinet, however, continued to feel ill at ease with him; nor did the Allies show any willingness to work with him, as revealed by the increasing denunciation of him by the British Broadcasting Corporation (BBC). Among other things, and on the basis of material compiled by the British legation in Tehran, the BBC strongly condemned the Shah for his dictatorial conduct and deviation from the Constitution. Such transgressions had not previously concerned the British officials, who considered them fully consonant with the "oriental mind" and the "Persian character." Comparing Reza Shah with Peter the Great, and admiring his "ardent and driving patriotism," the British minister in Tehran had in 1936 noted:

> His faults are faults without which he could not govern this country and his justification of them is the universal admission that no one understands Persia better than he does. This in itself explains his determination to keep all sources of power in his hands, financial, military and political, his ruthlessness, the ready awakening of his suspicions, his injustices and often his brutality. These are vices inherent in the race and cannot be left out of the make-up of the Sovereign.[4]

Beginning its Persian-language broadcasts to Iran in late December 1940 to rival broadcasts from Berlin, the BBC had added to the panic in the Iranian security and police forces, which sought to monitor and control those who purchased radio sets or listened to foreign broadcasts, particularly in the wake of attacks against the Shah from Berlin in the spring of 1940.[5] As Reza Shah's position grew less tenable, government ministers contemplated requesting his abdication, which was, in the event, precipitated by the news of the imminent arrival of Allied forces in the capital. The beleaguered Shah was not spared veiled denunciation by several deputies who not only had gained their seats with his blessing but had been among his ardent supporters. Forced into exile by the Allies, he was eventually allowed to reside in South Africa, where he died in 1944.

The Anglo-Soviet invasion of the country again demonstrated the acute vulnerability of Iran, and resuscitated bitter memories of past humiliations and the country's division into spheres of influence. Iranian nationalism suffered a severe blow. Soon after the start of the invasion, the British enumerated the transgressions of their Soviet allies in Iran, which included "disarming of all police and gendarmerie, combined with a refusal to accept responsibility for the protection of life and property; the stripping of Persian civilian lorries of essential parts required by Russian forces, such as tyres; the confiscation of property necessary to railway working; interference with civilian traffic; the retention of arrested Persian officers."[6] The proximity of Soviet troops, Bullard reported, rendered Tehran "morally crushed and materially hampered."[7] The Soviet forces, eradicating Iranian sovereignty in areas they controlled, aggressively exploited Iranian infrastructure and resources, harassed the population, disrupted commerce, obstructed the flow of goods from the northern provinces to the south, encouraged incipient secessionism in Azarbaijan, and actively assisted the formation of groups and parties likely to further their aims. Their presence and activities were deeply resented by the populace.

The British fared no better in the public perception. The sudden upsurge of British propaganda castigating the Shah as a tyrant and a thief reinvigorated Iranian cynicism and a deep-seated belief in British hypocrisy and sinister intentions. In the eyes of many Iranians, the British had treated the Shah respectfully as long as he was cooperative, but vehemently turned against him when he failed to comply promptly with their demands. Inveterate proponents of conspiracy theories, who attributed the rise and demise of Reza Shah entirely to British machinations, felt vindicated. Belief in the mythical scale of British influence was revived. Real or putative anglophiles, who had long kept a low profile, received a major boost. Again the British legation (later embassy) and consular offices became, or were seen as, foci of unusually consequential political brokerage, where careers were made or unmade. The British concentrated on cultivating supporters, renewing old ties and forging new ones; they bribed journalists and secured the suppression of newspapers critical of Allied policies; they began to influence key appointments, including those of cabinet ministers and prime ministers, and showed little respect for the revived constitutional procedures. Once again the perception of British influence, resting on collective memories of a powerful imperial presence in Iran, became a tangible reality in the country's politics. A belief in the ubiquity of British influence was resuscitated as an article of faith in the Iranian political culture. This perception both reflected and reinforced the reestablishment of the overlapping British oil and diplomatic presence in Iran as an institutional component of Iranian domestic politics. As the oil crisis of the late 1940s would reveal, despite the end of the British empire in India and the decline of their influence in the Middle East, the British continued to ignore or denigrate Iranian nationalism and Iran's rights as a sovereign nation.

In its socioeconomic impact on Iranian society, the occupation was highly disruptive and damaging. Effective central government authority virtually disappeared in much of the south and west, as well as the north, occupied by the British and the Soviet forces respectively. Severe shortages of foodstuffs, high prices, inflation, and unemployment caused great public distress, particularly among the lower classes. The dwindling income of the salaried classes and bureaucratic disruption provided further grounds for corruption and abuse of office. In various parts of the country, bread shortages and the adulteration of flour had started well before the occupation. In its aftermath the worsening shortage of bread, and its poor quality when available, often provoked protests and near-riots. The crumbling apparatus of autocratic repression was unleashing new forces and giving rise to new expectations and problems. In the words of a noted writer witnessing the situation, the removal of Reza Shah

liberated the enchained [political] forces in the country. The toiling masses were being pushed to the front stage of politics. The problems of political and social life were reaching city squares and factories. In the civil service and the university, the young were becoming increasingly agitated. Adventurers of various brands were busily enlisting the simple-minded to their own cause. The bazaar was gripped by the fever of high prices and hoarding. Everything was beyond reach—sugar, cloth, medicine, tires, rice, etc.—and everything was being greedily bought and sold. Every commodity . . . was being exchanged ten or twenty times a day, profit was added to profit, misery to misery. Typhus and inedible bread . . . were two prevailing calamities, and rationing coupons the foundation stone of windfall riches.[8]

The virtual disappearance of state authority in large parts of the country, the breakdown of administrative control, and disorder in rural areas and among pastoral-nomadic populations, together with the resurgence of highway robbery, aroused fears that the country could revert to the conditions prevailing in the pre-Pahlavi era. Allied war-related activities and the use of the country's roads and railway network to carry supplies from the Persian Gulf to the Soviet border created some employment and business opportunities but put a great strain on the system. Iranians saw the occupation as a calamity, and some inevitably longed for the order and certainty of the Reza Shah era. Although the end of authoritarian rule was widely welcomed, the occupation inevitably gave rise to a growing sense of humiliation. With the collapse of the military, many feared the outbreak of unmanageable disorder throughout the country. Yet the political elite, whether politicians or civil servants, apprehensive about the fate of the country, endeavored to reempower the government, which scrambled to gain the cooperation or assent of the occupying powers in reclaiming its authority, to maintain public order, and to revive the military and security forces.

In the wake of Reza Shah's abdication the Allies were not enthusiastic about the accession of the crown prince. The British toyed with the idea of restoring the Qajars, but no viable candidate was found, and Forughi counseled against measures likely to cause a constitutional crisis and sociopolitical disruption; he favored the retention of the existing Constitution, which allowed for a smooth succession.[9] The British and the Soviets reluctantly agreed to give the twenty-two-year-old Mohammad Reza the chance to succeed his father, subject to certain conditions, including "good behaviour."[10] The new Shah, noted Colonel Fraser, the British military attaché, "is not credited with much strength of character, which, if true, may suit the present circumstances . . . In any case, no alternative presented itself, nor could any have been without considerable delay and a welter of intrigue. The present Shah, if unsuitable, can be got rid of later. In the meantime it should be possible to prevent him from doing much harm."[11] The Shah, according to a different account, "had given assurances that the Iranian Constitution would be observed, that the properties taken by his father would be restored to the nation and that he would undertake the carrying out of the reforms considered necessary by the British Government."[12] In an atmosphere in which Reza Shah's autocratic rule was becoming the target of growing denunciation, the new Shah had no choice but to distance himself from his father, undertake to act as a constitutional monarch, and seek to redress the wrongdoings of the past.[13] The continuation of the dynasty and the Shah's accession to the throne had occurred almost by default; by invoking constitutional provisions and underlining the expediency of observing them, Forughi had played a key role in making it possible. The new Shah was constitutionally required to take a formal oath before the parliament in order to accede to the throne. The Constitution proved indispensable in furnishing legitimacy to the young Shah, the process of succession, and the consolidation of his reign.

The Shah's authority was as precarious as his accession had been fortuitous. Having reluctantly remained in the capital, he was at the mercy of the Anglo-Soviet forces. But although he was youthful, inexperienced, and shaken by the fate of his father, he retained considerable residual power, which he gradually enhanced: he reestablished the links forged during his father's reign between the crown and the armed and security forces; the court remained the chief dispenser of patronage; and the monarchy's institutional strength remained undiminished, enabling the Shah to exploit and promote the political disarray of the constitutional arrangements. Inherently imbued with an authoritarian political culture, the monarchy's structural tendency was to strive to reinvigorate itself and to reestablish its domination of the political process.

The democratic legacy of the Constitutional Revolution, even if largely unrealized, was, however, resilient, and after the occupation the Pahlavi monarchy was not in a position to unravel it. Yet the new Shah only grudgingly acquiesced in a situation in which the country was no longer a patrimonial domain of the court. Despite his publicly reiterated commitment to democratic governance, the Shah missed no opportunity to undermine it. He favored or tolerated only servile prime ministers and relentlessly sought to manipulate the parliament by playing a role far greater than any sensible reading of the Constitution or requirements of prudence would prescribe. This situation was starkly incongruent with the antiautocratic ethos of post–Reza Shah Iran and with the revived Constitution, which had in effect saved the Pahlavi throne.

The role that the young Shah would play in the political arena was determined not simply by the peculiarities of his character but primarily by the institutional salience of the monarchy, which largely rested on the army and the court clientele. Refusal to take advantage of the vast opportunities afforded by the political fragility of the constitutional arrangements would have required exceptional qualities of character. The credibility of a true constitutional monarch rested primarily on demonstrated avoidance of corruption, hubris, and extravagance; a genuine commitment to the rule of law; and a capacity for exerting moral authority in times of crisis. These would ensure that he would not be held responsible for the failings of the government. There was, of course, a middle ground between admittedly unattainable benevolent detachment and the Shah's obsession with enhanced personal power at the expense of the vulnerable constitutional arrangements. The Shah's machinations and maneuvers for increased power could not, however, proceed smoothly in the boisterously antiautocratic political milieu of post–Reza Shah Iran. In addition to the revived constitutional procedures, a burgeoning press, proliferating political parties and associations, and other social forces militated against royal schemes. A rumbustious civil society was reemerging.

## Revival of Political and Civil Society

After the abdication of Reza Shah, his repressive policies became the subject of scrutiny and condemnation, and a handful of notorious members of his security apparatus were tried and punished. Left-wing activists released from jail and a host of other intellectuals were at the forefront of the wave of criticism. Few, however, fundamentally questioned the reform measures of the Reza Shah era. The developments of recent decades, particularly the expansion of modern education, had transformed the urban sociopolitical landscape. The physical and cultural character of cities had also changed. Tehran, with its many modern buildings, paved and lit streets, restaurants, cinemas, theaters, bookshops, and cafés frequented by intellectuals, including former students sent to Europe by the government, was far removed from the dusty town of the pre–Reza Shah era. The city had acquired a metropolitan ambiance. The traditionalists' efforts to restore the veil persisted but were only partially successful. Women were, of course, no longer coerced by the government to appear unveiled in public. An ongoing, albeit implicit, secularization facilitated the coexistence of different tastes and preferences. Visible expressions of religiosity were no longer met with intolerance. Nothing, however, could reduce the consternation of the traditionalists, who, encouraged by the conciliatory gestures of certain politicians, mounted a campaign to restore their influence and to revive ritual practices prohibited under Reza Shah. In their eyes, Iranian society had become perilously permissive; a moral decadence had crept in, and nothing symbolized it as much as the policy of banning the veil in public, which they blamed for the erosion of family values, modesty, and the chastity and dignity of women. Such sentiments continued to be a rallying cry of the traditionalists and others who wanted to reverse many of the modernizing measures of the Reza Shah era. Such a reversal, however, seemed virtually unimaginable.

The spread of left-wing trends provided further impetus for members of the traditional and pious classes, including many bazaar merchants, to favor the public revival and political salience of religiosity. Ayatollah Sheikh Hosein Qomi, who in May 1943 returned from Iraq (where he had resided since 1935), did not succeed in bringing about a drastic reversal of the secular tenor of education; he was able to obtain only an affirmation of government neutrality regarding veiling in public. Qomi's limited success did not deter others from pursuing similar objectives. The elevated and uncommon title of *ayatollah* (sign of God) was increasingly employed to bestow added distinction and an aura of sanctity to distinguished men of religion, as a counterbalance to the prestige-conferring modern titles of "doctor" and "engineer" ostentatiously used by highly placed members of the intelligentsia. Despite a rise in the fortunes of the exponents of religious orthodoxy there was a reassuring, almost complacent, confidence among the intelligentsia that modern and secular practices would persist and withstand challenge.

The advent of mass communications, helped by the Persian broadcasts of foreign radio stations and the establishment of Tehran radio in April 1940, as well as by the publication of a sizable number of newspapers, journals, and books, no longer hampered by strict censorship, contributed to the growing political consciousness of the urban populace. The abolition of police permits for domestic travel facilitated mobility. Public debate, conducted through formal and informal societies, clubs, newspapers, in tea and coffee houses and cafés frequented by the intelligentsia, signified the resurgence of a public sphere. Certain cafés became important venues for intellectual gatherings, centered around writers such as Hedayat and other cultural figures, including leading left-wing activists. Though beset by a proclivity for conspiratorial thinking, a weak sense of civic responsibility, and an inadequate appreciation of the prerequisites of the rule of law, the political culture was proving adept in reconciling itself with ideological pluralism.

The emerging civil society was, of course, the consequence not of the voluntary withdrawal of an enlightened, institutionally robust state, but of the temporary paralysis of the authoritarian edifice. In the wake of the sudden collapse of authoritarian rule, the transition to a pluralistic political and civil society and a smoothly working constitutional government needed mental and emotional adjustments that would have been difficult to achieve in ordinary circumstances, let alone during an occupation. Close to two decades of repressive rule had ensured that the scope and meaning of liberty, and the assumptions regarding the requirements of effective governance, would remain contested, and that the existence of a lively civil society would appear irreconcilable with law and order. Inevitably, political inexperience and reaction to the stifling restrictions of the immediate past meant that the expression of newfound liberties would sometimes verge on lawlessness. Even well-versed advocates of political and civic liberties seemed to lack any immediately effective formula for securing such liberties while affirming institutionalized governmental authority. To the impatient, the goals of ensuring efficient and honest administration of the country while observing the Constitution, respecting the rule of law, and ensuring individual freedoms continued to appear irreconcilable. For some, the upsurge of numerous associations and parties indicated social vibrancy; others viewed it as signaling fragmentation and malaise.

The post–Reza Shah era witnessed the burgeoning of a variety of secular, religious, professional, and political associations. The Association of Engineers, which emerged in March 1943, established itself through a successful strike aimed at instituting a transparent merit system as the basis of promotion. University professors as well as physicians supported the strike; in early June the government agreed to accept the demands of the engineers and those of the academics, who advocated autonomy and self-administration for the university. Several potentially viable political parties also emerged, some of which, such as the Iran Party—consisting of engineers, lawyers, and other prominent members of the intelligentsia—espoused and helped to promote social-democratic values. Many of the parties were, however, barely more than vehicles for promoting the interests of their few key founder members. They were ideologically amorphous and espoused no clear set of principles or a political program. In impact, significance, and intellectual vitality none could rival the Tudeh Party, founded in early October 1941 and comprising many left-wing intellectuals and activists, including most of those who had been imprisoned in 1938.

Reflecting the wartime alliance of the Soviets and the Western powers, the Tudeh Party, though created with active Soviet support, assumed a reformist and social-democratic character that significantly increased its appeal. It targeted workers as well as the intelligentsia; advocated the protection and expansion of political, civic, and social liberties; and supported constitutionalism and legislation beneficial to the poorer classes.[14] It vigorously denied that it was communist,[15] and advocated forming a broad coalition with other reformist parties. Though relentless in its condemnation of Reza Shah, it campaigned against groups seeking to roll back the process of modernization or to restore traditionalist practices and mores. It denounced the revival of the veil.[16] In its various publications it persuasively analyzed the inequities of Iranian society and proffered appealing remedial measures.

The party leadership was heterogeneous; it included those who genuinely cared for the independence and prosperity of the country and the well-being of its poorer classes, as well as those who considered Iranian interests to be closely identified with, if not subordinate to, those of the So- viet Union, which they loyally sought to promote. Eight party members were elected to the fourteenth parliament (1944–1946), mostly from areas under Soviet control, and the party continued to portray itself as an advo- cate of constitutionalist government. After the Soviet victory over the Ger- mans at Stalingrad in February 1943, however, the party's commitment to the Soviet Union deepened, and toward the end of the war it became even more pronounced. In defiance of nationalist sentiments, the party advo- cated granting an oil concession to the Soviet Union, and to this end marched in the streets of Tehran flanked by occupying Red Army soldiers.

The party's influence and latent identification with Soviet Communism had alarmed the ruling elite and the propertied classes in general. The ba- zaar merchants nurtured the formation of anti-Tudeh parties, such as the National Will Party, formed by Sayyed Zia, the former prime minister and co-perpetrator of the coup of 1921, who had returned from a long exile abroad in September 1943 to serve as a member of parliament. Sayyed Zia was in many respects an eccentric traditionalist sympathetic to premodern agrarian and pastoral-nomadic mores. Elected to the fourteenth parliament, he supported parliamentarianism and the limitation of royal prerogatives. Above all, he established himself as a political broker, an intermediary be- tween the state and the vulnerable elements of society, and attracted a var- ied following. He viewed British influence in Iran as a necessary safeguard against Soviet Communism. His views resonated with other traditionalists and opponents of communism. An ardent anglophile, from the outset Sayyed Zia became the most trusted Iranian confidant of the British em- bassy. The British saw him as a most desirable prime ministerial candidate; he offered them detailed advice on how to conduct their affairs in Iran and how to maintain and enhance their influence. Like other key anglophiles, Sayyed Zia benefited from the lingering and invigorated Iranian belief in a vast and insidious British influence. Capitalizing on close links with the Brit- ish brought him notoriety but also considerable clout. Many, including the Shah, saw him as the unofficial but authoritative mouthpiece of the British.

Traditionalist opposition to communism and modernity found more ve- hement expression in the Fada'iyan-e Islam, a Shi'ite fundamentalist group founded in 1945 by Sayyed Mojtaba Mir-Lauhi (known as Navvab-e Safavi), a man in his early twenties with little or no formal Islamic education. Based

*Sayyed Zia al-Din Tabataba'i, collaborator with Reza Khan in the coup of 1921. In the years after 1941 he became a major political broker, unsuccessfully groomed by the British for the premiership.* (Courtesy of the Institute for the Study of Contemporary Iranian History, Tehran)

mainly in Tehran, the Fada'iyan consisted largely of young men of lower-class origins, limited education, and traditional occupations. A fringe group with no mass base or political agenda that could resonate with the Iranian public, it endeavored to tap the resentments of the lower- and underclass urban elements and used terrorism as a means of gaining prominence and compensating for its marginal status. The group's defining features, together with its challenge to the ruling elite, enabled it to acquire a significance disproportionate to its size. Ideologically resembling the Muslim Brotherhood in Egypt, the Fada'iyan espoused a literal reading of Islam; they abhorred what they considered to be decadence resulting from irreligion. Striving to counter modernity, secularity, communism, pluralism, and civic-nationalism, they sought to eliminate those whom they regarded as obstacles to their agenda or as stooges of foreigners; yet they were not averse to questionable though politically useful alliances. Pronouncing their primary goal to be the establishment of Islamic law (shari'a), they envisaged a crucial sociopolitical role for the clerics.

Unsettled by the controversial essays and polemics of Kasravi, particularly his criticism of traditional or folk Shi'ism, Safavi masterminded his assassination in March 1946. Safavi had used Kasravi's views on Shi'ism as a rallying cry to form the Fada'iyan. The assassination of Kasravi and his secretary, which took place in a courtroom where he was being questioned, was accomplished with the blessing or help of certain leading clerics.[17] The murder of Kasravi, who has been described as "one of the greatest figures in the contemporary intellectual history of Iran,"[18] the almost supine reaction of the intelligentsia to it, and the complacent attitude of the ruling elite, which resulted in the eventual release of his assassins, revealed the deep vulnerability of secular intellectual trends and institutions to mobilized religious fervor.

A primary target of the more broadly defined traditionalists was the Tudeh Party. Though committed to secular ideas, it pursued an expedient or utilitarian attitude to religion; sympathetic critics such as Kasravi chastised it for paying "extensive homage" to Ayatollah Qomi.[19] But the party's strategy of not provoking the religious forces did not mitigate the animosity of right-wing traditionalists. In response to the rise in the party's fortunes and its increasingly explicit pro-Soviet stance, Sayyed Zia and his acolytes spearheaded a sustained anti-Tudeh campaign, and to this end formed the National Will Party in early 1945. In their anti-Tudeh efforts they received considerable help from British diplomatic as well as intelligence personnel in Iran, including Robin Zaehner and Norman Darbyshire, both of whom would later play a crucial role in efforts to roll back the nationalization of the oil industry and to overthrow the government pursuing it. In turn, the Tudeh Party resorted to a relentless campaign against Sayyed Zia and the British. This confrontation cast a shadow over Iranian politics and civil society. It poisoned political debate and hindered the rise of a tolerant and sturdy ideological pluralism.

The charges of subservience to the Soviet Union in no way deterred the Tudeh Party's increasing ideological reliance on and close organizational links with the Soviet Communist Party. The refusal of the Red Army to vacate Iranian territory after the end of the war, and its actions in instigating and sustaining "autonomy movements" in areas it controlled, particularly Azarbaijan, deeply unsettled the central government.[20] Its continued presence also provoked intense anxiety among all Iranian nationalists. The party's attitude to the Azarbaijan crisis and its willingness in 1946 to cooperate with the government of Ahmad Qavam—not known for prosocialist leanings but perceived as amenable to Soviet demands—caused unease among some of its leaders and other members, who wished it to follow a more independent or patriotically sensitive approach. Internal demands for reform of the party's structure and for a more open and accountable leadership remained unaddressed. In January 1948 several key party members broke away with the aim of forming an alternative, more genuinely socialist party. They naively expected that their move would earn them the blessing of the Soviet Communist Party, which in the event excoriated them. This experience and the barrage of denunciatory Tudeh propaganda against them impelled the dissenters to abandon their plans, but also freed them from their residual illusions and the Stalinist spell. Many abandoned leftist politics altogether; others, represented by Khalil Maleki, the prime target of Tudeh invective, eventually made common cause with the civic-nationalists. To this end, after an abortive alliance with the anticommunist Toilers' Party, they formed their own Third Force Party in October 1952.

The departure of leading dissenters deprived the Tudeh Party of considerable talent and dented its ideological power but made it more homogeneous. This development intensified the acrimonious war of words be-

*From right, seated, Prime Minister Ahmad Qavam, Mohammad Reza Shah Pahlavi, and his twin sister, Princess Ashraf, in the mid-1940s.* (Courtesy of the Institute for the Study of Contemporary Iranian History, Tehran)

tween the party and its various opponents, including pro-British groups. Despite occasional tactical alliances among adversaries, ideological rifts and bitter recriminations increasingly marred Iranian intellectual and political life. Few Iranians believed in the intellectual autonomy and integrity of activists, or accepted that genuine left- or right-wing leanings could exist independently of links with the Soviet or British embassies. Such an atmosphere made it imperative to develop a political stance demonstrably opposed to both Soviet and British influence. It is in the context of the ideological polarization of postwar Iran that the emergence and growing relevance of civic-nationalism can be understood. Although it ended autocratic rule, the Allied occupation of the country had wounded nationalist sensibilities and had painfully demonstrated that the country was still weak and vulnerable. This realization strengthened a belief that national sovereignty could be safeguarded only if the people themselves felt committed to defending it.

Civic-nationalists such as Dr. Mohammad Mosaddeq, the veteran constitutionalist of widely recognized stature and reputation, sought to redefine and reinvigorate the values of patriotism, constitutionalism, national and popular sovereignty, and the promotion and protection of the civic and political rights and entitlements of all Iranians. Civic-nationalism combined leftist liberal or social-democratic leanings with nationalism; it advocated political neutrality in relations with foreign powers; it was anti-imperialist, cognizant of indigenous cultural, moral, and religious sensibilities but fully committed to the values of qualified modernity. It promoted an inclusive and nondiscriminatory approach to the nationalist values of solidarity, belonging, and loyalty. It did not confuse political freedom with national self-determination; it advocated national self-determination as well as freedom from domestic oppression.

Civic-nationalist values appealed not only to the modern educated intelligentsia but also to other politically discerning segments of the urban population, whether modern or traditional. Promoted by a number of leading figures, political parties, and groups, such values were increasingly identified with the political beliefs and conduct of Mosaddeq and a sociopolitical movement that he both led and was inspired by. The movement aimed at championing the sovereignty of the Iranian people by exercising effective control over both the shape of domestic politics and the country's sources of wealth, particularly oil. The civic-nationalists concentrated their efforts on promoting political and civil liberties and a recognized space for responsible oppositional politics. An equally significant challenge, but one that they did not adequately address, was the crafting of a viable structure of governance. The apparent impunity with which the Fada'iyan were able to assassinate not only a leading intellectual but also several prominent politicians demonstrated the fragility and incompetence of the government and its inadequacy to enforce the nation's laws. It also indicated that civil society was threatened less by the intrusions of the state than by social forces hostile to key political, civic, and social liberties.

The government was undeniably ill equipped to ensure law and order. At the same time, its efforts to assert its authority were invariably denounced or portrayed as dictatorial by groups or individuals who often had little or no understanding of or concern for the prerequisites of order and freedom. Though able to rely on martial-law regulations, particularly in the capital, the government was not in a position to root out acts or threats of violence or to contain abuses of press freedom. The years after 1941 witnessed an upsurge of newspapers and periodicals, some of which were of considerable literary and journalistic significance. Most of the newspapers were small and highly partisan promoters of narrow causes, functioning as mouthpieces of their proprietors or editors. Rarely displaying a developed sense of journalistic and civic responsibility, some papers readily abused freedom of expression.

An extreme yet not entirely untypical example was *Mard-e Emruz* (1942–1948), edited by Mohammad Mas'ud, who had studied journalism in Belgium thanks to the patronage of Ali-Akbar Davar. Mas'ud was not merely a sensational polemicist but also a popular novelist capable of vividly delving into the context and determinants of aberrant behavior. Using his acerbic pen, total irreverence, and vitriolic denunciation of the ruling class, including the royal family, to attract an avid readership for his intermittently published newspaper, he was undeterred by frequent detentions or by suspensions of publication, which merely added to its popularity. In October 1947 he printed a formal and unequivocal personal pledge to pay a large reward to anyone who would assassinate the then prime minister, Qavam, whom he accused of treason.[21] Ironically, Mas'ud himself was assassinated in February 1948, and his death was attributed to his enemies, particularly the Shah's influential twin sister, Princess Ashraf, one of Mas'ud's prime targets. It later turned out, however, that leading members of the Tudeh Party had arranged his murder, in the expectation that the court, which had been a main target of Mas'ud's invective, would shoulder the blame.[22] The phenomenon of Mas'ud, the public receptiveness to his relentless vilification of the ruling class, belief in the validity of his charges, together with his personal fate—intended to further muddy the political waters—exposed some of the predicaments facing the prevailing mode of governance and the political and civic culture.

## Resuscitating Constitutionalism

The unseating of Reza Shah ushered in a new era of constitutional government, marked by an upsurge of public interest in politics and democratic participation, and symbolized by the resumption of the active celebration of Constitution Day (August 5/14 Mordad), which had faded during Reza

Shah's rule. As one future prime minister remarked, the "shock" of the occupation awakened the people to the perils of personal rule and the necessity for "government of the people over the people" and arrangements to
ensure that "no one occupied a formal position of power unless the people
had freely empowered him and were in a position to supervise and determine the length of his incumbency of the office."[23] The twelve years between the abdication of Reza Shah and the coup of August 1953 are regarded as the most important period of sustained experimentation with
constitutionalism, a period in which the viability of constitutional monarchy was put to the test. Many Iranian writers and journalists who lived
through this critical juncture, though cognizant of its flaws, referred to it as
an era of democracy. In the aftermath of the coup of August 1953, this period was to be remembered with considerable nostalgia and an emotionally
charged, almost tragic, sense of loss. These feelings rested on the assumption that had constitutional arrangements endured longer and encountered
fewer domestic and foreign impediments, they could have evolved into a viable parliamentary system.

Several factors adversely affected the functioning of the semimodern
state apparatus, which survived Reza Shah's fall, and the workings of the revived parliamentary arrangements. Most immediately, the presence of occupying forces severely challenged the authority of the central government.
Concomitantly, the fragility of the constitutional arrangements was exacerbated by, and at the same time facilitated, the increased role of the British,
American, and Soviet embassies in Iranian politics, which persisted beyond
the formal end of the occupation. Fear of growing foreign influence and its
ramifications, and of the revival of forces and ideas that militated against
national unity and a centralized state, preoccupied many Iranian statesmen.
Echoing such concerns, Taqizadeh was convinced that Iran needed a constitutional and at the same time strong and centralized state. In his view, the
major challenge facing Iranian politicians consisted in ensuring that the
country had a capable military yet remained immune from the tyranny of
rule by a military officer—that a centralized state capable of maintaining
order throughout the country did not degenerate into despotism.[24]

Governing and maintaining order and national unity while adhering to
the constitution were primarily the tasks of the government, which was

institutionally weak, while the parliament, though fractious and vulnerable, was constitutionally enabled to exert considerable power. In July 1943 Mohammad Sa'ed, foreign minister and later prime minister, complained:

> The parliament is preoccupied with factional disputes and with engineering a new cabinet every few months; the level of cooperation and amity that at this juncture should exist between the parliament and the government is nonexistent, so that in order to proceed in its expected tasks, every head of government needs to spend most of his time negotiating and wheeling and dealing with deputies . . . who leave him no opportunity to spend any time attending to the fundamental problems facing the country.[25]

The emergence of a measure of consensus over what constitutionalism implied and required was hampered by ideological conflict, the rivalry of competitive networks of patronage, the machinations of various vested interests, and the activities of antidemocratic social forces. The democratically inexperienced populace was ill served by the existing political parties and dejected by the authorities' efforts to rig elections. Despite professions of adherence to constitutional governance, the majority of the political elite readily branded any gesture of deference to public opinion as sheer demagoguery. They barely distinguished opposition from sedition or public debate from chaos, while those in opposition castigated the incumbents with scant attention to the constraints they faced.

More immediately significant, the government and the parliament could be both thwarted and manipulated by the court. From the outset the Shah wanted to assume a leadership role and circumvent the government. Soon after assuming the throne he sent a secret message to Bullard expressing a desire to see him "fairly often without the knowledge of politicians"; Bullard's response was that "it would not be possible to be received without knowledge of Persian Government and my Soviet colleague."[26] Undeterred, the Shah remained adamant in playing an active role in politics and in preventing the emergence of capable prime ministers with sources of sustained support outside the court or unwilling to defer to it. To the detriment of the very foundations of constitutional governance, if the Shah could not personally control the government effectively, no one else would have the opportunity to govern either.

The parliament, on the other hand, though containing a large number of royalist deputies, and in spite of factional divisions, procedural constraints, and foreign pressures, was collectively intent on asserting its constitutional authority. Having automatically passed bills or artificially debated them, it took the parliamentarians some time to accustom themselves to spontaneous debate and to developing a shared understanding of the scope of their rights and duties. Nevertheless they were determined to take their deliberative and legislative tasks seriously and to play the primary role in forming, maintaining, or undermining governments. The Shah's refusal to acquiesce in this situation meant that governments rarely enjoyed both parliamentary and royal support. Representing intricate, even conflicting, interests, governments remained institutionally fragile and scarcely able to perform their functions, a state of affairs that in turn enabled the Shah actively to intervene in the process of governance. A parliamentary majority was rarely able to sustain a government, while a small but vocal minority often succeeded in undermining it. The parliament could not normally engineer and maintain a strong government, nor could it easily afford to tolerate an ineffective one. Consequently, in the course of twelve years, twelve prime ministers formed seventeen cabinets, which underwent twenty-three major reshuffles.[27]

The first prime minister who attempted to assert the authority of the executive independently of the court was Qavam, the renowned patrician and a prime minister in the pre-Pahlavi era. Qavam's first cabinet (August 1942–February 1943) was undermined by both royal and parliamentary opposition.[28] Most of Qavam's successors—men of far less force of character assigned the task of governing against numerous odds—were ineffectual. Facing a drastic decline in the administrative effectiveness and authority of the central government, they had no choice but to attempt to appease the court, the parliament, the occupying powers, the press, and the public.

The first parliamentary elections to be openly contested in some seventeen years were those for the fourteenth parliament (1944–1946). The outcome was influenced by the court, the governing elite, local notables, constitutionalist figures, chiefs of the guilds, the leaders of the bazaar and the crowds, as well as informal alliances, associations, political parties, the press, and certain foreign embassies, notably the British and the Soviet. In Tehran and several other cities the elections proved far more difficult to manipulate than elsewhere, and many candidates there won their seats with real public support. Having failed to exert the degree of influence over the elections that he wished, the Shah considered declaring the elections null and void, but the British warned him against such a move.[29] Though beset by factionalism and continued pressure from the occupying powers and the court, the fourteenth parliament was able to play a crucial role in the political process and in safeguarding Iranian sovereign rights.

With the end of the war in sight, the British possession of a lucrative oil concession in Iran and their influence over the ruling class were openly resented by the Soviets. Prompted by the efforts of American oil companies to obtain oil concessions in Iran, the Soviet government mounted strong pressure to gain an oil concession of its own. This situation led Mosaddeq, Tehran's first deputy (the candidate with the highest number of votes) in the fourteenth parliament, to sponsor a bill banning the granting of oil concessions to foreigners. The bill passed with overwhelming support. Having failed to obtain the concession, the Soviets exerted pressure by undermining Iran's territorial integrity and refusing to withdraw their troops from the country.

The crisis created by the Soviet refusal to evacuate Iranian territory resulted in the reinstallation of Qavam as prime minister (January 1946– December 1947), the only premier with whom the Soviets were prepared to negotiate. Because the term of the fourteenth parliament expired soon afterward, and because elections had been postponed pending the evacuation of foreign forces, Qavam was able to proceed unhampered by either the parliament or the Shah, who saw no alternative to him. But Qavam was able to remain in power only as long as the crisis persisted; the evacuation of the Soviet forces and his cunning elimination of the autonomy movements undermined the *raison d'être* of his government. Even his formation of a seemingly powerful political party—the Democratic Party of Iran— which manipulated elections for the fifteenth parliament (1947–1949), failed to consolidate his position. Soon after the opening of the new parliament and prompted by the court, a large number of deputies affiliated with Qavam's party deserted him in favor of the royalist camp. Faced with the resignation of his ministers at the royal behest, Qavam was forced to resign and to face charges of abuse of office.

Qavam was succeeded by a number of royalist premiers. Although he was in a position to outmaneuver prime ministers with ease, the still dissatisfied Shah had been preoccupied at least since 1945 with the idea of revising the Constitution and formally increasing his prerogatives. He had worked persistently to enlist the support of the British ambassador for such a move. Having publicly condemned his father's anticonstitutional conduct, the British were hesitant to condone the Shah's designs against the Constitution. Exploiting an attempt on his life on February 4, 1949, the Shah, marshaling his royalist supporters, launched a protocoup to suppress, banish, or silence his opponents, implicate and officially ban the Tudeh Party, and formally enhance his powers. Finally overcoming Anglo-American reservations, he convened a constituent assembly (April–May 1949) that amended the Constitution to increase the prerogatives of the monarch, granting him the right to dissolve the parliament and specifying an arrangement for further constitutional amendment. At the same time the parliament approved a bill submitted a year earlier for the formation of a senate. Constitutionally envisaged but not previously established, the senate, with half of its members directly appointed by the Shah, would considerably enhance royal influence.

The Shah's bid to increase his formal powers did not go unchallenged. In a bold open letter, Qavam denounced the Shah's tampering with the Constitution. This provoked the Shah to instruct his court minister, Ebrahim Hakimi, to respond by excoriating Qavam personally rather than attempting to provide a reasoned rebuttal.[30] A more vigorous challenge to the Shah's desire to formalize his domination of the political process came from Mosaddeq. As a deputy in the sixteenth parliament (1950–1952), Mosaddeq spoke forcefully against royal bids to undermine the Constitution; he also succeeded in frustrating the Shah's plan to acquire further powers, particularly the right to suspend bills adopted by the parliament.

## Civic-Nationalism Ascendant

The Shah was prevented from immediately benefiting from his increased powers when the oil issue began to dominate Iranian politics. In October 1947 the parliament rejected a draft agreement between Prime Minister Qavam and the Soviet ambassador promising the Soviets an oil concession with the aim of securing the withdrawal of their forces from the country.

Simultaneously the parliament empowered the government to redeem the nation's impaired rights to its sources of wealth, particularly its southern, British-controlled oil resources. This move, partially aimed at placating the Soviets, placed the issue of the British oil concession at the top of the political agenda. This increasingly salient issue dominated the elections for the sixteenth parliament. Mosaddeq and other civic-nationalists maintained that the Shah and his close aides wanted a parliament that would settle the oil dispute to the satisfaction of the British. Indeed, as he informed the British ambassador, the Shah wished to prevent the election of deputies with "subversive" intentions.[31] Similarly the pro-British court minister Abd al-Hosein Hazhir, who overshadowed the prime minister, wanted the elections rigged by the government in the interest of a speedy resolution of the Anglo-Iranian oil dispute.[32]

Efforts to this end eventually failed. In October 1949, for the second time during the reign of Mohammad Reza Shah, protesters took sanctuary in the royal palace to publicize the rigging of elections. They intended to expose the Shah to focused public attention in order to force him to embrace publicly the role of protector of constitutional principles. Though not immediately successful, by November the Mosaddeq-led protesters constituted the nucleus of the National Front (Jebheh-ye Melli), a coalition aiming to counter foreign influence and autocratic trends. More immediately, the Front advocated freedom of the press, free and fair elections, and an end to martial law. Mosaddeq pronounced these measures—highly pertinent at the time—essential to the preservation of democracy in Iran.[33] The assassination of Hazhir in early November 1949 at the hands of the Fada'iyan-e Islam was a major setback for the Shah, the court, and the government. Ironically, Hazhir had helped to secure the freedom of Kasravi's murderers. Despite concerted efforts against them, Mosaddeq and seven of his supporters were eventually elected to parliament, where they constituted a vocal group with an influence and moral authority far exceeding its size. Mosaddeq had once again won the highest number of votes cast in the capital.

By November 1950 Britain's failure to meet or seriously consider Iranian demands regarding the country's iniquitously low share of the oil profits provoked a call for nationalization of the oil industry. This move was spearheaded by the National Front, which now represented a broad civic-nationalist movement *(nahzat-e melli)*. The Front maintained that only a constitu-

*Parliamentarian and Prime Minister Dr. Mohammad Mosaddeq.*
(Author's collection)

tionally legitimate government that enjoyed public support could safeguard national interests, particularly with regard to control of Iran's oil. In February 1951 the British began grudgingly and belatedly to make real concessions, while the Front, riding the growing tide of public support, found itself unable to accept any measure short of nationalization. Legitimately claiming to speak for the nation, the Front derived its growing influence from its ability to link the assertion of national sovereignty, symbolized by the nationalization of oil, with insistence on popular sovereignty as the core principle of constitutionalism. On March 7, 1951, Prime Minister Haji-Ali Razmara, a capable former general with reformist intentions who was favored by the Americans, the British, and initially by the Shah, was assassinated by the Fada'iyan-e Islam. Soon afterward both houses of parliament approved nationalization of the oil industry, which Razmara had opposed. By late April 1951 Mosaddeq had left his parliamentary seat to replace Hosein Ala, Razmara's stopgap successor, as prime minister. Mosaddeq's premiership followed the revival of the "vote of inclination"—the practice of expressing prior parliamentary approval for prime ministerial candidates—which the Shah had disregarded since November 1948, but which Mosaddeq demanded. To the chagrin of the incredulous Shah and the British, the civic-nationalists had succeeded in forming a government with a solid popular base, dedicated to restraining the Shah and ending Britain's inordinate influence in Iran.

The rise in the political fortunes of civic-nationalism and the emergence of a politically active public was unwelcome to the traditionally elitist politicians, whether royalist or anglophile, whose chief political *modus operandi* was to exploit or manipulate the masses. They dismissed Mosaddeq and his colleagues as dangerous demagogues, as did the Shah, who regarded Mosaddeq's premiership as an insuperable obstacle to his bid for increased power. Mosaddeq had always maintained that the monarch's proper constitutional role was to reign, to refrain from hampering the government's authority to rule, and to use his residual authority and ceremonial functions beneficially to facilitate parliamentary government.[34] The Shah, Mosaddeq believed, should be prevented from subverting constitutionalism.

Having established himself primarily as a prominent figure of opposition, with his unexpected acceptance of the overly encumbered premiership, Mosaddeq found himself thrust into the role of a head of government exposed to a scale of opposition and pressures far greater than those experienced by his predecessors. From the outset his government faced concerted foreign and domestic opposition. Assisted by the anglophiles and resorting to various subversive measures, the British wasted no time in undermining his premiership. He also faced the relentless opposition of royalists and right-wing religious activists, as well as the officially banned but virtually unhampered Tudeh Party. The party promoted disaffection with the existing order and ridiculed reformist measures. Dismissive of civic-nationalism, which it saw as an ideological rival, the party leadership attempted to disrupt and derail Mosaddeq's efforts, denouncing him as seeking to salvage the existing order through minor reforms. Mosaddeq, the party propaganda maintained, wanted to substitute American imperialism for that of the British. The party's activities—whether disruptive opposition or occasional tactical support—did much to harm Mosaddeq's government.

From the opposite end of the political spectrum, the Fada'iyan vilified

Mosaddeq for not suppressing the Tudeh Party. Though deeply distrusting the civic-nationalists, the Fada'iyan had inadvertently helped them by assassinating Hazhir and Razmara, two of their leading opponents. Some of Mosaddeq's earlier supporters had links with the Fada'iyan, but neither he nor any of his like-minded colleagues could in any way support or condone the activities of the group. Yet, until Mosaddeq's assumption of the premiership, the civic-nationalists seemed far less concerned with threats from such a group than with the efforts of the royalists and their allies to undermine the fragile constitutional order.

Soon after his assumption of office, the Fada'iyan resorted to intimidation of Mosaddeq and his cabinet ministers and demanded the establishment of *shari'a* laws. Refusing to give in to these demands, in June 1951 Mosaddeq antagonized them further by ordering the detention of Safavi, the group's leader. The Fada'iyan's relations with Ayatollah Abolqasem Kashani—a leading proponent of nationalization of the oil industry—had also become strained as a result of his support for Mosaddeq, but by mid-1952 the group had resumed its ties with Kashani, who had begun to oppose Mosaddeq. In February 1952 the attempted assassination of Mosaddeq's dynamic colleague Hosein Fatemi, undertaken by the Fada'iyan, left him severely injured and effectively disabled. The Fada'iyan collaborated actively or tacitly with Mosaddeq's domestic opponents, particularly Mozaffar Baqa'i, who had deserted the National Front to become one of its fiercest and least scrupulous opponents, encouraging or condoning the Fada'iyan's use of violence and intimidation against it.[35] In the last six months of Mosaddeq's premiership, the level of Fada'iyan hostility to his government led the American and British secret services to count on the group to help oust the premier.[36]

Although Mosaddeq enjoyed the backing of a number of senior clerics who sympathized with his aims, most leading clerics tended to support the Shah and feared any weakening of the monarchy. Chief among them was Ayatollah Mohammad Behbahani, a high-ranking, flamboyant, and wily cleric linked to both the royalists and the anglophiles. In late February 1953 Behbahani and Kashani, who had openly turned against the civic-nationalists, played key roles in instigating a pro-Shah mob that attacked Mosaddeq's residence, severely testing his government. Behbahani and Kashani also crucially contributed to the success of the coup of August 1953.

The highest-ranking religious authority in the country, Grand Ayatollah Hosein Borujerdi, was on good terms with Mosaddeq, and in his espousal of quietism refused to support the Fada'iyan or Kashani's political activism. But toward the end of Mosaddeq's term of office, Borujerdi too in effect sided with the Shah. The political, civic, and social liberties advocated by the civic-nationalists were unpalatable to the clerical establishment and traditionalist groups. Concomitantly, Anglo-American propaganda, emphasizing that the continuation of Mosaddeq's premiership would lead to the abolition of the monarchy and the triumph of communism, also played a role in provoking active clerical opposition to him.

In addition to threatening Iran militarily, declaring it a pariah state, and preventing it from marketing its oil internationally, the British resorted to a variety of overt and covert measures to bolster and mobilize opposition to Mosaddeq. Such measures included wide-scale bribery of parliamentarians, journalists, and other politically consequential figures. In seeking to incapacitate, destabilize, and unseat the government, the British concentrated on manipulating parliamentary procedures. Enjoying popular backing, Mosaddeq was able to frustrate the British-backed parliamentary opposition, but the absence of sustained organizational support rendered his government vulnerable. Expecting Mosaddeq's government not to last long, and encouraged by the anglophiles, the British showed no real willingness to reach a settlement with him. In their various proposals they paid lip service to nominal nationalization of the oil industry but refused to accept any arrangement approximating real nationalization, which in Mosaddeq's view was the indispensable affirmation of Iranian national sovereignty. Though committed to the payment of just compensation to the AIOC, Mosaddeq abhorred the disguised return of the company, the idea of giving half of the Iranian oil revenues to it, or accepting its control over the production and management of Iranian oil.

Mosaddeq also faced numerous intractable problems in his efforts to revitalize constitutionalism and demonstrate that parliamentarianism was compatible with effective governance. On the domestic front he initially proceeded cautiously and included a number of reputable traditional notables in the cabinet. These figures, however, rarely shared his key objectives and resented his reluctance to clamp down on leftist opponents.[37] Although the cabinet ministers gradually became a more cohesive body, with a greater sense of common purpose, the cabinet could not hope in only a year or two to achieve the level of institutional cohesion and empowerment needed for the challenges it faced. Mosaddeq had maintained that "the salvation of the country rests solely on faith in true democracy and the creation of a real government of the people by the people . . . which can be achieved only through free elections."[38] He had always advocated free elections, but conducting such elections, when well-placed opponents were determined to pull every string and use every loophole to pack the parliament with anti-Mosaddeq deputies, was an insurmountable task.

The situation was made more complicated by Mosaddeq's view that any efforts on his part, in his capacity as prime minister, to promote civic-nationalist candidates was incompatible with free elections. His narrow conception of electoral freedom was as much of a handicap as his inability to encourage and assist greater organization of his supporters. Mosaddeq's failure to prevent the court, the military, and hostile local notables from improperly interfering in the elections for the seventeenth parliament (1952–1953) led him to suspend the elections when only 79 deputies, and not the required 136, had been elected. Deeply dejected by the outcome of the elections and increasingly frustrated by, among other things, his lack of authority over the armed forces, Mosaddeq demanded that the Shah relinquish his control of those forces in favor of the government and agree to Mosaddeq's assumption of the War Ministry. The Shah's refusal led to Mosaddeq's resignation.

Mosaddeq was, however, returned to power as the result of a popular uprising on July 21, 1952 (30 Tir 1331). In addition to constituting a clear setback for the Shah, who acquiesced in the extension of Mosaddeq's authority over the armed forces, the uprising signaled the defeat of the convoluted British efforts, coordinated chiefly by the former diplomat and then Oxford academic Robin Zaehner, to engineer Mosaddeq's downfall. The aim had been to replace Mosaddeq, preferably with Sayyed Zia or any other candidate willing to agree to an oil settlement acceptable to the British. The four-day-long premiership of Qavam, who had gained concerted British and American backing but not royal support, proved to be an unmitigated fiasco. Mosaddeq's opponents tactically retreated and the parliament granted him extra powers, which strengthened his position but rendered him potentially vulnerable to charges of deviating from the Constitution. Mosaddeq's attempts to improve the performance of the existing parliamentary arrangements, expedite the legislative process, and alleviate the institutional weakness of the cabinet were frustrated. His new press bill did not curb the excesses of the press, and his public security act failed to stem antigovernment activities. Similarly, his conscious efforts to adhere to what he considered to be the "principles of democracy" regarding freedom of expression and association[39] led to charges of leniency toward the Tudeh Party without mitigating the Tudeh opposition to his government.

In the wake of the July uprising the British focused on toppling Mosaddeq through a coup. They concentrated on cultivating active U.S. support and persuaded the Americans to join them in their stand against the Iranian government. Despite their mediation efforts to settle the oil dispute, the Americans were no more prepared than the British to allow Iran to make its oil nationalization a sustainable success, as this development would have jeopardized their own oil interests elsewhere. In November 1952 the Central Intelligence Agency began collaborating with the British Secret Intelligence Service to unseat Mosaddeq. The threat of a communist takeover of the country would be used as justification.

An important component of the Anglo-American plan was to destroy Mosaddeq's parliamentary majority as a prelude to toppling him. This would be achieved by bribing parliamentarians to act as collaborators. Aware of such moves, Mosaddeq astutely preempted them in August 1953 by resorting to a referendum to dissolve the parliament; this was to be followed by fresh elections on the basis of his new electoral law. However, after more than two years of relentless destabilizing moves, which reached their peak in the last two months of his premiership, Mosaddeq's hold on power had become increasingly tenuous. Taking advantage of the prevailing atmosphere of freedom, including a free press promoted by Mosaddeq's government, the CIA and its British counterpart resorted to intensive covert operations and a massive psychological campaign of disinformation and deception aimed at defaming, disorienting, and immobilizing Mosaddeq's supporters, fostering and exploiting royalist sentiments, and spreading fear among the populace that the country was on the verge of succumbing to communism.

Mosaddeq's abhorrence of violence and his refusal to appeal to the public crucially helped his antagonists, who left no stone unturned in their efforts to unseat him. Yet even if Mosaddeq's government had survived the onslaught of August 1953, in the prevailing Cold War milieu, and in the face of Anglo-American determination to dislodge his neutralist and defiant government in favor of a subservient one, its chances of successfully remaining in office and fulfilling its objectives were negligible. Had he appealed directly to the public, Mosaddeq might have been able to foil the almost fortuitous victory of his Anglo-American-backed opponents in August 1953, but by refusing to do so—and thus averting bloodshed—he upheld the moral legitimacy of the democratic and anti-imperialist principles and aspirations which he represented and which his opponents had tirelessly sought to discredit.

The domestic opponents of Mosaddeq, encompassing a wide range of variously motivated forces, were powerful, but they would not have achieved their aims without the concerted support of Britain and later the United States. Nor could the Anglo-American operations have succeeded without significant domestic collaboration. The operations to unseat Mosaddeq constituted a sordid tale of Anglo-American readiness to protect their own interests by manipulating, degrading, and sacrificing others. The Anglo-American operations in Iran aimed at nothing short of restoring Western hegemony and subverting the guiding principles and foundations of the Iranian struggles to achieve what the British and the Americans duplicitously claimed to value—representative, accountable, and decent governance.

In addition to domestic and foreign hostility, Mosaddeq's government suffered from weaknesses inherent in the very structure of prevailing constitutional arrangements. His premiership demonstrated that in the specific circumstances of Iran, liberal democratic constitutionalism was more congruent with political opposition than with governance. It was far easier to oppose violations of the Constitution and denounce election rigging than to govern constitutionally or conduct free elections. Veteran opposition figures such as Mosaddeq and his senior National Front colleagues had not seriously entertained the possibility of ever assuming power and were unprepared for doing so. This situation partially explains some of the problems that Mosaddeq encountered as prime minister. It also accounts, at least to some extent, for the eventual disintegration of the National Front, which, being intrinsically imbued with an oppositional spirit, could not function as an effective instrument of governance.

More significantly, political and civic institutions that could have facilitated and structurally strengthened the democratic tenor of Mosaddeq's rule were underdeveloped. An adequate and reliable bureaucratic, judicial, security, and intelligence infrastructure sustaining the state independently of the court was virtually nonexistent. Although the civic-nationalists did not lack support among the military and security forces, the ethos of the military and security establishment was unmistakably royalist. Therefore, the government could not feel reassured that these forces would not act against it. Maintaining order, enforcing the law, and detecting and countering subversive moves remained major challenges. Popular support partially compensated for this situation, but undermining such support was one of the key aims of opponents, whose efforts received a major boost from the activities of disgruntled former supporters such as Kashani.

The momentum of the civic-nationalist movement had been maintained by combating imperialism and autocratic monarchism simultaneously, but the structural means of sustaining achievements in these areas remained absent. With eroding national solidarity, and a parliament and a press susceptible to foreign financial inducements and manipulation, the combined efforts of Mosaddeq's foreign and domestic opponents could be countered only by drastic action, which might include abandoning or suspending key ethicolegal civic-nationalist principles. The Mosaddeqists were, however, neither willing nor readily able to adopt such a course of action. The domestic and foreign hostility that the civic-nationalists faced had helped sustain their sense of purpose and relative cohesion, but the scale and configuration of such opposition was inimical to their continued hold on power. And these problems were compounded by the Shah's residual power to thwart them.[40]

No prime minister had been as successful as Mosaddeq in marginalizing the court and curbing the activities of the royal family and the Shah. But the Shah was always potentially in a position to act against him. Mosaddeq's British-backed opponents failed, during his first year of office, to unseat him partly because of their inability to enlist the active support of the Shah, who felt unable to oppose a man popularly regarded as the anti-imperialist champion of Iranian nationalist aspirations. Mosaddeq's frustrations were a result not only of his deadlocked oil policy but also of active or passive royal enmity. Even a personally timorous monarch could play a crucial role as the incumbent of an institutionally powerful office. Perhaps more than any other statesman, Mosaddeq had realized that such extensive power institutionally vested in the monarchy was integrally linked to, and indeed accounted for, the chronic weakness of parliamentary government and was incompatible with such a form of government. It is in this context that Mosaddeq's simple *idée fixe*—that the Shah must *reign*, not *rule*—more than any other dictum captured the spirit of the Constitution. Reigning, in Mosaddeq's view, did not imply a merely idle and redundant role, as royalists assumed. A reigning monarch, Mosaddeq believed, acted as a detached umpire, a symbol of national unity, a bearer of moral authority dedicated to facilitating the success of the government. The Shah had, however, long demonstrated that he was ill suited for this task; nor was the institutional weight of the monarchy conducive to such a function.

In March 1953 an eight-man parliamentary committee confirmed the constitutionality of Mosaddeq's insistence on the fundamental disjuncture between reigning and ruling, and on the essentially ceremonial nature of royal authority, a reading of the Constitution in which other prominent statesmen such as Qavam and Taqizadeh concurred.[41] Mosaddeq's royalist opponents, however, bolstered by the desertion of several of his key supporters, were able to prevent parliamentary approval of the committee's report. In October 1952 Mosaddeq's supporters in the parliament had been able to push through a bill that dissolved the increasingly antigovernment senate by reducing its term from four years to two. This move constituted a major blow to Mosaddeq's royalist and other opponents, who now concentrated their efforts on the lower house, turning it into a potent instrument for frustrating Mosaddeq's efforts to govern effectively.

In addition to manipulating parliamentary procedures, the British, later joined by the Americans, had sedulously sought to enlist the Shah's active support for anti-Mosaddeq measures. The Shah was, however, deeply hesitant to collaborate, as CIA documents were later to confirm.[42] He feared that doing so would, in case of failure, disgrace the monarchy and terminate his reign and even the dynasty; even a successful outcome would, upon disclosure, mar his credibility and legitimacy. Anglo-American efforts to enlist the Shah's collaboration proved to require enormous pressure and barely disguised threats. Throughout virtually the entire span of the oil crisis and Mosaddeq's premiership the Shah had felt obliged and had found it expedient to maintain a low political profile and to act only indirectly and discreetly against the premier. And yet he had never abandoned his desire to play the key role in Iranian politics. He gave the impression of being prepared to abandon the throne rather than accept the role of a figurehead. In late May 1952 the Shah had made the following statement to the U.S. ambassador, Loy Henderson:

> The British had thrown out the Qajar Dynasty, had brought in his father and had thrown his father out. Now they could keep him in power or remove him as they saw fit. If they desired that he should stay and that the Crown should retain the powers given to it by the Constitution he should be informed. If on the other hand they wished him to go he should be told immediately so that he could leave quietly.[43]

If reported accurately, this intriguing statement is revealing in several respects. First, it sheds light on the precarious mental state of the Shah—who had long maintained that the Constitution granted him extensive prerogatives—at a political juncture when Mosaddeq had radically marginalized him. Second, the Shah was, among other things, sending a message to the British that he regarded them as culpable for much of what had gone wrong in recent Iranian history, implying that they should make amends through expiatory measures. Finally, and most significantly, he was indicating to the British and the Americans that he was not prepared to remain a titular figure, that his continued role as Shah or any cooperation they expected from him was conditional upon retaining the powers that he believed the Constitution had granted him.

The constitutional issue had clearly remained the central problem in Mosaddeq's relations with the Shah. Mosaddeq had continued to regard his commitment to ending British hegemony in Iran as integrally linked to the creation of a democratic polity, a task that in his view required disentangling the constitutionally empowered and accountable government from the unaccountable and essentially ceremonial monarchy. For the Shah and the royalists, in the absence of active royal involvement in the process of governance, the parliamentary arrangements could only generate stalemate. Mosaddeq, on the other hand, blamed governmental stalemate largely on unwarranted interventions by the Shah, which hampered the steady evolution and institutionalization of the parliamentary order. A monarch who enjoyed no inordinate influence upon the process of governance could not be used by foreign powers or domestic clusters of vested interests to further their aims. Forcing the Shah to submit to constitutional restraints was, in Mosaddeq's judgment, a vital step in establishing the authority and credibility of the government and in fulfilling the cardinal objective of the Constitutional Revolution. Ironically, it was Mosaddeq, the main protagonist of this seminal but ultimately doomed enterprise, who was later tried, along with a number of his supporters, and convicted on charges of having violated the Constitution.[44]

Mosaddeq's premiership was a crucial episode in the history of Iran's experiment with democratic governance. It revealed the vexed ambiguities, antinomies, and inadequacies of the Constitution if literally interpreted. It underlined the virtual impossibility of transcending the intrinsic constraints of the existing mode of constitutional monarchy, which was structurally disposed to generate weak governments directly or indirectly controlled by the Shah. It highlighted how a democratic interpretation of the Constitution, favoring a strong executive branch independent of the court, could be construed and opposed as a violation of the Constitution. Maintaining that the "spirit" and purpose of the Constitution were unmistakably democratic, Mosaddeq refused to condone its prevailing, ultimately royalist, interpretation.[45]

Mosaddeq and his supporters lacked the opportunity to devise and implement a viable alternative to the existing arrangements. But their insistence that legitimate and credible constitutional governance must be both independent of the court and demonstrably dedicated to upholding such independence continued to inspire the opponents of royal autocracy. Only a democratic reading of the Constitution, Mosaddeq maintained, could promote the national and the public interest. As a desirable form of government and sociopolitical organization, democracy, he contended, could be achieved and sustained only through patient and persevering practice.[46] Democracy needed not only laws and institutions but also dedicated democrats endowed with vision and conviction, personal integrity, and a spirit of public commitment. In Mosaddeq's political cosmology, no socioeconomic objectives, however important, could justify or mitigate the dangers of disregarding or suppressing democratic aspirations.

Mosaddeq's term of office revealed that a democratically minded, popularly backed government could not but be responsive to public opinion and to freely expressed, rather than paternalistically surmised, public needs and expectations. In its attitude to the public, Mosaddeq's government practiced a politics of recognition at odds with the ruling class's habitual contempt for the people. Viewing urban or literate citizens as having a greater opportunity to engage in informed participation in political life, when referring to the people Mosaddeq primarily meant the inhabitants of the cities, particularly the middle classes. But this understanding did not imply a belittling or ignoring of the poor, whether urban or rural. Despite the numerous odds and challenges, particularly financial constraints, that he encountered while prime minister, Mosaddeq did not neglect the welfare of needy citizens. In addition to a law regarding national insurance, measures for building cheap housing and regulating rents were adopted to combat rural poverty and to assist the urban poor. Undeterred by the variety of ways in which existing freedoms were exploited to destabilize the government, it remained committed to respecting and promoting various liberties, particularly freedom of expression and association; it also enacted bills to promote grassroots democracy and deliberative councils. It took steps to reform the judiciary and to ensure the independence of the Lawyers' Association, and introduced a host of other measures aimed at building the infrastructure essential to a civil society.

The civic-nationalist movement had been animated by the interrelated struggles against imperialism and autocracy. It had endeavored to mobilize public support through a nationalist agenda and relied on such support in order to strengthen the democratic cause and impede the expansion of royal powers. It was dedicated to promoting meaningful national as well as popular sovereignty, and enlisted public trust through adherence to integrity and principle in political conduct, transparent policies, and respectful treatment of citizens. Committed to a collective endeavor to end informal British imperial domination over Iran, and in the face of a British oil embargo, it introduced measures to counter the country's dependence on oil revenues by stimulating other exports. It sought to foster national and civic self-confidence and, despite enormous opposition, promoted a real sense of national solidarity and civic pride essential for bridging the gap that traditionally separated the rulers from the ruled.

Mosaddeq was a pioneer in promoting the rights of Third World peoples in terms of the universalist premises of international law. He led one of the most significant postwar anti-imperialist movements, which served as an inspiration to other leaders in the Middle East and beyond. His term as prime minister constituted a crucial moment in the Iranian people's struggle for a decent government, and a momentous stage in their continuing constitutional revolution. The defeat of the movement was a watershed that marked renewed antagonism between the rulers and the ruled, as well as intensified abhorrence of Western imperialism. An increasing number of Iranians came to believe that Mosaddeq could not have been toppled without concerted Anglo-American action designed to restore Western hegemony, that the aim of the United States and Britain was not simply to defeat a recalcitrant leader and his government but to discredit the very ideals and aspirations associated with the civic-nationalist movement, and that the West enabled the Shah to become what he had always aspired to be—the unchallenged ruler of the country. By embracing that role, the Shah was defying the aspirations of his compatriots while remaining beholden to and compliant with his Anglo-American supporters. This widespread perception would signal the beginning of the irreversible erosion of the Shah's, and eventually the monarchy's, legitimacy and standing with the public.

# Part II

# Authoritarian Supremacy: Consolidation and Collapse

(1953–1979)

"If God gives someone an office, he also gives him the necessary brains" is an old joke that no one would take very seriously these days.

—G. W. F. Hegel, *Philosophy of Right*

Tyranny is overthrown by the peoples because it is abhorrent, degrading, etc. The real cause of this is that it has become superfluous.

Hegel, *Realphilosophie II,* quoted in Shlomo Avineri,
*Hegel's Theory of the Modern State*

# 4

# The Trajectories of Monarchism

## Reign and Rule

A few days after the ousting of Mosaddeq, the Shah, having left the country, returned in triumph to become the coup's chief domestic beneficiary. A crucial turning point in the history of modern Iran, the coup had a stifling impact on Iranian civic-nationalist and democratic aspirations and derailed the constitutional evolution of the country. The stratagems that contributed to the coup's success left an indelible mark on Iranian perceptions of the United States and Britain and their supporters in the country. By restoring foreign domination over Iran and its oil resources, the coup also dealt a blow to Iranian national sovereignty. It adversely affected the Iranian political culture, lending greater plausibility to prevailing assumptions regarding an insidious British and now American influence. The coup would be ingrained in the collective memory of most politically discerning Iranians as an imperialistically induced defeat, a humiliating violation, and a stark reminder that Iranians were not in control of their own fortunes.

The coup irrevocably altered the character of the Pahlavi monarchy, casting a shadow over its legitimacy. It had a transforming impact on the Shah, driving him in an increasingly autocratic direction and toward greater dependence on foreign support. The painful awareness that his return to power was the consequence primarily of foreign operations was detrimental to his self-image. On the other hand, he felt reassured that the British and the Americans unequivocally wanted him on the throne and saw him as indispensable to a pro-Western, stable, and orderly Iran. He perceived his restoration as a clear vindication of his long-held belief that without him firmly at the helm, constitutional arrangements in Iran were conducive only to stalemate and chaos, which benefited communism.

Certain that his political preeminence had been endorsed by the Western powers, the Shah increasingly sought to embrace the role of the country's chief decisionmaker and agenda-setter. Sustaining such a role required subverting constitutionalism and averting the revival of civic-nationalist and leftist ideals. It entailed pursuing a repressive or exclusionist policy against any contender, group, or ideology questioning the rule of the Shah or the desirability of a wholeheartedly pro-Western regime. The interconnectedness of royal objectives meant that Western support for any one of them would in effect be support for all.

The coup and the premiership of General Fazlollah Zahedi, the only viable contender that the British and American secret services had been able to muster to succeed Mosaddeq, resulted in an extensive crackdown on the opposition. Military governors firmly controlled the cities and suppressed any form of resistance. Less than two months after the coup there were, according to some estimates, 13,000 political prisoners in Iran, consisting of supporters of Mosaddeq and of the Tudeh Party. Many military personnel affiliated with the Tudeh Party were put on trial; some were executed and others sentenced to various terms of imprisonment. Zahedi crushed pro-Mosaddeq unrest in the bazaar of Tehran, the capital's economic and political nerve center. Prominent civic-nationalist civilian and military personnel were purged and key Qashqa'i tribal chieftains loyal to Mosaddeq sent into exile.

Against the counsel of some of his foreign and domestic advisers, who were concerned about the resultant adverse publicity, the Shah decided to have Mosaddeq tried for treason. Mosaddeq and later several of his colleagues were brought before a military tribunal; the prosecutor sought in vain to discredit them by invoking a host of spurious charges. Mosaddeq's success in outmaneuvering and discomfiting the prosecutor with witty and candid rebuttals turned the trial into an event of immense public interest. Mosaddeq used the tribunal as an effective platform not only for a robust defense of his political objectives and record as prime minister, but also for a powerful indictment of the legitimacy of the coup and of the regime that followed it. Some of his colleagues received various terms of imprisonment; Foreign Minister Fatemi (incapacitated as a result of an earlier Fada'iyan attempt on his life and a severe beating by police-sponsored thugs) was executed. Mosaddeq himself was condemned to three years in prison and subsequent house arrest outside Tehran for the rest of his life. This treatment not only failed to obliterate him from the collective memory; it enhanced the significance of the Mosaddeq factor in Iranian politics.

Once the domestic situation had been stabilized, one of the Shah's first objectives was to discard Zahedi as prime minister. Zahedi's role in saving the throne had been considerable; by rooting out supporters of Mosaddeq and the left, he had helped to secure and consolidate the monarchy. This record would not, however, endear him to the Shah, who disliked the image of Zahedi as savior of the throne. More significantly, the Shah was eager to dismiss him because he had not personally chosen him and because Zahedi was not totally dependent on the court, as he enjoyed foreign as well as parliamentary support. The elections for the eighteenth parliament (1954–1956), controlled by Zahedi as well as the court, had provided the prime minister with a considerable number of supporters. Zahedi's parliamentary supporters knew that, unable to rely on royal backing, he needed them and could not disregard them. However, in the face of royal determination to oust him by, among other things, emphasizing the scale of his personal corruption, they failed to save him.

With the parliamentary ratification in October 1954 of the Consortium Agreement, the vexed oil issue was settled to the clear disadvantage of Iran and by the reversal in all but name of the Nationalization Act of March 1951. This, together with the coup that had made it possible, enabled the United States to supersede Britain as the predominant power in Iran. Mosaddeq had dealt a major blow to the British imperial aura, but British influence, though diminished, persisted: Britain received 40 percent of the shares in the consortium, 40 percent went to American oil companies, 14 percent to Shell, and 6 percent to the Compagnie Française des Pétroles. Although it lost full control over Iranian oil, Britain received the exorbitant compensation of nearly $1.5 billion.[1] Once the Consortium Agreement had been ratified, Zahedi's British and American supporters considered that he had accomplished the tasks expected of him. They no longer insisted on his retention, and in the face of mounting royal pressure he felt obliged to resign and leave the country as a virtual exile.

Zahedi was succeeded in early April 1955 by the elderly Hosein Ala, who had long served the Shah as court minister and who was better known as a loyal and well-meaning royalist rather than as a man of guile or cunning or a skillful administrator and effective head of government. Nevertheless, viewing Ala as a key figure in the regime, in mid-November 1955 the Fada'iyan made an abortive attempt on his life, which resulted in the execution of Navvab-e Safavi, the group's leader, and three of his colleagues two months later. As prime minister, Ala would be no more than a figurehead, while the Shah exerted extensive control over the entire process of governance, acting through court protégés such as Asadollah Alam, the upstart and scheming minister of the interior. Claiming to espouse reformist ideas, Alam had for some time gathered around himself a group of men, including a number of parliamentarians; often sardonically referred to as "the royal socialists," they antagonized established and conservative deputies.

As a result of residual support for Zahedi or an aversion to the Shah's flagrant efforts to overshadow the government and tamper with the parliamentary process, many parliamentarians were not as readily cooperative as the Shah expected. At the same time, the majority of deputies and senators did not wish to antagonize the court and thus jeopardize their chances of reelection. "The parliament," confided the Shah to the British ambassador, was a "relatively insignificant body . . . he could deal with them."[2] Yet the Shah experienced considerable difficulty in controlling the houses of parliament. Even the senate was not a tame body; its president, Taqizadeh, and a handful of senators close to him exerted considerable opposition to the Shah's cavalier autocratic drive.

The scandalously stage-managed elections for the nineteenth parliament (1956–1960) enabled the Shah to exclude troublesome political figures and further undermine the residual credibility of the parliament. Those who were to be "elected" had been picked by the Shah; the public responded with a virtual boycott; the U.S. embassy estimated that in Tehran only 10,000 to 15,000 people voted, but "organized multiple voting by government employees and simple ballot box stuffing raised the total ballots cast to 87,324. The same pattern was followed in the provinces."[3] The "elections," the extent and manner of royal control over the government of Ala, and the overall conduct of the Shah and his protégés demonstrated that constitutionalism had been unceremoniously reduced to a mere façade. Embittered and frustrated, some Iranian politicians vented their feelings to American and British diplomats. Abolhasan Ha'erizadeh—a former deputy who had deserted the Mosaddeqist camp, done much to contribute to the coup of August 1953, and was subsequently rewarded with a seat in the nineteenth parliament—confided to one American diplomat:

> The main fact of this government is that the Shah is ruling through men who are no better than his personal servants. Of course his servants combine among themselves . . . and stab one another in the back and lie about one another. This sort of thing is of no importance. No matter which one of these people gets the Shah's favor temporarily, the Shah will make sure that he has a rival working against him, a political counterweight. No matter who the Prime Minister is, the faults and virtues of this Government will remain the faults and virtues of the Shah. If any of these men cease to be loyal servants and bootlickers, they will leave the Government. Were the Shah to retire from active politics, none of them, with the possible exception of Taqizadeh, would have even third-class political status.[4]

In early April 1957 Ala resigned and resumed his position as court minister, which had been occupied by Manuchehr Eqbal. A French-educated physician and high-ranking politician, Eqbal was appointed prime minister. Though a royalist who had long been grooming himself for the premiership, Eqbal was privately critical of the Shah's dominant political role and advocated strong government headed by the prime minister. He initially gave the impression of intending to revive the authority of the government and announced some measure of press and associational freedom. Yet in his desire to act as a credible prime minister he encountered the same problems faced by all his predecessors. He soon discovered, as he confided to the U.S. embassy, that his "biggest problem" was "maintaining the confidence of the Shah"; the embassy officials doubted that the Shah would ever give Eqbal "a real opportunity to govern."[5] Persistent in his efforts to win the trust of the Shah or at least not to provoke him, Eqbal gradually succumbed to cynical resignation and public displays of abject servility toward the Shah. He set a new record in the display of obsequiousness, frequently referring to himself as the Shah's slave-servant *(gholam)*. At the same time his attitude to the parliament was characterized by gratuitous arrogance and contempt; he openly pronounced parliamentary procedures to be irrelevant.[6] As one British diplomat noted, Eqbal exposed, with "quite unnecessary blatancy, the fact of the direct imperial autocracy."[7] The U.S. embassy concurred: "Eqbal is an extremely vain man who is apparently more interested in being Prime Minister than [in] struggling with conscience."[8] Both in his servility to the Shah and in his contempt for the constitutional processes, Eqbal would have many successors.

Packed with mostly pliant deputies, the parliament was no longer able to influence the processes of governance significantly or to initiate and control legislation; despite occasional displays of vigor, its normal practice was to acquiesce in endorsing government bills after perfunctory debates. In the words of a British ambassador not known for sympathy with constitutionalism in Iran, the Shah, aided by Eqbal, had "gratuitously degraded and discredited" the parliament.[9] Despite the undeniable erosion of constitutionalism, the Shah was adamant in maintaining a constitutional façade. Having in effect eradicated all independent political entities, he now abandoned his aversion to party politics and endorsed the establishment of official political parties. In April 1957 he told senators that now that "traitors and foreign stooges had been eliminated," the Iranian people could enjoy the "blessings of democracy," attainable through a two-party system.[10] Less than a month later Alam formed the People's (Mardom) Party, which claimed to espouse progressive policies. In February 1958 Alam's staunch rival and opponent Eqbal, having overcome his barely disguised earlier reluctance, formed the more conservative Nationalists' (Melliyun) Party. The Shah intended Mardom and Melliyun to be parties of opposition and government respectively; they were of course barred from broaching foreign-policy, oil, internal-security, and other significant issues pertaining to the Shah's autocratic rule.

It soon became obvious that the Shah had no intention of allowing even the tame official parties, headed by two of his most loyal henchmen and consisting of tested loyalists, to acquire any semblance of credibility. After an audience in August 1958 the British ambassador reported that the Shah had made it "quite clear" that the official party arrangement was "a mockery" and that he had no intention of allowing the two parties to engage in anything other than "a shadow battle" or to represent "any real principle or policy."[11] Similarly, the U.S. embassy observed: "almost everyone will admit that the two parties are phonies and rather than aiding the regime by serving as first steps in developing a democratic government, their very transparency as window-dressing serves to feed the dissatisfaction of many politically sophisticated Iranians."[12]

Publicly the Shah continued to profess his commitment to democracy, party politics, free elections, and the campaign against corruption.[13] Yet the Shah's rhetoric, when contrasted with his political behavior, proved counterproductive. The conduct of the Shah and his close subordinates alarmed many of his domestic and foreign critics as well as his supporters. The parliamentarian Dr. Hosein Pirnia echoed widely shared sentiments when he told the British ambassador:

> Even a genuine dictatorship . . . was better than a fraudulent democracy. The present system, by which elections were cooked and politicians were forcibly enrolled into fake parties, was worse than a sham; it was corrupting and degrading the whole standard of public life and filling every Iranian who had any concern for the healthy evolution of his country with black despair . . . the basic complaint of every Iranian against the present Government was that they were powerless to influence its policy or actions in any way. They had no part or share in it.[14]

There was a growing sense of apprehension in Iranian political circles about the consequences of the Shah's unchecked power. Venting their fears and frustrations to the staffs of the American and British embassies, many Iranian politicians attempted to alert them to the dangers of autocracy and encourage them to restrain the Shah. The British and the Americans occasionally lamented his style of rule, but they rarely questioned the necessity or inevitability of the Shah's central role in the political process. In essence they saw no viable alternative to the existing regime. By joining the anti-Soviet Baghdad Pact (October 1955) alongside Iraq, Pakistan, Turkey, and Britain, Iran had formally committed itself to the West. Uncertainty and apprehension in the region, provoked by the Iraqi revolution of 1958 and the growing influence of Nasserism, enhanced the significance of Iran as a strategic ally of the West, lending substance to the Shah's claim to be a key contributor to regional stability. This situation further entrenched the Shah in his autocratic hold over Iranian politics. The underlying premise of the coup of August 1953 had been that stability under a pro-Western and anticommunist regime in Iran superseded what a British diplomat in Tehran described as "the luxuries of democracy."[15]

The creation in 1957 of SAVAK (the Persian acronym for the State Security and Intelligence Organization), established with American, British, and Israeli assistance, resulted in more-effective monitoring and control as well as suppression of opposition. Throughout this period the Tudeh Party and the National Resistance Movement—formed soon after the coup of 1953 and consisting of Mosaddeqists—had been incessantly targeted with the aim of organizationally crippling them. The National Resistance Movement had reached the peak of its strength in 1956 and 1957, but SAVAK repression and internal dissension gradually weakened it. Confident that the opposition had been effectively contained and would continue to be undermined by SAVAK, the regime ended martial law in Tehran in March 1957. Resistance to the oppressive and corrupt autocracy continued, however, and expressed itself in a variety of ways. Despite the official hold on the media and ceaseless efforts to persuade the public that the Shah and his protégés were running the country in a competent and nationally beneficial manner, public opinion, particularly in the capital, remained unfavorable to the regime. The Pahlavi clan was viewed as strategically placed and enabled to enjoy the greatest benefits resulting from the Shah's personal rule. Deputy Fathollah Forud told a U.S. embassy counselor:

> Nobody is going to tell the Shah what his greatest weakness is with regard to public opinion. It is the rapidly spreading conviction that he and his family are crooked, and are milking the country for money to be placed in foreign banks. This happens to be untrue or exaggerated, but the fact that the people feel this way is still very dangerous. It nullifies almost anything good and useful that the Shah does.[16]

Throughout his rule, the Shah failed to address or successfully counter this highly damaging public perception.

The regime was equally unsuccessful in countering public disapproval of its overall manner of governance. This disapproval was reflected in support for oppositional causes and in the invariably strong public aversion to official candidates during elections. Despite the extensive restrictions to which they were subject, civic-nationalists remained able to muster considerable support among the urban population. The regime was unable to convince the public that the Shah and his protégés were politically competent and well intentioned and that their rule was conducive to the common good. Foreign observers occasionally took note of Iranians' perceptions of the regime and attempted to analyze them. According to Victor Wolf, a member of the U.S. embassy staff writing in July 1957:

> Iranians do not recognize many developments today which they would call successful. Iranians do not have an increased feeling of justice and security since the Shah started to rule personally. Iranians do not feel that the economic development program is more successful since the Shah took the reins of power. The Shah's lack of success probably stems from two causes: (1) The Shah is indecisive to an alarming degree. He does have the power, for now, to direct the course of Iranian events; he does not seem to have the ability to make up his own mind. The formidable image of Reza Shah dominates him and he seeks to imitate it; yet his personal characteristics inhibit. (2) The Shah is probably the most isolated man in this country. He has no personal staff he feels he can trust and his most frequent contacts are with a corrupt Court group which seeks to influence him in its own personal behalf. The wide variety of opinions, rumors, and suggestions which pour in on him in this isolation combined with an innate tendency to intrigue continually probably leave him hopelessly confused and unsure of whom to trust.[17]

Perhaps because of the prevailing public disapproval of its conduct, the regime increasingly assumed the character of a police state in which coercively enforced political conformism or silent disengagement was viewed as consent, and stagnation mistaken for stability. The flagrantly arbitrary apparatus of coercion and its growing identification with the Shah were clearly at odds with real and enduring political and economic stability. Yet in the eyes of the Shah's Anglo-American supporters, the advantages of a pro-

Western Iran ruled by a cooperative autocrat outweighed the advantages of any alternative arrangement. It was far easier to work with an amenable autocratic regime than one complicated by effective constitutional and legislative processes. Any form of credible representative government in which elected officials were responsive to their constituents was bound to resist Anglo-American demands, interests, and influence. In this sense and as far as the West was concerned, there was, indeed, as one British ambassador concluded, no viable alternative to the Shah's pro-Western and stable, but otherwise less than desirable rule.[18] Thus Cold War assumptions and the imperative of perpetuating Western hegemony in Iran helped sustain autocratic monarchism to the detriment of democratic institutions and aspirations.

## Tactical Retreat

In 1960, in response to cumulative public pressure and restlessness, the regime announced that the elections for the twentieth parliament would be "free." This promise, together with the relaxation of press censorship, galvanized the public. At the same time the Shah told the American ambassador that it was "premature to think in terms of free elections . . . in Iran."[19] In fact the regime had no intention of holding free elections; it could not afford to do so. Exposed daily by the unmuzzled press, clumsy rigging during the August elections provoked public agitation, which alarmed the Shah. The increasingly unpopular government of Eqbal resigned in late August after three years and four months in office; Ja'far Sharif-Emami, a mild-mannered royalist, was appointed prime minister. The Shah then secured the mass resignation of the elected deputies, who had failed either to win over the public or to gain the endorsement of the Shah; whereas the electorate rejected the elections as insufficiently free, the Shah rejected them as insufficiently controlled. New elections in early 1961 were more discreetly rigged by SAVAK. Yet the newly constituted parliament again failed to reassure the Shah of its compliance or to satisfy the public, who had grown more confident that the regime could be forced to make greater political concessions. By promising free elections and relaxing press censorship, the regime had raised expectations and stimulated demands that it could neither meet nor easily control. On May 6, 1961, in an effort to contain the crisis, the Shah invited Ali Amini, a French-educated scion of the Qajars, former minister, ambassador to the United States until March 1958, and a high-profile and dynamic advocate of free elections, to assume the premiership. This move was followed three days later by the Shah's dissolution of the new parliament, which had lasted less than three months.

Amini assumed the premiership against a background of public restlessness and sociopolitical crisis, including a teachers' strike, which he ended by accepting the strikers' demands. His appointment indicated that the Shah had felt obliged to abandon his preference for submissive prime ministers and resort to a tactical retreat. American pressure for change had also become difficult to resist or deflect. The Shah and royalists such as Alam considered Amini as having been virtually "imposed" by President John F. Kennedy.[20] The Americans did indeed regard Amini as "one of the three or four really able men in Iran."[21] The circumstances that led to his appointment as prime minister were, however, more complex. Amini himself had played an important role in precipitating the crisis leading to his premiership by actively campaigning to expose the regime's deviation from constitutionalism and, more specifically, its rigging of elections. The Shah, though never genuinely trusting Amini, had agreed to his premiership in the expectation that this move would neutralize him as an opponent and might help restore government credibility, defuse the prevailing tensions, and initiate reforms that would be credited to the Shah.

As premier, Amini inherited the legacy of several years of maladministration. Despite his sometimes radical rhetoric, he was a flexible pragmatist; yet his policies threatened too many vested interests. His determined efforts to assert the authority of the cabinet and the prime minister, and his insistence that ministers report to him rather than to the Shah, dismayed the monarch. His efforts to implement socioeconomic reform, establish honest government, and confront and contain corruption antagonized both the privileged classes and the military. Chief among his policies was land reform, proclaimed in January 1962 and championed by the dynamic and dedicated agriculture minister, Hasan Arsanjani, who had long advocated a radical land distribution program. Favoring land reform, the Shah described it as one of the most revolutionary measures in the 3,000 years of recorded Iranian history. Like Egypt soon after 1952, and Syria and Iraq in 1958, the Iranian state launched a program of land reform intended to demonstrate the regime's reformist, justice-oriented objectives and concern for the least privileged. The program was to be accomplished in stages;

it would break up the power base of the landowners, a traditionally influential class not keen on royal autocracy, and would create a landholding peasantry beholden to the regime. It was also a means of integrating the peasants into the state-sponsored national culture.

Amini also alienated the Mosaddeqists, who in July 1960 had formed a new National Front, which in May 1961 proved itself capable of mobilizing considerable public support, particularly in the capital. The Front insisted on the indispensability of the rights and liberties guaranteed by the Constitution and the Universal Declaration of Human Rights. It advocated democratic constitutionalism and insisted on free elections, which Amini had indefinitely postponed in defiance of the Constitution as well as his own earlier vocal proconstitutionalist stand. Tactical cooperation between the Mosaddeqists and Amini, even if feasible, was likely to provoke the Shah, who would not tolerate it and was able to thwart it. Amini had little choice but to attempt to neutralize the Mosaddeqists and avoid antagonizing the Shah, who retained control over the military and security forces. Becoming "embroiled in an open quarrel with the Shah," the U.S. embassy noted, would render Amini "totally ineffective as Prime Minister and very likely would soon make him jobless."[22] To the delight of the royalists, Amini and the National Front turned against each other despite their common views regarding royal autocracy. The outbreak of serious disorder at Tehran University in January 1962, for which a host of opponents, particularly leading Mosaddeqists, were blamed and arrested, further worsened relations between civic-nationalists and Amini. The unprecedented brutality of the police and soldiers in suppressing the students damaged Amini's image, but the episode enabled him to justify a firmer stand against his opponents and for some time carry the Shah with him. Persuading the Shah that the aim of the opponents had been to launch a coup, Amini muzzled the press and secured the exile of General Teymur Bakhtiar. Formerly the feared military governor of Tehran, and then chief of SAVAK, Bakhtiar—a cousin of the Shah's second wife, Sorayya—had over the years amassed enormous wealth and influence. He had been intriguing against Amini, and right-wing activists such as the Rashidian brothers (Asadollah, Seifollah, and Qodratollah)—whose *agents provocateurs* had contributed to the unrest among the students—had sought to bring about the premiership of someone like Bakhtiar.[23]

If pro-Mosaddeq students had aimed to undermine Amini and strengthen the National Front, they achieved the opposite. In any case, the grip of the older generation of Mosaddeqists over the younger, particularly students, was tenuous. Though committed to broad civic-nationalist aims, the Mosaddeqists were not homogeneous: old-fashioned constitutionalists and moderate Islamists joined cause with social democrats and socialists, who advocated appropriating the land reform initiative as part of their own strategic agenda, relegating elections to secondary importance, and refraining from undermining Amini. Many of the younger Mosaddeqists favored widespread change while their older counterparts, including leading figures, avoided radical sociocultural issues and demanded the establishment of what they called "legal government." Faced with intractable royalist hostility, they felt in no position to alienate traditionalist and religious forces while working to secure broad popular support. The Mosaddeqists did not reject socioeconomic reforms as such, but opposed them as a substitute for democratic objectives. Viewing U.S. policies as having a crucial impact on Iranian domestic politics, many of them considered the Kennedy presidency as facilitating the advancement of their reformist agenda. At the same time they were concerned that tolerating Amini indefinitely would adversely affect their public standing, eliminate the political momentum created by the electoral fiascos, and produce no political dividends. Supporting Amini's reformist moves, they feared, would imply condoning the royal agenda of suspending constitutionalism in the name of reform.

Amini was apprehensive that the court and a host of other influential figures whom he had antagonized, such as landowners or high-ranking officers prosecuted for corruption, would ensure that the next parliament would frustrate his reformist and anticorruption measures, thereby forcing him out of office. Conversely, to hold no elections and govern without a parliament was no less problematic. Regardless of the merits of his private reasoning, Amini failed to provide a publicly defensible justification for his failure to live up to his earlier constitutionalist stand.

In his inevitable confrontation with the Shah, Amini had no means of mustering domestic support. His defiance of the constitutional process rendered him vulnerable to the challenge of forces such as the National Front, other constitutionalists, and those who tactically invoked the Constitution. His efforts to appease the clerics and the traditionalists did not pay off. He was under pressure from all sides and provoked student activists as well as right-wing opponents of reform. His government persisted in its anti-corruption drive and measures to reform the administrative machinery. At least two of his colleagues—Arsanjani and the justice minister, Nur al-Din Alamuti—advocated far-reaching policies. In order to justify his radical agenda, his government had to assume a quasi-revolutionary posture; the opposition that this move provoked gave Amini further justification to maintain that the country faced a state of emergency that required suspension of normal constitutional procedures. Amini had advocated restoring governmental credibility, which implied restraining the Shah in accordance with the spirit of the Constitution. Yet, paradoxically, by governing without a parliament he had to rely on the Shah and remain at his mercy in order to retain office.

The Shah would tolerate Amini only so long as the latter enjoyed Anglo-American support, which eventually evaporated as a result of relentless royal ploys and pressures. Given Amini's reformist agenda and the continued support he received from the American and British embassies, the Shah could not prematurely turn against him and at the same time claim to share and support his reformist objectives. Amini had not been able to reverse the autocratic trends set in motion by the Shah. The Shah had used him to de-rail the antiautocratic movement, manifested in the popular demand for free elections. His implacable royalist opponents used the breathing space provided by his premiership to regroup and rethink their strategies. By suspending constitutional processes in the name of reform or combating corruption, he inadvertently helped to provide a precedent and justification for the Shah's later reformist but anticonstitutional transgressions. Yet Amini was the last prime minister to govern with a real measure of effective authority independent of the court, to allow a degree of political freedom, and to give the impression that the government genuinely sought to combat corruption and injustice. The Shah would appropriate and continue the reformist agenda of Amini's cabinet, but without the tempering political skill and acumen that Amini had provided.

## On the Offensive

By the summer of 1962 Amini had exhausted his political utility and created numerous enemies; the Shah no longer needed to tolerate him. Disagreement with the Shah over the budget of the military precipitated Amini's resignation on July 17 and his immediate replacement with the Shah's protégé, the staunchly royalist Alam, who was widely regarded as pro-British. Prompted by the Shah and mindful of being viewed as too pro-British by the Americans, Alam concentrated on winning the confidence of the U.S. embassy. Later during his term of office he also worked to improve Iran's relations with the Soviet Union. His premiership signaled an era in which, in his own words, the Shah, with his "unrivaled power," was "the absolute ruler."[24] But while giving the impression of being unfailingly subservient to the Shah, Alam was capable of exerting considerable influence on the ruler's political conduct. The implementation of land reform, which had begun in February 1962, proceeded. Arsanjani was retained as agriculture minister in the new cabinet in order to give credibility to the regime's intentions regarding land reform. The obstinate Arsanjani was of course not the docile minister that the Shah and Alam preferred; he had also grown popular with the peasants, and was therefore removed in March 1963, being dispatched as ambassador to Rome. Ambassadorial appointments had become a form of exile for politically troublesome politicians.

Inevitably, land reform and similar measures, together with the Shah's increasingly authoritarian tendencies, resulted in determined opposition from, among others, a number of leading clerics. Having failed to reverse the modernizing trends set in motion during the Reza Shah era or to hinder the rise of secular, particularly leftist ideologies after his abdication, the activist clerics, relying on their links with the traditional classes, sought to reassert their sociopolitical influence. They sided with the Shah in his conflict with Mosaddeq, fearing the triumph of leftist or republican tendencies and viewing the monarchy as more likely to abide by the tenets of the official religion. They also appear to have believed that the Shah, having benefited from their backing and in need of their continued support, would not readily contravene their influence and interests. An issue that could be exploited to constrain the regime and focus public attention on its level of commitment to safeguarding the official faith was its attitude to the Baha'is.

The Baha'i faith had emerged in the 1860s as an outgrowth of Babism to become an international movement. Its prophet and leader, Mirza Hosein-Ali Nuri (1817–1892), known as Baha'ullah, "Splendor of God," had been a disciple of Bab. Baha'ism emphasized the unity of mankind and opposed prejudice arising from race, creed, nationality, or gender. Considered hereti-

cal by the Shi'ite establishment, adherents of the Baha'i faith in Iran generally led an unobtrusive existence but continued to be viewed as a threat. A
clerically inspired anti-Baha'i campaign in the mid-1950s soured relations between the regime and the politically astute and generally quietist Grand
Ayatollah Hosein Borujerdi, who had headed the clerical establishment
since 1947.[25] Yet the Shah took care not to antagonize him unnecessarily;
in the aftermath of the Iraqi revolution of 1958, the regime wanted to
strengthen its ties with the Shi'ite establishment as a countervailing force to
the revolutionary regime in Iraq.

At the same time the government had continued its intrusion into the
clerics' patrimonial sphere; it had expanded Tehran University's School of
Theology and established classes to train itinerant preachers to be sent to
the rural areas—an activity previously monopolized by seminaries. The regime's purpose, according to Ann Lambton, professor of Persian at London
University and a former press attaché at the British embassy in Tehran who
visited Iran in the summer of 1956, was "to control and use the religious
classes for its own ends, the result of which is likely to strengthen the existing tyranny, and ultimately to weaken the religious institutions."[26] Borujerdi
was alert to the regime's intentions; in February 1960 he raised objections
on Islamic and constitutional grounds to a land reform bill. Though failing
to prevent the bill's adoption by the parliament, he played a major role in
impeding its implementation.[27] He had also opposed any discussion of
equal or improved status for women. With Borujerdi's death in March 1961
the Shah no longer felt constrained to delay the reform program. He
attempted to influence the choice of Borujerdi's successor, preferring the
Iraqi Ayatollah Mohsen Hakim, a divine comparable in standing to
Borujerdi but residing in Najaf. As the U.S. embassy noted, the Shah wished
"to rid himself of the annoyance of an alternative focus of loyalty for the
masses" inside Iran.[28]

The issue of land reform presented the clerics with a dilemma: on the
one hand, they did not wish to be seen as allies of those portrayed by the regime as the privileged and exploiting classes; on the other, they saw the authoritarian tenor of the state as detrimental to their status and influence.
They detested the intrusive attempts of the state to reorganize the traditional order of life and undermine its underpinning moral code. The clerics,
landowners, and other propertied classes feared that the momentum of the

land reform would intensify and property rights would be subverted. Land-owners constituted a significant component of the urban notables who, to-gether with the clerics, had long acted as intermediaries between the state and large segments of the population, and had tried to counter the state's absolutist tendencies. The landowners knew that the expropriation of their lands would result in rapid erosion of their political clout. Fearful of the de-cline of their own influence, the clerics were also concerned about losing control over the revenue-generating piously endowed lands. In the autumn of 1962 the regime announced that the rights of small landowners would not be infringed and income from charitable endowments would be safe-guarded; yet anxiety and opposition continued. With few exceptions the clerics opposed the land reform. They also rejected the enfranchisement of women as threatening female chastity and norms of domesticity, and her-alding further moves toward secularity.

In October 1962 a cabinet decree regarding the election of district and provincial councils provoked considerable clerical protest. The decree had omitted to specify adherence to Islam as a condition for voting and can-didacy; the article pertaining to the oath to be taken by elected candidates had not mentioned the Koran; more significantly, it had implicitly extended the franchise to women. Attempts to enfranchise women, initially at the level of local councils, had started with Mosaddeq in 1952 and was quietly but partially implemented under Amini despite strong clerical opposition. Alam's October 1962 cabinet decree was in substance the same as the one implemented by Amini. The clerics protested the decree, portraying it as a move aimed at undermining Islam. Among other things, they sent Alam and the Shah a barrage of telegrams. The formerly proregime Ayatollah Behbahani warned Alam of "grave consequences"; Ayatollah Ruhollah Khomeini, an emerging opponent of the regime, pronounced the measure contrary to Islam and the Constitution. Mounting clerical objections even-tually resulted in the cabinet's rescinding the decree in late November.

Having mishandled the whole episode, the Shah and the regime suffered a serious loss of face, while the clerics were emboldened. Determined to compensate for this setback, and increasingly adopting a radical posture, the Shah pressed ahead with the broader reform program, irrespective of the misgivings even of Alam. In the words of the British ambassador: "The Prime Minister is, I know, alarmed at the pace at which the Shah is moving and is trying to restrain him. The Shah, on the other hand, is obsessed with the need for haste and, as he told me himself at my last audience, is determined that no one (and he meant Dr. Arsanjani) shall be out ahead of him in courting the newly emancipated peasantry, representing 75% of the population."[29]

"The Shah," reported Julius Holmes, the U.S. ambassador (1961–1965), is "deadly serious about being a revolutionary monarch."[30] In the absence of the parliament the regime was more vulnerable to the charge of having discarded even sham popular representation and of openly disregarding the Constitution, while the Shah needed some kind of legitimacy for his reform program. Inspired by the example of President Charles de Gaulle in France, the Shah contemplated a referendum. He sought the advice of the American and British ambassadors, who had misgivings about a referendum, as did Alam, but decided to proceed with the plan, as he felt he had no other option. On January 9, 1963, in a mass rally organized by Arsanjani, bringing together 3,000 peasants from various parts of the country, the Shah announced that he would resort to a referendum. Some two weeks later the Shah's six-point reform program, known as "The Revolution of the Shah and the People" or "The White Revolution," which included measures such as land reform and the creation of a literacy corps, was put to a referendum. The fact that some ten years earlier the royalists had denounced Mosaddeq's use of such a measure as unconstitutional was conveniently ignored. The Shah had told the British ambassador that there was no constitutional provision for a referendum, and had admitted that "in fact, nearly every recent act of the government had been outside the Constitution."[31]

Less than a month before the referendum, the National Front had held its first congress in Tehran, lasting eight days. General Hasan Pakravan, the chief of SAVAK, had reportedly persuaded the Shah to allow the congress to take place, believing that it would publicly reveal the extent of internal fragmentation in the Front and would thereby benefit the regime.[32] Alam also maintained that the Front was too divided to be a threat to the regime but considered that it might assume a significant role in the future, and thus sought to maintain links with its leaders. The Americans and the British had left no doubt about their position and advocated continued "firmness" vis-à-vis the National Front.[33] Yet, regarding it as politically expedient, Alam personally took the initiative of negotiating with the Front. As Harrison, the

British ambassador, noted, Alam's approach involved "a substantial element of political manoeuvre." The Shah told Harrison on December 5, 1962, that he had no intention of reaching an accommodation with the Mosaddeqists, adding that the only group that "was completely outside the pale, so far as he was concerned, was the National Front."[34]

Not surprisingly, Alam's overtures to the Front did not result in a rapprochement. In the prevailing politically inhospitable milieu, dissension among the Mosaddeqists, actively stimulated by SAVAK, became more evident; the Front failed to create a cohesive structure, but it succeeded in gaining considerable publicity, which it could not otherwise have achieved. It established itself as the only national entity dedicated to promoting democratic objectives and, if allowed, capable of mustering extensive public support. But efforts to build on the publicity thus gained were interrupted by the arrest of many of those who opposed the Shah's referendum, particularly leading Mosaddeqists. The Front remained adamant that its democratic agenda should not be eclipsed or compromised and that reform should not be used as a ploy to justify autocracy.

A month after the January referendum and despite persistent clerical opposition, the franchise was extended to women. For some years groups of women in the large cities had been agitating for equal political status and rights. In January 1959 a question posed in the senate regarding this issue had provoked a strong rebuke from Borujerdi, prompting a visit by Prime Minister Eqbal to reassure him that no step would be taken in such a direction. By February 1963 the political situation had markedly changed. The enfranchisement of women was undoubtedly a crucial and overdue step in countering gender inequality and enabling women to play an important role in public life. But the full significance of this measure was overshadowed by the eroded credibility of the electoral process. Alam pronounced the principles of "The Revolution of the Shah and the People" to be Iran's new constitution, ominously implying that the old Constitution was defunct.[35] Reformist rhetoric acquired a new salience in justifying autocratic rule. The Shah's moves added to the ranks of the enemies of the regime, antagonizing in particular the beneficiaries and custodians of the traditional socioeconomic and moral order. The presumed strength and commitment of the regime's newly won or would-be supporters remained uncertain.

In the spring of 1963, opposition to land reform and the intrusive and heavy-handed actions of the state resulted in serious tribal unrest in the southern province of Fars, especially among the Boir-Ahmadis. The army suppressed the lingering rebellion only after suffering considerable casualties and a number of serious reversals. A more severe test for the regime and the armed forces came in the form of clerically inspired rioting in Tehran and several other large cities in June. Having boycotted the referendum, the clerics continued to oppose the Shah's policies. Aiming to undermine their opposition, the Shah went on the offensive, intensifying a propaganda campaign to vilify his clerical antagonists. This campaign, reaching its peak in his speech of January 24, 1963, in the compound of the shrine at Qom, provoked equally sharp responses from the clerics, indicating that the rift between the regime and at least one crucial segment of the traditionalist forces had grown dangerously wide.

Measures to silence the vocal clerics included a March 1963 assault by security forces, disguised as peasants and workers, on the Qom seminary, which was becoming a hotbed of clerical activism. The military draft was also extended to seminary students. These developments intensified clerical resentment and solidarity. The anger provoked in Qom and other cities culminated in an uprising triggered by the arrest of Khomeini on June 5. Two days earlier—on the occasion of Ashura, the day of the most intense fervor in the Shi'ite calendar—he had fiercely denounced the Shah in an exceptionally blunt and fearless speech at the Qom seminary. Seeking to expand the antiregime movement, Khomeini directly or indirectly pressured other leading clerics not to remain inactive. He was also asserting his leadership role and political primacy in the void that had persisted since the death of Borujerdi. Several senior clerics, including those not favorable to Khomeini, denounced his arrest or expressed solidarity with him. Some referred to him as a "source of emulation" for the faithful (marja'-e taqlid), as this elevated status gave him greater immunity from harsh treatment by the regime. Ayatollahs such as Mohammad-Reza Golpayegani and Kazem Shari'atmadari played an important role in securing his eventual release.

The disaffection of leading clerics, signaling and reinforcing the cumulative resentments of the traditional classes, not to mention wider opposition to royal autocracy, had provided grounds for antiregime protests. A major public outburst involving segments of the pious middle classes as well as subaltern and underclass elements, the uprising in Tehran started in and engulfed the traditional heart of the city around the bazaar. There was also rioting in a number of other large cities. SAVAK unpersuasively blamed foreign provocation, particularly from President Jamal Abd al-Nasser of Egypt. The government's determination and willingness to use violence, in contrast to the Shah's initial vacillation, proved crucial in suppressing the uprising and saving the regime. Alam claimed that ninety people had died in the clashes;[36] others have given much higher figures for the deaths in Tehran, Qom, Shiraz, and Mashhad. Large numbers were also arrested, and leading ayatollahs such as Shari'atmadari and Hadi Milani were subjected to restrictions. In the meantime, measures to terminate lingering antiregime activities continued, and the military government imposed on Tehran and Shiraz was not lifted until the autumn. The scale and ferocity of the uprising shook the regime to its foundations, damaging its image of unshakable stability; yet the loyalty of the armed forces and security apparatus was demonstrated in their willingness to confront and defeat the clerically instigated uprising and the pastoral-nomadic rebellion in Fars.

Besides clerics, a number of street leaders formerly close to the regime had turned against it, playing a leading role in the uprising. Yet the state's links with the traditional classes or the public at large had not been wholly eroded. Moreover, while ferocious, the challenge was not sufficiently pervasive, sustained, or coordinated to dislodge the regime. Though startling to the Shah, the episode eventually strengthened his autocratic resolve; however, he learned less from this experience than did Khomeini, who came to understand where the regime's fault lines were and how they could be exploited. Deeply alarmed by what had occurred, a number of respected establishment figures privately expressed concern about the wisdom of the Shah's policies. They included the well-meaning and loyal court minister Ala; Abdollah Entezam, the respected former foreign minister who had headed the National Iranian Oil Company (NIOC) since May 1957; and Mohammad-Ali Varasteh, a reputable former senator. Contemptuously dismissing their views, by October 1963 the Shah sacked Entezam and Ala, who was appointed a senator, while Varasteh became persona non grata.

The concerns of monarchists such as the veteran politician and man of letters Ali Dashti, "an active supporter of the Shah's role in government affairs," also fell on deaf ears.[37] Reacting with bewilderment to the June uprising, Dashti, then Iran's ambassador to Lebanon, wrote to the Shah expressing alarm at the antagonism of the clerics, who, he said, traditionally supported the monarchy. Blaming Eqbal, Alam, and the Shah's entire entourage, Dashti considered it exceedingly dangerous that the Shah should personally have become the target of opposition, openly vilified in the streets. Khomeini, Dashti argued, emerged in the context of concrete public grievances, and his "credibility and prestige rests on his audacious willingness to articulate the people's unexpressed aspirations." Dashti counseled "an accommodationist policy" and reliance on "argument, law, justice, and impartiality" and a measure of "royal forgiveness."[38]

The Shah and his entourage, however, felt that slowing the pace of reform would deprive them of the rationale for suspending constitutional formalities and embolden their opponents. Undifferentiating and dismissive toward them, the regime showed no willingness to address their concerns. The Mosaddeqists had avoided embroilment in the June uprising; nor had they responded positively to the wooing gestures of tribal leaders in the south. It was in this context that in the autumn of 1963, despite having failed to win over the National Front leaders in December of the previous year, Alam again tried to seek an understanding with them. In exchange for endorsing the Shah's political role and program of reform, the Front's leaders, incarcerated from January to early September 1963, were to be allowed to engage in political activity and freely compete to gain a limited number of seats in the parliament. Alam did not have the full support of the Shah in this initiative, nor did the Mosaddeqists prove amenable. The prerequisites of any meaningful cooperation between them and the regime were fundamentally lacking.

Failing to co-opt the Mosaddeqists, the regime came increasingly to see them and all other opponents as enemies. The Shah continued to castigate his clerical opponents as "black reactionaries" who, along with "red reactionaries," namely the left, were opposed to reform. Despite his reckless outbursts, a combination of insecurity and complacency led the Shah to avoid harsh treatment of senior clerics. Their near-deferential detention contrasted starkly with the unceremonious imprisonment of senior Mosaddeqists—who had advocated or endorsed no violence against the regime—and clearly indicated, but also reinforced, the salience of religiosity and the social influence of the clerics. Undeterred by moves to silence him, but sensitive to the charge of being regressive, Khomeini avoided challenging the Shah on avowedly religious grounds and emphasized broader issues. The regime prevented a recurrence of the June 1963 uprising by resorting to punitive and repressive preemptive measures. The Shah and the younger royalists surrounding him seemed increasingly confident that they had once and for all neutralized the clerics. The structural basis of the clerics' social and ideological power or influence was not, however, successfully undermined and was in some respects strengthened. Those grievances that they could exploit not only remained essentially unaddressed but increased.

Having overcome a series of challenges, the regime felt confident and able to resume parliamentary formalities. After nearly two and a half years of government without a parliament, elections were held in September 1963. According to a pattern to be followed in two future elections (1967 and 1971), parliamentarians were "elected" from a carefully vetted list prepared by confidants of the Shah and approved by him. In effect no one unacceptable to the government could be a candidate. The old notables having been discarded, over 80 percent of the elected deputies, including eight women, were serving for the first time. Less than one-fifth of the electorate voted; virtually no member of the lower house was nationally known, and some were barely known in their constituencies. By early October the twenty-first term of the lower house and the fourth term of the senate were convened by the Shah. In the wake of a violent episode that had revealed the frustrations of the disenfranchised, the regime resurrected the façade of constitutionalism but made it increasingly meaningless.

## Impairment of National Sovereignty

Alam was succeeded by Hasan-Ali Mansur in March 1964, when the regime seemed to have regained its composure and restored security. Mansur was to revive the bungled experiment with official party politics and form a party government that could implement reforms more effectively. A minister in Eqbal's cabinet and son of a former prime minister, Mansur and his friend and protégé Amir-Abbas Hoveyda, who was from a humbler social background, were among the key members of an informal study group and political association formed in 1961 with the Shah's blessing. Comprised of some 200 individuals and known as "The Progressive Circle," it became "a vehicle to promote the personal fortunes of Ali Mansur."[39] It constituted the nucleus of the New Iran (Iran-e Novin) Party (NIP). Formed in December 1963 and led by Mansur, the party replaced the defunct Nationalists' (Melliyun) Party. Encouraged by the Shah, it actively groomed itself to become the party of government; it constituted a reservoir from which trusted office seekers acceptable to the Shah could emerge and become a much more powerful instrument of elite control and mobilization than its predecessor.

Mansur had cultivated, and boasted about enjoying, active American support; he was indeed widely regarded as being an American nominee; some saw him as an American stooge.[40] He also remained close to the British embassy. Mansur and his predecessor Alam, noted one British ambassador, were "the last of the old school of Prime Ministers who, from fear of our power and respect for our wisdom and experience, sought our views."[41] Mansur was effectively the last prime minister who thought it imperative to consult and seek the support of foreign ambassadors. Also like many of his predecessors, he constantly feared losing the trust or support of the Shah or provoking the antagonism of more-established rivals. Though committed to the Shah's commanding political role and vision of what was in Iran's national interest, he seemed less than fully confident in his ability to meet the expectations of the Shah. He also felt ill at ease in his position as a faithful servant to a mercurial monarch who wanted to rule, determine policy, and make as many decisions as possible regardless of who held the nominal office of prime minister. Concomitantly, to those who regretted the turn of events in Iranian politics Mansur's very appointment as prime minister indicated that he lacked any compelling qualities of character or leadership.

Mansur and the aspiring "technocrats" whom he represented were bent on collective self-promotion through royal patronage and advocacy of a steady modernizing drive. By seeking to place socioeconomic development more firmly on the agenda of Iranian politics and to expedite its implementation, they hoped to bypass, ideologically disarm, or render irrelevant the civic-nationalist and other opponents of the regime. They also hoped to co-opt as many pliable Mosaddeqists as possible while dismissing more determined opponents as "fifth columnists." Mansur and his acolytes began an overhaul of the civil service; for the first time women were appointed to senior positions. The government of Mansur attempted to foster an air of optimism that at last there were sufficiently capable and organized personnel dedicated to fulfilling the Shah's vision of development. Mansur's own political and administrative skills were, however, markedly unimpressive. "Mansur," the British ambassador commented, "has, like his predecessor, proved to be an obedient servant, but he lacks popular appeal or administrative drive."[42]

Mansur's term of office was punctuated by a development that demonstrated the inherent problems of a merely managerial approach to the complexities of governance, and dealt an enormous blow to the very foundations of the Pahlavi monarchy. In March 1962 the U.S. government had demanded that the Iranian government extend immunity from trial under Iranian law to all American military advisory and technical personnel serving in Iran. American advisers paid by their own government already enjoyed such immunity, but the new demand would have extended immunity to Americans who were technically employed and paid by the Iranian government. It might have been possible to settle the matter quietly between the two governments by extending the provisions of the Vienna Convention on diplomatic relations to all American military personnel in Iran, considering them members of the U.S. embassy staff. In early October 1963, Alam's cabinet had agreed that such an arrangement could be made once the parliament had ratified the Vienna Convention; it had, however, proceeded to refer the matter to the legislature for consideration and approval. Mansur's government also felt that the issue was too significant not to be referred to the parliament, but assumed that it would be easily ratified. On July 25, 1964, a bill regarding the Vienna Convention, with an amendment to extend its provisions to American military personnel employed by the Iranian government, was rushed through the senate, which had prevaricated for over six months. Two and a half months later, on October 13, the bill was submitted to the lower house, with Mansur and his foreign minister assuring the Americans that it would be smoothly ratified.

Accustomed to taking parliamentary cooperation for granted, Mansur's government failed to mount a compelling defense of the bill. Instructed by the Shah, it had taken steps to mobilize members of the governing NIP to ensure the smooth adoption of the bill but "advised the Shah against sending direct instructions to the Parliament."[43] The expected overwhelming support did not materialize, and the bill was strongly attacked, but Mansur insisted on an immediate vote. The bill passed narrowly: some seventy deputies supported it, more than sixty voted against it, and around fifty absented themselves.[44] The assumed cohesion of the governing party had proved illusory, while the public perception of Mansur's dependence on the Americans, which had handicapped him from the outset, was reaffirmed. Both Mansur and the Shah, having complacently expected nothing short of the customary compliance and endorsement of the bill, were taken by surprise. Neither could disclaim responsibility for the disastrously clumsy mishandling of such an explosive issue, which publicly resurrected the ghost of the reviled capitulations.

The privileged status thus formally granted to the Americans was virtually unprecedented. Unlike agreements governing U.S. servicemen elsewhere, the Status of Forces Agreement with Iran gave the United States exclusive and permanent jurisdiction over all U.S. military and civilian employees of the Department of Defense and their dependents stationed in Iran and freed them from Iranian legal control. The U.S. embassy refused to shoulder any responsibility and blamed Mansur and the Shah for having mishandled the situation and having failed to marshal or manipulate public opinion.[45] Yet, as Phillips Talbot, U.S. assistant secretary of state for Near Eastern and South Asian affairs, admitted, this "highly unpopular measure" was "rammed through the Iranian Parliament" by the Shah at "our insistence and with considerable risk to his domestic position."[46] Irrespective of the domestic political risks involved, the Iranian government, having succumbed to steady pressure from the Americans, did its utmost to appease them, particularly as they had proved unwilling to provide Iran with military supplies without full payment. By pushing through the immunities bill the regime revealed the extent of its ignorance of or indifference to public opinion. For a regime that had reduced the constitutional processes to a mere rubber stamp, placing the bill before the tame and routinely pliant parliament had not seemed a major blunder. Yet the matter had been inadvertently transformed into an issue of great public concern.

Refusing to countenance the genuine unpopularity of such a bill, and the existence of boundaries that even his carefully handpicked parliamentarians could not cross, the Shah was enraged. He detected a "plot" and blamed Alam, the anglophiles, and ultimately the British for having instigated opposition to the bill. Many who had voted against the bill were, or were believed to be, pro-British; there were others who were not. The Shah wanted the recall to London of one member of the British embassy regarded as the prime culprit; but the ambassador, Sir Denis Wright, having found it "disturbing to realise how much the Shah's whims and fancies can make policy," worked hard to persuade the Shah that the British had no reason to seek to derail the bill or to undermine U.S.-Iranian ties.[47] The brief diplomatic wrangle faded away, but the immunities issue decisively strengthened the opposition's case against the Shah, further aggravating the undercurrent of nationalist resentments.

The adoption of the bill and the publication of its text, together with the attendant parliamentary discussions, provoked public indignation, which, in the prevailing repressive milieu, could not be overtly aired. However, a forceful excoriation came from Khomeini, who had been released and allowed to return to Qom in April after ten months of house arrest in Tehran. Seeking to extirpate the charge of being reactionary, in late October he castigated the Shah for having forfeited Iranian national independence, sovereignty, and dignity by reviving the capitulations. He denounced the ever-growing influence of the United States and Israel in Iran, and linked the passage of the bill to the approval of a $200 million credit from American banks requested by Iran to be used on the purchase of U.S. arms. Khomeini also dismissed the Shah as an American stooge determined to end the influence of the clerics and thereby proceed with his policies unopposed; he bemoaned the elimination from public life of patriotic statesmen and warned the Shah to change his conduct or await a dire fate.[48]

This speech resulted in Khomeini's arrest and exile to Turkey, which he would soon leave to begin a long exile in Iraq. With the suppression of all secular opposition, the most effective protest had come from a cleric who had already made his mark as a staunch opponent of the regime. Khomeini's implacable confrontation with the Shah enabled him to become a figure of growing national renown. By invoking the Shah's demonstrated disregard of nationalist sensibilities and constitutional and legal processes, Khomeini skillfully attacked the Shah where he was most vulnerable. There was widespread agreement among the regime's opponents that the bill was an affront to Iranian national dignity, a gratuitous forfeiture of the sovereign rights of an independent nation with an adequately modern legal system. It was seen as a humiliating concession to the Americans, who "rewarded" it with a loan of a paltry $200 million. From being branded by the regime as a reactionary opponent of reform, Khomeini had, in the popular imagination, transformed himself into not only a constitutionalist but also an advocate of Iranian sovereignty. The regime did much to contribute to this transformation.

The significance of Khomeini's opposition to the Shah was not lost on the Americans. The government, observed the U.S. embassy, "has lent him [Khomeini] a new aura of martyrdom and has quite likely raised his stature among the Iranian contenders for Shia paramountcy . . . Should he return he would no doubt find a more enthusiastic following than he did before his exile." The religious opposition had "obtained a new lease of life by having become an ally of the nationalist opposition."[49] Similarly, according to a U.S. State Department account, "Khomeini's exile has aroused dormant nationalist feelings. The Shah and the United States have been branded as both anti-nationalist and anti-religious. This new attitude has tarnished our formerly favorable image, poses a threat to our interests in Iran, and will certainly make our task there far more difficult."[50]

Undeterred by recent events, on November 23, 1964, the government suddenly doubled the price of petroleum products, causing widespread public anger and an unrelenting strike by taxi drivers. This move once again demonstrated the cavalier attitude of the Shah and his compliant prime minister to the public. Intended to generate additional funds for military purchases, the measure had to be almost totally reversed, to the regime's considerable discomfiture. It was, however, the bungled handling of the immunities issue that primarily accounted for the irreparable damage to the Shah's standing and professed nationalism, and for Mansur's tragic end. He was assassinated in January 1965 by affiliates of the Fada'iyan-e Islam, which had been disbanded in late 1955. Shocked by the fate of Mansur, the Shah felt the need to reiterate his nationalist credentials. In a long radio broadcast he emphasized his tireless championing of nationalist causes, particularly in confronting British influence.

## Authoritarianism Ascendant

The death of Mansur led to the prompt appointment as prime minister of his confrere Hoveyda, who had acted as finance minister and the NIP's deputy secretary general. Even more of a political nonentity than Mansur,

Hoveyda assumed the premiership sooner than he expected and by default, but remained in office for an unprecedented twelve and a half years (January 1965–August 1977), far longer than any other prime minister. Having started his career as a diplomat, he cultivated the patronage of, among others, the reputable statesman Abdollah Entezam, who did not, however, seem to have had a high opinion of his administrative skills.[51] Above all, it was royal favor gained through association with Mansur that expedited Hoveyda's political rise; in addition to friendship and close political ties, Mansur and Hoveyda were related by marriage.

Though personally secular, Hoveyda was the son of a well-known Baha'i diplomat; while his meteoric rise indicated how far Iranian politics had moved from the officially tolerated anti-Baha'i agitation of the 1950s, his putative religious affiliation could be exploited against him, making a "reconciliation with clerical elements more difficult."[52] To counter this situation, Hoveyda made a pilgrimage to the shrine of Imam Reza in Mashhad, sent his mother to Mecca, and through an intermediary contacted Ayatollah Mohammad-Taqi Qomi in an attempt to establish a "close rapport" with the clergy; Qomi reportedly "declined to assist in this endeavor."[53] Yet Hoveyda continued his gestures of demonstrating his faith in Islam, avoided unnecessarily provoking the clerics, and persisted in his efforts to win them over if possible. Using the discretionary secret budget available to his office and funds from the endowment department attached to it, he tried to appease amenable clerics but failed to influence those who supported Khomeini. In 1967, in an uncompromising letter, Khomeini sternly rebuked Hoveyda and the regime. Among other things, Khomeini wrote: "While invoking constitutionalism, you have created the worst form of tyrannical and arbitrary government," adding that "violation of the Constitution is a sign of backwardness; the illegal and fraudulent referendum is a sign of backwardness, the refusal to let the people freely chose their representatives, and the appointment instead of disreputable individuals, on orders from above and without the participation of the people—this too is a sign of weakness and backwardness."[54] The Shah's efforts to secure the return of Khomeini to Iran, on the condition that he abandon politics, had failed;[55] the latter showed no sign of lessening his hostility to the regime. Both Hoveyda and the Shah preferred, however, to follow a strategy of avoidance, tempered by qualified appeasement, vis-à-vis the clerics.

Hoveyda was a far more capable administrator than Mansur; the U.S. embassy praised him for his "blending of humility, tact and frankness."[56] Ambassador Wright of Britain was less enthusiastic, describing him as "clever, likeable and highly intelligent but also emotional, excitable and somewhat unreliable."[57] Wright's successor would be more positive, describing Hoveyda as a "nimble and clever personality" who possessed "a flair seemingly lacking in other Iranian leaders."[58] Hoveyda showed dedication, tenacity, and a noncomplacent attitude to his tasks. He did of course assume the office of prime minister when it had become more politically subservient to the royal court than at any other juncture since 1941. His premiership completed a process that had begun with Ala and, in particular, Eqbal. The Shah had never willingly tolerated an able prime minister concerned with asserting his constitutional authority. Hoveyda was entirely willing to embrace and affirm the prime ministerial role as defined by the Shah, and would in effect readily act as the Shah's executive assistant. This was the primary reason for his political longevity, and also the main reason for his denunciation by his constitutionalist opponents.

During Hoveyda's term of office the Shah was more visibly in charge of governance than ever before. A failed attempt on his life in April 1965—by a member of the Imperial Guard affiliated with a group described as British-educated, pro–Chinese Communist students—did not dent his apparent self-confidence. It made him more determined in his autocratic drive. This incident, together with Mansur's assassination, prompted the idea of establishing a Regency Council. The Shah grudgingly agreed to the appointment of his wife, Farah, as regent in the event of his death and the minority of the crown prince (due to end in October 1980). The designation of Farah as regent was formalized in the fall of 1967, when she was also crowned empress. As regent, however, Farah was to have far less formal power than the Shah.

Having muzzled the domestic opposition, the Shah attempted to preempt, deflect, or silence foreign criticism; he did not hide his dislike for the unsolicited advice of the U.S. or British ambassadors. "The Shah," reported the American embassy, "does not listen readily to advice on how to run his country, especially if it implies criticism."[59] "He himself," the Shah pointedly told the British ambassador, "will never forget how the Americans had tried to appoint his Government for him in 1962; he hoped they had now learned their lesson and would treat Iran as a truly independent country. He remembered, too, how we in the past had sought to interfere in the elections of deputies, etc."[60] Aiming to prevent any criticism of his handling of parliamentary elections, for instance, he informed the British and American embassies that "they should not expect the 1967 elections to be like those in the West and that he did not wish to see any foreign interference."[61]

To the Shah's relief, the British and the Americans were no longer particularly concerned about the domestic implications of his unfettered authoritarian conduct and were increasingly hesitant in volunteering to advise him on his handling of Iranian politics. Yet at the same time they were unwilling to allow him to act too independently, and in any event they could rely on key pro-Western politicians to exert pressure on him. In 1966 the Shah threatened to procure arms from the Soviet bloc should the West prove insufficiently cooperative; he also put intense pressure on the oil consortium to increase the production of Iranian oil. On both occasions, even before he had been appointed court minister, Alam, fearing a deepening crisis, "played a useful role in bringing the Shah back to a saner course," while Hoveyda supported or encouraged the royal demands.[62] As court minister for almost eleven years (November 1966–August 1977), Alam played a crucial role in both assisting the Shah and tacitly influencing his decisions.

As compliant aides to the Shah, both Alam and Hoveyda seemed devoid of any ambition other than facilitating implementation of the royal program of development. Both professed wholehearted commitment to the Shah's vision of the country's national interests, and both purported to be able to surmise royal wishes even before they were fully articulated. In contrast to Alam, who had long been a devoted friend of the Shah and whose role was less explicit and whose responsibilities were often ill defined, Hoveyda was a newcomer, a virtual outsider with a more or less formally defined and much more demanding role. He had explicit responsibility for implementing royal directives in governing the country and for ensuring the smooth operation of the administrative machinery. Assisted by cabinet colleagues who were on the whole equally dedicated to serving the Shah loyally and efficiently, he had as his prime tasks mobilizing and supervising the required personnel and creating a stable environment in which a strong socioeconomic infrastructure could be built, the industrialization drive could continue, and commerce and business could thrive. Especially in his earlier years as premier, he may have entertained the illusion of relying on a team of competent administrators and eventually modifying the Shah's authoritarian role or reducing the need for it. He may indeed have seen himself and many of his colleagues as contributing to the eventual emergence of a more reasonable and decent polity. In practice, however, he and his colleagues not only affirmed royal authoritarianism but facilitated and augmented it. By fully embracing a role that undermined any credible notion of constitutional monarchy and underscored its current starkly autocratic form, Hoveyda also unwittingly paved the way for the monarchy's eventual collapse.

## An Entrenched Functionary

As a politician, Hoveyda was both theatrical and serious, nonchalant and persistent, timorous and ruthless, well-meaning and devious; he could combine melancholy with exuberance, chilling cynicism with relentless profession of belief in the Shah's leadership. He was both nationalistic and disdainfully insensitive to the nationalist sensibilities of his opponents. His unabashed elitism contrasted with his empty populist gestures. Fully sharing the Shah's contemptuous dismissal of constitutionalist and other opposition, he seemed confident that development would render the regime less vulnerable to such opposition and would undermine its protagonists. A *bon vivant* with an affected stylishness and cultivated avuncular demeanor, he could not conceal his clear preference for a Europeanized life style, which contrasted with his undisguisable indifference to Iranian cultural sensibilities. He "had no idea about the Iranian people."[63] Despite his intellectual pretensions he showed little intrinsic respect for intellectual values or political and civic rights. Flirting with the intellectuals, he often claimed to be shielding them from the consequences of royal disfavor; he sought to lure, cajole, and co-opt them into serving the regime or not opposing it, but failed to address any of their real grievances. Despite paying lip service to the necessity of criticism, he disliked critics and relished praise however spurious it may have been. He was familiar with European intellectual and political traditions but possessed little grasp of the Iranian literary and cultural heritage.

An avid reader of French detective novels, Hoveyda may have turned to such a genre not merely for pleasure or escapism but also for making sense of the tangled world of Iranian politics and its bewildering byzantine ambience. Such a world, which he himself had done much to create, flourished on seemingly spontaneous and internalized but highly choreographed displays of respect for the Shah, predictable pretensions, concealment of one's inner thoughts, and the search for the real intentions and tactics of rivals. Such a world was not conducive to trust, truth, idealism, and principle. Hoveyda's prolonged experience of office could produce only cumulative cynicism. His feigned continued adherence to political idealism became increasingly hollow, unpersuasive, duplicitous, and counterproductive. In any case, whatever guiding principles, values, or political creed Hoveyda and his acolytes may have espoused, they carefully avoided any course of action likely to displease the Shah and jeopardize their careers. Hoveyda relished the trappings of office, which he utilized to consolidate his control over the administrative machinery. Yet he seemed unconcerned about the consequences of his commitment to a mode of politics that increasingly appeared opportunistic and bereft of moral impulses and recognizable attachment to principle.

For political technicians such as Hoveyda and his cohorts the Constitutional Revolution was a dim memory and its legacy little more than an essentially cosmetic and ceremonial framework—a set of empty rites and procedures. They affirmed the royalist invocation of "the Constitution" as emphasizing no other entrenched principle than the Shah's pivotal role in the political process. A demonstrated acceptance of this contrived norm was the overriding prerequisite of inclusion in the top echelons of government. Hoveyda's primary strategy vis-à-vis the unofficial opposition was to dissolve it through co-optation. He tried to co-opt not only the Mosaddeqists but also lapsed or penitent Tudeh Party members and any other worthwhile opponents as long as they at least implicitly embraced the unquestionable leadership role of the Shah. Relying on largesse and the resources available to his office, he attempted to buy off anyone who could be bought. Unable to grasp why opponents of the regime were not as flexible in abandoning their principles or reprioritizing their aims as he, Hoveyda dismissed them as "negation mongers," as the Shah himself habitually did.

At every opportunity Hoveyda echoed the Shah's disdain for those who sought to revitalize constitutional arrangements or for democracy in general; he seemed to believe that despite the propaganda of implacable and "unpatriotic" opponents, the people would indefinitely acquiesce in the existing mode of politics; they would see the overall balance sheet of the regime as positive, and would accept or gradually resign themselves to believing that the Shah and his elite were fully committed to the higher interests of the nation. For his part, Hoveyda tolerated every humiliation from influential rivals and opponents such as Alam and particularly Ardeshir Zahedi, the cabinet's rogue foreign minister (1966–1971), whose openly contemptuous treatment of Hoveyda revealed the level of disrepute to which the office of the prime minister had sunk. Hoveyda was able to neutralize Alam's maneuvers and to pave the way for Zahedi's eventual removal by the Shah. Clinging to office, he displayed a strangely cheerful mood of stoic, even fatalistic, resignation; for him the rewards and advantages of retaining office far outweighed any indignity.

Hoveyda's unassertiveness vis-à-vis powerful opponents who had the Shah's ear contrasted with his often aggressive attitude toward lesser antagonists or potential rivals. He showed little patience with the mild criticism of his policies by the "opposition" People's Party; he was even less restrained in his treatment of the equally self-effacing press, which he often claimed to shield from the royal wrath. Mindful of the impact of pro- and antiregime propaganda, he frequently admonished journalists to highlight the Shah's positive achievements and thus refrain from providing ammunition for "the enemy." In August 1966 he nominally removed censorship, but this move did little to change the laudatory tone of the tame press and routinized self-censorship. In the summer of 1974 the government ordered the closure of more than sixty newspapers and journals in Tehran and sixty-five elsewhere, claiming that their circulation was too small to be viable. This move ensured that the two official papers, *Keyhan* and *Ettela'at,* became even more politically interchangeable, while self-respecting journalists felt more demoralized than ever.

Hoveyda cautiously arrogated to himself as much power as possible. While the Shah concentrated on policymaking, foreign policy, the military, oil, and security, Hoveyda was able inconspicuously to make many decisions and to exercise considerable power. He "sought to rule as much as possible."[64] He was, according to the U.S. embassy, virtually free to choose his cabinet colleagues, after they were vetted by SAVAK. The task of issuing final clearances and recommendations on all candidates for political office was performed by Parviz Sabeti, chief of SAVAK's much-feared Third Department, in charge of internal security. Shunned by the Shah but close to Hoveyda throughout his adult life, Sabeti enabled him "to obtain clearance for several individuals of questionable background whom he has installed in his Cabinet."[65] The U.S. embassy described Sabeti as "perhaps Hoveyda's closest personal friend, he is also both beholden to and devoted to the Prime Minister. Sabeti despises the imperial family to the point of fanaticism. He has long shared Hoveyda's belief that imperial power must be limited."[66]

Hoveyda may have indeed believed in the desirability of reducing royal power, but his public conduct, no doubt in the interest of his political survival, affirmed the contrary. The Shah was confident that he had fully grasped Hoveyda's psychology; he considered Hoveyda one of those politicians who responded readily to firmness and who needed to be resolutely reined in by power.[67] "When treated forcefully," the Shah told Alam, Hoveyda "belittles himself more than my personal servants," but "if our power declines nothing will restrain him."[68] Clearly, the Shah did not unequivocally trust Hoveyda, but he knew that the prime minister would serve the powerful monarch loyally. For his part, Hoveyda had contrived his own cunning way of unobtrusively influencing and manipulating the Shah and the very structure of decisionmaking. He appeared nonchalantly to acquiesce in delegating all major acts of decisionmaking, and even the activity of thinking politically, to the Shah. Yet, to the chagrin of his influential rivals such as Alam, who considered him incompetent,[69] Hoveyda retained considerable power. He exerted real, albeit indirect and discreet, influence in defining the range of options available to the Shah. Hoveyda, Alam observed, could persuade the Shah to believe that what he (Hoveyda) wanted or had done was nothing other than what the Shah himself had commanded.[70] Hoveyda had, Alam remarked, "deceived" the Shah, or the Shah pretended "to have been deceived."[71] "In Hoveyda," one of his more perceptive ministers remarked, "there was an inherent contradiction. On one level, he was but a pliant tool of the shah; yet midway through his tenure as prime minister, his tentacles reached deep into all layers of Iranian society. He had become an institution himself."[72]

By constantly reiterating that his chief responsibility was merely to im-

*Prime Minister Amir-Abbas Hoveyda greeting the Shah and the queen.* (Courtesy of
the Institute for the Study of Contemporary Iranian History, Tehran)

plement royal commands, Hoveyda hoped to deflect any criticism from
himself and to direct credit as well as blame to the Shah. He would often
rhetorically and disarmingly retort to critics that surely they could not presume to have a deeper understanding of issues than "His Majesty." Readily
invoking the Shah's name to muffle his own critics, he often invited them to
accompany him in an audience with the Shah, which had the effect of
roundly silencing them. In lionizing and eulogizing the Shah and helping to
affirm and sustain his self-image, Hoveyda was particularly skillful; he could
not allow any key official, including Alam, to outstrip him in the ongoing
marathon of sycophancy. Hoveyda benefited immensely from playing a crucial role in enabling the Shah to become the undisputed arbiter of Iranian
politics and in nurturing his *folie de grandeur.* By constantly affirming that
only the Shah was in the position of command and uniquely entitled to be
so, he condoned the public demeaning of the office of prime minister more
than anyone else. During his term of office, the Shah's whims became government policy subsequently embellished and justified by various experts;
the foreign minister was as removed from foreign policy as the director
of the NIOC was unaware of oil negotiations. Ministers reported separately
to the Shah and received orders without Hoveyda's knowledge.[73]

While wholly ingratiating himself with the Shah, Hoveyda invoked the Shah's extensive powers and the watchfulness of SAVAK to justify his own actions or inaction. He behaved as though the Shah's commanding role and his own subservient position were unalterably determined by the forces of destiny. In response to critics who wondered why he did not resign, he would retort that as a servant of the Shah he could not resign but only await dismissal—which, of course, he did his utmost to avert. He would claim that in the current circumstances any other prime minister would have to perform essentially the same role as he did, and that his departure would make little difference. He would also contend that he was more dedicated to development, more attentive to the public interest, and less tolerant of corruption than any other prime minister would be. At no point did he reveal a clear appreciation of the immense burden of responsibility he bore for the prevailing political predicament as the incumbent of the office of prime minister. However constrained he was, he had sufficient power to act differently.

## The Power of Perseverance

Opponents of Hoveyda such as Alam scornfully dismissed him as doing little more than muddling through, if not floundering.[74] Hoveyda possessed the means, in terms of both personal skills and institutional resources, to gain a more accurate picture of the country's realities than did the Shah; yet he opted to ignore and not act upon his responsibilities, "to the detriment of the country, himself and the Shah."[75] At the same time he missed no opportunity to maintain or extend his influence, promote his own agenda, and marginalize or drive to resignation ministers who disagreed with him. Favoring active intervention in the economy, particularly to regulate prices, brought him into disagreement with the veteran economy minister Ali-Naqi Alikhani—a friend of Alam—who advocated a market economy and greater scope for the private sector. Such differences of view, Alikhani recounts, together with growing unease between the two and Hoveyda's increasing appeasement of court protégés, eventually led the minister to resign in July 1969.[76]

Hoveyda's eventual complete control over the NIP enabled him to cultivate a large clientele, consisting of an extensive network of the upper echelons of the civil service, who saw themselves as politically indebted to him.

Becoming a vast dispenser of patronage, the NIP was not a political party in the usual sense but an organization for mobilizing elite support for the government. It was well funded and linked to a considerable number of industrialists and others in the private sector. Those who joined the official parties, particularly the NIP, were mostly government employees who felt compelled to do so; they wished to avoid trouble or hoped to benefit from the support of those in power. By 1974 the NIP had over 200,000 dues-paying members; some 230 of the 268 parliamentary deputies and half of the 60 senators were affiliated with it, and it controlled official unions and rural cooperatives; it had a large network of cells throughout the country; its budget was supplemented by SAVAK. Hoveyda had succeeded in dominating the party by undermining leaders of whom he disapproved; he instigated purges of leadership cadres and in 1969 became the party's secretary general and chairman of its politburo. The party had achieved "a degree of patronage power formerly reserved only for the court."[77]

Hoveyda used his position as premier and at the apex of the NIP not for inordinate personal gain or material self-enhancement, but for accumulating a political and symbolic capital that he invested in the cultivation of friends, protégés, and cronies of various standing and functions who enabled him to outmaneuver or neutralize the incessant machinations of powerful foes and rivals. Hoveyda's cabinet colleague, rival, and successor as prime minister, Jamshid Amuzgar, who was not a member of the NIP, lacked a comparable network. Hoveyda's clientele could and did complicate Amuzgar's tasks as premier. Cultivating such a clientelist bureaucratic nepotism rendered Hoveyda far more powerful than he appeared to be. He had even, Alam feared, bought off the queen's retinue.[78] In addition to his firm control over the NIP, Hoveyda determined who was to lead the minority People's Party.[79] But he continued to project an image of being merely the coordinator of a vast, routinized bureaucratic structure dedicated to unquestioning execution of the will of the Shah.

In his compulsive desire to retain office, Hoveyda was left with little choice but to facilitate or condone the ubiquitous corruption of the Pahlavi clan and virtually ignore the corruption that saturated the regime. The prevailing corruption should not be understood narrowly or merely as wrongful material self-enrichment, but more broadly as widespread abuse of office in contravention of stipulated laws, norms, and procedures. The prime minister's secret budget and his access to other financial resources, as well as his key role in the allocation of lucrative positions, important promotions, transfers, and other material or symbolic rewards, ensured that his often discreetly exercised power and influence was far more tangible than is commonly assumed. He had a vested interest in perpetuating a system that had enabled him to retain a strategic position in the prevailing power structure. Such a system could not in any way have been, or have easily become, a constitutionally legitimate, accountable, and transparent one.

The most glaring failure of Hoveyda and his ministers—mostly recycled royalist cohorts who were also largely loyal to him—was their inability to perceive or their willingness to ignore the inevitably tragic consequences of their ostentatious disregard of any notion of meaningful constitutionalism. They thus irretrievably eroded the residual legitimacy of a regime of which they were an integral part. They perpetuated the myth, and seemed to have succumbed to the illusion, that the system that they had helped to create was invincible; that it rested on sound socioeconomic foundations and had the requisite paraphernalia of strength, success, and continuity. In practice, they had crucially contributed to the ever closer and progressively undisguisable identification of the entire state with one man. In the name of creating a more viable socioeconomic foundation for the state they unwittingly uprooted it. By obediently basing state policies on the edicts, whims, and fancies of the Shah and facilitating the increasingly personalized exercise of state power, they helped to render the entire edifice of the state intrinsically vulnerable.

During Hoveyda's term of office, state power expanded vastly. Coercively maintained stability and increased oil revenues enabled a reasonably competent personnel, unencumbered by effective parliamentary oversight, to carry forward the rapid development program. Loyally served by a powerful military and dedicated officials, the Shah felt more firmly entrenched than ever. Through the SAVAK chiefs and other officials who regularly reported to him he gained a picture of the country at once distorted and reassuring. He embarked on ever more grandiose schemes irrespective of the costs and ignored the question of how long a disenfranchised public was to remain quiescent. The behavior of the regime implied that what was realistically feasible in Iran was no more than the formal trappings of a constitutional polity, none of which functioned in a manner likely to inspire public confidence. The occasional, innocuous, and often stage-managed criticism of the government by the official opposition party was of little consequence; yet even this criticism was not tolerated. The last two secretaries general of the People's Party, Ali-Naqi Kani and Naser Ameri, had been summarily dismissed when their criticisms irritated the Shah or Hoveyda. When Ameri fell out of favor, Hoveyda even cut the party's government stipend.[80]

The governing NIP appeared to be an indispensable component of governance and its role clearly defined. Yet it, too, was becoming a liability; it had become unwieldy and too closely associated with Hoveyda, whose growing influence, the Shah felt, needed to be checked. The party's corruption had also proved uncontrollable. The party's authority was tacitly challenged by the White Revolution Study Group, established on the Shah's orders and headed by Houshang Nahavandi, a former finance minister, who had become the chancellor of Tehran University. Though a party member, he reported directly to the Shah and, to Hoveyda's consternation, refused to make the study group a party affiliate. The group was an establishment "think-tank," whose formal assignment was to explore the ramifications and amplify the content and scope of the monarch's reformist program and ideas. It was to address the neglected need for a measure of deliberation and expert advice long ignored and resisted by the Shah despite the urging of advisers such as Alam.[81] The group initially took its work seriously. In the opinion of the U.S. embassy, it produced "extraordinarily frank reports" critical of the government program and suggested ways of dealing with problems.[82] Not surprisingly, Hoveyda resented the group, fearing that Nahavandi could become a rival.[83] For his part and not uncharacteristically, the Shah considered the whole project "a good entertainment for the young."[84] It was meant to be no less frivolous than other bodies he had established. In the public eye, the group provided little more than a meek and admiring audience to be lectured by the tediously grandiloquent Shah. Its primary task was to demonstrate that all problems could be addressed within the confines of the existing regime. It also aimed to rationalize and justify the monarch's aims and whims while affirming and celebrating his endlessly publicized wisdom and foresight.

The main potential challenge to Hoveyda came from his rival and cabinet colleague Amuzgar, who had particularly impressed the Shah during the oil negotiations with the consortium. As interior minister, Amuzgar formally headed the civil service and was expected to implement the "administrative revolution" advocated by the Shah; he was also charged with conducting "freer" elections, which were likely to weaken the NIP. The failure of Amuzgar was bound to diminish his position vis-à-vis Hoveyda, a fate that some felt Hoveyda had planned for him.[85] Amuzgar had long been tipped as the next prime minister, but his chances for success as premier were limited by Hoveyda's control over the NIP. Although as interior minister Amuzgar was in a position to influence the elections scheduled for 1975, the NIP network was likely to make his task exceptionally difficult.

A drastic way out of these difficulties, which reduced Hoveyda's power and reconfigured the reservoir of influence that he controlled, was found by the Shah. Ignoring his previous denunciation of single-party systems, in March 1975 the Shah discarded the existing official parties in favor of the single and all-encompassing Resurgence (Rastakhiz) Party. He had, he told Alam, been pondering the question of forming such a party for five months without telling anyone.[86] All "patriotic" Iranians were called upon to join the new party, thereby affirming their allegiance to "the Constitution," the imperial system, and the principles of the "Revolution of the Shah and the People," or leave the country. The Resurgence Party, the Shah declared, was to be the most nationally inclusive and popularly based organization in the whole of Iranian history and a vehicle for broader participation. The NIP, and thus Hoveyda's large clientele, joined the Resurgence Party en masse, and Hoveyda became the new party's secretary general. He began to install individuals loyal to himself in key positions and remained strategically well placed to outmaneuver rivals such as Amuzgar, who was a leading party member but could not muster even a remotely comparable level of clientelist support.

The Resurgence Party's constitution discouraged one-man control.[87] Moreover, intending to forestall a repetition of the experience with the NIP, the Shah divided the new party's leadership, ensuring that rivals were placed in key positions. By royal design the party contained wings or factions; it had a "progressive" and a "liberal" wing led by Amuzgar and Hushang Ansari—another influential cabinet minister—respectively. Some, like Alam, considered it ill advised to have both these positions occupied by men who were widely viewed as pro-American.[88] Characteristically, the Shah had appointed the two without their prior knowledge, and nor were they entirely sure what agendas they were specifically expected to promote. Ideological differences between the two wings remained ill defined, even spurious. Parliamentarians sought royal guidance regarding which wing they should join but were given vague or contradictory signals.[89]

The NIP had controlled the 1967 and 1971 elections, ensuring its domination over the parliament and leaving little scope for the "opposition" People's Party. In the June 1975 parliamentary elections, the electorate was given the seemingly greater choice of voting for prescreened Resurgence Party candidates who competed with each other but were all equally acceptable to the regime. The task of vetting and approving candidates was assigned to General Hosein Fardust, the Shah's personal intelligence chief, and not to Sabeti, Hoveyda's close friend in SAVAK. This was plausibly viewed by the U.S. embassy as a move "perhaps intended to undercut" Hoveyda.[90] Determined pressure was put on the electorate to register to vote. Reportedly, fewer than seven million people registered, but, contrary to government claims, fewer than half of these voted. For a population of some thirty million, this was a dismal turnout; despite the scale and intensity of official pressure and propaganda, the general public had refused to endorse the regime. The elections were not even procedurally free; an official of the Interior Ministry told the U.S. embassy that 10 percent of them were rigged through the influence of Alam.[91] Alam admitted that half of the 42 reelected former NIP members were his friends, but claimed that these and other reelected deputies enjoyed local standing.[92] The elections were, however, significant, as they drastically changed the composition of the parliament. Only 48 of 268 incumbent deputies had been reelected, and only one-third of the elective senators.

When Amuzgar suggested that the attitude of the newly elected deputies could not be easily anticipated, he was severely rebuked by the Shah, who expected all deputies to follow the party line. Having incurred the royal anger, Amuzgar was petrified with fear.[93] No one was to be allowed to entertain any illusion about real change; nor would anyone be allowed to forget that the imperial system was primarily a person-centered regime and not a political entity sustained by a party or an ideology. Whether the regime was informally committed to one party, as in the recent past, or formally relied on one made little real difference. Whereas the function of the old government party was to organize the elite, the new party's task was ideally to mobilize the whole population in support of the regime. Not surprisingly, the proclaimed objective—that the new party would give greater leverage to the parliament and the press and would serve as a forum for meaningful, publicly appealing debate—was not realized. After his loss of the throne, the Shah acknowledged that forming such a party was a mistake.[94]

One of the main purposes in forming the Resurgence Party was to restrain Hoveyda's inordinate power, and indeed the overwhelming defeat of former NIP members in the parliamentary elections signaled the beginning of the erosion of his influence. As Alam frequently noted, Hoveyda saw the formation of the new party as a personal blow; yet he was able to adapt to the new situation. Having discomfited older and more powerful rivals, Hoveyda was too resilient and well entrenched to relinquish his privileged position in the face of new contenders. In the summer of 1974 the U.S. embassy had noted that Hoveyda was "not well," reportedly suffering from "severe gout and uremia."[95] Yet his energy seemed undiminished. However, toward the end of his astonishingly long term of office the political and economic situation appeared disconcerting even to the regime's most stalwart supporters. In January 1976 Abd al-Majid Majidi, head of the Plan Organization—a government body that since 1949, and more effectively since 1955, had been in charge of preparing and implementing development plans—complained bitterly to Alam about economic mismanagement and waste, presenting a picture that Alam thought "should ordinarily result in a revolution." Adding to the causes of concern was some $2 billion in loans given to foreign countries while the Iranian economy itself was in trouble. Accusing Hoveyda of treason, Alam believed that the Shah had been deliberately kept in the dark about the situation.[96]

The Shah did not, however, abandon Hoveyda, who continued not only to resent but to counter the interventions of powerful figures such as Alam and Farah. In July 1976 Richard Helms, former CIA director and U.S. ambassador to Iran (1973–1977), described Hoveyda as "Iran's most consummate politician."[97] By sheer longevity as premier he had rendered himself virtually indispensable. The Shah, it seemed, was reluctant or could not afford to replace him. He carefully avoided giving the Shah any pretext to remove him, and fully adhered to the Shah's approach to the present and to his vision of the future. He had always shared the Shah's fondness for nationalistic postures and reiterated his rhetoric. Hoveyda had, for instance, told the British ambassador, Sir Peter Ramsbotham (1971–1974), to use the term "Persia" rather than "Iran," as he found it more evocative of the country's past glories. A desire to revive such glories led the Shah in March 1976 to sanction the abandonment of the Iranian-Islamic calendar (starting with the prophet Mohammad's migration from Mecca to Medina in 622 C.E.) in favor of an imperial one dating back to the beginning of the reign of the Achaemenid emperor Cyrus (circa 550 B.C.E.). This move, together with extravagant ceremonials marking the fiftieth year of Pahlavi rule, as well as other measures which were seen as detrimental to the Islamic components of the Iranian national culture, provided the Islamist forces with powerful rallying points. No measure of responsibility for these actions would, of course, be accepted by Hoveyda. By invoking the commanding role of the Shah, he had cultivated the art of wielding considerable power without admitting any responsibility.

# 5

# Revolution:

# Chronicle of an Implosion

During the final year of Hoveyda's premiership, particularly from the spring of 1977 onward, the regime began to relax constraints on freedom of expression and association. The incipient policy of controlled openness had accompanied the rise in the fortunes of the Democrats in the U.S. presidential elections, a development always unwelcome to the Shah. The election of Jimmy Carter, whose political agenda highlighted respect for human rights, led many Iranians to anticipate American pressure on the Shah. Perceiving a direct correlation between developments in Iran and in the United States, the regime's critics viewed the greater openness as an effort by the Shah to appease the United States and to preempt American criticism. The Americans had played no more than a passive role in the liberalization. "The U.S.," wrote its ambassador, William Sullivan, "is not directly involved in this process of increased criticism, nor should it be . . . It will [however] do no harm and some positive good to express our approval of the opening up process and reinforce the thinking that has led to it," but, he added, the United States must avoid moves that could be "misinterpreted by either critics or supporters of the present regime, or both."[1] Political openness was primarily a response to manifest or latent domestic sociopolitical pressures. It revealed the regime's efforts to adjust itself to changing domestic and international exigencies; it also signified its self-confidence. The Shah had been pondering some form of openness for some time; by the spring of 1977, criticism within the Resurgence Party was more openly tolerated; the

Shah saw liberalization as an effective way to enlist the support of the newer segments of the elite brought to the fore by the party. The sessions of the Royal Commission, formed in November 1975 to investigate wasteful measures and other forms of official mismanagement, were broadcast on television with the aim of showing that the regime was willing to espouse a real measure of transparency. Through these strategies the Shah and the elite sought to contain all opposition within the boundaries of the existing political system and futilely attempted to manufacture an opposition that was loyal but credible.

Managing the implications of even limited political openness was a daunting task for a regime unaccustomed to and unprepared for it. Political openness, if meant or taken seriously, was bound to strike at the roots of the Shah's pivotal role, as well as the continued tenure of Hoveyda and the majority of the political elite. The parliament, packed with supporters of the regime and its constitutional role thoroughly discredited, could not be easily reinvigorated to command public respect. The Shah did not intend, nor could he afford, a radical restructuring of the regime and the prevailing modality of exercising power. At the same time, political openness, without commensurate change in the structure of power, in the political conduct and composition of key officeholders, and in the acceptance of free and fair elections, was bound to prove counterproductive.

Perceptible political openness resulted in and was in turn inspired by the circulation of "open letters" addressed to the Shah or Hoveyda. Writing and distributing open letters was an effective age-old strategy by which renowned public figures aired their concerns and criticisms not so much to the nominal addressees but to the public at large. In March 1977 the veteran essayist and intellectual Ali-Asghar Haj-Sayyed-Javadi published an open letter addressed to the Shah and critical of the regime. This letter would often be cited as marking the beginning of liberalization. Of greater political significance was an open letter sent to the Shah in mid-June, signed by three leading Mosaddeqists—Karim Sanjabi, Shapur Bakhtiar, and Daryush Foruhar—in which they cogently criticized royal autocracy and underlined its dangerous consequences.[2] This was followed two days later by a letter addressed to Hoveyda from forty leading writers warning the regime about the consequences of stifling "creative thinking," promoting "cultural decadence," and harassing writers and intellectuals. These and similar letters emphasized human rights and the need for the rule of law. The regime initially reacted with silence or scorn; Daryush Homayun, a leading official of the Resurgence Party and Ardeshir Zahedi's brother-in-law, dismissed the Mosaddeqists as passé.[3] Yet there was a noticeable unwillingness to use force to curb the growing voices of criticism. In the early autumn a "poetry reading" festival organized by the Goethe Institute (Iran-Germany Cultural Society) and the Writers' Association became a gathering of noted poets, other writers, and a large audience, who over ten unprecedented nights defied and condemned repression and demanded an end to censorship.

Having barely disguised his disdain for intellectuals,[4] the Shah was now constrained to tolerate them. Intellectuals, human rights campaigners, lawyers, and a variety of opposition politicians and activists began to organize; they agitated for the promotion and protection of civic and political rights, the revival of constitutional governance and constitutionally guaranteed rights and entitlements, and the removal and punishment of high-ranking officials who over the years had systematically violated political and civic rights, acted against the public interest, and abused their official positions. Not surprisingly, the regime felt unable to address or respond to such demands, as doing so would have radically transformed its configuration. The Shah would prevaricate for as long as possible; confining himself to gestures, promises, and halfhearted concessions aimed at mollifying opponents and deflecting their criticism, he refused to forfeit any real components of his extensive powers. Such forfeiture was, however, at the very heart of the opposition's demands.

High-level corruption was an issue the Shah himself had vocally invoked at various junctures since 1953. After the establishment of the Resurgence Party and resorting to one of his favorite populist gestures, the Shah castigated the corrupt and the rich as having no place among parliamentary candidates. A number of well-known and wealthy businessmen were arrested, and in January 1976 a committee headed by key establishment figures, including Hoveyda, Amuzgar, and Ansari, was assigned the task of curbing corruption. An inconvenient issue that the regime could neither afford to ignore nor publicly address was corruption at the royal court. Many members of the Pahlavi clan were among the chief perpetrators of corruption, which took a variety of often intractable forms. They not only were involved in a variety of lucrative private enterprises but also, and more significantly, enriched themselves through their influence over the management of government-run public enterprises and assets. The unbridled misconduct of the Pahlavi clan undermined the Shah's proclaimed commitment to combating corruption and seriously damaged his credibility and stature. Measures to put an end to the abuses of the Pahlavi clan were adopted only when it was too late.

Hoveyda's response to growing open criticism of the regime was one of nonchalant or mocking dismissal. He had come to symbolize much of what the opponents considered wrong with the regime; his retention could in no way be reconciled with the much-vaunted political openness. In the first week of August 1977 and in the wake of signs of serious economic difficulties, Hoveyda was replaced by Amuzgar, but was in effect promoted to the position of court minister, succeeding the dying Alam. Alam, who regarded Hoveyda as having led the country to the brink of disaster, could only have considered this move as an ultimate affront, a clear sign of royal betrayal. Relying on his flair for tactical moves, the Shah failed to realize that the situation demanded a strategic response. His political redeployment of establishment figures indicated that he failed to appreciate the deep undercurrents of oppositional politics. He shunned a timely accommodation of opposition demands, which in effect called for a democratic reconstitution of the state.

The new prime minister, Amuzgar, the son of a former senator, brother of a former minister, and a U.S.-educated engineer, had started his career working for the American Point IV program—an arrangement based on a U.S.-Iranian agreement of October 1950, under which the United States provided Iran with technical and economic aid. He had become a cabinet minister in August 1958. He had earned a reputation as an efficient administrator more concerned with transparency and principle than Hoveyda, but few regarded him as an effective or inspiring politician. He enjoyed royal support, was close to Alam, and was "possessed of formidable energy."[5] Yet he exuded little personal magnetism and lacked the requisite skills for attracting devoted protégés. Despite his long political career, he had not been able to create a clientele remotely comparable to that of Hoveyda, who had enjoyed the sustained organizational support of the NIP and close links with SAVAK. Upon assuming the premiership, Amuzgar resigned his position as secretary general of the Resurgence Party, which he had held since November 1976.

Amuzgar could not feel confident that Hoveyda's supporters would not seek to undermine him, or that as court minister Hoveyda would refrain from aggravating his problems. Nor was he immune from maneuvers by SAVAK and other vested interests to thwart him. The policies pursued under Hoveyda were bound to haunt his successor. Moreover, the premiership had become a more challenging position at a time when the regime felt obliged to respond to powerful pressures for political change and political problems had become far less manageable. With the Shah's endorsement, Amuzgar promised to adopt a policy of transparency and to continue with political openness. Aiming to contain growing economic problems, his cabinet pursued an austerity program designed to reduce public expenditure, and combatted inflation and various shortages while trying to increase tax revenues. The program was, however, unpopular even among the regime's supporters, long accustomed to generous public spending. Opponents of the regime, relentless in enumerating its failings and unimpressed with the new cabinet, pushed for greater freedom.

The country was gripped by political convulsions that the regime neither fully appreciated nor could effectively address. In addition to the pressures from intellectual and secular opponents, the regime also increasingly faced challenges that were inspired by or couched in religious terms and took a variety of forms. Instances of these, according to a U.S. embassy report, included "increased use of the *chadour* among college-educated women as a sign of opposition to the government, resistance to women's rights legislation (almost amounting to pressure group lobbying), and the spread of unflattering jokes about the Shah."[6] In mid-August 1977, soon after Amuzgar's assumption of the premiership, the eleventh Shiraz arts festival, annually held in the presence of Queen Farah, caused a stir. According to the British ambassador, Anthony Parsons, an avant-garde theatrical piece, performed in the main shopping street of Shiraz in full view of passersby, involved "a rape which was performed in full (no pretence) by a man (either naked or without any trousers . . .) on a woman whose dress had been ripped off by her attacker."[7] Khomeini, whose statements were being smuggled into the country, and other clerics seized on such events to denounce the regime. By early autumn Islamists in the universities were more assertively agitating against what they saw as lax relations between the sexes and the immodest attire of female students.

Opponents of different persuasions used various opportunities to assert themselves and test the regime's resolve; they no longer seemed overly concerned with possible reprisals. One such opportunity arose in October 1977, when news of the death in Iraq of Khomeini's eldest son, Mostafa, reached Iran. Commemoration services were held in Qom, Tehran, and other cities, at which preachers defied the taboo of mentioning Khomeini's name and openly paid homage to him. A service organized at one of Tehran's main mosques, Masjed-e Ark, was attended by academics, opposition politicians, and activists of various persuasions. SAVAK estimated the number of participants at 8,000.[8] Similar occasions provided opportunities for the utilization of religious venues, networks and organizations, symbols and rituals for unmistakably oppositional political aims. These gatherings helped to generate solidarity, exert pressure on quietist clerics or those unsympathetic to Khomeini, and engage in publicity on his behalf in clear defiance of the regime. Engraved in the collective memory since the 1960s, Khomeini's name was rapidly emerging as a byword for opposition to the Shah.

Among known political forces, one group stood out, namely the Iran Freedom Movement, founded in May 1961 by academics such as Mehdi Bazargan and Yadollah Sahabi, and Sayyed Mahmud Taleqani, a civic-minded clerical activist who espoused a combination of religious faith and moral socialism. Active in oppositional politics since 1953 and having endured terms of imprisonment, these leaders saw themselves as faithful to Mosaddeq's legacy, but considered a combination of civic-nationalism and a moderate and essentially ethical version of Islam to constitute an ideology of wider public appeal. The formation of this group marked the growing salience of political Islam and worried the secular Mosaddeqists. The emergence of the group had signaled a rift between secular and nonsecular supporters of Mosaddeq—a development welcome to the regime. In due course the Freedom Movement would to varying degrees ideologically nourish different religiously minded activist opponents of the regime, and would even partially succeed in transcending the religious-secular divide.

Certain secular Mosaddeqists had come to believe that a tactical alliance with the Freedom Movement and other supporters of Khomeini would create a powerful instrument for exerting pressure on the regime and extracting greater political concessions. Similarly, in the eyes of some pro-Khomeini activists, such an alliance could be used to strengthen their claims that they were attentive to civic-nationalist and democratic concerns.

Viewing the clerics as indispensable tactical allies in confronting the regime, many active Mosaddeqists failed to take seriously the prospect or consequences of possible clerical ascendancy in the antiregime protest movement. The essentially reformist Mosaddeqists did not envision the easy or imminent collapse of the regime. The regime itself seemed to consider its secular opponents, whether Mosaddeqists, left-wing groups, or university students, more immediately dangerous than its religious antagonists, and showed greater willingness to counter and suppress them. In November 1977 a meeting of some 1,000 Mosaddeqists, convened to discuss the formation of an opposition alliance, was violently broken up by 700 agents of the regime, referred to by SAVAK as "patriotic youth."[9] This incident revealed the clear limits of political openness.

The Shah's worries about the ramifications of Carter's human rights policies had proved unfounded; in practice American policy toward Iran remained unchanged. This state of affairs was symbolized and confirmed by Carter's brief visit to Tehran on the last day of 1977. Overwhelmed by the hospitality of his imperial host at a lavish New Year's Eve party held in his honor, the slightly intoxicated Carter diverged from the prepared text of his speech. Praising the Shah's leadership, he described Iran as "an island of stability in one of the more troubled areas of the world."[10] Reassured by American support and confidence, the Shah adopted a less tolerant attitude toward the opposition. A week after Carter's speech, incensed by the antiregime pronouncements of Khomeini and intending to undermine his image, the Shah had a poorly written article offensive to Khomeini planted in a mass-circulation newspaper.[11] The article, titled "Red and Black Colonialism" and published under a false name, had been prepared under the auspices of Court Minister Hoveyda, who could not shrug off his share of responsibility for it. Both the Shah and Hoveyda drastically underestimated the consequences of planting such an article; Hoveyda may also have mischievously considered the article helpful in furthering his own political aims, as it was certain to damage the position of Prime Minister Amuzgar.

The publication of the article was a catastrophic failure of judgment on the part of the Shah and Hoveyda. Provoking protests in Qom and elsewhere, it set in motion a chain reaction involving ever more violent and bloody confrontations, deaths, and funerals, which generated a surge of emotion. It proved to be one of the chief triggers of a revolutionary process that within one year destroyed the monarchy. According to a SAVAK informer, "seminary students believe that the government itself wants to provoke chaos and agitation in the country since it knows that if such material is planted in the press, the people will protest. Seminarians were quietly attending to their education; one person published something in a newspaper and plunged the seminary into convulsion."[12]

The article generated growing public recognition of Khomeini as the regime's chief antagonist and provided his supporters with a timely *casus belli* that they put to maximum use to mobilize the discontented traditional segments of the population and push forward their own agenda. They expanded the scope and scale of the protests beyond intellectual and middle-class circles by introducing new slogans, tactics, and rituals, and worked to overtake and outmaneuver secular protesters. Even those clerics who had grave reservations about supporting Khomeini felt obliged to add their voices to the protests. Encouraged by these developments, Khomeini openly advocated the overthrow of the Pahlavi dynasty. While trying in vain to subdue and contain the increasingly violent religious-traditionalist protests in several cities, the regime also had to confront student and other secular protesters who had grown more radical in their antiregime pronouncements and tactics. With opposition mounting, whatever the regime did only worsened the situation and promoted greater solidarity among the wide spectrum of its opponents.

Journalists, long complicit in the regime's apparatus of propaganda and further damaged by the use of a newspaper to attack Khomeini and instigate violence, joined the chorus of protest. In March 1978, in a move that could be seen as either expiatory or aimed at self-rehabilitation, ninety journalists published an open letter addressed to the prime minister. While demanding full implementation of constitutional provisions, they complained that sycophantic exaggerations had ensured that even the positive achievements of the government were viewed with cynicism. They added that government-imposed restrictions on the press had resulted in journalists' being viewed by the people as both mendacious and culpable.[13] In April a letter signed by ninety-four other journalists affirmed the views of their colleagues.[14]

In the face of the growing crisis, the Shah vacillated between firmness and leniency. In June 1978, as a concession to the protesters, he replaced the reviled SAVAK chief General Ne'matollah Nasiri with General Naser Moghaddam, head of the Second Department (in charge of intelligence) of the Supreme Commander's Staff. At the same time, this move was aimed at restructuring SAVAK and making it more effective in managing and diffusing the crisis; Moghaddam also acted as a conduit between the regime and its opponents. Nasiri's removal and the intended changes in SAVAK were measures likely to lower the morale of the increasingly cornered security service without mollifying the regime's opponents, who were heartened by the course of events, including desertions from the Resurgence Party. The widening gap between the people and the regime ensured that virtually all forms of provocation or violence would invariably be blamed on the regime; a notorious case was an arson attack on a cinema in the southern city of Abadan in August 1978, which was widely believed to have resulted in the death of up to 400 people.

Eventually, in late August, Ja'far Sharif-Emami was summoned to head a government of "national reconciliation." But the current perilous situation was a far cry from the crisis of the early 1960s, when the Shah had also called upon Sharif-Emami to form a cabinet: this time he would prove to be a far more unsuitable choice. Though representing the gentler self-image of the regime, Sharif-Emami was a key establishment figure: a grand master of the Freemasons, a veteran president of the senate, head of the Pahlavi Foundation, and a royal confidant. In view of his religious lineage and links with a number of clerics, in appointing him the Shah aimed to respond to pressures from certain religious quarters. He could find few politicians whom he trusted, yet in these explosive circumstances his rationale for turning to a routine royalist defied common sense. Sharif-Emami took a number of steps to appeal to secularists, including the elimination of censorship and hastening the dissolution of the Resurgence Party. Emphasizing his clerical lineage, he also made conciliatory gestures toward the clerics. Among other measures, he abolished the imperial calendar, established two years earlier, and closed down casinos and night clubs. Such moves, however, were seen both as hypocritical and as encouraging indications of the growing weakness of the regime. Khomeini denounced conciliation, and other leading clerics felt unable to disagree with him. No major opposition figure or group seemed willing to counsel reconciliation, knowing that it would not resonate with the protesters. The opponents intensified their demonstrations and disruptive tactics, leading the regime to impose martial law in Tehran and eleven other cities.

On September 8, 1978 (known as Black Friday), a day after the imposition of martial law, the military clashed with demonstrators in Jaleh Square, in a lower-class area of Tehran; the majority of the demonstrators were apparently unaware of the curfew regulations. The ensuing bloodshed, the gravest since the beginning of the crisis, marked a watershed in the tumultuous relations between the regime and the radicalized population, who began more unanimously and persistently to demand the Shah's overthrow and, exhorted by Khomeini, to resort to paralyzing stoppages, strikes, and other tactics to undermine the very foundations of the regime.

A day after Black Friday, Hoveyda resigned as court minister; although he may have advocated a different approach from the one pursued by the Shah, he seemed no less pathetically out of touch with the realities of Iranian society and the unfolding convulsions. Hoveyda's self-inflicted insularity and naiveté led him to misunderstand what had happened. Mistaking the revolution for a revolt, he continued until the very end of the monarchy to await a royal "master scenario" or a royalist military coup to retrieve the regime. Hoveyda was replaced as court minister by Ali-Qoli Ardalan, a reputable senior diplomat and former foreign minister. Prompted by Ardalan, the Shah ordered members of the royal family to refrain from a host of mainly commercial activities. The collapse and dismantling of the Resurgence Party, so clearly identified as a foundational edifice of royal power, served as another powerful symbol of the autocracy's reversal of fortune. Not unexpectedly, in the face of increasing unrest, violence, and subversive activities, the "national reconciliation" government was faltering. It was becoming evident that by entrusting the task of defusing the mounting crisis to Sharif-Emami and his colleagues, the Shah had made a costly strategic miscalculation; he wasted precious time, and squandered perhaps the last opportunity to spare the country from what was to follow. Yet the appointment of Sharif-Emami was not an ordinary error or lapse of judgment. It revealed deeper failings: the Shah's tragically inadequate grasp of the depth of the crisis, and his vain hope of weathering the storm and retrieving his position without making drastic and timely concessions.

There was an inverse relationship between the growing assertiveness of the opponents and the eroding self-confidence of the regime, between the defiant single-mindedness of Khomeini and the desperate disorientation of the Shah. The ease with which Khomeini's messages reached Iran and his stark denunciation of conciliation, coupled with his calls for the regime's overthrow, provoked the Shah to press the Iraqi government to silence or expel him, leading to Khomeini's departure from Iraq. Turned down by Kuwait, he arrived in Paris on October 12, 1978, where, as an exotic and ascetic divine, an elderly spiritual visionary and unconventional revolutionary, he attracted extensive media attention. Such attention and such freedom to air his views were unprecedented for an opposition leader unequivocally preaching the overthrow of his country's government, a government friendly to France. Assisted by an assortment of seasoned opponents of the Shah and encouraged by the ease with which he could communicate his messages to his followers, particularly through the Persian broadcasts of foreign radio stations, chiefly the BBC, he found France a congenial haven.

Strangely, Khomeini's sojourn and unrestricted activities in Paris, where he arrived with a valid Iranian passport, not only provoked no strong objection from the Iranian government but in effect met with its acquiescence. The French would have expelled Khomeini to Algeria or Libya had the Shah explicitly asked them to do so. But the Shah wanted the French to take the initiative without implicating him. The regime had never been relaxed in its attitude to those deemed determined to undermine it. It had, for instance, relentlessly sought to eliminate the former chief of SAVAK, General Teymur Bakhtiar, fearing that he was attempting to organize an anti-Shah coup. Exiled in 1962, Bakhtiar later turned against the Shah; he eventually found refuge in Iraq, where he was assassinated by SAVAK agents in August 1970. The regime's attitude to Khomeini was radically different from the very outset. It is difficult to explain or understand the Shah's calculations, complacency, or resignation in this regard, and to make sense of his failure to take seriously the evident implications of Khomeini's presence and unrestrained activities in France. The Shah may have despairingly believed that Khomeini's departure from France would make scant difference to the situation, or that it might antagonize the latter's supporters even further. He may have hoped that exposure to the moral laxity of French society would tarnish Khomeini's aura of sanctity. In any case, evincing deep despondency, he appeared reluctant to be held responsible for having harmed or even restricted Khomeini or secured his expulsion from France.

The hapless premier, Sharif-Emami, continued his conciliatory efforts. On October 24 he ordered the release of more than 1,100 political prisoners, some of whom had been imprisoned for long periods. Most of those released promptly joined the ranks of the antiregime revolutionary agitators. On November 4 a bloody confrontation between students at Tehran University and security forces, captured by television cameras, sealed the fate of Sharif-Emami's government, which resigned the next day. Having bungled the conciliatory approach, the Shah opted for what appeared to be firmness: he entrusted the task of governance to the military commanders and appointed General Gholam-Reza Azhari, chief of the Supreme Commander's Staff since July 1971, as prime minister. Like his fellow generals, the affable but ineffectual Azhari was unaccustomed to taking the initiative or acting unguided by the Shah. The Shah's high-ranking generals had no clear vision or approach of their own as to how to handle the crisis. By forming a military government the Shah was embarking on a fateful strategic step of openly relying on the military as a last resort in his efforts to roll back the revolutionary wave. The military had, of course, already been deployed to enforce martial-law measures but without tangibly positive results. It was unclear how the new government, politically inexperienced and unversed in the tactics of countering and containing civil unrest, would act to achieve its objectives.

Unable to receive consistent and clear advice and assurances from his foreign friends, to whom he increasingly turned, the Shah's erratic behavior and disorientation increased. Any wavering or vacillation on his part would surely defeat the whole purpose of installing a government run by the military and expected to handle the situation resolutely. However, on the very day that he appointed his military cabinet, the Shah made an emotional televised appeal to the nation; among other things he said:

> I pledge that past mistakes, lawlessness, injustice, and corruption will not only no longer be repeated, but will in every respect be rectified. As soon as order and calm have been restored, I undertake to set up a national government to establish fundamental liberties and [arrange] for elections so that the Constitution, which is the blood price of the Constitutional Revolution, can be fully implemented . . . I guarantee that in future the government in Iran will be based on the Constitution, social

justice, and the will of the people, and will be free from despotism, injustice, and corruption.[15]

Paradoxically, in recognizing the legitimacy of revolutionary aspirations
and at least indirectly admitting his own culpability, the Shah was implicitly pleading to be given another chance. His desperate plea and diffident,
apologetic, even pathetic tone, so starkly in contrast to his erstwhile imperial arrogance, were as perplexing to his supporters, including his hapless
generals, as they were reassuring to his implacable enemies, who rightly
concluded that the Shah had crumbled and was in no position to unleash
the military in a major crackdown. There were, of course, also those who
saw the speech as a perfidious maneuver designed to buy time. Khomeini
rebutted the Shah by emphasizing that he had often made such pleas and
promises only to break them later; that he had not made "mistakes" but had
always acted deliberately. The Shah had started his reign by promising to redress the mistakes and injustices of his father's era and was now, as he was
losing his hold on power, promising to rectify the mistakes and injustices of
his own reign.

Considering the Shah's formal reliance on the military to restore order,
which implied firmness, his surprisingly conciliatory speech was ill timed
and likely to prove counterproductive. Of course, neither the Shah nor his
new prime minister had worked out a viable approach for handling the
deepening political crisis; nor did they indicate any serious intention of vigorously containing disorder. Within days following its appointment and in
the hope of placating the opposition and deflecting blame from the Shah,
the Azhari government arrested a number of leading functionaries of the
regime, including Hoveyda and the former SAVAK chief General Nasiri.
Such steps, however, did not have the desired effect on the opponents, who
dismissed them as merely tactical. The ill-equipped government was incapable of sustained vigor or of devising any strategy to counter the growing
civil disobedience. It could not deal with demonstrations, strikes, and the
opponents' psychological tactics aimed at corroding the morale of the soldiers confronting civilian protesters.

The government's demonstrated lack of ability and political will encouraged its opponents. Khomeini denied the Shah any respite; he tirelessly reiterated his *idée fixe* that the Shah and the entire regime must be toppled.

Such an objective resonated with a wide spectrum of left-wing forces who had long preached revolutionary radicalism. Bazargan, who flew to Paris on October 21, 1978, to visit Khomeini, was apprehensive about the prevailing unbridled and simplistic militancy, and feared the consequences of a sudden collapse of the state. In the absence of any clear plan or preparations for a successor regime, Bazargan and other moderate activists wanted to proceed through the existing constitutional mechanisms and procedures without retaining the Shah.[16] They were, however, overruled and outmaneuvered by Khomeini and the uncompromising revolutionary fervor that he had done much to instigate.

Karim Sanjabi, a leading figure in the revived National Front—which did not at the time include all active or senior Mosaddeqists—and a former Mosaddeq minister who also visited Khomeini in Paris, shared Bazargan's misgivings. Yet he formally affirmed Khomeini's view that the existing monarchy had forfeited its legality and committed himself to Khomeini's program of noncooperation with the Shah. Khomeini received Sanjabi's statement passively; the ayatollah increasingly exuded an air of dismissive indifference toward all other claimants to the nation's leadership. Sanjabi's statement created no tangible obligation or reciprocal commitment for Khomeini. A number of other Mosaddeqists, then and later, seriously questioned Sanjabi's wisdom and motives. Apparently convinced that Khomeini's success was certain, Sanjabi may have hoped that by joining him he would be able to play a role in influencing the course of events.[17]

Sanjabi's stance meant that he had in effect withdrawn from the small pool of senior Mosaddeqists whom the Shah, in the wake of the evident failure of the military cabinet, was belatedly considering for the premiership. For some time the Shah had been consulting a number of elder statesmen whom he had previously discarded, including the former premier Amini and politicians Entezam and Varasteh, shunned since 1963. The chronic marginalization of statesmen of this stature, as well as the senior followers of Mosaddeq who were now being wooed, was, of course, one of the main precipitants of the prevailing crisis. Prompted by these advisers, the Shah had eventually turned to the Mosaddeqists, although there was clearly little ground for optimism that anyone who now ventured to assume the premiership could ward off the revolutionary tidal wave and salvage the monarchy. The invitation had come too late.

Having hoped to form a government that ideally had the approval of both the Shah and Khomeini, Sanjabi would eventually refuse to cooperate with the Shah. He also opposed any rapprochement between other leading Mosaddeqists and the Shah on the issue of forming a government. Yet, following several meetings with the Shah, by mid-December 1978 Gholam-Hosein Sadiqi, Mosaddeq's minister of the interior and a widely respected academic and man of integrity, agreed to consider forming a government despite overwhelming odds. In Sadiqi's view, the dangers facing the country warranted such a move on his part; he was not deterred by pressure from Sanjabi and others, whom he readily rebuffed. He did, however, put forward a number of conditions, chief among which was that the Shah abandon his plans for leaving the country. The Shah himself admitted that Sadiqi was the only political leader advising him not to leave.[18] Sadiqi believed that the Shah's departure would precipitate further paralysis and rapid disintegration of the military, with grave consequences for the country. It was likely to result in the widespread arming of militants and the outbreak of serious disorder, thereby providing opportunities for the country's enemies.[19]

By this time the Shah's position had become desperately precarious. The political situation demanded a self-assertive sovereign leadership, acting autonomously and resolutely irrespective of foreign preferences or advice. The Shah, however, seemed more than ever to rely on and need the expressed backing of the Americans and the British. His opponents portrayed such professions of support as vindicating their claims that the Shah had always been dependent on foreign powers. Sadiqi had reminded the Shah that continued public expressions of Anglo-American support were counterproductive and humiliating to the Iranians. The desperate and paranoiac Shah tended to seek clues to his likely political future in the nuances of his foreign supporters' statements. He took any indication of diminished commitment from American and British leaders to maintaining his throne as a personal blow and a betrayal. By ceaselessly consulting with and seeking the advice of American and British officials he wished to implicate them in the outcome of his actions or inaction, sharing with them the burden of responsibility for any risks taken.

Unwilling to accept Sadiqi's conditions and commit himself to remaining in Iran, in late December the Shah turned to another senior Mosaddeqist, inviting Shapur Bakhtiar, the spirited sixty-three-year-old leader of the Iran

Party, to form a government. Bakhtiar was a suave, French-educated civic-nationalist whose father, a Bakhtiari tribal chieftain, had been executed by Reza Shah. In contrast to Sadiqi, Bakhtiar was willing to try to form a government on the condition that the Shah left the country. He hoped to resurrect democratic constitutionalism; his thirty-seven-day premiership (January–February 1979), however, came too late to stem the tide of revolution.[20] Bakhtiar's willingness to form a government prompted rebukes from his National Front colleagues, particularly Sanjabi, who spearheaded his expulsion from the Front, while Sadiqi praised him for his "courage," adding, "We all have a duty to assist him."[21]

A number of royalists, including Princess Ashraf, had maintained that the only solution to the crisis was a royalist military coup and massive crackdown on the opposition. Some American officials also favored such a course of action if all else failed. However, the military was barely capable of such a task. It had served as the main instrument of sustaining the regime, but the prolonged exposure of soldiers to a situation of incipient civil war had corroded their morale; nor had the commanders remained unscathed. All vestiges of political authority and the sinews of the state's sovereign powers had been seriously undermined. Prolonged civil unrest, disobedience, disruption, violence, and the paralysis of the economy through widespread strikes had created a situation whose reversal could not be attempted except with massive counterrevolutionary violence. The outcome of such violence was incalculable and unpredictable. The Shah was unable and unwilling to condone it, and the military was incapable of carrying it through. The generals had grown increasingly disillusioned with the Shah. Confiding to U.S. Ambassador Sullivan, Azhari, who toward the end of his ill-fated premiership had suffered a heart attack, complained bitterly about the Shah's contradictory decisions and orders, and blamed the collapse of the state on the Shah's chronic indecision.[22]

The military was expected to support and sustain Bakhtiar, and also to work out a contingency plan for intervention to restore order should Bakhtiar fail. And yet the rumors of the imminent departure of the Shah had an adverse effect on the already beleaguered armed forces. Unaccustomed to obeying and reporting to anyone other than the Shah, the generals did not find it easy to submit to a civilian former opponent of the regime. Significantly, the Shah had not clarified the relationship between

Bakhtiar and the generals, confining himself to generic exhortations that they should cooperate with him. The Shah had, in fact, refused to delegate control of the military to the prime minister, a measure that both Sadiqi and Bakhtiar, as well as other moderate opponents, had demanded. In refusing to relinquish his control over the military, the Shah was encouraged by aides such as Zahedi, who had recently returned to Iran in the hope of stiffening the Shah's resolve and assisting him in retrieving the political situation. In the words of the U.S. embassy's political attaché, "Zahedi's ultimate effect was extremely pernicious. He was unable either to engineer a compromise or to unite the military to strong action, yet he disrupted the only real compromise efforts which might have brought forth a controlled transitional government."[23]

Despite severe difficulties in finding competent and untainted colleagues, Bakhtiar formed a cabinet after receiving the parliamentary "vote of inclination," redundant for over twenty-five years. The cabinet did not, however, include any well-known opposition figures, and Bakhtiar's inability to present himself as having control over the military severely vitiated his authority and credibility, particularly vis-à-vis moderate opponents. The Shah acted as though he did not trust Bakhtiar or genuinely wish him to succeed in his gargantuan task. Bakhtiar had hoped to convince the capable General Fereydun Jam—who had in 1971 been relieved of his duties as chief of the Supreme Commander's Staff and sent into political exile as ambassador to Spain—to head the military or join the cabinet as war (defense) minister. Bakhtiar's hopes were dashed, however, as the move was unwelcome to the Shah, and nor did it appeal to Jam. Indeed, until the very end the Shah tried to ensure that the military remained his exclusive domain. Without consulting Bakhtiar, he appointed General Abbas Qarabaghi as chief of the Supreme Commander's Staff. In justifying his failure to act with the full knowledge or consent of Bakhtiar, Qarabaghi maintained that the Shah had neither placed the military under Bakhtiar's control nor specified the precise relations between Bakhtiar and the military command.

Espousing a social-democratic agenda, Bakhtiar pledged, among other things, full commitment to the implementation of the Constitution, human rights, and measures against injustice and corruption; he also undertook to abolish SAVAK. Relying on his Mosaddeqist credentials and long career in opposition, he concentrated on finding ways of containing or defusing the prevailing crisis and exploring all possibilities for a negotiated settlement. He hoped to do so by persuading the opposition that his premiership marked a radical rupture with the past. He believed that the departure of the Shah would strengthen his case and free his hand. He did not need to persuade the Shah to leave, as he had already decided to do so, following the establishment of a Regency Council.

Not unexpectedly, however, Khomeini strongly denounced Bakhtiar, as did some of his former National Front colleagues. Imbued with a heightened revolutionary fervor and an enthusiastic expectation of impending victory, the whole spectrum of the opposition seemed unanimous in wishing to waste no time in toppling Bakhtiar by intensifying the violence and war of attrition against the embattled government. Although the U.S. administration supported Bakhtiar, his relations with Sullivan were uneasy; Sullivan was pessimistic about the political prospects of Bakhtiar, whom he dismissed as a "quixotic" character, and saw no possibility of Khomeini's coming to terms with him.[24] Sullivan's attitude was in conflict with the views and mission of General Robert Huyser, who arrived in Tehran on January 4, 1979, soon after Bakhtiar had assumed the premiership. Huyser maintained that he had been instructed by Carter "to make every effort to help" Bakhtiar's government.[25] He was to encourage the military to support Bakhtiar and if necessary resort to direct action to sustain him. He was also to support a military takeover if the government collapsed, and in any event help prevent the military's disintegration.[26]

The departure of the Shah for Egypt on January 16, 1979, which was widely celebrated in the streets of Iranian towns and cities, further weakened the morale of the military commanders. Some of them viewed it with stoic indifference; many treated it as an inglorious abdication of responsibility, a flight marking the beginning of the regime's end. By stopping in Egypt the Shah perhaps hoped to allay such concerns; he also hoped that his presence in the area might encourage and facilitate a coup on his behalf, an unlikely repetition of August 1953, long hoped for by aides such as Zahedi. The departure of the Shah rendered far less likely any sustained cooperation among top military commanders. The military command structure had been fashioned by the Shah in such a way as to preclude the possibility of coordinated action in his absence. The incalculable risks of drastic action, serious doubts about its efficacy, uncertainty about the support of the rank and file, together with contradictory pressures—whether threats or conciliatory promises made by Khomeini—militated against any move such as a coup.

Even though a successful coup was unlikely, the very threat of it, Bakhtiar and U.S. officials such as Zbigniew Brzezinski believed, could be used to intimidate Khomeini and provide Bakhtiar's government with a breathing space to consolidate its position. In direct or indirect contacts with Khomeini, American officials invoked the threat of a coup, maintaining that undermining Bakhtiar would provoke the military and result in widespread violence. Khomeini and his supporters resorted to counterthreats, asserting that any violence by the military would be blamed on the Americans. Meanwhile, by making conciliatory gestures toward the generals, the Khomeinists drove a wedge between them and the Bakhtiar government; at the same time, by continuing to avoid divisive issues, Khomeini maintained the momentum of popular unity. The cause of constitutional monarchy was dealt a severe blow and the Khomeini camp further emboldened when, within a week after the Shah's departure, the head of the Regency Council, the religious-minded veteran politician Sayyed Jalal al-din Tehrani, resigned his position. Having compromised with the Khomeinists, he announced that, in compliance with "public opinion" and Khomeini's edict (*fatwa*), he now considered the council to be illegal.

Despite Khomeini's reassurances regarding his commitment to moderation, democracy, social justice, and a policy of positive neutrality,[27] American officials remained uncertain about Khomeini's real objectives. They differed in their assessment of his aims and the feasibility of his ill-defined program. They disagreed about the extent to which he intended or would be able to involve himself and the clerics in the actual running of the country. Differences among U.S. officials were even sharper on the question of how the Bakhtiar government should handle the crisis. Treated with contempt by Sullivan,[28] Bakhtiar more than reciprocated. Denouncing Sullivan for incompetence and complacency, he bitterly complained about the incoherence of Carter's policy toward Iran, his lack of resolve, the squabbles and lack of coordination of U.S. officials, and the contradictory signals being sent to the Shah.[29] Bakhtiar's account is corroborated by Gary Sick, the principal presidential assistant for Iran during the revolution: "Throughout the crisis, discipline within the U.S. government had been deplorable at almost every level. Policy was constantly contradicted or undermined by leaks, unattributed comments by 'insiders' who had a particular axe to grind, and bureaucratic sniping."[30]

Though deeply angered by Sullivan's dismissal of some of his policies regarding Iran, Carter was unable to replace him in the midst of the crisis. While Huyser had been trying to rally the military to support Bakhtiar, Sullivan and his British counterpart, Parsons, dismissed the army as a paper tiger.[31] Brzezinski clearly advocated military intervention to ward off a Khomeinist victory; Sullivan, however, thought that "it was better for the military forces to step aside, let the political forces fight it out among themselves, then accept whoever won." Sullivan was optimistic that the drift of an Islamic republic would be toward democracy, while Huyser felt it would be toward the left and an eventual Communist takeover.[32]

The demeanor and resolve of the generals was hardly threatening, yet Bakhtiar continued to invoke both the prospect of a military crackdown and a Communist takeover to intimidate Khomeini's supporters and persuade them to negotiate. Unmoved by such threats, Khomeini in turn invoked the prospect of violence, chaos, and leftist ascendancy in order to deter the Americans from instigating a coup or supporting Bakhtiar.[33] Khomeini would settle for nothing less than the unconditional capitulation of Bakhtiar, who even offered to visit him in Paris for talks. Khomeini, however, demanded his prior resignation. Clearly, hard-line Khomeinists were bent on opposing and derailing all mediation efforts and conciliatory moves.[34] The death on January 26, 1979, of a number of demonstrators agitating for Khomeini's return provoked the latter to excoriate Bakhtiar as a criminal. Any possibility of negotiation was now more remote than ever.

Bakhtiar resisted the rising public clamor for Khomeini's return. The rebellion of a group of low-ranking air force officers in support of Khomeini augured ill for Bakhtiar; a proconstitutional demonstration in Parliament Square slightly bolstered him, but paled in comparison with the massive opposition crowds. In a disorienting atmosphere in which the military and SAVAK chiefs were negotiating with Bazargan, who acted on Khomeini's behalf, Bakhtiar was barely in control of the situation, yet he could not afford to appear devoid of initiative. Shifting his position, he announced on January 29 that Khomeini's return would no longer be blocked. He also abandoned a plan to divert Khomeini's plane and arrest him. It was clear that he had neither the means nor the will to thwart Khomeini any longer or to resort to drastic action against him. He hoped that upon the ayatollah's return to Iran, Khomeini's more moderate and politically perceptive supporters might prevail upon him to avoid a final showdown.

Following his triumphal return after fourteen years in exile, and a wildly enthusiastic reception from massive crowds, the seventy-seven-year-old Khomeini defiantly denounced Bakhtiar while exhorting the military to join the people. Many supporters of Khomeini had concentrated on enlisting the cooperation of the military or neutralizing it, realizing that success in either would expedite their takeover of power with little bloodshed. Moderate collaborators of Khomeini continued to work to avoid further violence and other consequences of confrontation with the military, including the looting of arms and ammunition, masterminded by left-wing groups. They also hoped to enable the military and Bakhtiar to give up without a total loss of face.

Confident of the irresistible appeal of unbending resolve, and aware of the visible cracks in the resolve of the military commanders, as well as the shaky position of Bakhtiar, Khomeini refused to relent. He appointed Bazargan as prime minister of a provisional government to work with a shadowy revolutionary council. The expedient appointment of Bazargan, long known for his civic-nationalist attachments and barely disguised opposition to the political supremacy of the clerics, was a reassuring gesture intended to allay misgivings and fears about radicalism and revolutionary vengeance.[35] By a quirk of misfortune, the two old Mosaddeqist comrades were now reluctantly plunged into a tragic confrontation that they had wished to avoid. The Speaker of the parliament attempted unsuccessfully to orchestrate a vote of no confidence against Bakhtiar's government so that Bazargan's cabinet could be voted in constitutionally. Khomeini, however, had denounced the legality of the entire edifice of the crumbling regime.

With his residual authority fast eroding, the beleaguered Bakhtiar's only hope lay with the military, which, following months of constant exposure to violent street clashes with civilians and an exhausting war of nerves, seemed deeply demoralized and on the verge of collapse. The demoralization of the commanders was compounded by desertions from the ranks, the increasing fraternization of the soldiers with demonstrators, and the growing paralysis of the political system and economic infrastructure. Nationwide strikes and the disruption of the transportation system had left the military without an adequate supply of gasoline and diesel fuel. In addition to these problems, Bakhtiar's relations with several generals, in particular Qarabaghi, had been strained. Qarabaghi had threatened to resign and had to be dissuaded by Sullivan.[36] Huyser vacillated between trusting Qarabaghi and questioning his reliability; he did, however, reassure Carter that in a crisis the military would be reliable.[37] Yet Qarabaghi's conduct remained puzzling and his commitment to the continued resistance of the army uncertain. According to U.S. sources, he had been "instrumental in opening the lines of communication with the religious forces."[38]

A number of events, including clashes between the Imperial Guards and prorevolutionary cadets in the air force supported by armed left-wing activists, revealed that fears about the possibility of the military's disintegration were not far-fetched. Several military commanders had also made overtures to or joined the opposition on their own initiative. Eventually, on the fateful morning of February 11, the twenty-seven generals attending the council of the commanders of the armed forces concluded their deliberations with a public declaration of neutrality. This move, together with the retreat of military units to their barracks—made without consulting Bakhtiar—signaled the unequivocal victory of the revolutionaries. The military's neutrality did not stop attacks against police stations, army barracks, ammunition depots, and similar facilities, in the course of which arms and ammunition were looted, particularly by the Mojahedin-e Khalq (People's Warriors) and the Fada'iyan-e Khalq (People's Devotees), armed revolutionary guerrilla groups crucially involved in bringing down the regime. A large quantity of weapons had also been handed out to the revolutionaries by mutineers in the military. The capitulation of the military abruptly ended the tortuous tenure of Bakhtiar and conclusively sealed the fate of the Pahlavi monarchy.

The collapse of the reviled monarchy was widely celebrated not only as the end of the prolonged repression that had provoked turmoil and trauma, but also as the dawn of an enticingly promising new era. Many secular opponents of the Shah viewed such celebrations as premature; they were deeply concerned about the activities of mushrooming revolutionary committees, the uncertain future course of events, the fate of secular values and forces, and, most immediately, the rule of law. The first executions—of key military commanders—started within a few days of the collapse of the monarchy, to be followed by those of members of the former political elite, opponents of the revolutionary government, and those considered as moral delinquents. Those who had only hesitantly or tactically supported Khomeini and those who had suspended their disbelief in the face of his shrewdly ambiguous but reassuring pronouncements soon found themselves disappointed. Yet Khomeinist revolutionaries continued to maintain that an era of virtue, justice, cultural authenticity, and freedom from both foreign domination and domestic oppression had indeed begun.

Bakhtiar went into hiding, eventually to reside in exile in France; he later denounced the military chiefs, particularly Qarabaghi (who also found refuge in Paris), claiming that had they not surrendered, he would have forced Khomeini to negotiate.[39] The validity of such a claim is, of course, impossible to ascertain. Qarabaghi accused Bakhtiar of anticonstitutional moves, of intending to establish a republic, and of exacerbating the prevailing crisis.[40] Like Bakhtiar, the Shah later denounced Qarabaghi, adding that his treasonous behavior prevented the military from acting against Khomeini.[41] Accusations of treason are notoriously difficult to assess, but the Shah was hardly in a position to blame others for vacillation, lack of resolve, and spineless capitulation. Moreover, he rarely showed any gratitude to those who, in his desperate moments, responded to his call. Having failed to place Bakhtiar in charge of the military forces, the Shah undeniably contributed to his failure. He also later characteristically commented that he had agreed to appoint Bakhtiar as prime minister only reluctantly and under foreign pressure.[42]

# 6

# The Edifice and Emplacements of Royal Rule

## The Domestic Constellations of Support

Spanning fifty-three years, the Pahlavi dynasty was, compared with its predecessor, short-lived. Reza Shah entered the political scene through a coup d'état, remained a military man comfortable only in uniform, and relied primarily on the army and the police to maintain his hold on power. Having received some early military training in Iran in addition to secondary education in Switzerland, Mohammad Reza Shah was equally at ease in a uniform or civilian dress. He too cultivated and relied on the military and the police, but also more clearly on foreign support, entrenching himself through a coup launched on his behalf. The Pahlavi monarchy failed to develop a solid social basis of power; it did not rely on a dependable "aristocracy" of blood or even service, and its sociopolitical legitimacy remained tenuous. Nevertheless, by cultivating a large political clientele, carefully controlling the distribution of political spoils, rewarding loyalty, and elevating proven royalists, the Pahlavi clan ensured itself a strategic position at the apex of the upper class. The Shah's power was thus not without its domestic roots. Moreover, to its privileged supporters a powerful monarchy represented stability, continuity with the past, maintenance of the existing order, and territorial integrity, as well as opposition to radical ideologies.

Those who had opposed Mosaddeq, including much of the clerical establishment, had contributed to the Shah's resumption of power. For some time following the coup of 1953, the Shah felt obliged to defer to or at least not ignore the demands and expectations of the landowning and mercantile notables as well as senior clerics who had bolstered him against his left-wing and civic-nationalist opponents. Yet he resented any mention of his indebtedness to such forces, whom he increasingly saw as opposed to his reformist objectives and autocratic drive. The Shah's attitude to the elite and to the people in general had been deeply affected by the experience of August 1953. Although the coup was celebrated annually as a "national uprising" and the Shah often referred to as an "elected monarch," he grew increasingly wary, distrustful, and dismissive of the people and of public opinion. This attitude was shared by many royalists, who disparaged as a demagogue anyone who expressed other views. The Shah was at the same time determined to ensure that no one would be allowed to acquire a popularity, prestige, and authority comparable to Mosaddeq's. Elections would be closely controlled to prevent the success of "undesirable" candidates. A host of statesmen, chiefly Mosaddeqists but also other constitutionalists, were thus effectively barred from political participation. Despising "negation mongers," by which he usually meant the Mosaddeqists, the Shah also became increasingly impatient with moderate well-wishers who hoped to restrain his conspicuous authoritarianism.

Before the land reform of the early 1960s, the upper class traditionally consisted of urban notables, including extended wealthy landowning families, high-ranking civil servants, big merchants, and tribal-regional magnates, drawn together by ties of kinship, convivial links, and shared interests and perceptions.[1] Relying on lineage, renown, and wealth, they enjoyed their own sources of support; they cooperated with the state but also attempted to exert a controlling influence over it; they endeavored to use the residual authority of the parliament to check the royal power. The post–land reform era marked the growing autonomy of the state. The last remnants of tribal opposition were rooted out. Landowners, the Mosaddeqists, the traditional left, as well as the clerical establishment, were conflated and castigated as forces of reaction opposed to the development measures championed by the Shah. Development, the Shah and his royalist supporters believed, would render the regime's opponents redundant.

The political predominance of the Shah accelerated a rift between the regime and its traditional supporters, whether veteran notables or senior clerics. The disillusioned and alienated traditional elite neither readily accepted abandoning their own bases of power nor welcomed the Shah's alarmingly autocratic role. Yet, unable to mount a sustained counterchallenge, they were increasingly marginalized. The traditional class of landowner politicians gave way to a new elite that had no real power base other than royal patronage. To their chagrin, the influential notable families were no longer able to restrain the Shah, particularly as he displayed ever-increasing conspicuous contempt for the traditional modalities of political conduct. Such modalities were rooted in a conception of politics as an intricate system of negotiation, recognized reciprocity, consultation, bargaining, and brokerage, involving influential clusters of notables able to maintain a fragile balance of power among themselves. The Shah also increasingly shunned elder statesmen; there were many such figures who enjoyed unassailable reputations and were highly competent. Nonetheless, as a class concerned with safeguarding its vested interests, the traditional notables could scarcely offer a viable approach to the pressing problems of Iranian society and politics. Their predominant values and modes of conduct were not readily congenial with political equality and other requirements of a modern representative and reformist political system. They were, however, analogous to what thinkers such as Hannah Arendt and José Ortega y Gasset have described as "ancient political classes," a kind of aristocracy whose disappearance or marginalization expedited the decline of politics to the banausic and even the banal, and created a political void that would end in the rise of a malleable mass society.

The elite that gradually replaced the notables was attuned to the exigencies of the new era and unwilling or unable to question the focal role of the Shah. Lending itself to thorough domestication, it embraced and facilitated the decline of politics into mere routinized administration. It gradually transformed itself into a quasi-aristocratic entity differentiated from the old notables by its technocratic qualifications and claimed managerial skills. The percentage of cabinet ministers with degrees in economics and technical and scientific subjects had been on the rise since the early 1960s, in con-

trast to earlier ministers, who tended to have backgrounds in law and related subjects.[2] The new elite presented itself as technocratically competent
to devise and implement development projects, which would be credited to
the Shah. It endeavored to ensure that by producing tangible public benefits, by addressing undeniable socioeconomic problems, royal autocracy—
masquerading as benevolently public-minded leadership—would be seen as
politically efficacious and conducive to the common good. Benevolent autocracy, it was believed, would be accepted because it worked and produced
results, in contrast to the ineffective and nonviable old-fashioned constitutionalism.

Members of the new elite were mostly Western-educated; graduates of
American universities were increasing in number; nevertheless, between
1963 and 1979, 36 percent of ministers were French-educated compared with
26 percent who had received their degrees in the United States.[3] Ministers
and other members of the new elite came from privileged backgrounds;
they had close kin and other social ties with the old elite but differed from
them in political and cultural orientation. Customarily mindful of the time-
honored etiquettes and civic norms of public conduct, the old elite was
generally well-versed in traditional Iranian cultural and literary values. Unconcerned with, if not dismissive of, those norms and values, the new elite
often displayed a shallow grasp of Iranian culture and boasted instead of its
Western technical-professional expertise. In line with the Shah's views, as
well as the views of many influential Americans concerned with Iran, the
new elite sought to increase the viability of Iranian socioeconomic and political structures and to broaden the social basis of Iranian politics by appealing to peasants and workers, and especially to the growing middle class.
By attempting to win over the middle class in particular, the new elite
hoped to overshadow and undermine the Mosaddeqists; but it remained severely handicapped in this regard. The royalist elite was unable to address
and respond to the political aspirations of the disenfranchised public, particularly the middle class, who continued to be drawn to the values and practices advocated by supporters of Mosaddeq.

The network of notable families did not of course disappear; adept at
coping with changes in the political milieu, the old notables maintained
links with the court and their presence in the diplomatic corps; they continued to serve in the upper echelons of the civil service. Through ties of mar-

riage they conferred prestige upon members of the new elite while facilitating their own access to the nexus of power and safeguarding their material and symbolic advantages. Though not averse to co-opting the old notables, the Shah was, however, determined to extirpate their political culture and influence. He did not hesitate to discard or marginalize those members of the traditional political elite who for whatever reason, including a sense of pride or dignity, disbelief in the Shah's leadership qualities or concern for the country and its direction, found it difficult to condone royal autocracy. As a result, all statesmen, even loyal but principled monarchists, who might have had the temerity to disagree with the Shah, tell him unpalatable truths, and lend a degree of public credibility to the regime were eliminated in favor of a service nomenklatura consisting largely of obedient, opportunistic, and self-seeking sycophants who, in the interest of retaining their positions, increasingly came to tell the Shah only what he wanted to hear.

The emerging new elite was both dependent on the Shah and sustained him. Embedded in a complex nexus of connivance, its chief task was to reaffirm the focal role of the Shah not only as inevitable, given the political circumstances of the country, but also as politically desirable and conducive to tangible public benefits. It continued to take for granted and act upon the undeclared but fully operative central premise of the regime—that old-style constitutionalism had reached an impasse and was irretrievable. Increasingly aloof from Iranian society, the new elite, in its reckless and outlandish conduct and self-confident modernizing drive, proved insensitive to the democratic aspirations of the urban population and to the sensibilities of its pious or traditional segments. The new elite enabled the Shah to play the roles of chief decisionmaker, leader, and archmanipulator of the elite more effectively than ever. Anyone aspiring to high office needed his blessing. Even those officials who resented his style of rule continued to serve the regime and often did so obsequiously. In the interest of retaining their positions, members of the new elite increasingly vied with one another in ingratiating themselves with the Shah.

## Cronyism and Complicity

Under both Pahlavi rulers, but particularly during the reign of Mohammad Reza Shah and at the height of his power in the 1960s and 1970s, the Pahlavi court became the nerve center of the Iranian state. An enclave of privilege sustained by a battery of loyal servants, the court was also a theater of deference and duplicity, intrigue and neuroses, conformity and eccentricity. It nurtured a culture of deception and pretension, connivance and collusion, hierarchy and dependency. It was an arena of carnivalesque sycophancy, opportunism, cronyism, and supplication. The Shah received his obeisant and dispensable officials in an atmosphere of contrived rituals and elaborate ceremonials. No one was left in any doubt that his or her political fortune and destiny depended on the Shah's whims. Access to the Shah, parsimoniously controlled by veteran courtiers such as Alam, was the most highly sought-after prize and privilege. The most intractable of problems could be resolved through such access. The influence peddling of even minor courtiers was often staggering. The court was a vast political and bureaucratic complex dedicated to promoting the vested interests of the Pahlavi clan. It was the chief dispenser of patronage, the epicenter of lucrative brokerage, the matrix of powerful alliances. Access to the material or symbolic largess dispensed by the court required the blessing of the Shah and the Pahlavi clan, but not necessarily direct access to the progressively aloof and secluded Shah. A few may have believed that they had the Shah's ear; he did grant audiences but increasingly made a point of candidly indicating that he was above listening to or consulting any Iranian.

The court bureaucracy was greatly extended under Alam, with his many deputies and subordinates, as well as the Shah's large number of civilian and military adjutants and retainers. Combining the seemingly sublime with the vulgar, merciless intrigue with excessive decorum, the court under Mohammad Reza Shah to some extent underwent what Norbert Elias has described as the transmutation of violence into etiquette.[4] Yet the veneer of sophistication and civility remained thin, and crudeness and violence, actual or threatened, were never far from the surface. Etiquette in turn degenerated into sycophantic obeisance, which became an institutionalized rite of passage to career advancement. The extent of the royal penchant for, if not addiction to, flattery alarmed the Shah's twin sister, Princess Ashraf, as well as Queen Farah, who complained that everyone was unctuous even toward the Shah's dog.[5] Realizing how appealing it was to the Shah, many foreign officials, even leaders, also treated him with unusual deference and lavished him with praise.

The court or the inner circle of the elite increasingly repelled self-respecting men of principle and candor, who had long come to believe that attempting to influence the Shah was an exercise in futility and humiliation. Averse to capable independent-minded statesmen, the Shah forced them out of active political life; he then invoked the absence of such statesmen to justify his own preponderant political role. Unhesitant in banishing any politician worth consulting, the Shah would often disingenuously bemoan the absence of anyone to consult. He sought only the services of yes-men, whom he then derided for being yes-men. Any official seen as too successful in his position would be moved to another post; none would be allowed to become in any sense indispensable. Indispensability was solely a royal entitlement. Relentlessly stimulating rivalry among key government officials, the Shah used them purely instrumentally. His manipulative and contemptuous treatment of his subordinates was in turn privately reciprocated within the ruling class. Consequently, the Shah became an irredeemably friendless figure surrounded by obsequious cronies. By the mid-1970s Alam believed that, blissfully unaware, the Shah was habitually lied to and surrounded by a group of treacherous people.[6] Yet the Shah remained confident that the reports he received were accurate and truthful.[7] Toward the end of his reign he came to realize the disastrous consequences of lacking devoted and dependable support, but failed to recognize or admit that his own conduct was primarily to blame. When the Shah desperately needed sound advice, few were left to provide it.

The ruling elite that gradually emerged in the years after 1953, and particularly after the White Revolution, became essentially an extended entourage of the Shah. It was not devoid of factionalism, ideological rifts, and other divisions. Besides loyalty to the Shah, its success in status advancement depended on which clusters of influence its various segments were affiliated with. Political survival required a flair for unraveling the hidden intentions of rivals, and timely preemptive moves. It depended above all on retaining royal favor. The elite saw its vested interests as best served by ingratiating itself to the Shah and by demonstrating its desire to assist him in consolidating and perpetuating his autocratic rule and rearranging the contours of Iranian politics. The Shah's success in doing so depended on the conformity and complicity of his subordinates. Although the Shah viewed himself as above any power and treated all his subordinates as dispensable, and although he alone conferred favor and honors, he and the elite were mutually dependent. Arbitrary rule had clear limits in terms of both the domestic and external factors affecting it. The Shah set the rules of the political game but he was also constrained by them. His absolute power was a myth conveniently invoked by a conniving elite to justify its lucrative compliance. The very politicians who were turned into mute personal retainers were themselves complicit in their subordination.

There was, of course, no doubt that those who wavered in their unquestioning loyalty would be discarded or marginalized irrespectively of how crucial a position they occupied. Those who appeared steadily loyal were allowed to acquire and retain key positions of power, again often irrespectively of merit or capability. Regardless of what they felt privately, the inner circle of the elite appeared unhesitatingly dedicated to following the royal lead and fully convinced of the wisdom of their conduct. Without their servility and adulation, the Shah, possessed of a fragile ego, would not have been able to achieve the degree of misplaced, unjustified, and dangerous self-confidence and self-righteousness that he did. Yet beneath the surface of unreserved deference, few seemed genuinely to believe in what they were engaged in; if the opportunity arose, the ostensibly servile supporters in the parliament and the press turned into vociferous critics. The cynicism that lay at the root of servility was either not fully perceived by the Shah, or he felt there was no alternative to it. The duplicity endemic to the regime undoubtedly contributed to the Shah's disdainful treatment of his subordinates, including men who had served sincerely but had also spoken their minds, such as Ala, Entezam, Ebtehaj, and Arsanjani.

In 1964, in a revealing report, Martin Herz, the U.S. embassy counselor for political affairs, remarked on the serious problems facing a regime that had "so few convinced supporters." Evidence of this state of affairs was apparent

at every turn: Prominent members of the New Iran Party who express the belief, quietly and privately, that their party is a sham and a fraud and that no political party can be expected to do useful work as long as the Shah's heavy hand rests on the decision-making process; handpicked Majlis members who deplore "American support" for a regime which they term a travesty of democracy; Civil Adjutants of the Shah, who belong to his most devoted supporters, yet who express the belief that Iran will never be able to solve its problems as long as there is no freedom of expression, no delegation of authority, and so little selection of personnel for merit; prominent judges who declare, with surprising lack of circumspection, that the anti-corruption campaign cannot get anywhere as long as it is known that certain people are immune from prosecution; military officers who tip off the National Front regarding actions planned against its demonstrators; Foreign Ministry officials who privately advise against courses of action they are officially urging on the U.S. with respect to the treatment of opposition spokesmen in the United States. These are *not* members of the opposition. They are members of the Establishment who, even while loyal to the Shah, are suffering from a profound malaise, from lack of conviction in what they are doing, from doubts whether the regime deserves to endure.[8]

Undoubtedly there were officials who were apprehensive about the consequences of many aspects of the Shah's conduct. They commended his objective of wishing to lead the country toward greater prosperity but doubted the wisdom of many of his policies, approaches, and tactics, and the competence and credibility of the key personnel on whom he relied. There were many who regretted the discrediting of all constitutional procedures and feared for the country's future. Nevertheless, for whatever reason, they eschewed airing their concerns publicly. To this extent they shared responsibility for what later befell the country. Throughout most of Reza Shah's rule, ministers and other high-ranking civilian and military personnel legitimately feared for their lives. In an atmosphere permeated by fear, when a move misinterpreted by Reza Shah could result in death, high-ranking officials could not easily extricate themselves from the regime or resign without inviting serious retribution. The situation under Mohammad Reza Shah was different. Officials did fear incurring the Shah's displeasure, which might lead to the reversal of their political and material fortunes. The lives of high-ranking officials were in many respects closely controlled. For instance, all high-ranking officials, including the retired, were required or expected to seek royal permission to travel abroad; but this situation also often entitled them to the perquisites of a diplomatic passport. Openly turning one's back on the regime or a politically loaded resignation was undoubtedly risky but did not result in death. Such moves could even on occasion earn the resigning official public acclaim.

Although the Shah's more immediate entourage appeared dedicated to his vision, for many years it revealed no serious commitment to reform, which had become the regime's chief ideological leitmotif. In 1964 the U.S. embassy described the inner circle as being "almost completely devoid of genuinely dedicated reformists."[9] Nor was it likely to lend credence to the regime's anticorruption propaganda. Two key members of the royal entourage who were considered reputable—Ala, the veteran court minister and prime minister, and Sharif-Emami, former prime minister and later president of the senate—readily used their political links for material gain. Ala had long complained about the conduct of the Shah's sisters, and particularly of his mother, whose protégés he described as "all corrupt."[10] In the aftermath of the coup of 1953, Ala advocated measures aimed at restraining the Pahlavi clan and improving the court's image.[11] Failing in his efforts, he was forced into servility but remained in the Shah's service, as it ensured him his considerable wealth. Ala was involved in a number of business activities; among others, Habib Sabet, the wealthy businessman and an influential member of the Baha'i community in the country, enjoyed "very close financial connections" with Ala and his wife.[12] Sharif-Emami also had extensive business links, including financial arrangements with Princess Ashraf. By joining the Freemasons in the early 1960s, he further enhanced his political and business connections and the opportunity to forge closer ties with the Shah. On the Shah's instructions, he created the Iran Lodge, incorporating some eighteen existing lodges linked to Masonic lodges abroad,[13] thereby severing their outside links and bringing them under effective royal control. As "grand master," Sharif-Emami was instrumental in placing Freemasonry in the service of the Shah, and also making it a more lucrative network, both politically and financially.

Other prominent members of the royal entourage were distinguished mainly by their loyalty. They included General Motreza Yazdanpanah[14]—who had also dutifully served Reza Shah and subsequently held many influential positions, including heading the Royal Inspectorate—and Ardeshir Zahedi, son of the former prime minister, an active player in the coup of 1953, and the Shah's son-in-law from 1957 to 1964. Zahedi served in the key positions of ambassador to Britain and the United States, as well as foreign

*Foreign Minister Ardeshir Zahedi (1966–1971) initiating the practice of kneeling to kiss the Shah's hand, after the fashion of the court of Louis XIV.* (Courtesy of the Institute for the Study of Contemporary Iranian History, Tehran)

minister. Like Alam, Zahedi was devoted to the Shah; he had a reputation of being uncouth and intellectually shallow but far more candid than most other royal servants. He was, in the words of a former Iranian diplomat, "fair-minded, fearless, effective, free from complexes, and supportive of his subordinates."[15] Chronically acrimonious relations with Hoveyda eventually led the Shah to remove Zahedi as foreign minister and to dispatch him as ambassador to the United States, where, relying on the abundant financial resources available to him, he concentrated on winning friends in the highest places, including the White House, through lavish gifts and parties.

Others closely linked to the court included the Rashidian brothers, influential businessmen with extensive investments in banking and land development, veteran political brokers, skilled fixers linked to Britain, and deeply involved in the activities that had led to the coup of August 1953. Their political and business influence extended even over the Tehran taxi drivers' cooperative. There were also court bureaucrats, including Soleiman Behbudi, who had served the Pahlavis since the beginning of the dynasty. He was

*Influential political brokers in a traditional gymnasium (zurkhaneh) in Tehran in
the 1950s. From the right, in suits: Mohammad Ali Mas'udi, a parliamentarian and
expert in election rigging; General Teymur Bakhtiar, military governor of Tehran
and later chief of SAVAK; and Asadollah Rashidian, a wealthy businessman-
politician who, together with his brothers, collaborated with British intelligence
in the coup of 1953. Members of the zurkhaneh were often used by such figures
for political purposes.* (Courtesy of the Institute for the Study of Contemporary
Iranian History, Tehran)

identified by the CIA in the early 1950s as a British agent.[16] Another notable
courtier was General Abdolkarim Ayadi, the Shah's personal physician, who
had vast business interests and wielded enormous influence, considered inordinate even by Alam.[17] A CIA report described Ayadi as apparently "the
major channel through which the Shah dabbles in financial affairs." It added
that "Ayadi, a Baha'i, is credited by one observer with being one of those
who protect the sect against persecution by the more fanatical Iranian Mos-

lems."[18] He was instrumental in helping the rapid rise in fortune of his coreligionist Hozhabr Yazdani, an upstart businessman.[19] These and a host of other confidants, advisers, bureaucrats, and relatives constituting the royal entourage could not, as the U.S. embassy correctly observed, be relied upon to be truthful in what they reported to the Shah.[20]

The military members of the entourage were no more likely to depict a veracious picture of the country's situation. The Shah's security advisers included Generals Hasan Pakravan, Hosein Fardust, and Ne'matollah Nasiri. Prominent among his military advisers was General Amir-Mohammad Khatami, the Shah's brother-in-law and his American-trained private pilot since 1946, who had flown the Shah and his wife to Baghdad during the coup of August 1953. Appointed commander of the air force in 1957, Khatami wielded considerable influence among the royal entourage until his mysterious death in a gliding accident in September 1975. The Shah treated Khatami's death with apparent indifference and revealed secrets about him to Alam that the latter found too sensitive to record in his diaries.[21] Khatami had been shunned by the Shah for some months before his death, a circumstance that may have led him to take his life; or he may have been killed by SAVAK. The Americans had viewed him, probably without his knowledge, as a capable pro-U.S. officer likely to play a crucial role in the event of the Shah's death, and a probable leader in such a contingency. Joseph Farland, the U.S. ambassador, had, for instance, reported in 1973 that if Queen Farah should have to face the task of ruling as regent, she would need "supporters and/or protectors. One such could be [Khatami] who is ambitious, clever, and reportedly corrupt . . . and would be likely to rule Iran through Farah."[22] Somehow learning about American views of Khatami's possible political role may have led the Shah to suspect him of involvement in a plot. Khatami's death removed a capable officer from the political scene. Believing that his wealth amounted to some $100 million, the Shah for some time contemplated confiscating it.

Another influential figure among the Shah's military advisers was General Fereydun Jam, son of a former prime minister and the Shah's former brother-in-law. Jam became chief of the Supreme Commander's Staff in the late 1960s, but his independence of mind resulted in his dismissal in July 1971. Officers such as Jam and Pakravan differed from others, in terms of both caliber and conviction, but as the U.S. embassy justifiably concluded as

early as 1964, "All in all the group of military officers having regular and frequent contact [with the Shah] seem most likely to tell the monarch what
they assess he wants to hear rather than what they may honestly believe he
should be told."[23] The composition of the royal entourage changed over the
years, but all its members grew ever less able to act assertively or conscien-
tiously.

At the core of the court stood the Pahlavi clan, an extended nexus of kin
and a source of irritation to the Shah. He often resented his family members and on more than one occasion described them as "moronic" *(khol)*,[24]
and yet he made no serious or timely attempt to control them. All the
Shah's relatives pursued their own ambitions, often without regard to how
their activities affected the royal image. Princess Shams, his eldest sister, had
become a devout Catholic, living in luxury but, to the Shah's satisfaction
and unlike the flamboyant Ashraf, unconcerned with politics. Farah's
mother, Farideh Diba, pretended to be an ascetic but constantly asked for
favors, from luxury cars to honorific titles. The Shah mocked her but gave
in to many of her demands, as he needed her help in restraining Farah's objections to his ceaseless philandering. Too accommodating an attitude to
Farideh would, he confessed to Alam, have provoked his own mother.[25] The
court was the setting for the vicious but also burlesque intrigues of the
Shah's many relatives, a stage for farce and melodrama; the royal family was
far from a model family.

Influential members of the Pahlavi clan included the Shah's brothers,
particularly Prince Abd al-Reza; the Shah's mother, Taj al-Moluk (Reza
Shah's second and most influential of four wives); Shams; Farah; and, most
significantly, his twin sister, Ashraf. From the outset of the Shah's reign,
Ashraf played a key political role; resolute and impetuous, she worked to invigorate the Shah and to undermine his opponents. Exiled by Mosaddeq,
she took an active part in securing his overthrow and upon returning to the
country resumed the unbridled pursuit of her political ambitions and personal pleasures. She was connected with a host of officials, civilian and military, who were widely regarded as being corrupt. Her activities negated
much of the regime's anticorruption rhetoric. For instance, in the early autumn of 1958 she was detected smuggling currency across the French fron-
tier; this much-publicized incident resulted in her "open disgrace."[26] Yet, according to a U.S. embassy report, "despite the constant talk and occasional

direct complaints to the Shah, no one dares act against Ashraf as long as the Shah refuses to acknowledge her wrongdoing."[27] According to another report, Ashraf's "palace intrigues with Queen Mother against all three of the Shah's wives and against her half-brother Abdorreza were once notorious, but during the decade of the sixties, as the Shah found himself and grew in confidence, he curtailed her political and personal activities which had helped to besmirch the Pahlavi name."[28] But the Shah's success in restraining Ashraf remained limited.

A chief promoter of cronyism, at various stages in her life Ashraf patronized a coterie of aspiring men, some of whom were able to assume key positions in Iranian politics, among them Prime Ministers Hazhir and Razmara. Her protégés were often immune from challenge by powerful figures such as Alam, who was critical of Ashraf's flagrant profiteering. The Rashidians were among her closest friends. Mehdi Pirasteh, a staunch royalist, not only owed his parliamentary seat in the 1950 elections to Ashraf, but in the summer of 1958 became deputy interior minister on her recommendation and without the interior minister's knowledge.[29] The U.S. embassy identified Parviz Radji, a principal adviser to Hoveyda and Iran's last ambassador to Britain under the monarchy, as a "clever 'graduate' of Ashraf's stable of young men."[30] Ashraf continued to engage in high-profile activities on behalf of the regime, headed diplomatic and international missions, several times led the Iranian delegation at the United Nations and chaired the UN Human Rights Commission. Relying on funds from the Pahlavi Foundation, she competed with Farah in promoting charitable and development activities, and supported entities such as the Imperial Organization for Social Services and the Iranian Women's Organization. Her charitable activities did little, however, to improve her image. Upon hearing of Ashraf's intention to establish her own charitable foundation, the enraged Shah told Alam that "the Iranian people will not be fooled" by such pretensions.[31] The life style and activities of Ashraf and her son, Shahram, remained an "embarrassment to the Pahlavi dynasty."[32]

A staunch rival of Farah, whose prominence had increased considerably after her crowning as empress and designation as regent, Ashraf was considered by the U.S. embassy an impediment to a stable succession.[33] She could muster far more support than Farah among key officials, including Hoveyda and the chief of SAVAK. There were many people personally be-

holden to Ashraf, such as Ali Reza'i, a wealthy industrialist, whom she protected "when he was accused of huge corrupt land transaction in
Khuzistan."[34] In contrast to Ashraf, Farah had built no real coterie of influential protégés. She had her own assistants and advisers who were liked by
neither the Shah nor Alam.[35] Alam was convinced that Hoveyda had bought
all her retinue and some of her servants, and viewed this as a dangerous development.[36] Similarly, the American embassy reported that her secretariat
seemed not fully under her control. Karim-Pasha Bahadori, chief of Farah's
personal office, led "a group of courtiers said to have been placed under
Farah by Hoveyda and Ashraf more to keep watch over the Queen and control the flow of information to her than to assist her in her duties."[37]

Unlike her two predecessors, Fawziyya (daughter of a former king of
Egypt) and Sorayya Esfandiari, Farah had married the Shah when he was
more politically involved and consequential than ever before. Also, unlike
the other two, she bore him a son and heir and took her political tasks more
seriously. Assuming a more active role, particularly after 1967, Farah toured
provinces and engaged in the promotion of philanthropic and cultural
causes. "Farah," observed the U.S. embassy, "is the beneficiary of a carefully
orchestrated program of image making."[38] Though not free from extravagance in her life style and tastes, she was, according to another embassy report, "genuinely popular among the Iranian people, the only member of
the Pahlavi family who could make such a claim."[39] She feared that the activities of the Shah's sisters and relatives might endanger the succession of
the crown prince.[40] She also tried to exert a moderating influence on the
Shah and to curb aspects of his conduct that she considered politically damaging. Alam praised her as a factor militating against "corruption of power"
and for raising issues that no one else dared broach.[41] But her attempts to
counter the distorted picture the Shah was given of political realities often
seemed only to arouse his irritation.

Undoubtedly some courtiers, personal friends, and individuals with
known or putative links with Anglo-American diplomatic or intelligence circles were tacitly able to sway the Shah. Yet ordinarily, few among the high-
ranking civilian and military personnel who were considered members of
his inner circle appeared to be in a position to influence him. These formal
or informal confidants included Eqbal (the former prime minister and director of the NIOC since October 1963), Hoveyda, and key ministers such as

Amuzgar and Ansari. Also in this category were the well-connected Swiss-educated lawyer and Tehran's official prayer leader Hasan Emami (Emam-e Jom'eh), a handful of parliamentarians, and military and security chiefs. The most notable in the latter group was the unpretentious and elusive General Fardust, a former classmate of the Shah, deputy director of SAVAK from 1962 to 1973, head of the Royal Inspectorate, chief of the Shah's Special Intelligence Office, and his devoted servant and security adviser. The daunting task of attempting to influence the Shah significantly was, however, performed primarily by Farah, who was in competition with Ashraf and Alam, all three pursuing different, often conflicting, agendas.[42]

Alam was the only Iranian man who could disagree with the Shah with impunity. Scion of an old royalist, patrician family, Alam had from the outset of his political career enlisted the favor of the Shah, dedicating himself to serving him. In his typical manner, the Shah appointed Alam court minister without consulting him.[43] A self-proclaimed slave-servant *(gholam)* of the Shah, as court minister Alam relied on his large and carefully cultivated clientele, his knowledge of Persian poetry and anecdotes, as well as common sense, experience, and guile, to don a mantle analogous to that of a medieval chief minister *(vizier)* and a court chamberlain *(hajeb)*. If his diaries are in every respect to be trusted, he served as a selfless and devoted adviser to the Shah, often candid in expressing his views when he believed the Shah was wrongly informed or was treading a wrong course. Alam's influence as court minister far surpassed that of the prime minister and was even envied by Farah. He described himself as second only to Farah—albeit far behind her—in being able to tell the Shah "everything."[44]

Though suffering from leukemia since 1968, Alam continued to work energetically in running the court. He took no step without royal permission, but jealously controlled the much-sought-after access to the Shah, whom he saw daily. His formal and informal tasks were numerous and included tackling problems resulting from the activities of members of the Pahlavi clan, especially Ashraf and the Shah's unsavory cronies; overseeing the purchase of arms; managing various official celebrations; liaising with high-ranking foreign dignitaries and ambassadors of key countries on the Shah's behalf; cooperating with the Israelis to improve Iran's public image in the United States; and supervising the security of the Shah's foreign trips. He combined the roles of a reliable friend, an obedient servant, an exalted pimp, an

*Court officials, headed by Court Minister Asadollah Alam (seen kissing the Shah's hand), in an audience with the Shah.* (Courtesy of the Institute for the Study of Contemporary Iranian History, Tehran)

unctuous jester, and an efficient functionary who did his utmost to cater for all royal needs and fancies.[45] A cultivated opportunist, he sponsored extravagant projects and events to please the Shah, heaped lavish praise on him, viewed him as no less than Napoleon, called him a "true ayatollah and ascetic *(darvish),*" and equated him with Iran itself.[46] By way of praise, Alam considered the statement "L'état c'est moi" as wholly applicable to both the Shah and his father, who were the very "embodiments or manifestations" of Iran, a view with which the Shah fully concurred.[47]

Devoid of the personal ambition that might alarm the Shah, Alam was devoted to him until the end of his life; he remained unaware of the gravity of the Shah's illness, nor did he for many years realize the seriousness of his own disease. Though aware of his dispensability and unwavering in his dedication to the Shah, Alam was often cunningly successful in influencing or manipulating him. He also readily lent himself to being used by the Shah to counterbalance other key officials. Through a mixture of persuasion, manipulation, submission, and firmness, he was entirely successful in neutral-

izing rivals. Many of those seeking redress, protection, employment, and
other favors appealed to him; the highest-ranking officials, including the
prime minister, when needing to convey an important message to the Shah
came to Alam. Those who lost in the elections of 1975, his own relatives,
and people from the region of his birth constantly besieged him for favors.[48]
He relished his unique position and enjoyed its numerous perquisites;
wealthy to begin with, he used his position to enrich himself further and to
reward his friends and protégés, placing them in key positions. These
protégés included Mohammad Baheri, a law professor who became Alam's
chief deputy; and Nosratollah Mo'inian, a former journalist and civil servant who was in 1966 appointed the Shah's private secretary.

Alam was one of those associates of the Shah who contributed immensely to the consolidation of autocracy. His very position and role as the
second most powerful man in the country, accountable to no one other
than the Shah, both signified and reinforced the prevailing structure of
domination. Though deploring the Shah's liking for flattery he was himself
a master flatterer. He complacently believed that the regime had vanquished the clerics. He shared the Shah's proclivity for dismissing as demagogic most efforts in Iran and elsewhere aimed at winning public support.[49]
Yet he often, if rather flippantly, lamented the absence and extolled the virtues of a measure of popular participation and democracy.[50] He regretted
the fact that the Shah arrogated not only policymaking but also thinking
about politics and the national interest entirely to himself. As early as 1973,
he had compared Iran to Iraq before its 1958 revolution.[51] Primarily blaming
Hoveyda, Alam lamented the regime's treatment of the people. In telling
the Shah of the rift between the people and the regime, Alam felt thwarted
by the Shah's inattention and the zeal of others to present only a reassuring
picture of the political situation. His worsening illness led the Shah in early
August 1977 to ask for his resignation; to his horror and disbelief he saw
Hoveyda appointed as his successor. Alam had increasingly come to fear a
sudden implosion of the regime. Long dismayed at the Shah's growing un-
responsiveness to advice, in March 1978, just before his death, he warned
the Shah of the likelihood of a widening crisis, but was dismissed as having
lost his mind.[52] Though not a man of exceptional intellect or force of character, he revealed greater spirit and a sounder grasp of what was politically
sensible or prudent than other high-ranking royal servants such as Hoveyda

and most of his colleagues, whom by 1976 Alam had come to castigate as traitors.

In many respects, Alam was temperamentally more in tune with the old notables while Hoveyda was an archetypal exponent of the new elite. As premier and a key member of the Shah's entourage, Hoveyda occupied an extensive space of formal and informal decisionmaking effectively vacated by the Shah, who was increasingly unable to pay attention to the myriad issues involved in governing a complex society like Iran. Politicians such as Hoveyda were, however, always able to invoke the ultimate royal authority in order to downplay their own responsibility as no more than mere functionaries in the routinized, predictable and banausic administrative machinery exclusively controlled by the Shah. They, or their apologists, implied that their removal from office would make little real difference while their continued political role partially constrained the regime's more overbearing conduct. Neither these politicians nor indeed any reasonably intelligent member of the elite's inner circle could fail to recognize the Shah's evident failings and follies; none, however, wavered in pandering to his vanities and paying obsequious homage to his "farsighted" leadership. The elite's opportunism or self-deception and the Shah's self-righteousness reinforced each other at the expense of any residual public confidence in the regime. The extent of the elite's conspicuous endeavors to affirm the Shah's belief in the soundness of his convictions and his self-image of sagacity baffled the public and exacerbated their cynicism and alienation. In the eyes of discerning citizens, the behavior of the elite, if sincere, revealed an alarming failure of judgment, and if insincere, indicated repulsive cynical opportunism.

After his final departure from Iran, the Shah reportedly complained to President Anwar Sadat of Egypt that his advisers had created a rift between him and the people; true to character, he ignored the fact that he had personally selected these advisers. At the height of his rule, the Shah almost single-handedly controlled the apex of a vast and complex political-administrative nexus, making key policy decisions and issuing all important orders. Matters of significance were dutifully referred to him and implemented by unquestioning and seemingly dedicated officials. Yet the byzantine edifice of rule that he had crafted, together with the paranoia that such a system and his own traits of character generated, meant that the Shah barely trusted and had scant regard for any of his servants. He demanded from them unswerving loyalty without any reciprocation. In his monologic "conversations" with government officials, he gave orders without seeking their opinions or granting them an opportunity to air their real views without fear of retribution. They did, however, provide, at the very least, the tacit contours, attitudinal ambience, and data and information needed for royal decisions while mindful of furthering their own agendas. The Shah had come to expect the implementation of his decisions by an acquiescent officialdom, which in carrying out his orders practiced political dissimulation as compulsively as it shunned the ethic of bureaucratic rationality.

The Shah, the elite, and their critics and opponents all strongly maintained that they loved the country and wished to see it prosper. The Shah and his opponents, however, readily impugned each other's patriotism; they disagreed fundamentally about what was in the interests of the public and the nation, who was best qualified to determine and promote such interests, and what arrangements were most conducive to them. The Shah, the Pahlavi clan, and the royalist elite confused vainglorious paternalism with prudent leadership, governing with owning. They acted as though the country was a royal patrimony or fiefdom. They failed to realize that any reasonably broad agreement regarding the public interest required a secure space of dialogue and deliberation in the public sphere, credible representative bodies, a viable civil society. No consensus on the contours of the common good could be coercively superimposed from above, as the Shah and the royalists had avowedly attempted to do. A domesticated and servile elite, acting as the Shah's personal retainers, lacked the credibility to sustain its claims that it did, or meant to, serve the country. In the eyes of the public, the rampant and cynical opportunism of high-ranking officials did not make sense except in terms of their ample opportunity for self-enrichment. The ruling elite's conduct eroded public trust in the state and undermined belief in the integrity, honesty, and sense of duty of politicians and senior civil servants.

## Corruption

The loyalty of the Shah's immediate entourage as well as the broader civilian and military elites was procured largely through formal rewards of office and the tolerated abuse of office for personal gain. Corruption in its broad sense was intrinsic to the functioning of the regime. The issue of corruption had been on the agenda of Iranian politics at various junctures. During bouts of contrived populism, the Shah felt obliged to speak about his determination to uproot corruption. He could not have failed to realize, however, that a certain measure of implicitly licensed or condoned corruption practiced by civilian and military elites was a necessary incentive to enlist and sustain their support. There was, therefore, a hollow ring to the anticorruption pronouncements of the regime. Moreover, not only the Pahlavi clan and those associated with it but also the Shah himself had long been involved in practices that he publicly repudiated and condemned. In 1958 the British ambassador reported that the Shah promoted schemes in which he had "a personal interest, financial or otherwise." It was necessary to enlist "his support (often through middlemen of dubious reputation) to obtain priority treatment, cut through red tape and secure finance." The Shah operated "through trusted nominees or servants such as Meybud, [Mohammad Ja'far] Behbehanian [deputy court minister in charge of finance], or the Court Minister Ala, or his own family, who themselves are said to benefit in proportion." The Shah also conferred "favours to family . . . and friends who have merited favours or whose favour is sought." Many members of the Shah's family "profited singularly"; his conduct "had the effect of attracting to the Court a number of highly undesirable hangers-on whose unscrupulous exploitations of whatever crumbs may fall has earned the Court a bad name."[53]

By the 1970s the endemic high-level corruption, striking some foreign observers as more rampant than elsewhere in the Middle East, militated against the regime's declared aim of administrative reform. Corruption had become an institutionalized practice. The line of demarcation between legitimate and illegitimate services rendered for material gain had become blurred. Foreign companies coming to Iran discovered "a bewildering array of informal, extra-legal methods of conducting their relations with the Government of Iran and even with other companies."[54] There was a whole battery of brokers of varying status and influence whose informal or semiformal services had become indispensable for the successful conclusion of a deal. Influence peddlers, fixers, arrangers, and advisers had, or claimed to have, contacts at the highest levels—cabinet ministers, the Pahlavi clan, Alam, and even the Shah. Companies promised a certain percentage of their sales to such brokers, viewing them as legitimate agents. Other middlemen knew lower-level officials and could expedite matters or provide advice or information about how to proceed in concluding deals. By readily paying bribes to win lucrative contracts, Western companies and businessmen promoted and invariably benefited from the corruption; they were not, as they claimed, merely at the receiving end.

Despite the adoption of various anticorruption measures, the U.S. embassy reported in 1973 that all such initiatives had proved "futile."[55] Viewing corruption as little more than illegitimate or improper material gain, over the years the regime had succeeded in prosecuting a number of culpable high-ranking officers; the Shah, however, expressed disappointment, as very few high-ranking civilians had been indicted.[56] Not only bribery but other, more resented and by no means less rampant, manifestations of malfeasance and abuse of office—nepotism, cronyism, favoritism—persisted and remained virtually ignored. Clearly, the autocratic-clientelist configuration of a financially resource-rich state free from parliamentary accountability and media scrutiny had increased both the opportunity for and intractability of corruption. The grandiose aims of the regime, its extravagant prestige projects, and particularly its growing military expenditure wasted the country's newly acquired wealth and fed corruption. In the post-1973 oil boom and in the absence of careful planning, adequate accountability and proper auditing, the volume of Iran's military purchases, and the scale and nature of the transactions created a bonanza for foreign dealers and brokers selling their hardware to Iran at inflated prices; the bonanza also provided considerable opportunity for abuse by domestic actors.

The key civilian and military personnel associated with the Shah were widely viewed as the primary perpetrators and beneficiaries of corruption. Those to whom the Shah assigned the task of investigating and uprooting corruption were themselves often viewed by the public as indistinguishable from the culprits. The Pahlavi clan, indelibly associated in the public mind with corruption, had ensured that the Shah lacked the necessary moral authority or the will to give teeth to his anticorruption campaign, which, in any case, given the configuration of the system, was unlikely to succeed. The regime's anticorruption measures deepened public cynicism as the root causes of corruption remained unaddressed. By early 1976 Hoveyda was appealing to Alam to intercede with the Shah, as he feared that the anticorruption campaign was becoming counterproductive; it generated negative publicity and was internationally damaging to the regime. Concurring with Hoveyda on this matter, Alam viewed the anticorruption campaign as having become banal.[57] Yet the Shah wanted it to continue, expecting it to reflect well on him and to elicit a positive public reaction.

The expected public response did not materialize, since the Shah failed to appear genuinely concerned about the abuses and corruption of those close to him, or resolute in restraining the Pahlavi clan and ensuring that equality before the law remained a credible idea. Those with the right connections remained able to flout laws and rules and enjoy extensive extralegal advantages and exemptions. Corruption in its broad sense continued to corrode the foundations of a regime that seemed intrinsically geared to rewarding a privileged class of key civilian and military personnel. In the end, its undeniable complicity in sustaining the authoritarian rule of the Shah would result in a deep-seated loathing of this class. No one could deny that under the auspices of Pahlavi rule, a privileged segment of the population, epitomized by the Pahlavi clan, enjoyed ample opportunity to empower itself at the expense of the rest, whom it chronically sought to patronize and silence. No doubt, in addition to the ruling class, the propertied and other segments of the middle class had also benefited from the prevailing regime, but those upper- and middle-class strata that continued to support the regime were not in a position to rush to its defense or in any sense counter its opponents.

## The Military

The military elite was more immediately responsible than any other group for sustaining the Shah's authoritarian rule and his self-image of invincibility. The military was the single institution on which the Shah most relied and which he treated as his exclusive patrimonial domain. Loyal, obedient, and politically unambitious officers were allowed to rise to high ranks and positions of command, to amass wealth, and to enjoy influence, patronage, and a life of luxury and privilege. Meteoric rise in the military was one of the most effective paths to material enrichment. The Shah had always and, particularly after 1953, tirelessly concerned himself with expanding and equipping the military. In the 1960s a variety of factors—including strained relations with Iraq, which after the 1958 overthrow of its monarchy had become a major cause of concern to the Shah—accounted for his growing obsession with building a powerful military. Steadily rising oil revenues facilitated this objective, increasingly enabling Iran to procure large quantities of modern weapons from various countries, including the Soviet Union.

The military continued to enjoy the lion's share of the national budget. The funds allocated to it constituted by far the largest item in the national budget and were often supplemented with foreign loans for further arms purchases. By 1973 the military consumed some 23 percent of the national budget, or around 12 percent of the gross national product, and a "significant part of the Shah's time."[58] In 1972 Iran's military comprised some 265,000 personnel, and by 1977 it had increased by less than 100,000. However, according to one account, in the same period Iran's defense budget increased by 680 percent, and by 1977 the military and security establishments in the country absorbed over 40 percent of the national budget.[59] In 1977, in proportion to its gross national product Iran spent twice as much as Turkey on its military and considerably more than Iraq. Thanks to President Richard Nixon and his national security adviser, Henry Kissinger (two of the Shah's closest U.S. allies, who visited Iran in late May 1972), the Iranian military was able to purchase whatever advanced nonnuclear weapons and equipment it wanted.

In early 1974 the government employed a major U.S. firm to establish electronic eavesdropping facilities in the Persian Gulf. Noting that $600 million had been allocated to finance this project, Alam boasted that Iran would become the real policeman of the Persian Gulf.[60] The British had been allowed to set up similar facilities in the Caspian region to monitor Soviet communications. Iran was not only playing a major policing role in the Persian Gulf and helping the ruler of Oman to quell a left-wing rebellion, but was also developing a strong interest in the defense of the Indian Ocean. Yet, failing to establish an advanced domestic weapons industry, the country remained dependent on imported, particularly American, hardware. The quadrupling of Iranian oil revenues by 1974 intensified the pace of its military buildup, making Iran the chief purchaser of U.S. weapons. U.S. military sales to Iran increased tenfold between 1972 and 1977;[61] the value of U.S. military sales to Iran in this period amounted to over $16 billion.[62] This situation involved greater reliance on U.S. expertise and increased employment of American personnel. On the eve of the monarchy's collapse the country had more jet fighters than trained pilots; there were also some 50,000 Americans in the country, up to 80 percent of whom worked with the military. The number of such advisers had tripled in the course of six years.

The Iranian military had long developed a collective vested interest in sustaining the Pahlavi monarchy, which had shown an unfailing commitment to its expansion and strength and to the needs of the officer corps. Under Reza Shah, the military's principal function was to suppress internal disorder. Under Mohammad Reza Shah, however, the military had grown to become a defensive force of regional significance. Yet, unlike in the years following 1953, when many key positions of power were occupied by military men most of whom originated from or were linked to the old notables, by the late 1960s the military's political influence or presence in formal politics was visibly on the wane. The military was no longer the main enclave of privilege; it did not attract superior talent; there was a noticeable decline in the caliber of its commanding officers. Nevertheless, it continued to furnish status and opportunity; some 500 senior officers could be counted as an important segment of the elite. The military not only constituted a key pillar of the regime but also functioned as an important agency of control and socialization: since the early 1970s on average between 60,000 and 80,000 young men and women were conscripted into military service annually. Yet, firmly harnessing the military, the Shah kept it out of politics. Officers too popular with their subordinates or capable of threatening the regime were watched and purged; loyalty to the Shah had long become the primary guarantor of survival and advancement.

As the political crisis intensified in the last year of his rule, the Shah was forced to rely primarily on the military, which he had not imagined would one day be called upon to safeguard the throne against a sustained popular insurrection. But the military, particularly its lower ranks, could not be expected to continue indefinitely to confront massive civil unrest. Such a confrontation, involving potentially extensive bloodshed and constant exposure to the unnerving tactics of civilian protesters, would be emotionally taxing and demoralizing for the largely conscript army. No less significantly, the military's command structure had been designed in such a way as to allow only the Shah to be in a real position of command. The chief of the Supreme Commander's Staff did not have the authority to issue orders to the commanders of the three forces; he merely acted as a conduit for the Shah's orders; the three commanders reported directly to the Shah (as did the chief of police and commander of the rural police) and received their orders from him, before informing the chief of the Supreme Commander's Staff.[63] By establishing himself as the sole coordinator of the armed forces, the Shah sought to ensure that key officers would not be able to cooperate with one another in a sustained manner except through his watchful and detailed involvement. Concomitantly, in order to forestall exploitable disgruntlement or coups, the Shah had done everything possible to ensure that the monarchy would be viewed as fully committed to the collective and institutional interests of the military. Curiously, the only known coup attempt against the Shah—led by General Mohammad-Vali Qarani in the winter of 1958—was a halfhearted and ill-fated plot not to overthrow the Shah but to force him to confine himself to his constitutionally designated role.

The "Qarani Affair" was used by the Shah and the royalists to increase surveillance activities and monitor and deter "unusual" contacts among key civilian and military personnel, as well as their interaction with foreign nationals, including the staffs of the U.S. and British embassies. SAVAK would play a major role in this regard. Together with military intelligence, SAVAK increased its vigilance in monitoring the spread of oppositional ideologies among army officers and worked to forestall the formation of politically motivated cliques likely to launch or support a coup. The Americans and the British, too, carefully monitored the military to detect signs of any possible move against the Shah. Thanks to their well-placed advisers, the Americans were in a position not only to watch the Iranian military but also to exert considerable control over its conduct.

For his part, the Shah missed no opportunity to assert publicly his personal control over the military. When, in May 1969, relations with Iraq reached a crisis point, awareness of inadequacies and inefficiency in the military prompted the Shah to remove the chief of the Supreme Commander's Staff and the commander-in-chief of the army. Three months later, seven of the eight admirals of the navy were removed. In July 1971 the chief of the Supreme Commander's Staff, General Jam, an officer of recognized ability and integrity, was replaced by the more pliant General Azhari. A year later several army commanders were replaced. The Shah wanted to leave no doubt that he was ultimately in command and that the commanders' continued service depended on his favor.

The Shah's divisive and manipulatory tactics and his cultivation of a culture of docility in the armed forces had ensured that high-ranking officers would not be men of unusual ability or imagination capable of real initiative and independence of mind. The Shah himself, as he told Alam in December 1973, viewed the military's top brass as men more of pretension and false bravura than of valor and substance.[64] The responsibility for this situation, General Jam later asserted, rested solely with the Shah, who "had emasculated all officers; no officer enjoyed the authority accruing from his position. Everything had to be referred to and approved by the Shah—even the leave of absence of junior officers . . . junior appointments and so forth." Jam adds that he "repeatedly reminded the Shah of the defects of the prevailing system . . . [emphasizing] that no commander had authority, that all were stripped of power, devoid of will, and incapable of initiative, and that if there were a significant development and [for whatever reason] the Shah was not able or willing to issue orders, everything would disintegrate."[65]

Jam was in no doubt that the eventual collapse of the military, and by implication also what happened to the country, was rooted in the manner in which the Shah handled and controlled the armed forces. The war minister, Jam noted, did not control the chief of the Supreme Commander's Staff, nor had he the authority to interfere in the affairs of the military. The military did not obey the government and was not answerable to it; it was "the Shah's private army and not the army of the country and the nation." Such a military force was incapable of facing and surviving a crisis. The manner in which it disintegrated and the conduct of its last chief, General Qarabaghi, was, according to Jam, reprehensible but not surprising. The Shah "wanted obedient servants and not responsible commanders."[66] In a similar vein, the U.S. embassy had been concerned that the Shah's attitude and conduct, the close scrutiny of officers by SAVAK, and purges of those whose loyalty was suspect had resulted in a flawed military leadership. Subordinates were unwilling "to make even simple decisions," and loyalty and obedience took "precedence over proficiency, energy, and initiative."[67] The views expressed by Jam and the U.S. embassy are corroborated by several other Iranian officers and by the U.S. envoy General Huyser, who identified the "major weakness" of the Iranian military commanders as being their "dependency on rigid central leadership," having been "trained this way, from the lowest to the highest ranks, by the Shah himself."[68]

The Shah had endeavored to mold the military in his own image. He had once pronounced: "I am the military," implying that he saw himself as personifying the armed forces.[69] Such a symbiotic identification with the military meant that if he faltered in the face of mounting revolutionary unrest, the armed forces would also be likely to collapse. In the final months of his rule, the Shah, a demoralized, beleaguered, and reviled leader ravaged by debilitating illness and paralyzing indecision, was in no position to raise the morale of his military commanders. Bereft of real leadership qualities, the commanders had obeyed the Shah dutifully and with a sense of awe, and were long accustomed to look to him for leadership and guidance. They could only have felt disheartened by the Shah's willingness to sacrifice any of his senior subordinates, civilian or military, in order to placate the opposition, and particularly by his willingness to abandon ship. The Shah's departure from the country was the military's coup de grâce; it dealt the severest blow to the armed forces, exacerbated the commanders' disorientation, and expedited the concomitant collapse of the military and the monarchy.

## SAVAK

The task of safeguarding the regime from foreign espionage and subversion and from domestic challenges was to be performed by SAVAK, which was designed to ensure, together with the police and other security and intelligence entities, that antiregime activities were closely monitored, plots uncovered, and active opponents deterred or neutralized. The establishment of SAVAK—portrayed as equivalent to the legitimate security, counterespionage, and intelligence service indispensable to any state—had been opposed in the Iranian parliament and among the old notables. From the very beginning, and under the auspices of its first chief—the flamboyant, politically influential, and notoriously ruthless General Teymur Bakhtiar—SAVAK was used for a whole range of activities, from rigging elections and summary detention or banishment of those who opposed official candidates, to infiltrating opposition circles and spying on key individuals, Iranian or foreign. It used a variety of tactics to spread disinformation, stimulate discord and distrust in the ranks of the regime's opponents, defame and discredit them, and ensure that some of them were viewed as suspect by their comrades.[70] In focusing on harassing and bullying the opposition and stifling all criticism of the regime, SAVAK eroded any residual public belief in the rule of law; it came to be widely, and justifiably, seen as an instrument of oppression and extrajudicial violence.

Bakhtiar's replacement by General Pakravan in March 1961 appeared to be a move to improve SAVAK's image. In contrast to his predecessor, Pakravan had a reputation as a learned and thinking man; he was interested in probing the causes of discontent rather than merely suppressing its manifestations; he also cautiously sympathized with moderate or liberal-minded opponents of the regime. "Pakravan," reported the U.S. embassy, "is known to be periodically in despair about the situation because he feels that repression is not a solution to the principal problem of government in Iran, which is to obtain a broader popular consensus."[71] Pakravan was also unwilling to tell the Shah only what he wanted to hear. He "exhibited sophistication and discretion on occasion and sometimes seemed to be able to give the Shah a reasonably objective view of events even when that view revealed some unpleasant facts."[72]

With the regime facing powerful challenges from various quarters, whether civic-nationalists or clerical and traditionalist forces, under Pakravan SAVAK attempted to show greater tact and flexibility. Without abandoning its basic strategy of diffusing or countering opposition to the regime, it resorted more to divisive or manipulatory ploys and remedial tactics. It also helped to sustain political entities useful to the regime. For instance, according to U.S. sources, in May 1964, ordered by the Shah, it supported Mohsen Pezeshkpur, the leader of the fringe chauvinist Pan-Iranist Party, in launching a campaign against Arab nationalism and President Nasser. The party was allowed to have a newspaper and to win five seats in the lower house of parliament. Although the party had virtually no constituency, "membership in it brought tangible rewards."[73]

SAVAK's strategy was, of course, ultimately determined by the Shah and implemented by its chiefs; but if Pakravan indeed doubted the efficacy of repression in uprooting dissent, his tenure as head of SAVAK was bound to be brief. In late January 1965, following the assassination of Prime Minister Mansur, Pakravan was replaced by General Nasiri. Nasiri's brutality

*Generals Teymur Bakhtiar (left) and Ne'matollah Nasiri, the notorious first and*
*penultimate chiefs of SAVAK.* (Courtesy of the Institute for the Study of
Contemporary Iranian History, Tehran)

matched or exceeded that of Bakhtiar, but he lacked both Bakhtiar's intelligence and independence of mind and Pakravan's finesse. Pakravan enjoyed
respect among his colleagues and in the political establishment. One general praised him as "one of the most distinguished, patriotic, knowledge-
able, humane, and honest officers in the Iranian military," while describing
Nasiri as "very simple, superficial and impressionable, but incredibly loyal
to the Shah, an officer whose military and general knowledge was below average and whose appointment to positions such as chief of SAVAK was astonishing."[74]

During Nasiri's tenure as chief, which lasted until June 1978, SAVAK became more brutal and more subservient to the Shah's whims. As commander of the Imperial Guards, Nasiri had assisted the Shah in his confron-

tation with Mosaddeq; he was not only unrefined and ruthless but also corrupt, and by the early 1970s was believed to have become, next to the Shah, the biggest property owner in the Caspian region. Under Nasiri, SAVAK came to be increasingly feared even by officials close to the Shah; the regime's staunchest supporters were also spied on by SAVAK and avoided antagonizing it. In reporting to the Shah or the U.S. and British intelligence agencies, SAVAK presented a reassuring picture of the country's domestic situation. Its surveillance had long restricted contact between British and U.S. embassy staff and members of the opposition. Government officials sometimes warned the two embassies about the harm SAVAK was doing to the regime. The U.S. embassy, however, confined itself to occasionally describing SAVAK as "overzealous" or to expressing concern that its conduct could harden the attitude of antigovernment guerrillas and their supporters.[75]

Contrary to the projected image, the regime's reliance on the putatively efficient and effective SAVAK was more a sign and source of weakness than an indicator of strength or a guarantee of survival. This reliance became a political and moral liability for the regime and a resonating rallying point for the opposition. SAVAK's tactics and its public image ensured that the regime, particularly in its last decade, acquired the notoriety of being unusually intolerant, cruel, and oppressive. Of SAVAK's eight departments, which had a variety of functions, including counterespionage, the third—responsible for domestic security and surveillance—was the most culpable. It was, among other things, responsible for the notorious ill-treatment of political prisoners. A senior official of the Third Department since 1966 and later its head, Sabeti, was a close friend of Hoveyda. This association made the latter at the very least partially responsible for the department's conduct. The Third Department's intrusive surveillance and relentless harassment of opponents, together with its widespread use of torture and callous suppression of dissent, resulted in SAVAK's being seen as the embodiment of everything that was abominable about the regime.

Regardless of its departmental divisions, SAVAK as a whole had come to be publicly reviled. It functioned inadvertently as an instrument of creating rather than containing antiregime opposition. It overreacted to student unrest, adopted an iron-fist policy in silencing criticism, raided student dormitories and houses, and assaulted and detained anyone found possessing left-wing literature or material deemed harmful to the regime. It created a deep sense of vulnerability and intimidation and fostered a Kafkaesque atmosphere in which suspected opponents or critics were arrested on the flimsiest evidence. It helped encourage a belief in the ubiquity of its informants. At the same time, mere suspicion of collaborating with SAVAK resulted in ruinous opprobrium and stigma. SAVAK's tactics of disinformation, its reliance on *agents provocateurs,* and its real or putative infiltration of student organizations, surreptitious opposition circles, and politically motivated informal gatherings contributed to an atmosphere saturated with paranoia, distrust, and bitterness. It poisoned the wellspring of civil society.

As radical opponents of the regime turned more and more to violence, SAVAK intensified its preemptive measures to hunt them down. Reports of bloody confrontations, arrests, and executions marred the image of tranquil stability projected by the regime both at home and abroad. When, for instance, in the winter of 1976, thirteen members of the Mojahedin-e Khalq organization were executed, Alam feared the impact on Iran's image abroad. The Shah, however, seemed no longer particularly concerned about image.[76] For him, failure to contain and uproot guerrilla violence was clearly of greater consequence. In the hope of deterring actual or potential violence, the regime grew more repressive and appeared intent on portraying itself as more of a ghastly police state than it actually was. Few doubted that SAVAK's tentacles extended into every facet of public and even private life, and it was widely believed that countless political opponents were languishing in prison, horrifically treated.[77] This perception was partly a result of opposition propaganda, but, paradoxically, the regime also found it useful to cultivate an ominous image, inspiring fear and relying more on the threat of cruelty than on its actual deployment. Clearly, the pervasive shadowy fear of SAVAK aided the objective of demoralizing, managing, and manipulating the populace. The regime mounted no serious or sustained effort to refute or repair SAVAK's image.

As an agency partly in charge of monitoring opposition activities, including what was taking place in mosques and other religious venues, SAVAK was not as ineffective as has sometimes been claimed. Published SAVAK documents indicate that its middle-level functionaries were capable of reasonably competent intelligence gathering and surveillance of opposition activities, including those of Islamist opponents. Informers often provided detailed accounts of such activities. It is not clear, however, whether these reports ever reached the Shah or in what form they reached him. It appears that higher-level analysis of the collected intelligence was seriously inept.

The Shah did not of course rely exclusively on SAVAK; according to the U.S. embassy, he maintained "at least six separate and competing information services reporting directly to him as well as numerous personal contacts in all elements of society. He is always aware, however, that any of these sources may slant their reports to suit their own interests and he alone must be the final arbiter of which reports are worthy of further consideration. He believes this intensely and believes also that such leadership is necessary for the national good."[78] The Shah sought detailed information, for instance, on the private lives of ministers and senior officials to be used against them if necessary.[79] He did not, however, show much enthusiasm for his intelligence chiefs' analysis of the collected material on less interesting subjects. Since the overriding priority of all royal sources of intelligence or information was to keep their jobs, almost until the very end of the regime they avoided alarming or displeasing the Shah with unpalatable news. Concomitantly, the regime's self-confidence fostered considerable complacency in attempting to make sense of and address the existing, often unambiguously expressed, political resentments.

# 7

# Elective Affinities:

# Western Imperial Interests and Authoritarian Monarchy

## Involvement

The circumstances relating to the forced abdication of the Shah's father and to his own largely fortuitous accession to the throne, which he almost relinquished in 1953 and retrieved only with Anglo-American support, left an indelible mark on him. After the consolidation of his power in the 1930s, Reza Shah normally avoided receiving foreign ambassadors and abhorred seeking their advice. In contrast, Mohammad Reza Shah relished personally liaising with the British and American ambassadors, enlisted their support for his autocratic drive, and, during the greater part of his rule, sought and heeded their advice. Yet he retained a deeply ambivalent attitude to his American and British supporters; he viewed them with suspicion but considered their support indispensable. He maintained that the monarchy was secure unless foreign powers turned against it, and that he retained his throne as long as those powers wanted, but otherwise would relinquish it.[1] Despite the public persona that he tried tirelessly to foster, he was unable, particularly in the face of a chronic crisis, to appear or to see himself as self-reliant. Reacting to powerful nationalist trends and impulses in Iranian society, both Pahlavi rulers endeavored to act as ardent nationalists. Yet the paradox of Pahlavi nationalism was that it remained handicapped by the fact that both rulers had, at a crucial stage in the their political careers, relied on influential foreign powers. In the context of broader Iranian nationalism, neither Pahlavi ruler fully succeeded in extirpating from the collective memory the residual image of cooperation with or dependence on foreign powers.

Convinced of the pivotal role of the monarchy in the Iranian body politic, the Anglo-American sponsors of the 1953 coup forced the vacillating Shah to act decisively against Mosaddeq. For the Shah, Western backing for his retention of the throne indicated an affirmation of and commitment to his domination of the political process, which enabled him to ensure that no future challenge to his power would be allowed. In the post-1953 era, cognizant of the extent of Anglo-American influence in Iran, a host of politicians, including prudent monarchists, pleaded with the U.S. and British embassies to help steer the Shah away from personal rule; they rarely hid their serious doubts about his leadership capabilities. The British and American diplomatic personnel did not deny the justifiability of their interlocutors' concerns, which they regularly conveyed to their superiors. They reported on extensive election rigging, the Shah's unfettered control of cabinets, his selection and sponsorship of key officials, his manipulation of both supporters and tame opponents, his stimulation of rivalry among top civilian and military personnel, and an array of other moves designed to sustain his autocratic domination. Yet the ambassadors concurred that Iran was not ready for democracy or saw democracy as dangerously inappropriate for Iran considering the threats posed by instability, communism, civic-nationalism, and any form of neutralism, not to mention the "character" of the Iranian people.

Reflecting on the extent and style of the Shah's autocratic rule, British and U.S. diplomats at times feared its outcome. For a number of years they thought it expedient for the parliamentary arrangements to retain a degree of credibility. Yet a parliamentary polity was credible only if it allowed a real measure of press and associational freedom, and the emergence of various political parties that would inevitably oppose or question the focal role of the Shah and the country's close alliance with the West. A constitutional government hoping to inspire public confidence and support could not afford to falter in upholding national sovereignty; it would resist undue foreign influence, insist on real Iranian control over the oil industry, and prevent the country from becoming a growing market for Anglo-American goods and weapons. As Mosaddeq had repeatedly emphasized, the emergence of such a government was not in the interest of the Western powers, despite their rhetoric. Major foreign powers, statesmen such as Mosaddeq maintained, found it incomparably more convenient and effective to deal with one man, the Shah, than to contend with an often unruly and recalcitrant parliamentary government.

## A "Special Relationship"

The United States emerged as the hegemonic power in post-1953 Iran. For many years the country remained dependent on U.S. economic aid, but it was primarily in military and security matters that it relied increasingly on U.S. assistance. The expectation of greater assistance in these areas was an important factor in Iran's adherence to the Baghdad Pact (renamed the Central Treaty Organization after the Iraqi revolution of 1958). In early 1959, for a variety of complex reasons, including dissatisfaction with Western assistance, the Shah began secretly negotiating with the Soviets toward a nonaggression pact. These negotiations were aborted as a result of Western pressure—a development that incensed the Soviets but hastened the signing a few months later of the Mutual Defense Agreement between Iran and the United States. This agreement signaled greater Iranian dependence on the United States and further embroiled Iran in the Cold War. U.S.-Iranian ties were dubbed a "special relationship"; key figures in the Iranian government increasingly sought U.S. assistance and advice on important matters. The United States, its Tehran embassy admitted, maintained "advisory groups with all of the [Iranian] security forces" and was "associated in the public mind with the work of the security forces . . . So far, however, the short run advantages in strengthening internal security, combating Soviet pressure and internal communism, and strengthening the Shah's regime outweigh the one major disadvantage in this United States activity—the adverse public opinion."[2]

The Iranian public increasingly resented U.S. predominance, manifested, among other things, in the growing visibility of its advisers, and viewed the regime as sustained by the United States. Aiming to counter this image and the neutralist legacy of Mosaddeq, the Shah invoked "positive nationalism" and sought to emphasize his independence of action. Few, however, doubted that through its aid and other measures the United States helped sustain not only an unrepresentative regime in Iran but also a dependent one. This asymmetrical relationship was forcefully criticized by Abolhasan Ebtehaj, the able director of the Plan Organization (1954–1959). In September 1961, addressing the International Industrial Conference in San Francisco, Ebtehaj enumerated the pitfalls of "bilateral aid" and as an example singled out Iran, where, "now after more than $1 billion of loans and grants, America is neither loved nor respected; she is distrusted by most people, and hated by many."[3] Such views, together with Ebtehaj's integrity and nonservility, contributed to his marginalization and prosecution on spurious, politically motivated charges.

U.S. officials were not unanimous in their support for royal autocracy. In the early 1960s, viewing the Shah's regime as nonviable, some American policymakers even contemplated his removal. Many more, however, favored retaining the existing regime while helping to revitalize it through encouraging a program of socioeconomic development. Voices critical of the Shah were brushed aside, and the regional situation, whether instability in Iraq or convulsions in Turkey, provided added incentive to the U.S. foreign policy establishment to favor a stable, reform-minded Pahlavi monarchy. The regime could not hope to justify its authoritarian tenor domestically or to retain vital U.S. support without initiating reform measures, whose urgency was underlined by the Kennedy administration. The Shah grudgingly appointed a government led by Amini, which he viewed as imposed by the United States and incongruous with his autocratic rule, but sought to establish himself as the chief proponent of reform. Concomitantly, Iran's rising oil income, its ability to purchase weapons from other countries, diminished U.S. economic assistance from 1962 onward, and the Shah's continued need to be seen as independent affected the relationship. Yet reliance on the United States continued.

To counter its nationalist and other opponents, the regime needed to portray itself as fully independent; however, attempts to manufacture such an image received a devastating blow in October 1964, in the wake of the granting of immunities to U.S. Department of Defense personnel in the country. Despite this concession, U.S. officials disliked the implications of what they referred to as the Shah's "new independence." In January 1965 a senior U.S. State Department official candidly spelled out the rationale of

*The Shah and President Dwight D. Eisenhower.* (Courtesy of the Institute for the Study of Contemporary Iranian History, Tehran)

U.S. predominance in Iran: "Our security interests are too compelling for us to allow favorable indications of Iran's increasing self-reliance to obscure its continuing vulnerability and basic weakness or to conclude too early that U.S. objectives can be achieved without significant participation in Iranian affairs."[4]

American officials viewed the Iranian desire for independence, partially symbolized by the Shah's "positive nationalism," as largely rhetorical.[5] Similarly, few politically minded Iranians doubted that the American embassy was deeply involved in Iranian domestic politics and in promoting particular individuals or agendas. The conduct of some U.S. officials lent credence to such assumptions. For example, in the early 1960s the CIA station chief in Tehran, Gratian Yatsevitch, sounded out certain Iranian politicians for cabinet posts or even the premiership.[6] Others, such as the senior diplomat Stuart Rockwell, sought to interfere in the parliamentary elections on Mansur's behalf.[7]

The United States continued to be increasingly seen as sustaining the re-

gime by both its supporters and its opponents, whom the United States
tended to dismiss rather brashly. In June 1964 the U.S. embassy described
the opposition to the Shah as "thoroughly inchoate" and as giving vent "not
to ideas but to frustration." Yet it admitted that the Shah's regime was regarded as "an unpopular dictatorship not only by its opponents but, far
more significantly, by its proponents as well." It was widely believed in Iran,
the embassy observed, that without U.S. support "the Shah and his government would be swept away in short order." The Shah himself, the report
added, also believed in this "myth"; the embassy "had authoritative reports
of his profound worries at the beginning of the Kennedy Administration
and again, especially, when Ngo Dinh Diem was removed from power.
What the American Ambassador says in public or in private is given the mi-
nutest scrutiny." In the embassy's view the Americans were given "credit"
for power to influence the situation in Iran which they did "not actually
possess" and were blamed for "deficiencies" that they were "in no position
to prevent or remedy."[8] Belief in inordinate foreign influence, though a
deep-rooted component of the Iranian political culture, had been reinforced
by recent experiences. The embassy failed to acknowledge the profound impact of the coup of 1953. Its indignant professions of innocence were deeply
disingenuous. Among other things, as the immunities issue and its consequences indicated, the U.S. government cared little about manifestations of
Iranian nationalist aspirations and sense of dignity, which it dismissed as
merely indicating "frustration." American policy toward Iran, the embassy
maintained, should not be seriously influenced by "the tendency of Iranians
to make foreigners responsible for the frustrations and shortcomings of
their condition"; it added that "at present there exists no realistic alternative
to our support of the Shah."[9]

The claim that there was no "realistic alternative" to supporting the Shah
had been a salient theme of both American and British foreign policy discourses at least since 1953. Convinced of the absence of an alternative, U.S.
Ambassador Loy Henderson (1951–1954) had done much to embolden the
Shah to confront Mosaddeq and to act as a "leader," as he had done, according to Henderson, during the Azarbaijan crisis of 1946. Any American or
British pressure exerted on the Shah was aimed not at persuading him to
rein in his autocratic proclivities but at initiating socioeconomic reform that

would, in their view, render the country less vulnerable to communism. The Americans and the British not only supported the regime's anticommunist measures but also condoned the political exclusion and suppression of the Mosaddeqists, whose constitutionalist and civic-nationalist programs they regarded as unrealistic and dangerous. Close ties between the regime and its Anglo-American supporters remained unaffected by vicissitudes in the relationship. In the first half of the 1960s a variety of factors adversely affected U.S.-Iranian ties. The Shah resented the failure of the United States to assist Iran adequately, to understand the logic of his desire to have a powerful army, and to sell it weapons at reduced prices. He felt that the Americans were seeking to frustrate his approaches to the Soviets to build a steel mill in Iran, and were soft on Nasser. From the mid-1960s onward U.S.-Iranian relations grew steadily closer. Ambassador Armin Meyer (1965–1969), described as virtually "a public relations officer" for the Shah,[10] worked hard to persuade the U.S. government to accommodate the Shah's demands for weapons on credit and at discounted prices. Assisted by diplomats such as Meyer, the Shah's perseverance, ploys, and implicit threats to turn to the Soviets paid off; he was able to achieve most of his objectives regarding weapons.

By the 1970s, as its embassy reported in January 1973, the United States was "deeply involved in the growth of Iran's military program." It had had a significant team of military advisers in Iran since World War II. By 1972 more than 11,000 Iranian military personal had received training in the United States; Iran had received $840 million in grant assistance and another $1 billion in credit for hardware and services. The United States was strategically placed to maintain enormous influence over the Iranian government.[11] Its influence permeated "all levels of Iranian military structure."[12] The U.S. embassy justified the Iranian military buildup by asserting that "if we don't sell items to them some one else will." U.S.-Iranian relations were described as being "as soundly based as they can be imagined." Carefully monitoring the conduct and attitude of military officers, the embassy was optimistic about the continued support of the military for the Shah. It saw no "ground for concern about close US identification with the Iranian military" and asserted that even during an uncertain period of political transition "our long and close collaboration with the military elite should pay dividends." The embassy summarized the mutual benefits of close U.S.-Iranian ties as follows:

> The benefits we derive from the relationship are: important intelligence facilities; the only secure air corridor from Europe to Southeast Asia; good markets, a friendly investment climate for US business, and direct contributions to our balance of payments; a current and future reliable source of oil to our allies, and perhaps to us; a staunch political ally in regional and world councils; and an increasingly strong and stable territorial entity standing in the way of Soviet ambitions in the strategic Persian Gulf and Indian Ocean areas. For Iran, the United States is the leading source of military equipment and technological assistance, a friend whose political and psychological support can be relied upon and, of overwhelming and fundamental importance, the sole power in the world strong enough to thwart Soviet designs on Iranian territorial integrity and independence.[13]

"Special ties" with the United States did not necessarily mean strained relations with the Soviets. The Shah had remained able to use the Soviet card skillfully to get what he wanted from the West. Also, better relations with the Soviet bloc could be seen as an indication of Iran's more independent course of action. In September 1962, with the aim of improving relations with the Soviet Union, Iran undertook not to allow foreign missile bases on its territory. Though committed to the Western alliance, the Shah attempted to pursue a pragmatic approach to foreign policy. But there were clear limits to the degree of closeness between Iran and the Soviets. The Shah considered Soviet weapons insufficiently sophisticated and did not welcome large numbers of Soviet technicians and advisers. Despite good relations with the Soviets and improved relations with China after 1972, the Shah was concerned about the spread of communism in the region, the close ties between the Soviet Union and India, the future of Pakistan, and the dangers of communist-instigated separatism among minorities in Iran. The anti-Iranian attitude of the pro-Soviet Iraqi regime unsettled the Shah. His trip to Moscow in October 1972 reduced his fears in the short run, but the antimonarchist coup of July 1973 in Afghanistan, and the gradual ascendancy of pro-Soviet forces in that country, confirmed his fears. Yet, thanks largely to close ties to the United States, his confidence in the stability of his own regime remained unshaken.

## A "Good Risk" for Britain

British influence had deeper historical roots. Although it was dealt a severe blow by the oil crisis of the early 1950s and Mosaddeq's premiership and seemed to be in decline after the Suez debacle of 1956, next to the United States Britain was the most influential country in Iranian foreign policy and domestic politics. The British were no less consequential than the Americans in enabling the Shah to assume political ascendancy without any illusion about his capacity to be an enlightened ruler. Some Foreign Office officials maintained that what the Iranians "undoubtedly need is a benevolent dictator on the pattern of [Portugal's] Dr. Salazar."[14] Few, however, considered the Shah an ideal candidate for such a role. Ann Lambton, who had long-standing links with the British political establishment as well as with the older Iranian political notables, never harbored a high opinion of the Shah and frequently shared her views with her former colleagues at the Foreign Office. "There is nothing worse," Lambton observed, "than a dictator who does not dictate." Reiterating the old-school British advocacy of relying on the veteran anglophile Sayyed Zia "as the most likely man to pull Persia out of her present slough," she suggested that the Shah "might profitably take a long holiday in the south of France."[15] Lambton's contacts and trips to Iran increased her gloom and concern about the discontent caused by the Shah's close identification with the West, corruption, waste, lack of freedom, visible foreign influence, and the growth of radicalism.[16]

The predominant British view was, however, to eschew any misgivings and support the Shah. It not only placed "stability" before "the luxuries of democracy" but maintained that "with all his shortcomings the Shah is the only element of stability here today; for better or worse we must stick with him."[17] In August 1958 the British ambassador, Sir Roger Stevens (1954–1958), asserted that the Shah was

> psychologically incapable of surrendering power or presiding over a genuine popularly-based Government; even were he able to do so, his

name is now so thoroughly associated with authoritarian rule that it is unlikely that he would ever be accepted by public opinion as fulfilling the necessary conditions . . . I would not deny that in a vague way he has the welfare of his people at heart, difficult though it is to reconcile this with the way he lives, the antics of his dreadful family, the syco-phants who surround him or alarming signs of increasing corruption in high places, including the throne itself. He is, I fear, incapable of formu-lating, let alone executing, a really constructive policy of any kind. His domestic policy—surrender of estates, charitable activities, manipula-tions of Parliament, creation of parties, making and unmaking of Gov-ernments, advocacy of honesty in administration—is, on present show-ing, a hollow sham.

In Stevens' judgment, as long as the Shah remained on the throne stability would be "both tenuous and spurious," and there would be no "decent" government, let alone "social justice."

On the other hand, if he were to be removed, there would be no cer-tainty, indeed little likelihood, of any better government . . . I suppose we must adjudge the Shah's government from our point of view as distinctly the lesser evil and cooperate with it, especially in the inter-national field, as best as we can. But we should not deceive ourselves about the sort of man, or the sort of regime, with which we are deal-ing.[18]

Stevens had earlier noted that Western-style constitutional democracy in Iran was impractical and "might prove disastrous."[19] Stevens' successor, Sir Geoffrey Harrison (1958–1963), echoing many of his predecessors, consid-ered the "Iranian character" an impediment to democratic rule. He also firmly believed that no conceivable alternative regime was likely to be as fa-vorable to British interests as the current one.[20] A corollary to such a view was an increasingly more positive assessment of the Shah, his conduct and objectives.

Observing how British views regarding "political stability and the mainte-nance of the flow of oil" in the Middle East were "broadly speaking identi-cal with Iran's," and how "at long last" the Shah seemed "satisfied that we

do not meddle in his country's internal affairs," Harrison's successor, Sir
Denis Wright (1963–1971), noted at the outset of his mission that the Shah

> regularly seeks our advice, both directly and through encouraging close
> personal contact between this Embassy and his Prime and Foreign Min-
> isters. He also seeks American advice, though I should say he is more
> suspicious of this than he is of ours these days. It is fortunate that with
> admirable Julius Holmes as my American colleague the advice he gets
> from us both has usually been synchronised and is the more likely to
> make some impact on his doubting and brooding mind.[21]

By the mid-1960s British influence seemed tangibly on the wane. Yet Britain
remained a significant player in Iranian politics, thanks to the lingering
memories of its past status, the resilience of influential and well-placed
anglophiles, and the widely held belief in British guile and capacity for devious mischief. Fully sharing this belief, the Shah avoided antagonizing them.
British agents such as Asadollah Rashidian played important roles as members of the wider royal entourage. There were also other agents and political and business brokers such as Shapoor Reporter, who enjoyed close ties
with the court, Alam, and Zahedi, among others, and worked in various capacities—MI6 agent, *Times* correspondent, teacher of English. When necessary, the British used such figures to ensure that the Shah did not act in a
manner injurious to British interests. He did, however, display increasing assertiveness. "Today I doubt," wrote Ambassador Wright in 1971, that the
Shah "would be taking any notice of our views once his mind was made up.
He both trusts and distrusts us, and when things go wrong his subconscious
tells him that the British lie somewhere behind the troubles. He is unlikely
to rid himself of this complex which should not be ignored in our dealings
with him." While commending the Shah's reformist drive and his firmness
vis-à-vis "reactionary Mullahs," Wright added that "Ministers run in fear
and trembling of the Shah and take few decisions without his blessing. Such
a state of affairs does not make for good government, though it does mean
that certain things get done quickly. I wonder how much longer he can continue to carry this heavy burden."[22]

Concerns of this nature did not dampen optimism about the future and
praise for the Shah's domestic achievements. A 1969 British embassy assess-

ment described Iran as "the most stable, prosperous and steadily developing country in the Middle East and a 'good risk' politically and commercially. This should be good for Britain."[23] Wright's successor praised the Shah as a "farsighted autocrat" who had transformed Iran from an "underdeveloped country into a modern industrialized state," a leader motivated by "a desire to wipe out past humiliations, a determination to proclaim Iran's present achievements and to expand them, and a concern about the future."[24] Like the Americans, the British aimed at ensuring that despite the Shah's desire to demonstrate a real measure of independence in Iran's foreign relations, the country remained firmly in the Western camp, friendship with the Soviet Union was circumscribed, and Iranian pressure to extract more money from the oil consortium—in which British Petroleum, which replaced the AIOC, had a 40 percent share—did not exceed tolerable limits. Maintaining close commercial ties between the two countries, and increasing the export of British arms and the opportunity for investing and winning lucrative contracts for British companies, assumed primary significance.

In 1970, following intense secret Anglo-Iranian negotiations, the Shah abandoned Iran's long-standing claims regarding the Persian Gulf Island of Bahrain, officially designated as the country's fourteenth province. To counterbalance this move, in late November 1971 Iranian forces occupied three small islands in the Persian Gulf, declaring them vital for Iran's security. The Shah wanted the issue of the three islands to be decided between Iran and Britain, and Iran's renunciation of its claim over Bahrain to be compensated by recognition of its sovereignty over the three islands. But in the face of unrelenting Arab objections the sovereignty issue was shelved; the Shah saw occupation of the islands as tantamount to sovereignty. The British worked to convince the Shah that after the December 1971 departure of their forces from the Persian Gulf, security in the area should be maintained through Iranian, British, and Arab cooperation. The Iranian government, on the other hand, had been preparing to replace Britain as the dominant power in the region. Yet it behaved less arrogantly toward the Persian Gulf rulers than the British had feared.

Following the islands settlement Anglo-Iranian ties steadily grew closer. In 1972 British exports to Iran were considerably more than the previous year. The immediate future caused little concern. The ambassador noted that "for the next five or six years, and barring accidents, there is unlikely to be any fundamental upset to Iran's stability . . . But, in the long term, the Shah will have to find a way out of the dilemma he has faced himself with by his refusal or inability to delegate authority to better people."[25] Some British officials did not discount "storms ahead for the monarch"; they presciently feared that by 1978, when, among other military items, the last batch of 800 Chieftain tanks that Iran had contracted to purchase were delivered, they could well fall into "the hands of a revolutionary govern-ment."[26] But concerns about "trouble" in the future were outweighed by more optimistic assumptions. Britain wished to replace the United States as the main supplier of arms to Iran but knew that the Americans were de-termined to prevent this. British envoys continued to view the regime's prospects with optimism; they were aware of "the revolution of rising ex-pectations" but, like their American counterparts, saw the possibility of a revolution as negligible, considering the loyalty of the military and the se-curity forces.

## A Regional Petro-Power

The fall of the Iraqi monarchy in 1958 had caused immense anxiety in the Iranian political establishment, providing greater impetus for pursuing poli-cies to strengthen the Shah's position, including a development program. From the late 1960s relations with the Ba'thist regime in Iraq deteriorated. In December 1971, in the wake of continued border disputes and attempts by both regimes to conspire with or assist each other's opponents—includ-ing a bungled effort by Iran to instigate a coup in Iraq—diplomatic relations between the two countries were broken off. Iraq expelled 40,000 Iranians. Although the Shah was on good terms with conservative Arab states, rela-tions with radical regimes and certain rulers of the Persian Gulf region were often strained. By the mid-1960s the Shah's dislike of Nasser had turned into an obsession, often stimulated by Israeli intelligence, which maintained close links with SAVAK. Nasserist propaganda in the Persian Gulf and efforts to stir up the population of the southern province of Khuzestan deeply alarmed the Shah. Even after the massive Arab defeat in the June 1967 war with Israel, the Shah's obsession with Nasser persisted. His fear of Nasserism and his desire to play a leading role in the region and to check the ambitions of the Iraqi regime contributed to his determination to build as strong a military as possible and to maintain closer ties with the West.

In 1970, just before Nasser's death, Iran resumed diplomatic relations with Egypt after a rupture of ten years. Yet the Shah continued to view the predominant Arab attitude to Iran as ultimately unfriendly. Despite clerical objections, he cultivated close and more or less open ties with Israel, which after the 1967 war the Shah came to admire greatly. Israel provided Iran with intelligence, advice, and weapons; helped dampen criticism of the Iranian regime in the United States; and engaged in public relations on its behalf, in exchange mainly for oil. During the Arab-Israeli war of October 1973, Iran maintained its close ties with, and sold oil to, Israel. Iran's growing regional power ensured that even states that resented it tried to come to terms with it. By March 1975, after a meeting in Algiers between the Shah and the Iraqi leader Saddam Hussein, problems that had long bedeviled relations between the two countries were resolved. Among other things, the Iraqis renounced their claim to the whole of the Shatt al-Arab and accepted the *thalweg* (the median of the river's navigational channel) as the common border along the entire river. Acting as one of the most influential leaders in the Middle East and beyond, the Shah not only strengthened relations with Israel, the other regional power propped up by the United States, but also developed strong ties with Nasser's successor, Anwar Sadat. The Shah became a close friend of Sadat and mediated between him and the Israelis. He engaged in concerted efforts to bolster Oman, Pakistan, Morocco, and Jordan militarily. Having established close relations with Pakistani leaders, particularly Prime Minister Zulfiqar Ali Bhutto, the Shah told Alam that by 1976 Iran had given Pakistan more than $1 billion.[27] Clearly, with the British departure from the Persian Gulf, Iran had become a major regional power and harbored political and military ambitions beyond the region. It was also playing an important role in exercising greater control over its oil, which was a major issue in its relations with the United States, and particularly with Britain.

Compared to many other products, the price of oil had increased negligibly between 1950 and 1968, when prices began to rise steadily, along with a rapid growth in the Western demand for oil. Though mindful of the constraints and risks involved, the Shah had begun to insist on greater revenues for Iran. In 1966 he pressed the consortium to increase oil production by 17.5

percent, considerably more than it was prepared to accept. The Americans were also refusing to sell Phantom jet fighters to Iran at reduced prices. The Shah threatened to turn to the Soviets for jets and to act unilaterally against the consortium. Eventually, with Alam's help, a compromise was reached. The Shah played a key role in the negotiations. The British embassy considered the Shah's handling of the arms and oil issues "disquieting," adding that "in both cases he put on a brilliant performance in brinkmanship which paid handsomely." The embassy feared the playing of "this game" too often by an "authoritarian ruler of mercurial temperament," as it could risk not only "Iran's Western alignment" but also, in the longer term, the Shah's "own position."[28]

The Arab-Israeli war of 1967 triggered a far greater increase in oil production than the Shah had expected, but he missed no opportunities to press the consortium to increase production still further. Lashing out at the oil companies had become a favorite royal tactic to demonstrate his nationalist claims and to gain domestic credibility as well as increased revenues. When former prime minister Amini (who as finance minister had negotiated the Consortium Agreement of 1954) was seeking allies in his opposition to autocratic rule, the Shah denounced him as a "servant of the oil companies."[29] Such a posture left the Shah unable to appear too soft in his attitude to the companies. In 1970 a confrontation with the consortium again resulted in a victory for Iran and more revenues. Soon afterward, in February 1971, the Tehran Agreement between the Organization of Petroleum Exporting Countries' Persian Gulf producers, led by Iran, and representatives of the international oil industry promised Iran an additional $3.6 billion in oil revenues in the following five years.

By the early 1970s the Shah was contemplating arrangements whereby Iran would guarantee the supply of oil to oil companies for a period of twenty years, while they would formally act as contractors in Iran and their role would gradually wither away. In the spring of 1973 Iran announced the cancellation of the 1954 Consortium Agreement, due to expire in 1993, and its replacement with the twenty-year Sale and Purchase Agreement along lines envisaged by the Shah. This appeared to be a major step toward effective nationalization of the country's oil industry, attempted unsuccessfully some twenty years earlier. Yet the rights of the consortium were not radically affected, and Iran's freedom of action was less than the regime claimed; the amount of oil the country produced, for instance, would still be ultimately determined by the oil companies. By the end of 1973 Iran's oil revenues had quadrupled, reaching some $20 billion a year and enabling the Shah to spend far more on the military and development than he had anticipated. With its oil-dependent economy, Iran could be seen as a typical *rentier* state, in the sense that it received the bulk of its income from abroad, paid by the international oil industry. Reliance on oil income and the negligible impact of taxes or public contributions to state revenues reinforced the structural basis of authoritarian rule, reducing the state's need to rely on key social classes while enabling it to spend money on development. However, inflationary tendencies and other movements of the economy also became more difficult to control. Nor, indeed, could the key role of significant social forces, such as a political elite and an expanding civil service, be underestimated in the state's pursuit of its objectives.

## Enabling and Disabling Ties

Over the years the Shah tended to overestimate British clout and cunning. Conversely, referring to the Americans as "naive" had become a royal refrain.[30] The perceived American naiveté was no less troubling to the Shah than the presumed British guile; he clearly trusted neither of his chief foreign allies. The Shah viewed any change in the attitude of politicians such as Amini toward himself as merely reflecting the U.S. attitude.[31] Concealing but failing to overcome his insecurity and paranoia, he continued to fear British and American intrigues and hidden agendas in a manner unbefitting his projected image. He remained deeply sensitive about the coverage of Iranian politics by the British press and the BBC—whose views he regarded as representing British policy—as well as the London-based Amnesty International's criticism of the regime's human rights record.

The Shah's many failings, combined with his unbridled pursuit of autocratic power, had made his domestic and foreign detractors apprehensive about the future. Western concerns were overshadowed, however, as the Shah, having secured political ascendancy, accelerated the reform program. With a contrived aura of autonomy and authority, he attempted to manipulate his Anglo-American backers. Exuding an air of imperious gravitas, he saw himself as supported by key Western leaders, such as President Nixon, because he was an indispensable partner deservedly worthy of support, a strategic Cold War ally, a pillar of communist containment, a major stability-promoting player in the regional politics of the Middle East and even on the world scene, an antidote to Arab radicalism, whether Nasserist or Ba'thist.

The Shah's domestic position remained closely linked to his relations with influential outside powers, particularly the United States and Britain; he saw his handling of Iranian foreign relations, particularly the cultivation of powerful allies, as crucial to his continued grip on power at home. He had long used his by no means straightforward links with the United States and Britain to impress his domestic supporters, buttress the authoritarian structure of the regime, and lend substance to his later claims of political invincibility. Iran had escaped formal colonial domination, but foreign influence, or the widely held belief in its pervasiveness, had permeated every facet of Iranian political life. In the eyes of the civilian and military elites, who viewed foreign favor or support as the essential ingredient of success in Iranian politics, the Shah's close ties with foreign powers guaranteed the monarchy's continuity, rendering cooperation with it more expedient. Yet such ties could not be easily reconciled with the proclaimed unencumbered independence of the Shah.

Having consolidated his domestic position, the Shah, who had specifically designated foreign relations, oil, defense, and national security as areas of policy directly under his control, intensified his efforts to eradicate the image of subservience to the West and to play the role of a truly independent-minded world leader in the mold of the French president, General de Gaulle. Key development projects often proceeded with an eye to foreign policy considerations; a steel mill was being built by the Soviet Union in exchange for natural gas; gas pipelines were constructed with Western participation, and the Americans were asked to take part in establishing a petrochemicals industry. Although the United States was the main provider of weapons to the country, trade, including the purchase of weaponry, was also conducted with other major partners—West Germany, Japan, Britain, France, Italy, the Soviet bloc, Israel. By early 1970 Iran was playing a dynamic and prominent role on the international scene; without abandoning old allies such as Britain it was increasingly turning to West Germany and Japan as prominent trade partners.

Iran in the 1970s, with its ample oil revenues and stability, was a growing market for foreign, particularly Anglo-American, arms and goods. In addition to strategic and military issues, British and American diplomats became more concerned with commercial considerations—with winning lucrative contracts for their respective governments or nationals and ensuring the Shah's goodwill—than with delving into or reporting unpalatable realities. Relying on SAVAK for coverage of domestic events, in their failure to reach beyond officialdom and probe other layers of Iranian society the British and American diplomats showed a steady willingness, despite occasional mild reservations, to accept and affirm the regime's self-projected image. Assisted by the Israelis and various political brokers, and through a variety of activities, including lavish displays of largesse and extensive public relations exercises, the Iranian regime was successful in winning a host of influential friends in the United States, Britain, and elsewhere. The Shah's many trips to the United States and Europe, as well as frequent visits to Tehran by Western dignitaries, businessmen, pundits, public relations specialists, and politicians from the Soviet bloc, helped strengthen the Shah's international links and sustain his vaunted stature as a world leader respected abroad and entrenched at home.

If, in the end, the Anglo-American friends of the Shah found themselves surprised by the turn of events in Iran, they could not merely blame the Shah and his domestic supporters. The domestic factors and forces sustaining autocracy had long been reinforced by foreign interests and concerns. The peculiar autocracy of the Shah would not have persisted without extensive domestic and foreign complicity. By facilitating or condoning so enormous a concentration of power in the hands of a leader with evident failings, his domestic and foreign supporters could not expect to avoid the harsh judgment of posterity. Paradoxically, by empowering the Shah to erode the constitutional framework, and enabling him to undermine the foundations of the monarchy's legitimacy, they had in effect weakened him. Few Iranians doubted that the United States and Britain had played a key role in bolstering the Shah in the interests of Western strategic, oil, and commercial considerations, and to the detriment of Iranian democratic aspirations. At the peak of royal power Iran was far more than a passive client state of the United States, but with the onset of the revolutionary crisis it came increasingly to be seen in this light. In moments of strength, the Shah seemed determined to be the unchallenged master of his realm. In the end, the charges of his opponents that he was a foreign "puppet" became a self-fulfilling prophecy as he helplessly sought Anglo-American advice and support to weather the storm of revolutionary upheaval. Inadvertently or otherwise, the Shah missed few opportunities to lend substance to the charges of his opponents that he was inordinately subservient to foreign powers. For instance, he blamed the appointment not only of Amini but also of his last prime minister, Bakhtiar, on American pressure, seemingly without realizing the damage such assertions did to his own prestige.[32] He repeatedly attributed the measures that precipitated his departure from Iran mainly to American but also to British pressure. Curiously, he never saw the need to explain why he felt obliged to submit to such pressures so passively.

# 8

# The Architecture of Royalist Hegemony

## Character and Cosmology

The Shah, the antihero of the Iranian revolution, owed his political longevity not only to structural factors but also to contingent ones—mainly to *fortuna,* but, unlike his father, not to any particular *virtú* (in the Machiavellian sense). He had been helped by propitious or permissive circumstances and an abundance of luck, but did not possess the wisdom and guile of a virtuoso leader or the qualities of character that his assumed role demanded. His lack of *virtú* became woefully evident in adverse circumstances when *fortuna* seemed to have mysteriously deserted him. Even many sober monarchists, though sympathetic to the Shah personally, felt uncertain about his capacity to be the kind of leader he obsessively sought to be. They considered him ill equipped to run the country prudently, to enlist the services of men of ability and integrity, to play the traditionally sanctioned role of a guide and arbiter, using his political and moral authority to ensure the smooth functioning of state institutions and hold in check the bickering, corruption, and inefficiency of officialdom. Yet he projected himself exactly in this light—as the embodiment of the institution of monarchy and a benevolent ruler who firmly controlled the otherwise quarrelsome and self-seeking politicians. Indeed, he behaved as though he had fully internalized this self-image. The manufactured myth of a selfless king, a lone champion with a sense of mission, surrounded by knaves of various descriptions, appealed to the Shah's hubris, which was the obverse of his fragile self-confidence and a sublimation of his insecurity.

The Shah was self-absorbed, vain, devious, deceitful, often ruthless, but not viciously cruel. His imperious demeanor and cultivated gravitas masked an innate shyness and diffidence. Anguished and melancholic, he was too prone to agonizing self-doubt and bouts of debilitating paranoia and indecision to display the steady self-assertiveness of a successful dictator. He did, of course, eventually reinvent himself as such a dictator but remained devoid of many of the requisite dictatorial qualities—sustained resolve, a large measure of self-reliance, audacity in the face of danger, a stomach for violence. In no way could he be meaningfully compared with the likes of Iraq's Saddam Hussein or Syria's Hafez al-Asad. He lacked not only their guile but also their ferocity and penchant for unhesitant and large-scale cruelty. His regime had no qualms about the harassment, intimidation, or incarceration and torture of opponents; many opponents, particularly if they resorted to violence, met the death penalty, but he had no taste for blood. The Shah wished to be seen, and perceived himself, not as a typical Third World military ruler, but as a dignified and well-meaning, if misunderstood, monarch; a sovereign representing the authority of the historically rooted imperial Iranian traditions combined with a modern reformist vision. Though lacking the intrinsic qualities of autocratic leadership, the Shah often convincingly improvised them. Yet substance remained eclipsed by pomp, prudence by stratagem, resolve by feigned determination, foresight and knowledge by selective information and doctored statistics. The Shah was decisive when hesitation and consultation were needed, and indecisive when decisiveness was imperative. He could cope with minor setbacks but, in the face of prolonged adversity, severely faltered, even crumbled. He proved to be the cornerstone of the regime, and also its Achilles' heel.

By surviving the challenge of Mosaddeq, the Shah had overcome the greatest test of his early career. He showed determination not to allow anyone or any situation to result in a repetition of 1951–1953. Having withstood the challenge of 1963 and preempted possible military coups, he also narrowly survived several assassination attempts and flying accidents; these events helped to make him near-complacent, fatalistic, and curiously religious in his apparent conviction that he enjoyed providential protection.[1] Yet the Shah's office and role were unequivocally secular. Like other Persian kings, but unlike some earlier European counterparts, he made no pretense of enjoying thaumaturgical powers. Unlike certain other kings in the region, such as those of Jordan and Morocco, he could claim no sacred lineage; nor indeed could he claim any constitutionally envisaged religious authority. Yet he seemed confident that the Iranian monarchy's mystique not only was rooted in ancient traditions but rested on the sacred, that he had been anointed by the divine, that his enemies would perish one after another.[2] His fatalism could also verge on defeatism and resignation. Faced with a protracted crisis, the Shah felt abandoned, succumbing to paralyzing anxiety and hesitancy. Paradoxically, he both suspected convoluted foreign designs or a conspiracy to unleash a crisis against him, and sought foreign advice on how to handle the crisis.

The Shah seemed more modern than traditional in outlook. His insularity was, however, deeper than his pretensions of cosmopolitanism, despite his early Swiss education, command of French and English, extensive foreign trips, and contact with world leaders. His cosmology comprised a farrago of selective traditionalism and a skewed understanding of modernity; lacking psychological depth and intellectual breadth, it ensued from, and in turn allowed, a distorted perception. The Shah evinced no more than a thin grasp of societal change—a culturally undernourished understanding of how societies evolve and respond to misrule, well-intentioned or otherwise. He saw himself as an expert on international, strategic, oil, financial, and military issues. His technical knowledge of such matters impressed his interlocutors, but he was a man of limited education and modest intellect; his political instincts and imaginative capacity were unexceptional. Despite his appearance of reflective composure, he was capable of acting in an impulsive and erratic manner. He failed, for instance, to realize that in his often quixotic efforts to tarnish the image of former officials by invoking the pressure foreign powers might have exerted on their behalf, he damaged himself. His dearth of diplomatic finesse sometimes resulted in blunders necessitating careful damage limitation by servants such as Alam. The Shah demonstrably lacked an intuitive grasp of his real public standing; he either imagined himself popular or willfully avoided pondering his standing with the public.

The Shah had contrived a twisted narrative of the past and his own imagined "heroic" role in events such as the eviction of the pro-Soviet regime from Azarbaijan and the confrontation with Mosaddeq. He also harbored grand illusions about the near future, when Iran was to become comparable to advanced European states. He seemed confident that at the very least the continued socioeconomic revitalization of the country would generate enough prosperity to diminish the scope for discontent and to appease or disarm the politically disenfranchised. The royalist conventional wisdom took it for granted that modernization weakened or substantially delayed the need and demands for political development, that is, for civic and political openness and participatory politics. Having tenaciously discredited and marginalized the civic-nationalists and other moderate and secular opponents, the Shah purported to prove that there was no viable alternative to his regime. No alternative was conceivable to him.

The Shah appeared to entertain few doubts about what kind of government best suited Iran: whatever its formal designation, it would be a government that upheld his uncontested executive as well as politico-spiritual leadership. Regardless of who was formally in office, he would be firmly in power. The inevitable conflict between this situation and the actual requirements of a constitutional monarchy—and the ideal of a real measure of democracy that it entailed—seemed, however, to trouble the Shah, as did the implications of being part of the "Free World." During the last two decades of his rule, he made many inconsistent remarks regarding democracy. Sometimes he spoke positively about it, but maintained that because of widespread illiteracy or the people's lack of mental and spiritual readiness, democracy was inappropriate for Iran: it could be easily abused and was likely to degenerate into political fragmentation or chaos, to the obvious benefit of the Communists and other "enemies."

The Shah often sternly denounced "enemies," including foreign powers and oil companies, when appealing to the domestic audience. Yet, despite his sometimes inflated rhetoric concerning domestic and particularly international issues, his seemingly inflexible championing of Iranian national interests, and his idealistic or ideological pretensions, the Shah was a staunch pragmatist. He invariably acted cautiously vis-à-vis foreign powers. He worked, for instance, to diversify Iran's sources of arms, but knew that the country's ultimate dependence on the United States severely limited his room for maneuver. Domestically, however, he showed little flexibility in his autocratic convictions, asserting that his vision of empowering the Iranians to enjoy the fruits of development and progress could not be reconciled with the constraints of democracy. The Shah regarded Western democracy as conducive only to "the rule of a minority and encouragement of treason";[3] it was the epitome of "demagoguery"—a cardinal sin in the royalist discourse. Viewing democracy as a "ludicrous" encumbrance, he fully approved of its suspension in India by Prime Minister Indira Gandhi.[4] The Shah not only often publicly belittled Western democracies but confidently predicted their imminent demise. He sometimes astonishingly claimed that by having economically empowered the Iranian people, he had helped them to achieve true democracy. He would claim that his "crusade for national reconstruction" was "implemented within a democratic framework" without encroaching upon "individual freedom, private ownership and personal initiative."[5] In August 1976 he contended that "we" have attained "real" democracy, adding that "apparent" democracy entailed no progress.[6] One year later, when political liberalization was already under way, he would still contend that democracy was beneficial only in the form that existed in Iran and was not a commodity to be imported from abroad.

Inevitably, as the crisis facing the regime surfaced, the Shah began to speak of the desirability of constitutional democracy and the urgent need to move toward it. By then, however, few were prepared to take his *volte-face* seriously. In the end, the Shah's long-voiced claim that Iranians were unprepared for democracy seems to have become self-fulfilling. The Shah and his servile elite appeared neither to have reflected on how Iranians were to be "prepared" for democracy nor to have pondered who was responsible for their lack of practical experience of it. The Shah and the royalists had avoided dwelling on the consequences that the lack of such an experience inevitably entailed.

The Shah's often mocking dismissal of constitutional representative democracy was an indication that at the peak of his power he could not imagine or accept that there was anything wrong with his style of rule. Opponents and critics were disparaged as incorrigible malcontents who malevolently ignored what had been accomplished under his leadership. The

Shah had come to believe that on the basis of their ancient imperial traditions, Iranians viewed their king not as a figurehead or ordinary head of
state but as a spiritual father destined to act as a guide and a leader. As a paternalistic ruler personally credited for every achievement, he felt justified
in viewing himself as the country's proprietor.[7] His lax attitude toward the
abuses of the Pahlavi clan stemmed at least partially from the belief that
they were entitled to the privileges they enjoyed. Paternalism was at the
root of his tendency to treat his subjects as minors.

At the same time, exuding an air of cultivated insouciance, he increasingly betrayed little or no empathic understanding of the wants, expectations, anxieties, and collective psychology of his compatriots. To his ultimate peril he underestimated their reaction to chronic humiliation. He
proved viscerally incapable of reflecting on the consequences of his cavalier
rejection of a politics of recognition. In his self-righteous and sanctimonious paternalism, the Shah was confident that he alone was equipped to
determine what was in the country's and the people's best interest. He was
answerable only to God and "History." "He has been," wrote a British ambassador, "increasingly informed by a messianic sense of duty and destiny";
his "brooding sense of a manifest destiny is one which comes to autocratic
rulers at a certain stage of their power—that on their brow alone is the
mark of intimacy with the fates of their people. The Shah has fully identified himself with Iran. He is, in many respects, becoming an oriental de
Gaulle, but without the latter's saving grace of irony and humour."[8] By portraying himself as the infallible master of his people, the condescending
monarch unwittingly antagonized them. Failing to pay attention to the dangerous and growing rift separating him, and indeed the entire ruling class,
from the people, he self-deceptively denied such a rift. In order to rule he
found it imperative to divide his supporters; he also disarmed his actual or
avowed friends while uniting his enemies.

The Shah's steadily nurtured illusion of power was reinforced by an internalized illusion of knowledge: he and his technocratic elite seemed to
believe that they "knew" the Iranian people thoroughly and acted accord-
ingly. The Shah once told Court Minister Alam that "the Iranian people are
such a lot that if you give in to their demands you are finished, but if you
stand your ground you will prevail."[9] Alam was privately inclined to favor a
less nakedly autocratic rule, holding that in the modern world autocracy

was neither sustainable nor acceptable.[10] He feared the future but maintained that the Shah, in view of his unique qualities, was exceptional. He thus concurred with the Shah, typically arguing that

> a shah agreeing merely to reign will seal his fate, as had Ahmad Shah Qajar. The people are not mature enough to deserve democracy. As the *Shahanshah* [King of Kings] says, if we were to have real democracy in Iran, twenty-seven million Iranians would cast twenty-seven million different and contradictory ballots . . . the only option in Iran is to have an intelligent, perceptive, enlightened, wise, fair-minded and just king, with whom we are at present fortunately blessed.[11]

The Shah thus saw the Iranians as unruly, fickle, immature, fissiparous, bereft of civic spirit and the capacity for cooperation and solidarity—a people helplessly needing the firm control and guidance of a virtually all-knowing and demonstrably benevolent paternalistic king. Thus the people's failure to identify their interests along the official lines or to see themselves through the official prism resulted from ignorance, false consciousness, or groundless resentment provoked by the sworn enemies of orderly progress. The imbricated discourses of the knowledge of the rulers and the ignorance and gullibility of the disenfranchised ruled, and the smug conceit that sustained such discourses, were at the root of the regime's drastic failure of perception, banal bureaucratic complacency, and ultimately self-defeating arrogance. In contrast to its supercilious treatment of the people, the elite's seemingly unflinching confidence in the Shah—referred to by Alam as "the great leader," and by Hoveyda as "guru" and "master"—indicated profound duplicity, self-deception, or both.

In 1972 the Shah remarked to Alam with a sense of satisfaction that ministers would often inform him that they found themselves wholeheartedly convinced by his every utterance.[12] No doubt many were dissimulating, but the Shah, intoxicated by flattery, had fabricated a grandiose image of his own stature that many of his subordinates appeared to share. The Shah resented excessive praise of anyone else, even his own father. Since the queen's assumption of the regency, the Shah had shown considerable sensitivity about her receiving inordinate publicity. Only he was to be the object of copious displays of obligatory deference. Yet his expectation of unfailing reverence and unconditional loyalty induced no commensurate response in him; it contrasted starkly with his indifference to the plight of his subordinates, whom he readily turned into scapegoats if doing so served his interests. The inevitably duplicitous nature of flattery reinforced his contempt for his subordinates and, by extension, for his compatriots in general. He rarely showed himself capable of revealing the level of affection and magnetism expected of a charismatic leader. An essentially lonely figure, the Shah attempted to disguise his friendlessness as splendid imperial solitude. He increasingly mistook narcissistic self-enclosure for aura and mystique. His demeanor rarely suited affective projections; with his listless eyes and solemn scowl he radiated little warmth; nor did he generate genuine conviction. As the U.S. embassy observed in 1975, there was "very little of a human being about him"; there were "no humanizing stories as was the case with Kennedy," nor was he "the butt of dirty jokes as was the case with Nasser." By 1975 he had largely lost whatever residual popularity he may have enjoyed with segments of the lower classes. Not only was he unpopular among the middle class; there was also, the embassy noted, an "erosion of support" for him among the upper classes.[13]

Earlier in his reign the Shah had realized that he could not afford to ignore the need to relate to the public. In the 1950s, aiming to win popular support, explain his views and plans, and counter and refute his opponents, he intermittently engaged in concerted public relations exercises. During his reformist campaign of the 1960s he addressed the public more frequently. His poor oratorical skills and mangled syntax reduced his effectiveness as a communicator, but he laboriously and sententiously repeated his mantra that his personal championing of reform was motivated by a unique sense of patriotic dedication. Sometimes posing as a populist revolutionary, even a socialist, the Shah castigated the privileged classes as parasites while praising and claiming to champion the "barefooted," the downtrodden, and the toiling peasants whose support he endeavored to win. As he grew more secure as monarch, his sporadic efforts to communicate his views to the public diminished or became insipidly didactic. He more readily impugned the patriotism of anyone who failed to share his vision, which he viewed as self-evidently conducive to the common good. Without showing any sustained interest in ascertaining what the public really believed or wanted, he continued on occasion to claim that his autocratic rule was genuinely sanctioned by the people. Yet his often scornful disregard for the opinions, sentiments, and reactions of the Iranian people contrasted sharply with his undue concern about even cursory comments by the foreign media. Distrustful or dismissive of the views of even top-ranking generals or senior ministers, he was more willing to listen to his foreign interlocutors or to confide his inner thoughts to them than to the shrinking number of his Iranian friends.[14] This attitude produced a corrosive spiritual void. After his departure from Iran in January 1979 to begin a period of desperate wandering around the world before dying in Cairo in July 1980, the Shah seemed more willing to trust his newly acquired foreign confidants than his long-standing Iranian servants.[15]

By the twilight years of the monarchy it was increasingly clear that the Shah and his elite had cocooned themselves in an impenetrable web of collective self-deception. Perceiving the danger to the regime as stemming mainly from communism, civic-nationalism, and later from "Marxist" Islam, the Shah and the elite were overconfident about their vigilance, the efficacy of their co-optive and coercive measures, and the abundance of resources available to them to crush any challenge. Confident of the success of their modernization drive, they failed to realize how uneven and problematic it was in the absence of commensurate political change, and how the sociocultural strains that it had caused had remained undetected. They could not grasp how anomalous the prevailing autocracy had become; nor were they capable of comprehending the genesis of Islamism or the phenomenon of Khomeini, whose popularity they found deeply puzzling. The Shah's contempt for the clerics, shared by other key officials, particularly Alam, had helped delude them into believing that all forms of clerical influence had been eradicated. The Shah's political cosmology seriously constrained his ability to understand how an elderly mullah, whom the royalists had long considered regressive and destined for oblivion, could emerge to take charge of an overwhelming popular movement for change, defy royal power, and demand the abolition of the monarchy. How could the people, the baffled Shah and the royalists wondered, turn against him with such rancor and ingratitude, in spite of everything he had done for the country? In their eyes, the shocking public revulsion against the monarchy represented a malevolent rebellion rooted in foreign conspiracy and domestic treason.

The scale of the public discontent and the reasons for the massive mobilization of opposition challenged but did not profoundly change the Shah's

distorted and complacent assumptions regarding the country's political realities. He felt that the regime's accomplishments had not been adequately
communicated to the public. The Shah and the elite were in every respect
ill equipped either to make sense of what was happening or to deal with it.
Unlike in 1953, when the monarchy was used to symbolize social order,
anticommunism, and the protection of religion, and when the clerical establishment and traditional classes had helped the Shah to retain his throne,
now almost everyone opposed him. Even the British and the Americans,
who had in 1953 pressed him to stay in the country, were now counseling
him to leave. Later the Shah blamed his ouster on foreign, mainly American, machinations or failings. This claim was partly tactical, a bid to disclaim or minimize his own pivotal role in the genesis and success of the revolution; and a sense of self-righteous victimization and martyrdom suited
his essentially tragic character. Yet at a deeper level he seemed genuinely incapable of comprehending what had gone wrong.

At the peak of his power the Shah was ensnared in an illusion of invincibility, a belief that the imperium he had fashioned was unassailable and
incomparable to other monarchies. He solicitously patronized and subsidized deposed European royalty, including the former kings of Albania and
Greece. His largesse led the king of Spain to request a contribution of $10
million "to strengthen the Spanish monarchy." He supported the exiled king
of Afghanistan with a monthly stipend of $10,000 and other subsidies.[16]
Concerned about the stability of Pakistan, he bolstered its leaders materially and militarily. Generously assisting the kings of Jordan and Morocco, he
often worried about the future of the monarchy in those countries; he
feared that the house of Saud would soon succumb to revolutionary officers. Yet his confidence in the future prospects of the Iranian monarchy
and the security of his own tenure remained undiminished. Embracing a
constructed mythic narrative of the traditionally sanctioned role and function of the ancient Iranian monarchy and its attendant imperial glories, he
believed that they could be revived, and actively sought to do so. The Shah
found refuge in a fanciful universe of grand illusions, in part to escape the
grim realities of the police state over which he presided.

Despite his evident flaws, traceable to the very beginning of his reign, it
can be argued that had the Shah died, for instance, in 1975, the course of Iranian history and the judgment of posterity on him would have been very
different. A former British ambassador to Tehran who knew the Shah well

later plausibly observed that the Shah lived far too long and that his political longevity proved ruinous to the dynasty and the monarchy.[17] In the final years of his rule, greater foresight and wiser and more timely steps might have produced a different outcome. A less clumsy management of political liberalization, less erratic conduct, and a determined demonstration of autonomy from foreign powers might have helped to avert the revolutionary upheaval in favor of a more orderly political transformation. But such steps would only have been taken, or the need for them would not have arisen, had the Shah been a different man. The fact that the Shah, as he was, had, against numerous constraints and odds, retained the throne and remained in power for so long was by any account a remarkable record; it was fortuitous but also unfortunate.

To emphasize the character of the Shah or to argue that his role in precipitating the revolutionary displacement of the monarchy was crucial is not to ignore the structural context in which he acted. Such a context included a matrix of coercive power, an array of domestic and foreign forces on which he relied, the permissive circumstances that helped him to succeed, as well as his own mental and psychological dispositions, which negatively or positively constrained him to behave as he did. But structurally situating the conduct of the Shah or identifying the complex of factors determining or influencing that conduct does not amount to stating that he could only have acted as he did. To speak meaningfully and coherently of the *power* of the Shah is to maintain that he had the power or the ability to act differently. His own enormous responsibility for what he did or failed to do must not be underestimated. To those Iranians steeped in the values and aspirations of the Constitutional Revolution, it was utterly unjustifiable and unfortunate that the destiny of so many had come to be determined by the whims and dictates of one man, whatever his strength or weaknesses. Others, who doubted the possibility of a smoothly functioning constitutional order in the country and favored a strong monarch, could not deny that the tragedy of Iranian politics was that so much had come to depend on a man so ultimately undependable.

## The Constitution of Royal Rule

The autocratic political arrangements that emerged under Mohammad Reza Shah could not have survived his demise or even the relaxation of his firm grip. Acknowledging this fact, in 1975 the U.S. embassy described Iran as "a police state, a very sophisticated police state, which except for an assassin's bullet, has effectively eliminated every real political threat to the regime." Though emphasizing the monarchy's "mystique" in explaining its resilience, the embassy also observed that "the current system of absolute rule cannot survive Mohammad Reza Pahlavi." It pointedly added that "there is a great convenience in dealing with one man, and we probably are not going to enjoy it much longer."[18] Of course, with steady U.S. and British connivance, the Shah had long contended that anything short of his overarching control over the political process would be tantamount to governmental and parliamentary stalemate, suspension of the development drive, general disorder, and communism. Royal rule thus came to be presented as the only situationally feasible, politically viable, order-generating, and publicly beneficial polity. Sustaining such a claim required occluding alternatives and defeating or discrediting opponents and rivals; it also necessitated underlining the impracticability of constitutionalist principles, which had to a large extent been a consequence of the Shah's own obstructive meddling.

The continued use of formal, merely ceremonial constitutional procedures had no extenuating impact on the authoritarian character of the state, and did little to satisfy even partially the expectations of a muzzled but potentially lively political-civil society and the aspirations of a disenfranchised public. Parliamentary elections continued to be held but were flagrantly rigged or carefully stage-managed. Whenever elections were not completely manipulated, large segments of the urban population were galvanized to express their disapproval of the regime and its cronies by voting for civic-nationalist or independent candidates. Not even a controlled measure of popular participation or credible elections at local government or municipal level was allowed or their necessity recognized. A tame opposition had also proved unsustainable, as any criticism of government policies became in effect opposition to the Shah. No public space for even controlled voicing of criticism or venting of anger was deemed necessary. Formal associational life remained impoverished; no independent, effective political party or association was tolerated. No politician or group associated with the state was allowed to acquire a power base independent of the court. Not surprisingly, the officially sanctioned political parties failed to sway the public or disguise the autocratic character of the regime; they further demonstrated the hollowness of the regime's constitutional and parliamentary pretensions.

Militarily the Shah could boast that he enjoyed enormous power and unchallenged control over the apparatus of the state. His regime failed, however, to generate remotely comparable ideological power or a cultural capital that could help to sustain his claims to legitimate power. In the 1970s "constitutional" monarchy was increasingly overshadowed by what the Shah and the regime's publicists came to dub the "imperial system" *(nezam-e shahanshahi)*. The Shah portrayed himself as not just a head of state and a leader but also a "commander" *(farmandar)*. Concomitantly, and invoking the imperial traditions of pre-Islamic Persia, as described by the Danish scholar Arthur Christensen, the Shah proclaimed himself to be both a teacher and a spiritual guide.[19] He resorted to conspicuously lavish spectacles, pageantry, and invented traditions to justify and consolidate his new style of authoritarian rule and to maintain that monarchy had an aura, a mystique, and deep roots not only in Iranian culture but also the Iranian psyche. In 1965 the celebrations of the twenty-fifth year of his reign increased his belief in his genuine popularity. The lofty title "The Aryan Sun" *(Aryamehr)*, conferred upon him on that occasion by the dutiful parliamentarians, particularly appealed to him, evoking as it did the image of Louis XIV, the Sun King, to whom the Shah was sometimes compared.[20] In 1965 the U.S. embassy remarked that increasingly "the Shah is the Government," a point Alam often reiterated.[21] The Shah wholeheartedly approved of being identified with the very edifice of the state but otherwise described himself as "a revolutionary leader" while dismissing Louis XIV as "the kernel of reaction."[22]

The Shah's "revolutionary" posturing and rhetoric did not, however, prevent him from seeking to recast the splendor of European royalty in a highly embellished local form. His sumptuous 1967 coronation was a clear case in point and an indication of a newfound self-confidence. The extravagant celebration in 1971 of twenty-five centuries of Iranian empire allowed him to present himself as an heir and modern counterpart to the legendary Achaemenid emperor Cyrus the Great, the founder of the Persian empire. Such a self-image enabled the Shah to see his task as restoring the grandeur of ancient imperial Persia not just by emphasizing his own contrived imperial image and prerogatives but also by fashioning a modern, strong, and prosperous industrial society. The new imperial system heralded an imminent "Great Civilization," which meant that Iran would become a highly developed industrial society, and Iranians, as an Aryan people, would be comparable to Europeans. Though fearful that the corruption pervading the system might undermine progress toward his envisioned Great Civilization, he nevertheless believed it achievable by the end of the 1980s. The imagined glorious beginning of the Persian empire was linked to the envisaged splendor of the Great Civilization depicted by the Shah as Iran's destiny.

The Shah confidently embraced the heroic reformer's burden, as he saw it, to uplift and truly "civilize" his subjects. His conception of civilization entailed quantifiable and conspicuous material progress but not a qualitative civilizing process anchored in the growth of liberty, civic virtues, and meaningful citizenship. His vision did not in any way incorporate his subjects' variously voiced demands and aspirations; they would simply be led or coerced to embrace the promised civilization, which they would then surely and gratefully recognize as fulfilling their dreams. The perilous arrogance of the Shah and the elite was not lost on all royalists; Alam claims that in April 1972 he told the Shah: "we treat the people as though we are a victorious army . . . and they, the inhabitants of a vanquished country"; Ashraf concurred with this assessment.[23] Yet the Shah was unperturbed; how the deep alienation of a disenfranchised public was to be overcome did not overly concern him, how the moral squalor of a police state would give way to a "great civilization" remained unexplored. The Shah's frequent invocation of the myth of a great civilization indicated his steady loss of grip on the realities of Iranian political life.

The genesis of the discourse of the "Great Civilization" coincided with greater repression and more intrusive state control of public life. The establishment of the Resurgence Party was, among other things, intended to strengthen the regime by allowing a controlled measure of pluralism within clearly defined boundaries. It failed in this objective, as even limited debate could easily impinge on the royal power. Perceived not only as accentuating the authoritarian character of the Pahlavi state but as taking it in a totalitarian direction, the party further antagonized the regime's opponents. The single party's efforts to organize the elite, and more broadly state employees, and to mobilize a pool of public support in the state's

favor were cut short by the onset of revolutionary unrest. The Shah's jealously maintained domination over the key loci of power ensured that the
state, despite its apparent invincibility, remained structurally fragile. The
evident discrepancy between the extensive socioeconomic change taking
place in Iranian society and the personalized exercise of repressive state
power could not remain indefinitely unaddressed. The state structure had
grown too complex and the bureaucracy too large and cumbersome for one
man to presume to pull all the strings and to do so successfully. Government employees had numbered less than 700,000 in 1966; by 1976 there were
close to 1.7 million. Yet the Shah, unprepared to recognize any fault in the
substance or style of his leadership, persisted in refusing to delegate authority and responsibility or to accept the necessity of meaningful consultation
and deliberation.[24] Considering the constraints of time and the sheer volume of work involved, the Shah's insistence on personally supervising all
major affairs of the state could only mean the cursory consideration of
complex issues resulting in perfunctory and ill-considered orders.

The royalist deployment, to use the language of Antonio Gramsci, of
force and consent, with an interjection of corruption and fraud to disarm
or eliminate antagonists, had seemed successful. The regime's intermittent
offensives and retreats, its tactical fusion of coercion and concession, collision and collusion, banishment and co-optation, could have continued, in
the context of the fear-induced disorientation and fragmentation of the
opposition, to keep recognizable challenges at bay. The Shah's flair for manipulation and inducement, and his capacity to stimulate, exploit, and hold
in check the petty rivalries of his docile subordinates, could in normal circumstances have continued to bear fruit. Sustained by foreign support, a
formidable military, and an extensive security apparatus, he could have
retained his power. Yet the regime's idiosyncratic political structure rendered it intrinsically vulnerable. Enabled by his institutional position as
king, by his power of patronage, and by his political longevity, the Shah had
crafted a system that only he, in normal circumstances and when enjoying
robust physical and mental health, could manage and control. When circumstances became extraordinary and the Shah's physical health and mental state deteriorated, control from the top, and its associated matrix of gen-
eralized fear, dwindled; no one else was in a position to step in to salvage
the regime. Having long been lionized as an Olympian, near-infallible, and

extraordinary ruler, the Shah could no longer resume the earthly demeanor of an ordinary constitutional monarch. His promises to modify his style of rule could not inspire confidence. The identification of the Shah not only with the institution of the monarchy but with the very foundations of the state meant that the removal of the Shah or his serious loss of credibility would not spare the state.

The Shah had been terminally ill since 1974, although this fact was kept a secret for a considerable time from his closest confidants, foreign allies, and even from himself. The Shah's illness could be construed as a metaphor for the decay of the royal body politic. For a leader who had become indispensable to the system he had crafted, awareness of the severity of his illness and intimations of death must have been overwhelming. The medications he took may also have had an adverse effect on his alertness.[25] Yet he had never shown any real capacity for handling a momentous crisis. Shocked by the extent of the vocal opposition to his rule, the Shah began to lose his will for political survival. He had failed to convince his opponents that he intended to abandon his autocratic grip on power; he also failed to show that he was determined to save the regime. The Shah's metamorphosis from a boastfully imperious *Shahanshah* into a timidly tolerant, disoriented, and accommodating monarch inevitably involved a drastic diminution of aura and power. Structured to respond only to royal control, in the face of the Shah's failing leadership the state's various organs could not function in coordination. Without the harmonizing, coercively enforced royal domination, the regime lost its coherence and sense of direction.

The tragedy of constitutionalism in Iran was that it gave rise neither to an effective and credible parliamentary government nor to a socially rooted, structurally robust, impersonal state. By the eve of the monarchy's collapse, the country had made undeniable strides in the direction of modernity, yet its structure of rule was anomalously premodern. It had proved inimical to constitutionally sanctioned rights and entitlements, to real party politics, to an active civil society, and to any real measure of popular participation. It rested primarily on patronage, on the assumed loyalty of a domesticated elite readily willing to assist the Shah in his personal arrogation of political power, and on the assistance of a coterie of amply rewarded henchmen. It enjoyed foreign backing, abundant oil wealth, and the support of an extensive machinery of coercion, surveillance, and punishment that aimed at

promoting fear rather than respect. Like all autocracies, it fostered paranoia; it could neither readily trust its supporters nor fail to monitor them
and thus keep them divided. Its fear of the public was naturally far deeper;
it relentlessly sought to eliminate and incapacitate its opponents or perpetuate their fragmentation; it hoped to prolong the apparent apathy of the coercively silenced and depoliticized masses.

## "The Constitution" as Ideology

All four monarchs who reigned in the era of constitutional monarchy, that
is, between 1907 and 1979, died in exile. This rarely noticed but highly significant fact starkly highlights the deeply problematic nature of attempting
to reconcile monarchy and constitutional governance in the specific circumstances of Iran. Constitutionally, the greater part of Pahlavi rule amounted
to an undeclared state of emergency. Though adhering to a formal procedural façade of constitutionalism, Reza Shah showed scant concern for its
substance. From the very outset of his reign in 1941, Mohammad Reza Shah
aspired to emulate his father, despite pledging otherwise. Yet, unlike his father, who simply bypassed the Constitution, Mohammad Reza Shah sought
to manipulate and tamper with it in order to achieve his aims. Contrary to
unwarranted assumptions about his earlier democratic inclinations, he had
at no time been free from an obsession with enhancing his own political
role. From the very outset of his reign, the Shah had attempted to maintain
direct and secret links with the British, bypassing the normal ministerial
channels. Incessantly complaining about his powerlessness and the dysfunc-
tional nature of the country's parliamentary arrangements, he strove to increase his constitutional prerogatives, which he eventually succeeded in for-
malizing through the Constituent Assembly of 1949.

The Constitution had unequivocally associated power with accountability, thereby barring the unaccountable monarch from exercising effective
power. During the reign of Mohammad Reza Shah the contrast between
monarchism and constitutionalism revealed itself not only in the Shah's all
too clear subversion but also in its frequent invocation of "the Constitution." The Constitution was thus used both to undo constitutionalism and
as an ideological justification for the endeavor. Even politicians sympathetic
to the Shah and his aims had long feared that such conduct undermined the

credibility of the Constitution as the monarchy's legal foundation, and ulti-mately focused all responsibility for the omissions and commissions of the government on the Shah alone. The identification of governance with the Shah meant that anti-Shah sentiments would be unmistakably directed against the very foundations of the monarchy. Yet the Shah proved unre-lenting: he not only wielded enormous power but also presented the Con-stitution as endorsing the centrality of a powerful monarchy in the Iranian body politic. The Constitution became the primary means of consecrating the pivotal role of the monarchy. Respect for the Constitution was pro-claimed to imply the inviolability of the monarchy and to affirm its all-encompassing prerogatives. The Constitution would indeed be seen as de-fining the rights and entitlements of the Shah and delimiting the duties and obligations of his subjects. It would also, the Shah hoped, ensure continuing autocratic Pahlavi rule after his demise.

In 1973 the Shah told the British ambassador that he intended to rule for another decade, when he would be sixty-four years old, and then delegate power to the crown prince.[26] According to the U.S. embassy, the Shah had prepared a will that "allegedly liberalizes politics in Iran and limits the pow-ers that his son will exercise as Shah."[27] Yet in November 1973, in a confiden-tial address that, as Alam recounts, amounted to the Shah's political will, the monarch admonished the country's top civilian and military leaders to ensure the continuity of his style of rule in the event of his death. He par-ticularly urged the military to uphold the version of the Constitution that he promulgated and to make certain that, as the country's "higher inter-ests" required, his successor enjoyed the same "legal prerogatives" that he had. Nor should the military ever accept the changing of a system that had resulted in "such a degree of advancement and progress." The Shah empha-sized that his control over the executive, which was an "exclusive royal do-main," had resulted in advances in the country that "astonished and sur-prised the world—and this was only the beginning."[28]

This understanding and usage of the Constitution, negating its spirit and also a substantial number of its entrenched clauses, characterized the greater part of the Shah's reign. The maximalist royalist view of the mon-arch's constitutional prerogatives was taken as self-evident. No debate was tolerated, let alone fostered, regarding its purported constitutional plausibil-ity, or whether any constitutionally justified royal authority could be construed and reconciled with the imperative of parliamentary governance. The royalist abuse of the Constitution and opposition to its legitimate employment to justify and sustain an effective court-independent parliamentary government had far-reaching consequences. Paradoxically, it strengthened an alternative approach to constitutionalism that, perhaps inevitably, assumed an aridly legalistic and predominantly oppositional character, inattentive to and not easily reconcilable with the exigencies of effective governance.

Democratic constitutionalism could not be reconciled with an institutionally powerful and interventionist monarchy. Constitutionalism, by its very nature, implied the taming of authority, the maintenance of checks and balances, and an effective mechanism of accountability, the establishment of institutions and procedures for promoting and safeguarding essentially egalitarian political and civic rights. It represented modern values and involved the emergence of a framework for public deliberation. It required sustained and reflective debate about institutions, rights, laws, values, culture, identity. It defined or affected norms, rules, and practices pertaining to the whole gamut of political and civil life. It necessitated rational and critical evaluation of inherited traditions; it entailed a modern, forward-looking vision and a break with the past. Monarchy, on the other hand, by refusing to submit to constitutional taming, represented the rejected past. Firmly embedded in premodern values, it sought to perpetuate unencumbered authority, privilege, hierarchy, patronage, deference, and elitism. Its ethos was inherently incompatible with the civic and political egalitarianism implicit in constitutional representative democracy. Unable to adapt itself to the constraints of constitutionalism, the monarchy sought, among other things, to pronounce it impractical. Royalists would contend that constitutionalism was inimical or irrelevant to the more urgent needs of order, national regeneration, and socioeconomic reforms, promoted by a benevolently autocratic king. Yet autocracy was the very antithesis of the struggles and aspirations that characterized the Iranian Constitutional Revolution. Indeed, the key objective of that revolution had been to depersonalize the exercise of state power.

An authoritative or legally justifiable reading of the Constitution had long been a contentious issue in Iranian politics. Prime ministers such as Qavam and Mosaddeq, who had tried to govern with a real measure of authority, found themselves vulnerable to charges of deviation from the Constitution. However, what constrained the authority of capable prime ministers and enabled the Shah to play a preponderant role was not constitutional provisions as such, but the institutional weakness of the executive and legislative branches of the government in contrast to the strength of the monarchy. Such weakness was of course exacerbated by the inadequacies of the Constitution if literally interpreted. Even before 1953, the Shah was institutionally enabled to manipulate the entire constitutional process, to influence elections, and to affect factional alliances, the conduct of parliament, and the composition of the cabinet. The monarchy's institutional salience ensured that the Shah was inordinately capable of taking advantage of the opportunities provided by the disarray of the constitutional arrangements, which he himself had a key role in aggravating. Given the permissive sociopolitical context, the availability of ample opportunities, as well as the pressures and expectations of the vast royalist clientele, only a virtuous and wise monarch—characterized as "civilized" by statesmen such as Mosaddeq—could resist the temptation to abuse his position, and confine himself to the role of a benevolent arbiter of the political process. He would, within the confines of the Constitution, strive to harmonize the various institutions of the state, harness his autocratic impulses, and resist the temptation to don the mantle of a recklessly impatient modernizer.

Neither of the Pahlavi monarchs displayed the qualities of character valued by the constitutionalists; nor did they adequately reflect on the consequences of their excesses or refusal to recognize any alternative between being either a redundant figurehead or an outright autocrat. By retaining the constitutional framework, they recognized that ultimately no other effective legitimizing mechanism existed. They tried to ensure that constitutional formalities were more or less observed, but by systematically undermining meaningful constitutionalism they perilously deprived themselves—and ultimately the monarchy—of the very legitimacy that, particularly in moments of crisis, they sorely needed. They took the need for an authoritative state to mean the need for an authoritarian state. By invoking and exaggerating the inevitable problems of parliamentary politics, and by declaring the country unprepared for full-fledged democracy, they subverted the residual credibility of constitutional procedures and all other forms of political accountability.

## Authoritarian Developmentalism as Legitimation

Foremost among various rationales proffered for authoritarian monarchism was the need for the efficient implementation of reform. Reiterating a familiar royalist contention, the Shah asserted that "to carry through reforms, one can't help but be authoritarian."[29] Under Reza Shah, the revitalization of the socioeconomic life of the country was held to be attainable only coercively, with the result that his rule degenerated into tyranny. After the coup of 1953 Mohammad Reza Shah moved in a similar direction. By dispensing with the last vestiges of real constitutional legitimacy, the Shah and the state, which he increasingly personified, needed new sources of legitimacy. Thus the royalists came to invoke the rhetoric of development and advocated socioeconomic modernization.

Chief among the proclaimed development objectives, which became a central component of the "White Revolution" of the 1960s, was land reform, an aim long on the agenda of Iranian politics. Championed by Hasan Arsanjani (minister of agriculture, May 1961–March 1963), who also played a crucial role in implementing its first, and radical, stage, land reform was appropriated by the Shah to lend substance to his "revolutionary" claims. Despite its considerable dilution after 1963, it had a major impact on sociopolitical life in both rural and urban areas. Its first stage in particular could be seen as a bona fide distributive project infused with a recognizable notion of social justice. Another measure with potentially wide-ranging consequences was the literacy drive. Parviz Natel-Khanlari (education minister, July 1962–March 1964) later maintained that he had initiated the literacy corps, and complained about bureaucratic barriers and corruption marring his efforts, which were also relentlessly undermined by SAVAK.[30] Another significant step was the extension of the franchise to women, which, at least as a strong aspiration, was traceable to the early phase of Iranian constitutional politics.

Most measures undertaken by the regime, regardless of how effectively they were implemented, were steps that any country with comparable problems and resources would have adopted in one form or another. A less paternalistic government would have proved more successful in initiating pertinent reforms that the public recognized as genuinely intended to promote the common welfare. In the absence of public debate, a free press, and parliamentary accountability, development priorities remained arbitrary; thoughtful strategy and coherence suffered, sociocultural sensitivities were ignored, and opportunities for corruption abounded. Not unexpectedly, the autocratic modernizing drive provoked a backlash. Unconcerned, the Shah confidently persisted in his projected role of a benevolent absolutist ruler. Yet absolutism, even if benevolent in intention, was rarely benevolent in consequence; it was invariably accompanied by unchecked high-level corruption and increasing public disaffection.

State planning, which began in 1949 under the auspices of the Plan Organization, constituted a program to transform the country's socioeconomic infrastructure. The increase in oil revenues in the late 1960s and the 1970s ensured that development projects in the areas of education, health, welfare, communications, urbanization, and industrialization gained momentum. Projects included the expansion of the university system and the public health infrastructure and the construction of roads, railroads, airports, hotels, a modern air transportation system, and other communications facilities. The construction of major dams and the development of hydroelectric power proceeded, along with the establishment of the petrochemical industry and the laying of gas pipelines to the cities. In addition to oil and gas, the country was endowed with other natural resources, including copper, large reserves of which were discovered near Kerman in 1967. The Tehran stock exchange opened in October of that year. The fourth development plan, which started in 1968, focused on rapid industrialization. Coexisting with an interventionist state, the private sector continued to grow. By 1969 the regime boasted economic growth of 12 percent; stability and economic opportunities attracted foreign investment. In 1972 a steel mill began operating near Esfahan, and heavy machinery and aluminum plants also opened. The government claimed that Iran's economic growth was second only to that of Japan. In 1974 Iran began building nuclear reactors in the southern port of Bushehr, with completion expected by 1980;[31] assisted by West Germany, France, and particularly the United States, Iran was actively pursuing an extensive nuclear energy program. By early 1976 preliminary steps for constructing a subway network in Tehran were under way.

The development of agriculture lagged far behind, but it was to be boosted by the fifth plan (1973–1978). As the U.S. embassy observed in 1975, "Iranians were net exporters of agricultural products until the land reform program . . . [which was] a political and sociological success but an economic disaster since it sanctified small agricultural plots and spawned legislation which made private agricultural investment very unattractive."[32] In the fiscal year 1975 Iran imported approximately a billion dollars' worth of agricultural goods.[33] Clearly, the government had failed in the long run to sustain agricultural productivity or to devote adequate resources for the creation of an effective infrastructure to support the peasants. The decline of agriculture also deleteriously accelerated urbanization and depleted the agrarian workforce. The growing population and falling agricultural productivity continued to increase the need for food imports. A massive increase in government spending, a building boom, and uncontrollable property speculation, particularly in Tehran, resulted in sharp inflation and social distress. From 1970 on, inflation threatened continued economic growth. In 1972 inflation was at 7–8 percent; by the spring of 1973 it had reached 10–15 percent.[34] The official indices, however, tended to understate the inflation rate.

The shortage of rental accommodation in the cities and exorbitant property prices and rental costs began to affect lower-income groups. Foreigners, mostly Americans, living in salubrious areas of cities like Tehran and Esfahan, aggravated the situation, as they were able to live lavishly and afford high rents. The overcrowded capital was beset by lack of affordable accommodation, power outages, an inadequate piped water and sewage system, traffic congestion, and deficient public transport. The appearance of makeshift dwellings and the shortage and high cost of basic foodstuffs such as sugar and meat, which primarily affected the lower classes, indicated deep structural problems. The infrastructure, particularly the capacity of ports and roads to handle goods and traffic, remained inadequate. Administrative inefficiency worsened the situation. The lack of an adequately trained workforce, whether physicians, teachers, or truck drivers, was acute. Medical doctors were concentrated in Tehran and other major cities; beyond these there was one doctor for every 16,000 people. The educational infrastructure, particularly at the primary level, had remained glaringly inadequate and outmoded; by 1976 there was a scandalous shortage of schools, and overcrowded classes necessitated a three-shift school day. Geared to learning by rote, the educational system failed to develop analytical and creative thinking in students. Despite efforts to combat it, illiteracy, estimated at 50 percent, remained a major handicap and an embarrassment; average life expectancy was fifty-two years. In both areas, Iran fell well below Turkey.

In the face of rising inflation, exacerbated by uncontrolled public spending, the government targeted symptoms rather than causes; it blamed small shopkeepers and middle-income bazaar merchants for high prices, causing acute resentment. Corruption, inefficiency, and the often cosmetic nature of government measures to deal with inflation made the situation worse. Government policies also adversely affected the morale of the private sector. Segments of the upper middle class resented policies that tampered with their wealth. Pressuring industrial concerns to sell 49 percent of their shares to their employees or to offer them as stock failed to produce desired results. Lower-income Iranians were more harshly affected by the regime's policies. The absence of independent unions and adequate labor laws left workers vulnerable; the government's policy of allocating workers a portion of the profits made by their employers or giving them company shares failed to lessen their burden. They contrasted themselves indignantly with the *nouveaux riches* and the well connected, with their abundance of wealth and privileges. The opportunities for rapid self-enrichment both encouraged domestic parasitism and attracted an army of international contract seekers, adventurers, brokers, and venture capitalists, as well as sycophants and publicists of various colors, all seeking to make a quick profit. Brokerage, the exchange of favors, bribery, and the payment of "commissions" by foreigners dealing with Iran and their Iranian contacts became a lucrative and effectively tolerated, if not officially condoned, business.

Modernization was intended primarily to increase the viability of the regime. It involved the establishment of a more effective bureaucratic machine ostensibly dedicated to promoting public welfare but in effect geared to enhancing the state's coercive and exploitative control over society and national resources. The primary beneficiaries of modernization were the ruling elite and the emerging *nouveaux riches* associated with them. In a broader perspective, modernization signaled and reinforced the interrelated processes of state formation and nation-building steadily under way since the Constitutional Revolution and intensifying under the Pahlavis. Such processes required both effective leadership and strong institutions; the structure of the state suffered as a result of zealously nurtured dependence on one man. Modernization was bound to generate a greater urge for a public space of debate; it could not but contribute to the emergence of a more extensive oppositional matrix. At the same time, by helping to remove the residual traditional and constitutional restraints on the conduct of the state, it rendered its opponents increasingly vulnerable.

By the mid-1960s the royalist discourse, iconography, rhetoric, and ceremonials were employed increasingly to craft a new image of kingship as the promoter of the public good. Authoritarian monarchy was portrayed not only as sanctioned by Iranian cultural traditions, but also as the only political system capable of promoting modernity and prosperity. Undoubtedly the Shah wished to build a modern, prosperous Iran, but his vision of prosperity was tragically narrow. Former premier Amini believed that although the Shah undoubtedly loved his country, the love did not extend to the people.[35] Not surprisingly, far from obliterating the appeal of democratic and civic values and institutions, socioeconomic development accentuated the need for them. The unintended and unanticipated consequences of socioeconomic development heightened tensions and public resentments rooted in the systematic disregard of democratic aspirations.

With the quadrupling of oil revenues, careful and competent management of the Iranian economy and the wise handling of such revenues to contain their dangerously destabilizing impact became vital. Yet the state failed to forestall the overheating of the economy. Instead it spent lavishly and accelerated the growth of its grandiose military and prestige industrial projects. Yet the country remained a market for mainly Western manufactured goods, while inflation continued to erode the income of the lower classes. By 1976, when oil revenues began to decline, wasteful measures and policies, including loans to other countries, inordinate military expenditure, and the regime's mindless largesse, had limited its room for maneuver. It was unable to devote adequate resources to crucial areas such as housing and urban infrastructure; many publicly beneficial projects had to be shelved. In the last decade of Pahlavi rule, overall prosperity had undoubtedly increased, but policies and mechanisms for addressing the issues of distributive justice remained erratic and haphazard. Among the lower classes in particular a strong sense of relative deprivation was on the rise. The life-style and intelligibility gap between the seemingly modern and extravagantly Westernized dominant minority and the rest of society had dangerously widened.

Efforts to alleviate structural bottlenecks often made them worse. Focusing the blame for high prices on shopkeepers and bazaar merchants deeply alienated them without appeasing the low-income consumers. The state-sponsored Chamber of Guilds and the Committee for Consumer Protection did not appear able to resolve their squabbles.[36] Complaints and charges of wrongdoing, particularly against high-ranking officials, were addressed not only through conventional legal mechanisms but also by court-sponsored bodies such as the Royal Inspectorate and the Royal Commission. The people staffing these bodies, which were essentially mere public relations vehicles for the monarch, were incapable of addressing the huge volume of complaints and instances of uncovered or reported injustice, and thus of inspiring public confidence.

Although many measures were aimed at improving the regime's public image, they were at the same time intended to address existing socioeconomic problems and attend to lingering inequities in areas such as the social position of women. Legislation aimed at improving women's rights, revising the divorce laws, and limiting polygamy was introduced; a family protection law sought to secure greater entitlements for women. The entry of women into the higher echelons of government had clearly helped to bring gender issues to the fore. Steps were also taken to create a more modern cultural infrastructure. With the rise in royal self-confidence and resolve, and the increasing resources available to the state, many significant areas of cultural life, including printing and publishing, libraries, research and teaching institutions, and museums and exhibitions, received considerable attention, as did the Iranian cultural heritage, folklore, the performing arts, Persian as well as Western music, and cultural and academic exchanges. The material and institutional foundations of urban popular as well as high culture continued to develop. By the second half of the 1960s Tehran was becoming the site of increasing geographic and social mobility. The affluent inhabitants of Tehran and other major cities enjoyed greater opportunity for foreign travel, which helped widen horizons but at the same time increased awareness of the country's shortcomings. Emerging as a distinctly cosmopolitan city, Tehran attracted a host of foreign visitors; it became a venue for international conferences on topics such as Persian art and architecture. Tehran's population had increased from 200,000 at the turn of the century to nearly three million by the end of the 1960s; by the eve of the revolution it was close to five million.

Since 1967 the French-educated wife of the Shah had endeavored to act as a role model for modern Iranian women. She showed particular interest in artistic, cultural, and architectural projects. Although her support for outlandish artistic expression at times revealed egregious inattention to local sensibilities, her sponsorship and supervision of cultural projects expedited their completion. She was, for instance, the moving spirit behind the establishment in 1974 of Tehran's Museum of Contemporary Art, which housed an exceptionally rich collection of modern and contemporary Western art. Elitist cultural life came to be in many respects imbued with a modern ethos, but secular sociocultural institutions catering to the needs of the less privileged received little attention. Social liberties became more meaningful and extensive; religious minorities, though to a far lesser degree assertive ethnic ones, felt more secure in their sense of belonging and citizenship.

An institution central to a public life of order and security, as well as to constitutionalism, was the judiciary. Although autocracy was essentially incongruent with the rule of law, the gradual development of a modern judiciary created a real measure of legal security and predictability; its success in institutionalizing impersonal and rational legal norms throughout the country was by no means negligible. The emerging legal system, though not immune to bureaucratic inefficiency and to pressure, influence, and abuse, was capable of considerable effectiveness and impartiality. Thanks to the elaborate codification and reasonable clarity of the laws, established legal procedures, the probity of many judges, and the skill of attorneys, the opportunity for fair settlement of disputes and for legal redress was considerable. The integrity of certain judges verged on the legendary and conferred considerable celebrity. Generations of lawyers, trained mainly at the School of Law, which had been incorporated into Tehran University, helped the consolidation and institutionalization of a uniform nationwide legal order. Even military tribunals followed well-regulated and predictable procedures, and severe punishments were reserved for clear-cut and extreme cases. The judiciary was not a means of intimidating or terrorizing opponents and silencing dissent. Such tasks were performed by SAVAK.

Applicants for public service knew—as it had become a routine fact of life—that they had to be carefully screened and endorsed by SAVAK. There was, however, no institutionalized system of discrimination. In most cases the absence of a recent record of opposition to the regime was adequate; loyalty would not be formally tested, and there was no need for any positive demonstration of ideological commitment to the regime. There was no systematic positive discrimination in favor of the regime's supporters, such as, for instance, in the allocation of university places. Overall achievements in improving the quality and standard of living were below what the regime claimed but were by no means negligible. Yet the regime, despite or because of its machinery of propaganda, was not able to capitalize on its accomplishments convincingly. The vast but inept and cumbersome public relations apparatus of the state, including the government-run media, remained hampered by relentless and effusive adulation of the Shah, stale platitudes, chronic mendacity, and routine disingenuousness. The people tended to disbelieve official pronouncements and viewed most state-sponsored measures with cynicism. The regime's paternalistic refusal to concern itself with public opinion and perceptions, its defiance of accountability and transparency, and its elimination of mechanisms through which real public opinion and sentiments could be articulated or gauged inevitably overshadowed its achievements.

Achievements in the sociocultural and judicial spheres found no commensurate parallel in the political arena and were marred and distorted by political repression and the regime's failure to tolerate, let alone engage, even its moderate and politically responsible opponents. The erosion of civil society and credible parliamentary institutions hampered the emergence of an informed citizenry capable of smoothly adapting itself to the demands of participatory politics in the event of the regime's abandonment of its authoritarian drive. The parliament, the central edifice of constitutionalism, underwent a gradual but irreversible decline in the years after 1953. Under the presidency of the respected elder statesman Taqizadeh, the senate had remained able for some time to play an effective role. With the presidency of Sharif-Emami, starting in 1963 and coinciding with the consolidation of royal autocracy, the senate became an insignificant body. In the same vein, the public standing of the lower house of parliament reached a nadir under the unimaginatively dull Speakership of Abdollah Riazi, who also assumed this position in 1963, retaining it for fifteen years. Riazi, a professor of engineering, was not at all comparable in stature or effectiveness to his accommodating but shrewd and in no way docile veteran predecessor Reza Hekmat (Sardar Fakher). Riazi's unquestioning deference toward the Shah contrasted sharply with his disdainful attitude toward the deputies, whom he treated virtually as schoolchildren. Yet the substantial parliamentary opposition in 1964 to the immunities bill revealed that even a packed and muzzled parliament could not be overly cavalier in defying national interests or public expectations. Thereafter the parliament would not be allowed to act except in a compliantly endorsing capacity. In the last year of the monarchy the parliament resumed its assertive role, but by then it was too late: the deputies and senators could no longer in any sense claim to represent the people, and the parliament as an institution had almost irretrievably lost its credibility.

The royalists had long assumed that socioeconomic development could be achieved only through royal leadership, at the expense of constitutionalism. Even if this assumption was remotely plausible, the cost was too high. Authoritarian monarchy was bound to degenerate into oppressive misrule with no legitimate basis. If the government had even partially tolerated the constitutionalist opposition, had adopted a less repressive attitude toward its critics, and had not so systematically eroded the credibility of the constitutional arrangements, the fate of the regime and the country would have been different. Perhaps the pace of certain development projects would have been slower, but corruption and extravagance would have been held in check through parliamentary accountability and through public scrutiny by the media. The regime would certainly not have so drastically undercut its own legitimacy; citizens participating in the political process would have rallied to its support or would not have readily turned against it; calls to overthrow the regime would not have so overwhelmingly resonated with an antagonized or alienated public. Clearly, toward the end of the monarchy's rule whatever capacity it had previously mustered for reproducing legitimacy by invoking the discourse of development had been lost.

The regime persisted in seeing development as achievable only at the expense of a full-fledged democratic process and incompatible with meaningful political accountability. It assumed that the disenfranchised public would accept a trade-off between material prosperity and democratic aspirations. The opposite happened. The promised or partially delivered material well-being did not provide an antidote to political resentment or a substitute for political freedom and participation. Thus the nation ended up paying a high price for an uneven authoritarian developmentalism that was financed by squandered oil revenues and was far less extensive and qualitatively satisfying than it could have been. By portraying political and civic liberties as anathema to development, the regime not only denied the public those liberties but deprived itself of any positive impact that its development policies might have had on its public standing. Recognition of an intrinsic link between meaningful development and freedom was not alien to civic-nationalist thinking; such a link—emphasized in recent years by prominent development economists such as Amartya Sen—was, however, ignored, denied, or rejected by the technocratic royalist elite.[37]

The Shah cherished Iran's military strength and its key regional and international position. He aspired and worked for the country's steady socio-economic development, envisaging the fulfillment of his promised "Great Civilization." It was, however, the docile, politically myopic, and culturally distant technocrats, seemingly dedicated to implementing the Shah's vision of beneficent social engineering, who were to be the harbingers of the "Great Civilization." The imperative of ascertaining and taking into account the uncoerced views, aspirations, and judgment of the people themselves lay beyond the royal conception of governance. The Shah and the royalist elite ignored or dismissed the crisis of representation that had engulfed Iranian public and political life. They feared that their hold on power would be jeopardized if they replaced scornful dismissal by genuine attempts to address the grievances and arguments of their opponents. Authoritarian rule, and the privileges of those who sustained it, could obviously not be reconciled with embracing a politics of recognition. Any affirmation that citizens, as distinct from subjects, were entitled to political and civic rights and real opportunities to participate in shaping their destiny had far-reaching consequences. In the specific circumstances of Iran, however, the continuation and peculiar configuration of the royal authoritarian regime, which systematically and myopically undermined civil society, secular democratic forces, and the very possibility of a politically mature citizenry, guaranteed that its successor regime would also, tragically, be authoritarian. The royalists could never disclaim or shrug off their enormous responsibility not just for the collapse of the monarchy but also for the character of the regime that followed it.

# 9

# A Culture of Confrontation

## The Crippling of Civil Society

From 1953 onward the institutions of civil society gradually faded. Independent trade unions, associations of guilds, and autonomous professional associations were disbanded or not allowed to emerge. Bodies such as the Association of Journalists and the more resilient Lawyers' Association came under effective government control. Press freedom was increasingly curtailed. Independent political parties were no longer tolerated. No opposition group was allowed to present itself as a politically responsible player in public life and a potential alternative to the government. The Mosaddeqists' efforts to organize themselves and engage in open political activity provoked harassment and imprisonment. Following their release from eight months of imprisonment in September 1963, the exhausted National Front leaders failed to regain the initiative and revive their organization. By May 1964 the leadership of the veteran civic-nationalist Allahyar Saleh had been discredited. He had become politically inactive and, along with like-minded colleagues, felt that they had reached an impasse. Interrelated factors such as the weakness of leadership, fragmentation, failure to accommodate Mosaddeq's insistence on a more inclusive organization,[1] and, most significantly, the highly inhospitable political milieu left no room for the Front to survive, let alone flourish.

*Allahyar Saleh, leader of the second National Front in the early 1960s.* (Courtesy
of the Institute for the Study of Contemporary Iranian History, Tehran)

The civic-nationalists were denied the opportunity for intellectual self-
renewal and experience-based revision of their ideas. In their tenacious
constitutionalism, they seemed unperturbed by the crucial question of the
practical feasibility of their political vision. Their royalist antagonists saw
them as espousing unreconstructed, legalistic, and impractical ideas. They
were vulnerable to the charge of having ignored the need to develop a reform program to rival that of the regime. Prominent in voicing this charge
was Khalil Maleki, a former Tudeh Party leader who had joined the civic-
nationalists and become one of their most incisive exponents. A trenchant
critic of the strategy and tactics of senior Mosaddeqists in the post-1953 era,
and of their approach to reviving the National Front, he was shunned by
them. With his residual Marxian premises, and without ignoring the significance of principles and ideals, Maleki saw politics more in terms of ide-

ology, interest, class, and organization. He advocated active leadership and management of public opinion rather than deferring passively to the public. The Front, he maintained, needed to appropriate an agenda of socioeconomic reform more far-reaching than that of the regime, and to distance itself from traditional or conservative forces. Overestimating the immediate difficulties facing the regime, he assumed that it was willing to make significant concessions to reach a rapprochement with the Mosaddeqists.[2]

Skeptical about such an approach, mindful of both their traditional and modern constituencies, and distrustful of the Shah, senior Mosaddeqists remained wary of significantly modifying their strategy. They continued to think primarily in terms of the constitutional imperatives of restraining the Shah and ensuring electoral, press, and associational freedoms. The regime portrayed disagreements among the Mosaddeqists as revealing inherent fissiparity, but to a large extent they indicated serious internal debates on how to adapt to the new circumstances or respond to the regime's reformist rhetoric. Measures such as land reform had strong supporters among them. Rather than opposing reform as such, what they deplored was the regime's strategy of invoking it in order to eliminate or occlude the constitutionalist agenda and render democratic politics redundant. The political approach adopted by senior Mosaddeqists left them with little room for maneuver and ended in virtual inactivity; given the political circumstances, they saw no path that would allow them to survive and pursue their objectives.

The Mosaddeqists enjoyed considerable support among the urban middle class—teachers, engineers, lawyers, journalists, clerks, bazaar merchants—which was broadly identified with civic-nationalist aspirations. Expansion of the public and private sectors and of institutions such as the Plan Organization, universities, the National Iranian Oil Company, banks, and insurance companies provided new opportunities for employment, thereby broadening the base of actual or potential National Front support. Yet the modern middle class—largely employed by or otherwise subordinated to the state, whose political leverage had increased along with oil revenues—felt unable to reveal its political preferences. Thus a potentially vital constituency, including the more vocal segments of the intelligentsia, continued to resent its politically disenfranchised status and its inability to support openly entities such as the National Front. Cut off from their constituency, bereft of charismatic leadership, and barred from maintaining a formal political presence in the public sphere, the Mosaddeqists were in effect gradually relegated to the political wilderness. Some National Front activists would regret their refusal to cooperate with Amini during his premiership. As a critic of royal autocracy, Amini would also, in the mid-1960s, try to form an alliance with them, but the regime was determined to thwart all such coalitions.

Though trying to co-opt the Mosaddeqists, the regime had taken no steps that might have enabled even the most moderate among them to claim that cooperation could benefit their cause. The Mosaddeqists were left in no doubt that they would be tolerated only if they accepted the royalist agenda *in toto* and affirmed that the Shah not only reigned but also ruled the country. Such an acceptance would have been tantamount to abandoning the foundational principles of their political existence. No segment of the Mosaddeqists could afford to be accommodating on this issue; they could not contemplate an understanding with the regime without tangible gains in furthering their democratic agenda. The regime's tactic of co-opting National Front elements continued; the United States, by no means favorable to the National Front collectively, endorsed such attempts, which resulted in recruiting no more than a few individuals—people such as Fereydun Mahdavi, who was soon elevated to ministerial rank.[3] The tactic failed either to lend respectability to the regime or to diminish the appeal of Mosaddeqist ideas. Although the Mosaddeqists' ideals and their principled refusal to be co-opted assured them a continuing moral and political standing, by the 1970s the younger generation of Iranians—even many younger activists—systematically deprived of knowledge about recent history, knew little about them.

Non–National Front constitutionalists were no more acceptable to the regime than other opponents. The regime's exclusionist policy toward moderate opponents, with whom it shared a modernist idiom if not values, so alienated them that a "loyal" opposition became an impossibility. Barred from forming or joining formal oppositional associations, opponents had to rely on the age-old *daurehs*—convivial gatherings in private houses that in Iran often functioned as a substitute for absent civic venues and formal political clubs or parties—to discuss matters of common interest. However, SAVAK surveillance increasingly curtailed the number, scale, and effectiveness of these gatherings. Many participants felt obliged to shun any direct discussion of politics. The state's repressive intolerance encouraged the appeal of satire, jokes, gossip, and rumor as a means to counter and defy the regime. By eliminating all viable secular constitutionalist alternatives, the regime effectively helped to create or strengthen radicalized forces bent on dismantling it. If the older generation of constitutionalists, including Mosaddeqists, were marginalized, the younger generation of opponents were catastrophically deprived of the opportunity to acquire political experience.

Post-1953 Iran increasingly became a theater of the Cold War in the political as well as the ideological sphere. The Leninist-Stalinist legacy weighed heavily on the discourse of the radical left, widely seen as subservient to the Soviet Union, while independent socialism, social democracy, and liberalism remained ideologically weak and identified with bourgeois mores and the values of the capitalist West. For over a decade civic-nationalists and leftists maintained an active presence among the urban intelligentsia, particularly in the universities; but by the mid-1960s the Mosaddeqists and the radical leftist opponents of the regime in particular were increasingly cornered. They remained active abroad, most notably among Iranian university students in Europe and the United States, who in 1961 already numbered some 16,000 and by the eve of the revolution well over 50,000. From 1965 onward the Confederation of Iranian Students, operating abroad, became a radical revolutionary organization.[4] Viewing revolution and reform as conflicting incarnations of good and evil respectively, the organization was, in the words of one activist, founded on "utter negation."[5]

Through a variety of tactics, SAVAK attempted to counter student activities abroad and severely curtail them at home. Moreover, through its socioeconomic reformist measures the regime was in part trying to steal the limelight from the left; but the appeal of radical leftist ideas and sentiments continued to rise, thanks largely to the regime's relentless efforts to suppress them. Antileftist propaganda, including exaggerated claims regarding the influence of left-wing forces, produced the very opposite of its intended aim. In addition to its commitment to the Soviet Union, the Tudeh Party's advocacy of the political and socioeconomic transformation of Iranian society ensured that there was no real possibility that the party would be tolerated by the regime. The civic-nationalist followers of Mosaddeq, on the other hand, espoused a seemingly more feasible and limited agenda: the restoration of the constitutionally guaranteed rule of law and accountable government. They could justifiably be seen as a viable alternative to the regime. For this very reason the Shah, chronically and viscerally haunted by the specter of Mosaddeq and the stigma of restoration by the CIA, was relentlessly hostile to the Mosaddeqists, often derisively describing them as more dangerous than the Tudeh Party.

The adverse political circumstances ensured that the Mosaddeqists' political and symbolic capital would consist less of intellectual and political-theoretical inventiveness than of publicly acclaimed moral propriety and principle-based integrity. In the absence of a solid organizational base of support, they felt that they had no choice but to be overly concerned with safeguarding their public image, which was bound to restrict their room for political maneuver. Yet, despite the disabling constraints to which they were subject, they remained able to inspire considerable public confidence; Mosaddeq's name had long been politically taboo, but it had continued to be symbolically evocative. In view of this situation, toward the end of his rule, in a desperate attempt to save the regime, the Shah turned to the Mosaddeqists. Had the Shah's appeal to them been made sooner, the course of Iranian history might have been significantly different.

At the onset of the monarchy's unraveling and as a result of its policies, the systematically enervated Mosaddeqists were left with only their painfully retrieved personal reputations to rely on. They were mentally unprepared and organizationally ill equipped to achieve much in the face of the rapidly unfolding revolutionary fervor. Confronted with the regime's chronic aversion to genuine political change and with the concomitant growth of political radicalism, principled reformists faced a dilemma. They feared the consequences of the prevailing radicalism but did not trust the Shah or wish to be seen as acting to save a regime that had brought about the current impasse. Nor were they certain that their actions could avert the impending political deluge. The growing conviction that the regime was politically unregenerate and impervious to structural political reform had undermined reformist agendas. Opponents of various persuasions had come to believe that any concession by the regime was tactical, insincere, temporary, and designed to buy time. This perception, together with the catastrophic political fragmentation and inexperience of the enfeebled secular reformist opposition, was among the primary factors accounting for the appeal of extremist and maximalist ideas promulgated by many publicists and intellectuals.

In Iran, as in France or prerevolutionary Russia, ideas, intellectual discourses, and ideologies inspired passionate interest and commanded widespread attention. Iranian intellectuals comprised politically engaged writers, poets, and other noted individuals actively involved in the world of ideas and culture. They enjoyed moral authority and social prestige, which they owed largely to having maintained a critical and oppositional stand, a conspicuous albeit in many cases ostensible political purity, and an aversion to unequivocal co-optation by the state. Although privately the Shah used derisory terms in referring to them,[6] the regime did not abandon its attempts to win them over. The expansion of literacy and urbanization ensured that there was an ever-widening audience for their ideas. The growth of secondary and university education was yielding an increasing number of young activists who could be recruited to support a movement for change. University students in particular were greatly attracted to critical or oppositional discourses and causes, articulated or championed by intellectuals. Censorship, frustration, and discontent increased the resonance and receptivity of critical ideas, which, despite various restrictions, often easily reached their target audience. The scope for open discussion and examination of ideas and ideologies was, however, drastically limited, as was the opportunity for developing the requisite skills for formal associational life. Too fissiparous and prone to ideological rifts, personal rivalry, and factional bickering, the Association of Iranian Writers, formed in 1968 and revived in 1977, was unable to act effectively as a collective body, but pursued its commitment to countering censorship. Intellectuals, including writers and poets, remained capable of exerting considerable influence in the public sphere.

Iranian intellectuals suffered a major setback with the 1953 defeat of the Mosaddeq government and suppression of the Tudeh Party; the ensuing bouts of imprisonment, internal exile, and other forms of ill-treatment had a lasting effect. The disjuncture between being an intellectual and serving the state became more pronounced, and identification with the regime became increasingly a source of public opprobrium. The Shah's renunciation of any pretense of neutrality in foreign relations affirmed the West's sustained commitment to him; it also helped to deepen the gulf separating the Mosaddeqist and leftist intelligentsia from the regime. The state's predominant strategy of seeking only to co-opt and thus neutralize its opponents vindicated them in their rejectionist stance. By the second half of the 1960s both the Mosaddeqists and the Tudeh Party were in serious disarray. SAVAK repression and infiltration, ideological splits, and improved relations between the regime and the Soviet Union rendered the party weaker and more fragmented. "The communist movement in Iran," noted the U.S. embassy in late 1966, "offers no immediate threat to the regime."[7] Defeating its old opponents organizationally did not, however, mean eradicating their ideological influence or success in portraying any cooperation with the regime as an outright betrayal.

## The Poetics of Revolution

*The curious logicality of all isms, their simple-minded trust in the salvation value of stubborn devotion without regard for specific, varying factors, already harbors the first germ of totalitarian contempt for reality and facticity.*

—Hannah Arendt, *The Origins of Totalitarianism*

Since 1953, university students, particularly in Tehran but also elsewhere, had been at the forefront of opposition to the regime. One particular day, December 7, 1953 (16 Azar 1332), when student unrest in Tehran was quelled by the police, resulting in the death of three students, would be annually commemorated. The growing authoritarianism since the mid-1960s provided greater impetus for student unrest, which broke out on various occasions and pretexts. In January 1968 Iran's widely celebrated wrestling champion, Gholam-Reza Takhti, a member of the National Front's Central Council in the early 1960s, was officially declared to have committed suicide but was widely believed to have been killed because of his pro-Mosaddeq sympathies. Though almost entirely ignored by the media, the large attendance of university students as well as the wider public at his funeral indicated strong antiregime sentiments. During another large gathering forty days after his death, slogans in support of both Mosaddeq and Khomeini were chanted, Takhti was declared a martyr, and his suicide denied by the participating students.[8] The students also protested unpopular government measures, particularly price increases, in the hope of attracting greater public sympathy. SAVAK remained unable to prevent student unrest, which grew in frequency in the 1970s. The student disturbances were often suppressed and sometimes defused by concessions to some of their more tangible demands. Yet the underlying causes of student unrest both at home and abroad persisted.

In the second half of the 1960s, provoked by the political intransigence of the regime and disillusioned by what they viewed as the quietism of older and moderate opponents, the students began to favor increasingly radical measures. Some left-wingers, animated by revolutionary idealism and romantic populist yearnings, and inspired by the theorists of guerrilla warfare, the struggles of the Vietnamese and the Palestinians, and events in Latin America, supported armed struggle. They advocated the violent overthrow of the monarchy and hoped that they would win over segments of the peasantry and other exploited classes to launch a sustained insurgency against the regime. By the early 1970s various guerrilla groups, estimated to have some 2,000 members and enjoying support among the students, had become more active; SAVAK considered some of them to have received training in Iraq or from Palestinian guerrillas.[9] They clashed with security forces and threatened key functionaries of the regime, as well as its American advisers, with assassination.

One group, the Fada'iyan-e Khalq, established in 1971, subscribed to a narrow form of Marxism combined with other radical revolutionary ideas. It fervently resented any accusation of ideological affinity with the Tudeh Party and projected itself as ushering in a new communist movement.[10] It viewed violence or armed struggle as essential for triggering a popular movement against the regime. By the early 1970s another group, the Mojahedin-e Khalq, which had emerged in 1965, was also resorting to violence. The Mojahedin combined leftist and Islamist ideas before splitting in 1975 into Islamist and Marxist-Leninist factions. Guerrillas used violence against the regime and their own vocally dissenting cadres. Even in the case of the Fada'iyan, which had attracted a number of intellectually talented leaders, the constraints of ideological dogma and circumstances ensured that their theoretical perspectives and analyses remained rudimentary and schematic.[11] In their antiregime operations, which were primarily of symbolic significance, the guerrillas showed dedication and single-mindedness but suffered dire reprisals at the hands of the security forces, who killed or incarcerated most of their leadership.

Out of touch with the young and unable to comprehend or deal with what alienated or antagonized the students, the regime saw no alternative to a suppressive policy, which inevitably meant a greater constriction of civic and political life. Between 1971 and 1973 some 3,000 people, mostly students, suspected of supporting guerrilla activities were arrested.[12] Despite official propaganda to the contrary, the guerrillas had created a sense of insecurity; they damaged the regime through a number of assassinations and acts of sabotage such as bank robberies, attacks on police stations, and other disruptive measures, as well as a psychological campaign. They marred the Shah's claim to have established a secure environment in the country, but enabled him to take seriously or invoke the threat of communism while neglecting other challenges to the regime. They were seen by the authorities as a serious source of nuisance and harassment, and by the public as inexplicably willing to sacrifice their lives for largely incomprehensible ideas. They had no chance of instigating a mass revolutionary movement, but by provoking further repression and more intrusive SAVAK operations—particularly against university students, who were their main sympathizers and targets of recruitment—the protagonists of armed struggle helped to deepen public resentment against the government.

In the last decade of the Shah's rule various forms of leftist ideologies dominated the universities, coexisting or in conflict with religious orientations. Some leftist activists advocated or took part in antiregime activities, which invariably ended in detention or incarceration by SAVAK. Many leftists, however, confined themselves to sloganeering and occasional demonstrations; they, too, and even those who distributed or merely read left-wing literature, faced detention. This state of affairs did little to dampen interest in such literature, and in fact stimulated it. Students wrongly arrested for harboring leftist ideas ended up embracing them while in prison or after their release. The more the regime sought to uproot leftist tendencies, the more appealing they became. Politically inactive or indifferent students and those regarded as "pleasure loving" were harassed by both the left and the right. In contrast to the irresistible allure of militancy, moderation was despised as bourgeois decadence. Those stigmatized as being liberal suffered. As a political-philosophical system, liberalism was little understood; it had not attracted serious intellectual attention in Iran. Translations of the works of thinkers such as John Locke and John Stuart Mill found few inspired readers compared to dogmatic leftist tracts or often-incomprehensible Hegelian philosophy.[13] Liberalism was conventionally taken to involve no more than affirmation of rapacious capitalism. Moderate Hegelian Marxism and social democratic leanings were also scorned by radicals. There was an evident failure to recognize and affirm individual autonomy, the dignity of the person, and the sanctity of the private sphere as the constitutive components of any worthy notion of civility. Radical leftist discourse revealed scant appreciation of the necessity for a public space of dialogue and mutual recognition free from harassment, stigmatization, and fear as the prerequisites of meaningful civic and political life.

Traditionally the left in Iran spanned a wide spectrum of tendencies, including socialism and social democracy. A generic, ideologically inchoate, oppositional left rooted in a moral revulsion against corruption, injustice and erosion of principle in political and public life had long been a major component of intellectual life. It overlapped with civic-nationalist sensibilities and outweighed in significance the role of various leftist organizations and ideologically distinct trends. Though highly differentiated, the left as a movement had contributed to the greater resonance of social justice, a keener awareness of inequality and exploitation, the need for unionism and rights of workers, women's rights, and gender issues. It had influenced the focus or orientation of literary and intellectual sensibilities away from stale traditional or mundane pursuits and toward realism and social criticism. The left had helped to fashion the idiom for recognizing, analyzing, and eradicating social ills.

However, at least partly in consequence of the Cold War atmosphere and political repression, the ideological leftist voice became increasingly radical and Stalinist in tenor. It remained intellectually shallow and theoretically impoverished. Combining rigid dogmatism with tactical flexibility, it both selectively subsumed and dismissed generic socialist and civic-nationalist sensibilities. With its inherent abhorrence of liberal ideals, willingness to ignore conventional moral norms, and acceptance that noble ends justified ignoble means, it sometimes degenerated into leftist fascism. It was fervently ready to excoriate, stigmatize, or demonize opponents and to justify violence, particularly against the "enemies of the people."

Eradication of imperialism—which they never adequately defined and barely differentiated from "decadence" and modernity, but broadly identified as Western domination—emerged as the primary ideological leitmotif of the radical leftists. Without acknowledging it, they found much in common with radical religious activists, to the detriment of more thoughtful leftists, civic-nationalists, and liberals, who viewed them as having formed a Faustian pact with their ideological antagonists. The tactics, slogans, and even idioms of the two groups often overlapped or converged. Both valorized an intemperate politics of heroic sacrifice and martyrdom and an ethic of purity; both detested what they considered to be the regime's morally lax attitude to, and deliberate encouragement of, sexual license as a deterrent to political engagement and struggle. Their joint aim was to radicalize the universities and beyond to the detriment of all forms of moderation. Thanks to them, moderation, prudence, and particularly compromise became despised terms. Politics as the art of the possible found no place in the maximalist cosmology of the radical left and extremist Islamists. For the majority of the radical left, ideology was theological; it was a surrogate religion.[14]

Naive but resonant radical leftist propaganda had long been disseminated in unsuspected forms and through unlikely venues. Samad Behrangi (1939–1967), an elementary school teacher in rural Azarbaijan and a writer mainly of children's stories, played a major role in surreptitiously indoctrinating the young. He died by drowning but was widely believed to have been murdered by SAVAK. Behrangi's influence far outlived him. In his often ostensibly innocuous stories he preached the value of a selfless pursuit of noble ends, justifying heroic sacrifice; he combined indirect but uncompromising demonization of the regime with reverence for a life of political struggle and an abhorrence of all moderate and gradualist approaches. The little black fish in his famous allegorical children's tale of that title can be construed as symbolizing a guerrilla.[15] Behrangi's ideas were unwittingly propagated by state institutions such as the Center for the Intellectual Development of Children and Youth and hundreds of youth cultural centers.

Nourished by a variety of sources, the dazzling myth of a total and redemptive transformation of society through collective violent action animated a growing number of young people. Gripped by wishful enthusiasm, they seemed confident that a society free from all evils and exploitation was both possible and within reach. The Shah's regime was increasingly viewed as the embodiment of evil, and its successor, baptized by cleansing revolutionary violence, the incarnation of good. In the prevailing milieu, posing inconvenient questions was avoided and skepticism unwelcome. Those who had strong misgivings failed to air them; they feared the all-too-common accusation of either being agents of the regime or wishing to salvage it. The radical leftists emphatically maintained that the violent overthrow of the existing order and the elimination of imperialism inevitably paved the way for a good society. Similarly, for the radical Islamists, the elimination of the morally defiled monarchy, with its West-inspired licentiousness, and the implementation of "true" Islam would rapidly eradicate social ills. Neither the radical leftists nor their Islamist counterparts wished to temper their exuberance by pondering the complexities of politics, society, and economy in the modern world.

Many radical leftist activists tended to believe that clerics were uninterested in or incapable of ruling, and that secular forces would be the inevitable heirs of the monarchical regime. They thus ignored their own weaknesses and divisions and overestimated their capabilities while underestimating the Islamists and turning a blind eye to their unmistakable countersecularity. The facile assumption that the Islamists were inherently unable to rule, or that their rule would inevitably be short-lived, cost the secular forces dearly. An important segment of the activist left naively believed that they could use the Islamists to unseat the Shah, and with this aim in mind readily provided them with revolutionary tactical and organizational guidance and assistance. The Islamists welcomed such a collaboration, but saw any alliance with secular, particularly leftist, forces as only tactical. During the Constitutional Revolution it had been the intellectuals who had manipulated the clerics; now the clerics were doing the manipulating with the well-camouflaged aim of recovering lost ground.

As the revolutionary movement spread, an increasing number of secular opponents of the Shah, leftist or otherwise, grew concerned about the likely ascendancy of the Islamists and feared the kind of polity they would wish to fashion. They nevertheless justified siding with the Khomeinists by concluding that they had no real choice: neither neutrality nor inaction was a viable option; failure to go along with the revolutionary flow could be viewed as siding with the crumbling monarchy and could result in irreversible marginalization. "The massive power of the popular deluge," wrote one renowned leftist writer, "engulfs and carries along everyone regardless of religious, philosophical, or political orientations. Resistance is impossible; legs move spontaneously, and faster than brains. A revolution is but the sight of unanimity at the moment of destiny. All are intoxicated—revolutionary and counterrevolutionary."[16] The Tudeh Party, operating from Europe, repeatedly declared that Khomeini's political program was fully in accord with its own.[17] Prominent leftists inside the country, including party supporters, erstwhile or otherwise, were more prone to skepticism but fully agreed that "international imperialism" had to be radically uprooted and that "salvation lies in the overthrow of the calamitous monarchical regime."[18] Few could deny that Khomeini's leadership had become unchallengeable, and his role in the unraveling of the monarchy indispensable. Regardless of serious misgivings about the future and the political shape of the monarchy's successor regime, few among the secular opponents of the Shah believed that retrieval of the monarchy was possible or desirable. Some secularists persisted in their residual optimism, persuading themselves that clerical rule was improbable, anachronistic, and anomalous. Many seemed to believe that even if the clerics attempted to rule, they could be easily undermined or inevitable failure would force them to quit.

The more politically astute opponents of the Shah feared that the dismantling of royal authoritarian rule could result in an even more ruthless, intractable, and intrusive form of authoritarianism. Few of them, however, either ventured to speak up or to do so vigorously. There were, of course, notable exceptions; even before the Shah's final departure from the country, Mostafa Rahimi, a prominent intellectual and lawyer, incisively denounced the concept of an Islamic republic as an oxymoron and insisted that by rebelling against the monarchy, the Iranian people aspired to affirm an inclusive notion of popular sovereignty as opposed to royal or clerical tutelage.[19] Yet, on the whole, those intellectual or opposition activists who feared the current extremism and the course of the future rarely aired their thoughts, believing that they would fall on deaf ears or make them the targets of excoriation. Skeptics knew that in the prevailing moment of enthusiasm for radical change and optimism about its consequences, few were prepared to entertain any doubts that the future would be anything but better.

In the eyes of its more reflective critics, the most damning indictment of the regime was its failure to anticipate the consequences of the constriction of political and civil life, which was at the root of the growing radicalization of opposition. Self-deceptively boasting about its success in radically modernizing the country, the regime had failed to realize how chronic authoritarian rule had undermined some of the key signifiers of civic and political modernity in the country. A disenfranchised populace, having been denied the opportunity to acquire political and civic experience, could not instantly become an informed citizenry capable of a measured assessment of the costs and consequences of collective political action. Persistent repression had ensured that when restraints on free speech began to collapse, most people had lost the necessary skills for the intelligent exercise of freedom. Abandoning its seemingly fatalistic apathy and cynical resignation, the urban public had assumed the collective persona of a restless, emotionally charged, massive crowd increasingly responsive to revolutionary calls and blissfully confident or unconcerned about the future.

Nor did the seemingly modern-minded segments of the population, whether in Tehran or in other cities, escape the revolutionary cathexis. Many of them succumbed to the casuistries and vague promises of those whose democratic credentials and adherence to modern values were suspect. The regime's vast paraphernalia of propaganda and its unimaginative efforts to socialize the people into the dominant state-sanctioned values had proved dismally ineffective. The scale of the regime's loss of credit and the abysmal but not surprising failure of its edifice of public relations became fully apparent when its opponents succeeded in convincing a vast number of Iranians that any regime would be infinitely better than the Shah's. An entrenched clause in the political creed of the leftist revolutionary intellectuals and activists, shared by many other groups, was that history moves only forward, and that no one could block or defy the logic of inexorable historical progression.

The unfolding revolutionary leftist activism had resulted from and in turn aggravated the regime's relentless quasi-fascist antipathy to the left. Despite or because of its repressive measures, the regime had failed to placate or subdue the university students. By attempting to depoliticize them and the public in general, it had in effect overly politicized them. By denying Iranians the opportunity to air their resentments and articulate their wants and demands through the institutions of credible parliamentary politics, the regime had rendered them vulnerable to simplistic remedies and demagogic inculcation. Unable to channel and express their energies, emotions, and aspirations through legal political avenues, the public, particularly the young, had been driven to act as an impressionable mass susceptible to psychological pressures, manipulation, facile slogans, and eschatological proclamations. In reinforcing or not questioning the current simplistic assumptions and in failing to provide sober moral leadership, leftist intellectuals did their compatriots a lasting disservice. Yet they themselves were as much molded by the prevailing political-oppositional climate as they had helped to shape it. They were no less deluded than those whom they were meant to lead.

Saturated by the recycled idiom of a Leninist provenance, the discourse of the leftist revolutionary intellectuals and activists was readily conducive to confident certainties and schematic and distorted views of the unfolding crisis. Ideologically self-righteous, and often displaying a disquieting closed-mindedness, they took much for granted, examined little, and failed to validate their self-referential assumptions. Their intellectually relaxed premises contrasted sharply with their rigid conclusions; their radical zeal was impervious to counterargument or refutation, and anathema to anguished contemplation. Their ideologically sealed cast of mind constrained their ability to anticipate or even perceive many issues. A tyranny of elevated clichés and slogans had left little room for critical discursive thought. Counterintuitive thinking was equally in short supply, as was the wisdom resulting from reflectively pondering the history of the recent past.

The predominant intellectual complacency can be explained only in the context of prevailing circumstances. The cloistered society and the watchful police state that had evolved after 1953 provided few opportunities and resources for open debate and the examination of ideas. Leftist books and tracts, banned by the authorities and coveted by students, acquired the aura of sacred texts, just as any officially proscribed topic or idea became instantly attractive.[20] Intellectuals who sought to cultivate a wide student audience tapped into and affirmed voguish ideological discourses. Despite appearances, premodern modes of thinking and the tradition of accepting ideas on grounds of authority and deference had persisted, giving rise to a milieu readily congenial to dogmatism of any kind. The collective oppositional mentality, in spite of its variations, was suffused with a narrow range of concepts and assumptions some of which were even shared by the Pahlavi elite. Among such assumptions was a confident belief in progress. In their celebratory contention that they had irreversibly established modernity and defeated the forces of regression, the Shah and the technocratic elite revealed a shallowness as disquieting as that of the regime's least cultivated opponents. The regime was indeed no better equipped to ponder the fragility of the prevailing sociocultural modernity. Illusions of an ineluctable forward march had been internalized by both the regime's supporters and its secular opponents.

The fact that the Shah had called his reform program a "revolution" reflected the cachet that the concept of revolution had acquired in the Iranian political culture. The radical opposition, however, construed a "true" revolution as by definition cataclysmic. Optimism about success in bringing down the monarchy nourished and was in turn inspired by the allure of revolution as a violent and radical rupture with the immediate past. Thanks largely to the virtual hegemony of radical leftist discourse, reinforced by Shi'ite messianism, revolution acquired an increasingly seductive appeal; the poetics of revolutionary redemption conquered the collective imagination. Revolution was seen as an apocalyptic panacea, the catalyst for a just social order, the path to political salvation. The regime's capacity to counter its inspired opponents on intellectual and ideological grounds was negligible. The people had come to disbelieve and distrust the regime to such an extent that they unquestioningly accepted the revolutionary propaganda. Such propaganda successfully maintained that if the people were to relent, the Shah would recover his nerve and composure, revitalize his authoritarian rule, and even exact revenge.

This situation was not surprising given the fact that the paternalistic autocracy had reduced even its own high-ranking officials to virtual servitude. By closing all avenues for the emergence of a responsible opposition and by depriving even moderate dissenters of a voice, the regime could not meaningfully expect opponents different from those who emerged. Both the pious middle classes and the urban lower classes, whose ranks were swelled by continued rural-urban migration, felt increasingly ill at ease with the secular tenor of the regime. Yet the pervasive abhorrence of the Shah and the ruling class was rooted primarily in their chronic indifference to the growing demands for a more open and equitable society, and in the alienation of those who felt excluded from the political process. The regime's refusal to treat the people as worthy of respect, as individuals whose sense of self-worth was to be nurtured rather than paternalistically undermined, could not but provoke rage. Accustomed to a docile, long-suffering, and acquiescent populace, the regime neither expected nor was it prepared to counter massive public defiance. Its illusory promises had long been met with disbelief. Its ability to inspire paralyzing fear was rapidly on the wane; its vacillations and conspicuous loss of nerve, together with its failure to address and counter the corrosive public distrust of those in power, benefited the radical opposition. The regime's erratic postures and responses led the restless public to grow in confidence, to defy and taunt the overwhelmed SAVAK and other security forces, and eventually to overthrow monarchical rule.

A dynamic sociocultural life, an essentially subterranean civic life, and particularly democratic aspirations, though battered, had persisted beneath the vast shadow of the monarchy, which had failed to subdue the spirit of resistance and to impose any real political conformity. Democratic struggle succumbed, however, to insular leftist radicalism and an inchoate and barely understood Islamism that selectively borrowed democratic ideas and idioms to advance its own exclusionist agenda. Cunningly redirected away from this agenda to focus solely on overthrowing the existing regime, the revolutionary fervor produced immense solidarity. Yet in addition to marked differences arising from social class, ideology, belief, ethnic and regional ties, and the rural-urban divide, the Iranian public was also divided along generational lines. The urban youth had proved to be far more receptive to revolutionary ideas than the older generation. This receptiveness was rooted not in fear of the future or in concern for issues such as job prospects but in sublime hope. It was inspired by youthful revolutionary romanticism.

By suppressing knowledge of recent history and substituting for it a highly distorted official narrative interspersed with Pahlavist hagiography, the regime had ensured that the younger generation knew little about the recent past, the trajectory of postconstitutional history, and the social forces involved in promoting or impeding political, civic, and social liberties. Lack of such knowledge had further limited the intellectual resources needed for determining which courses of action were feasible and wise in building a better future. The rank-and-file revolutionaries, whether secular leftist or

Islamist and regardless of class affiliation, were overwhelmingly young, inexperienced, and inattentive to the sober misgivings of the older generation. To those who knew something about the past, about the frailty of human endeavor, and about the worrying possibility of regression, the revolution seemed like a children's crusade, a harbinger of uncertainty, chaos, and the loss of everything that those in the autumn of their life cherished. The old regretted what they saw as youth's innocent idealism or naive ideological zealotry, while the young dismissed the conservatism or cynicism of the aged. Dedicated to nothing short of the radical unraveling of the existing order, the young only looked forward to a future which they saw as infinitely better than the past.

## Relative Deprivation and the Moral Economy

*A nation trampled by despotism, degraded, forced into the role of an object, seeks shelter, seeks a place where it can dig itself in, wall itself off, be itself . . . But a whole nation cannot emigrate, so it undertakes a migration in time rather than in space. In the face of the encircling afflictions and threats of reality, it goes back to a past that seems a lost paradise.*

—Ryszard Kapuscinski, *Shah of Shahs*

With the steady increase in oil revenues and the growth of both the public and private sectors since the late 1960s, industrialization became a strategic goal, and the social structure underwent major transformation. Economic growth increased overall prosperity; the standard of living, particularly in the areas of diet, health, and sanitation, continued to improve. The urban upper-middle class, whether modern or traditional, including entrepreneurs, merchants, professional strata, and the higher echelons of the civil service, grew in size and significance. The line of demarcation between social classes and differences in life style and life chances became more pronounced. Greater entrepreneurial opportunities facilitated the emergence of a self-confident, status-conscious, and ostentatious class of *nouveaux riches;* the size and income of the middle classes increased, widening the gap between them and the lower classes. The opulence of the upper class, directly or indirectly associated with the state and identified in Iran as "the one thousand families," grew faster. "In Iran," asserted the U.S. embassy in 1973, "3% of the people control some 78% of the wealth."[21] If these figures were even remotely accurate they indicated the staggering, interrelated disparities of wealth and power and the coercively safeguarded structure of unjustifiable inequality that had come to characterize Pahlavi rule.

In the capital, the privileged upper class and the emerging *nouveaux riches* generally inhabited the salubrious, leafy northern part of the city, while the modern and traditional lower-middle classes such as middle-income bazaar merchants and shopkeepers, middle-level state employees, and teachers lived in its central quarters. The lower classes—artisans, small shopkeepers, petty clerks, and laborers—were mostly concentrated in the congested southern quarters. An underclass of urban poor—the semiemployed or jobless, drug addicts, beggars, pickpockets, prostitutes, and pimps—also lived in this area. Those rural migrants who worked in the northern part of the city as domestic servants, gardeners, or laborers lived in crowded and ramshackle rented dwellings in the south. Relative anonymity, together with the erosion of traditional restraints, increased delinquent behavior in the capital.

The socioeconomic policies of the regime in the 1960s, particularly land reform, accelerated the dislocation of the traditional contours of Iranian society. The lure of the cities, in contrast to the isolation and desolation of the villages, and the prospect of better-paid work increased social mobility and life chances, hastening rural-urban migration. In 1976 urban dwellers still constituted only 47 percent of the population; yet they had been less than 32 percent in 1956. The population of Tehran in this period had, however, increased from some 1.5 million to over 4.5 million. Although the inhabitants of the rural areas were by and large far poorer than the city dwellers, they showed little hostility to the regime and in some cases seemed willing to defend it. Over time, however, the rural and small-town migrants to the cities would become a significant component of the revolutionary upsurge. The revolutionary restlessness had its roots firmly in the cities, where discontent—born of relative deprivation, an inability to influence the regime's policies, envy, and revulsion against the ruling elite—was on the rise.

The growth of class consciousness in the cities, particularly Tehran, was a consequence of socioeconomic change, which had created both new opportunities and new problems. There was an inevitable rise in expectations as well as frustrations. Discontent was no longer confined to the agonistic intellectuals, who, according to the regime's ideologues, had turned discontent into a vocation. The lower-middle and subaltern classes were also feeling increasingly indignant at the conspicuously unequal distribution of wealth and privilege. They had long been deeply ill at ease with the flamboyant insensitivity of the regime's modernity. They no longer felt able to tap the protection of traditional notable patrons or turn to leading publicly recognized men of integrity whose word still carried weight with the rulers. Moreover, in the last few years of the monarchy, there was a lingering anxiety that traditional values were in danger, that injustice was approaching intolerable levels. Concomitantly there was a sense, inchoate or otherwise, that even if the rulers were concerned with securing the material amenities of everyday life for the populace, they were guilty of dereliction in their duty of providing an emotionally reassuring public environment.

Resistance to oppressive or neglectful misrule had taken various forms, from bread riots in Tehran in 1912 and again in the years after 1941, to taking sanctuary in an attempt to publicize and rectify an injustice. There were also silent protests, such as refusing to vote. A potent form of protest was the strike, which, in the absence of real trade unions and as a result of SAVAK's vigilance, had become difficult to organize and very risky to participate in. Nevertheless, the 1960s and 1970s saw a number of major strikes. There was a widespread taxi drivers' strike in late November 1964 in protest at increased petrol prices, forcing the government to retreat. In February 1970 students led strikes and protests against the tripling of bus fares, leaving the government no choice but to reverse the measure. A year later there were major strikes in Karaj and Abadan. In July 1972 bus drivers went on strike; in the same year a strike in response to an overnight doubling of meat prices forced another reversal by the government. In September 1973 there was an unprecedented four-day strike among the Abadan oil refinery workers objecting to rising prices. In almost all cases the government more or less relented; triggered by what were considered to be unjust price increases, strikes unmistakably assumed political dimensions.

Clearly, the urban poor, including recent rural migrants, had grown resentful about their own status and prospects. The failure of rural migrants—mostly young men—to integrate into urban society or to achieve an adequate standard of living intensified their sense of outrage at massive socioeconomic inequality. When inflation and the rising cost of living increasingly burdened the urban poor, the regime could not convince them that it genuinely sought to address their wants and expectations or to lessen their burdens by, among other things, setting just wages and prices. Striving to curb inflation and price increases, the government had pursued a draconian antiprofiteering campaign since 1975. A major consequence of this campaign, which targeted bazaar merchants and shopkeepers, was to provoke their widening animosity. In 1977 and 1978, enraged by the municipal authorities' demolition of their makeshift dwellings, which contravened municipal regulations, segments of the urban underclass in Tehran put up a stiff resistance. The authorities' failure to relocate those who had lost their homes created growing rancor, which spread among the urban poor, facilitating their mobilization against the regime.[22] The resentments of these vulnerable social strata had immediate and specific reasons unrelated to any direct attachment to traditionalism or religiosity. Yet a pervasive sense of alienation, stemming from a consciousness of relative deprivation and social injustice, underlined the rejection of the regime. It also accounted for revulsion against the perceived depravity of modern life and stimulated interest in traditional religious attachments and values. Cognizant of and wishing to tap such interest, the religious and traditionalist opponents of the regime and their pious middle-class supporters sought to deepen it. They promoted a politicomoral discourse centering upon the interrelated ideas of injustice, oppression, and the moral decadence of the existing regime and its privileged supporters. Invoking the threatened disintegration of traditional values and bonds, they worked to mobilize anxieties and fears. To its more conservative critics, the regime's undiscriminating promotion of foreign culture and its belittling of local mores were deeply alarming. There was a growing anomie, rooted in the regime's failure to substitute modern for premodern norms perceived to be seriously endangered.

Abhorring the ostentatious life style of the privileged and their perceived libertinism, and resentful of the sociopolitical arrangements that made such a situation possible, the pious and the poor increasingly embraced religious and traditional ties and sentiments. In their search for equality, brotherhood, and moral conduct, they turned to mosques, shrines, and other religiously based communal venues. They saw these venues as the indispensable loci of communitarian ties, solidarity, and meaning; as familiar, comforting, and reassuring antidotes to anomie, anonymity, and the dispiriting meaninglessness of metropolitan life. Religiosity provided the receptive poor with solace and a deeply resonating sense of self-worth. Since 1953 the urban population had witnessed a massive increase in the construction of mosques and other centers of religious congregation. Rural migrants were adopting the habits, practices, and orientations that the nonmigrant urban masses were relinquishing. Thus, as elsewhere in the Middle East, a traditional mode of life was being perpetuated.[23] In addition to their specific devotional or spiritual functions, mosques and other venues of religious congregation such as *hoseiniyehs* were used as community centers, places of charity, and sociopolitical clubs, as well as loci of politicoreligious indoctrination and mobilization. *Hoseiniyehs* were built or used by *hay'ats* (informal religious associations organized mainly with the purpose of annually commemorating the martyrdom of the third Shi'ite Imam, Hosein); they were traditional communal entities formed, among others, by guilds, city quarters, and migrants from other towns. Religious commemorations, festivals, spectacles, and symbols affirmed traditional values and a politics of identity in which Islam figured most prominently. To paraphrase E. P. Thompson, the people had remained attached to values and customs even as the economy was changing. They were using cultural attachments to intervene actively in an attempt to alter economic as well as sociopolitical conditions. Premodern values provided a cultural lens through which change was both interpreted and acted upon.

By the eve of the revolution, the consequences of the massive increase in oil revenues since late 1973 had accentuated sociopolitical strains in the cities. A sense of foreboding, sometimes verging on panic, had come to dominate the traditionally minded; skillfully provoked and exploited by the Islamists, it would help furnish the emotional milieu for revolutionary restlessness. It was feared that religious and moral norms of decency and chastity and the dignity of marriage were fast eroding; that family values and the traditional authority of the family, particularly the authority of fathers, were being seriously compromised. The regime was seen as intent on removing the residual traditional restraints upon relations between the sexes.

The extension of conscription to females had been deeply unsettling. The conspicuous extravagance and the gratuitous insensitivity of the regime and the upper classes continued to alarm traditional Iranians. The putative immorality of the upper classes, their ample opportunities to indulge their pleasures, carnal and otherwise, contrasted sharply with the austere lives of the deprived poor, who, even if unconcerned about religious restraint or moral rectitude, lacked the means or opportunity to enjoy remotely similar pleasures. The politically opportune circumstances ensured that the cumulative resentments, frustrations, and anxieties of the urban poor could be exploited by those who fervently denounced the decadence and moral depravity of the ruling class and sought to revive ethicoreligious propriety.

The nonexistence of conventional political vehicles for venting discontent and articulating political wants had facilitated the task of the mosques and other religious institutions in filling the oppositional organizational vacuum. Seemingly nonpolitical religious associations of various kinds had largely supplanted the banned secular associations. In the absence of viable rivals, modes of solidarity rooted in religious sensibilities and concerns or couched in religious terms had overshadowed or saturated civic life. No one could deny that by eliminating or paralyzing the secular democratic opposition, the Shah had paved the way for the ascendancy of uncompromising opponents of the regime, whether secular or Islamist. He had particularly facilitated the rise of a religiously inspired and led opposition whose political genesis, configuration, feasibility, and prospect of success had eluded him and his supporters. This opposition expressed itself partly in terms of an activist Islamic modernism but also, and more significantly, in a radical traditionalist or revolutionary religious idiom. For some time the regime tolerated student religious activism as an antidote to the left; it could not fathom that such activism represented deeper sociocultural undercurrents nurtured by the transformed demographic and socioeconomic configurations of Iranian society. Socioeconomic change had also given rise to attitudes and expectations that rendered increasingly unpalatable the dominance of an arrogant and self-serving elite committed to authoritarian royal rule and the privileges of a segment of the population at the expense of the rest. The state was ultimately challenged by social forces that were largely created, sustained, or strengthened by the intended and unintended consequences of its own policies, consequences that the regime had proved singularly ill equipped to anticipate.

The relative roles of various social forces and classes in the revolutionary process have been a matter of some disagreement. According to one scholar, the peasantry played no role in the revolution but, with the exception of the industrial working class, all other segments of the urban population did.[24] Another emphasizes the "bazaar-clerical-intellectuals' alliance" and "the crucial role played by a variety of cities."[25] Others have argued that "from the beginning to the end, the driving force of the revolution came from three significant social groups—the clergy, bazaaris, and students and teachers. Other social forces—government employees, workers, peasants and the urban poor—joined the revolution in its final stages and following the first three groups."[26] The topic has been approached from a range of heuristic angles. However, weighing the specific roles of various social classes or groups requires detailed and extensive empirical investigations that have not as yet been attempted. On the basis of existing evidence, there seems to be little doubt that the revolution which unraveled the monarchy embraced the majority of the urban population regardless of class affiliation. Acting with unprecedented solidarity generated by defiance of the Shah, activists of diverse ideological leanings, the lower echelons of the intelligentsia, students, clerics, women, workers, and other urban lower and underclass Iranians committed themselves to collective action to bring down the regime. The most powerful monarchy in the Middle East was unseated primarily by the power of the powerless.

## The Discourse of Authenticity

If the ruling class had become the object of loathing, so had the ruling modernist ideology, which was being challenged from various intellectual perspectives, including reinterpreted political Shi'ism. In the intellectual and the ideological spheres the regime had failed to offer any appealing alternative to what its opponents advocated. It was particularly vulnerable to the charge of commitment to perpetuating Western political hegemony and cultural ascendancy at the expense of a real measure of Iranian political and cultural autonomy. The West's unmistakable identification with and support of the Shah's autocracy had resulted in a backlash not only against Western double standards and hypocrisy but also against Western values. Western claims of respecting democratic norms while at the same time condoning and aiding their disregard in countries such as Iran had helped to engender disillusionment with the universalist Western paradigm of modernity and the legacy of the Enlightenment.

Jalal Al-e Ahmad (1923–1969) was one writer who forcefully articulated such disillusionment. A member of the Tudeh Party's Tehran provincial committee, who deserted the party in early 1948 and later joined the pro-Mosaddeq camp, Al-e Ahmad came from a traditional religious background (his father and elder brother were clerics). A high school teacher by profession, as a stylishly laconic and engaging writer and fearless critic he became a notable figure in Tehran's intellectual circles. Al-e Ahmad was a man of conflicting impulses and incompatible intellectual allegiances. A restless activist and passionate moralist, he seemed rarely concerned about the coherence or rigor of his ideas; nor did he sufficiently reflect on their implications.

Al-e Ahmad followed Western, particularly French, intellectual trends and admired writers who were critical of Western imperialism. As his published letters reveal, he never wholly abandoned his essentially secular, social democratic convictions or admiration for Maleki, his socialist, anticlerical guru.[27] Yet Al-e Ahmad had become disillusioned with the efficacy of secular ideas and movements in Iran and renounced European modernity in favor of oriental values. Embracing a nostalgic, quasi-Luddite populism, in a controversial, tersely written tract titled *Gharbzadegi,* covertly published in 1962,[28] he turned to "the essential conflict between Iranian traditional social institutions and [a process which,] in the name of development and progress, but in effect as political and economic imitation of Europe and America, is turning the country into a colony."[29] For Al-e Ahmad, the threatened Iranian national and cultural identity could be salvaged only by relying on local traditional culture and particularly Shi'ism. He regretted the quietism of the clerics, whose influence he considered a countervailing force to the decadent and shallow modernity of the regime and Western cultural encroachments.[30] Despite censorship, Al-e Ahmad's work reached a wide audience. Secular fellow intellectuals did not at the time take his ideas seriously, and some dismissed them as facile and retrograde. Regardless of the broader ramifications of his views, they were widely seen as an indictment of the regime and its Western supporters, a denunciation of the prevailing imitation and celebration of the often banal manifestations of Western customs and fashions.

Al-e Ahmad recognized the darker side of the domineering Western technological civilization; its irresistible tendency to colonize, subjugate, and manipulate the nonwhite peoples; and its lack of moral resources to ponder or care about the traumatic implications of its policies. The preoccupation of Al-e Ahmad and like-minded intellectuals elsewhere in the nonwestern world was to explore ways of countering Western political and cultural hegemony. This perspective often involved privileging a certain strand in Western thought—in Al-e Ahmad's case, socialism or Sartrean existentialism—in order to challenge other Western ideas. More significantly, it entailed imagining an often-romanticized, pristine folk culture that could be revived and employed to confer self-respect and provide a self-sufficient locus of authentic identity, in contrast to an alien or borrowed identity. For intellectuals such as Al-e Ahmad, the fear of being overwhelmed by alien cultural influences was particularly intense, as these influences were perpetuated by political, military, and economic power, which could result in near-colonial subjugation and the traumatic triumph of rapacious capitalism.

How to appropriate pertinent modern ideas and values without succumbing to Western subjugation had long occupied many Middle Eastern intellectuals. In their encounter with modernity, they attempted to probe the question of how to revitalize, or halt the erosion of, the local culture and sense of identity. Which components of the local culture, they would ask, were salvageable and which irredeemable? How were these components to be identified, and who was qualified to identify them? There were of course many other questions that these writers, sincere though they were in their quest for a local normative blueprint of a decent polity, barely explored: On what grounds should local cultures, and especially their self-proclaimed protagonists, be relied upon to provide a viable alternative to the borrowed culture? How was viability to be ascertained? Were all forms of borrowing equally objectionable? Were the shackles generated or justified by local traditions any more bearable because they were local? Was a fully homegrown authoritarianism any more palatable than one sustained by external forces? How could cultural hybridity be avoided, and was cultural authenticity really possible in an age characterized by cultural interpenetration and cross-fertilization? These and similar questions rarely concerned most critics of modernization, who were justified in seeing it as synonymous with Westernization but who tended to consider nearly all political and sociocultural ills as primarily externally induced. Regardless of the merits of the alternatives they proffered, critics such as Al-e Ahmad could be seen as providing an intellectually prosaic but politically appealing indictment of the Western imperialist record and of Western hubris in seeking to set the agenda of worldly salvation for the whole of humanity.

Sharing and extending Al-e Ahmad's critique of Westernization and the prevailing secular disdain for the Islamic components of Iranian culture was Ali Shari'ati (1933–1977). A French-educated sociologist, a gifted speaker and publicist, Shari'ati was an affiliate of the Freedom Movement. He relied on a selective reading of Marxism, French existentialism, and Third Worldist ideas to transform Shi'ite Islam into a viable ideology of mobilization and liberation. Like Methodism, Shi'ism furnished inspiration for both action and inaction. It provided emotional comfort and fostered a sense of community; it could also severely limit important individual civic and social liberties. It encouraged accommodationist tendencies and expedient dissimulation of beliefs, as well as defiance and rebellion; it could be both revolutionary and reactionary. Clearly, Shari'ati chose to interpret Shi'ism in a way that highlighted its uplifting revolutionary potential.

Shari'ati's lack of philosophical depth and coherence contrasted with his power of oratory and rhetorical skills. He emphasized the necessity of intellectually transcending the routine traditional preoccupations of clerics and dealing with issues relevant to the modern world. He hoped to ensure that as an ideology Shi'ism would appeal to members of a younger generation who were deterred by the secular contours of other radical ideologies and repelled by the intellectual aridity of traditionalist Shi'ism. By imaginatively reinterpreting Shi'ism, impregnating it with new ideas, and extirpating from it what he regarded to be the inessential or congealed accretions of past centuries, Shari'ati crafted a discourse that could be employed both for making sense of the world and for changing it. It could enable its adherents to think and act as autonomous agents unhampered by the literal scripturalism and paternalism of traditional clerics. True Shi'ism, Shari'ati contended, was incompatible with clerical tutelage and the strictures of traditionalist Shi'ite discourse.

Shari'ati's project of intellectually reformulating Shi'ism and salvaging it from clericalism did not endear him to the clerics, while his objective of turning Shi'ism into an ideology of political liberation eventually antagonized the regime. Through lectures delivered at the religious-educational Hoseiniyeh-ye Ershad Institute from 1969 until its closure in 1972, he was remarkably successful in spreading his ideas. He aspired to turn the Hoseiniyeh into a center for the modernist rethinking of Shi'ism, in contrast to the traditionalist teachings of the seminaries. As he had correctly assumed, segments of the younger generation, particularly among university students, felt ill at ease with secular ideologies. Equally averse to unreconstructed traditional versions of Shi'ism, they found Shari'ati's alternative politically enabling and spiritually uplifting. When he was finally banned from lecturing, the illegally printed versions of his lectures were widely disseminated and read. The regime's efforts to ban such writings only helped to fuel interest in them. Shari'ati has often been regarded as paving the way for Khomeini.[31]

In their political approach to Shi'ism, both Al-e Ahmad and Shari'ati were preceded by Mehdi Bazargan, a French-educated professor of engineering, a pious Muslim, a Mosaddeqist, and the leading figure in the Freedom Movement. Bazargan's concern with a liberal reading of Islam as essential for both personal and sociopolitical renewal went back to the early 1940s. Though rejecting the separation of politics and religion, he abhorred the manipulation of religiosity and its instrumentalist use by lay or clerical political groups to further their political aims. A prudent man of conviction and common sense, Bazargan denounced extremism and ideological excess; he represented like-minded activists who, by the early 1960s, had concluded that secular constitutionalist forces by themselves could no longer mount a viable challenge to the regime; in their view an ethicopolitical Islam, insistent on political freedom and combined with civic-nationalism and reformist objectives, constituted a more potent countervailing force.

Other influential exponents of Islamic reform included Morteza Motahhari (1920–1979), an academic-cleric, a former pupil of Khomeini and his trusted adviser. A philosophically minded ideological architect of Islamist polity, Motahhari also sought to revive Shi'ite Islam through reinterpretation and to address a number of current intellectual discourses while seeking to refute and counter the influence of Marxism and Western materialist thought among the intelligentsia. Both Bazargan and Motahhari were eclipsed in their influence on students and the lay intelligentsia by Shari'ati. In their diverse ways, they and several others sought to rely on and give greater attention to reinterpreted indigenous religious culture as a means of warding off outright Western ideologies while coming to terms with the challenge of modernity.

Ironically, the monarchical regime promoted its own discourse of authenticity. In the ranks of its ideologues and formal or informal publicists, the regime had several denouncers of the West or Western humanism, Marxism, liberalism, and secular values and institutions, who also advocated a return to "authentic" Iranian-Islamic cultural and spiritual values. In fact, abstract criticism of the West was by no means unwelcome to the regime, which detested leftist ideologies and dismissed Enlightenment-inspired ideas pertaining to civic and political rights and democratic liberties. Sayyed Hosein Nasr, a pious high-ranking academic and political mandarin who headed the Imperial Iranian Academy of Philosophy, advocated the promotion of traditionalist Islamic norms, values, and modes of thinking as an antidote to secular trends. In April 1977 he recommended basing the country's educational system on Islamic principles. Ehsan Naraqi, a sociologist with extensive political links, contended that many ideas and practices that Iranians sought in Western civilization could be readily found in the native culture.[32] The philosopher Daryush Shayegan located pertinent spirituality and intellectual resources in Asian values.[33] Such ideas were more intensely, if obliquely, advocated by Ahmad Fardid, who had provided the initial inspiration for Al-e Ahmad's conception of *gharbzadegi*.

An eccentric teacher of philosophy at Tehran University, Fardid rarely committed himself to writing, but attracted captivated disciples who mistook pedantry and incomprehensibility for philosophical depth. Fardid crafted an arcane and pretentious language dotted with turgid neologisms to denounce "the West"—with its intrinsic nihilism, scientism, materialism, and cult of technology—and embrace "the East" and its spirituality. Paradoxically, he invoked a Western philosopher, Martin Heidegger, to support his antiwestern onslaught. Unconcerned with conceptual coherence and analytical clarity, he employed elusive verbiage to mask an essentially obscurantist set of ideas. Though virtually inscrutable, such ideas centered on hostility to rational thought and the philosophical premises and implications of humanism and modernity. Supporting the Shah and his professed advocacy of "spirituality" *(ma'naviyat),* Fardid wrote a prologue for the official ideological formulation of the Resurgence Party. Later, however, he allied himself with the more extreme segments of the Islamic republic and helped to lend an air of quasi-philosophical justification to their feverishly antiliberal impulses. He openly advocated the elimination of liberal and secular forces. In recognition of his contributions as "the chief source of ideological inspiration," upon his death in 1994 his house was purchased by the Islamic Republic of Iran to serve as the seat of the newly established Fardid Foundation.[34]

The Pahlavi regime's desire to uphold its own version of an authentic Iranian identity and polity was best represented by attempts to portray the monarchy as an ancient and traditionally sanctioned institution, and to insist on the alleged cultural affinity and deep-rooted historical links between the Iranian people and paternalistic kingship. The proclaimed "imperial system" was portrayed as the true representation of genuine Iranian political values and traditions. Through a number of lavish spectacles, the Shah and the elite emphasized the centrality of the monarchy in what they portrayed as a quintessentially unchanging and timeless Iranian political culture. The extravagant spectacles failed, however, to mobilize the public in support of the regime or to engender any results beneficial to the rulers. Nor was the regime able to produce an appealing intellectual alternative to the antiwestern or anti-imperialist discourse of its opponents or to persuade its critics that it had grown any less dependent on the West.

The Shah's version of an authentic Iranian system of rule did not directly impinge on Islam, to which the regime frequently paid lip service, describing it as a "progressive" religion. The court maintained links with amenable clerics and sponsored ceremonies on major religious occasions. Sometimes during these observances, while emphasizing the Shah's devotion to Islam and unfailing dedication to the good of the country, preachers blamed any shortcomings or excesses of the government on his subordinates. By the last years of the monarchy, however, the tactic of blaming the Shah's subordinates while praising him had ceased to produce the desired result. Similarly, royal gestures of appealing to the faithful invariably proved counterproductive, as they were generally viewed as hypocritical. In line with the prevailing conventional political wisdom, the Shah and the royalist elite seemed to fear the left and the civic-nationalists more than they did the Islamists, whom they viewed as too regressive and marginal to constitute a viable force. Ironically, this view was also shared by many intellectuals, who, along with other opponents of the Shah, could not in their heart of hearts have believed that the regime would collapse so rapidly.[35]

On the eve of the fall of the monarchy, the secular intellectuals, despite their continued impact on shaping the political idiom, had become less socially influential than they or the regime assumed. The co-opted among them enjoyed no public credit, while the impact of those who had remained defiant had been curtailed. Islamist ideologue-activists had emerged to compete with, if not outmaneuver, their secular counterparts, selectively appropriating from them ideological notions that they recast to suit their own constituency. They contended that the polity they envisioned self-evidently represented a culturally authentic and spiritually fulfilling alternative to the status quo. Islamist and leftist opponents converged on a rejection of the existing order; their consensus was the result of variegated but focused ideological hostility to the imbricated systems of discourse and power that had sustained royal authoritarianism. The revolutionary momentum thus generated did not seek merely to unseat the Shah but to unravel the foundations of the regime, its accompanying political culture, and its paradoxical conflation of Westernization and imperial nativism.

## The Archaeology of Khomeinism

The anxieties, resentments, and wants of the urban masses and their reactive traditionalism were shared, and in certain instances aggravated, by segments of the clergy—a sartorially distinct hierarchical status group ranging from high-ranking ayatollahs to local preachers. The leading clerics enjoyed social status and prestige; they collected large sums of money, most of which they disbursed in stipends for seminary students and charitable purposes. The regime had failed to undermine the symbolic and cultural capital of the clerics and had helped to consolidate their standing as a powerful counterelite untarnished by open collaboration with the rulers. The clerics' cultural capital rested on controlling the transmission and reproduction of religious learning. Clerical power was consecrated by theological knowledge and qualification, and reproduced through well-funded networks of seminaries. The clerical elite maintained its privileged status by its credentials and a carefully nurtured aura of pious spirituality, which also enabled it to maintain its social prominence and its influence over the public space of

culture. In life style the clerics did not significantly differ from the pious segment of the traditional middle class, with whom many had kinship ties. In
the face of the prevailing secularizing trends and with the aim of safeguarding their status, senior clerics had welcomed, if not readily adopted, the title
*ayatollah*. By doing this they aimed to counter the modern, educationally
based, prestige-conferring titles of their secular counterparts, and in effect
fostered a more distinctly hierarchal clerical structure.

During the greater part of the Shah's reign, the clerics, led by influential
quietist or accommodationist divines such as the Grand Ayatollah Borujerdi,
had worked out a *modus vivendi* with the monarchy. They generally ab-
stained from and disapproved of direct or overt involvement in politics,
while ensuring that their collective interests and the constitutionally sanctioned status of Shi'ism remained undisturbed. This stance by the Shi'ite establishment had helped to ensure that more conspicuously political ayatollahs such as Kashani were not able to derail or overtake the broadly secular
Mosaddeq-led civic-nationalist movement. Concomitantly, the configuration and political dispositions of the urban population made it receptive to
modern secular or cautiously secular sensibilities. Thus the appeal of civic-
nationalism overshadowed the brand of Islamic-nationalist activism represented by Kashani. Similarly, the Fada'iyan-e Islam and their violently intolerant Shi'ism failed to attract mass appeal or to enlist the blessing of
Borujerdi, who disapproved of weakening the monarchy. It was the desire
to preserve the monarchy, and fear of the alternative, that in 1953 had led
virtually the entire clerical establishment, including the generally prudent
Borujerdi, to side with the Shah.

Indebted to the clerics for the retention of his throne and in need of their
continued support, the Shah for some time felt unable to take any measure
injurious to them. He found their enmity toward the left and their largely
disapproving attitude toward the Mosaddeqists politically useful. He even
felt obliged to condone the anti-Baha'i campaign of the mid-1950s, spearheaded by preachers such as the wily, spellbinding Mohammad-Taqi Falsafi,
whose sermons were broadcast over the state radio. Falsafi had close links
with leading clerics, particularly Borujerdi, whom he claimed to represent.
Since its emergence in Iran in the 1860s, Baha'ism had been a bête noire of
the Shi'ite establishment. But the anti-Baha'i campaign of the 1950s, which,
among other things, warned against the rising influence of the Baha'is in

the civil service, was a byproduct of the complex prevailing political situation. The Shah and his supporters could not allow the campaign to get out of control, particularly as they were under American and British pressure to curb it; nor could they afford to be seen as soft on Baha'ism. Gauging the Shah's vulnerability on this issue, certain politicians who were alarmed by the extent of royal manipulation of parliamentary procedures used the mobilized anti-Baha'i sentiments in an attempt to restrain the Shah's autocratic drive.

Officially condoned anti-Baha'ism soon waned; many clerics felt frustrated or betrayed despite the fact that the episode had done much to enhance their ideological profile and sociopolitical influence. It had proved that with the help of effective ploys and alarmist tactics the clerics could easily arouse popular phobias and anxieties in order to promote specific political agendas. With the death of Borujerdi, mutual restraint and accommodation between the regime and the activist clergy began to erode. The regime's development drive, beginning in the early 1960s, further alienated some of the Shah's former clerical supporters, including Ayatollah Behbahani. The most implacable opponent of the Shah, however, turned out to be the little-known Ayatollah Khomeini. According to one account, in terms of political outlook he had been close to the conservative Behbahani.[36] However, Khomeini's combative demeanor and fearlessness distinguished him from other senior clerics, bringing him considerable public attention. Deeply sensitive to any personal slight, his hostility toward the Shah was traceable to developments preceding the uprising of June 1963.[37] Khomeini came to prominence as an opponent of reform, but thanks to U.S. insistence on acquiring immunities for its military personnel in Iran and the gross mishandling of this issue by the regime, he became, as the Americans themselves admitted, "a national hero."[38] The Pahlavi regime had long employed cultural nationalism as an important component of its anticlericalism. In his opposition to the immunities bill, Khomeini also implicitly but unmistakably utilized a nationalist discourse to challenge the Shah.

The overall secular ethos of Pahlavi rule had a detrimental impact on the public influence of the clerics. The establishment of theology as an academic discipline, which encroached upon the work of the seminaries, the extension of state control over the management of the pious endowments, and the creation of the Religion Corps in October 1971 were only some of the measures regarded by the clerics as highly intrusive. Over many decades the clerics had instigated or supported moves to ban alcoholic beverages, but no such prohibition had proved sustainable. Above all they had failed to roll back cultural Westernization and the slow but steady erosion of the constraints of custom and tradition upon the lives of women. Considering the setbacks and loss of prestige suffered under the Pahlavis, the clerics, wrote Bazargan, were primarily concerned with recovering their lost position and status.[39] Deeply angered by the decline of clerical influence, but careful to avoid charges of obscurantism, Khomeini invoked a broad range of pertinent issues to attack the Shah. He assailed him for subverting Islam and spreading immorality, for his unfettered autocratic rule, for chronic violation of the constitution, and for his subservience to foreign powers in defiance of Iranian national sovereignty and dignity. Khomeini's enumeration of such criticisms, though aired to various degrees by other opponents of the Shah, particularly the civic-nationalists, resonated with virtually all opponents of the regime. Transcending narrow religious and traditionalist concerns, Khomeini castigated the Shah in sociopolitically effective populist terms. Regardless of Khomeini's real intentions and the subtext of his denunciations, other opponents of the regime could fault few of his assertions or fail to concur with him.

In contrast to Khomeini, several quietist, traditionalist, or politically prudent high-ranking divines such as Ayatollahs Sayyed Abolqasem Kho'i—who resided in Iraq and had the largest following in the Shi'ite world—Shari'atmadari, Milani, Golpayegani, and particularly Sayyed Ahmad Khansari, had maintained working relations with the regime.[40] Khansari often interceded on behalf of detained religious activists, and refused to condemn those dubbed by the regime as "Islamic Marxists."[41] Echoing the Shah and confident that clerical power had been conclusively destroyed, Alam viewed the clerics as no longer meriting much attention.[42] When ayatollahs such as Golpayegani and Khansari objected to the adoption of the imperial calendar, Alam recommended ignoring them, as he believed that the clerics no longer enjoyed social status and political clout.[43] The quietist clerics silently and to various degrees disapproved of the regime or its policies, but did not vocally oppose it. The regime tended to view the clerics' support or hostility as equally inconsequential.

The quietist clerics had come to disapprove of or reject the conflation of religious concerns with militant rhetoric and confrontationist politics. They hoped to maintain their social prestige through piety, noninvolvement in formal politics, and the pursuit of traditional religious preoccupations. Khomeini, on the other hand, spoke out defiantly, adopting a denunciatory populist approach in circumstances in which a significant portion of the secular opposition was also increasingly leaning toward radical rejection of the regime. By the mid-1970s Khomeini's influence in the country and among segments of Iranian students abroad was growing, and SAVAK feared that with the death of Kho'i, Khomeini might emerge as the leading contender to succeed him. However, even one year before Khomeini's triumphant return to Iran in 1979, SAVAK did not seem to view him as a major threat to the regime. SAVAK's recommendation for thwarting Khomeini was simply to support rival ayatollahs.[44] The regime's largely inept and ill-conceived efforts to stem Khomeini's influence failed, and some of the measures designed to damage his reputation had the opposite effect. Even many left-wing opponents of the regime had come to embrace Khomeini's leadership of the anti-Shah opposition. The Shah had frequently spoken of the unholy alliance of "red and black reactionaries," that is, communists and clerics. If such an alliance came into being, the Shah could blame only himself for having unwittingly brokered it.

Khomeini had appropriated most of the criticisms leveled against the Shah by his various opponents, recasting them in simple but effective language. Significantly, he appealed to the nation or the people and not to the community of the faithful or the broader Islamic community. He tapped both religious and nationalist sentiments and utilized modern methods of challenging and paralyzing the state, such as strikes. He also fully understood that what sustained his aura and image was noncompromise, a universally compelling value in the Iranian oppositional subculture. Compromise was increasingly perceived as politically polluting. Khomeini had realized that the more unrelenting and decisive he proved to be, the more despondent and desperate the Shah became. The Shah's stark hopelessness fed the unconcealable helplessness of his scattered supporters. Khomeini's strategy of noncompromise heartened and psychologically uplifted his followers. It appealed to the maximalist aspirations and strategies of the left as much as it demoralized the Shah and his supporters, and disarmed and overwhelmed the moderate reformers.

In a society in which opponents of the regime had been habitually humiliated and belittled, Khomeini was able to counter the arrogance of the Shah with unflinching audacity, obstinacy, and a commensurate overconfidence. His demonstrated stoic composure contrasted with the Shah's debilitating emotional vicissitudes. He was the very antithesis of the Shah: immune to self-doubt and relentlessly single-minded in the pursuit of his objectives regardless of the cost. His gravitas, enhanced by formidable resolve, pugnacious confrontation with the regime, and long exile, was more potent than his undistinguished oratorical skills. A philosophical mystic, recluse, and activist, he was an atypical member of the *ulama*. With his aura of sublime spirituality he seemed too unworldly to harbor personal political ambitions; nor did his age and fragile health appear conducive to such ambitions. A somber and quiet man, too stolid to provoke a torrent of emotional energy, he seemed an unlikely agitator. Yet he was capable of vocalizing the heated denunciations of a self-righteous, confidently oracular, indignant, and inspired moralizer.

The fact that an ostensibly simple and unpretentious man of religion—a man who in his austere demeanor, frugal life style, and provincial dispositions and accent differed little from the ordinary men of piety among the capital's rural and small-town migrants—had been able to defy and confront the Olympian Shah was exhilaratingly uplifting to the urban subalterns. For the downtrodden, those self-consciously aggrieved by the arrogance of the ruling elite, and those marginalized or unsettled by the regime's extravagant modernity, Khomeini's determination to unseat the Shah was mesmerizing. His indomitable persona touched the imagination of the masses, who saw in his achievements the vicarious fulfillment of their own suppressed aspirations.

Khomeini deftly refused to share with any other opposition leader the credit for engineering the Shah's rapid descent from invincibility to helplessness. For Khomeini, the smallest compromise would have undermined his unique status and benefited either the Shah or the moderate forces that wished to retrieve the 1906–1907 Constitution as the basis of a democratic polity. A number of Khomeini's moderate supporters feared the collapse of the monarchy in the absence of viable arrangements to succeed it. Khomeini revealed no anxiety about an imponderable future. In his self-confidently reassuring and stark ethicopolitical message, he seemed convinced that all problems could be easily overcome. For Khomeini and his brand of faith-based conduct and conviction politics, the task of governance or management of the economy posed no formidable challenge.

Taking charge of the country, he believed, required little more than enabling men of religious faith and determination to assume key positions of power, liquidate undesirable domestic elements, eradicate foreign influence, and reverse as many policies of the royalist regime as possible. Relevant knowledge, experience, and administrative skill were of marginal significance. Espousing a distinctly uncomplicated conception of governance, Khomeini and most of his fervent followers resisted marring the dazzling clarity of their vision. Adhering to a self-validating sense of certainty, they refused to encumber their minds with unsettling reflections about the complexities of governance. Had they done so they might have faltered; their cohesion and determination would have seriously suffered.

Whereas Khomeini's followers interpreted him literally, his skeptical sympathizers did so metaphorically. His admirers saw his every word and move as imbued with deep meaning and wisdom. His detractors perceived him at best as an atavistically engrossed providential visionary who was crafting the blueprint for a pristine "Islamic polity" that was ill defined, impractical, and at odds with the spirit and requirements of the modern world. If indeed Khomeini had a clear political program for the future, he was careful to avoid any elaboration that might have seriously alarmed secular or moderate forces. A successfully cultivated ambiguity about the specific configuration and policies of the future regime was essential for ensuring revolutionary cohesion, which rested more on rejection of the monarchy than on any informed agreement about its successor. Khomeini's insistence on unanimity *(vahdat-e kalameh)* in rejecting the monarchy was intended to prevent fragmentation of the revolutionary forces and to forestall or postpone debates about the future. While the Shah had succeeded in uniting virtually everyone against himself, despite their misgivings about the course of events, Khomeini was able to unite everyone in his support regardless of their doubts and concerns.

A remarkable gift for captivating supporters and generating conviction among the less committed, together with a unique instinctive grasp of crowd psychology and the techniques of mass mobilization and manipulation, enabled Khomeini to assume a decisive leadership role in unseating the monarchy and in the ensuing developments. However, Khomeini's charisma and political skills accounted only partially for his success and the resonance of his message. The regime's policies provided the broader structural context for his ascendancy, and its blunders furnished the catalysts needed to launch the revolutionary upheaval. Largely as a consequence of the regime's suppression of secular political organizations, religious activists had been able to take advantage of the absence of organized rivals. A loose coalescence of politically militant, organized or semiorganized clerics and traditional Islamists, including remnants of the Fada'iyan-e Islam, constituted the Khomeinist core. Together with advocates of Islamic reform, particularly those inspired by Shari'ati, and supporters of the Mojahedin-e Khalq, they worked ceaselessly to ensure Khomeini's triumph, crucially assisted by segments of the secular opposition.

A combination of religious piety, particularly of the traditional middle classes, and a nationalist-communitarian belief in the authenticity of the native culture as represented by these classes and their clerical spokesmen— in contrast to the alien Western culture ascribed to the regime—had generated an antimodern, volkish mentality. This constituted the broader context of Khomeinism and furnished its emotional and ideological underpinning. Nourished by the resentments of the marginalized, who had long been denied access to formal political outlets to articulate their aspirations, Khomeinism represented a backlash against the chronic belittling of the powerless by the Westernized elite. In its salvationist rhetoric and tactics, Khomeinism—a hybrid construct—relied more heavily on the modern myth of revolutionary redemption through mass mobilization than on any chiliastic yearnings of activist Shi'ism. In its formative phase it was little more than an improvised, simultaneously right- and left-wing populist call for reviving faith-based virtues and communitarian ties; it sought to rehabilitate what it regarded to be a morally degenerate, culturally contaminated, and spiritually debased nation. It elevated religious and spiritual revival of the nation over democratic and civic considerations, Shi'ite particularism over universal values. It inspired a religiously consecrated sense of volkish unity, and increasingly reflected and fostered a set of agonistic attitudes and a mood of indignation. A preoccupation with retribution, punishment, and correction, and a sharp differentiation between friend and foe, true believers and hypocrites, became Khomeinism's hallmarks, its chief operational leitmotifs.

Though ideologically inchoate, Khomeinism sought to create a new meaning system. It aimed at nothing short of a normative reconstitution of society, the conquest of the public sphere and the entire domain of cultural and aesthetic life. Committed to a stern ethical monism, it wanted to launch a campaign for the moral cleansing of society, to act as the undisputed custodian and enforcer of morals. Such aims could be accomplished only by taking over the reins of power and pursuing counterpluralism and exclusion. The constraints of governance both modified and radicalized Khomeinism; inevitably it relinquished much of its dogmatic zeal in favor of pragmatic considerations. Yet, ever bold in its objectives, it sought a fusion of Islamist-ideological and political power in the service of an Islamic state that was the embodiment of the sacred and subordinated the religion itself.

Ideologically, Khomeinism lent itself to serve as a vehicle of both opposition and domination, but its functions overlapped. In its oppositional phase, infused with a seemingly benign vision of moralized social engineering, Khomeinism promised to promote a politics of recognition and empowerment aimed at the pious middle and lower classes. Celebrated as an iconoclast, an "idol-smasher," Khomeini launched his populist campaign as a denunciation of the arrogance of power and ascriptive privilege represented by royalty, and an affirmation of the worth of the common people. He was widely seen as promising an inclusive, just, humane, and tolerant society; but from the very beginning, though purposefully opaque, he left little doubt that the polity he desired to fashion was inspired solely by Islam, which he pronounced to be the solution to all existing problems. He fervently denied any suggestion that such a polity, anchored in Islamic law, would rest on exclusionary values and practices. In rendering this denial plausible Khomeini was greatly helped by the fact that few had any clear idea about what was specifically meant by Islam or what an Islamic polity might actually involve. The majority of those taking part in the revolution understood an Islamic polity to entail political arrangements that constituted a vastly superior alternative to the monarchical regime. Islamic symbols and idiom had come to dominate the revolutionary discourse and process, but their meaning was by no means clear or uncontested. Nor was their practical feasibility taken seriously.

Captivated by the internalized illusion of near-total and irreversible liberation, radical left-wing forces seemed the least perturbed by the possibility of an Islamic polity, and were the least intellectually equipped to grasp its implications. If an attempted Islamic polity turned out to be unjust, oppressive, and insufficiently hostile to imperialism, they would fight it; many of them believed that, assisted by History, they would be able to defeat it. Significant segments of the moderates, despite their misgivings, supported Khomeini in the hope of being able to influence the future course of events. They tried to ensure that rejection of the Shah would in no way entail affirming a nondemocratic alternative. But the Khomeinists and the left, converging on the need for drastic measures and the radicalization of society, promoted a psychological atmosphere in which dissent was stigmatized and moderates increasingly cornered, thereby severely limiting their scope for maneuver and forcing them either to quit active politics or to swim with the current.

## The Crisis of Authority

The long premiership of Hoveyda potently symbolized unmistakable defiance of all credible constitutional modalities of legitimacy and accountability. It was an era marked by the mutual and deepening estrangement of the regime and the public. The regime's exercise of power had not in substance been as recklessly arbitrary and absolute as its opponents claimed, and nor in its often erratic demeanor was it as consistently inflexible as it presented itself. Yet its marginalization even of moderate opponents had greatly boosted radical oppositional impulses, which in turn contributed to the regime's diminished capacity for political flexibility. By 1975 there were signs that the Shah was concerned with finding ways of opening up the political system without losing his grip on the reins of power. He wanted to overcome the perception of Iran as a mere client of the United States, and domestically, according to the U.S. embassy, he was "intellectually committed to broadening of democratic practices." He was "striving to create a workable system" that would "incorporate both participation and control." The U.S. embassy considered such a system, "in combination with continuing economic growth," to be "flexible enough to ensure the survival of the Pahlavi dynasty following the death of the present Shah."[45]

Regardless of whether there were or were not any premeditated and clear plans for opening up the political system, what actually happened was a haphazard, grudging, and ineptly handled policy of decompression that, thanks to gross blunders, precipitated a crisis which steadily acquired its own momentum. The Shah reluctantly made concessions but, hoping to weather the growing storm, and failing to ascertain the extent of the regime's vulnerability and unpopularity, confined himself to inadequate measures. He remained unable to convince his opponents that he intended to abandon his personal grip on power; he also failed to demonstrate that he was resolutely determined to ward off the collapse of the regime.

If, instead of establishment figures such as Amuzgar or Sharif-Emami, the Shah had called on a publicly respected statesman to form a government capable of asserting its authority and determination to bring about change, he might have averted the revolution that removed him from power. Autocracy had become untenable and change inevitable, but Iran might have escaped violent upheaval by going through a more orderly political transformation. Among other things, such a transformation required a radical overhaul of the authoritarian structure of power and the configuration of the state, real change in the composition of the ruling elite, and genuine commitment to democratic principles and procedures. Overtaken by events, the Shah merely reacted, forgoing vital initiatives and squandering many opportunities. So long as the autocratic framework of the regime remained virtually intact and key officials retained their positions, liberalization would inevitably be counterproductive and was sure to prove unmanageable. As a result of liberalization, some functionaries who had been complicit in the regime's repression, corruption, and mendacity became advocates of liberty, tolerance, and criticism. Some of them even began to castigate the very regime that they had helped to sustain and from which they had benefited. Such a situation only increased public cynicism.

Political liberalization at any stage during the Shah's authoritarian rule would have proved deeply problematic. As early as 1964, Counselor Martin Herz of the U.S. embassy had perceptively noted:

Concessions made to popular (or rather, middle class opposition) pressure, for instance by way of giving leeway for freedom of expression and assembly, are quite likely to be the very thing that might set off a revolution in Iran. There are many examples in other dictatorships where a relaxation of the repressive apparatus gave heart to pent-up opposition and impelled especially the young people to ask—and fight— for more freedom than the regime could safely grant. The Shah, in other words, is riding a tiger from which he cannot safely dismount.[46]

Although such an assessment may have sounded implausible for Iran in 1964, it shed a clear light on the predicament of its rulers in the second half of the 1970s. By then the authoritarian regime, despite its apparent overwhelming might, had grown more structurally vulnerable; it was doomed if it did not liberalize and doomed if it did. Any measure of liberalization had become an exercise in irreversible brinkmanship. Having totally discredited the constitutional processes, it could not revive them without undermining itself. It was incapable of managing the crisis of liberalization and surviving it. The strategic management of liberalization was the single most crucial challenge facing the regime and clearly beyond its capabilities, particularly as it seemed utterly incapable of generating public trust, conviction, and goodwill. Liberalization was intended to be a controlled, gradual, halfhearted decompression; it resulted, not accidentally or unexpectedly, in explosion. In the same vein as Counselor Herz, the social theorist Leszek Kolakowski observes:

A typical and by no means exceptional phenomenon is revolutionary disorder in oppressive systems at the time of their relative "liberalization"; times of relaxation and moderation are—as has often been since Tocqueville's time—the most dangerous for a tyranny. Ruthless, brutal, and self-assured despotism may enjoy long impunity. Woe betide it, however, if it tries to humanize itself or to show the world a human face: instead of conciliating society with its various smiles, it emboldens its critics and puts into motion a self-propelling mechanism of ever-more-audacious and ever-further-advanced claims, the pressure of which can eventually shatter it.

Kolakowski adds: "it does not follow that a sympathetic adviser could simply recommend to despotic authorities: don't change anything, don't slacken oppression, don't try to ease poverty, don't weaken the police and the army, respond mercilessly to all disobedience, and so on."[47] Kolakowski's seemingly paradoxical observation—that attempted conciliation of society by a tyrannous regime often unleashes its own demise—seems readily applicable to the Shah's Iran.

The Shah's authoritarian rule rested above all on visible and invisible coercion, on fostering fear as a deterring and demoralizing factor. The significance of implicit fear in enabling a ruler to transform force into authority and maintain his personal grip on power was noted by Machiavelli, among others. Drawing on Machiavelli, the social theorist Richard Sennett observed that a "crisis of authority which in any way loosens the bonds of fear will altogether destroy [an autocratic ruler]—like a fatal crack however small in an engine."[48] Political liberalization quickly eroded "the bonds of fear"; it provoked extensive criticism of the establishment, and soon—and inevitably—the primary direct or indirect target of such criticism became the Shah. He had long been viewed as chiefly, if not solely, responsible for the deeds and misdeeds of the regime. Open criticism soon demystified the Shah; the aura of imperial authority, invincibility, and irreproachability quickly waned; the Shah's long-cultivated mystique, image, and self-image rapidly crumbled. This was nothing short of a symbolic decapitation of the regime. A political system long accustomed to apparent public docility, deference, indifference, and numbing fear, and lacking the requisite political and civil society institutions for the management of conflict, was unable to cope with fearlessly vocal, cumulative public assertiveness. The discredited servile elite, the rubber-stamp constitutional procedures, the laudatory and compliant media lacked the requisite authority to reassure and convince the people that capricious and arbitrary autocratic rule had come to an end in favor of the rule of law and constitutional government.

Collective memory militated against the reassurances and promises of a culpable officialdom. Without a corresponding fundamental, rapid, and tangible change in the very constitution of governance, one that also radically affected the key incumbents of positions of power, political liberalization was bound to be publicly perceived as insincere, tactical, cosmetic, and provisional. Even seasoned opponents who feared radical change did not rule out the possibility that reconciliation might enable the regime to overcome the crisis without any significant change in its structure and mode of ruling. The opposition, or its more politically active segments, were determined to use the opportunity presenting itself to extract as many concessions from the regime as possible, while the prospect or possibility of unseating the regime and the existing ruling class was becoming increasingly tantalizing. The demands for change were real and needed to be vigorously addressed by the autocratic ruler who, by addressing them, would inevitably undermine the very position that he had so obsessively sought to acquire and sustain. By bringing about a genuinely constitutional and reformist government early on, the Shah would have had to forfeit his power and prerogatives. He would not have been able to save himself, but he might have spared the country from the looming trauma.

In any event, the regime would have had tremendous problems in warding off revolutionary change. All those who could have assisted the Shah had long been rendered incapable of playing effective political roles. He could find few capable aides untainted by association with the worst features of the regime. Having long before lost the ability and skill to win the people's hearts and minds, the regime was unable to mobilize any sizable segment of the population to rally in its support. It had confined itself largely to manipulation, fraud, and co-optation of amenable opponents—who thus lost public credibility—and to purchasing loyalty or extracting feigned expressions of support. It had routinely relied on coercion, surveillance, and fear, but lacked the capacity and the requisite political imagination to generate support and mollify the alienated public.

Despite its vast resources, the regime had irretrievably lost the public relations war. The Shah had unfailingly provided as much ammunition for his opponents as he had totally disarmed his would-be supporters. The floundering, cumbersome machinery of propaganda had long become counterproductive as habitually mendacious official pronouncements ensured that the people believed the reverse of what they were told by the regime. The regime expended far more effort on improving its image abroad than on improving it at home. In May 1974 Alam boasted that Iran "virtually controlled the entire future apparatus of public relations in France."[49] The absurdity of such a claim was demonstrated during Khomeini's four-month sojourn in that country (October 1978–January 1979). Even outside Iran the regime lacked a clear vision of the image it wanted to project. Assisted by the Israelis, it enlisted the services of an American public relations firm, but beyond vague generalities centering upon the principles of "the revolution of the Shah and the people," it furnished few ideas regarding its desired image. The Shah's primary objective in the regime's public relations exercise was self-aggrandizement; by the mid-1970s many foreign and domestic publicists had been employed to write about the Shah, his achievements, and the Pahlavi dynasty. Although the issue of image had become less important with the Shah's increasing self-righteousness, he still cared about how he was perceived both abroad and at home. The domestic press had, of course, long been reduced to hagiographic chronicling of royal deeds. Yet even the servile proprietors of the two largest, and tame, daily newspapers, *Keyhan* and *Ettela'at,* would be rebuked for failing to suppress the slightest insinuation that displeased the Shah.

In the absence of outlets for reflecting popular wants and grievances, the regime had come to see itself as successful in engineering consent. The need for monitoring or paying attention to real popular reactions, sentiments, and aspirations had received scant attention. In October 1972 Court Minister Alam had told the Shah with a tone of bafflement, "Whoever wants to ingratiate himself with the public shuns us; I don't comprehend the meaning of this."[50] There was nothing particularly puzzling about the need to shun the regime in order to retain or win public confidence. Yet the regime operated on the basis of a fundamental assumption that disgruntlement was not widespread or rested on false consciousness—that the mass of the people, if properly informed, and freed from superstition and pernicious propaganda, would be grateful for what the regime had benevolently done for them. If the need arose, the regime could take the privileged inhabitants of the neighborhoods of northern Tehran to represent the entire Iranian people. Long unchecked, and obsequiously nurtured, such illusions had led the Shah to believe that he was steering the country toward a "Great Civilization," but as it turned out, he had brought it to the edge of a historic abyss.

Toward the end of the Shah's reign, the unwieldy royal autocracy could no longer bear its own weight; it could be undone by a mere accident; sooner or later change was inevitable. The Shah's removal, death, or abdication would have had a transforming impact on the configuration of the state. Succession was likely to be problematic. The transition to a "constitutional monarchy" would have proved tumultuous; the Constitution, if unrevised and unreconstructed, provided no recipe for a strong and stable parliamentary system. A substantially revised Constitution could make a difference, or a republican form of government could emerge. The eventual dismantling of the autocratic monarchy would have come about even if there had not been the cataclysm of revolution; yet with the Shah on the throne, peaceful transformation became elusive. Acting as the very embodiment of governance, and overshadowing the vast complex of impersonal political processes, the Shah provided the mass revolutionary struggle with a personal and concrete focus as calls for his removal came to connote demands for the end of authoritarian rule. The Shah and the elite could have averted a revolutionary upheaval only if they had paused to reflect on the consequences of their policies and had acted in time, not with the aim of retrieving their hold on power but in the interest of saving the country. Such a project, of course, was inimical to the very nature of the regime; in any event it required a degree of foresight, courage, resolution, and patriotism scarcely on display among the functionaries of the regime and rarely fostered in the milieu of the Pahlavi court.

Having played a major role in enabling the Shah to amass inordinate power, his foreign friends were in no better position to predict the coming revolution or help him to avert it. In 1973 the U.S. ambassador, Joseph Farland (1972–1973), had confidently asserted that "the days when a clergy/ bazaari alliance could directly precipitate significant political change are over."[51] But by the summer of 1976 Farland's successor, Richard Helms, was expressing concern about the "complex problems" facing the regime, from the discontent of various groups to the negative consequences of the army's lack of "discretionary decision-making power" and the inadequate "political institutionalization." He was also aware of the activities of "the group of religious conservatives, both clergy and laity," and noted that SAVAK exerted "a great deal of effort monitoring religious activities of even those mullahs friendly to the regime." Though admitting that "there is probably less information available to foreigners about the dynamics of this sociological strata than about any other," Helms was fairly confident about the future of the regime.[52]

In trying to make sense of the growing restlessness that had swept the country, by September 1978 U.S. officials faulted the Shah for lacking "charisma to convince his people of the benefits of his desire to modernize Iran"; noting that "expectations have risen faster than benefits," they were concerned about "ostentatious displays of wealth and pervasive corruption at the highest level."[53] Yet as late as the end of September 1978, some four months before the collapse of the monarchy, the Defense Intelligence Agency reported that the Shah "is expected to remain actively in power over the next ten years."[54]

Reza Shah's autocracy came to an end with foreign occupation, and Mohammad Reza Shah's with a popular revolution; both father and son had failed to envisage that, by identifying themselves with the very edifice of the state, they would expose themselves and the country to grave dangers. Both displayed a curious fatalism born of a paranoiac belief in intractable enemies resolved to unravel the Pahlavi dynasty. Both displayed a hubris nurtured by illusions of invincibility, self-inflicted isolation, an almost heroic sense of mission and achievement, a self-righteous dismissal and belittling of others, whether friend or foe, and an unimaginative and flawed grasp of the changing realities of Iranian society and the world. Their insular world was populated by servants, sycophants, jesters, spies, secret service men, but no real friends or conscientious and brave advisers. Reza Shah antagonized foreign powers at the wrong juncture; the population gleefully welcomed his removal and did not lift a finger to save him. Mohammad Reza Shah antagonized the Iranian people but wooed foreign powers, which were unable to save him. The country benefited from socioeconomic transformation under the two rulers, but ultimately paid a high price for their misrule.

# Part III

# The Eclipse of Popular Sovereignty: Iran since 1979

Men never do evil so completely and cheerfully as when they do it from religious conviction.

—Blaise Pascal, *Pensées*

. . . the periods which were the most bound by tradition were also those which took the greatest liberties with their true heritage. It is as if, in a curious compensation for an irresistible creative urge, they were naturally led, by the sheer force of their veneration of the past, to invent it.

—Marc Bloch, *The Historian's Craft*

# 10

# The Unfolding of Clerical Rule:

# Oligarchy by Divine Right?

### Process of Elimination

The residual optimism of the monarchy's liberal opponents did not outlive its overthrow. The rise in the fortunes of Islamist exclusionism provoked deep disillusionment among moderates, whether religious or secular, while leftists persisted in their wishful exuberance. The head of the provisional government, the urbane and witty Bazargan, had been plunged into a political fray for which he was utterly ill suited; he found himself unable to promote law and order, national solidarity, or common sense. Several key figures associated with the Bazargan-led Freedom Movement, particularly Ebrahim Yazdi and Sadeq Qotbzadeh, both active outside the country, had played key roles in assisting Khomeini while in France. Yet Bazargan and his colleagues were only barely able to exert a restraining influence on the Khomeinists, who had used them to reassure those who feared clerical ascendancy and the total eclipse of civic-nationalism. Overshadowed by the Revolutionary Council, which included a number of key clerical and non-clerical confidants of Khomeini, Bazargan found his government increasingly thwarted. Endeavoring to lead a government that included moderate secular figures, he provoked the intractable enmity of radical Islamists and leftists alike. Leading clerics associated with Khomeini were grooming themselves for power through organized cliques or formal entities such as the Islamic Republican Party (IRP). Confronted by a plethora of clerically controlled bodies—revolutionary committees, Islamic tribunals, various militias, "charitable" foundations, Islamic societies—the authority of government was highly tenuous.

The radical secular left provided or significantly affected the content of much of the revolutionary idiom in use—counterrevolutionary, feudal, liberal, opportunist, conciliationist, imperialist. They advocated revolutionary trials, expropriation of the lands and property of wealthy counterrevolutionaries, the establishment of workers' councils, and other measures designed to usher in an anti-imperialist socialist order. Their hostility to other secular forces benefited the Khomeinists, who also used many tactics and slogans of the left but introduced their own counterversion of the revolutionary idiom—"combatant against God" (mohareb), "idol-worshipper" (taghuti), "hypocrite" (monafeq), "perpetrator of corruption on earth" (mofsed fel arz), "disinherited" (mostaz'af), "arrogant" (mostakbar). The Khomeinists were also much encouraged by the squabbles, ideological fragmentation, and political inexperience and ineptitude of the secularists.

Inevitably, during 1979–1980, Iran was a society in flux and crisis; beset by the absence of a deeply rooted democratic culture, political order was fragile, as were the improvised new institutions of governance. Revolutionary activists of various ideological leanings pursued their own radical agendas; there were heated debates, sharp disagreements and clashes about the past, particularly the explanation of the revolution, and also about the future. Not surprisingly, from the very beginning there was no informed and broad consensus on the meaning and scope of liberty, order, justice, and other foundational notions and requirements of a decent society. Secular forces remained disparate and fractious; the dogmatic radicals on the left continued their denunciation and harassment of "liberals" and moderates, who in turn derided the leftists. There were no secular leaders remotely able to compete with Khomeini. Led by Khomeini, segments of the clergy, dismissing the contributions of other forces, were laying exclusive claim to the revolutionary spoils. They were not only determined to deny others the opportunity to marginalize them, as in the aftermath of the Constitutional Revolution, but were bent on outmaneuvering and discomfiting their rivals and opponents.

Having appropriated the long legacy of struggle by diverse political forces, the Khomeinists gradually but steadily worked to displace and eliminate them. The assassination in May 1979 of Motahhari, head of the Revolutionary Council, deprived the Khomeinists of a reform-minded cleric ca-

*Mehdi Bazargan, prime minister of the postrevolutionary provisional government, reporting to Khomeini; future president Rafsanjani is seated, left.* (Courtesy of the Institute for the Study of Contemporary Iranian History, Tehran)

pable of exerting a moderating influence on his less intellectually cultivated colleagues. By the summer of 1979 a constellation of secular opposition forces was beginning to bear the brunt of a clerical offensive. These forces included the National Democratic Front, which had emerged some six months earlier with the aim of transcending the limitations of the old National Front, combining a spectrum of leftist and social democratic tendencies with Mosaddeqist civic-nationalism. The older Mosaddeqists fared no better than their younger critics: their opposition to the imposition of *shari'a* laws brought a charge of apostasy, and effective banning. The political clerics had begun crafting and institutionalizing an exclusionist polity intrinsically inimical to pluralism. The vibrant civil society of the last year of the Shah's rule and the year or so after his ouster gradually faded in the face of the emergent regime's determined monopolization of political and ideological power. According to Bazargan, of the main revolutionary groups, the clerics emerged as the winners of the revolution.[1]

Chastised by Khomeini as weak, the beleaguered Bazargan had grown more conscious of the frailty of moderate political endeavor. Barely able to hide his frustration, he aptly described his government as a knife without a blade. A manufactured crisis that facilitated clerical ascendancy was the 444-day-long hostage saga, which began on November 4, 1979, when a group of "students" claiming to "tread Khomeini's [political] path" stormed the U.S. embassy and took its diplomats hostage. Condoned by Khomeini, the crisis precipitated the resignation of Bazargan, who continued for some time to work with the regime but gradually became one of its most candid and trenchant critics, until his death in January 1995.[2] Ostensibly provoked by the Shah's arrival in the United States and by fears that the Americans might try to organize a coup similar to that of August 1953, the hostage crisis was used to create a state of emergency.[3] By maintaining that the country faced determined U.S. animosity, the clerics were able to advance their exclusionist agenda, move against moderate forces, and unravel fragile political and civil liberties. The hostage crisis served to affirm the clerics' anti-imperialist posture and steal the limelight from the radical left. Though crucially helpful to the clerics' political aims, the crisis proved disastrous for Iran's national interests. It not only provoked the freezing of Iranian assets in the United States but turned Iran into an international pariah. The financial settlement following the resolution of the hostage crisis was highly disadvantageous to Iran. It involved the early repayment to American banks of loans negotiated by the Shah's government at favorable rates, as well as numerous lawsuits brought against Iran at a special claims tribunal at The Hague.

On April 1, 1979, following a referendum in which 98 percent of the electorate indicated their approval, the country was formally designated an Islamic republic, but the political and legal configurations of such a polity were yet to be clarified through a constitution. Khomeini was willing to accept a draft constitution prepared by the cabinet and the Revolutionary Council—which contained no provisions regarding hierocratic authority—to be put to a referendum. He may have taken such an authority for granted, or perhaps he did not view its formal inclusion in the Constitution as necessary or prudent. Failing to anticipate the probability of Khomeinist ascendancy in a constituent assembly and on grounds of principle, Bazargan and some of his colleagues wanted the draft constitution debated by an elected constituent assembly. This step was also demanded by secular forces, as well as by the democratically inclined Ayatollah Shari'atmadari, who had a considerable following in his native province of Azarbaijan and among several moderate groups.

In lieu of an envisaged 350-member assembly, Sayyed Mahmud Taleqani, the cleric close to Bazargan, suggested a smaller assembly of some 70 members. Having grown increasingly impatient with demands for an unencumbered democratic constitution, Khomeini found this proposal acceptable.[4] A 73-man body—the "Assembly of Experts"—was elected in July 1979 with limited popular backing; consisting primarily of ardent supporters of Islamist government, it included more than 50 clerics. The elections for the assembly were boycotted by virtually all political groups except the IRP, which came to dominate it. Unlike the earlier draft, the constitution adopted in mid-November by the assembly formally enshrined clerical ascendancy.[5] One of its entrenched clauses, based on an idea developed by Khomeini some ten years earlier, was the Guardianship of the Islamic Jurist (*velayat-e faqih*), whose incumbent would also be referred to as the Leader.[6] Aiming to retrieve the original draft, the Bazargan government had tried to undermine or restrain the assembly only to provoke a stern rebuke from Khomeini, who had fully embraced an Islamist constitution. The death in September 1979 of Taleqani had silenced a voice increasingly at odds with the emerging monological clerical ascendancy. By early December, when the draft constitution was to be put to a popular vote, the continuing hostage crisis enabled the clerics to outmaneuver their opponents with greater ease.

The new Constitution contained antinomies that reflected the conflicting forces, interests, and aspirations involved in the revolution. The Constitution's republican components, though opaque and subdued, indicated the democratic yearnings underlying the revolution. The symbolically significant choice of a republican form of government revealed a recognition of democratic aspirations, which were among the core motivating ideals of the revolution. However, meaningful republicanism would in practice prove incongruent with the leading role and privileged status of the clergy as the unchallengeable heirs of the revolution. Republicanism was eclipsed, if not abrogated by, the Constitution's theocratic tenor, which was designed to ensure clerical hegemony.[7] Advocates of democracy saw the institutionalization of clerical tutelage as tantamount to treating citizens as minors, denying them a sphere of self-determination essential to citizenship and thus effectively negating the concept of citizenship. The politically enforced religious paternalism required guiding the people on how they ought to lead their lives and more crucially on what meaningful life amounted to. Thus, there was a real setback not only in the area of popular sovereignty but also in the domain of personal and civic autonomy.

Replicating the constitutional antinomies, the envisaged governmental apparatus rested on a fundamental and irresolvable structural contradiction. It purported, on the one hand, to defer to and represent the will of the people and sought to embody popular sovereignty. On the other, it constructed a theocratic edifice in which a leading cleric would be empowered to accumulate and exercise vast political and ideological power; he would guide, oversee, and overshadow other state institutions while avoiding any real measure of accountability. Such an arrangement provoked dissent even among leading clerics, who were silenced or neutralized along with other political forces. Besides the use of coercion to silence dissent, character assassination emerged as a favorite tactic. "Documents" taken from the U.S. embassy—renamed "the nest of spies"—were selectively published, often in a mistranslated form, and utilized to defame opponents, accusing them of improper or treasonous contacts with embassy personnel.

## Consolidation of Clerical Tutelage

The first president of the Islamic Republic, Abolhasan Bani-Sadr, a French-educated activist who combined revisionist Islam with strong Mosaddeqist tendencies, was not a cleric. The idea of a cleric as president was still anomalous and did not appeal to Khomeini. Despite winning 75 percent of the popular vote and enjoying the favor of Khomeini, who also appointed him commander-in-chief of the armed forces, Bani-Sadr soon found himself facing problems far exceeding his personal ability and room for maneuver, including the hostage crisis. More significantly, he had to assert his authority and restrain the exclusionist trends that were gaining momentum, spearheaded by the IRP. To Bani-Sadr's chagrin, Khomeini entrusted the party leader, the influential cleric Mohammad Beheshti, with the tasks of controlling and Islamicizing the judiciary, further dashing the hopes of secularists. Temperamentally and intellectually Bani-Sadr found it difficult to reconcile himself with the expectations and political conduct of the rising clerical elite. Having failed to organize or capitalize on his widespread popular support or to neutralize his clerical and doctrinaire (maktabi) religious opponents, he clumsily tried to co-opt or disarm them, vacillating between vain defiance, dismissive avoidance, and reluctant cooperation. He collaborated with them in launching the Cultural Revolution in April 1980, which effectively ended meaningful political pluralism, led to the expulsion of hundreds of faculty and thousands of students, closed down universities for two years, and disrupted academic and cultural life for much longer. The elections for the first Islamic parliament in May 1980, in which his clerical opponents held the upper hand while he enjoyed little support, increased his problems. Finding a prime minister acceptable to both the president and the parliament proved a major challenge.

The outbreak of the war with Iraq in September 1980 temporarily reduced the friction between Bani-Sadr and his clerical opponents, most of whom were affiliated with the IRP. The war provided Bani-Sadr with a diversion from his grinding political tasks, exacerbated by the hostage crisis and by rebellion in the Kurdish areas. More crucially, it provided him with an opportunity to establish himself as a dedicated patriot and a war leader; by spending considerable time at the front he also hoped to disarm, restrain, or circumvent his clerical opponents. Yet the rift with them was only widening. He denounced them as corrupt, incompetent, and authoritarian, and they more than reciprocated. Khomeini's attempts at reconciliation bore no fruit. The IRP mobilized all its forces against Bani-Sadr; the parliament considerably reduced the scope of his authority as president; his refusal to submit provoked an outcry against him as a "dictator."

Bani-Sadr's deteriorating relations with his clerical adversaries rallied most secular forces around him, including the well-organized and well-armed Mojahedin-e Khalq and many Mosaddeqists. These forces were countered by the clerically organized vigilante group hezbollah (partisans of God), which consisted of gangs of underclass elements and street fighters. The parliament declared Bani-Sadr unfit to be president; Khomeini promptly endorsed the move and dismissed him (June 22, 1981) after seventeen tumultuous months in office. By late July Bani-Sadr had fled to Paris, together with the leader of the Mojahedin. June 1981 marked a watershed in the early phase of the Islamic regime, with the outbreak of a cycle of remorseless violence between the regime and the Mojahedin. An explosion at the IRP headquarters in Tehran in late June killed some seventy of the party's leaders, thus eliminating key members of the new elite. It unleashed an intensified onslaught against the Mojahedin, who resorted to a variety of violent countermeasures, ending in the elimination or incarceration of a large number of the organization's members.[8] A key group among the opponents of the monarchy, the Mojahedin enjoyed considerable following among the younger generation. Many surviving members of the group found refuge in Iraq, establishing a military base there in the hope of overthrowing the Iranian regime.

Clerical tutelage evolved gradually. It drew its legitimacy from the revolution, which it portrayed as solely, emphatically, and self-consciously Islamic. It also relied on Khomeini's charismatic leadership in order to consolidate and institutionalize itself. The three key revolutionary mottos—independence, liberty, and an Islamic republic—which had been assumed to be interconnected and mutually reinforcing, continued to be relentlessly repeated. Yet liberty was reduced to an empty slogan and a chimera, republicanism remained a diluted formality, and independence failed to produce the much-promised self-sufficiency and prosperity for all. Regardless of how salient the idea of independence or national self-determination was as a guiding principle for the rulers, it produced little positive change in the lives of ordinary citizens.

The regime was structurally fragile, vulnerable to intra-elite conflict, and beset by the lack of a high-caliber, professionally competent, and experienced cadre. Yet it had a reservoir of dedicated supporters and could rely on loyal armed revolutionary bodies and on Khomeini's resolve, which enabled it to survive attempts to decapitate it. In October 1981, despite the reservations of a number of influential clerics who objected to the clerical assumption of the presidency, Sayyed Ali Khameneh'i, long active in the Islamist movement, was elected to this office.[9] The role of the IRP as the ruling party was now confirmed beyond question or challenge: its members now filled the three highest positions in the government—Khameneh'i as president, the Islamist engineer Mir-Hosein Musavi as prime minister, and the influential cleric Ali-Akbar Hashemi-Rafsanjani as the Speaker of the parliament.

In postrevolutionary Iran, creating political order had become the greatest challenge; yet neither the regime nor its radical opponents offered a viable blueprint for achieving it. Resistance to clerical rule provoked suppression, brutalization, a spiral of violence and revenge, a dehumanizing atmosphere of terror fueled by religious or ideological zeal. It also invigorated the regime, which seemed to thrive on crisis and confrontation. The scale of opposition facing the regime had led it to conclude that it could not survive without a massive crackdown.[10] Estimates differ as to the number of those killed by the regime; according to one account, more than 10,000 active opponents, whether radical leftists or liberals, would be eliminated in the years after 1981—ten times more than the number of royalists executed in the early phase of the revolution.[11] Nor were prominent clerical opponents of the regime spared persecution. The dissident Ayatollah Shari'atmadari had distanced himself from his rebellious, powerful constituency in Azarbaijan and was unable to prevent the dissolution of a political party that he had sponsored. Implicated in an antiregime plot, he was—in an unprecedented move—"demoted," publicly humiliated, and treated in a manner unbefitting a high-ranking Shi'ite divine.[12]

Having effectively eliminated nearly all liberal and radical leftist forces, the regime turned against the last surviving organized secular force, the Tudeh Party. The party had consistently displayed its goodwill and subservience to the regime, even to the extent of assisting it in suppressing other secular opponents. Constrained by internalized ideological assumptions and dependence on the Soviet Union, the party's conduct was not entirely inexplicable. Yet, even to its most charitable opponents, the party was guilty of allowing itself to be cynically exploited and then unceremoniously discarded by the regime. The suppression of the party in February–May 1983 marked the effective end of an organization that had been a resilient player in Iranian politics since the early 1940s. The loyally pro-Soviet party had opposed the secular, prowestern monarchy but had found it expedient to collaborate with the Islamic regime. Both the regime and the party were hostile to "liberalism." Yet in the eyes of the party leaders, and by implication the Soviet leadership, the Islamic regime's chief redeeming virtue, despite its professed antagonism to both the East and the West, was its antiimperialism, that is, its opposition to the United States.

The outbreak of the war with Iraq greatly facilitated the regime's repression of its opponents. In the context of steadily deteriorating relations between the two countries, and taking advantage of the political disarray and isolation of the Islamic Republic, the Iraqi regime launched a massive offensive. Though crippled by the revolutionary turmoil, by May 1982 the Iranian army and revolutionary forces had liberated the southwestern city of Khorramshahr, repelling the Iraqis. This event signaled the clear victory of Iran, which could now extract substantial reparations from Iraq and its fearful Arab backers, particularly the Saudis, desperate to check Iranian advances and end the war. Yet, hoping to punish and even topple the Iraqi regime and export the revolution, and grossly misconstruing the regional and international situation, the Islamic regime opted to fight on. It let it be known that if an Islamic state emerged in Iraq, Iran would forgo demands for reparations. Among other things, and as a precondition for ending the war, the Islamic Republic insisted on a Security Council resolution condemning Iraq as an aggressor, which Iran was unlikely to achieve given its international status. Until May 1982 Iran had been fighting Iraqi aggression, engaged in a war viewed by the Iranian public as patriotic and just. The continuation of the war beyond that date changed everything. Iraq and its supporters now saw the war as an attempt by Iran to export its revolution and destabilize the oil-producing Arab states.

Despite its devastating impact on Iranian society and economy, the war helped to consolidate clerical rule and in effect rescued and invigorated the regime. Although the war would be described as "imposed," it would also be referred to as the "sacred defense," even as "a providential gift." It gave greater resonance to the emotive rhetoric of martyrdom and sacrifice that dominated the regime's public pronouncements. The regime seemed committed to fighting to the bitter end regardless of the cost, particularly in human terms. A war to punish a reviled enemy was used to undermine growing public demands and pressures for a more open and rational society; it helped divert attention from mounting domestic problems. The exigencies of war were invoked to explain away such problems and justify or conceal the rulers' failings. A war-generated state of emergency enabled the regime to suspend the residual amenities of normal politics and to silence dissent. The overthrow of the Iraqi leader, Saddam Hussein, became an obsession in circumstances in which the Arab states and the West were determined to deny Iran a victory. With virtual stalemate on many fronts, Iraqi attacks against Iranian shipping and oil installations, the use of poison gas, and indiscriminate attacks on Iranian cities beginning in 1985, over time the situation became utterly hopeless.

The ruling clerics could no longer remain unresponsive to growing public disquiet and pressure, nor could they appear indifferent to the death and misery engulfing both Iranian soldiers and civilians. The cost of continuing the war, in terms of human lives and material resources, was proving enormous. Considering the level of international opposition to Iran, any expectation of an evenhanded approach or active concern from the United Nations was naive. The United States and other major powers would not allow Iran a victory. By mid-July 1988 the Iranian regime's fortunes and morale had plummeted. Iraq had intensified targeting Iranian cities with Scud missiles, and the Iranians attempted to reciprocate; Iranian forces had retreated from some of the positions they had held, and the United States—increasingly embroiled in the conflict by openly siding with Iraq—had damaged or destroyed most of the Iranian navy in the Persian Gulf. No longer in a position to fight, exhausted, and lacking essential material resources, particularly military hardware, on July 18, 1988, the Iranian regime accepted a UN-brokered cease-fire.

While Iran was isolated internationally, Iraq was backed by its rich Arab neighbors, the United States, and other Western powers. The result was a stark contrast between the volume and quality of military equipment and other kinds of assistance available to Iraq and Iran. Iran's stigmatization as an outlaw state cost the country dearly. International, particularly Western, reaction to the extensive bloodshed caused by the war, the Iraqi use of poison gas, and the downing of an Iranian civilian aircraft over the Persian Gulf by a U.S. warship in early July 1988—killing all 290 passengers and crew—was dishearteningly mute. As in the case of the hostage crisis, the regime acted too late to secure a less costly outcome for the country. Moreover, it adamantly refused to allow its war record and policies to be subjected to public debate or scrutiny.

As a Shi'ite state the Iranian regime continued to have limited ecumenical potential and appeal among the Islamist movements of the wider Islamic world, and the hope that the Shi'ites of Iraq would rise up to join their Iranian brethren remained unfulfilled. The fact that a Shi'ite state had relentlessly fought another Muslim state with a majority Shi'ite population militated against the pan-Islamist claims of the Islamic Republic. Such claims also overshadowed the region's recognition of Iranian nationalism; yet nationalism had been a key, if unacknowledged, inspiration in repelling the Iraqi army. Domestically, instituting Shi'ism as the ruling ideology of governance proved inimical to the interests of Iran's religious and ethnic minorities. Externally, Iran's rhetoric of exporting its revolution provoked Saudi Arabia, which, with U.S. endorsement, began to export its own rigidly conservative and virulently anticommunist brand of Islam. Focused on Iran as the real source of danger, Western leaders myopically saw Saudi Wahhabi proselytizing activities as unthreatening to Western interests.

Viewing itself as sufficiently consolidated, and despite the ongoing war, at the end of 1982 the regime relaxed some of its draconian policies. A decree issued by Khomeini affirming respect for certain individual rights and entitlements resulted in less wanton and arbitrary treatment of individuals. Institutional juridical fairness and predictability, legal security, and due process, however, remained elusive. The regime's surviving opponents were still vulnerable to arbitrary treatment. Both the Iraqi and Iranian regimes had cultivated and assisted organized opposition to each other in their respective territories. In July 1988, in the wake of the cease-fire ending the war, Mojahedin-e Khalq units stationed in Iraq started an ill-fated invasion of western border areas of Iran, which reignited the Iranian regime's violence against the remaining, mostly incarcerated, members of the group. Within some two months thousands of prisoners—Mojahedin and other leftists—who were deemed not to have genuinely repented were summarily executed despite having previously been sentenced to terms of imprisonment.[13]

Though in many respects helpful to the regime, the war was an overwhelming burden, often leading the rulers to desperate measures. In 1985–1986 the need for military equipment embroiled the regime in covert, convoluted, and ultimately ill-fated contacts with the United States, and indirectly with Israel. In exchange for its assistance in the release of U.S. hostages in Lebanon, arms were sold to Iran and the proceeds diverted to the pro-U.S. Nicaraguan rebels who were fighting their left-wing government. When the matter—known as the Iran-Contra affair—came to light it badly damaged the Iranian regime's vaunted image of integrity. The affair was reminiscent of the putative deal of October 1980 between Iran and the representatives of Ronald Reagan, the Republican presidential candidate. It has been contended that the deal, known as the "October Surprise," was to delay the release of the U.S. embassy hostages until after the presidential election. In exchange, and in the event of Reagan's victory, Israel would sell military hardware to Iran.[14] Ironically, by their actions the Iranian revolutionaries helped destroy Carter's chances for reelection, while the Iranian royalists continued to blame him for having helped to weaken the monarchy and facilitate the success of the revolution through his human rights policies. The relentless anti-Carter hostility of the Khomeinists contributed significantly to the election of the indefatigably right-wing Reagan.

The management of the war and governing a complex society proved to be daunting challenges to the clerics. While recognizing no other group as competent to make valid pronouncements on Islam, they paradoxically saw no area of expertise into which they could not intrude. Despite a cunning instinct for power they were ill equipped for the task of governance; their trustworthy nonclerical accomplices were no more politically and administratively competent. The political blunders and squabbles of the inexperienced elite were compounded by the regime's explicit preference of ideologically correct commitment over professional expertise. This resulted in extensive and costly mismanagement and glaring bureaucratic inefficiency. Since assumption of, or promotion to, high office was dictated by avowed ideological commitment, loyalty, and factional affiliation and patronage, the morale of the professional secular civil servants who had survived various purges dwindled. A bureaucratic hierarchy based primarily on nonrational criteria commanded little respect among subordinates, who often showed their discontent by deliberate inefficiency, which in turn added to public frustration.

Yet, against all odds and thanks largely to Khomeini's pivotal role, which partially compensated for the many blunders of the Islamic regime, it proved more resilient than its proponents and certainly its opponents imagined. Khomeini not only ultimately sanctioned the policies of the regime but gave it a sense of cohesion and direction. Though vulnerable to conflicting advice and factional machinations, he assiduously sought to curb and control factionalism. Much of his energy was spent on mediating among cliques vying for greater influence and turf. In the pursuit of his chief aim of establishing and preserving an Islamic polity, he regarded all other objectives as secondary and no one as indispensable. Defying him could be unimaginably costly. Despite his single-mindedness, Khomeini fully understood the limits of inflexibility. He proved willing to drink the "poison chalice" of ending the war with Iraq short of overthrowing the Ba'thist regime. He did not go out of his way to support distributive measures; a radical program of land reform that he had sanctioned was abandoned following clerical opposition and rural disorder. No other political cleric possessed Khomeini's capacity for self-righteous leadership, or his ability to combine tenacity of purpose with shrewd tactical flexibility. The factors motivating or informing Khomeini's conduct were bound to be open to conflicting interpretations, as were the contours of his political legacy. The immediate challenge for Khomeini and his key followers was, however, to ensure that his successor was fully committed to his vision of an Islamic polity.

## Decline of Zeal: The Post-Khomeini Era

Irrespective of the theological genealogy of ideas regarding the clerics' role in Islamic governance, Khomeini was the architect of the Guardianship of the Islamic Jurist, which, Bazargan observed, was an apt designation for the political regime emerging under Khomeini. "Jurist" implies the implementation of juridical Islam by a privileged clergy, and "guardianship" denotes a relationship analogous to "tutelage over minors and the mentally incompetent." "Transcending laws, rules and responsibilities, the Guardianship of the Jurist involves doctrinaire patriarchy and tutelary power over the nation and the state, the religion and all affairs of the country." Yet this position, Bazargan added, was "a cloak tailor-made" for Khomeini; it was unlikely that any other person would have his "background, authority, and initiative" or be treated with "the same degree of devotion and obedience."[15] Aiming to ensure the continuity of this mode of rule beyond his own life, Khomeini resorted to a number of measures.

In January 1988, intending to extend the authority of the Jurist/Leader, he introduced the notion of the "Absolute Guardianship of the Islamic Jurist." This implied that safeguarding the Islamic state, which took precedence even over the observance of Islamic law, was the primary task of the Leader. He was, in effect, solely entitled to determine what was in the state's interests and what policies and measures were needed to protect it; he alone could invoke *raison d'état* and act on it.[16] The epithet "absolute" strengthened the notion of guardianship as the pivotal institution of clerical rule, but in practice changed little, as absolutism was already implicit in the earlier conception. Soon afterward, in February, Khomeini created the Council for Ascertaining the Interests of the [Political] System, commonly known as the Expediency Council, to assist the Leader and arbitrate disagreements between the parliament, the government, and the powerful Council of Guardians. The last body consisted of six Islamic jurists appointed by the Leader and six lay Muslim lawyers selected by the parliament from a list provided by the head of the judiciary. The chief task of the Council of Guardians was to ensure conformity of parliamentary legislation with Islamic law, which was determined by the council's jurist members. It had the authority to interpret the Constitution and to ascertain the acceptability or "competence" of candidates for the presidency and parliamentary seats, and saw itself as answerable only to the Leader. Khomeini seemed clearly concerned that with his death, the eccentric and fragile political arrangements that he had crafted might crumble as a result of structural weakness, lack of institutional coordination, and the rivalries of cliques that directly or indirectly controlled those arrangements.

Interinstitutional conflicts, exacerbated by factional and ideological differences between the predominantly "leftist" second parliament (1984–1988) and cabinet and the right-wing Council of Guardians, at times severely tested the regime. With Rafsanjani as Speaker since July 1980, the parliament, despite its institutional weakness, had become more effective but was still vulnerable to the dictates of the council. The existence of bodies such as the Council of Guardians and the Expediency Council indicated that clerical politics resembled a politics of village elders, which privileged patriarchal authority and gerontocratic wisdom; it flourished on intra-elite negotiations and on improvised mediated solutions. The conduct and the ethos of the Islamic regime demonstrated that the parliament was essentially a consultative body with limited legislative authority; it did not embody popular sovereignty, which figured dimly in the regime's legitimizing apparatus.

Concern about the future of the regime also played a crucial role in Khomeini's decision to discard his designated successor, Ayatollah Hosein-Ali Montazeri, the iconic veteran revolutionary figure and one of the founding fathers of Islamic governance. Montazeri had retained the egalitarian populism of his revolutionary activist phase and its attendant concerns about moral rectitude, justice, and political transparency. He had grown increasingly critical of the conduct and policies of the ascendant clerics and had developed closer ties with Bazargan's Freedom Movement. By criticizing the intolerance, lack of principle, and political greed of key figures in the regime, by denouncing the execution of incarcerated Mojahedin, by defending human rights, and by criticizing the conduct of the war he had angered Khomeini and made enemies, who dismissed him as "naive" and lacking the requisite political acumen and skills to succeed as Leader. Certain key officials of the regime feared the consequences of the removal of Montazeri and the resulting absence of a high-ranking jurist to succeed Khomeini. Yet, irrespective of such concerns, Khomeini procured Montazeri's resignation (March 28, 1989). Efforts were also made to undermine his image, yet despite subsequent harassment Montazeri remained a bold critic of many aspects of the regime's conduct.

In April 1989, some two months before his death, Khomeini established a twenty-five-man Council for Constitutional Amendment. Khameneh'i and Rafsanjani played key roles in this process. By the time the council, most of whose members were appointed by Khomeini, had accomplished its task, he had died and had been promptly replaced by Khameneh'i, who resigned the presidency. Khomeini had been able to harmonize or harness different cliques, but with his death, as he had anticipated, the need for greater coordination between various institutions was paramount. The new Leader had to be able to overcome stalemate and to forestall prolonged discord. The constitutional amendments were formalized through a referendum in late July 1989. The Expediency Council became a formal institution of the state, and the stipulation that in the absence of a single qualified leader there could be a leadership council was abandoned in favor of a single Leader.

Most important of all, the office of the Leader was institutionally redefined and strengthened. In addition to continuing to act as commander-in-chief of the armed forces and appointing and dismissing key officials such as jurist members of the Council of Guardians, the head of the judiciary, the director of state radio and television, and the commanders of the armed and security forces, the Leader determined the general policies of the regime and oversaw their proper execution. He also regulated relations among the three branches of the government and resolved their differences. The office of the prime minister was abolished and the responsibilities of the president were extended, but not his authority, which in certain respects was diminished to the benefit of the Leader. The Leader was now more than ever not only the head of state but also the head of the government; he was the ultimate decisionmaker and arbiter. In every respect, the office of the Leader was formally far more powerful than the monarchy had been: the monarch's authority had been secular, and his proper constitutional role essentially ceremonial.

Like Khomeini, Khameneh'i was referred to as both the Leader of the Islamic Republic and the Leader of the Islamic Revolution. This designation could imply that the Islamic revolution was a continuing process. Khameneh'i could rely on his credentials as a committed follower of Khomeini and a key figure in the Islamic state who was linked to revolutionary institutions or to those who controlled them. He was elevated to the rank of ayatollah, but there was a general shift away from recognized religious status and learning in favor of temporal knowledge and political and administrative skills. The Leader as a jurist of the highest rank (source of emulation) gave way to the Leader as a competent jurist-statesman.

Despite the authority conferred on the incumbent by the redefined office of Leader, succeeding Khomeini was undoubtedly a major challenge. As Leader, Khameneh'i had to play a role not only befitting the office that he inherited but also satisfactory to the disparate constituencies that he had to take into account. He was expected to harmonize and control factions with differing views and interests, protect the legacy of Khomeini, and ensure that the regime did not stray from the "straight path." In due course the institutional centrality of his office, together with his long tenure and the vast resources available to him, would enable Khameneh'i to nurture an extensive patronage network, dispense material and symbolic rewards, and win over or silence many would-be opponents among the clerics. Yet the characterization of the Leader as "absolute" would rarely be invoked, as it contravened even the flimsiest notions of republican governance and was at odds with growing demands for political openness and with the requirements of a society struggling to revitalize its economy and improve its international status. The fact that the regime survived the demise of its founding leader indicated undeniable resilience.

Both Rafsanjani and Khameneh'i had survived assassination attempts (in

May 1979 and June 1981 respectively). They were considered among the most dedicated leaders of the Islamic state and had played important roles in its consolidation. In July 1989 Rafsanjani was elected to replace Khameneh'i as president. With a newfound self-confidence the regime began to move away from its ideologically driven policies toward greater pragmatism. It favored a wider scope for the private sector and foreign capital, an improved international image, and trade with the West. It sought to distance itself from the stultifying legacy of the immediate past and viewed a degree of social tolerance as essential to its survival. After Khomeini and later Khameneh'i, Rafsanjani was the second most powerful man in the country. Even before becoming president he had played a significant role in the conduct of the war, diplomacy, the Iran-Contra affair, and the management of crises facing the regime.[17] In the eyes of his critics, he was a wily and manipulative oligarch with an almost regal self-image and conduct, a veritable *éminence rouge*.[18] In the eyes of his supporters, he was endowed with the stature, vision, and skills to overcome relentless factional squabbles; a leader keenly attentive to Iranian nationalism and dedicated to socioeconomic development, which would pave the way for a more prosperous and open society.

The emotionally exhausted population saw Rafsanjani as possessing both a greater understanding of the realities of the modern world and a determination to heal the wounds caused by repression, war, and chronic mismanagement. He enjoyed close ties with Khameneh'i, other leading clerics, and the main institutions of the Islamic state. With his presidency it seemed that at last a statesman had emerged whose personal abilities and strong links with the main loci of power gave him an authority and opportunity far greater than that which the office of the president formally allowed.

Supporters of Rafsanjani expected that he would immediately address the lack of consensus about how to run the country and about Iran's overall priorities, as well as the need to cultivate competent administrators. Rafsanjani encouraged the rise of a "technocratic" elite with proper Islamic credentials. However, organizing and sustaining political support remained a challenge. The IRP, which had acted as the party of government, had, despite its domination by clerics, remained ideologically heterogeneous and organizationally fractious. The intensification of conflict between the party's radical and pragmatist factions contributed to its formal dissolution in early June 1987. This outcome reflected the continuing difficulties afflicting formal party politics, even a single-party system, in the Iranian political culture. There would, of course, be surrogate groups or parties with various agendas. Rafsanjani himself encouraged and enjoyed the support of, among others, a group espousing socioeconomic reform. Yet neither the dissolution of the IRP, the decline in the number of clerics elected to the parliament, nor any similar development would change the configuration of the prevailing politics—a politics premised on the unchallengeable rule of the clerics and their nonclerical but like-minded or loyal allies, with Islam serving as the legitimizing ideology. No group or party would be allowed to contest or even question the ideologically enshrined clerical-Islamist domination.

For Rafsanjani and his political cohorts, the imperative of coordinating and homogenizing the regime's decisionmaking and administrative structures involved purging or marginalizing groups or individuals considered opposed to the pragmatist agenda. Thus, an association of clerics known as the League of Combatant Clerics was gradually eased out of the ruling institutions, including the parliament. Though ideologically inchoate, the league advocated distributive policies and active state intervention in the economy, and opposed large-scale privatization, which the pragmatists considered essential for economic recovery.

On the opposite side of the political spectrum stood the Association of Tehran's Combatant Clergy, which was ideologically no more coherent than its rival but favored free enterprise, was broadly traditionalist, and was linked to the bazaar merchants. In the 1990s this group and its nonclerical allies dominated the fourth and fifth terms of the parliament. Yet, despite its ideological affinity with Rafsanjani, the parliament was not consistently cooperative. One reason was the persistence of personal rivalries—for instance between Rafsanjani and Ali-Akbar Nateq-Nuri, the Speaker of the parliament and an influential cleric. Hard-liners, too, continued their efforts to undermine or dilute Rafsanjani's policies or to win him over. Despite Khomeini's remedial measures before his death, the Islamic regime remained vulnerable to cliquish conduct and fissiparity arising from ideology, personal differences, conflicts of interest, and patronage ties. The situation was further complicated by competition or discord both among and within state institutions that proved resistant to either exhortation or pressure.

The chief challenge facing the government of Rafsanjani was revitalization of the ailing Iranian economy. He and his supporters understood that the regime's indifference to everyday suffering had proved counterproductive, and its earlier emphasis on the worthlessness of life in this world as opposed to the next had long ceased to have a palliative impact. As a state, the Islamic regime needed to attend to the needs and expectations of the people. It could not expect to survive without redefining its mandate and fashioning a new source of legitimacy by focusing on development and public welfare. It had to deal with the reconstruction of the war-ravaged areas, revitalize the economy, and revive many projects pursued or envisaged by the previous regime.

The Islamic state's takeover of many private enterprises following the collapse of the monarchy, the distributive objectives associated with the revolution, and war-related needs had resulted in a form of state "socialism." This étatist policy appealed to the lower classes and was favored by radical politicians such as the former prime minister, Musavi, who had been close to Khomeini's son Ahmad. But the state's control over the economy and its distributive measures were anathema to the conservative or traditionalist clergy and bazaar merchants. During the war years, rationing, shortages, inflation, and shrinking incomes had promoted a flourishing black market, which needed to be contained. With the end of the war, the poorly managed state "socialism" looked less than viable; the state's control of the economy was gradually but steadily diluted by capitalist measures. At the same time the government focused on postwar reconstruction. The main priority was rebuilding the country's socioeconomic and industrial infrastructure, badly damaged by the war and years of neglect. Equally urgent were the reconstruction of war-ravaged cities and the relocation of their uprooted inhabitants. Yet the regime could not ignore or avoid a host of daunting contradictory challenges: how to remain attentive to the needs of the lower classes, which it publicly claimed to represent, while embracing unfettered capitalism and privatization; how to reconcile the requirements of social justice with the inequities intrinsic to capitalism; how to alleviate the excessive economic hardships suffered by the salaried as well as the lower classes—who were overwhelmed, indeed pauperized, by uncontrollable inflation and the regime's inept economic policies; and how to reward its key supporters while avoiding large-scale corruption and systematic abuse of office.

Hasty privatization and the erosion of subsidies on basic foodstuffs would leave the lower classes, who had made enormous sacrifices during the war, more vulnerable. The "disinherited," whose fortunes were to be radically transformed through a nonwasteful "Islamic" economy and distributive measures, remained as vulnerable as ever. The charitable foundation that bore their name did little to empower or unburden them. It did, however, lavishly benefit those who claimed to speak on their behalf. Enterprising supporters of the regime were able to amass large fortunes. A decline in manufacturing industries and a growing demand for consumer goods, together with the lucrative profits coveted by proregime entrepreneurs, resulted in opening the country to foreign imports. The imbalance between imports and exports spiraled out of control. Lip service continued to be paid to "Islamic" economics and banking, but the purported "Islamicization" of the economy and banking had no lasting consequence. The much-proclaimed objective of national self-sufficiency remained a dream. Abandoning many of its earlier policies, the regime saw no alternative to greater economic privatization; it concentrated on attracting foreign investment and encouraged diaspora Iranians to return and invest in the country. Responding to economic pressures, and in an effort to control population growth, the regime revived family planning, which it had unwisely abolished in 1980.

The shift away from the morally austere étatism of the earlier phase of the revolution and toward increasing privatization could also be gauged by the changing composition of the parliament. The economically leftist clerics and activists of the first parliament gave way in later parliaments to conservative or right-wing technocrats advocating free enterprise. Similarly, earlier revolutionary denunciations of material indulgence and luxury, and efforts to promote thrift and ideological zeal, proved unsustainable. The idealistic puritanism and frugality of Islamist revolutionary activists untainted by power would prove, as Ibn Khaldun, the fourteenth-century Muslim thinker, had observed, incongruent with the consolidation and routinization of governance and the material and symbolic rewards associated with high office. Gradually the mellowing effects of power, privilege, experience, and age would ensure that puritanical fervor and ideological radicalism gave way to defensive conservatism.

During Rafsanjani's two-term presidency (1989–1997), despite remedial efforts, the economic problems facing the regime, particularly rampant inflation and unemployment, and mounting foreign debts, in addition to chronic rural-urban migration, remained intractable. The regime embarked on many infrastructural projects, although most of the significant projects undertaken had been planned or started before the revolution. Completing them successfully or on time proved to be a major challenge. The development process remained uneven, and the postwar reconstruction fell far short of revitalizing the economy or society. Despite the fact that Iran is a resource-rich country, the record of the regime in promoting economic development and self-sufficiency, industrialization, job creation, welfare, and self-confidence born of real success was unimpressive. According to one account, between 1970 and 1995 no country comparable to Iran experienced a similar regression in its development.[19]

Clearly, after the sacrifices and hardships of the war years and in the context of rising expectations, satisfying or not alienating various constituencies had proved difficult. By promoting pragmatism, Rafsanjani provoked those who had remained loyal to or invoked the earlier revolutionary ideals. The economic privatization of the postwar era intensified social rifts, contributing to a potentially dangerous backlash. In the first half of the 1990s the regime faced serious lower-class unrest, which it suppressed; yet the underlying causes of discontent were not adequately addressed. Mercantile and entrepreneurial support was cultivated, and real estate speculation and other opportunities for self-enrichment gave rise to a class of well-connected *nouveaux riches* with real or feigned Islamist pedigrees or commitment. A vast and growing number of people, however, including the salaried middle and lower classes, saw themselves becoming increasingly and helplessly impoverished. In the absence of political transparency and accountability or a reasonably free press able to scrutinize the conduct and record of the government, instances of dereliction of duty, various forms of corruption, including nepotism, cronyism, favoritism, and other abuses of office that rewarded the undeserving and the unmerited, became widespread. The impact on the public perception of the regime was corrosive.

Politically, too, the regime seemed unable to resolve the incongruence between its attempts to continue modernizing the country's infrastructure and its resistance to political and cultural change. It could not successfully defuse the prevailing crisis of legitimacy without allowing the existing parliamentary and representative procedures to acquire credibility. However, it could not accomplish the latter without also irrevocably altering the "Islamic" character of the state and undermining clerical domination over the key edifices and apparatus of power, privilege, and coercion. With the end of the war, demands for political freedom and pluralism were on the rise. Yet the constitutionally stipulated, and subsequently reaffirmed, freedom to form political parties was officially ignored. When the grudgingly tolerated Freedom Movement and "liberal" Islamists close to it demanded political openness, they were arrested and imprisoned in large numbers. They were barred from candidacy in the elections for the fourth parliament in 1992.

Intellectuals and activists expressing criticism of the regime continued to be denounced, harassed, or worse. A multi-installment television program called *Identity (Hoviyat)* sought to defame some of the top scholars and intellectuals in the country. The regime made it patently clear that limits on organized oppositional activities and control over the resurgent civil society were to persist. The result was a considerable dwindling of support for Rafsanjani, who was blamed for condoning or failing to oppose repressive moves. Yet civic and sociocultural life had acquired a dynamism that could not be easily controlled or arrested. Universities remained politically and intellectually boisterous. The publication and translation of books, and interest in modern sociopolitical thought, continued to flourish, and various journals emerged to respond to the growing interest in such topics. Iranian cinema acquired an international stature. Stimulated by the momentous revocation of a postrevolutionary ban, music, particularly classical Persian music, previously favored mostly by the upper echelons of society, found a growing audience among all classes. Learning to play a musical instrument became a favored activity among the young.

Despite Rafsanjani's efforts to normalize the country's relations with the outside world—essential for economic recovery—relations with the United States remained strained or deteriorated. Iraq's occupation of Kuwait and its eviction and defeat by the U.S.-led international forces benefited Iran, which attempted to recover its regional influence. However, in 1993 the U.S. government resorted to a policy of containing both Iran and Iraq, and two years later imposed strict oil and trade sanctions on Iran, which it regarded as a "sponsor of terrorism" seeking to develop nuclear weapons and hostile to the Israeli-Palestinian "peace process." This was a further step in the long-standing U.S. policy of isolating and weakening the Iranian regime, which turned increasingly to European countries; but its tarnished international image could not be easily repaired. The Khomeini decree of February 1989 imposing a death sentence on Salman Rushdie, the Indian-born British writer and author of *The Satanic Verses,* a novel considered blasphemous to Islam, continued to complicate the task of the government. Benefiting the hard-liners, the edict had dealt a major blow to Rafsanjani's efforts, preceding his presidency, to improve relations with the West. The regime's international image continued to be adversely affected by its abuses of human rights; it also suffered gravely as a result of the assassination of a number of its opponents abroad.

## Khatami: Mandate Unfulfilled

After his second term as president, Rafsanjani was appointed head of the Expediency Council by Khameneh'i. The establishment's candidate to replace Rafsanjani as president was Nateq-Nuri, the Speaker of the parliament. The other viable contender from a small pool of officially sanctioned candidates was Sayyed Mohammad Khatami. The fifty-four-year-old cleric was not an outsider: he had been a member of the first Islamic parliament, had managed a proregime newspaper, had been appointed minister of culture and Islamic guidance in 1982, and had assumed the same position in Rafsanjani's cabinet in 1989. Viewing him as too tolerant, the conservatives forced him to resign in 1992, but he was appointed cultural adviser to the president as well as director of the National Library. In contrast to the relatively unknown Khatami, not only did Nateq-Nuri enjoy the formal or informal endorsement of the leading figures in the establishment, but the entire official propaganda apparatus was mobilized on his behalf. In response, voters turned out in overwhelming numbers to support Khatami; whereas in the presidential elections of 1993 just over half the electorate had voted, on May 22, 1997 (2 Khordad 1376), nearly thirty million people, some 80 percent of the electorate, turned out to vote, and over twenty million voted for Khatami. This event—a turning point in the history of the Islamic regime—symbolized the emergence of a popular movement that came to be known as "the Second of Khordad Movement" (henceforth referred to as the May Movement).

The large number of votes cast for Khatami were, as many observers at the time noted, cast against the old-guard clerical establishment and their traditionalist and mercantile allies. The vote for Khatami, in which the younger generation, including women, figured prominently, signaled an overwhelming repudiation of the status quo and an affirmation of change; it was a rejection of authoritarianism and a clear indication of the scale and strength of democratic aspirations in the country. Khatami had campaigned on a platform of political reform. Exuding warmth and sincerity, and emphasizing governmental accountability and transparency, the rule of law for both the rulers and the ruled, and respect for the rights and dignity of the individual, he appeared committed to a politics of recognition. His invocations of "civil society" and "Islamic democracy" aroused optimism both inside and outside Iran. He had studied modern philosophy as well as Islamic theology and favored a reflective reconciliation of faith and freedom. Distancing himself from the prevailing ossified and monolithic religious ideology, he advocated viewing Islam as both a multifaceted system of religious belief and a vibrant complex of spiritual and moral values indispensable for meaningful individual and communal life. He proclaimed his desire to promote civility, honesty, and dialogue, as well as mutual trust and respect between the rulers and the ruled.

The May Movement was a spontaneous, cathartic, and powerful outburst of popular desire for change; Khatami came to symbolize it and benefited from it, but failed to lead it effectively or to sustain its momentum. The movement embraced forces, from outside as well as inside the orbit of the regime, that felt vindicated by the magnitude and implications of the popular vote for Khatami. By the mid-1990s many of those formerly known as radicals had come to support piecemeal political reform and openness. Together with a large number of disillusioned former revolutionaries, they coalesced to assist and sustain Khatami and ensure that he did not waver in his commitment to the reformists' agenda. Activists and politicians who stepped forward to lay claim to the leadership of the May Movement or to direct or represent the movement could not represent all its dimensions, nor were they capable of fulfilling its explicit or implicit aspirations. They appropriated from the secular democratic opposition much of their political idiom, as well as ideals that they knew they could not in practice uphold, given the existing political constraints. Yet the wider voicing of such ideals attested to and contributed to their growing public resonance.

Postrevolutionary Iranian factional-ideological politics has been far too convoluted to lend itself to neat classification along consistent lines. It has encompassed an abundance of dogmatic zeal and deeply held beliefs, as well as veiled or overt pragmatism; groups, factions, and individuals who have been moderate in some respects and radical in others. Moderates, radicals, reformists, and conservatives alike have often shifted positions and have even recycled one another's discarded tactics and rhetoric. Sectarian, sectionalist, cliquish, clientelist, and other ties and situationally specific considerations have either overlapped with ideological affiliations or have reinforced or replaced them. In Iran as elsewhere, real or feigned principles and convictions, opportunism, and cynicism have been endemic in political life. Few activists and politicians have remained constant or consistent in their political beliefs, yet they have continued to lay claim to consistency and adherence to strong principles.

Some of Khatami's key supporters and sympathizers had no reassuring record in defending moderation, let alone democratic principles. They backed him more out of enmity toward his conservative opponents than out of genuine affinity with his proclaimed political reforms. The conservatives, despite their differences of outlook and factional affiliations, were mostly authoritarian, illiberal, or hostile to political liberalism and its philosophical premises. They were averse to any reform that threatened to diminish clerical sociopolitical control. Their illiberal or antiliberal impulses overlapped with those of the religious left. Yet the May Movement signaled a reorientation of the religious left toward certain aspects of political liberalism. Most of those who now favored an open society had previously opposed it. Whatever their past political affiliations or orientations, the majority of those who supported Khatami were consciously rejecting practices that they had come to regard as wrong or counterproductive. They had realized that the regime's simplistic and rigid policies and conduct were at odds with the changing realities of Iranian society and the world. They had come to regret what had emerged in the name of ideals they had once espoused. They had concluded that only commitment to political reform would save the country from the prevailing hopelessness and alienation. They considered the mounting ineptitude and corruption of the power holders, who had sustained one another through mutually reinforcing factional alliances, as detrimental to a viable polity and deeply corrosive of the very foundations of the state.

Advocates of change believed that in view of Khatami's overwhelming popular mandate, his reformist objectives could not be easily thwarted by the establishment; the presence of several known reformers in the cabinet provided further reassurance. Khatami began to promote civil servants sympathetic to his aims, appointed a number of women to key positions, attempted to exert presidential control over the Islamic Revolution Guard Corps (Revolutionary Guards) and the security forces, relaxed official control over the press, traveled to various parts of the country, and in general gave the impression that he genuinely sought to forge a firm link between the rulers and the ruled and thereby reverse the process of popular disaffection. He addressed matters of concern not just in the capital but also in the provinces, and began improving the country's international image.

Gradually recovering from their initial shock and setback, Khatami's conservative opponents, who controlled key government institutions, particularly the judiciary and the Council of Guardians, began to regroup and react. They concentrated on the broad strategy of restricting Khatami's room for maneuver and denying him the opportunity to succeed; more specifically, they focused on undermining Khatami by removing or disabling his key colleagues and supporters. The conservatives failed to prevent pro-reform candidates from winning local elections, but turned their attention to hindering their future electoral successes. For some time the conservatives avoided confronting Khatami openly, fearing a public backlash. They also feared that in a premature showdown the forces on whom they expected to rely might prove unreliable. Bodies such as the Revolutionary Guards, a well-equipped component of the armed forces, together with the officially organized militias *(basij)*, remained committed to safeguarding the Islamic Republic. Yet among the rank and file of these bodies were many who shared the prevailing hopes for improvement.

To the chagrin of supporters of reform, Khatami, unprepared for the mandate he had received and lacking a clear strategy, allowed the momentum generated by the popular vote to slip away. His efforts to promote a free press remained only partially successful. He could not but be committed to upholding the Constitution and the existing laws that left the boundaries of freedom and the scope of rights heavily circumscribed. His emphasis on the rule of law was problematic when laws were indeterminate, insufficiently institutionalized, or at odds with international norms. Conservatives remained capable of closing down or harassing the reformist press, which was the chief signifier and promoter of openness and a key gauge of its success. They also resorted to other moves, direct or indirect, to damage the reformers.

During the first eighteen months of Khatami's presidency the mysterious death of a number of political activists and writers cast a dark shadow over the political atmosphere. The gruesome killing in November 1998 of the veteran Mosaddeqist, former Bazargan minister, and vocal critic of the regime Daryush Foruhar, along with his activist wife, was the most notorious example. Although the government pledged a full investigation, "rogue" middle- and low-level secret service agents were held responsible for the crimes. The public remained unpersuaded by the official account, attribution of responsibility, and promise of further investigations. The conviction grew that key officials wanted the matter forgotten and that those who wished to suppress the issue had gained the upper hand. In a program called *The Beacon (Cheragh)*, the state radio and television network blamed Khatami supporters for the murders. With the blessings of the Leader, the network was fully committed to the conservative agenda, and all attempts to subject it to parliamentary scrutiny were frustrated.

The conservatives also attempted to punish or harass pro-Khatami figures. One instance was the arrest and trial in 1998 of Gholam-Hosein Karbaschi, the mayor of Tehran, on charges of corruption and abuse of office. A flamboyant and self-assured protégé of Rafsanjani, Karbaschi had been the leading figure in the "Promoters of Reconstruction" (Kargozaran-e sazandegi), a group consisting of Islamist "technocrats" who had supported Rafsanjani and now favored Khatami. Karbaschi had actively supported Khatami in the presidential elections. As Tehran's mayor he had combined cavalier recklessness with engaging zeal to give the capital a facelift— including the construction of many high-rise buildings, which some admired but other, more discerning citizens abhorred. The televised trial of Karbaschi, which led to his conviction and imprisonment, became a gripping and extensively watched spectacle. Whatever harm this episode was intended to do to Khatami was dwarfed by comparison to the damage it did to the regime in its entirety. It revealed the extent of corruption and other abuses of office since the late 1980s, in contravention of the regime's projected image, as well as the proper norms and ethics of bureaucratic conduct. It also indicated how structurally permissive the regime was of corrupt practices. The case of Karbaschi provided a clear indictment of the regime's efforts to promote a reform-minded technocratic elite in the absence of transparency and agreed norms of rational meritocracy. The trial and conviction of Karbaschi corroded the morale of the "technocratic" elite. It also provided much ammunition for the regime's opponents.

A development more damaging to Khatami was the conservatives' success in June 1998 in arranging for the parliamentary impeachment of Abdollah Nuri, Khatami's minister of the interior and one of his most credible reformist colleagues. Khatami's failure to defend Nuri vigorously and thwart his removal by the conservatives was a turning point, signaling the reversal of the reformer's political fortunes and the beginning of the end of the May Movement. Khatami lost the initiative sooner than his opponents and supporters might have expected. The removal of Nuri emboldened the conservatives immeasurably. In the autumn of 1999, accused of a host of charges largely related to articles he had written in *Khordad*, the newspaper he edited, Nuri was tried by the Special Clerical Court and condemned to five years' imprisonment.[20]

From the outset, another key reformist, Ata'ollah Mohajerani, minister of culture and Islamic guidance, faced determined opposition by the conservatives, who seemed more concerned with the policies of this ministry than with any other. One group, the Coalition Association (Jam'iyat-e mo'talefeh)—a loosely organized right-wing party associated with bazaar merchants, other traditionalist entrepreneurs, and conservative clerics—spearheaded the opposition to the cabinet and its culture minister's pursuit of tolerant policies. In early May 1999 Mohajerani narrowly survived a motion of interpellation in the parliament. Undeterred, he continued his relaxation of state control over cultural activities; he also attempted to conciliate, and on occasion to honor, writers and artists long vilified or ignored by the regime. According to one account, between March 1999 and March 2000 the publication of books reached well over 20,000 titles a year, 5,000 more than two years earlier. In the same year the number of print media reached nearly 1,500, more than double what it had been four years earlier.[21] Cumulative pressure from the conservatives eventually led to Mohajerani's resignation in October 2002.

An outbreak of unrest at Tehran University in July 1999 indicated growing disillusionment with the pace, scope, and seriousness of reforms in the context of stimulated but frustrated expectations and incessant maneuvers by the right-wing conservatives. The trigger came in the form of a protest at the closure of *Salam,* a pro-Khatami newspaper. Unrest turned violent when official or semiofficial proconservative forces attacked the main dormitory of the university. With the spread of unrest to other cities the situation became tense and dangerous. Khatami, who had done much to raise student expectations, was unable to defend them, nor was he able to defuse the situation, which had alarmed not only the conservatives but also many reformers. Having initially vacillated, he blamed the students for their unruly conduct. The student unrest, which could have spiraled out of control in response to the provocations of proconservative forces, sobered the rulers. They realized that whatever their disagreements, they had to defend and preserve the Islamic regime. Khameneh'i adopted a soft approach and resorted to moves such as replacing the head of the judiciary, who was a hard-liner and a vocal opponent of political reform. Khatami, too, modified his more radical statements and showed less enthusiasm about defending his supporters. Despite differences in political allegiance, style, and tactics, the rulers had shown that they would not hesitate to confront and suppress challenges to the authority of the regime.

Khatami's aim was primarily to modify and revitalize the regime. Yet what such a task involved and what strategy was best suited to it remained contentious. An *idée fixe* of the opponents of political reform was the primacy of economic development—an old and sterile debate in Iranian politics going back to the authoritarian developmentalism of the 1960s and 1970s, and invariably invoked to disparage or derail democratic demands. The Khatami government was by no means negligent of the economy. Yet, despite efforts at diversification, the economy remained totally dependent on oil; the privatization drive continued, but its advocates complained that the economy remained dominated by an inefficiently managed state sector. The fact that one third of the population was below the age of fifteen put enormous pressure on the economy; unemployment continued to be a major problem. Statistics, particularly during the latter years of Khatami's second term in office, showed a decline in the rate of inflation and an economic growth rate of around 7 percent; but the daily lives of most people told a different story, and lower-income and vulnerable classes felt ever more financially burdened.

Social justice, one of the canonical notions of the revolutionary era, had become increasingly irrelevant. The state had not been able to generate the economic resources or the requisite political will to create even a rudimentary welfare state. The regime's failure to handle the issue of social justice beyond rhetorical lip service, together with the intensification of relative deprivation, corroded the moral foundations of the Islamic Republic. The problem of how to generate economic growth through free market practices without pushing more people below the poverty line persisted. Khatami had many advisers who gave him conflicting advice on such matters. His supporters also differed on the shape and pace of economic reform, but steps to overhaul the economy continued. Attracting and facilitating foreign investment remained a key priority; the more tangibly relaxed political ambiance helped efforts in this direction, but the possibility of political instability militated against them.

The segmentary nature of Iranian politics and the factional diffusion of power ensured that orchestrated incidents by forces outside the orbit of formal government could always derail or overshadow the endeavors of the government to improve the country's image. Violations of human rights also continued to cast a shadow over Iran's international image. Yet, measured against Afghanistan under the Taliban, Iran was an incomparably free and modern society, and its political record appeared no worse, if not noticeably better than, that of many other Middle Eastern countries. Blaming the failings and inadequacies of the government entirely on the obstructive tactics of the opponents of reform, Khatami continued to enjoy considerable sympathy and goodwill abroad, particularly among Europeans. Also, many Islamist reformers around the world looked to Iran as a beacon of hope, an example proving that an Islamic government could embrace both democracy and modernity. Khatami's advocacy of a "dialogue of civilizations" resonated widely. The Rushdie affair was formally declared to be a closed chapter as far as the state was concerned.

Relations between Iran and the United States, however, remained deadlocked, and by the late 1990s, despite earlier optimism and efforts, no breakthrough seemed likely. As always, the Palestinian-Israeli conflict and Iran's support for groups opposed to Israel figured prominently in factors militating against improved U.S.-Iranian relations. There was also the issue of Iran's nuclear program. U.S.-Iranian relations had, of course, long been a contentious component of Iranian domestic politics. The right-wing conservatives were apprehensive that improved relations with the United States would ideologically disarm them by removing the much-vaunted "enemy" essential for sustaining their political cosmology. Seeing or portraying the United States as an intractable foe had become a key ingredient of the regime's sense of identity and proclaimed ideological purity. Many conservatives also feared that Khatami's domestic and international stature would be boosted by better relations with the United States.

The establishment's intolerance of public discussion of U.S.-Iranian relations revealed severe limitations on free debate. It also indicated a real handicap faced not only by the public at large, but also by members of the parliament in debating, let alone determining, what was or was not in the national interest. The reform movement was often denounced by its right-wing opponents as instigated and supported by the United States; Khatami could therefore not afford to appear enthusiastic about improving relations with Washington. Nevertheless in 2003 his government made overtures to the United States; the fact that they were not reciprocated worked to the advantage of hard-liners in both countries. Iran's success in improving its relations with European countries indicated that the U.S. policy of isolating the country had not proved wholly effective. Yet strained U.S.-Iranian relations were economically and otherwise costly to Iran and adversely affected the government's efforts to attract international investment and improve foreign trade. From 2001 to 2003 Iran was 136th out of 140 countries in terms of attracting direct foreign investment.

In the runup to the parliamentary elections of February 2000, for whatever reason, the Council of Guardians did not disqualify any large number of reformist candidates, who went on to win a majority of seats in the assembly. The conservatives were soundly defeated; even Rafsanjani, though advocating moderate reform, failed to win a parliamentary seat. Once again the conservatives were dejected and disoriented by the massive public rejection. Facing the prospect of a president backed by an overwhelmingly supportive parliament, they retaliated. Against a mounting conservative offensive, which included the attempted assassination in March 2000 of Sa'id Hajjarian, one of the main reformist ideologues, Khatami's countermeasures remained feeble. The parliament and Khatami suffered a major blow when moves to reform the press law—a highly significant measure that the reformist majority in the parliament was intent on passing—were aborted because of an unprecedented last-minute order issued by Khameneh'i. Khatami's muted public complaints and hollow and increasingly discredited threats to resign became counterproductive. He seemed to be haunted by the fear of losing control of the situation and triggering violence, and numbed by the apprehension that his opponents were trying to provoke a major crisis in order to oust him.

Khatami could, of course, no longer blame the parliament for being ob-structive, but instead of being obstructive the parliament became ineffective as the Council of Guardians consistently rejected important bills. In June 2001 Khatami was reelected to a second term as president with close to 77 percent of the votes. Clearly, the public had renewed his mandate in the hope of invigorating him and sending another clear message to his oppo-nents. Yet despite this outcome and a supportive parliament, Khatami mus-tered no real resolve; he found his tasks no easier, and in some respects more difficult. His considerable oratorical skills, reassuring sense of com-mitment, and personal charm became increasing ineffectual. His compro-mises irretrievably vitiated his ability to generate conviction. His conserva-tive opponents continued to blame him for much of what they viewed as wrong with the regime. Most of his well-wishers and supporters no longer looked to him as able and willing to stand up to the old guard; they did not hide their frustration at his seemingly radical pronouncements and invari-ably tame and lackluster conduct.

Khatami's opponents had long realized that he was not likely to resign in protest or to resort to gestures that could provoke public unrest. His in-action and passivity, in contrast to his continued rhetorical flair, alienated the public and eroded the support of those who still looked to him as the spokesman of political reform. His chief talent had been to avoid con-frontation. His politics was the art of the possible, sharply demarcated. He operated deftly in a political milieu in which, despite grand declarations of principle, pragmatism, realpolitik, and the pursuit of narrow interests were the chief modalities of conduct. He inhabited a political space in which factional ties were fluid and ideological positions interchangeable and modifiable in the light of changing circumstances and roles; yet he was aware, perhaps too keenly, that there were red lines that one crossed at one's peril. Despite earlier difficulties he seemed to have worked out a *mo-dus vivendi,* albeit an uneasy one, with the chief holders of power. Many major objectives thus remained elusive. Civil society, as a public space free from intrusive and undue interventions by the state, proved a chimera; the press could be easily muzzled; the judiciary continued its harassment of the regime's critics.

Yet, to the displeasure of some traditionalist clerics, the regime could not but relax its rigid policies in many areas of social life. Consistently repressive social control had proved impossible to sustain, and counterproductive; the consequences of restlessness among the frustrated youth could be ruinous. Developments in the areas of art and culture, particularly publishing, also continued. There was considerable freedom of expression, particularly during Khatami's first term of office, and several newspapers emerged to cover and discuss critically a wide variety of issues of public interest rarely probed previously. Yet those who transgressed certain limits or took the sustainability of such freedom for granted often paid a heavy price. Judicial arbitrariness and the absence of a well-defined rule of law meant that a Damoclean sword hung over journalists and writers who persisted in antagonizing vested interests or appeared too impertinent in airing their criticisms. In defense of those of his supporters who provoked the wrath of the conservatives, Khatami could do little more than express mild indignation and sympathy.

The beleaguered Khatami wanted to distance himself both from his right-wing opponents and from the more radical critics of the regime who invoked the ideals of the May Movement. Continuing his plea for greater tolerance, he castigated the perpetuation of the wartime intolerance and state of emergency (1980–1988), which, he complained, had become virtually the norm. What was needed, in his view, was to end social polarization and recognize the need for greater reconciliation of faith and freedom. Denouncing his right-wing opponents as fascists, he maintained that the purpose of the revolution had not been to impose, in the name of Islam and revolution, a "fascist mentality" on Iranian society. Both a "fascistic" and a "liberalist" reading of Islam, he argued, should be abandoned in favor of an interpretation allowing for an "Islamic democracy," which constituted the only alternative to the collapse of the existing political arrangements.[22]

Fascism, in Khatami's view, was a system that combined autocracy or oligarchy with criminalization of political dissent; it rested on the promotion of hatred, totalitarian tendencies, and the idea that any means were permissible to achieve the desired end. Most of the conflicts engulfing the country, Khatami contended, were not between religiosity and irreligiosity, but between liberalism and fascism.[23] Though appearing intellectually well disposed to a generic liberal outlook, he repudiated liberal politics and its secular implications in favor of "Islamic democracy." Addressing his various detractors, including his disillusioned former supporters, he asserted that "there is no chance of a secular republic emerging in Iran."[24] However, the structural preconditions, institutional requirements, and constitutional basis of an Islamic democracy remained ill defined, and Khatami provided little guidance on how they should be achieved. Moreover, crucial lacunae and ambiguities in his conception of Islamic democracy remained unaddressed: Could such a democracy meaningfully affirm equal citizenship for all? Could any reading of the existing Constitution lend itself to such an affirmation and allow the inclusive and nondiscriminatory representation and political equality essential for any notion of democracy? Of course, "Islamic democracy" was the only kind of democracy that Khatami, as president of the Islamic Republic, could speak about. To expect him to favor democracy in its broad sense would have been unrealistic.

Though highly articulate, Khatami tended to confuse smooth rhetoric and fustian verbosity with conceptually rigorous argument. His mode of thought and conduct involved many antinomies and paradoxes. He combined unusual flexibility with professions of consistent adherence to principles. Tirelessly preaching the virtues of tolerance, greater freedom, dialogue, and civility, he offered no practical strategies to fulfill his ideals. Lacking the requisite determination and capacity to push for real reform, he often appeared to act as the leader of the opposition rather than as the head of the government. He conceded to his antagonists at every step and was bullied and obstructed by them at every turn. As his frequent threats to speak out or resign remained unfulfilled he lost ever more ground; his public standing suffered, and his opponents were heartened. His failure early on to utilize his massive public support to outmaneuver his initially disoriented opponents and respond to the expectations of those who keenly supported him was astounding. The risk-averse Khatami seemed to fear that pushing too hard for reform could undermine the regime or unleash uncontrollable violence. His abstract, sometimes ponderous ruminations on the desirability of political reform were thus bound to backfire. The inevitable inadequacy of his didactic, cautious, and piecemeal approach alienated many of his supporters, including the disillusioned former revolutionaries who had pinned their hopes on him. Reformist rhetoric became increasingly hollow and anemic.

The record of the reformist movement, including its parliamentary representatives, was no more impressive. Reformist groups were not united in every respect, nor did they consistently identify with Khatami, who continued to vacillate between acting as a populist loner and as a hesitant leader. As always, organizing and sustaining effective political support remained a problem. Groups that backed or constituted the organized core of the reform movement included the "radical" League of Combatant Clerics and the pragmatist group Promoters of Reconstruction; there were also the small but influential Organization of the Islamic Revolution's Mojahedin and later the Islamic Participation Front (Jebheh-ye mosharekat-e Islami), a party headed by Mohammad Reza Khatami, the president's brother and deputy speaker of the sixth parliament. Hoping to establish itself as a party of government, and adhering to the president's vision, the Participation Front maintained that the only viable and realistic form of democracy was one that was "mindful of religious principles."[25] But as the presidency and the parliament remained ineffective, and the prospects for fulfilling reformist promises looked increasingly elusive, the party's public image and prospects waned. The reformist parties faced the opposition of conservative groups such as the Coalition Association, the Association of Tehran's Combatant Clergy, and the Association of Instructors of the Qom Seminary. These groups were far from cohesive parties, but acting together in opposition they could be effective, particularly as they seemed faithfully to represent the ideological underpinnings of the regime.

In order to retain their position the reformers had to reiterate their commitment to the foundational notions of the ruling ideology, albeit in a qualified version. This very commitment, however, together with their increasing ineffectiveness, resulted in the estrangement of many of their would-be supporters. The reformers came to be widely seen as simply another faction of the regime, intent on perpetuating it. They were accused, for instance, of practicing their own brand of exclusionism, of attempting to control the government as well as the opposition, and of putting themselves forward both as government and opposition.[26] They lost much of

their public support without real success in appeasing or positively influencing the conservative ruling clique, who exploited the reformers' loss of public standing to taunt, humble, discomfit, and eventually engineer their exclusion from the parliamentary elections of February 2004. The failure of
Khatami and his parliamentary supporters to prevail upon the conservatives
not to disqualify reformist candidates signaled a conclusive defeat. Khatami
eventually withdrew bills he had submitted to the parliament aimed at restraining the Council of Guardians' control over the elections and clarifying
and extending the authority of the president. The bills had been thwarted
by the Council of Guardians.

In May 2003, in an unprecedented open letter addressed to Khameneh'i,
127 reformist parliamentarians had provided a frank litany of what the conservatives had done to derail and defeat the reform movement. The letter
referred to the Council of Guardians as the biggest obstacle to the functioning of the parliament and described it as a vehicle for "discrediting Islamic
law and the constitution." It reiterated Khatami's well-known complaint
that on average he faced one manufactured crisis every nine days. The parliamentarians went on to list

> Serial murders, the Tehran University dormitory crimes, newspaper
> closures, the detention of political activists, suppression of university
> students and lecturers, public enforcement of unprecedented judicial
> sentences, neutralization of parliamentary legislation and governmen-
> tal decisions, transfer of power to institutions such as the Council of
> Guardians, the Expediency Council and the Council of the Cultural
> Revolution.

The letter called upon the authorities "to apologize to the people sincerely
for all their failings and ill-advised policies"; it affirmed "the establishment
of real democracy and respect for the freedom and dignity of citizens" as
the only way to avoid serious crises in the future.[27] There was no doubt
that the reformist parliamentarians felt deeply frustrated and impotent. As
in the past, their warnings elicited no positive response. Soon afterward, in
June 2003, a broader sense of public frustration resulted in ten days of unrest in Tehran spearheaded by university students. The rumored impending
privatization of universities, subsequently denied, had provided the trigger.

Voicing their profound disappointment with Khatami, the protesters seemed confident that the regime had reached an impasse and was highly vulnerable; they received active or tacit support from many citizens. The arrest of student leaders brought the situation under control, but as before the underlying reasons for the protests remained unaddressed. The episode further weakened Khatami's cabinet; Mostafa Mo'in, the minister in charge of higher education and one of the last credible reformers in the government, resigned in protest at the mistreatment of the students.

In a different political setting, the reformers' control of the presidency and the parliament would have heralded significant change. In Iran, however, unelected bodies could easily undermine the authority of the presidency and the formal government as well as the parliament. The president often resembled the tame prime ministers of the monarchy, while the parliament never achieved the stature and authority it had enjoyed during the first two decades after the Constitutional Revolution or in the 1940s. Nor did the distinguished parliamentarians of the past find many peers among the deputies of the post-1979 era. Parliamentary immunity remained tenuous, and the deputies seldom commanded extensive public attention; with few exceptions their popular standing rarely exceeded that of other functionaries of the regime. The parliament itself was allowed an effective role only if its composition and ideology were fully in tune with the core of the establishment. It could be reduced to act either as a tame and routinely cooperative body or as little more than an ad hoc drafting committee whose bills were summarily rejected by the Council of Guardians or modified beyond recognition.

Having dashed the hopes he had untenably raised, Khatami disappointed not only his supporters at home but also moderate Islamists abroad. Yet for many such reformers, the ideals and values of the movement that sustained Khatami would continue to resonate as it attempted to overcome the impasse facing the Islamic regime in Iran. For these reformers the agenda of reconciling Islam—understood as a nonmonolithic faith—and democratic values was the only means of devising a viable political program. Such an agenda would enable moderate Islamists to overcome the dilemma of having to live with either an authoritarian government that used religion as a legitimizing ideology or with a secular representative government that treated Islam as a constant and serious threat to democratic values. In the eyes of Islamist reformers, the failure of Khatami and his supporters was not necessarily the failure of their aspirations. Yet it was not enough, many Muslim reformers as well as their critics would argue, to contend that Islam and democracy were compatible; such a claim needed to be concretely and persuasively demonstrated.

A compassionate and reasonably tolerant religiosity, mindful of the exigencies of the modern world and receptive to democratic sensibilities, has a fairly long pedigree in Iran. An emphasis on spiritual values and on the ethical and cultural as well as religious components of Islam, rather than merely on Islamic law, did not start with Khatami and will not end with him. Yet Khatami's popular mandate as president in 1997 enabled him to symbolize such a conception of Islam, which resonated widely in Iran and beyond. It stimulated hope among Muslim reformers worldwide that a modern and tolerant Islamist approach to governance could produce a political alternative to the rigid paternalistic authoritarianism that is usually fashioned in the name of Islam.

The sociopolitical arrangements crafted in Iran by the traditionalist opponents of political reform have had little appeal for those who wished to be both believing Muslims and practicing democrats. Those seeking to inhabit a spiritually satisfying, humane, and modern world maintain that Islam must be interpreted as compatible with sensible pluralism; it should not be manipulated as a coercive ideology of exclusionist and intolerant rule. With the failure of Khatami, Iran forfeited an opportunity to provide a model for Islamist reformers everywhere, particularly among reform-minded practicing Shi'ites beyond Iran's borders. For the custodians of the Islamic establishment in Iran, the fulfillment of the ideals that Khatami had come to voice seemed clearly incongruent with the continuation of the existing political order. For the Iranian proponents of reform, however, the Khatami interlude demonstrated conclusively that regardless of whether Islam and democracy are compatible, the prevailing regime in Iran had proved itself inimical to democratic ideals.

In early May 2004 Khatami issued a public statement titled "A Letter for Tomorrow," addressed to the young. In this rambling, didactic statement, Khatami reiterated his credo and tried to provide a justification for his conduct and for his government's shortcomings. Placing the May Movement in the broader context of Iranian history, he implicitly compared the problems he faced with those encountered by Mosaddeq. Khatami blamed the persistent legacy of "despotism" in Iran, which in his view affected the conduct of government, the opposition, and intellectuals. Criticizing blind attachment to "fossilized habits," rigid traditionalism, and the unreflective tendency to either love or loathe the West, he castigated "superficial reactionaries," myopic opponents, and "impatient friends." He insisted on the indispensability of reform in a spirit of "moderation, flexibility, rationality, and patience"; warned against defying popular aspirations; and rebuked the Council of Guardians, the judiciary, and others who invoked a theocratic reading of the Constitution in order to oppose liberty by portraying it as synonymous with moral depravity. Condemning those who promoted "violence instead of logic" and saw "values" as incompatible with progress, Khatami appealed to the cultural elite not to remain indifferent when freedom was being "stolen," and urged the youth not to succumb to passivity.[28]

The reform movement, Khatami asserted, aimed at the "modernization of religious culture" in order to render it compatible with democracy; it wanted to create a "free, prosperous, and happy" country. For more than a century, he argued, Iranians had demanded "liberty, independence, and progress," and despite numerous setbacks had not relented in pursuit of these aims. Though readily admitting to his own errors and unfulfilled objectives, Khatami nevertheless contended that the achievements of the reform movement were not negligible. Even its opponents, he claimed, were now obliged to speak the language of law, reform, and democracy and to shun myopic views; violations of the private sphere were much less frequent than before. He did, however, have considerably more to say about "the flourishing economy" since 1997 than about positive achievements in other areas.[29]

Detecting unpersuasive or implausible claims in Khatami's statement is not difficult. Among other things, the statement replicated a confusion regarding the notions of "government" and "the state," which in Persian are usually rendered interchangeably. The state as the institutional embodiment of indivisible sovereignty was not headed by Khatami; though notionally the president, he merely acted as the head of an institutionally fragile executive whose authority was ill defined and in practice heavily circumscribed. Without probing the question of how *republican* the Islamic Republic really was or could be, Khatami reiterated that his objective had been to rectify it, clearly implying that this was possible. He expressed fear that the opportunity for reform could slip away if the unreflective assumptions of his opponents made reform from within appear impractical. The Iranians, he contended, did not seek "liberty, independence, and progress" outside the Islamic Republic, which they wanted to retain but also to reconcile with their historic democratic demands—an unverifiable claim in the absence of a credible referendum, a measure demanded by many of those associated with the May Movement.

The structural constraints that Khatami faced cannot be underestimated. Yet from the outset he demonstrated a singular inability to seize the initiative and build on the strength of the mandate that had brought him to office. Politicians are judged by their actions and the consequences of those actions and rarely by their good intentions. Too compromising an attitude emboldened the very forces that Khatami had been mandated to restrain. He failed to empower those who supported him or in any significant way to diminish the prerogatives of the old guard. His posture as a public intellectual, a promoter of dialogue both within Iran and among civilizations, an enlightened Muslim modernist exhorting his compatriots and his coreligionists to uphold and promote the more urbane ideals and practices of their religious creed, failed to produce adequate results. His accommodationist resilience was viewed as capitulation even by many of his own supporters.

Khatami has had his charitable admirers and cynical detractors. In retrospect, many will remember his dignified elegance and refinement, and view him as a sincere reformer whose efforts were systematically thwarted by the vested interests of powerful establishment figures. They might see him as a man who injected new ideas into the stale discourse of the rulers, attempted to set a new agenda, change the rules of the political game, promote transparency, accountability, and other democratic and civic values, and make a dent in the grim exclusionist clerical politics. Others might see themselves as justified in having doubted Khatami's competence or statesmanship, and even his sincerity as a dedicated reformer. Denouncing his surfeit of words and dearth of action, they might dismiss him as having at best lent himself to manipulation by those he purported to oppose, and at worst as guilty of manipulating and disappointing, even betraying, supporters of reform and reformist aspirations. In the eyes of such critics,

Khatami's promises to promote civil society—which he later said was modeled on the City of the Prophet *(madinat al-nabi)*—and Islamic democracy inevitably proved illusory, while his socioeconomic policies placed an increasing burden on the poor. For some antiregime opponents, Khatami was, from the very outset, cynically camouflaging himself as a reformer while actually intent on prolonging the life of the regime through cosmetic and halfhearted measures.

Irrespective of whatever view is vindicated by posterity, the failure of Khatami and of the reform movement more or less associated with his name indicated the limitations of political reform in the prevailing circumstances of Iran. It revealed that the regime lacked the capacity for rational adaptability to the expectations of the citizens and faced a serious crisis of legitimacy. Concomitantly, it showed that Iranian society was gripped by a chronic crisis of representation, seeing itself increasingly at odds with those who claimed to represent it, whether politically, socially, or culturally. These crises could render the country vulnerable to domestic unrest or externally induced turmoil.

Regardless of the repeated admonitions of the likes of Khatami, the parliamentary elections of February 2004 and the extensive disqualification of reformist candidates reaffirmed the establishment's resistance to and resentment of even the limited political and civic liberties and entitlements advocated by a loyal opposition. The conservatives' strategy had been to incapacitate and neutralize the reformers prior to discarding them. Indeed, the failure of the reformist deputies had undermined their residual popular support and facilitated their exclusion, which provoked little public outcry. Many of these deputies had been branded by the conservatives as "infiltrators" *(nofuzi)*. When they protested their exclusion from standing for reelection, they were dismissed as "bullies" *(gardankoloft)*. The parliament was routinely eclipsed by other bodies and its bills rejected, yet it still needed to be packed with deputies firmly committed to the ruling ideology. Though themselves divided along factional lines, the hard-liners broadly agreed on the parameters of inclusion and exclusion, and on what was in the regime's best interest. Defeating the enervated reformers, who sought to modify the regime from within, was a short-term gain, not an indefinitely sustainable strategic achievement or a moral victory. This was a move likely to aggravate the already deep public alienation and apathy, and strengthen the conviction that the existing political arrangements were hopelessly archaic and impervious to real reform.

Few now believed that the Islamic Republic, any more than the monarchy before it, could tolerate active democratic dissent or organized attempts to promote alternative visions of the public good. The Islamic Republic sought at best to promote a loyal "technocratic" elite with Islamic credentials advocating socioeconomic reform. Again, as in the prerevolutionary regime, economic development, viewed as a legitimacy-generating strategy, continued to be regarded as vital, while a credible measure of political development—that is, the emergence of democratic practices and institutions and the expansion of political and civic liberties—continued to prove incongruent with oligarchic paternalism, just as it had proved incompatible with paternalist royal autocracy. As in the past, far from supplanting political development, socioeconomic reform, whether actual or promised, would only stimulate and widen demands for far-reaching political change that would prove impossible to suppress or ignore. The failure of even a cautious and moderate effort to reform and politically revitalize the regime from within could only lead to a more resilient and ambitious movement for change.

## Ahmadi-Nejad: Inventing a Neo-Khomeinist Populism

Having established their control over the parliament, the hard-line conservatives sought to take over the executive and to ensure the election of a president closely identified with the establishment's core ideology. Though more fractious than they appeared, they experienced little difficulty in further emasculating Khatami's presidency. In the interest of gaining credibility and regardless of its composition, the parliament was bound to try to assert itself institutionally—across the board and not just vis-à-vis the enfeebled presidency. Hoping to avert complete marginalization, the reformers attempted to put forward a viable presidential candidate who commanded public respect and around whom they could rally; success in doing so would have helped to galvanize their supporters and perhaps the wider public. However, their favorite would-be candidate, the former prime minister Musavi, refused to reenter active politics. His similar refusal in 1997 had paved the way for Khatami's candidacy.

In the controversial presidential elections of June 2005, the Council of Guardians disqualified some 1,000 would-be candidates and approved the candidacy of 7. For the regime, a presidential election with ostensibly real competition was a welcome development; it posed no threat to those entrenched in positions of power. If Khatami's successor was a conservative, the regime would be strengthened; if he was not, the council would have little difficulty incapacitating his government. Many politically discerning citizens vacillated between boycotting the elections and voting for a least objectionable candidate, such as Mostafa Mo'in, a physician and former minister. Initially disqualified, Mo'in was reinstated at Khameneh'i's behest, a development that politically embarrassed him. For many the election of a reformer like Mo'in would have meant the perpetuation of the ongoing stalemate, as his authority would have been disputed at every turn. Yet it was widely believed that Mo'in and Rafsanjani, the former president, would emerge as the final contenders. The little-known Mahmud Ahmadi-Nejad was perceived as no more than a marginal candidate.

Despite extensive and in certain cases expensive campaigns, in the absence of real political parties, contenders invoked ill-defined issues and relied on loose ideological-factional alliances. Though viewed by observers as exaggerated, the official figure for voter turnout for the first round was 62 percent, with Rafsanjani winning 6.1 million votes, Ahmadi-Nejad 5.7 million, and Mehdi Karrubi, the former parliamentary Speaker, in third place with 5 million votes. Karrubi publicly and vigorously alleged large-scale irregularity and fraud, implicating the Revolutionary Guards and militias as well as the highest-ranking officials; other reformist candidates concurred; Rafsanjani publicly spoke of "organized intervention." In certain areas the number of those reported to have voted was too high; in regions with a sizable Sunni population, for instance, the electorate was unlikely to have voted overwhelmingly for Ahmadi-Nejad.

In the second round, 27 million citizens were declared to have voted—17 million for Ahmadi-Nejad and 10 million for Rafsanjani. A nonthreatening and appealing candidate as far as the key ruling figures and loci of power were concerned, Ahmadi-Nejad's surprising and unexpected election would have been unlikely without the active blessing of Khameneh'i and the mobilization of proregime forces on his behalf. The role of the Revolutionary Guards and the militias proved crucial in this process. Thus the fact that the right-wing and hard-line conservative forces had been fissiparous and unable to agree on a single candidate did not affect Ahmadi-Nejad's prospects. The failure of the reformers to coordinate their strategy and concentrate on one candidate had clearly harmed them; the second round proved to be a major setback not only for the reformers but also for moderate conservatives.

In the second round virtually all moderate reformist parties, personalities, and groups, fearing the victory of Ahmadi-Nejad, whom they regarded as dangerously unqualified, retrograde, and authoritarian, declared their support for Rafsanjani, who was running on a moderate reformist agenda. Undeterred by his failure to win a parliamentary seat in the elections of February 2000, he hoped to win over large segments of both conservatives and reformers. Perceived as a uniquely placed pillar of the establishment, he was widely expected to win. Appearing reluctant to enter the race and indifferent to success, he refused to visit the provinces and addressed the international media and foreign policy concerns more than the issues of immediate relevance to the majority of Iranians. Though making broad promises, ranging from social justice to sociopolitical liberties, he wanted to be seen as motivated by a sense of duty to check the drift and crisis of authority pervading the regime—the man best capable of improving the economy and handling relations with the United States, as well as the nuclear issue.

Regarded as the most consummate and resilient statesman of the Islamic Republic, the seventy-year-old Rafsanjani enjoyed support among the affluent urban middle classes and the upper echelons of the intelligentsia. The reformers were attracted to him primarily because of his personal clout and his ability to stand up to Khameneh'i and revitalize the enervated institution of the presidency. Given his stature and his understanding of the inner workings of the regime and its key players, he could not be easily thwarted or bullied by the hard-liners in the parliament and other bodies. The underprivileged and the marginal, however, feared that a Rafsanjani victory would ensure their own continued neglect. In addition to blunders during his electoral campaign and the concerted defamatory propaganda against him, Rafsanjani's defeat was rooted in his identification with the status quo and his widely perceived association with the unjustifiable concentration of wealth and power. In spite of suffering a damaging humiliation, Rafsanjani continued in his previous capacity as head of the Expediency Council, with increased authority as compensation.

In contrast to the clerical patrician Rafsanjani, Ahmadi-Nejad was a political novice, a forty-nine-year-old engineer of proletarian provincial origins (he is the son of a blacksmith). He joined the Revolutionary Guards in 1986 and was associated with the *basij*. Having served as governor-general of Ardebil, in the spring of 2003 he became mayor of Tehran. His constituency included the poorer urban and rural masses, the *basij,* the Revolutionary Guards, organized vigilante groups, and the right-wing activist clerics epitomized by Ayatollah Mohammad-Taqi Mesbah-Yazdi and his disciples and students, who had supported Ahmadi-Nejad from the very outset of the elections. Irrespective of the authenticity or procedural fairness of the elections, for those who actually voted for him his chief virtue lay in his not being politically tainted or identified with the existing interconnected structures of power, wealth, and patronage. To support him was to reject the hierarchy of privilege, the new class structure, the growing rift between the rich and the poor. It was a rejection of the practical, though not rhetorical, occlusion of social justice in the conduct and policy preferences of the Islamic Republic.

His rise also reflected a demographic shift resulting from the continuing influx of rural populations into the cities, particularly since the 1990s. This movement of people had accentuated the ruralization of urban sensibilities and steadily eroded the already fragile urban ethos. Ahmadi-Nejad's ascendancy can be viewed as a provincial conservative backlash against the social liberties and social ills associated with the Khatami era. It can be seen as representing a conflict between the modern-minded urban middle classes and the poor, whether in the cities or beyond. The elections revealed the intensification of the very class polarization in Iranian society that the revolution was supposed to overcome. The social divide and the consciousness of relative deprivation had been sharpened by the policies of the Rafsanjani and Khatami eras. The wielders of power in the Islamic regime themselves largely originated from underprivileged backgrounds. Yet in their attachments to the spoils of office, they were often quick to forget the hidden injuries of others afflicted by poverty.

Ahmadi-Nejad espoused a messianic neo-Khomeinist populism with a strong right-wing authoritarian content and faint leftist overtones; it was regressive and forward looking, denunciatory and affirmative, coarse and conciliatory; above all, it purported to be committed to rectifying inequity. This stance, together with his unassuming and plebeian demeanor and advocacy of piety and frugality, enabled him to craft an image of a dedicated, principled, and simple man of the people. It was essential, he maintained, that the ruled should trust the rulers as committed to public service on the basis of genuine Islamic principles, which provided the solution to all problems. Consistent in his views, he displayed an alarmingly uncomplicated approach regarding governance, the economy, and the modern world. He capitalized on his ostensible disassociation from the existing networks of power and patronage. Representing a desire to return to the fervor and early idealism of the revolution, he employed ideas, slogans, and sentiments that still appealed to the poor and the deprived lower classes. Justice in general and social justice in particular were notions that during the revolution most forcefully resonated with the majority of Iranians, transcending otherwise sharp ideological differences among various groups. Having invoked justice as a pivotal notion almost defining its *raison d'être,* the Islamic regime proved singularly unsuccessful in establishing a more just and equitable society. Promising to redress this situation was at the heart of Ahmadi-Nejad's rise.

Ahmadi-Nejad's election could be seen as an indication that the U.S. government's assertions of supporting democracy in Iran had proved counterproductive. He was a candidate most likely to alleviate the hard-liners' anxieties about the repercussions of improved relations with the United States; his election was a defensive, inward-looking move. More momentously, it signified a defeat for the strategy, if not the discourse, of the advocates of political reform. It manifested deep public disaffection, a rejection of the existing socioeconomic and political state of affairs, and a desire for change. The elections could be seen as revealing the political despair of most voters regarding the possibility of political reform within the contours of the existing arrangements and a lowering of expectations in favor of more immediate concerns.

The reformers confused the conditions of June 2005 with those of May 1997; they overestimated the role of urban women, students, and the intelligentsia and ignored a shift in the public's political priorities and expectations, rooted in their own failure. Fragmented, intellectually complacent, and unfocused, they had failed to develop an effective strategy or to counter their detractors vigorously. They were unable to point out tangible successes recognizable by the poor and other marginal segments of the public. Having shown themselves unable to improve the lot of the lower classes, they became vulnerable to attacks by their right-wing opponents, who portrayed their efforts to promote political and civic liberties as irrelevant or conducive to decadence and immorality. By concentrating on slogans that appealed primarily to the urban middle classes, the reformers ignored or underestimated the less privileged segments of the population and the mass of voters on the periphery. Their increasingly anemic slogans could not genuinely inspire even their own disheartened and exhausted supporters.

Of the forty-seven million people eligible to vote, both those who voted and the twenty million who did not rejected the status quo. Abandoning the well-known figures more or less identified with the regime unmistakably implied an indictment of its record and policies. The election of Ahmadi-Nejad, who denounced rampant corruption, wasteful practices, political clans (qabileh), and the existing structure of power for having failed to live up to its Islamic claims would, paradoxically, be portrayed as vindicating popular support for the regime. Yet the key question was not openly broached: Why was it that after more than a quarter of a century a "true" Islamic government had not emerged and the existing disparities of power and wealth—or what Ahmadi-Nejad himself called "pinnacles of wealth"— had been allowed to arise?

Ahmadi-Nejad's election, as well as the composition of his cabinet, indicated a greater ascendancy of the security and intelligence forces; it could also be seen as a victory for Khameneh'i. Not only was the new president unlikely to challenge the prerogatives of the Leader, but he was also ideologically close to him, as both advocated revitalizing Islamic values and cultivating the poor. With the aim of gaining credibility and distinguishing himself from his ineffectual predecessor, Ahmadi-Nejad would attempt to assert a real measure of executive authority. Yet major policies and decisions would continue to be made not by the president but by the Leader, in coordination with other loci of power. With this further diminution of the presidency, the structure of power appeared to have acquired an autocratic character. Yet its oligarchic constitution was unlikely to be radically modified, being consonant with the segmentary nature of sociopolitical power and the intricate system of reciprocity underlying it. Though chiefly responsible for thwarting the reformists' agenda, Khameneh'i remained mindful of the exigencies of modernity and the changing nature of Iranian society. More pragmatic than is often assumed, he seemed unconvinced of the desirability or feasibility of attempting to roll back the modest social and civic liberties that helped to defuse social tensions and increase the viability of the Islamic regime. Ensuring that formal electoral procedures continued to be operative, he remained alert to the indispensability of popular participation, no matter how truncated, in furnishing legitimacy for the regime.

After the election of the new president, the key institutions of governance appeared ideologically and even factionally more homogeneous and coordinated than at any other time since 1979. Of course, relative political and ideological homogeneity—as enjoyed by the regime during the Rafsanjani presidency, for instance—was by itself no guarantee of enduring success. It was not the achievements but more the crises of the Rafsanjani era that had created the impetus for political reform, bringing Khatami to the fore. Yet now the political environment seemed in important respects more permissive than during the Rafsanjani era or when Khatami became president. Among other things, the government anticipated few problems in securing parliamentary approval for its bills; whenever beleaguered, it could rely on Khameneh'i to intervene to prevent the president from faltering or from seriously losing face. Many moderate conservatives would view Ahmadi-Nejad as impulsive and regret his reckless flouting of diplomatic etiquette, but the right-wing hard-liners appeared to be behind him. The vanquished reformers could only await an erosion of conservative unity. The path seemed clear for the government to implement its agenda; concomitantly, excuses for failing to deliver would prove difficult to concoct. Predictably, Ahmadi-Nejad lost no time in blaming the political elite long involved in governing the country as working to derail his efforts.

Despite the ideological affinities among Ahmadi-Nejad and the majority of parliamentarians, their relations were likely to be adversely affected by the systemic, albeit fluctuating, institutional discord between the parliament and the presidency and by conflict over the contours of institutional power and turf. This state of affairs largely accounted for the parliamentary rejection of the president's three nominees for the Oil Ministry. Ahmadi-Nejad showed a tendency to select his colleagues primarily on the basis of loyalty and ideological reliability rather than technical and managerial competence. There were, however, limits to how much this approach could be tolerated by the otherwise supportive parliament. The deputies could not afford to appear indifferent to issues affecting the national or the public interest; nor could they ignore the cost and consequences of the alienation, demoralization, or insecurity of the experienced upper echelons of the civil service, or the adverse impact of unfulfillable promises. With Ahmadi-Nejad as president, the reduction of politics to administration—a recurring theme in the Iranian culture of politics—was once again reaffirmed, this time more noticeably, at the expense of bureaucratic rationality, administrative competence, and expertise.

At the same time, messianic beliefs appeared to have gained greater ground since Ahmadi-Nejad's election. For complex socioreligious as well as political reasons, belief in the possibility of inducing the positive intervention or even the return of the Hidden Imam (Mahdi)—believed by the Twelver Shi'ites to be in occultation since 874—has been on the rise in recent years. A well and a mosque in the village of Jamkaran, near Qom, have attracted much attention: on the basis of the epiphanic dream of a local, they have long been viewed as a sacred site linked to the Hidden Imam. Hosts of supplicants visit the place and drop letters of entreaty into the well in the hope of receiving the Imam's help in overcoming their problems. High-ranking clerics such as Ayatollah Naser Makarem-Shirazi have denounced certain practices associated with Jamkaran as superstitious, but it is widely believed that Ahmadi-Nejad and his colleagues are among the avid believers and promoters of such practices. After the parliamentary elections of February 2004, Ayatollah Ali Meshkini, head of the Assembly of Experts, the body that selects the Leader, claimed that successful candidates had enjoyed the endorsement of the Hidden Imam; similar claims were also made for Ahmadi-Nejad.

The ideas and rituals associated with the Hidden Imam as the savior have a central place in Twelver Shi'ism. They have long existed at the intersection of folklore, theology, esoteric beliefs, and popular messianic longing rooted in socioeconomic distress and despair at the inefficacy of temporal solutions. However, their revival at the current juncture, and the way in which they are used for political purposes, have alarmed advocates of modernist Shi'ism. Traditionally, beliefs concerning the Hidden Imam and his reappearance, inaugurating the dawn of a just society, increased accommodationist or nonpolitical tendencies among the clerics, because his advent was to be awaited passively. More recently such a traditionalist attitude has been associated with Sheikh Mahmud Halabi, a charismatic cleric who in the 1950s created the Hojjattiyeh Association to counter Baha'ism. Pressured by SAVAK, it undertook to abstain from political activity but had a major impact on the ideological formation of the future elite of the Islamic regime. Politically quietist, the association advocated patiently waiting for the appearance of the Hidden Imam and discouraged action aimed at hastening his return or crafting an Islamic polity in his absence. This approach was denounced as conservative by the Khomeinists, who supported struggle aimed at creating an Islamic polity in the absence of the Hidden Imam, maintaining that this would be likely to hasten his appearance. By the spring of 1984, following the expressed disapproval of Khomeini, the association was formally disbanded. Though moribund, it is believed to have survived in various forms, and clerical disciples of Khomeini have often warned about its potential revival and its continued threats to revolutionary Shi'ism. Unlike their quietist predecessors, however, some of those who now appear to believe in the imminent reappearance of the Hidden Imam and who see themselves as contributing to it see no reason to be sociopolitically pragmatic.

Messianic longings, and more tangibly the public resonance of social justice as demonstrated during the 2005 presidential elections, signify glaring inequalities and rifts in Iranian society. However, given the imbrication of wealth, power, and privilege, the existing inequities and divisions cannot be tackled without adversely affecting many vested interests and antagonizing influential political clans within the wider ruling class. Conversely, the conservatives' control of all branches of government and the dramatic rise in oil revenues since 1999 should have led to unusually permissive conditions.[30] Nevertheless, there were no signs to indicate that Ahmadi-Nejad's government would succeed in implementing its distributive agenda and would not experience serious problems in attempting to improve the lives of the poorer classes. Containing inflation, which by the end of Khatami's presidency was well above the official 15 percent, and reducing the excessively high interest rates, which have ruined many small businesses, are major tasks, as are the creation of jobs, ending the dire shortage of affordable housing, and ensuring that the incomes and expenditure of average households are proportionate. Entrepreneurs and bazaar merchants were deeply unsettled by Ahmadi-Nejad's election; however, his rhetoric of social justice did not hinder his espousal of neoliberal economic policies. Maintaining that 80 percent of the Iranian economy was controlled by the state and was mostly unprofitable, he promised to support the private sector. Yet doing so and also addressing issues of equity and welfare, which require active state intervention, are not easily reconcilable. Attempting to tackle economic problems without adversely affecting investment and enterprise or precipitating a flight of private capital from the country is a daunting task. From the start Ahmadi-Nejad did not seem to have a coherent economic policy; among other challenges, he had to find a way of spending the increased oil revenues without exacerbating inflation. As some economists warned, slogans such as "bringing the oil wealth to people's tables" would "only increase expectations and tensions" that could prove unmanageable, as happened in the last years of the Pahlavi era.[31]

Setbacks in pursuing the president's domestic agenda were partially compensated by fervent rhetoric, symbolic radicalism, and ultimately counterproductive repressive moves. The issue of nuclear energy continued to be exploited to tap nationalist sensibilities and deflect attention from domestic problems. Successful handling of this issue, and that of Iran's influence in Iraq, required tremendous skill, finesse, and foresight, the absence of which could harm the country and even prove disastrous. Economic failure could fast erode Ahmadi-Nejad's base of public support to the advantage of advocates of political reform and democratic development. Similarly any increase, albeit unlikely, in general prosperity and the material and emotional uplifting of the lower classes, far from rendering democratic concerns redundant, was certain to underline their urgency and benefit the advocates of democratic politics.

Despite Ahmadi-Nejad's promises to respect freedom of expression and social liberties, his opponents braced themselves for measures aimed at subduing civil society and imposing a more restrictive sociocultural life. Through their failings and blunders the reformers inadvertently deprived the key concepts associated with democracy and civil society of their resonance. This result made it easier for their opponents, particularly Ahmadi-

Nejad, to be dismissive of democracy and, paradoxically, to forget that he won his position through "elections." Considering his attitude to democratic aspirations and the political struggles of the last 100 years, many have viewed his election as signifying the failure of the democratic agenda; it should, however, not be seen as more than a temporary setback. The salience of distributive justice does not mean that demands for political, social, and civic liberties and democratic governance have been abandoned or have become less pressing. Those who refused to vote or did not support Ahmadi-Nejad, that is, some thirty million people, the majority of the electorate, cannot be ignored, nor can many components of the reformists' aims be publicly disowned. Disregarding or deflecting demands for change in the configuration of governance will only deepen the crisis of representation. Ahmadi-Nejad's authoritarian tendencies and policies have not gone unchallenged by civil society forces, particularly students, and threaten to provoke a deeper sociopolitical backlash.

Political alignments in Iran remain fluid; contenders for power can converge on substantive issues but stridently differ over secondary ones. Mobilization of partisan passions can mask existing similarities and accentuate differences. The bifurcated view of Iranian politics, and the use of dichotomous categories such as conservatives and reformers, has always been an oversimplification often readily employed by the contestants themselves. Those broadly identified as right-wing conservatives are now at the helm, but with the political exclusion of the reformers, they cannot sustain their fragile cohesion. There could be a realignment of factions resulting in a new coalescence of pragmatic and centrist elements. The pragmatic or hard-line segments among the conservatives could be driven to replay some of the political drama of the Khatami era. Forced by circumstances, the conservatives could prove more amenable to certain aspects of the reformers' agenda than they appear. The excluded reformers, too, though fragmented, could regroup, revise their strategy, and reenter the political fray. Many advocates of political reform face a dilemma: to continue to work within the existing system, or to attempt to create a movement from outside it, with the aim of seeking to amend the Constitution and bring about radical political change, as advocated by long imprisoned activists such as Akbar Ganji. Some reformers will less hesitantly embrace unfettered democratic republicanism.

In the event of a major domestic crisis the establishment could once again relent, make minor concessions, and try to negotiate its way out of the crisis. The rulers could draw on their controlled but inexhaustible flair for improvisation, tactical flexibility, and realignments. Yet, given the regime's overall record of experimenting with political reform from within, it seems unlikely that the public could again be overwhelmingly won over. Khatami's presidency, if successful, would have tangibly altered the regime's political contours. His failure and the marginalization of the reformers have also affected the regime. The Islamic Republic faces a dilemma: it cannot survive far-reaching political reform, and it cannot survive without it. Despite the greater readiness of the rulers to resort to preemptive repression, it seems unlikely that the relative openness of the Khatami era could be radically reversed; the more circumspect conservatives find it advisable to maintain at least a façade of openness. Some of them might even try to steal the limelight from their former rivals and pursue relatively lenient policies. Right-wing, coercive, and vigilante forces could find themselves freer in attempting to combat what they perceive as vice but might also show greater political restraint. In any event, the regime has remained unable to extinguish the conviction that it cannot meaningfully tolerate even mildly dissenting reformist leaders from within its own midst. It cannot shake off the perception that its authoritarian configuration defies sustained modification and openness.

If recent history can provide a frame of reference, it is clear that the issue of justice, distributive and otherwise, can be efficaciously addressed only in circumstances in which the institutional prerequisites for effective public scrutiny, accountability, and transparency are securely in place. Without them, even politicians of demonstrated goodwill and integrity will ultimately forfeit public credibility. Justice and equity cannot be secured at the cost of liberty but only through transparent institutions permeated by and dedicated to promoting liberty. Efforts to reduce socioeconomic inequity, vital though they are, cannot supplant demands for political equality and meaningful suffrage. Genuinely elected officials are far more likely to be responsive to the needs of their constituents than are the self-appointed custodians of the public good. Without democratic governance and deliberation, the rational rule of law, and public accountability, attempts to attain social justice or initiate socioeconomic reform are bound to mire in self-perpetuating corruption. Invoking the slogans of the past will not restore the conditions of the past. Despite attempts to resurrect the political zeal, moral certainty, and social austerity of the revolutionary era, Iranian society is radically different from what it was in 1979. Far from detracting from the significance of civic and democratic values, the Ahmadi-Nejad interlude is likely to render them more urgently appealing.

# 11

# The Culture of Politics:

# The Presence and Absence
# of the Past

The mode of rule emerging in the aftermath of the 1979 revolution was anomalous in the history of authoritarianism in Iran, intermingling as it did the sacred and the profane, soulcraft and statecraft, stern moralism and realpolitik, exclusive castelike clerical dominance, embellished by an often obscure argot, with a populist ideology of plebeian mobilization. It created a polity in which popular sovereignty, the foundational principle of the Constitutional Revolution, was all but abrogated; the ideal of an independent judiciary and a meaningful separation of powers was similarly eclipsed. In an age of republican and democratic sensibilities, in a country that had been a pioneer in the Islamic world in launching a constitutional revolution, and in the wake of a massive rejection of royal autocratic misrule, self-righteous paternalism seemed glaringly out of place.

In significant respects, Iran's authoritarian political culture persisted or was invigorated after 1979. The postrevolutionary state, despite its proclaimed radical rupture with the past, not only retained many characteristics of its predecessor but displayed an even greater propensity for repression. Not surprisingly, the revolution failed in the objective of taming the state through more rigorous constitutional structures and strictures. The postrevolutionary state, as Tocqueville had observed in the case of the French Revolution, turned out to be stronger, more vigorously coercive, than its predecessor. The state's treatment of dissent and opposition became more heavy-handed; its coercive and intrusive character accounted for the continued weakness of associational life. As before, mass-based organized political parties failed to emerge. Factionalism, clan politics, and patronage remained pervasive. Opposition parties vanished or became dormant; whatever proregime parties emerged remained organizationally weak, ideologically amorphous, and without a solid base of popular support. The regime was no more congenial to party politics than its predecessor had been.[1] The institution of the presidency enjoyed no more effective power than the premiership had under the monarchy. Unlike the premiers of the past, the presidents of the Islamic Republic were elected by popular vote, but if they sought to assert their authority and promote political reform they found themselves bereft of real power. Efforts to invigorate the presidency were denounced as dictatorial in the same manner that struggles to assert the authority of past prime ministers had been denounced. In the past, those who condemned as dictatorial the increased authority of prime ministers had often directly or indirectly augmented the prerogatives of the Shah; those who later favored a weak presidency wittingly or unwittingly shored up the preeminent position and power of the Leader.

The Islamic government behaved as master and proprietor of the people rather than as their servant and trustee. However, unlike the monarchy's unmistakably elitist culture of governance, the successor regime cultivated a decidedly plebeian posture. It showed a far greater affinity with the lower classes and could draw on their support. Yet it formally and informally treated the people as less than politically autonomous citizens with extensive rights and entitlements. Constitutionally the Iranians remained at best a semisovereign people. The regime's repeated professions that it enjoyed genuine popular support—as distinct from officially organized shows of support—could have been gauged only by allowing and facilitating free and fair elections involving real choice. In the eyes of its critics, the regime's aversion to such elections indicated a significant shrinkage in its base of support. In its authoritarian phase, the monarchy had blocked all political safety valves; whether inadvertently or otherwise, the Islamic regime would not do so. The oligarchic exercise of power and the multiplicity of factional clusters in the Islamic regime would make it, in certain respects, less vulnerable than its autocratic predecessor.

The segmentary constitution of clerical politics and the plurality of loci of power inevitably created some scope for political debate, but civic and social liberties remained severely circumscribed. The prevailing character and configuration of governance required that the ruled be treated as subjects rather than citizens; the ideal of a self-confident citizenry, imbued with civic pride and recognized as such by the rulers, remained elusive. Yet, in defiance of political impediments, the ruled persisted in seeking to act as citizens. Significantly, and as a result of the strength of the democratic aspirations underlying the revolution, avowedly democratic mechanisms and procedures of legitimation, including national and popular sovereignty, universal franchise, and parliamentarianism, were not, and could not be, abandoned. In most respects, however, they were radically diminished or diluted. For democratically minded opponents of the monarchy, the version of popular sovereignty upheld by the clerical government was manifestly retrograde.

Popular representation remained restricted and ineffective; candidates for the presidency or the parliament were selected by the Council of Guardians, itself an unelected body. The electorate was given only the choice of voting for candidates acceptable to the regime. There were no meaningfully free and fair elections, and for many the option of not voting was impracticable given official mobilization, coercive tactics, or threatened punishments of various kinds. The inconsequentiality of voting and the ineffectiveness of elected officials and bodies made elections tedious and unappealing. As in the past, however, voter participation became real and intense whenever people detected a relaxation, tactical or otherwise, in the familiar processes of electoral control and believed that their votes mattered. When the electorate realized that the authorities were not bent on, or capable of, resorting to extensive rigging and other corrupt practices, and concluded that the differences among candidates were more than cosmetic, they did not miss the opportunity to vote with the aim of revealing their grievances, demands, and preferences. They thereby sent a clear message to the rulers, evident in the presidential elections of May 1997, emphatically registering their support for popular sovereignty. The highly restrictive contours of the regime's electoral politics, together with numerous ways of tampering with the voting procedures, were further indications of the persistence of the authoritarian political culture.

Regardless of the officially sanctioned narrative, democratic aspirations had been among the most potent impulses of the revolution. Democracy is aptly characterized as a form of governance committed to respecting political equality and the full range of rights and entitlements of citizens; it protects minorities from the onslaught of the majority; it allows individuals to organize themselves or to join civic associations and political parties; it rests on free and fair elections involving real choice; it enables candidates to compete freely for the popular vote. In none of these senses could the legacy of the revolution be described as recognizably democratic. Conversely, the continuing struggles over key notions of popular sovereignty, democratic representation, and republicanism and the practices and procedures associated with them demonstrated the resilience of the democratic aspirations associated not only with the Constitutional Revolution and the civic-nationalism of the 1940s and 1950s, but also with the revolution of 1978–1979.

Yet the quest for democracy and the constitutionalist and civic-nationalist struggles against authoritarian rule were systematically deemphasized or occluded through a tendentious rewriting of history. The opponents and critics of the regime faced the possibility of being branded as opponents of Islam; dissent verged on unbelief. The state purported to embody the sacred and to promote commitment to "true" Islam, authentic cultural values, and moral righteousness. Opponents were portrayed as having succumbed to Western values, irreligion, hypocrisy, moral degeneracy, or outdated, congealed, eclectic, "liberal," or "Americanized" Islam. The theologization of politics inevitably involved a sharp demarcation between believers and nonbelievers, loyalists and nonloyalists, insiders and outsiders, friends and foes. The divide would, of course, not simply be between belief and unbelief, but between belief and "correct" belief; between Islam as a religion and Islam variously identified as an all-embracing ideology *(Islam-e maktabi)*, an ideology of clerical supremacy *(Islam-e feqahati)*, and the "pure Islam of Mohammad" *(Islam-e nab-e Mohammadi)*.

The combining of ideology and theology; charismatic leadership and popular, real, or manufactured cathartic fervor; a belief in the confrontation of the forces of truth *(haqq)* and falsehood *(batel)*, good and evil, God and Satan, resulted in an overarching religious and moral monism and an apocalyptic cosmology that sustained a degree of political self-righteousness unprecedented in Iranian history. A desire to eliminate impiety and impurity, to cleanse society of pollution and the polluted, inevitably resulted in justifying and acting upon the dehumanization of the other. A totalistic and absolutist religious and moral view fed a maximalist politics that shunned rational considerations and seemed impervious to norms of practical reason. Yet, behind the forbidding façade, there was always room for flexibility. Rigidity of belief or assertion was no barrier to flexibility of practice—an inevitable outcome of the experience of governing.

The ruling ideology underwent a tangible loss of intensity in the post-Khomeini era. Khomeini's legacy itself soon became a contested subject. Both those who emphasized the constitutional salience of the republican components of the regime, and those who did the opposite, invoked Khomeini. The ruling ideology was not fixed or static, nor was it as coherent and elaborate as it appeared to be. Disagreements concerning the legitimate range of interpretive perspectives on Islam, and the inevitable problems involved in adapting the religion to the requirements of governing a complex and evolving society, persisted. But the rulers' political outlook continued to be characterized by a conspicuous commitment to an ideologized, seemingly monolithic official Shi'ism, selective pragmatism, an aptitude for improvisation, and what often seemed like a battle to grasp the prerequisites of effective governance. While projecting a sanctimonious public persona, like all other politicians they presented themselves variously to various audiences and constituencies. The wheeling and dealing and theatricality of politics—for which they had a natural propensity—could not be easily reconciled with the aura of piety and moralism that they sought to cultivate.

Many clerics would, of course, realize that their brand of moralized or faith-based social engineering had proved no more successful than alternative brands in rooting out social evils such as addiction, sexual impropriety, and a variety of "deviant" conduct. Nor would they fail to recognize that their coercive enforcement of morals had not proved any more likely to eradicate what they viewed as immoral urges and practices. Yet they continued to harbor a static view of human nature and emotions, a formulaic view of morality as a set of prefabricated, virtually fixed codes overshadowed by and intertwined with the religious law. The self-righteous and pietistic soulcraft and the haphazard, crude, and often harsh statecraft practiced by the regime proved mutually antagonistic. The self-enrichment and other abuses of office prevalent among the regime's mandarins, key functionaries, and their supporters and clientele would prove corrosive to its moral fabric and authority and deepen the disillusionment of the public. This disillusionment would not be directed merely against the rulers but also, and more dangerously, against the very edifice of the religion and the morality closely bound to it.

Yet the postrevolutionary authoritarianism continued to rely, among other things, on the claim to represent an authentic moral vision and the authoritative version of Islam. By claiming to embody the sacred core of Islamic principles and ethicolegal norms, the regime would ensure that the most fundamental political issues lay outside the permitted scope of open debate. In its zeal to root out or suppress sin and unbelief, the regime would forget that conformism induced by fear or retribution was ruinous of spontaneous moral behavior. By subscribing to a paternalistic conception of rule and by claiming to be the unquestionable determinant and guardian of the true faith and correct moral conduct, it would strike at the very foundations of a viable civil society. Indeed, various civil society institutions that had emerged in the final year of the monarchy vanished soon afterward. The Lawyers' Association, which had remained free to elect its own officers throughout the Shah's rule, lost that freedom in 1980. Under the new regime there would also be a drastic shrinkage of the private sphere. In fact the curtailment of a whole range of social liberties and the arbitrary violation of the private sphere became the most conspicuous features of postrevolutionary life. The law and officially sanctioned morals would become virtually indistinguishable, a development in no way conducive to fostering civic and democratic sensibilities.

Despite later invocations of a culture of dialogue by politicians such as Khatami, the predominant mode of political communication rarely transcended patronizing preaching, lecturing, and perorating. Far from fostering compliance, preaching provoked recalcitrance. Sloganeering generated fatigue, while the moralizing constantly foisted on the public produced no commensurate increase in ethical conduct. Preaching was, of course, not only firmly embedded in the clerical subculture but also embodied in the constitutionally sanctioned institution of the Guardianship of the Islamic Jurist. Tolerance of a public sphere characterized by freedom of association and expression remained unfathomable to the rulers. Displaced and demoralized, the secular intellectuals, and active dissidents originating from within the orbit of the Islamist movements, bore the brunt of harassment and persecution.

Petitions, open letters, and other forms of protest by intellectuals and disillusioned former supporters of the regime continued, but the rulers were seldom visibly or positively responsive to such protests; they invariably dismissed them as instigated or manipulated by their foreign "enemies." Emphasizing the notion of the enemy remained a key component of the official strategy of delegitimizing or silencing dissent, in a manner reminiscent of the strictures of the right-wing German jurist and political theorist Carl Schmitt. For Schmitt, politics was founded on the friend/foe dichotomy; the task of the state was to oppose and confront enemies, to emphasize their ubiquity, and, if necessary, to invent them.

The universities remained a major arena of simmering and sometimes open challenge to the regime. The rulers had supported the politicization of the universities without realizing that this would not result in steady student support for the government but invariably the opposite. The reformist segment of the establishment hoped to ensure that the student movement would continue to operate within the confines of the prevailing Constitution. The majority of activist students, however, remained disgruntled and did not cease to agitate for democratic change.[2]

Religious intellectuals and a growing number of traditionalist or quietist clerics had long wondered whether the clerical takeover of power would not perilously entangle the transitory and mundane preoccupations of this world with the spiritual concerns of the next. Many came to believe that interweaving the sanctity of religious faith and the secular interests of the state had harmed both. Many clerics felt vindicated in their belief that Islam, as well as their own interests and social standing, was best served by asserting their financial and moral autonomy vis-à-vis the holders of power. They regretted the clerical assumption of political power as irrevocably damaging to the clerics' ability to exert moral authority and to enjoy public trust. Indeed, some of the most spirited debates in Iran have centered on rejecting a monolithic and ossified reading of Islam in favor of richer and more diverse interpretations. They have also focused on the question of whether the sacred spiritual values of Islam can escape unscathed from the failure of politicized Islam.

Many pious Muslims have resented and resisted the monopolistic fusion of religious and political authority, not because of any impact of secular ideologies but because of a growing belief that such a fusion has threatened the integrity of the faith and the well-being of the believers themselves.[3] Many Iranian Muslims also wonder whether the clerical assumption of power has not fundamentally violated the clerics' traditional role as mediators between the people and the state and as respected interceders on behalf of the oppressed and the victimized. Many more questions remain to be addressed: Does belief in Islam inevitably entail submission to the political supremacy of the clerics? Have the clerics proved particularly successful in transforming themselves into credible, skillful, and competent politicians? To what extent has the metamorphosis of Islam into an official ideology furnished a blueprint for successful socioeconomic development? Has it resulted in a viable and decent political order and a morally healthy society, that is, one free from the ills of modern or semimodern societies? Has the clerical government succeeded in creating an authoritative official version of Shi'ism, binding on every believer? Evidently the decentralized, state-independent traditions that have long rested on spontaneous public approbation of the high learning and demonstrated piety of leading clerics have persisted.

The regime has also been vulnerable to counterhegemonic religious-intellectual discourses and has failed to create its own intellectuals. Notable religious thinkers such as the clerics Mohammad Mojtahed-Shabestari (b. 1936) and Mohsen Kadivar (b. 1959), and the lay thinker and littérateur Abdolkarim Soroush (b. 1945), have long distanced themselves from the regime.[4] These writers, among others, have made significant contributions to a new understanding of Islamic religious and spiritual culture, as well as to the nature of religious knowledge itself. They have provided sacral justification for secularity, have critically probed and questioned the theological underpinnings of the current regime, and have broadly defended liberal-democratic values. While affirming that religion itself is divine and immutable, Soroush has argued that human knowledge of religion is indeterminate and changing. He has denounced rigid and monolithic approaches to the understanding of Islamic law in favor of a revisionist and fallibilist exegesis, and a historically situated and interpretively pluralistic jurisprudential knowledge. A trenchant critic of clerical politics, he has maintained that Islam is a "secular religion" in which the clerics cannot claim to mediate between God and the faithful or invoke any special religious privilege in order to rule over others. He has gone so far as to argue that, contrary to the prediction or "wishful thinking" of Ali Shari'ati—that a future Iran would see the emergence of an Islam free from clericalism—the reverse has actually occurred, a clericalism minus Islam.[5]

In Iran, the advocates of progress and the exponents of conservatism have on many occasions found themselves on the same platform or engaged in tactical alliances. The unreflective fusion of the intellectual horizons of modernity and traditionalism has at times proved maddeningly bewildering. Reacting to the misconstrued or muddled ideological discourses and ill-conceived political alliances of the past, many intellectuals have come to argue that logical and mythical modes of thinking must not be conflated. For such intellectuals, the line of demarcation between those who meaningfully and consistently embrace modernity and rationality and those who do not must be vigorously drawn. Others have come to maintain that a simplistic dichotomous contrast between modernity and tradition and between secularity and religiosity cannot capture the complex and textured intellectual and political orientations of existing political forces. Secularity, they add, can easily be illiberal, while religiosity in itself is no barrier to accepting pluralism. Such debates, and many others, indicate that Iranian society has remained intellectually vibrant and engaged.

Clearly, the experiences of the past twenty-seven years have been immensely instructive. The debates in the Iranian public sphere have become more mature and rationally grounded as they have become less ideological and doctrinaire. The main intellectual rift now seems to be between those who advocate an open, tolerant, and rational society and those who oppose it. Such a society is premised on the sanctity of freedom of conscience and inquiry, including unhampered investigation of the record of the rulers. To ensure the wider resonance of their message, the advocates of such a society must transcend the concerns of the affluent middle classes and develop a strategic social democratic vision to address the chronic socioeconomic problems afflicting the lower classes.

It has long been realized that sustained civil society, and the political and intellectual pluralism integral to it, cannot be meaningfully reconciled with governments that see themselves as embodying the sacred, as the sole determinants and custodians of what is good, virtuous, true, and authentic.[6]

An informed citizenry that rejects the ascriptive hierarchical values and practices associated with oligarchic paternalism has, however, emerged. It demands a government that is representative in the political as well as the sociocultural sense, a rational, meritocratic, and politically egalitarian government committed to treating its citizens with "equal respect and concern."[7] The Iranian public is fully cognizant of, and sees itself as entitled to, a whole range of concrete political, civic, and social rights, liberties and entitlements enjoyed in any decent society. If we are to judge by the history of the past 100 years, it will not be reconciled to submission or appeased by minor concessions.

In addition to invoking their revolutionary and antimonarchical credentials, the ruling clerics have projected themselves as endowed with the requisite Islamic learning to act as near-infallible custodians both of the true faith and morals and of culture. They would claim commitment to promoting both the society's moral health and its sense of dignity and identity. They see themselves as natural leaders of a national community defined primarily by faith—a community in which faith is the primordial locus of identity and the chief determinant of conduct. In the eyes of their detractors, however, they are culpable of neglecting or denigrating other crucial components of Iranian identity, and of acting as the self-appointed vicegerents of God and defenders of values and norms that they have unwittingly done much to undermine. Though often speaking about "Islamic compassion" (otufat-e Islami), the majority of clerics have adhered to a narrow, rigid, and not particularly compassionate reading of a multifaceted tradition in order to perpetuate their own guild, corporatist, or quasi-caste interests, while treating any far-reaching criticism of their conduct as hostility to Islam and God.

The Islamists relentlessly inveigh against secularity, which they habitually identify as anathema to religion. They refuse to admit, however, that the coercive enforcement of faith and morals and the instrumentalist use of religion for political purposes not only has failed to win over nonpracticing Muslims but has had an adverse effect on many self-respecting practicing Muslims. Secularity requires a pluralistic public sphere in which religion as a way of making sense of human experience, a set of cherished normative rules, a complex of rituals affirming a person's link with the sacred, and a significant component of the inherited culture can survive and flourish.

Secularity is not opposed to religion as spirituality; it is incompatible with religion as a totalizing discourse, an all-embracing and intrusive coercive code. Even granting that they act in good faith, those who oppose secularity but advocate democracy and republicanism forget that an officially sanctioned monolithic creed acting as the principal arbiter and coercive enforcer of right and wrong cannot be reconciled with meaningful civil society or democratic republicanism.

A far cry from democratic republicanism, paternalist clerical authoritarianism has provoked a culture of rejection and resistance that, despite the highly nonpermissive conditions, expresses itself in a variety of ways: urban unrest and protests of various kinds, particularly among university students; strikes and sit-ins; the circulation of open letters, satire, jokes, and rumors; and instances of civil disobedience. Rebelliousness is expressed through social behavior deemed unacceptable to the regime, defiance of the law, flouting of the dress code, and morally relaxed, if not indifferent, conduct verging on nihilism. Massive votes of disapproval, such as those cast in May 1997, signaled a more politically direct rejection of authoritarianism. The people continue to demand to be treated as citizens, with real respect and concern, and with due recognition of their rights and entitlements. The grievances saturating the Iranian public sphere reveal that discrimination and humiliation have been at the core of what the public particularly abhors. Nothing is more corrosive of the human soul than humiliation, which is anathema to any notion of a decent society.[8] The shabby treatment by governments that invoke spirituality leaves an even deeper scar on the human spirit.

# 12

# Predicaments and Prospects

Like other major political upheavals, the Iranian revolution meant liberation and empowerment for some and catastrophe for others. For its secular or moderate participants, its outcome was a far cry from the lofty ideals and sublime optimism voiced during the antimonarchist revolutionary struggle. The revolution unleashed forces, expectations, and passions that left little scope for practical reason and prudence. The winners tried to sustain the fervor, and ruled with an iron fist. Sloganeering was elevated to a national vocation and a lucrative pastime. The mobilization of prejudice and hatred remained a chief instrument for outmaneuvering opponents. The state's use of violence for control and repression, and also as a means of correction, purification, and salvation, persisted. Revolutionary populist reliance on "the people" gave way to reliance on officially mobilized, semi-professional demonstrators. The losers and the vanquished who escaped execution or survived incarceration, torture, show trials, public confessions, and other forms of ill-treatment either left the country or stayed and persevered in the hope that the regime would implode or a real reformist movement emerge. The tenacity of advocates of decent government rested upon a belief in the eventual triumph of sanity and the retrieval of the anti-authoritarian objectives and aspirations that had animated the revolution.

In the course of a century, Iran went through two revolutions and many widespread social movements. It is thus not surprising that Iranian society should reveal far greater attentiveness to social democratic values than have other societies in the region. To many, if not most, of its participants, the revolution of 1978–1979 sought to realize and extend the ideals and hopes that had inspired the Constitutional Revolution and the civic-nationalist movement led by Mosaddeq. The outcome of the revolution of 1978–1979 undoubtedly startled and disappointed all of those who had opposed authoritarian rule in the hope of achieving democracy. They would regret, and also suffer the consequences of, the loss or reversal of the central ideals of the revolution—social justice; egalitarianism; civic, political, and social liberties; rejection of undeserved privilege.

A century after the Constitutional Revolution, the pertinent issues and debates dominating Iranian public life have a persistent resonance: What does the rule of law imply and amount to, and how far has it prevailed? What are the preconditions of legitimate rule and the characteristics of misrule? What are essential features of decent government? What were the primary objectives of the revolutionary struggle to overthrow the monarchy? How politically sovereign are the Iranian people, and how representative is their government? Can bureaucratic rationality, administrative competence, and meritocracy be supplanted by or reconciled with clientelist loyalty and "correct" religious credentials? Can a credible notion of civil society be reconciled with a ubiquitous paternalistic and intrusive state bent on acting as the emanation of the divine, custodian of the sacred, and the sole arbiter of moral integrity and virtue?

The rulers have not ignored such debates. They have characterized the revolution as having been motivated solely by "Islam" and dedicated to creating an "Islamic state." Yet a fundamental challenge for such a state has been to justify and validate itself not merely in generic terms—of having secured "national dignity" or established "Islamic values"—but by demonstrating its commitment to crafting a prosperous and decent society. Indeed, the rulers have emphasized that they have sought to create a society consisting of a dynamic, self-confident, and dignified citizenry enjoying a wide range of rights and entitlements based on distributive justice, socioeconomic development, public welfare, and nondiscriminatory educational and employment opportunities. Having appropriated a republican façade and certain formally democratic procedures and rituals, the rulers have unhesitatingly claimed that the regime is soundly representative and firmly based on popular consent and support. What is significant about such claims is not their plausibility or otherwise, but the very fact that they are made and invoked. Such claims reveal the continued and growing salience of democratic and, more broadly, social democratic aspirations in the Iranian public sphere.

For those accustomed to a cursory look at the society, what seems to have survived the grand claims of the regime is little more than enforcement of the dress code for women, formally imposed in 1981, and the coercive upholding and valorizing of public norms of chastity. For more probing observers, the institutionalization of oligarchic clerical rule, resting on a narrow interpretation of Shi'ism, has had far-reaching consequences. With the abolition of the family protection law in March 1980, women became more vulnerable; many saw their agency and autonomy radically diminished or found themselves formally relegated to a position of subjugation. The symbolic significance of the dress code cannot be underestimated. Women found themselves in many respects among the losers of the revolution. Of course, the female franchise was not revoked, and women remained capable of playing an important political role. Divorce and inheritance laws were modified to compensate for their inferior legal status; other legislation designed to address some of their concerns was also introduced. Exemption from conscription, a diminution of prospects for early marriage, and a desire to compensate for lower social status gave them greater incentive to pursue their educational goals. Women would come to constitute a majority of the university student population: in 2004 they accounted for 64 percent of those entering university. They were able to distinguish themselves in a variety of professions, with notable exceptions, such as serving as judges. Yet literacy among women was lower; only 10 percent of women were employed, and belief in inherent gender inequality remained an integral component of the ruling ideology.

While gender-based discrimination was intrinsic to the legal system, men were no less affected by the drastic curtailment of social and civic liberties, the Islamization of the legal code, and the radical overhaul of the entire edifice of justice—developments that were among the most conspicuous outcomes of clerical rule. In contravention of the country's formal commit ment to respect human rights, the new legal code was in every respect discriminatory toward religious minorities. Punishment for a crime differed depending on whether the perpetrator was Muslim or non-Muslim. The judiciary amassed enormous power and enjoyed unusual prerogatives and resources to engage in a whole range of judicial and extrajudicial activities, including the investigation of wrongdoing, the administration of justice and punishment, formal or informal surveillance, and intimidation of suspects. The judiciary dealt not only with ordinary lawbreakers but also with vocal or active critics and opponents of the regime. The objective of creating a uniformly enforced and standardized system of justice remained a work in progress. Juridical imprecision and loopholes, and draconian laws enforced at the discretion of judges, aggravated legal insecurity. The tenuous or discretionary nature of legality and of the rule of law impelled Iranians to resort to a variety of inventive informal practices to cope with the situation. Political, social, civic, and cultural life continued to be marred by abuses of human rights; gross discrimination; extralegal punitive measures; the ubiquity of various agencies of surveillance, detention, and interrogation; the activities of authorized or "rogue" secret agents; the deployment of organized vigilante groups to attack and harass opponents or break up meetings and gatherings of the regime's critics. Evin Prison, Iran's Bastille under the monarchy, continued to evoke the same, if not a greater, sense of horror than before.

When in August 1999 Mohammad Yazdi, the head of the judiciary, was replaced by another cleric, Mahmud Hashemi-Shahrudi, there were expectations of change, as Shahrudi asserted that he had taken over a "ruin." These expectations, however, proved illusory. The judiciary remained one of the key instruments for frustrating the reformers' objectives; various forms of malpractice also continued. Ill-treatment and abuse had acquired a routinized, almost banal character in which the practitioners simply "did their job." In late April 2004 Shahrudi issued a directive banning all forms of torture, abuse, and ill-treatment of the accused and the imprisoned. Such a ban already existed on the statute books; the decree reiterating it indicated its widespread disregard. The sixth Islamic parliament (2000–2004) had tried several times to introduce legislation reinforcing antitorture measures, only to find its efforts frustrated by the Council of Guardians. The council rejected many similar measures passed by the parliament.

In May 2004, during its last days in session, members of the sixth parliament incorporated Shahrudi's directive in a draft law that they hoped the Council of Guardians would find difficult to reject, but the effort proved futile. Far from heeding criticism of its disregard for civil liberties, the judiciary was intent on increasing its actively intrusive role in society to an extent that alarmed even many conservatives. In November 2004 it launched its own intelligence-gathering agency and expanded its capacity for more-intense surveillance and control across the whole span of society, including city quarters, the bazaar, factories, seminaries, universities, schools, and women's associations. This entity, whose activities duplicated those of many parallel organizations, sought to monitor more effectively and combat not only crime but also "vice" and all other forms of conduct deemed detrimental to the regime.

Not only civic and gender equality, but also equality of employment opportunity remained elusive. Government employees, particularly at the senior level, were selected from among those with demonstrated religious credentials and commitment to the core ideology of the regime. Candidates from rural areas received preferential consideration. This policy compensated for their past chronic marginalization, yet these employees often brought with them a certain set of attitudes and expectations regarding office and its material or symbolic advantages. Many saw office as providing an opportunity not just to serve the regime but also to gain status and influence and to enjoy a variety of benefits, spoils, and trappings. Such attitudes exacerbated, and were in turn reinforced by, the consequences of the dearth of sufficient training, appropriate expertise, and managerial competence. Goodwill, commitment, and a desire to serve with integrity were not absent, yet few high-ranking officials or senior civil servants distinguished themselves by any exceptional accomplishments. This situation, rooted in the complex structures of loyalty, patronage, and factional ties sustaining the bureaucracy, militated against the rise of a capable civil service with a professional ethic. It was also a corollary to the regime's institutionalized and barely disguised discriminatory policy of cultivating a large clientele of ideologically reliable supporters and beneficiaries, with scant attention to the consequent alienation of vast segments of Iranian society.

Although the revolution was an urban phenomenon, the elite it gave rise to included many who came from rural areas or retained their provincial sociocultural outlook. The ruling elite aspired to sophistication and cosmopolitanism. It may indeed have achieved these in terms of visible lifestyle, material comfort, and a lavish culture of consumption; yet mentally it remained insular and continued to perpetuate its parochial sensibilities. A quarter of a century should have been sufficient for a class of skilled managers to emerge. Yet the system of bureaucratic recruitment, the criteria applied, and the mentality fostered have ensured that officeholders continue to lack credibility as well as confidence. Stories of incompetence or malpractice, abuses of office, and the amassing of riches abound. Regardless of whether they are true or fictitious, accurate or exaggerated, such stories, and the fact that they are repeated often, and perhaps widely believed, indicates a crisis of competence.

Besides radical changes in the political, administrative, civic, and judicial arenas, the structural transformation of Iranian society after 1979 was evident in areas such as social stratification and class rifts. The new ruling elite was characterized by avowed ideological commitment, broad similarity of social origins, and other social ties and affinities. In addition, a new class of *nouveaux riches* emerged which, thanks to its links to the ruling elite, amassed enough wealth to rival its royalist predecessor. The ruling elite, the *nouveaux riches,* and key bazaar merchants often overlapped, were interconnected, and constituted a quasi-plutocracy. Many other social strata, particularly lower-ranking employees, felt worse off, whether financially or in terms of social status. The urban poor remained highly vulnerable. Demoralized and consumed by resentment and despair, they often gave in to anomie and addiction and showed a greater propensity for millenarian yearnings. By 2004 unemployment stood at 16 percent; the average monthly income was no more than $100. The country's population of 70.7 million in 2005 had more than doubled since the inception of the Islamic regime, with some 70 percent below the age of thirty. Demographic growth and incessant rural migration exacerbated haphazard urbanization. Changes in the educational system, the bureaucratic culture, and the norms and standards of public behavior were no less conspicuous. No one could fail to notice a decline in traditional civic virtues such as courtesy, honesty, and respectful consideration of others. In addition to suffering routine inefficiencies, one rarely visited a government office without experiencing some form of humiliation. "The bureaucracy," noted one observer, "often makes you feel you are trying to run through mud up to the waist."[1] The quotidian experiences of the urban population did not make for a psychologically healthy or relaxed life; civic pride, happiness, even minimal contentment, remained more elusive than ever.

Despite or because of restrictive official policies, interest in Western cultural debates and intellectual trends persisted and was, in fact, on the rise. This trend led the authorities in the summer of 1992 to denounce what they dubbed the "Western cultural invasion." Revealing little understanding of the hybrid and heterogeneous nature of Iranian culture, the official view rested on the untenable idea that there was a timeless, authentic Iranian-Islamic culture that could be retrieved and safeguarded by exhortation or fiat. Yet in an age of expanding global communications, turning the country into a culturally self-contained fortress was impossible. No efforts could counter, let alone overcome, the impact of the Internet on the urban population at large, including the clerics, especially in Qom, and on the transmission of knowledge and information. Popular awareness of alternative modes of life rendered tight social control unachievable and counterproductive. Even in its early and more insular phase, the regime had felt obliged to rescind its ban on music and chess playing, which had stimulated tremendous interest in both. Increasingly, the public showed its defiance of the rulers by embracing any practice or attitude officially discouraged or banned. Thus, official anti-Americanism provoked pro-American sentiments among the populace. In defiance of the stern moralism of the rulers, the entertainment-starved youth displayed a growing appetite for the vulgar components of global, particularly American, popular culture.

The official emphasis on the primacy of Iran's Islamic identity had done much to revive strong interest in other components of the national culture. The regime would eventually be forced to recognize, and attempt to embrace, the non-Islamic aspects of Iranian identity. Inadvertently, the Islamic regime played a major role in reviving interest in Iran's specifically Persian and non-Islamic cultural legacy. Civic-nationalism, too, continued to grow in appeal among the urban population, and particularly the intelligentsia and university students. Despite its pan-Islamist rhetoric, the regime not only felt obliged to come to terms with Iranian nationalism but attempted to appropriate it. Clearly, just as ideologized Islam had transformed the Iranian political landscape, the process of governing had crucially changed political Islam, forcing the clerics to make many concessions.

Clerical rule also affected historically rooted practices and traditions in

Shi'ite Islam. The government attempted, unsuccessfully, to modify the clerical nomenclature and substitute the role of the officially designated Leader for that of an informally chosen grand ayatollah who owed his stature and role to the public acclaim of the faithful, for whom he was a revered model of learning and piety. Moreover, the regime remained unable to speak on behalf of the country's entire Shi'ite clerical establishment. Many clerics maintained their distance from the rulers and opposed or criticized them in a variety of ways. Vocally dissenting clerics were treated no less harshly than other critics.

Upon his return to Iran on the eve of the fall of the monarchy, Khomeini made an assertion of considerable significance: our fathers, he stated, were not our political custodians, entitled to determine our destiny or authorized to choose a form of government for us; we have the right to choose our own form of government.[2] The implications of Khomeini's statement were far-reaching: the legitimacy of a political system is provisional and in need of revalidation; it has to be periodically subjected to a formal or informal plebiscite and affirmed, modified, or rejected. Thus, every generation is, or ought to be, entitled to determine its own form of government. Within twenty-five years of the birth of the Islamic Republic, its opponents, including many disillusioned former supporters, would be echoing Khomeini and demanding that the destiny and popularity of the regime be subjected to a referendum.

Islamic governance was indeed formally legitimized when, following the collapse of the monarchy, the Iranian people were asked to participate in a referendum that involved simply affirming or rejecting an "Islamic republic." No alternative was provided, nor was the meaning of such a polity clarified. The people were thus given no real choice, nor the opportunity for careful reflection and an informed and meaningful decision on the future of the country. More than twenty-five years later all Iranians are certain about what an Islamic republic has meant in practice. Opponents of the regime view a properly conducted referendum on its future as a valid expression of informed public opinion and seem confident about its outcome. Those in power appear to share this assumption and are therefore unlikely to agree to such a test. Remaining inattentive to the evident signs of public disillusionment with the entire system, the rulers have thwarted the efforts of those who believe that reforming the regime is the only way to avert catastrophic collapse. Claiming to have learned from the past, the rulers sought to avoid repeating the mistakes of the monarchy; yet they tended to attribute the fall of the monarchy not to its heavy-handed clampdown on unrest but to its indecisiveness and leniency. Altogether they seem to have learned little about how regimes, self-deceptively or otherwise, see themselves as invulnerable—how they persist in alienating and antagonizing the public at their own peril.

Few observers would deny that the chronic crisis of legitimacy and representation and the attendant political disarray engulfing Iran constitute a serious threat to the moral fabric of its society. Apathy, cynicism, and hopelessness are compounded by anomie and pervasive forms of social malaise such as addiction, vagrancy, and crime, which are largely rooted in poverty. Promises of justice and equity, preeminent in revolutionary aspirations, have long rung hollow. Religion can no longer effectively function as a force for inner restraint; the prevailing indifference to moral qualms and to socioculturally sanctioned virtues is disheartening to most citizens. Coercive attempts to undo the secular ethos of the prerevolutionary era have set in motion a far-reaching process of secularization. Thanks to clerical rule and governmental appropriation of the sacred, the social process of secularization is probably more extensive in contemporary Iran than in any other Islamic society. Modernity has continued to move forward in every facet of life, and the clerics have felt obliged to come to terms with it. In reaction the regime has increasingly sought to promote beliefs and practices patently at odds with the dictates of reason and often dismissed as superstitious by learned clerics. The scripturalist and emotionally stern Shi'ism of such clerics has traditionally been at odds with cathartic popular Shi'ism. Similarly, efforts to fundamentalize Iranian Islam have contravened the long-cherished underlying tolerance of the country's lay religiocultural traditions. Such traditions had led the French ambassador to Tehran in the 1950s to describe Iranians as nonfanatical "Voltairian" Muslims.[3]

Revolution, an essentially modern phenomenon, combined with the most effective means of modern communication, was, paradoxically, used not only to overthrow the monarchy but to resurrect premodern modes of thinking and systems of values. Inventing a purportedly genuine, pristine Islamic tradition of governance involved a costly, concerted, and ultimately unsuccessful struggle to confront modernity, to reverse the process of disenchantment characterizing it, and to roll back the march of secularization. The failure of this undertaking is best exemplified in the unsuccessful efforts to combine and integrate universities and seminaries. Radical secularists celebrate what they view as the implosion of the myth of politicized religion as a vehicle for national salvation and regeneration. More prudent advocates of a disengagement between religion and governance, together with those who see religion, in the words of Charles Taylor, as one of the main "authoritative horizons" of life,[4] fear that the decline of religious faith has eroded the foundations of morality and weakened communal values. Many Iranians feel hopeful about the future, at least the distant future. Few, however, would regard the near future with the same degree of optimism.

More than a quarter of a century after its inception, the Islamic regime continues to face crises resulting from years of ill-conceived policies, poor management, and administrative inefficiency rooted in a lingering ideological-cliquish aversion to bureaucratic rationality and meritocracy. Such crises have manifested themselves in a variety of forms. The substitution of real or feigned ideological commitment to the regime for rationally ascertainable merit has cost the country dearly. Inefficient management, inadequate expertise, lack of bureaucratic coordination, and other structural constraints accentuated by deeper political problems account for a frustratingly slow rate of progress in the completion of development projects. The absence of coherent, clear, and sound economic policies has resulted in an economy marred by low productivity, uncompetitive domestic products, continued dependence on oil revenues, unemployment, inflation, and relative poverty for a vast portion of the population, engaged in an exhausting daily grind to make ends meet. An inadequate educational infrastructure, particularly at the higher level, has had a demoralizing impact on the young. In 2006 the available university places accommodated only one-fifth of the number of applicants, and even the relatively small pool of university graduates, including physicians, could not find suitable employment. Iran ranks first among developing countries in terms of a brain drain. The emigration of the educated, not unwelcome to at least some of those in office, has irretrievably harmed the country's scientific, technological, educational, and cultural infrastructures. Of course, if at some point and in the right circumstances even a small number of such emigrants should return, they would make a significant contribution to revitalizing the country.

Iran's underlying political, economic, and administrative problems, together with the dearth of imaginative, sound, and carefully implemented policies, have also largely accounted for many of the international setbacks suffered by the country. There has been no lack of skills for negotiating and haggling, or a flair for adopting tactically offensive or retreating postures as situations have warranted. The doctrinaire assumptions informing the country's foreign policy considerations have been more flexible than they have appeared; yet the country has lacked a clear, consistent, and effective foreign policy. Bereft of a strategic vision, it has remained virtually isolated, devoid of powerful allies, and unable to play the role befitting its historic regional significance, particularly in Central Asia, the Caspian region, Afghanistan, and the Persian Gulf. Iran is often seen as the chief beneficiary of the American misadventure in Iraq; the wise handling of its strategic advantages in Iraq requires skills greater than customarily displayed. But many challenges remain: how to reconcile issues of sovereignty, national security, and the right to develop nuclear technology as a source of energy while allaying international concerns about the military use of such technology, warding off external threats, and avoiding further sanctions and isolation. The implications of Turkey's efforts to join the European Union under an Islamist but unusually flexible and modern-minded government, though stalled, could only be unsettling to the regime in Tehran.

Domestically, the lingering crisis of authority and the routinized privileging of loyalty over merit have vitiated efforts to deal with bureaucratic ineptitude and various forms of corruption. The result has been a widespread disrespect for laws, regulations, and even culturally valued civic norms. Such disrespect, for instance, permeates the culture of driving and, together with inadequate roads and badly built, aged, and poorly maintained vehicles, results in an annual death toll of more than 20,000.[5] The polluted and congested but still expanding cities and the condition of the urban infrastructure reveal and symbolize deeper problems. Shoddily constructed and unsightly high-rises marring the Tehran skyline have enriched well-connected real estate speculators but greatly damaged the capital's aesthetic landscape. They reveal scant appreciation of the Iranian cultural-architectural heritage. Iran is catastrophically earthquake prone, yet few buildings in the country are designed to withstand a powerful earthquake. All the amenities of a modern society appear to exist, but quality and substance have invariably been compromised. Socioeconomic development has remained a key objective, but the kind of public scrutiny needed to ensure its thoughtful and beneficial accomplishment has been largely absent. Such scrutiny cannot be attempted without a secure public sphere of free expression and a broad range of fundamental liberties—in short, political development. Given its abundant natural resources, wealth, and trained manpower at home or abroad, Iran has a tremendous developmental potential, which has remained unfulfilled. This failure is inextricably intertwined with the crisis of representation and governance that bedevils Iranian public life.

A century after they first embarked on fashioning a constitutional representative government, the Iranian people continue to see themselves as lacking full sovereign status or equal citizenship. The old Constitution was tragically overshadowed by monarchism and abused by rulers who claimed extensive prerogatives. Yet, despite its inadequacies or ambiguities, which reflected historically specific issues that it had sought to address, the Constitution was in spirit committed to national and popular sovereignty and to a representative democracy. With careful revisions making it more coherent and workable while enhancing its democratic tenor and spirit, the Constitution could have served as the framework for the emergence of a functioning representative form of government. The Constitution of the Islamic Republic contains greater anomalies and contradictions; its entrenched theocratic clauses cannot be reconciled with a republican and meaningfully democratic form of government. The provisions of this Constitution are effective only within the confines of Islamic principles, which are, at least in theory, determined by the six jurists of the Council of Guardians.

Public demands for greater rights than those provided by the present Constitution or for a reading that emphasizes its more recognizably republican clauses would also force a revision of the official narrative. The clerics initially treated the prerevolutionary period as prehistory. They considered a radical break with the immediate past—in contrast to the distant past, with which they were intellectually and emotionally entangled—in every respect desirable and possible. Gradually abandoning this approach, they came to place themselves in the context of broader Iranian history. The regime's dismissal of the Constitutional Revolution as marking the beginning of the erosion of the country's sense of identity, and its lionization of obscurantist, anticonstitutionalist clerics, persisted. At the same time it constructed its own counternarrative, portraying the constitutionalist and civic-nationalist struggles as having been inspired and led primarily by clerics. Indeed, from the outset the regime had felt obliged to appropriate some key notions associated with those struggles, particularly as it had failed to generate ideas and vocabularies of its own that would resonate in the context of the modernizing tempo of Iranian society.

The quest for a viable and decent polity in Iran has since the late 1970s been more far-reaching than at any other time since the Constitutional Revolution and the civic-nationalist movement of the 1940s and 1950s. The ongoing struggle is infused with the aims, ideas, and idioms that the Constitutional Revolution interjected into Iranian political thinking. Such aims and ideas remain vibrant and pertinent, and thus the Constitutional Revolution continues. It is a revolution that is at times intense and on occasion barely perceptible; yet it goes on. It involves a sustained overt or covert struggle against obscurantism and paternalism, and for individual liberty and autonomy. It aspires to create a rational and democratic government committed to the rule of law, and a tolerant and open society. Despite bouts of despair, the forces of politicized civil society in the country remain hopeful that Iran is moving in that direction.

Without a doubt and contrary to the early optimism of secular intellectuals and its other detractors, the Islamic regime has demonstrated astonishing resilience. Yet, with its ideological power dwindling, it has been tangibly afflicted by a chronic crisis of authority. Toward the end of Khatami's presidency some feared that the domestic political impasse and regional conflicts might prompt the Revolutionary Guards to attempt a direct or indirect takeover of power. Others, however, maintained that the Guards, at least at the senior level, and the larger nexus of security and intelligence forces were already politically well placed, and thus unlikely to be uniformly supportive of such a radical venture. With Ahmadi-Nejad's presidency, many feared that the predicted political ascendancy of the Guards and the security forces had occurred. His assumption of office did not, however, have a significant impact on the routinized structure of oligarchic rule. The crisis of authority continues to be a salient feature of the regime and has in fact become more acute.

This situation creates considerable potential opportunities for the secular democratic opposition, which encompasses a wide spectrum of opinions.

The opposition, continuing to vacillate between despondency and buoyancy, has so far failed to assert itself and roll back public apathy and disillusionment resulting from the enormous blunders of the loyalist opposition. The diaspora opposition is even more politically, generationally, and culturally divided. Members of the older generation have had their lives torn apart by the corrosive melancholy of exile, loneliness, anonymity, and failure to adapt to the host culture, while the young seem insufficiently idealistic and display a thin grasp of their parental culture. Yet the fragmented opposition, both at home and abroad, has felt reassured that the movement for reform from within the regime has not rendered redundant the need for a broader and more vigorous opposition movement. The loss of optimism among intellectuals and activists at home regarding the prospect of reform from within could result in the informal coalescence of an invigorated democratic opposition. But whether such an opposition, deprived of the opportunity to organize itself, can make its mark depends on contingencies and crises that cannot be predicted, and on the success or failure of the regime to contain its crises and retain its exclusionist hold on power.

# Epilogue:

# The Resilience of Modernity

In 1978 the autocratic configuration of governance in Iran seemed anachronistic, ill-tuned to the complex administrative structure of the state and the burgeoning socioeconomic and cultural modernity of Iranian society. The most fundamental aim of the Constitutional Revolution—to create an impersonal and accountable state committed to the rule of law and constitutional representative government—had remained unfulfilled. The continuation of the constitutional struggle during the Mosaddeq era had also ended in failure, triggering an intensification of authoritarian rule. The systematic subversion of constitutionalism had provoked a crisis of legitimacy, rendering the Pahlavi state intrinsically vulnerable. Its intolerance of opponents and even of nonservile would-be supporters had antagonized many. Moderate secular opponents had long since succumbed to pessimism about the possibility of real political reform so long as the Shah remained in power. They had also been deprived of the opportunity to acquire cumulative political experience.

The monarchy's modernizing drive had unintentionally helped to create major sociopolitical strains. Most clerics and lay Islamists had become alarmed by the pace of modernization and the dangers posed to their collective interests and the privileged status of Shi'ite Islam. Rural migrants, lured to the cities by the prospect of better life chances, had become more conscious of the gulf separating them from the powerful and the prosperous. Unsettled by the putative decadence and alien culture and life style of the privileged classes associated with the regime, they sought refuge and solace in religious and traditionalist sensibilities. The universities and intellectual circles, on the other hand, animated by strong aversion to the regime and its antipathy to leftist ideas, showed increasing receptivity to radical left-wing tendencies.

Confident of its stability and aiming to defuse, partially address, or contain the growing political resentment, the regime grudgingly resorted to political liberalization. Yet the ruling elite's lack of credibility and the divide separating it from the populace ensured that such a move entailed unforeseen dangers; it would be widely perceived as a ploy to deflect or accommodate U.S. human rights concerns and to preempt domestic unrest while in effect perpetuating the nondemocratic, exploitative, and corruption-riddled regime. The Shah himself, perilously irresolute in moments of crisis, not only failed to manage the liberalization and its consequences but through blunders further antagonized his opponents. Having long cultivated an image as an august and invulnerable emperor, the Shah could not easily don the mantle of an accommodating constitutional monarch. He could not withstand the torrent of criticism leveled against the very foundations of the state that he had come to dominate and personify. The Shah's deficient judgment and imagination played a key role in widening the antiregime protests from intellectual and secular circles to encompass the urban masses. Beset by illness and shocked by the scale of his unpopularity, the Shah faltered. His failure to receive reassuringly clear signals from the U.S. administration, the paralysis of the political elite, and the dearth of credible statesmen able or willing to act in an effective executive or even advisory capacity, doomed any prospects for his continued rule.

With the Shah at the helm, the regime was structurally irreconcilable with sustained liberalization, which would have required a radical transformation of the state involving the dismantling of authoritarian rule. Given the scale of the opposition to it, the regime could neither address nor survive such a fundamental reorganization. Exposed to intense public protests and structured to respond only to royal control, when the Shah's aura vanished and his leadership collapsed, the servile inner circle around him lost all sense of cohesion and purpose, the state's institutions began to malfunction, and the regime inevitably succumbed to disarray. Many factors normally viewed as accounting for or contributing to the revolution—economic crisis or hardship, demographic changes, political discontent, cultural alienation, revulsion against modernity, the widespread espousal of a traditionalist or an ideologized Islam—were not specific to Iran. Unlike elsewhere in the Middle East, however, it was in Iran that a politically repressive state, having long defied powerful constitutionalist and civic-nationalist aspirations, resorted to a policy of political liberalization for which it was unprepared and which suddenly exposed its structural weaknesses. This was perhaps the single most important factor accounting for its implosion in the face of a sustained challenge.

Having increasingly acquired a militaristic cast, ultimately the regime had no solid foundation other than the military. No other state institution had been molded to the same extent in accordance with the whims and expectations of its royal commander-in-chief. The Shah had overseen the growth of an impressively well-equipped military; having catered faithfully to its needs and expectations, he in turn enjoyed its complete loyalty to himself. The assurance of the military's loyalty, together with continued U.S. support, had crucially helped to entrench the Shah in his position of power, but it had also greatly inflated his self-image of invincibility. But the military was even less capable than other institutions of functioning coherently in the absence of effective and clear royal leadership. And with no experience of intervening directly in domestic politics, as was the case elsewhere in the region, it was incapable of dealing indefinitely with a protracted, often bloody civil unrest and its accompanying war of attrition.

The increasingly bewildered and embattled Shah, unable to rely with confidence on his domestic power base, frantically sought the advice of the Americans and the British, a move that both revealed and augmented his indecision. Compounding his problems, a leader of unusual abilities emerged at this crucial moment, when a broad popular movement for change was rapidly taking shape. The combination of forces and circumstances that had helped to defeat Khomeini in 1963 had radically changed. Nineteen seventy-eight saw the emergence of an atmosphere of radicalized antagonism to the Shah that inspired Khomeini as much as he helped to instigate it. The regime's elimination of all other alternatives enabled Khomeini to become the sole leader and spokesman of the broad coalition of antimonarchist opposition, the Shah's nemesis, and all things to all men.

Unlike several other Middle Eastern countries, Iran lacked formally organized mass politicoreligious movements such as the Muslim Brotherhood.
The leading clerics were not united in opposition to the regime. Khomeini
emerged to lead a populist movement of broad appeal in the name of denouncing oppression, injustice, corruption, and subservience to foreign interests. His allusions to Islamic government were widely understood to connote an affirmation of spiritually sanctioned values and norms, underlying
a just and nonrepressive sociopolitical order. Animated by the rejection of
the Shah's authoritarian rule, perceived as the embodiment of despotism,
injustice, corruption, and inauthentic or alien values, the majority of Iranians did not envisage an Islamic polity as involving theocratic institutions
and clerical domination. In order to maintain and augment unity in rejecting the status quo, Khomeini avoided divisive and controversial statements.
He focused relentlessly on the overthrow of the monarchy as the incontro-
vertible leap into a self-evidently better future.

Few could imagine that the overwhelmingly antiauthoritarian aspirations
underlining the revolution would soon be betrayed. There was widespread
optimism that, with the Pahlavi state dismantled, the architects of the new
polity in Iran would embrace popular sovereignty and be committed to the
rule of law and political and civil liberties. For most of its participants, the
revolution of 1978–1979 was in crucial respects an attempt to fulfill the objectives of the Constitutional Revolution. Foremost among them was the
empowerment of the people to play a real role in determining their collective destiny and interests, through the establishment of a representative democracy and the institutionalization of political and civic liberties, rights,
and entitlements.

But Iran in 1978–1979 bore little resemblance to Iran on the eve of the
Constitutional Revolution some seventy-five years earlier. Thanks to the
central role of the state, the oil-rich country had been radically transformed, and modernity—with its vast cognitive, ontological, sociocultural,
and moral implications—had permeated Iranian society. Nationalism as a
powerful component of modernity had become an indelible feature of political, civic, and cultural life.[1] Paradoxically, in its autocratic configuration
the state had retained some of its chief premodern features and was thus
out of sync with the modern ethos it had fostered. Modernity also faced the
nostalgic rhetoric and longings of many detractors; yet it had come to stay.

In its sober and reflective form, modernity, in Iran as elsewhere, did not entail mindlessly negating tradition, but contextualizing and historicizing it; it entailed affirming a post-traditional society, characterized by a decline in the influence of authority and custom and a commensurate rise in status of the rational and the scientific. In spite of the institutional weight of the authoritarian state that inadvertently or otherwise promoted it, modernity sought to foster not a monolithic society but a multiplicity of coexisting traditions, beliefs, and values, a dynamic, multifaceted social identity. Of course, without a range of concrete liberties, the emerging modernity was flawed, yet it had the potential to reconcile itself with such liberties; its ethos was receptive not only to wide-ranging social liberty but also to meaningful civic and political pluralism. A reasonably functioning socioeconomic, legal, educational, welfare, and communications infrastructure, social and geographic mobility, expanding life chances, the growth of literacy, awareness of alternative and better modes of life, the appeal of individual autonomy, demands for gender equality, and the desire to participate in political and civic life and to enjoy political, civil, and social liberties—all were tangible and emblematic signifiers of the evolving modernity.

The revolution of 1978–1979 was itself in many respects the product of and a reaction to the complex process of the unfolding modernity, the consequence of both its enabling and unsettling impacts. The secularization process intrinsic to modernity provoked the mobilization of religious and traditional attachments with the aim of countering secularist trends or reversing a process analogous to what Max Weber had, in the Western context, identified as the "disenchantment of the world." Traditionalism and its attendant consciousness and reactive impulse, together with the ideologization of Islam and the utilization of the redefined religious idiom and symbols for revolutionary political purposes, were rooted in modernity. They constituted emotionally charged responses to modernity, which was at the same time the condition of their emergence. The entire conceptual and ideological apparatus and idiom underlying the revolutionary movement were deeply rooted in the process of encountering, appropriating, or rejecting modernity, as were the utilized techniques and means of modern communications and the tactics of mass mobilization.

In their hybrid revolutionary vision, the rank-and-file Islamists were simultaneously regressive and progressive, archaic and avant-garde; Janus-like, they looked both to the future and to the past; they sought to negate the immediate past but, on the basis of invented or imagined traditions, to reaffirm and revive the distant past, characterized by pristine Islamic values and norms. Their rhetoric was both liberating and restraining. They wished to restore and reassert what they viewed as the country's indigenous cultural identity vis-à-vis Western cultural encroachment. At the same time, they shared the forward-looking standpoint of other revolutionaries in their desire to counter imperialism, institute distributive justice, empower the powerless, and replace the monarchy, which intrinsically sanctioned privilege, with a more egalitarian republican form of government that purported to rest on popular sovereignty. The revolution was thus traditionalist in terms of some of its idiom, tactics, and inchoate objective of fashioning an "Islamic" polity—a polity based on reinstated canons of piety and equity and other assumed norms of proper religious conduct, whether in private, public, or political life. Simultaneously it was modern, in the profound sense of appropriating the vocabulary, strategies, and tactics of mass populist revolutions and the inspirational legacy of the Enlightenment. There was a sublime optimism that solidarity and purposive collective action would be the catalysts for a more equitable and decent society and polity, that the future would in every respect be better than the past. Freedom, not just from foreign control but also from domestic oppression, was the most inspiring revolutionary slogan. Ayatollah Montazeri, a leading revolutionary figure, would later often affirm a widespread belief, even among many clerics, that the revolution was inspired by a desire for freedom and a rejection of dictatorship.[2]

The overall results of the revolution have ensured that the seminal ideals and aspirations traceable at least to 1906 are bound, for the foreseeable future, to dominate the Iranian political agenda. Iranian history over the past century can be described as a continuous and resilient constitutional revolution rooted in a steady and irreversible, albeit problematic and uneven, process of coming to terms with modernity. Modern values have become inextricably intermingled with Iranian civic culture; efforts to undo such values have only helped to make them more appealing. With the consolidation of clerical ascendancy, democratic aspirations, civic-nationalist values, and Persian cultural nationalism suffered in the short run but emerged stronger and more resonant than at any other time in Iranian history. Not surprisingly, the process of secularization facilitated by cultural and socio-economic forces and trends, both domestic and global, has received an inevitable boost from the very clerical rule that intended to reverse it. The sacralization of politics has resulted in the desacralization of politicized religion.

Inevitably the postrevolutionary turmoil and trauma and the emergence of clerical rule have led many Iranians to indulge in selective remembering and forgetting; some have sanitized the prerevolutionary era as a gilded age destroyed by reactionary fanatics and ignorant or manipulated masses. All revolutions inspire nostalgia and foster regret: in the words of Leszek Kolakowski, "No revolution has ever succeeded without bringing bitter disappointment almost in the very moment of victory."[3] It should not, however, be forgotten that it was the disastrous conduct of the Shah and a servile elite, enjoying the shortsighted support of Western powers, that distorted and undermined Iran's constitutional political evolution and paved the way for the revolutionary upheaval. Revolutions also constitute sobering and soul-searching experiences; they dampen unwarranted illusions and facile hopes. The Iranian revolution has been such an experience; thus, to paraphrase Hegel, the tears shed have not been in vain. Regretting their simplistic assumptions, at least some former revolutionaries have blamed themselves for denouncing despots but failing to combat despotism, let alone understanding the mechanism and forces sustaining it.[4]

The revolution of 1978–1979 severely shook traditional Iranian cultural sensibilities, the political culture, and conventional wisdom. Together with the end of the Cold War, it helped to demystify the abstract ideological leanings that were inattentive to the specificities of Iranian society. Exploding many myths, it has paved the way for the greater invigoration and resonance of a critical and rationalist mode of thought. The Iranians have, of course, paid an enormous price, and the path to establishing a democratic polity continues to be studded with numerous obstacles. The country was able to withstand the overwhelmingly dislocating impact of the revolution because of its material and socioeconomic resources, not to mention the strength of Iranian nationalism. Such a revolution could not have taken place or succeeded in a less socioeconomically stable and resource-rich society. After the Bolshevik revolution, European nations learned valuable lessons from the fate of Russia; similarly, states in the Middle East and beyond learned from what happened in Iran. In the unlikely event that a revolution similar to the one in Iran seems imminent elsewhere in the region, the states and their allies, domestic and foreign, are on the alert and know what price will have to be paid for complacency.

One of the common illusions of radical opponents of the monarchy in its final years was that any successor regime would be preferable to the existing one, that in no way could the political situation worsen. Many opponents of the present regime may entertain similar views. It is not difficult to understand why such assumptions become pervasive, but it cannot be denied that worse political situations are imaginable and possible. In thinking about the future, one may envisage a variety of scenarios that may or may not be feasible or appealing. Proponents of democratic change in Iran must carefully explore the feasibility of various scenarios, refuse to succumb to wishful thinking, and avoid facile Manichaean dichotomies. They may have good reason to reject the status quo, but they should not blindly opt for just any alternative. All reasonable advocates of change realize that not every change is for the better, that change is not synonymous with inexorable progress. A Hobbesian nightmare of brutish disorder and lingering turmoil can haunt any society bereft of the peaceful means of political transformation. Yet even in the most politically undesirable circumstances, the advocates of change, particularly those inspired by an unflinching spirit of enlightened patriotism, can not afford to be cavalier. There are those who have looked to outside powers for deliverance; it is doubtful whether they have adequately comprehended the potentially catastrophic implications of what they favor. A sensible opposition must carefully ponder not only the ends it seeks to pursue but also the means of realizing those ends.

With its intolerance of any organized or meaningful opposition, the Iranian regime continues to face the challenge of politically containing the growing rift separating the rulers from the ruled. It cannot, however, do so without abandoning its exclusionist character, without genuinely working to overcome the public's apathy or cynical disengagement—in short, without democratic concessions. Such concessions, the regime plausibly fears, will unrecognizably change or undermine it. But not making them or continuing effectively to disenfranchise the citizens is even more dangerous, as it will provoke intractable animosity and could engulf the whole society in protracted violence. The trajectory of Iranian constitutionalism in the last

100 years indicates that indifference to democratic aspirations will breed dangerous disaffection and prove costly to the rulers and the ruled alike. It was the growing belief in the unreformability of the monarchy that precipitated its overthrow. It must by now be obvious that the claimed benevolence of an authoritarian state will in no way extinguish demands for democratic governance and will only deepen societal alienation. Modern states everywhere have to validate themselves democratically, or purport to do so, and the only publicly acceptable form of legitimation is a nonfraudulent democratic one. In the course of a century-long struggle for democratic governance in Iran, imperialism, whether British, Russian, or later American, found its interests best served by sustaining authoritarian regimes. To attempt to link the historically rooted demands for democracy in contemporary Iran with the agenda of a foreign power, as certain functionaries of the regime continue to do, will not work; nor will it detract from the legitimacy and urgency of those demands.

Iran today exists in a region that has become dangerously unstable, particularly on its eastern and western borders. In a unipolar world, the United States aspires not only to consolidate its presence in the area but also to create an informal empire in the name of spreading "democracy." Unencumbered by international law, it has shown itself willing to act either on its own or in the name of the "international community"—a euphemism for the United States and other Western powers—to bully, destabilize, even overthrow "rogue" states. It does not, however, require unusual perceptiveness to realize that declarations of U.S. government support for democracy in Iran are likely to help not its advocates but its opponents. These declarations, in the context of the Iranian regime's proclaimed championing of the country's sovereign rights to develop nuclear sources of energy, will enable it to use nationalist ploys to mobilize support. Exploiting the situation, the regime will increase its rhetorical belligerence to galvanize its base; it will attempt to divert attention from its failings and to stimulate popular anxieties and fear of anarchy and the disintegration of the state. By creating a fortress state or through an undeclared state of emergency, the regime will be in a better position to suppress civil society and will more readily accuse its critics of fraternizing with the enemy. All this, together with the state's enhanced capacity for violence and repression triggered by a siege mentality, augurs ill for the ongoing democratic struggles and aspirations.

The fact that in the Middle East regimes are predominantly authoritarian, their societies gripped by a crisis of representation, makes them vulnerable. The ultimate antidote to this vulnerability is to cultivate not a politics of fear and confrontation but a politics of recognition. States that do not fear their own citizens need not fear outside forces. Such states adequately respond and adapt to the demands of their citizens, cultivate genuine public support, and regularly renegotiate and consolidate their legitimacy through a credible democratic process. States that continue to defy the democratic aspirations of their citizens, particularly in societies in which such aspirations have been historically salient, must awaken from their self-induced political slumber. They need to recognize, without illusions, the imperative of real democratic representation as the only means of preempting an impending catastrophe. To do so will surely be costly to the power holders, but failing to do so will be enormously costly to their nations. Democratic representation is the only reliable bulwark against threats from without and within, against growing disaffection leading to unrest and ruinous violence.

Alarmists might contend that Iran is sitting on a time bomb, that despite an apparent sense of normality, the country is politically, economically, socially, culturally, and emotionally in crisis. Observers with a stoic cast of mind may argue that societies can continue to muddle through deeply unfavorable conditions. Societies can and indeed have done so, but always at enormous cost, paid by later generations. Many observers of Iranian politics are of the opinion that politically Iran is a country adrift, with little or no clear sense of direction, and averse to nurturing reflective reason and meritorious leadership. One may feel that on the surface, and on the grounds of conventional logic, the ruling apparatus in Iran has politically little to sustain and perpetuate it, as it has lost its ideological grip on society and has forfeited whatever hegemony it may have enjoyed. And yet the prevailing regime seems to have its own "logic," which may sustain it indefinitely. Iranian society is in equal measure deeply politicized and politically demoralized. It reveals that a society and a people can live with a multiplicity of contradictions. As Ernest Gellner has persuasively argued, certain rules, principles, or beliefs function not because they are rationally coherent or logically consistent, but because they are not, and indeed are the very opposite.[5] Those accustomed to thinking rationally may sometimes find themselves ill equipped to comprehend the convoluted grid of misrule. One should perhaps marvel not at the cunning of reason, but at the cunning of unreason.

Of course, muddling through, no matter how cultivated it may have become as a way of running a country, is not a real option in the context of the highly complex and relentlessly competitive postindustrial globalization. Every state must devise viable strategies to ensure its interrelated economic and political strength and success. Doing this ultimately entails enlisting the real support of the people it claims to serve and represent. To varying degrees, visible or invisible coercion, manipulation, and deception are structurally intrinsic to all states; yet the strength and success of a state rest on its ability to reinforce the people's conviction that they are sovereign. A successful state must be able to persuade the citizens, or enough of them, that it is their bona fide trustee and agent; that it treats them noncoercively, transparently, and decently; that it does not deceive and manipulate them, and is in power at their behest, in order to protect and serve them. Such a state must be persuasively able to claim real commitment to rectifying unjustifiable inequalities. Legitimacy can sometimes be generated through the invisible operations of power, yet no state can survive without sustainable claims to legitimacy, that is, without the capacity to persuade the people whom it rules that it is politically and socioculturally representative of them; that it is legally constituted, administratively competent, and morally authoritative and deserving to rule. Such a state can best be characterized as a modern democratic republic.

In the words of one astute scholar of politics, "Human beings have done many more fetching and elegant things than invent and routinize the modern democratic republic. But, in face of their endlessly importunate, ludicrously indiscreet, inherently chaotic and always potentially murderous onrush of needs and longings, they have, even now, done very few things as solidly to their advantage."[6] A growing number of Iranians, too, have come to believe that they can achieve a real sense of national self-worth, as well as political and civic equality and pride, and realize their potential as empowered citizens only by moving toward such a form of governance. Only such a polity, they believe, will enable them to overcome the crisis of representation that has marred their political life. They have long come to view democracy as the most rational mode of governance. The perpetuation of authoritarian rule inflicts a cost on Iranian society that, in the current interconnected and yet brutally competitive world, the country cannot afford without permanently succumbing to the status of a third-rate, insular, repressive, crisis-ridden, and thus ultimately unstable polity.

Politics is a site not just of conflict but also of cooperation, which can best be promoted by recognizing the diverse range of human purposes and desires, including the aspiration of citizens for autonomous self-development in sociopolitical circumstances that are permissive and indeed enabling. Paternalism, whatever its provenance and justificatory apparatus, is anathema to such a conception of politics, as it seeks to nurture mental servitude, stifle individual autonomy, and ignore social, cultural, and moral diversity. No matter how harsh the retribution, Iranians in the twenty-first century will continue to resist oppression and abhor misrule. They will continue to register their profound dislike of their nonsovereign status and to defy authoritarianism and divine-right paternalism. Only a law-abiding government that avoids a coercive, brazen, manipulative, and deceptive attitude toward the citizenry, and respects their wishes by submitting to their real collective verdict at regular intervals, can claim to be legitimate and expect to enjoy their loyalty and respect. The likely alternatives to submitting to the orderly replacement of the ruling elite through fair and free elections, and on the basis of a democratic constitutional framework, are growing public alienation, simmering civil strife, a costly war of attrition, and potentially catastrophic disruption and violence. The halfhearted deployment or cynical manipulation of quasi-democratic procedures will eventually prove counterproductive, as coercive and repressive measures cannot be indefinitely sustained.

The expansion of the middle class, growing literacy (estimated in 2005 to be 86 percent for men and 73 percent for women), an increasing consciousness of the rights and entitlements of citizenship, the political experience and practical wisdom accrued from living through the revolution and its consequences, and the commensurate waning of illusions have resulted in a sober and yet insuppressible public spirit. A corollary to this has been a tremendous rise in the appeal of democratic ideals and a resilient, albeit battered, civil society. Iranian civil society is sustained by students, teachers, lawyers, writers, artists, journalists, and a host of other civically minded, democracy-seeking activists. The cause of these activists, particularly in the areas of human rights and the rights of women and children, received a boost when the activist lawyer Shirin Ebadi won the Nobel Peace Prize in 2003. Despite the absence of permissive conditions, whether openly or half-concealed, assertive or in tactical retreat, civil society in Iran has not been, and will not be, successfully stifled. It is nourished by a widespread desire for democratic change; it inhabits a sphere of civic engagement that may look private but is quintessentially public. It manifests itself in trenchant debates, whether loudly aired or whispered. It has shown itself to be morally sensitive, conscious of the need for balance between rights and responsibilities and between individual aspirations and communitarian sensibilities. It represents and sustains vigorous demands for an open and decent society; it is ultimately drawn toward an unencumbered modern democratic republic.

Crafting such a form of governance cannot be envisaged without drawing upon and amplifying the democratic political-intellectual resources originating with the Constitutional Revolution, and without relying on the indigenous forces long aspiring to representative democracy. Efforts in this direction will be fully in tune with other successful or continuing movements for democratic rule in the nonwestern world that enjoy a good deal of international moral support. There is no need for the invariably counterproductive interventions of outside powers, which often cynically invoke ideals such as democracy to advance their own imperial interests and agendas. Democratic governance in Iran has to be created by the Iranians themselves, who will have to act through the mechanisms of an inevitably politicized civil society, and rely on the collective resources of a resilient national community that has long seen itself as a self-confident nation. A democratic polity thus created needs a strong institutional framework and foundations, which must be carefully devised and nurtured. It cannot be meaningfully democratic without promoting a voluntary and unconstrained civic life and affirming the moral, political, and civil equality of citizens, irrespective of their circumstances and ascribed identities. It must be fully cognizant of Iranian historical specificities and cultural and spiritual sensibilities, and at the same time be recognizably modern and universalist. It must be anchored in values, norms, and practices that are both conducive to and constitutive of a decent society, and valid across cultural and geographic divides.

Such a project should not be equated with Americanization or with an embracing of neoliberalism as signaling the "end of history." No society with a sense of its own enduring culture can afford to ignore the pitfalls of globalization and its ruthless culture of greed and consumerism. Of course, the question of what dimensions of a culture are or are not to be reconsidered, or revitalized and actively appropriated by a dynamic society, can be legitimately debated only in an unconstrained public sphere, which is the proper venue for such debates. Iran is endowed with a rich repository of cultural resources, including traditional civic virtues, which can be mined by the more reflective and critical advocates of modernity. These resources can be tapped as part of a strategy to counter the coarser aspects of the global culture. A modern democratic republic would be in harmony with the more commendable components of modernity as well as with the democratic transformation of numerous other societies in the past fifty years. It would also constitute the desirable culmination of Iranian democratic struggles that began a century ago. It is not far-fetched to view its prospects with measured, yet real, optimism.

Abbreviations

Notes

Index

# Abbreviations

| | |
|---|---|
| AIOC | Anglo-Iranian Oil Company |
| Alam | Asadollah Alam, *Yaddashtha-ye Alam* (Alam's Diaries), ed. Ali-Naqi Alikhani, 5 vols. (vols. 1 and 5, Tehran, 1992 and 2003; vols. 2, 3, and 4, Bethesda, Md., 1993–1995) |
| APOC | Anglo-Persian Oil Company |
| BBC | British Broadcasting Corporation |
| BMAIS | British Military Attaché's Intelligence Summary |
| CSH | Donald Wilber, *Clandestine Service History: Overthrow of Premier Mossadeq of Iran, November 1952–August 1953* (n.p., 1954) |
| EIr | *Encyclopaedia Iranica*, 14 vols. (London, Boston, and New York, 1982–) |
| FCO | British Foreign and Commonwealth Office |
| FO | British Foreign Office |
| FRUS | *Foreign Relations of the United States*, various vols. (Washington, D.C.) |
| Ghani | Cyrus Ghani, ed., *Yaddashtha-ye Doktor Qasem Ghani* (Diaries of Doctor Qasem Ghani), 12 vols. (London, 1984) |
| HIOHP | Harvard Iranian Oral History Project, edited by Habib Ladjevardi |
| IJMES | *International Journal of Middle East Studies* |
| IPD | *Iran Political Diaries, 1881–1965*, gen. ed. Robert M. Burrell, 14 vols. (n.p., 1997) |
| IRP | Islamic Republican Party |
| Mozakerat | *Mozakerat-e Majles-e shaura-ye melli: ruznameh-ye rasmi-ye keshvar-e shahanshahi* (Proceedings of the Parliament) (Tehran) |
| NIOC | National Iranian Oil Company |

NIP                         New Iran Party (Iran-e Novin)

SAVAK                       Sazman-e ettela'at va amniyat-e keshvar (the state se-
                            curity and intelligence organization, 1957–1979)

SAVAK Documents             Markaz-e barrasi-ye asnad-e tarikhi, *Enqelab-e Islami
                            beh ravayat-e asnad-e SAVAK* (The Islamic Revolution
                            according to SAVAK documents), 16 vols. (Tehran,
                            1997–2005)

# Notes

Prologue

1. Tom Nairn, *The Enchanted Glass: Britain and Its Monarchy* (London, 1990), 96.
2. Emmanuel Le Roy Ladurie, *The Ancient Regime: A History of France, 1610–1774* (Oxford, 1991), 512.
3. John Dunn, "Revolution," in Terence Ball, James Farr, and Russell L. Hanson, eds., *Political Innovation and Conceptual Change* (Cambridge, 1989), 350–351.
4. Lewis A. Coser, *Masters of Sociological Thought* (New York, 1971), 233.
5. Steven Lukes, *Power: a Radical View,* 2d ed. (New York, 2005). Also of interest to historians is the work of the English historical sociologist Michael Mann; see his *The Sources of Social Power,* 2 vols. (Cambridge, 1986–1993).
6. For useful discussions of democracy see David Held, *Models of Democracy* (Stanford, 1987); and Robert A. Dahl, *On Democracy* (New Haven, 1998).
7. Bernard Lewis, *The Shaping of the Modern Middle East* (New York, 1994), 59.
8. Ernest Gellner, "Civil Society in Historical Context," *International Social Science Journal,* 43 (August 1991), 509.
9. See for instance John Rawls, *Political Liberalism* (New York, 1996); and Jürgen Habermas, *The Inclusion of the Other* (Cambridge, Mass., 1998).

1. Constitutional Trial and Error

1. Fereydun Adamiyat, *Majles-e avval va bohran-e azadi* (Tehran, n.d.); Adamiyat, *Ide'olozhi-ye Nahzat-e Mashrutiyat-e Iran* (Tehran, 1976), 348–460.
2. Mas'ud Salur and Iraj Afshar, eds., *Ruznameh-ye khaterat-e Ain al-Saltaneh,* 9 vols. (Tehran, 1995–2000), 7: 4921.
3. *CSH,* app. A, 4–5.
4. Sheikh Ebrahim Zanjani, *Khaterat,* ed. Gholam-Hosein Mirzasaleh (Tehran, 2000).
5. Text in Mohammad Torkaman, ed., *Modarres dar panj daureh-ye taqniniyeh-ye majles-e shaura-ye melli* (Tehran, 1993), 44.
6. Adamiyat, *Majles-e avval,* 29–50.
7. Ehtesham al-Saltaneh, *Khaterat,* ed. Mohammad-Mehdi Musavi (Tehran, 1988), 590–657.
8. Letter of the parliament to Mohammad Ali Shah, in Iraj Afshar, ed., *Khaterat va asnad-e Mostashar al-Dauleh Sadeq* (Tehran, 1982), 144–148.
9. Adamiyat, *Ide'olozhi,* 393–423.
10. Adamiyat, *Majles-e avval,* 39, 65.

11. Ibid., 131–148, 203–243; Majd al-Eslam Kermani, *Tarikh-e enhelal-e Majles,* ed. Mahmud Khalilpur, 3 vols. (Esfahan, 1968–1972), quoted in Adamiyat, *Majles-e avval,* 141.

12. Sayyed Hasan Taqizadeh, *Tarikh-e enqelab-e mashruteh-ye Iran* (Tehran, 2000), 76.

13. Rahimzadeh Safavi, *Asrar-e soqut-e Ahmad Shah,* ed. Kaveh Dehgan (Tehran, 1989), 286.

14. Statement by the Shah, in *Tarikh-e bidari-ye Iraniyan,* pt. II, ed. Ali-Akbar Sa'idi-Sirjani (Tehran, 1970), 139–140.

15. Mohammad Ali Shah's letter to Zahir al-Dauleh, in *Asnad-e tarikhi-ye vaqaye'-e mashruteh-ye Iran: Namehha-ye Zahir al-Dauleh,* ed. Jahangir Qa'em-maqami (Tehran, 1969), 37–39.

16. Houshang Sabahi, *British Foreign Policy in Persia* (London, 1990), 5.

17. Cyrus Ghani, *Iran and the Rise of Reza Shah* (London, 1998), 31.

18. Norman to Loraine, December 25, 1923, Loraine Papers, FO 1011/126, quoted in Sabahi, *British Foreign Policy in Persia,* 50.

19. Cosroe Chaqueri, *The Soviet Socialist Republic of Iran, 1920–1921: Birth of the Trauma* (Pittsburgh, 1995), 376.

20. Yahya Aryanpur, *Az Nima ta ruzgar-e ma* (Tehran, 1995), 210–211.

21. The Soviet government made a number of concessions and revoked the tsarist claims but acquired the right to enter Iran militarily in the event of a third power's using Iran to threaten the Soviet Union.

22. He was killed in July 1930 after having been given a pledge of safe conduct.

23. *Mozakerat,* October 4, 1922.

24. Ibid.

25. Loraine to Curzon, October 11, 1923, FO 371/7810/10954; Loraine to MacDonald, February 16, 1924, FO 371/10145/2430, quoted in Sabahi, *British Foreign Policy in Persia,* 196; George Churchill, in charge of the Persian desk at the Foreign Office, had hoped that Reza Khan would "abolish" the parliament altogether; minute by Churchill, October 9, 1922, FO 371/7809/10723, ibid.

26. Loraine to Curzon, Tehran, May 21, 1923, *IPD,* 6: 657–660. Loraine later wrote: "For a man who joined the former Cossack Brigade as a stable boy at the age of 15, who can only read with difficulty and hardly write at all, he has shown exceptional ability in handling matters quite outside his own military sphere. He has much common sense and a breadth of mind unusual in a peasant, and probably developed by the roving life he has led during his career in the army"; Loraine to Curzon, Tehran, July 16, 1923, Persia, Annual Report, 1922, FO 371/9051/E8057/8057/34. The British documents cited in this book are from the National Archives in London (formerly the Public Record Office).

27. BMAIS, no. 47, for week ending November 24, 1923, *IPD,* 6: 634.

28. In 1923 the monthly wage of an Iranian worker in the southern oil fields was barely 10 tomans (approximately £2 sterling); in 1928 a teacher's monthly salary was only 20 tomans (£4).

29. Loraine to Curzon, July 16, 1923, Persia, Annual Report, 1922, FO 371/9051/E8057/8057/34; Loraine to Chamberlain, August 10, 1925, FO 371/10840/5210, quoted in Sabahi, *British Foreign Policy in Persia,* 196.

30. Salur and Afshar, *Ruznameh*, 9: 7316–18.
31. BMAIS, no. 25, for week ending June 21, 1924, *IPD*, 7: 78–79.
32. BMAIS, no. 29, for week ending July 19, 1924, *IPD*, 7: 89–91.
33. As prime minister and later as Shah, Reza Khan benefited from the reformed tax system devised by Millspaugh and his team, which provided the government and the military with a reliable source of revenue.
34. "Sooner or later," Loraine had noted, "we shall have to decide whether to oppose the policy of centralisation, implying the necessity of resisting it by force in the last resort; or to support it and endeavour to guide it into safe channels by the judicious use of our support. I am myself strongly in favour of the latter course"; Loraine to Curzon, Tehran, May 21, 1923, *IPD*, 6: 657–660.
35. He lived as a virtual prisoner, and British pressure to ensure that his affairs be settled by an "equitable arrangement" bore no fruit; ailing for many years, he died, or was allegedly killed, on May 25, 1936.
36. Loraine described Reza Khan's attitude toward the British legation as "uniformly of a most friendly nature"; Loraine to MacDonald, Tehran, March 4, 1924, Persia, Annual Report, 1923, FO 371/10153/E3362/2635/34.
37. Mohammad-Taqi Bahar, *Tarikh-e mokhtasar-e ahzab-e siasi-ye Iran*, vol. 2 (Tehran, 1984), 70.
38. Soleiman Behbudi, *Khaterat*, ed. Gholam-Hosein Mirzasaleh (Tehran, 1993), 218–270.
39. Ibid., 247.
40. Ghani, *Iran and the Rise of Reza Shah*, 366–367; in the words of Loraine, Britain "was nervous of a change lest it should lead to a land slide. Reza Khan was determined to have the change and avoid the landslide. He had therefore to ascertain definitely that England would not oppose a change and make sure that Russia could not create a landslide. A categorical reaffirmation of their neutrality by His Majesty's Government reassured him on the first point; for the second point he relied, successfully, on his own rapidity of movement and the sense of the country." On October 28 Reza Khan saw Loraine "and gave him clearly to understand that matters would very shortly be pressed to an issue, and promised him that when the crisis was safely over, British questions would be seriously attended to"; Loraine to Chamberlain, April 8, 1926, Persia, Annual Report, 1925, *IPD*, 7: 359–360.
41. BMAIS, no. 25, for period ending October 3, 1925, *IPD*, 7: 327–330.
42. BMAIS, no. 26, for period ending October 17, 1925, *IPD*, 7: 331–335.
43. Bahar, *Tarikh-e mokhtasar*, 18.
44. Yahya Daulatabadi, *Hayat-e Yahya*, vol. 4 (Tehran, 1982), 316.
45. Mohammad Mosaddeq, speech in the parliament, *Mozakerat*, October 31, 1925.
46. Davar, speech in the parliament, ibid.

## 2. Pahlavist Absolutism

1. Yahya Daulatabadi, *Hayat-e Yahya*, vol. 4 (Tehran, 1982), 320.
2. BMAIS, no. 31, for period ending December 26, 1925, *IPD*, 7: 351.
3. Wipert von Blücher, *Zeitenwende in Iran: Erlebnisse und Beobachtungen* (Biberach an der Riss, 1949), 218.

4. Clive to Chamberlain, Tehran, January 26, 1927, Persia, Annual Report, 1926, *IPD*, 7: 545–547.

5. Mohammad Mosaddeq, *Kapitolasion va Iran* (November 1914), reprinted in Iraj Afshar, ed., *Mosaddeq va masa'el-e hoquq va siasat* (Tehran, 2003), 39–78.

6. Von Blücher, *Zeitenwende in Iran*, 219.

7. Kaveh Bayat, *Shuresh-e ashayer-e Fars, 1307–1309 shamsi* (Tehran, 1986).

8. Clive to Henderson, Tehran, April 30, 1930, Persia, Annual Report, 1929, FO 371/4543/E2445/522/34.

9. It has been argued that enforced sedentarization in Lorestan, Fars, Azarbaijan, and Khorasan in 1933 and 1937 "took a very brutal and in some cases, genocidal, form"; Kaveh Bayat, "Riza Shah and the Tribes: An Overview," in Stephanie Cronin, ed., *The Making of Modern Iran: State and Society under Riza Shah, 1921–1941* (London, 2003), 217.

10. Baqer Aqeli, *Reza Shah va qoshun-e mottahed al-shekl, 1300–1320* (Tehran, 1998), 212–378.

11. Stephanie Cronin, *The Army and the Creation of the Pahlavi State in Iran, 1910–1926* (London, 1997), 155–157; Aqeli, *Reza Shah*, 258–269. Sheibani, commander of operations against the southern tribes in 1930 and governor general of Fars, was court-martialed in 1931 on charges "framed by the Shah" and condemned to two years in prison. According to the British legation, the Shah had not forgotten the refusal of Sheibani, "the best known officer in the army," to sign the warrant for the execution of Haim, which the Shah "was eventually obliged much later to sign himself"; Hoare to Simon, June 12, 1932, Persia, Annual Report, 1931, *IPD*, 9: 181.

12. Ali Asghar Zargar, *Tarikh-e ravabet-e siasi-ye Iran va Englis dar daureh-ye Reza Shah*, trans. Kaveh Bayat (Tehran, 1993), 136–139.

13. Clive to Chamberlain, Tehran, May 21, 1928, Persia, Annual Report, 1927, FO 371/13069/E2897/2897/34.

14. Ibid.

15. Iraj Afshar, ed., *Khaterat-e Sardar As'ad Bakhtiari* (Tehran, 1993), 206–217.

16. Hosein Makki, *Tarikh-e bist saleh-ye Iran*, vol. 4 (Tehran, 1982), 112.

17. Sayyed Hasan Taqizadeh, *Zendegi-ye tufani*, ed. Iraj Afshar (Tehran, 1993), 209.

18. Ne'matollah Mehrkhah, ed., *Reza Shah az zaban-e mardom, rejal, matbu'at, darbarian, omara-ye artesh* (Tehran, 1946), 116.

19. Mehdi-Qoli Hedayat, *Khaterat va khatarat* (Tehran, 1996), 386.

20. Clive to Henderson, Tehran, January 9, 1930, *IPD*, 8: 577–579.

21. Hoare to Simon, June 12, 1932, Persia, Annual Report, 1931, *IPD*, 9: 97–98.

22. Marion Rezun, "Reza Shah's Court Minister: Teymourtash," *IJMES*, 12 (1980), 132.

23. Zargar, *Tarikh-e ravabet*, 287–326.

24. Taqizadeh, *Zendegi*, 232–235.

25. As the British legation admitted, an article titled "Drop the Pilot" in *The Times* of January 9, 1933, contributed significantly to the Shah's suspicions; the war minister, who himself was later to lose his life on the Shah's orders, also believed that this article "had sealed" Teymurtash's fate. Hoare to Simon, February 24, 1934, Persia, Annual Report, 1933, FO 371/17090/E1620/1620/34.

26. Taqizadeh, *Zendegi*, 233.

27. Von Blücher, *Zeitenwende in Iran*, 289; Afshar, *Khaterat-e Sardar As'ad*, 236.

28. Von Blücher, *Zeitenwende in Iran*, 178.

29. Afshar, *Khaterat-e Sardar As'ad*, 223.

30. Mehrkhah, *Reza Shah*, 115.

31. Arsalan Khal'atbari, "Mas'ulan-e daureh-ye diktatori," *Ra'd-e Emruz*, February 28, 1944.

32. Reader Bullard to Viscount of Halifax, February 24, 1940, FO 371/24582, Y/W04702.

33. Ebrahim Khajehnuri, *Bazigaran-e asr-e tala'i* (Tehran, 1978), 97–104; Abolhasan Ebtehaj, *Khaterat*, vol. 1 (London, 1991), 30–31.

34. Hedayat, *Khaterat*, 370–420.

35. Allahyar Saleh, "Iran-e zaman-e Reza Shah," in Iraj Afshar, ed., *Parvandeh-ye Saleh* (Tehran, 2005), 48–58.

36. Clive to Henderson, Tehran, July 14, 1929, Persia, Annual Report, 1928, *IPD*, 8: 281.

37. Mallet to Simon, Tehran, July 14, 1933, *IPD*, 9: 436.

38. Hoare to Simon, February, 24, 1934, Persia, Annual Report, 1933, FO 371/17090/E1620/1620/34.

39. Ebtehaj, *Khaterat*, 51.

40. Mas'ud Salur and Iraj Afshar, eds., *Ruznameh-ye khaterat-e Ain al-Saltaneh*, vol. 10 (Tehran, 2001), 7719.

41. Gholam-Hosein Zargari-Nejad, ed., *Khaterat-e Sepahbod Ahmadi*, vol. 1 (Tehran, 1994), 293–294.

42. Von Blücher, *Zeitenwende in Iran*, 330.

43. Mehrkhah, *Reza Shah*, 122–123.

44. Charles C. Hart, dispatch 1339 (891.44/4), January 26, 1933, quoted in Mohammad Gholi Majd, *Great Britain and Reza Shah: The Plunder of Iran, 1921–1942* (Gainesville, Fla., 2001), 154.

45. Mehrkhah, *Reza Shah*, 22–23, 106.

46. In 1938 diplomatic relations with France were suspended because of criticism of the Shah in a French newspaper. Diplomatic relations with the United States had also been suspended in March 1936 following the brief arrest of the Iranian minister to Washington for speeding and the refusal of the U.S. authorities to apologize. Relations were eventually restored in January 1940.

47. Bullard to Viscount of Halifax, February 24, 1940, FO 371/24582, Y/W04702.

48. Von Blücher, *Zeitenwende in Iran*, 225.

49. Ibid., 282.

50. BMAIS, no. 16, for period ending August 9, 1941, *IPD*, 11: 378.

51. "Khaterat-e malekeh Turan," *Tarikh-e mo'aser-e Iran*, 2 (Spring 1990), 152–153.

52. Charles C. Hart, dispatch 282 (891.00B/36), January 1, 1931, quoted in Majd, *Great Britain and Reza Shah*, 148.

53. BMAIS, no. 23, for period ending November 5, 1938, *IPD*, 10: 568.

54. Hedayat, *Khaterat*, 403.

55. Von Blücher, *Zeitenwende in Iran*, 331.

56. Ali-Akbar Siasi, *Gozaresh-e yek zendegi*, vol. 1 (London, 1987), 76–77.

57. Ferdowsi has been described as "an actor of heroic stature, a poet of supreme ge-

nius who should be a living embodiment of the rebirth of Persian pride, of Persian self-respect, of Persian consciousness"; A. J. Arberry, *Classical Persian Literature* (London, 1994), 42.

58. Soleiman Behbudi, *Khaterat,* ed. Gholam-Hosein Mirzasaleh (Tehran, 1993), 395.

59. Universal free primary education was enacted by the parliament in 1943, but full implementation was a slow process.

60. The private schools run by various religious minorities were gradually brought under state control. According to one account, Baha'i schools in Tehran "enjoyed particular prestige" before and after Reza Shah's accession, enrolling children from privileged non-Baha'i backgrounds; Amin Banani, *The Modernization of Iran, 1921–1941* (Stanford, 1961), 96. Baha'i schools in Tehran and in several other cities were closed down by the Ministry of Education in December 1934 on grounds of having refused to obey an order not to close on December 6, the anniversary of the Bab's death. In Tehran more than 1,500 boys and girls were affected and "a much greater number in the provinces." The ministry sought to accommodate the students and teachers in non-Baha'i schools. Knatchbull-Hugessen to Simon, Tehran, February 5, 1935, Persia, Annual Report, 1934, *IPD,* 9: 657.

61. M. Hashem Pesaran, "The Economy in the Pahlavi Period," in *EIr,* 8: 145.

62. For a partial list of these factories see Arthur C. Millspaugh, *Americans in Persia* (Washington, D.C., 1946), 30. According to Millspaugh, "A government corporation supervised carpet manufacturing, handled the commercial side of the industry, and made progress in the rehabilitation of this ancient craft."

63. Salur and Afshar, *Ruznameh,* 8040–41.

64. Hedayat, *Khaterat,* 403.

65. Ahmad Kasravi, *Zendegani-ye man* (Tehran, 1944), 312–343.

66. Noting that Reza Shah hated "the idea of his country's backwardness" and longed "passionately to urge it forward," the British minister in Tehran added that the Shah "confessed to me on one occasion quite spontaneously that he could never go to Europe because he could not bear to see the contrast between Europe and his country"; Knatchbull-Hugessen to Eden, January 28, 1936, Persia, Annual Report, 1935, *IPD,* 10: 123.

67. Migration was not merely an ecologically determined activity but was intrinsic to the meaning-system defining the pastoral-nomadic way of life. In his discussion of the Basseri nomads of southern Iran, Fredrik Barth refers to migration as "the central rite of nomadic society," and to the "migration cycle" as "a primary schema for the conceptualization of time and space." He considers "the fact that many nomads, after the external disturbance of enforced sedentarization, resumed migratory life in spite of economic costs" an indication of their "emotional engagement" in the migration and in "*the meanings* implicit in the sequence of activities" associated with it. Fredrik Barth, *Nomads of South Persia: The Basseri Tribe of the Khamseh Confederacy* (London, 1964), 153.

68. Figures for casualties vary; officially the number of dead and injured was 28 and 60, respectively. The British estimated that 128 had died and up to 300 had been injured, while some 800 were arrested. BMAIS, no. 15, for period ending July 27, 1935, *IPD,* 10: 30. Later sources claim much higher casualty figures.

69. See further Touraj Atabaki and Erik J. Zürcher, *Men of Order: Authoritarian Modernization under Atatürk and Reza Shah* (London, 2004).

70. Yahya Aryanpur, *Az Nima ta ruzgar-e ma* (Tehran, 1995), 12–13.

71. In early August 1941 Churchill instructed the Foreign Office to revert to using "Persia" instead of "Iran"; in recent years the revival of the designation "Persia" has been spearheaded by Ehsan Yarshater, emeritus professor at Columbia University and editor of the *Encyclopaedia Iranica*.

72. Hoare to Simon, February 1934, Persia, Annual Report, 1933, *IPD*, 9: 527.

73. Clive to Chamberlain, Tehran, January 26, 1927, Persia, Annual Report, 1926, *IPD*, 7: 596.

74. The military proved to be more ill-prepared, ramshackle, and demoralized than even its severest critics anticipated. "The causes of the poor morale of the Persian troops," noted the British military attaché, "are not hard to find: their rank and file underfed and underpaid; senior officers corrupt, lack of training for modern warfare and in the use of the very good weapons they possessed; and conviction prevailing among certain officers that the war against Great Britain and Russia was a madness of the Shah"; BMAIS, nos. 18–20, for August 1941–September 24, 1941, *IPD*, 11: 387.

75. Even at the peak of the regime's repressive policies, strikes by students, for instance, did occur—in the spring of 1937 among students of the technical (German) school, and in November 1939 by medical students at Tehran University.

76. Salur and Afshar, *Ruznameh*, 7684–85.

77. Parviz Natel-Khanlari's address, *Nakhostin kongreh-ye nevisandegan-e Iran, 1325* (Tehran, 1946), 50.

78. *Majalleh-ye Museqi*, no. 1 (March 15, 1939), quoted in Aryanpur, *Az Nima*, 72.

79. Ruhollah Khomeini, *Kashf al-asrar* (n.p., 1941).

80. Anvar Khameh'i, *Panjah nafar va seh nafar* (Tehran, 1983), 25.

81. "He did things," observed Millspaugh, "to the people and for the people. Little was done by them"; his "most damaging failure lay in the means that he employed: dictatorship, corruption and terror"; Millspaugh, *Americans in Persia*, 35–36.

82. Ibid., 26.

83. Banani, *Modernization*, 41.

84. Behbudi, *Khaterat*, 395.

85. Mohsen Sadr, *Khaterat-e Sadr al-Ashraf* (Tehran, 1985), 379.

86. One writer has asserted: "It definitely cannot be denied that without the former Court Minister as an obstacle in their path, the actual task of convincing the Shah was made significantly easier for the British"; Rezun, "Reza Shah's Court Minister," 132.

87. Taqizadeh, *Zendegi*, 364.

88. Von Blücher, *Zeitenwende in Iran*, 231.

89. Ibid., 311.

90. On June 26 Tehran radio questioned whether attacks on the Shah reflected the views of the German government or of the announcer himself. The Germans blamed the announcer, Bahram Shahrokh, son of Arbab Keikhosrau Shahrokh, the prominent Zoroastrian member of parliament and head of the

Zoroastrian community in Iran. In early July the latter was found dead in a Tehran street.

91. Bullard to Eden, Annual Political Report, 1940, February 2, 1941, *IPD,* 11: 314.

92. BMAIS, no. 15, for period ending July 26, 1941, *IPD,* 11: 374–376.

93. Abbas-Qoli Golsha'ian, *Gozashteh-ha va andishehha-ye zendegi, ya khaterat-e man,* vol. 1 (Tehran, 1998), 381.

94. It was stated in the parliament that in its fourteen years of operation the fund had earned £31 million, of which £3 million had been used for the purchase of gold and the rest spent; Dreyfus (American Legation, Tehran) to the Secretary of State, October 1, 1941 (D. 128), 891.00/6363/Anglo-Iranian/50, National Archives and Records Administration, College Park, Md.

95. Bullard to Eden, Annual Political Report, 1940, February 2, 1941, *IPD,* 11: 308.

96. "It was humiliating," wrote Bullard, "to have to submit to such a blackmail but the demands came at a most difficult moment of the war and it was not thought worthwhile to precipitate a crisis which might perhaps interfere with our oil supplies"; ibid.

97. Ibid., 307.

98. Reader Bullard, *Letters from Tehran: A British Ambassador in World War II Persia,* ed. E. C. Hodgkin (London, 1991), 140. Prime Minister Churchill later wrote to the foreign secretary: "Sir Reader Bullard has a contempt for all Persians which however natural is detrimental to his efficiency and our interests"; ibid., 187.

99. Taqizadeh, *Zendegi,* 252.

100. Bullard to Eden, Annual Political Report, 1940, February 2, 1941, *IPD,* 11: 321.

101. Ebtehaj, *Khaterat,* 69.

102. Abbas-Qoli Golsha'ian, "Yaddashtha," in Ghani, 11: 530.

103. Ibid., 532–533; Bullard, *Letters from Tehran,* 69.

104. Bullard, *Letters from Tehran,* 75.

105. Golsha'ian, *Gozashteh-ha,* 443–486.

106. Mohammad-Reza Abbasi and Behruz Tayarani, eds., *Khaterat-e Nasrollah Entezam* (Tehran, 1992), 7–13.

107. Saleh, "Iran-e zaman-e Reza Shah," 53.

108. Golsha'ian, "Yaddashtha," 604.

3. Restoration of Parliamentary Politics

1. Abbas-Qoli Golsha'ian, "Yaddashtha," in Ghani, 11: 522–604; see especially 562. Bullard also reported that the Shah "has just ordered some useless building operation for himself to be continued and is asking whether he cannot send someone to the north to see how his estates are getting on"; Bullard to FO, September 14, 1941, in Reader Bullard, *Letters from Tehran: A British Ambassador in World War II Persia,* ed. E. C. Hodgkin (London, 1991), 79.

2. Allahyar Saleh, "Iran-e zaman-e Reza Shah," in Iraj Afshar, ed., *Parvandeh-ye Saleh* (Tehran, 2005), 58.

3. Golsha'ian, "Yaddashtha," 542.

4. Knatchbull-Hugessen to Eden, January 28, 1936, Persia, Annual Report, 1935, *IPD,* 10: 123. The same official had also noted that Iran will "never be blessed with an

organized form of government unless it has a strong man at the centre"; Knatchbull-Hugessen to FO, FO 371/E906/203/34, no. 279, January 1936, quoted in Marion Rezun, "Reza Shah's Court Minister: Teymourtash, *IJMES*, 12 (1980), 122.

5. In August 1940 the British had started broadcasting in Persian from Delhi, but could not compete with broadcasts from Berlin.

6. BMAIS, nos. 18–20, for August 24–September 24, 1941, *IPD*, 11: 388.

7. Bullard to FO, September 27, 1941, in *Letters from Tehran*, 84.

8. Mahmud E'temadzadeh, *Az har dari: Zendeginameh-ye siasi-ejtema'i*, vol. 1 (Tehran, 1991), 35.

9. Golsha'ian, "Yaddashtha," 603.

10. Bullard to Eden, Annual Political Report for 1941, June 17, 1942, IOR L/P&S/12/3472 A.

11. BMAIS, nos. 18–20, for August 24–September 24, 1941, *IPD*, 11: 385.

12. Memorandum of Conversation, by the Under Secretary of State (Welles), Washington, D.C., September 23, 1941, in *FRUS*, 1941, 3: 461–462.

13. Giving vent to the prevailing anti–Reza Shah sentiments, one writer referred to him as "the Mussolini of Savadkuh" (Reza Shah's birthplace); Ali Javaherkalam, *Ra'd-e Emruz*, January 30, 1944.

14. "Osul-e asasi-ye maram-e Hezb-e Tudeh," *Rahbar*, February 12, 14, 1943.

15. *Rahbar*, May 7, 1943.

16. Morteza Qasemi, "Hejab-e zanha," *Rahbar*, July 17, 1944; Naser Vosuqi, "Zaghha-ye siah," *Rahbar*, July 27, 1944; see also ibid., October 1, 1944.

17. Naser Pakdaman, "Dar bareh-ye qatl-e Kasravi," *Nameh-ye kanun-e nevisandegan-e Iran (dar tab'id)*, 2 (March 1990), 179–213.

18. Ibid., 203.

19. Ahmad Kasravi, *Sarnevesht-e Iran cheh khahad bud?* (1945; reprint, Cologne, n.d.), 33.

20. Recent research in the Soviet archives has confirmed that the autonomy movement in Iranian Azarbaijan was entirely engineered and sustained by the Soviet government and its proxies in Soviet Azerbaijan. Despite talks of autonomy it had clear secessionist aims and collapsed after the Soviets, having reached an understanding with the Iranian government, abandoned it. Jemil Hesenli, *Faraz-o-forud-e ferqeh-ye demokrat-e Azarbaijan*, trans. Mansur Homami (Tehran, 2004).

21. *Nasim-e Shemal (Mard-e Emruz)*, October 17, 1947.

22. Fereydun Keshavarz, *Man mottaham mikonam komiteh-ye markazi-ye hezb-e tudeh ra* (Tehran, 1978), 97–101.

23. Gholam-Reza Nejati, ed., *Shast sal khedmat va moqavemat: Khaterat-e mohandes Mehdi Bazargan*, vol. 1 (Tehran, 1998), 242.

24. Taqizadeh, letters to Qavam and Ala, in Iraj Afshar, ed., *Namehha-ye Landan* (Tehran, 1996), 7–17, 27–35.

25. Sa'ed to Taqizadeh, July 20, 1943, in Iraj Afshar, ed., *Namehha-ye Tehran* (Tehran, 2000), 249–256.

26. Bullard to FO, October 16, 1941, in *Letters from Tehran*, 89.

27. For more on this period, see Fakhreddin Azimi, *Iran: The Crisis of Democracy, 1941–1953* (London, 1989).

28. Ibid., 63–79.

29. Bullard to FO, January 20, 1944, FO 371/40186.

30. Ahmad Qavam, "Arizeh-ye sargoshadeh," *Bakhtar-e Emruz*, April 8, 1950; Ebrahim Hakimi, "Pasokh beh nameh-ye Qavam," ibid.; Qavam, "Pasokh beh nameh-ye Hakim al-Molk," *Bakhtar-e Emruz*, July 3, 1950.

31. Le Rougetel to FO, August 16, 1949, FO 371/75466.

32. Lawford to FO, October 13, 1949, FO 371/75466.

33. "E'lamiyeh-ye doktor Mosaddeq," *Bakhtar-e Emruz*, January 24, 1950.

34. Mohammad Mosaddeq, *Khaterat va ta'allomat-e Mosaddeq*, ed. Iraj Afshar (Tehran, 1986), 209–224, 237.

35. See *Jam'iyat-e Fada'iyan-e Islam beh ravayat asnad*, ed. Ahmad Gol-Mohammadi, 2 vols. (Tehran 2003), esp. vol. 2.

36. *CSH*, app. B, 21.

37. Mohammad-Ebrahim Amir-Teymur Kalali, *Nagoftehha-i az daulat-e doktor Mosaddeq*, ed. Morteza Rasulipur (Tehran 2001), 118–132.

38. Mohammad Mosaddeq, letter to the National Front, *Ahang-e Sharq (Shahed)*, December 31, 1949.

39. Mosaddeq, *Khaterat*, 288.

40. See further Fakhreddin Azimi, "Unseating Mosaddeq: The Configuration and Role of Domestic Forces," in Mark J. Gasiorowski and Malcolm Byrne, eds., *Mosaddeq and the Coup of August 1953* (Syracuse, N.Y., 2004), 27–101.

41. Qavam, "Arizeh-ye sargoshadeh" and "Pasokh be nameh-ye Hakim al-Molk"; Sayyed Hasan Taqizadeh, *Zendegi-ye tufani*, ed. Iraj Afshar (Tehran, 1993), 301–303.

42. *CSH*, 22–36.

43. Makins to FO, May 21, 1953, FO 371/104659.

44. Jalil Bozorgmehr, ed., *Mosaddeq dar mahkameh-ye nezami* (Tehran, 1990); *Doktor Mohammad Mosaddeq dar dadgah-e tajdid-e nazar-e nezami* (Tehran, 1986); *Doktor Mohammad Mosaddeq va residegi-ye farjami dar divan-e keshvar* (Tehran, 1988).

45. Mosaddeq, *Khaterat*, 218, 250.

46. Mohammad Mosaddeq, response to the leaders of the parliamentary groups Keshvar and Ettehad, *Bakhtar-e Emruz*, June 27, 1953.

## 4. The Trajectories of Monarchism

1. Mohammad-Ali Movahhed, *Khab-e ashofteh-ye naft*, vol. 2 (Tehran, 1999), 869.

2. Stevens to Shuckburgh, June 8, 1955, FO 371/114810.

3. Thomas L. Hughes to Secretary of the State, July 31, 1967, Pol.14 IRAN. Unless otherwise specified, the U.S. documents cited in this book are State Department documents obtained under the Freedom of Information Act.

4. Philip Clock, American Embassy, Tehran, to Department of State, July 3, 1956, D.5, 788.00/7-356.

5. American Embassy, Tehran, to Department of State, April 27, 1957, D.974, 778.00/4-2757.

6. Manuchehr Eqbal, speech in the parliament, *Mozakerat*, October 29, 1957.

7. Russell to FO, November 6, 1957, FO 371/12075.

8. American Embassy, Tehran, to Department of State, May 3, 1960, D.698, 788.00/5-360.

9. Harrison to Stevens, February 2, 1959, FO 371/140787.

10. *Keyhan,* April 24, 1957.

11. Stevens to Selwyn Lloyd, August 20, 1958, FO 371/133006.

12. American Embassy, Tehran, to Department of State, May 3, 1960.

13. Mohammad Reza Pahlavi, *Mission for My Country* (London, 1961).

14. Minute by Roger Stevens, August 18, 1959, FO 371/140789.

15. Russell to Selwyn Lloyd, October 27, 1958, FO 371/133007.

16. Charles Stelle, American Embassy, Tehran, to Department of State, March 5, 1958, D.791, 788.00/3-558.

17. American Embassy, Tehran, to Department of State, July 20, 1957, D.83, 788.0/7-2057.

18. Stevens to Selwyn Lloyd, March 24, 1958, FO 371/133004.

19. Harrison to Stevens, May 5, 1960, FO 371/149756.

20. Alam, 1: 368.

21. American Embassy, Tehran, to Department of State, May 14, 1959, D.839, 101.21-NIS/5-1459.

22. American Embassy, Tehran, to Department of State, July 29, 1961, D.64, 788.00/7-2961.

23. American Embassy, Tehran, to Department of State, February 8, 1962, D.368, 788.00/2-862.

24. Alam, 1: 368.

25. See also Chapter 8.

26. Miss A. K. S. Lambton's impressions of Iran—Summer of 1956, FO 371/120714.

27. A. K. S. Lambton, *The Persian Land Reform, 1962–1966* (Oxford, 1969), 56–58.

28. American Embassy, Tehran, to Department of State, December 29, 1962, A.404, 788.00/12-2-2962.

29. Harrison to Hiller, November 17, 1962, FO 371/164186.

30. American Embassy, Tehran, to Department of State, November 28, 1962, A.342, 788.00/11-2862.

31. Harrison to FO, November 29, 1962, FO 371/164186.

32. American Embassy, Tehran, to Department of State, January 14, 1963, A.446, 788.00/1-1763.

33. Minute by Goodchild, August 9, 1962, FO 371/164185.

34. Harrison to Hiller, December 15, 1962, FO 371/170373.

35. Jamshid Zargam-Borujeni, *Daulatha-ye Iran* (Tehran, 1971), 377–378.

36. Alam, 1: 206.

37. American Embassy, Tehran, to Department of State, May 14, 1959, D.839, 101.21-NIS/5-1459.

38. Dashti, letter to the Shah, June 1963, in Ali Dashti, *Avamel-e Soqut,* ed. Mehdi Mahuzi (Tehran, 2002), 181–192.

39. American Embassy, Tehran, to Department of State, February 14, 1962, D.374, 788.00/2-1462.

40. Alam, 2: 168.

41. Wright to the Secretary of State for Foreign and Commonwealth Affairs, April 20, 1971, FCO 17/1516.

42. Wright to Butler, 16 September 1964, FO 371/175712.

43. American Embassy, Tehran, to Department of State, October 27, 1964, A.303, DEF 15-3 Iran 2/5.

44. Mohammad Ali Safari, *Qalam va siasat,* vol. 2 (Tehran, 1994), 661–717.

45. American Embassy, Tehran, to Department of State, October 27, 1964.

46. Talbot to Rusk, December 19, 1964, U.S. Department of State, Central Files, FOL 15, Iran, in *FRUS, 1964–1968,* 22: 118.

47. Wright to Morris, October 1964, FO 371/175712.

48. Text in Hamid Algar, ed. and trans., *Islam and Revolution: Writings and Declarations of Imam Khomeini* (Berkeley, 1981), 181–188.

49. American Embassy, Tehran, to Department of State, October 27, 1964.

50. Paper prepared by Department of State, January 7, 1965, in *FRUS, 1964–1968,* 22: 123, 124.

51. American Embassy, Tehran, to Department of State, February 12, 1966, A.559, Pol.15-1.

52. American Embassy, Tehran, to Department of State, February 4, 1965, A.408, Pol.2-3 IRAN.

53. American Embassy, Tehran, to Department of State, February 12, 1966.

54. Open letter to Prime Minister Hoveyda, April 16, 1967, in Algar, *Islam and Revolution,* 189–193.

55. American Embassy, Tehran, to Department of State, August 17, 1965, A.105, Pol.2 IRAN.

56. American Embassy, Tehran, to Department of State, February 12, 1966.

57. Wright to Morris, January 30, 1965, FO 371/180781.

58. Ramsbotham to the Secretary of State for Foreign and Commonwealth Affairs, December 22, 1972, FCO 8/2049.

59. American Embassy, Tehran, to Department of State, May 3, 1965, A.567, Pol. IRAN.

60. Wright to Morris, September 1, 1966, FO 371/186664.

61. American Embassy, Tehran, to Department of State, February 20, 1967, A.448, Pol.2.3 IRAN.

62. Wright to Brown, January 23, 1967, FCO 17/351.

63. Ehsan Naraqi, Interview, *Tarikh-e mo'aser-e Iran,* 6, no. 24 (Winter 2002), 221; for Naraqi's account of Iran on the eve of the revolution see *Des palais du chah aux prisons de la Révolution* (Paris, 1991), pt. 1.

64. American Embassy, Tehran, to Department of State, April 16, 1975, A.75, P750 074-0998.

65. American Embassy, Tehran, to Department of State, July 10, 1975, A.151, P750 118-0729.

66. American Embassy, Tehran, to Department of State, April 16, 1975.

67. Alam, 1: 346.

68. Alam, 4: 52–53.

69. Alam, 1: 396.

70. Alam, 3: 37.

71. Ibid., 129.

72. Fereydun Mahdavi, quoted in Abbas Milani, *Persian Sphinx: Amir Abbas Hoveyda and the Riddle of the Iranian Revolution* (Washington, D.C., 2000), 275.

73. Alam, 1: 413.

74. Alam, 5: 216.

75. Mohammad Yeganeh, *Khaterat*, HIOHP (Tehran, 2005), 252–253.

76. Ali-Naqi Alikhani, *Khaterat*, ed. Gholam-Reza Afkhami (Tehran, 2002), 220–262.

77. American Embassy, Tehran, to Department of State, June 30, 1974, A.099, P74-73-135.

78. Alam, 2: 407.

79. Alam, 3: 98.

80. Alam, 4: 166.

81. Alam, 1: 413–414.

82. American Embassy, Tehran, to Department of State, June 30, 1974.

83. Alam, 4: 331.

84. Alam, 3: 34.

85. American Embassy, Tehran, to Department of State, June 30, 1974.

86. Alam, 4: 336.

87. American Embassy, Tehran, to Department of State, July 10, 1975.

88. Alam, 5: 190.

89. Ibid., 198.

90. American Embassy, Tehran, to Department of State, July 10, 1975.

91. Ibid.

92. Alam, 5: 136, 170.

93. Ibid., 135.

94. Mohammad Reza Pahlavi, *Answer to History* (New York, 1980), 124.

95. American Embassy, Tehran, to Department of State, June 30, 1974.

96. Alam, 5: 404.

97. American Embassy, Tehran, to Department of State, July 8, 1976, A.123, P760 105-0912.

## 5. Revolution

1. American Embassy, Tehran, to Secretary of State, Washington, D.C., July 25, 1977, A.124, P770 123-0763.

2. Bakhtiar was assassinated in Paris in August 1991; Sanjabi served briefly as foreign minister in the Bazargan government, but resigned and went into exile; he died in the United States in July 1995. Foruhar, a veteran political prisoner under the Shah, also acted as a Bazargan minister but became a vocal opponent of the Islamic regime; he and his wife were murdered in Tehran in November 1998.

3. Homayun was one of the officials detained on the Shah's orders, along with Hoveyda and Nasiri, in November 1978. His account of the regime contains incisive observations; Daryush Homayun, *Diruz va farda* (Washington, D.C., 1981).

4. Alam, 4: 313.

5. American Embassy, Tehran, to Department of State, June 30, 1974, A.099, P74-73-135.

6. American Embassy, Tehran, to Secretary of State, Washington, D.C., July 25, 1977.

7. Anthony Parsons, *Pride and the Fall* (London, 1984), 54–55; describing the play as a "bizarre and disgusting extravaganza" and a "grotesquerie" that "aroused a storm

of protest," Parsons recalled "mentioning it to the Shah, adding that, if the same play had been put on, say in the main street of Winchester (Shiraz is the Iranian equivalent of a cathedral city), the actors and sponsors would have found themselves in trouble. The Shah laughed indulgently."

8. SAVAK Documents, 1: 51–53.

9. Markaz-e barrasi-ye asnad-e tarikhi, *Jebheh-ye Melli beh ravayat-e asnad-e SAVAK,* vol. 1 (Tehran, 1990), 242–249.

10. Quoted in Mohammad Reza Pahlavi, *Answer to History* (New York, 1980), 152–153.

11. *Ettela'at,* January 7, 1978.

12. SAVAK Documents, 2: 5–7.

13. Mohammad Ali Safari, *Qalam va siasat,* vol. 3 (Tehran, 1998), 622–624.

14. Ibid., 624.

15. Text in Gholam-Reza Nejati, *Tarikh-e siasi-ye bist-o panj saleh-ye Iran, 1332–1358,* vol. 2 (Tehran, 1992), 132–134.

16. Ibid., 157.

17. Karim Sanjabi, *Khaterat: Omidha-va naomidiha* (London, 1989), 292–329.

18. Pahlavi, *Answer to History,* 168.

19. Author's interview with Sadiqi, September 1989.

20. Chapour Bakhtiar, *Ma fidélité* (Paris, 1982), translated into Persian as *Yekrangi* (Paris, 1982).

21. *Ettela'at,* January 6, 1979.

22. William H. Sullivan, *Mission to Iran* (New York, 1981), 211–212.

23. John D. Stempel, *Inside the Iranian Revolution* (Bloomington, Ind., 1981), 156–157.

24. Sullivan, *Mission to Iran,* 235–236.

25. General Robert E. Huyser, *Mission to Tehran* (New York, 1986), 24.

26. Ibid., 88; Garry Sick, *All Fall Down: America's Fateful Encounter with Iran* (London, 1985), 139; Cyrus Vance, *Hard Choices: Critical Years in America's Foreign Policy* (New York, 1983), 335.

27. Ebrahim Yazdi's account of discussions between Khomeini and Zimmerman, U.S. State Department representative, in Nejati, *Tarikh-e siasi,* 285–301.

28. Sick, *All Fall Down,* 143.

29. Bakhtiar, *Yekrangi,* 195–200.

30. Sick, *All Fall Down,* 153.

31. Ibid., 145.

32. Ibid., 151; according to Huyser, Sullivan had "decided that Khomeini was a 'Gandhi-like' figure whose accession to power, coupled with a change in government, would be the most suitable course for U.S. to pursue"; *Mission to Tehran,* 290.

33. Yazdi's account in Nejati, *Tarikh-siasi,* 297.

34. Abbas Amir-Entezam, *Khaterat: An su-ye etteham,* vol. 1 (Tehran, 2002), 19; Ehsan Naraqi, Interview, *Tarikh-e mo'aser-e Iran,* 6, no. 24 (Winter 2002), 236–239.

35. Khomeini later expressed regret about having appointed Bazargan; Ruhollah Khomeini, *Sahifeh-ye Nur,* vol. 12 (Tehran, 1982), 253.

36. Sullivan, *Mission to Iran,* 243–244.

37. Sick, *All Fall Down,* 140, 152.

38. Ibid., 140.

39. Shapur (Chapour) Bakhtiar, *Khaterat,* HIOHP (Bethesda, 1996), 117.

40. General Abbas Qarabaghi, *Khaterat [E'terafat-e general]* (Tehran, 1989), 363–364.

41. Pahlavi, *Answer to History,* 172–173.

42. Ibid., 170–171.

### 6. The Edifice and Emplacements of Royal Rule

1. Although the landowners traditionally constituted a powerful segment of the upper class, their socioeconomic position was less than fully secure. According to Lambton, "whereas the power and privileges of the landowning class have been relatively constant over a long period, its composition has undergone many changes. From time to time it has incorporated new elements into its ranks and lost others. Never, however, has a stable landed aristocracy, transmitting its estates in their entirety from generation to generation, emerged"; A. S. K. Lambton, *Landlords and Peasants in Persia* (Oxford, 1953), 259.

2. Zahra Shaji'i, *Nokhbegan-e siasi-ye Iran,* vol. 2 (Tehran, 1993), 347.

3. Ibid., 384.

4. Norbert Elias, *The Civilizing Process,* vol. 2: *State Formation and Civilization* (Oxford, 1982); Elias, *The Court Society* (Oxford, 1983).

5. Alam, 2: 145; 4: 34; 5: 494–495.

6. Ibid., 405.

7. Ibid., 407.

8. American Embassy, Tehran, to Department of State, June 15, 1964, A.702, Pol.1 IRAN.

9. American Embassy, Tehran, to Department of State, April 1, 1964, A.530, Pol.6 IRAN.

10. Ala to Taqizadeh, October 22, 1947, in Iraj Afshar, ed., *Namehha-ye Tehran* (Tehran, 1990), 266–268.

11. Ala's daily report to the Shah, *Tarikh-e Mo'aser-e Iran,* 1, no. 2 (Summer 1997), 123–174.

12. American Embassy, Tehran, to Department of State, May 14, 1959, D.838, 101.21-NIS/5-1459.

13. Ja'far Sharif-Emami, *Khaterat,* HIOHP (Tehran, 2001), 283–284.

14. Before 1953 Yazdanpanah did not hold a high opinion of the Shah, whom he described as surrounded by "spies" and "utterly indiscreet"; Ghani, 11: 367.

15. Hosein Shahidzadeh, *Rahavard-e Ruzgar* (Tehran, 1999), 211.

16. *CSH,* 23.

17. Alam, 2: 125. Alam later described Ayadi as medically incompetent but a good jester; Alam, 4: 359.

18. CIA, "Elites and the Distribution of Power in Iran" (by Ernest R. Oney), February 1976, 32–33, in *Asnad-e laneh-ye jasusi,* no. 7 (Tehran, n.d.).

19. Mohammad Yeganeh, *Khaterat,* HIOHP (Tehran, 2005), 188–234. The rapacious conduct of the likes of Ayadi irritated senior and reputable officials such as Yeganeh (director of the Central Bank, 1973–1976) and Alikhani (minister of the economy, 1962–1969); Ali-Naqi Alikhani, *Khaterat,* ed. Gholam-Reza Afkhami (Tehran, 2002), 246–254; Yeganeh, *Khaterat.*

20. American Embassy, Tehran, to Department of State, May 3, 1965, A.567, Pol. IRAN.

21. Alam, 5: 258.

22. American Embassy, Tehran, to Department of State, January 9, 1973, A.004, Pol.1 IRAN.

23. American Embassy, Tehran, to Department of State, April 1, 1964, A.530, Pol.6 IRAN / Pol.15-1 IRAN.

24. Alam, 1: 245.

25. Alam, 5: 500.

26. Russell to Selwyn Lloyd, October 27, 1958, FO 371/133007.

27. American Embassy, Tehran, to Department of State, May 14, 1959, D.838, 101.21-NIS/5-1459.

28. American Embassy, Tehran, to Department of State, January 28, 1975, A.119, P750027-2355.

29. British Embassy minute, September 1958, FO 371/133006.

30. American Embassy, Tehran, to Department of State, January 28, 1975.

31. Alam, 5: 441–442.

32. American Embassy, Tehran, to Department of State, January 28, 1975.

33. Ibid.

34. Ibid.; see also Yeganeh, *Khaterat*, 216–223.

35. Alam, 5: 209.

36. Alam, 3: 23.

37. American Embassy, Tehran, to Department of State, January 28, 1975.

38. American Embassy, Tehran, to Department of State, January 9, 1973.

39. American Embassy, Tehran, to Department of State, January 28, 1975.

40. Alam, 2: 43.

41. Alam, 2: 106; 5: 213.

42. In 1973 the Shah told the Italian journalist Oriana Fallaci: "Nobody can influence me, nobody. Still less a woman. Women are important in a man's life only if they are beautiful and charming and keep their femininity . . . You are equal [with men] in the eyes of the law but not, excuse my saying so, in ability . . . You've never produced a Michelangelo or a Bach. You've never even produced a great chef"; Oriana Fallaci, *Interview with History,* trans. John Shepley (Boston, 1976), 271–272.

43. Wiggin to Morris, November 12, 1966, FO 371/186665.

44. Alam, 2: 106.

45. Abundant evidence of Alam's services in procuring women for the Shah can be found in Alam's diaries.

46. Alam, 5: 68, 178, 389.

47. Ibid., 398–399.

48. Ibid., 323.

49. Ibid., 166.

50. Alam, 1: 340–341, 368.

51. Alam, 3: 352.

52. Author's interview with Sir Denis Wright, August 1994.

53. Roger Stevens to FO, August 7, 1958, FO 371/133022.

54. American Embassy, Tehran, to Department of State, June 20, 1972, A.105, INCO 15 IRAN.

55. American Embassy, Tehran, to Department of State, January 9, 1973.

56. Alam, 5: 469.

57. Ibid., 420–424, 435.

58. American Embassy, Tehran, to Department of State, January 9, 1973.

59. James A. Bill, *The Eagle and the Lion: The Tragedy of American-Iranian Relations* (New Haven, 1988), 202.

60. Alam, 5: 487.

61. Mark J. Gasiorowski, *U.S. Foreign Policy and the Shah* (Ithaca, 1991), 112–114.

62. Bill, *Eagle and Lion,* 202.

63. General Abbas Qarabaghi, *Khaterat [E'terafat-e general]* (Tehran, 1989), 157–158.

64. Alam, 3: 317.

65. General Feraydun Jam's letter to Ahmad Bani-Ahmad, January 23, 1993, *Negin,* no. 11 (2000), 39–40.

66. Ibid., 40.

67. American Embassy, Tehran, to Department of State, January 9, 1973.

68. General Robert E. Huyser, *Mission to Tehran* (New York, 1986), 288–289.

69. E. A. Bayne, *Persian Kingship in Transition* (New York, 1968), 186.

70. Ample evidence for this can be found in published SAVAK documents. See, for instance, Markaz-e barrasi-ye asnad-e tarikhi, *Jebhe-ye melli beh ravayat-e asnad-e SAVAK,* vol. 1 (Tehran, 1990).

71. American Embassy, Tehran, to Department of State, June 15, 1964.

72. American Embassy, Tehran, to Department of State, May 3, 1965.

73. Thomas L. Hughes to the Secretary of State, July 31, 1967, Pol.14 IRAN; American Embassy, Tehran, to Department of State, August 30, 1967, A.124, Pol.12 IRAN.

74. General Mohsen Mobasser, *Pazhuhesh: Naqdi bar ketab-e khaterat-e arteshbod-e sabeq Hosein Fardust* (London, 1996), 369.

75. American Embassy, Tehran, to Department of State, September 9, 1972, A.151, Pol. IRAN.

76. Alam, 5: 424–425.

77. After more than a quarter of a century and despite evident eagerness to expose SAVAK's extensive brutality, those who took charge of the organization's archives and other state documents have not produced evidence to support such a case.

78. American Embassy, Tehran, to Department of State, January 28, 1975. The Shah also received briefings on international affairs from the U.S. and British intelligence agencies; Alam, 5: 494.

79. Ehsan Naraqi, Interview, *Tarikh-e mo'aser-e Iran,* 6, no. 24 (Winter 2002), 210–212.

7. Elective Affinities

1. Ali Amini, *Khaterat,* HIOHP (Bethesda, 1995), 161.

2. American Embassy, Tehran, to Department of State, May 3, 1960, D.698, 788.00/5-360 HBS.

3. Abolhasan Ebtehaj, *Khaterat,* vol. 2 (London, 1991), 799–808.

4. Memorandum from the Deputy Director of the Office of Greek, Turkish, and Iranian Affairs (Howison) to the Assistant Secretary of State for Near Eastern and South Asian Affairs (Talbot), Washington, D.C., January 1965, in *FRUS, 1964–1968,* 22: 124.

5. Some U.S. officials would, however, later maintain that Iran's economic growth and the Shah's increased self-confidence and ambitions for "more rapid development" provided "the backdrop against which he could for the first time decrease his dependence on the US"; Intelligence Memorandum, Washington, D.C., June 5, 1967, ibid., 383.

6. Ebtehaj, *Khaterat*, 525–526.

7. Alam, 3: 119.

8. American Embassy, Tehran, to Department of State, June 15, 1964, A.702, Pol.1-I IRAN.

9. Ibid.

10. James A. Bill, *The Eagle and the Lion: The Tragedy of American-Iranian Relations* (New Haven, 1988), 173.

11. American Embassy, Tehran, to Department of State, January 9, 1973, A.004, Pol.1 IRAN.

12. American Embassy, Tehran, to Department of State, January 28, 1975, A.19, P 750 0027-2353.

13. American Embassy, Tehran, to Department of State, January 9, 1973.

14. Minute by Fry, June 16, 1955, FO 371/114810.

15. Minute by Samuel, July 18, 1955, FO 371/114810.

16. Minute by Hiller, November 3, 1960, FO 371/15759.

17. Russell to Selwyn Lloyd, October 27, 1958, FO 371/133007.

18. Stevens to Selwyn Lloyd, August 21, 1958, FO 371/133006.

19. Stevens to Selwyn Lloyd, September 29, 1956, FO 371/120714.

20. Harrison to FO, February 13, 1963, FO 371/170374. This assessment was broadly shared by the Foreign Office.

21. Wright to the Earl of Home, June 18, 1963, FO 371/170377.

22. Wright to the Secretary of State for Foreign and Commonwealth Affairs, April 20, 1971, FCO 17/1516.

23. Murray to the Secretary of State for Foreign and Commonwealth Affairs, January 19, 1970, FCO 17/1213.

24. Ramsbotham to Douglas-Home, October 11, 1971, FCO 17/1517.

25. Ramsbotham to the Secretary of State for Foreign and Commonwealth Affairs, June 17, 1972, FCO 8/2050.

26. Minute by Smith, June 16, 1972, FCO 8/1882.

27. Alam, 5: 414.

28. Wright to Brown, January 23, 1967, FCO 17/351.

29. American Embassy, Tehran, to Department of State, March 2, 1968, A.465, Pol.12 IRAN.

30. Alam, 2: 289.

31. Alam, 5: 349, 411.

32. Mohammad Reza Pahlavi, *Answer to History* (New York, 1980), 170–171.

8. The Architecture of Royalist Hegemony

1. Admitting to being fatalistic, the Shah asserted: "I'll stay alive until such time as I finish what I have to finish. And that day has been set by God, not by those who want to kill me"; Oriana Fallaci, *Interview with History* (Boston, 1976), 266.

2. Shah's speech, May 22, 1963, in *Sokhanan-e Shahanshah* (Tehran, n.d.), 130–133; Mohammad Reza Pahlavi, *Beh su-ye tamaddon-e bozorg* (Tehran, n.d.), 9–11. Claiming to be protected by an invisible "mystical force" and to receive "religious messages," the Shah asserted: "My reign has saved the country and it's saved it because God was beside me. I mean, it's not fair for me to take all the credit for myself for the great things that I've done for Iran"; Fallaci, *Interview with History,* 267–228; Alam, 1: 400; 2: 168.

3. Alam, 2: 280.

4. Alam, 5: 368.

5. R. K. Karanjia, *The Mind of a Monarch* (London, 1977), 226.

6. Mohammad Ali Safari, *Qalam va siasat,* vol. 3 (Tehran, 1998), 456.

7. Alam, 2: 265.

8. Ramsbotham to Douglas-Home, October 11, 1971, FCO 17/1517.

9. Alam, 2: 21.

10. Alam, 1: 368.

11. Alam, 2: 43.

12. Ibid., 239.

13. American Embassy, Tehran, to Department of State, April 16, 1975, A.75, P750 074-0998.

14. To officials, civilian or military, who ventured to make a suggestion disagreeable to the Shah, his response was always "And who are you to be saying this?" "The Shah," complained a high-ranking general, "did not consider us worthy of any attention, but whenever a foreigner spoke to him, he listened"; General Hasan Tufanian, *Khaterat,* HIOHP (Tehran, 2002), 114–117.

15. William Shawcross, *The Shah's Last Ride* (New York, 1988).

16. Alam, 3: 299; 5: 295.

17. Author's interview with Sir Denis Wright, August 1994.

18. American Embassy, Tehran, to Department of State, April 16, 1975.

19. Pahlavi, *Beh su-ye tamaddon,* 14–15.

20. *New York Times,* September 30, 1975.

21. American Embassy, Tehran, to Department of State, May 3, 1965, A.567, Pol. IRAN; Alam, 1: 212, 247; 2: 43, 142.

22. Alam, 5: 273.

23. Alam, 2: 199.

24. The Shah maintained: "if my son should become king before the required age, Queen Farah Diba would become regent. But there'd also be a council with which she'd have to consult. I, on the other hand, have no obligation to consult anyone, and I don't consult with anyone. See the difference?"; Fallaci, *Interview with History,* 272.

25. Alikhani maintains that the Shah had no clear idea about his illness until the start of the revolution, and that the medications he took had no adverse effect on his power of decisionmaking; Alam, 4: 17.

26. Author's interview with Wright, August 1994.

27. American Embassy, Tehran, to Department of State, April 16, 1975.

28. Alam, 3: 289–297.

29. Fallaci, *Interview with History,* 273.

30. "Khaterat-e Parviz Natel-Khanlari," *Ayandeh*, 16, nos. 5–8 (1990), 438–439.

31. Alam, 5: 354.

32. American Embassy, Tehran, to Department of State, April 16, 1975.

33. Ibid.

34. American Embassy, Tehran, to Department of State, November 7, 1973, A.166, E8-1 IRAN.

35. Author's interview with Amini, December 1981.

36. Safari, *Qalam va siasat*, 448.

37. Amartya Sen, *Development as Freedom* (New York, 1999).

### 9. A Culture of Confrontation

1. See further *Mokatebat-e Mosaddeq: Talash bara-ye tashkil-e jebheh-ye melli-ye sevvom* (n.p., 1975).

2. Khalil Maleki, *Dau Nameh* (Tehran, 1979); Maleki, *Namehha-ye Khalil Maleki*, ed. Amir Pichdad and Mohammad Ali Homayun Katouzian (Tehran, 2002).

3. American Embassy, Tehran, to Department of State, February 20, 1967, A.488, Pol.2.3 IRAN.

4. Hamid Shaukat, *Negahi az darun beh jonbesh-e chap-e Iran: Goft-o-gu ba Mehdi Khanbaba-Tehrani*, vol. 2 (Paris, 1998), 324–326.

5. Ibid., 338–339; also Hamid Shaukat, *Tarikh-e bist saleh: Konfederasion-e jahani-ye mohasselin va daneshjuyan-e Iran*, 2 vols. (Germany, 1993); on student activism abroad see Afshin Matin-Asgari, *Iranian Student Opposition to the Shah* (Costa Mesa, Calif., 2002).

6. Alam, 5: 313.

7. American Embassy, Tehran, to Department of State, December 31, 1966, A.357, Pol.12 IRAN.

8. Markaz-e barrasi-ye asnad-e tarikhi, *Jebheh-ye melli beh ravayat-e asnad-e SAVAK*, vol. 1 (Tehran, 1990), 391.

9. Author's interview with a SAVAK official, London, April 1989.

10. Maziar Behrooz, *Rebels with a Cause: The Failure of the Left in Iran* (London, 2000), 55; the author characterizes the Fada'iyan as Stalinist (61), along with most other "Iranian Marxist groups and organizations" (159).

11. Key texts included Amir-Parviz Puyan, *Zarurat-e mobarezeh-ye mosallahaneh va radd-e te'ori-ye baqa'* (n.p., 1970); Mas'ud Ahmadzadeh, *Mobarezeh-ye mosallahaneh* (n.p., 1970). An English-language translation of key writings by Bizhan Jazani, a Fada'iyan theorist, can be found in his *Capitalism and Revolution in Iran* (London, 1976).

12. Author's interview with a SAVAK official, London, April 1989.

13. Selections from the writings of Hobbes, Locke, and Mill translated into Persian were available in Mahmud Sana'i, *Azadi-ye fard va qodrat-e daulat* (Tehran, 1965). There were also two Persian translations of Mill's *On Liberty*. No adequate translation of any works by or on Hegel was available until Hamid Enayat's *Falsafeh-ye Hegel* (Tehran, 1968)—a translation of W. T. Stace's *The Philosophy of Hegel* (London, 1923)—and his later translations of works such as Hegel's *Reason in History*.

14. A provocative critique of the "theological" cast of mind of Iranian intellectuals of

various persuasions can be found in Aramesh Dustdar, *Derakhsheshha-ye tireh* (Cologne, 1991).

15. Samad Behrangi, *The Little Black Fish,* trans. Hooshang Amuzegar (Bethesda, 1997).

16. Mahmud E'temadzadeh (Behazin), *Az har dari,* vol. 2 (Tehran, 1993), 213.

17. The record of the Tudeh Party and some of its key figures has provoked much critical scrutiny among its former members; see, for instance, Babak Amir-Khosravi, *Nazari az darun beh naqsh-e hezb-e Tudeh-ye Iran* (Tehran, 1996); and Shaukat, *Negahi az darun.*

18. E'temadzadeh, *Az har dari,* 194.

19. Mostafa Rahimi, "Chera ba jomhuri-ye eslami mokhalefam?" *Ayandegan,* January 15, 1979.

20. With the exception of a translation of the Communist Manifesto (Moscow, 1951), no major text of Marx was available in Persian until the 1970s. The first volume of *Das Kapital* (trans. Iraj Eskandari, 1973) was followed a year later by the *18th Brumaire of Louis Bonaparte* (trans. Mohammad Pur-Hormozan). Both works were published by the Tudeh Party in Europe and were out of reach in Iran. Leninist tracts were more easily available; the leftist literature read by students comprised introductory works, extracts, or summaries, often poorly translated. Writings such as Amir-Hosein Aryanpur's *Dar astaneh-ye rastakhiz* (n.p., n.d.) and *Jame'eh-shenasi-ye honar* (Tehran, 1975) and pieces by the Tudeh ideologue Ehsan Tabari could more easily be found.

21. Helms, American Embassy, Tehran, to Department of State, November 7, 1973, A.166, E8-1 IRAN.

22. Farhad Kazemi, *Poverty and Revolution in Iran* (New York, 1980), 85–88.

23. Albert H. Hourani, *A History of the Arab Peoples* (Cambridge, Mass., 1991), 384–388.

24. Said Amir Arjomand, *The Turban for the Crown* (New York, 1989), 194.

25. Nikki R. Keddie, *Iran and the Muslim World* (New York, 1995), 75.

26. Ahmad Ashraf and Ali Banuazizi, "The State, Classes, and Modes of Mobilization in the Iranian Revolution," *State, Culture and Society,* 1, no. 3 (1985), 34–35.

27. Ali Dehbashi, ed., *Namehha-ye Jalal Al-e Ahmad* (Tehran, 1988); see also Jalal Al-e Ahmad, *Dar khedmat va khianat-e raushanfekran* (Tehran, 1978), 161–215.

28. Al-e Ahmad, *Gharbzadegi* (Tehran, 1962). The first critique of this tract, Daryush Ashuri's "Hoshyari-ye tarikhi," was published in *Barrasi-ye ketab* in February 1967 and revised and reprinted in *Ma va moderniyat* (Tehran 1997), 13–42. Several English terms have been coined to render *gharbzadegi,* including "Westoxication" and "Euromania"; for an English translation see Jalal Al-e Ahmad, *Occidentosis: A Plague from the West,* trans. R. Campbell, ed. Hamid Algar (Berkeley, 1984).

29. Jalal Al-e Ahmad, *Yek chah-o dau chaleh* (Tehran, 1964), 52.

30. Al-e Ahmad, *Gharbzadegi,* 35–36.

31. It has been claimed that "the massive and overwhelming response given by the Iranian people during the Revolution to the declarations and leadership of Ayatollah Khomeini is in part due to the extremely important influence of Dr. Shari'ati during the years of Ayatollah Khomeini's exile"; Hamid Algar, *The Roots of the Islamic Revolution* (London, 1983), 52. For more on Shari'ati, see Ali Rahnama, *An Islamic Utopian: A Political Biography of Ali Shari'ati* (London, 1998).

32. Ehsan Naraqi, *Ancheh khod dasht* (Tehran, 1976); Naraqi, *Ghorbat-e gharb* (Tehran, 1974).

33. Daryush Shayegan, *Asia dar barabar-e gharb* (Tehran, 1992).

34. For a debunking of Fardid see Daryush Ashuri, "Ostureh-ye falsafeh dar mian-e ma," www.nilgoon.com (2004), 3–57.

35. The rapid collapse of the regime also surprised its clerical opponents; see Ali-Akbar Nateq-Nuri, *Khaterat,* 2 vols. (Tehran, 2005).

36. Mehdi Ha'eri-Yazdi, *Khaterat,* HIOHP (Bethesda, 2001), 94–97.

37. Ibid., 102.

38. American Embassy, Tehran, to Department of State, December 22, 1964, A.327, Soc.12-1 IRAN.

39. Mehdi Bazargan, *Enqelab-e Iran dar dau harakat* (Tehran 1984), 125.

40. The November 1978 trip of Queen Farah to Najaf to seek the help of Kho'i—who was known for his opposition to Khomeini—in defusing the political crisis produced no positive result.

41. Alam, 4: 304; 5: 425.

42. Alam, 4: 72; 5: 426.

43. Alam, 5: 503.

44. SAVAK Documents, 1: 262.

45. American Embassy, Tehran, to Department of State, January 28, 1975, A.19, P750 027-2355.

46. Martin F. Herz, Counselor of Embassy for Political Affairs, American Embassy, Tehran, to Department of State, June 15, 1964, A.702, Pol. I-IRAN.

47. Leszek Kolakowski, *Modernity on Endless Trial* (Chicago, 1990), 216–217.

48. Richard Sennett, *Authority* (New York, 1980), 156.

49. Alam, 4: 79.

50. Alam, 2: 324.

51. American Embassy, Tehran, to Department of State, January 9, 1973, A.004, Pol.1 IRAN.

52. American Embassy, Tehran, to Department of State, July 8, 1976, A.123, P760 105-0912.

53. William G. Bowdler to Newson, Memorandum for Dr. Z. Brzezinski, September 18, 1978, P780 148-2210.

54. House of Representatives Permanent Select Committee on Intelligence, Subcommittee on Evaluation, Staff Report, *Iran: Evaluation of U.S. Intelligence Performance prior to November 1978* (Washington, D.C., 1979), 6, quoted in James A. Bill, *The Eagle and the Lion: The Tragedy of American-Iranian Relations* (New Haven, 1988), 258.

## 10. The Unfolding of Clerical Rule

1. Mehdi Bazargan, *Enghelab-e Iran dar dau harakat* (Tehran, 1984), 164–186.

2. The events of November 1979 have been referred to as a "clerical coup d'état . . . in the form of a direct takeover of the state by the clerically dominated Revolutionary Council"; Said Amir Arjomand, *Turban for the Crown* (New York, 1988), 139.

3. It has been claimed that policymakers such as Kissinger and Rockefeller—who were also leading officials in Chase Manhattan Bank, which held substantial Ira-

nian assets—fearing that the new Iranian regime might withdraw its funds and re-pudiate the former regime's loans, vigorously lobbied Washington for the admission of the Shah to the United States. They were fully aware that such a move would provoke a violent backlash in Iran, such as the takeover of the U.S. embassy, which would then result in the freezing of Iranian assets. See further James A. Bill, *The Eagle and the Lion: The Tragedy of American-Iranian Relations* (New Haven, 1988), 341–348.

4. Bazargan, testimony in court on behalf of his deputy Abbas Amir-Entezam, who was accused, among other things, of masterminding the dissolution of the Assembly of Experts; Amir-Entezam, *Khaterat*, vol. 2 (Tehran, 2002), 16–26.

5. The proceedings of the Assembly can be found in *Surat-e mashruh-e mozakerat-e majles-e barrasi-ye naha'i-ye qanun-e asasi-ye jomhuri-ye Islami-ye Iran,* 4 vols. (Tehran, 1985–1989).

6. According to the Freedom Movement, "the first suggestion" for the inclusion of this clause "was made by Hasan Ayat, an enemy of the legacy of Mosaddeq and civic nationalists"; Nahzat-e Azadi-ye Iran, *Velayat-e motlaqeh-ye faqih* (Tehran 1988), 151.

7. See further Asghar Schirazi, *The Constitution of Iran: Politics and the State in the Islamic Republic,* trans. John O'Kane (London, 1997).

8. Twenty-five hundred Mojahedin and other leftists had been executed by the end of 1981; Ervand Abrahamian, *The Iranian Mojahedin* (London, 1989), 220.

9. Ali-Akbar Hashemi-Rafsanjani, *Obur az bohran* (Tehran, 1999), 292.

10. An era of revolutionary terror had long descended on the country, epitomized by Sadeq Khalkhali, the "hanging judge." He presided over Islamic revolutionary tribunals in which the accused—officials of the former regime, various other opponents, and socially undesirable elements—faced charges such as being a "corrupter of the earth" or a "combatant against God"; they were executed with scant attention to any recognizable juridical procedures. Some insight on Khalkhali can be gained from his own "memoirs": Sheikh Sadeq Khalkhali, *Ayyam-e enzeva: Khaterat-e Ayatollah Khalkhali,* 2 vols. (Tehran, 2001).

11. Jean-Pierre Digard, Bernard Hourcade, and Yann Richard, *L'Iran au XXe siècle* (Paris, 1996), 169; according to another account, by 1985 the death toll exceeded 12,000; Abrahamian, 223.

12. Also, former Khomeini aide Qotbzadeh and some seventy army officers were executed for their alleged involvement in the plot.

13. For an account by Ayatollah Montazeri, see his *Khaterat* (Spanga, Sweden, 2001), chap. 10.

14. Gary Sick, *October Surprise: America's Hostages in Iran and the Election of Ronald Reagan* (New York, 1991).

15. Bazargan, *Enghelab,* 202–203.

16. For a powerful critique of the "guardianship of the jurist" and its "absolute" form, see Mehdi Ha'eri-Yazdi, *Hekmat va hokumat* (London, 1995); the author, a high-ranking Muslim jurist and philosopher, argues that, as a system of governance, the guardianship of the jurist has no basis in Islamic jurisprudence. He views it as a contradictory construct because, among other things, it considers the

people to be minors but at the same time purports to grant them the right to choose, and claims to be at least partially validated by their choice. See also Nahzat-e azadi-ye Iran, *Velayat*.

17. For Rafsanjani's political background, role, and views, see Ali-Akbar Hashemi-Rafsanjani: *Dauran-e mobarezeh*, 2 vols. (Tehran, 1988); *Obur az bohran* (Tehran, 1999); *Pas az bohran* (Tehran, 2001); and *Aramesh va chalesh* (Tehran, 2002).

18. Akabar Ganji, *Alijanab-e Sorkhpush va Alijanaban-e Khakestari* (Tehran, 1999), 122–222.

19. Digard, Hourcade, and Richard, *L'Iran au XXe siècle*, 213.

20. Abdollah Nuri, *Shaukaran-e eslah* (Tehran, 1999).

21. Sa'ideh Eslamiyeh, "Mohajerani: Mardi bara-ye tamam-e fasl-ha," *Negah-e Nau*, 47 (February 2001), 7–17.

22. Mohammad Khatami, speech in the Islamic parliament, text in *Yas-e Nau*, August 5, 2003.

23. *Hamshahri*, April 7, 2004.

24. Ibid.

25. *Yas-e Nau*, October 18, 2003.

26. Changiz Pahlavan, *Negahi digar beh dovvom-e khordad* (Hamburg, 2000), 38, 80.

27. Letter addressed to Ayatollah Khameneh'i, May 21, 2003, mimeograph.

28. Mohammad Khatami, *Nameh-i bara-ye farda*, www.president.ir (May 2004).

29. Ibid.

30. The price of oil increased from around eighteen dollars a barrel in 1999 to sixty dollars plus in 2006. However, the country's oil industry, providing some 85 percent of its export income, faced a crisis resulting from chronically inadequate investment and poor management. In 1974 oil production had reached 6.6 million barrels per day, but as a result of the revolution and war it plummeted to 1.3 million in 1981, recovering only slowly. In 2006 it stood at 3.8 million barrels per day, while domestic consumption had increased steeply.

31. Musa Ghani-Nejad, interview, *Sharq*, July 28, 2005.

## 11. The Culture of Politics

1. For more on the obstacles to political party activity in Iran, see Fakhreddin Azimi, "On Shaky Ground: Concerning the Absence or Weakness of Political Parties in Iran," *Iranian Studies*, 30 (Winter/Spring 1997), 53–75.

2. Not long after Ahmadi-Nejad's election, more than 1,000 students signed a letter denouncing exclusionist authoritarianism.

3. See further Sami Zubaida, *Law and Power in the Islamic World* (New York, 2003).

4. Mohammad Mojtahed-Shabestari, *Hermenutik, ketab va sonnat* (Tehran, 1996); Mohsen Kadivar, *Daghdaghehha-ye hokumat-e dini* (Tehran, 2000); Abdolkarim Soroush, *Qabz-o-bast-e te'orik-e shari'at* (Tehran, 1991); Soroush, *Reason Freedom and Democracy in Islam*, ed. and trans. Mahmoud Sadri and Ahmad Sadri (London, 2000).

5. Abdolkarim Soroush, lecture at Westminster University, London, June 13, 2003, reported by BBC Persian Service.

6. Ernest Gellner, *Conditions of Liberty* (London, 1996), 137–204.

7. The most elaborate discussion of political equality is contained in the work of Ronald Dworkin; see, for instance, his *Taking Rights Seriously* (Cambridge, Mass., 1977). In a later work, developing his egalitarian liberalism, which is committed to distributive agendas and to the full compatibility of liberty and equality, he considers "the sovereign virtue" and indeed the legitimacy of a political community to consist in treating the fate of all citizens as being of equal importance; see Dworkin, *Sovereign Virtue: The Theory and Practice of Equality* (Cambridge, Mass., 2000).

8. Avishai Margalit, *The Decent Society* (Cambridge, Mass., 1996).

### 12. Predicaments and Prospects

1. Jim Muir, BBC correspondent in Tehran (1999–2004), "Iran: A Place in My Heart," BBC News, August 12, 2004.

2. Ruhollah Khomeini, speech, February 1, 1979, in *Sahifeh-ye Nur,* vol. 4 (Tehran, 1982), 283–284.

3. Hardy (Paris) to Dixon, January 14, 1953, FO 371/104561.

4. Charles Taylor, *Hegel and the Modern State* (Cambridge, 1979), 159.

5. For a discussion of driving, traffic accidents, and cultural standards, see Norbert Elias, "Technization and Civilization," *Theory, Culture & Society,* 12 (August 1995), 7–42.

### Epilogue

1. For a discussion of the specifically modern context of nationalism, see Ernest Gellner, *Nations and Nationalism* (Oxford, 1983).

2. See, for instance, interview with Montazeri, *Bieler Tagblatt,* October 15, 2003.

3. Leszek Kolakowski, *Modernity on Endless Trial* (Chicago, 1990), 198.

4. Mohammad Maleki (former chancellor of Tehran University), message to students, August 20, 2003, mimeograph.

5. Ernest Gellner, "Concepts and Society," in Bryan Wilson, ed., *Rationality* (Oxford, 1970), 18–49.

6. John Dunn, *The Cunning of Unreason: Making Sense of Politics* (London, 2000), 363.

# Index